Granick → ~~Jeff~~ ac uk

— JDC

— Epilog 298-300
the extraordinary nature
of Jewish Philanthropy
as supported by
~ 15 NGOs so
highly rated by
AIP

— send email to Author
Granick (as ARNOVA
Review)

AIP is far more aggressive in its methodology
than Charity Navigator, BBB, etc.

International Jewish Humanitarianism in the Age of the Great War

In 1914, seven million Jews across Eastern Europe and the Eastern Mediterranean were caught in the crossfire of warring empires in a disaster of stupendous, unprecedented proportions. In response, American Jews developed a new model of humanitarian relief for their suffering brethren abroad, wandering into American foreign policy as they navigated a wartime political landscape. The effort continued into peacetime, touching every interwar Jewish community in these troubled regions through long-term projects for refugees, child welfare, public health, and poverty alleviation. Against the backdrop of war, revolution, and reconstruction, this is the story of American Jews who went abroad in solidarity to rescue and rebuild Jewish lives in Jewish homelands. As they constructed a new form of humanitarianism and redrew the map of modern philanthropy, they rebuilt the Jewish Diaspora itself in the image of the modern social welfare state.

Jaclyn Granick is Lecturer in History and Religion at Cardiff University.

Human Rights in History

Edited by

Stefan-Ludwig Hoffmann, University of California, Berkeley

Samuel Moyn, Yale University, Connecticut

This series showcases new scholarship exploring the backgrounds of human rights today. With an open-ended chronology and international perspective, the series seeks works attentive to the surprises and contingencies in the historical origins and legacies of human rights ideals and interventions. Books in the series will focus not only on the intellectual antecedents and foundations of human rights, but also on the incorporation of the concept by movements, nation-states, international governance, and transnational law.

A full list of titles in the series can be found at:
www.cambridge.org/human-rights-history

International Jewish Humanitarianism in the Age of the Great War

Jaclyn Granick

Cardiff University

CAMBRIDGE
UNIVERSITY PRESS

CAMBRIDGE
UNIVERSITY PRESS

University Printing House, Cambridge CB2 8BS, United Kingdom

One Liberty Plaza, 20th Floor, New York, NY 10006, USA

477 Williamstown Road, Port Melbourne, VIC 3207, Australia

314–321, 3rd Floor, Plot 3, Splendor Forum, Jasola District Centre, New Delhi – 110025, India

79 Anson Road, #06-04/06, Singapore 079906

Cambridge University Press is part of the University of Cambridge.

It furthers the University's mission by disseminating knowledge in the pursuit of education, learning, and research at the highest international levels of excellence.

www.cambridge.org
Information on this title: www.cambridge.org/9781108495028
DOI: 10.1017/9781108860697
© Jaclyn Granick 2021

First published 2021

Printed in the United Kingdom by TJ Books Limited, Padstow Cornwall

A catalogue record for this publication is available from the British Library.

Library of Congress Cataloging-in-Publication Data
Names: Granick, Jaclyn, 1986- author.
Title: International Jewish humanitarianism in the age of the Great War / Jaclyn Granick, Cardiff University.
Description: New York, NY : Cambridge University Press, 2021. |
    Series: Human rights in history | Includes bibliographical references
    and index.
Identifiers: LCCN 2020037945 (print) | LCCN 2020037946 (ebook) |
    ISBN 9781108495028 (hardback) | ISBN 9781108816830 (paperback) |
    ISBN 9781108860697 (epub)
Subjects: LCSH: Jews–Charities–History–20th century. | Humanitarian
    assistance, American–Europe–History–20th century. | Jews–United
    States–History–20th century. | Jewish diaspora. | World War,
    1914-1918–Civilian relief. | World War, 1914-1918–Jews.
Classification: LCC HV17 .G73 2021 (print) | LCC HV17 (ebook) |
    DDC 940.3/1–dc23
LC record available at https://lccn.loc.gov/2020037945
LC ebook record available at https://lccn.loc.gov/2020037946

ISBN 978-1-108-49502-8 Hardback

Contents

Figures

Maps

Table

Preface

When I began this research, I was seeking to discover what Jewish international politics looked like under the Minorities Treaties regime after the First World War. My archival research took me from Geneva to New York, Jerusalem, Washington, London, and Cincinnati. In governmental and privately held archives, I read papers in English, French, and Yiddish, though I frequently came across documents in Russian, German, and Hebrew. No researcher who is serious about transnational perspectives can content herself with a narrow archival approach, but as a historian facing Jewish archives, this problem is compounded. There are historic and ongoing questions about who and what creates and owns Jewish cultural production – the modern states presiding over places once populated by Jews, descendants of the creators, privately owned Jewish archival centers, or the State of Israel. Particularly after the targeted destruction and unmooring of this property in World War II, followed by the founding of Israel, a Jewish historian must traverse layers, or centuries, of geographical, cultural, political, and linguistic complexity. One must, in effect, retrace the multiple identities and contexts in which every actor, his predecessors, and his legacy lived.[1]

It is to sit in an unheated temporary building in Jerusalem over Christmas as wet snow falls outside, a room where rules and language change every day, depending on which archivist is in charge and whether they hail from (and catalog the papers of) French, Soviet, British, or MENA Jews. It is to greet security apparatuses placed at the door to deter antisemitism on one day, to look out over a placid Lake Geneva ringed with Alps on another; to sit in a bland cubicle at the offices of the Joint Distribution Committee with a microfilm reader posing as a computer the next, and to search for Jews and a reading spot in the immense holdings of the US National Archives. It is to struggle to learn a language known only in diaspora, whose accessible speakers are mostly over ninety years old. It is to feel one's heart drop when acquaintances are murdered in Pittsburgh by a gunman blaming Hias, wondering if things have come full circle, and are coming for me. It is to weep with despair in a library upon realizing that the whole world under one's study was completely destroyed within the lifetimes of its actors.

I approached these archives with humility, curiosity, and skepticism. If I was impatient, the papers revealed their nuances very slowly. I let myself get lost in the archives, ordering boxes and reels of material, choosing folders based on a name, a place, or year, and reading carefully, taking notes I did not yet understand. I never read enough, wrenching myself from each collection. If my plans were to write chapters as I traveled from archive to archive, finding correspondence split into collections across the globe made this impossible. As time went on, I began to understand the conversations occurring over telegram, letter, and minute notes. I knew the characters, understood their motivations, and saw their connections. My task was now to impose a narrative structure. As I sat down to write, piecing together the fragments of conversations a century old, I derived new questions as I realized that no conversation before me had taken place in isolation; each belonged to larger historical currents, and I would have to learn about these, too.

Thank you to my closest mentors, Professors Davide Rodogno, Pierre-Yves Saunier, Abigail Green, and James Loeffler, for working with me and your invaluable guidance and support along the way. Thank you to my many other dedicated professors, teachers, and mentors who encouraged me or otherwise prepared me to undertake and finish this project. I mention Tobias Brinkmann, Alexandra Garbarini, Marshall Ganz, Julia Irwin, Mara Keire, Rebecca Kobrin, Lisa Leff, Eli Lederhendler, Stephen R. Porter, David Rechter, Amalia Ribi Forclaz, Eszter Szendroi, Balazs Szendroi, Stephen Tuffnell, and Steven Zipperstein in particular. To my peer humanists, especially Sam Baltimore, Mary Cox, Anca Cretu, Nathan Kurz, Alice Little, Anat Mooreville, Francesca Piana, Rachel Rothstein, and Britt Tevis: You have all been crucial in shaping my thought and keeping me running. Thank you to Michael Watson and my team at Cambridge University Press, to my editors Daniela Blei and Jess Farr-Cox, and to my anonymous reviewers.

My thanks go to Seth Flaxman, my parents, sister, in-laws, grandfathers z"l, so many friends, and Ruben, for providing an indefatigable support network and loving nudges. I hope my children will read this book when they are grown and acknowledge their teachers.

Thank you to the many institutions and individuals who have funded my research. The University of Oxford and Cardiff University provided me with the resources and employment to see this book from thesis to monograph. Shelby Cullom and Kathryn Wasserman Davis gifted me with four years of doctoral training through the Graduate Institute Geneva. Thank you for graduate and postdoctoral research funding to the Fulbright Program; the Swiss State Secretariat for Education, Research and Innovation; the Rapoport family via the American Jewish Archives; Sophie Bookhalter via the Center for Jewish History; the British Academy for a Newton Fellowship; and the Rothschild Foundation Hanadiv Europe.

I had wonderful librarians and archivists who helped me find my way and many hospitable people who played host nearby over years of research. Thank you; it has been a pleasure. Of particular note, I mention Yochai Ben-Ghedalia, Hadassah Assouline, and David Assouline at the CAHJP; Fruma Mohrer, Gunnar Berg, Leo Greenbaum, and Ettie Goldwasser at YIVO; Richard Peuser at NARA II; Susan Woodland at AJHS; Melanie Meyers, David Rosenberg, Zachary Loeb, Christopher Barthel, and Judith Siegel at the Center for Jewish History; Linda Levi, Shelley Helfand, Misha Mitsel, Jeffrey Edelstein, and Naomi Barth at the JDC; and Kevin Proffitt, Gary Zola, and Dana Herman at the AJA. Thank you, Tamar Amsterdamer and Aleksandra Jakubczak, for archival assistance.

Earlier versions of Chapters 1 and 2 appeared originally in the following publications and are used here with permission:

"Waging Relief: The Politics and Logistics of American Jewish War Relief in Europe and the Near East, 1914–1918." *First World War Studies* 5, no. 1 (2014): 55–68.

"The First American Organization in Soviet Russia: JDC and Relief in Ukraine, 1920–1923." In *The JDC at 100: A Century of Humanitarianism.* Edited by Avinoam Patt, Atina Grossmann, Linda Levi, and Maud S. Mandel, 61–93. Detroit: Wayne State University Press, 2019.

Needless to say, this is hardly my work alone. I am humbled and awed by the significant investments in me made by my so many mentors, friends, and family, well beyond the aforementioned list. I do, however, take responsibility for any errors or faulty interpretations.

Terms, Acronyms, and Abbreviations

AEF	American Expeditionary Forces
AFSC	American Friends Service Committee, Quakers
Agro-Joint	The Joint Agricultural Corporation of the American Jewish Joint Distribution Committee (in Russia)
AJRC	American Jewish Relief Committee
Alliance Israélite	Alliance Israélite Universelle
Allianz	Israelitische Allianz zu Wien
ARA	American Relief Administration
ARC	American Red Cross
AZMU/HMO	American Zionist Medical Unit, Hadassah Medical Organization
CENTOS	Federation of Orphan Welfare Organizations in Poland, Centrala Związku Towarzystw dla Opieki nad Żydowskimi Sierotami, Farband fun di Tsentrales far Yesoymim-Farzorgung in Poyln
Central Relief	Central Relief Committee
chalutz(im)	Zionist pioneer(s)
CRB	Commission for Relief in Belgium
EKOPO	Evreiskii komitet pomoshchi zhertvam voiny, Central Jewish Committee for the Relief of War Victims
Emigdirect	joint migration organization of Ica, Hias, Werelief
Eurexco	Joint Distribution Committee's European Executive Council
Evobshchestkom	All Russian Jewish Public Committee, Jewish Social Committee for Relief among the Victims of Pogroms and Counterrevolution, Yidgeskom

Hadassah	Hadassah, the Women's Zionist Organization of America
Haskalah	the Jewish enlightenment movement, whose partisans were known as maskilim, related to the European Enlightenment, but centrally concerned with Jews' status and relationship to Europe
HC (The)	High Commissioner for Russian Refugees, Fridtjof Nansen
Hias	Hebrew Sheltering and Immigrant Aid Society
Hicem	joint migration organization of Ica, Hias, Emigdirect
Hilfskomite	Jüdische Hilfskomite für Polen
Hilfsverein	Hilfsverein der Deutschen Juden
HMO/AZMU	Hadassah Medical Organization, American Zionist Medical Unit
Ica	Jewish Colonisation Association, JCA, EKO
ICRC	International Committee of the Red Cross
IUSE	International Save the Children Union, l'Union Internationale de Secours aux Enfants
JDC or Joint	American Jewish Joint Distribution Committee
JFC	(Con)Joint Foreign Committee of British Jews
kassa	also known as a credit cooperative or a loan and saving society
kehile	traditional, organized, corporate Jewish community in a given Eastern European locality
KKS	Central Credit Kassa(s)
landsmanshaft(n)	Jewish hometown association and mutual aid society
LCRS	League of Red Cross Societies
League	League of Nations
Nansen Action	Fridtjof Nansen's International Committee for Russian Relief
NCJW	National Council of Jewish Women
NER	Near East Relief, American Committee for Armenian and Syrian Relief, American Committee for Relief in the Near East
NEP	New Economic Policy (Soviet Union)
OPE	Society for the Promotion of Enlightenment among the Jews of Russia, Obshchestvo dlia

	rasprostraneniia prosveshcheniia mezhdu evreiami v Rossii
ORT	Society for Artisanal and Manual Labor, Organization for Rehabilitation of Jews through Training, Obshchestvo remeslennogo zemledel'cheskogo truda sredi evreev v Rossii
OZE/OSE	Obshchestvo Zdravookhraneniia Evreev, Society for the Preservation of the Health of the Jewish Population, Oeuvre de Secours aux Enfants
PAKPD	Central Committee of Help to Children, Polish-American Children's Relief Committee
Pale	Pale of Settlement, the territories of the Russian Empire in which Jews were permitted to settle
PEC	Palestine Economic Corporation, Palestine Cooperative Company
People's Relief	People's Relief Committee
PZC	Provisional Executive Committee for General Zionist Affairs, Provisional Zionist Committee
RF	Rockefeller Foundation
shtetl(ekh)	small market town with a large Jewish population in the Pale
TOZ	Towarzystwo Ochrony Zdrowia Ludności Żydowskiej w Polsce, The Society for the Protection of Health of the Jewish Population in Poland
Tsisho	Tsentrale Yidishe Shul Organizatsye, Central Jewish School Organization
Werelief	World Jewish Relief Conference, Carlsbad Committee, Conférence Universelle Juive de Secours, Yidisher Velt Hilf Konferents, Jüdische Welthilfskonferenz
Yiddish	vernacular language of most Jews in Eastern and Central Europe before World War II, a Germanic language written in the Hebrew alphabet
Yishuv	the Jewish community in Palestine
ZOA	Federation of American Zionists, Zionist Organization of America

Introduction

"One cannot even imagine what hardship the Jews in Eastern Europe have suffered," wrote a youthful Lt. James Becker to his parents in Chicago. "Everywhere they have been plundered, driven out, homes destroyed, businesses ruined, until one is obliged to wonder if it ever will be possible to reconstruct these people. Personally I believe that a large percentage never will be saved or restored to their former position. And after all I am no pessimist. As a matter of fact I am generally quite optimistic. However, after having been given the chance to see the condition of the Jews in Poland, Galicia, Czecho-Slovakia, German-Austria, Roumania, Bessarabia and Bukovina you can believe me when I tell you that the burden of war has fallen on an undue and unbelievable proportion o[f] our coreligionists in all parts of Europe."[1]

James Becker, writing from Czernowitz,[2] was not a missionary, a businessman, nor a governmental official. This American-born, upper-middle-class Jewish twenty-five-year-old was working as a humanitarian delegate for the American Jewish Joint Distribution Committee (JDC). Traveling around Central and Eastern Europe in uniform after his US military service, he was having the education of a lifetime after his formal study at Cornell. Shouldering enormous responsibility alongside just a few other American Jews deployed by the JDC, he was supposed to be organizing humanitarian relief to save millions of European Jews from the ravages of war. Back in his home country, American Jews were raising millions of dollars and developing plans that he would have to try to carry out, balancing their instructions with his own inexperienced intuition regarding reality on the ground.

Without a state employing him, Becker's American looks and demeanor still took him far: He was the closest thing out there to an American Jewish emissary. Nevertheless, well-positioned and optimistic as he was, Becker was sobered by the intensive, overwhelming task of relieving the suffering of Jewish strangers. They were frustrating and quarrelsome at times, unreformed and wholly un-American, and yet, these strangers were his own "coreligionists" whom he understood to be like several million destitute kin. His was serious business.

1

Becker's humanitarian sojourn seems a familiar story, but upon closer inspection, it was rather unusual. It is not the story of American Jews arriving as US troops and liberating Nazi death camps, the story that sits at the center of our historical imagination regarding Jewish humanitarianism, especially where Eastern Europe is concerned. Rather, it took place a full generation earlier – his letter was composed in January 1920. Nor is it simply the romantic story of a hearty white American youth, off on a humanitarian adventure to feed the hungry children of Europe under Herbert Hoover's aegis for a short while. That story defined mainstream American humanitarianism of the moment. Becker and his peers occupied an ambiguous middle ground where worlds collided, precipitated by the Great War. This was international Jewish humanitarianism in action.

A Calamity of Stupendous Proportions

"The War was a calamity to the world at large; to the Jews it was a disaster of stupendous proportions."[3] Historian Abraham Duker's assessment of the Great War was published on the eve of the Second World War. And then, in the inconceivable horrors of the Second World War and the genocide of Jews, the Great War was promptly forgotten, never to be fully excavated. By exploring the birth of international Jewish humanitarianism in the age of the Great War, this book recovers a forgotten story. Put simply, the war sent the Jewish world into a tailspin. Jewish civilians and soldiers suffered terribly along the Eastern Front, which also happened to be where the majority of Jews in the world lived. Beyond untold deaths, it displaced more than a million Jewish refugees; created tens of thousands of Jewish war orphans; awakened intense anti-Jewish violence; and brought about the wholesale destruction of Jewish property, and with it, a way of life. In retrospect we can see that the Great War marked a crucial turning point in modern Jewish history, second only to the Holocaust.

In 1914, there were fourteen million Jews in the world, more than six million of whom lived in the Russian Empire. Large Jewish populations spanned Europe, the Middle East, and the Americas. There were nearly three million Jews in the United States, which meant that American Jews were poised to become the largest Jewish population in the strongest neutral country, outside a war zone. The Polish Partitions at the end of the eighteenth century had long reverberations in European Jewish history and demography, splitting the heartland of European Jewry into three empires (Prussian, Russian, and Austro-Hungarian) and launching its Jews onto three different yet interrelated trajectories. Jews who were legally confined in an area called the Pale of Settlement, which spanned the western provinces of the Russian Empire and part of Poland, suffered anti-Jewish violence and economic and legal oppression, particularly since the late nineteenth century. By contrast, Jews in the West, including Germany and Austria-Hungary, had been gradually emancipated since the French Revolution, and were increasingly acculturated and able to act with agency in domestic, imperial, and international politics. In many ways, the century leading up to the Great War was a golden age for Jews, with spreading emancipation, liberal immigration, and internal European peace.[4] Progress and emancipation for all of Europe's Jews seemed as much on the horizon as the possibility of war and destruction.

But war was what arrived in the summer of 1914 in the German Empire, Russian Empire, Habsburg Empire, and Ottoman Empire, borderlands sometimes called the "bloodlands" or the "shatterzone of empires."[5] Destruction and revolution followed. The Eastern Front overlaid the most densely Jewish places on earth, from Vilna and Poland, to Galicia in eastern Austria-Hungary, to Ukraine and Romania. Jews living within the shatterzone were exposed to the rampages of successive armies passing through their small urban dwellings as the front pushed west and east. *The Jews in the Eastern War Zone*, produced in 1916 by the American Jewish Committee, and based on careful research in several languages, noted that seven million Jews bore the brunt of the war, one million more than Belgium's population, which received much greater Western attention.[6] Jews fled in advance of armies, joining streams of refugees headed toward Siberia, Warsaw, Vienna, Budapest, and Constantinople, and estimates are that well over a million Jews became refugees. Although general civilian suffering from scorched-earth tactics, chaos, famine, cold, and disease was widespread along the Eastern Front, the wide acceptance of the antisemitic idea that Jews were or could become a danger to the conduct of the war proved particularly dangerous.[7] Jewish residents were deported from the front lines or targeted for violence by troops or other locals. Families were broken up, dispersed in different directions, and searched for one another, unable to reconnect.[8] From warring sides, Jews were charged with all manner of flimsy, antisemitic accusations, from well poisoning to hiding enemy soldiers, spying, speaking the occupiers' language (Yiddish, a Germanic language), to being Bolshevists.[9] Even where people survived, schools, synagogues, and homes were closed or destroyed. Occupying armies gunned and tore down for firewood buildings from which Jewish inhabitants had been driven.[10]

In Russia, military operations ordered the mass expulsion, region by region, of Jews from war zones in their westward drive across the Pale of

Settlement. Military authorities scarcely considered the logistical conditions or results of these deportation orders.[11] The one to two *million* Jews displaced from the front formed a mass humanitarian crisis. As they headed into Russia's interior, sent packing or forced into freight trains, they quickly overwhelmed Jewish social services in nearby cities. Romania's entry into the war in 1916 opened a bloody chapter of Romanian Jewish history that barely made headlines: targeted surveillance and abuse of Jewish soldiers, outlawing Yiddish, mass expulsions, pogroms "more or less organized by the authorities," and mass arrests and executions.[12] When the Russian Revolution overthrew the tsar in March 1917, Russian Jews were officially emancipated, which produced fleeting euphoria, until the Bolshevik Revolution in October of that year.[13] The Russian Revolution also sparked antisemitic backlash across the border in Romania, as Romanian Jews stood accused of treason and sympathizing with the revolution.[14]

The Central Powers meanwhile occupied Poland and Lithuania and marched across Galicia in the eastern reaches of Austria-Hungary. Jews escaping their small, vulnerable market towns crowded into Warsaw, Vienna, Prague, and Budapest, effecting an extraordinary acceleration of urbanization: Traditional Jews were suddenly visible in all of Central Europe's major cities. Estimates suggested that nearly a half million Jewish refugees moved within the Habsburg monarchy alone. Jews were granted freedoms under German occupation in Poland and Lithuania, but some were forcibly deported to work inside Germany proper.[15] As Catholic Poles sought to regain Polish independence as an outcome of war, they not infrequently turned against Jewish neighbors.[16]

The worst was yet to come. As militaries were defeated, empires crumbled and revolutions overthrew the political order. Civil and interstate wars were underway, making government protection utterly unreliable. The hardships of war – including severe food shortages, sometimes blamed on Jewish "middlemen," rather than on warring states – created a breeding ground for antisemitism. Pogroms took place across East Central Europe and Russia in 1918, reaching their height, but not ending, in 1919, killing or injuring hundreds of thousands of Jews and stripping survivors of their property. Alongside traditional interethnic hatreds, non-Jews were increasingly motivated by a concocted association between all Jews and the Bolsheviks.[17] These striking death tolls and the performativity of violence against Jews were unprecedented in modern times. In hindsight, these years look like some of the earliest examples of the mass interethnic violence that would characterize the twentieth century, and the bridge connecting the Russian pogrom to the Holocaust.[18]

Jews in the Ottoman Empire did not fare better. The economy of the Yishuv, the Jewish community in Palestine, depended on the receipt of *chalukah*, or charitable donations for scholars from the Jewish community abroad. This entire network fell apart immediately at the war's outbreak.[19] A volatile political situation already existed within the empire that opened the door to the mass murder of Armenians, another minority people, combined with high death rates from starvation and military service across the empire. In this context, Jews felt especially precarious without their usual means of outside support. The 1917 Balfour Declaration was a sign of great promise for Jews but also resulted in the suffering of Jews in lands still under the control of Djemal Pasha and the evacuation of the 9,000 remaining members of the Jewish population of Jaffa.[20]

Jews were not entirely passive victims in the war, but their participation did not go as planned. They signed up in record numbers for their countries' militaries, especially in Germany and Austria-Hungary, well above their proportions to the general population, displaying their loyalty and bravery to their homelands in the hopes that emancipation or further integration would follow on the heels of war. Jewish units were created within the framework of the British army.[21] Organizations sprung up to support Jewish soldiers and veterans, such as the Jewish Welfare Board in the United States.[22] Jewish women jumped into philanthropic activities to support the war, and men and women participated in civil and labor services.[23] Still others set about chronicling their experiences in the war, spurring a new genre of writing about anti-Jewish violence and producing a generation of Jewish ethnographers.[24] While war made coordination among Western European Jewish communities impossible, Western European Jews could take action on behalf of Jews within their own empires and across allied states.

At first, the war seemed to hold all kinds of possibilities for Jews. Even Tsarist Russia promised that Jews would gain full equality after the conflict. Few of these hoped-for gains on the battlefield came to fruition, except for the Zionist breakthrough of Jewish units in Palestine. Instead, Jewish soldiers suffered in social isolation in the trenches, died in the fighting, or were taken as prisoners of war, leaving behind women, children, and elderly Jews, who had to fend for themselves on the front lines of war. Jews in Galicia captured by the invading Russian army, for example, were women, children, and the elderly, who were raped and treated as enemies of state while their able-bodied men fought Austria-Hungary's battles elsewhere. The very destruction of total war then made it extremely difficult to publicize and keep records of it.[25]

The Great War rendered Jews a whole diaspora walking;[26] it was the most extensive and swiftest geopolitical displacement in Jewish history since late antiquity. Jews were not trapped and systematically murdered en masse as they would be just one generation later, at least not outside Ukraine. Still, Jewish refugees did not have a safe place to go or any government or military to protect them. The war upended "the search for physical security" that was a principal problem of modern Jewish life.[27] Contemporary documents show similarities with Holocaust-era writing: "Hundreds of thousands were forced from their homes ... the more fortunate being packed and shipped as freight— ... the less fortunate driven into the woods and swamps to die of starvation." "Orgies of lust and torture took place in public in the light of day." "Jews were burned alive in synagogues where they had fled for shelter."[28] The mass dislocation and disruption of Jewish life in the Great War must therefore be seen both as a distinct, meaningful event in Jewish history and also within the context of state-sanctioned or state-organized violence in the long twentieth century, especially in the shatterzone, often directed at long-marginalized civilian "others" and rarely ending in restorative justice of any kind. If the Balkan wars and the Armenian genocide opened a violent century, the Jewish disaster of the First World War continued it and presaged its tragic intensification.

The armistice in 1918 allowed the Great Powers of the West to come to a peace agreement, though on the Eastern Front violence intensified rather than receded.[29] Nationalism surged over the course of the war, and the borderlands of former empires were parceled out in Paris into a buffer zone of independent states. This had the effect of splintering a dispersed Jewish population into discrete ethno-religious minorities within their many new states. In 1922, more than 70 percent of the world's Jews lived under regimes that had not governed their place of residence before the war.[30] The "Jewish Question" hung over the peacemakers, dogging efforts to redraw the map of Europe according to US President Woodrow Wilson's Fourteen Points and promises made during wartime. The Jewish Question in European diplomacy had begun at the Congress of Vienna a century earlier and remained part of Great Power summits as Jewish notables in their midst sought to gain or assure the maintenance of rights on behalf of oppressed Jews.[31]

Eventually, a series of Minorities Treaties were appended to the peace treaty, largely based on the initiative of Jewish leaders who coalesced in Paris to lobby peacemakers.[32] The Minorities Treaties were designed to protect Jews and other national minorities (today one would say "ethnic minorities") under the guarantee of the new League of Nations. This political achievement, as well as the 1917 Balfour Declaration, which boosted the Zionist movement, were significant and offered reason for optimism. Both seemed to recognize the Jewish people as a coherent entity: The Minorities Treaty conceived of Jews as one national minority existing across and within many nation-states simultaneously and the Balfour Declaration envisaged Jews as forming a protonation.

"The Jewish Question" is a problematic slogan that has a long history of its own. The Jewish Question might be better thought of as "Jewish questions," a series of interrelated, hard to resolve issues around emancipation, antisemitism, Zionism, citizenship, labor, capitalism, and anti-Jewish violence, all of which fall under the larger question about how Jews fit into modern European society. In European diplomatic history, diplomats considered Jewish questions on multiple occasions, trying to figure out how to categorize Jews within and caught in between other political considerations. Often, Jewish notables brought Jewish suffering abroad to the attention of their own political leaders at international congresses or diplomatic summits in the hopes that their leaders would intervene, especially in far-flung lands where they had imperial influence. Nineteenth-century European politics produced several intractable social "questions," not the Jewish one alone – a context that can be helpful to remember.[33] The "Jewish Question" has also been used in a pejorative, antisemitic way to fundamentally question the place of Jews within Europe and for which the Nazis designed a "Final Solution." But Jews themselves also seized upon this label to collectively invoke their intractable political, social, and economic difficulties in modernizing, industrializing, nationalizing, and internationalizing Europe.[34]

Taken together, the war experience, American ascendancy, the Balfour Declaration, the Russian Revolution, the new states of East Central Europe, and new migration restrictions completely transformed Jewish life across Europe, the Middle East, and the Americas. International Jewish political leadership shifted irrevocably across the Atlantic. The disaster of stupendous proportions prompted an unprecedented international aid effort led by American Jews on behalf of their suffering kin. This humanitarian relief, of course, was also an extended act of Jewish agency in a war that caused much Jewish suffering. It was fundamental to the Jewish experience of the Great War, but we have known almost nothing about it. Not only did American Jews go to Paris in 1919 to see to it that Jews would be afforded rights after the war, but they also sent millions of dollars to Europe and the Middle East during the war and continued to in its wake. This would create long-lasting, systematic change across the Jewish world, which is the focus of this book.

The New Jewish Leadership

US Ambassador to the Ottoman Empire, Henry Morgenthau, first made Jewish leaders in New York aware of Jewish suffering in August 1914, when he sent an urgent telegram to prominent banker Jacob Schiff through the US State Department.[35] By early autumn, appeals from Jewish leaders from around Europe and the Mediterranean were pouring in for the American Jewish Committee (AJC). Louis Marshall, head of the AJC, busied himself responding to his colleagues overseas. Writing to the Alliance Israélite Universelle in Paris, appealing on behalf of Russian Jews stranded there, Marshall pledged American Jewish cooperation and action. "We are also confronted with the enormous problem which will undoubtedly be presented by the Jews within the Russian Pale, in Galicia, and in East Prussia," he wrote in September 1914.

When one thinks, that seven and a half million Jews are directly in the war zone, that there are upwards of 300,000 Jews in the Russian army, and perhaps half that number in the Austrian and German armies, it is evident that the Jews of the entire world will be called upon to co-operate for the relief of the inevitable and unspeakable suffering which these unfortunate cannot possibly escape.

That relief, however, could not include harboring Jewish refugees in the United States; after years of working as an immigration lawyer and leader of the American Jewish Committee, he knew that America's increasingly restrictionist initiatives would not permit such a plan.[36] Thus, relief would have to be sent overseas. Furthermore, the "Jews of the entire world" were soon drawn into conflict themselves. Before the calendar year came to a close, the American Jewish Joint Distribution Committee, which was founded in response to these appeals, sent $185,000 to Morgenthau directly, and to Vienna, Palestine, Russia, and to Americans stranded in Antwerp.[37] Tens of millions of dollars would follow.

Just a few months before, Jewish Americans had no idea that a protracted and gruesome war would overtake Europe and involve its alliances and colonies worldwide. No one did. Until this point, American Jews had no humanitarian infrastructure to speak of, nothing like that of their Jewish counterparts in Western and Central Europe. Like other Americans, Jewish Americans had only a practiced habit of running local communal and social institutions and undertaking associated philanthropic work. Foreign need precipitated by the Great War triggered the growth of American humanitarianism generally and of federated national and international American Jewish philanthropy specifically. Indeed, when the time came to turn these institutions outward to face the rest of the world – to the "old world" in Europe and the Eastern Mediterranean – American Jews generated the infrastructure and funds with remarkable speed, and with a resiliency that has lasted over a century.

American Jews had many overseas Jewish models to inspire their own organizations. Since the early nineteenth century, acculturated and wealthy Central and West European Jewish notables interceded on behalf of suffering Jews in the East, working with their imperial governments to build Western-style Jewish schools in colonies around the Mediterranean and helping Jews migrate to America. Emancipated European Jews were eager to appear in sync with their governments on questions of domestic as well as foreign and imperial policy, envisioning a mutually beneficial relationship.[38] Over the course of the nineteenth century, single intercessors and benefactors such as Moses Montefiore, Baron Maurice de Hirsch, Adolphe Crémieux, and the Rothschild family were replaced by organizations that grew up around them, especially after the establishment of the Alliance Israélite Universelle in Paris. These organizations included the Conjoint Foreign Committee of British Jews, the Alliance Israélite Universelle, the Hilfsverein der Deutschen Juden, the Israelitische Allianz zu Wien, and the Jewish Colonisation Association.[39]

These organizations had already generated three categories of activity to address the Jewish Question: improving the social and political position of Eastern Jews in situ; providing for the emigration of skilled workers to economically advanced regions; and initiating mass agricultural colonization.[40] Even in areas where Jews had not been granted full rights, like Russia, Romania, and the Ottoman Empire, by the early twentieth century, Jews had developed their own organizations that cooperated with, competed with, or called upon Western partners in times of need. By the turn of the century, these institutions – combined with additional transmigration relief societies and sheltering homes, agrarianization programs, anti-white slavery organizations, Jewish feminist social welfare organizations, B'nai Brith or other fraternal lodges, hometown associations in the New World, Zionist organizations, the chalukah collections for Palestine, and the traditional charitable organizations of local Jewish communities – formed a diffuse transnational network across the Mediterranean and Europe and to the Americas that mixed philanthropic and diplomatic functions.

The transatlantic connections of elite American Jews were rooted in the world of the private merchant bank. This small world of banking dynasties – the Rothschilds their most famous representative – emerged from west German lands. By the early twentieth century, they connected a small group of wealthy, intra-married Jews in ongoing transactions requiring a high level of trust across Central and Western Europe and to New York. The bank of Kuhn, Loeb, & Co. was the New York address for Jewish gentlemen banking at the turn of the century, with Jacob Schiff, Paul and Felix Warburg, and Loeb and Kuhn family members leading the way. Kuhn Loeb was the House of JPMorgan's "strongest competitor and an important collaborator," though it did not share the social background of the Morgans, who descended from early, white Protestant American settlers.[41] Other elite American Jewish merchant banks, including Seligman, Goldman Sachs, and Lehman Brothers, shared kinship and social networks with Kuhn Loeb. Kuhn Loeb's partners were German Jewish, and maintained close ties to Jewish banks back in Germany, notably, the Warburg brothers' bank M & M Warburg & Co.

These tight-knit American Jewish merchant bankers lived in mansions along Manhattan's Fifth Avenue. They were acculturated, and yet distinct from the rest of New York's high society. Though excluded from the most elite social clubs, they did not necessarily seek assimilation.[42] They were not just bankers but sometimes had major "merchant" aspects to their businesses, such as large department stores, manufacturing, and mining.[43] These bankers and merchants maintained close connections to politically oriented Jews whose personal and professional lineages connected them to the Habsburg Revolutions of 1848, such as Louis Marshall, Louis Brandeis, Stephen Wise, and Henrietta Szold.[44] Overlapping networks in civic and political organizations as well as the business world gave these "uptown Jews" access to the American elite, and bound them to many of the same structural and historical realities.[45] Thus, despite lingering separate Jewish and white Protestant spheres within America's elite, Schiff, Warburg, Rockefeller, and Carnegie shared practices and norms in business and similar commitments to philanthropy and a capitalist social order.

Uptown Jews dominated American Jewish social and political affairs at the turn of the century, funding and arranging for social service provision to Yiddish-speaking Russian Jewish immigrants. They were animated by antisemitism – Jacob Schiff consistently fought discrimination in the United States and confronted it abroad, especially attempting to undermine Tsarist Russia.[46] The Straus family, owners of R. H. Macy & Co, New York's biggest department store, included a committed Zionist and New York philanthropist (Nathan) who sponsored mass milk pasteurization and distribution programs for the poor; a career federal politician (Oscar) – US Cabinet Secretary, Ambassador to the Ottoman Empire, and founder of the American Society of International Law in 1906; and a

New York politician (Isadore) who died on the *Titanic*. The uptown group's social and economic capital among Jews, their deep connections abroad and international outlook, and networks that overlapped with those of America's elite could be mobilized in various ways.

Concurrently, Eastern European immigrants pieced together a vibrant institutional fabric of their own, including traditional synagogues, labor unions, political parties, mutual aid societies, cooperatives, and *landsmanshaftn* (hometown societies). One decade into the twentieth century, Eastern European Jews in America were multigenerational, but their networks were still *immigrant*. These immigrant networks, from the New World to the Old, maintained ties with family and friends back home as well as with other immigrants in America. Immigrants operated their own banks, sent remittances home, and bought steamship tickets. They lived and worked closely together in their adopted American cities, building new lives in constant dialogue with one another, with ethnic immigrant neighbors, and with their homelands. Crowding into New York's Lower East Side tenements and Garment District sweatshops, these were the "downtown Jews."

While downtown Jews benefited from the efforts of more established, Sephardi and Central European Jews in America, they could not tolerate their paternalistic nature. In their new country, immigrants had little power, and there was no coherent transnational political goal organized around their immigrant identity. Yet sending remittances and delegates boosted the homeland's economy and allowed them to weigh in on local political and social matters from a new, American standpoint. These prewar immigrant foreign relations patterns meant that a large number of American Jews still spoke the languages of their homelands, and regularly obtained precise, local information that covered piecemeal the vast territory in which Jews were still concentrated in Europe and the Ottoman Empire.[47] As Eastern European Jews adjusted to America, they insisted that they should also have a voice in running Jewish affairs. They set up competing institutions and a politicized Yiddish press. The desire of newly immigrated Jews to change American Jewish communal life on their own terms was often framed in terms of "democratization" of the "oligarchic" and "decorous" German Jewish elite leadership. "Democratic" was not necessarily the right descriptor for a movement with populist, Jewish nationalist tendencies, unaccustomed to operating within the norms of a Western liberal polity.

By the turn of the century, American Jews had consolidated into several considerable institutions that had the national agenda, or at least all of New York Jewry, in mind. The main organization the uptown crowd poured its capital into was the American Jewish Committee, founded for self-defense in 1906 in response to the Kishinev pogrom in the Russian Empire and shortly after an antisemitic riot in Manhattan's Lower East Side. Hiding behind a seemingly generic name was not only the confident expression of a hyphenated identity, but a statement that what was required was a "committee," a small group of carefully cultivated men appointed to negotiate such an identity on behalf of the whole. The AJC was much like an American version of the Alliance Israélite network. Like these other big international Jewish philanthropic organizations, it relied on a partnership between members of the Jewish financial elite and a more political type of Jewish elite, wherein the former bankrolled the latter as an essential structural feature.[48] Together, these men of the American Jewish Committee shared social networks with other uptown Jews, as well as with high-profile, non-Jewish politicians, lawyers, and civil servants. They were the kind of people who could write letters to the president of the United States and expect them to be read by him personally, who could call on the secretary of state, set up appointments with representatives of foreign governments, or make appeals before the US Congress. At a time when antisemitism threatened to deprive Jews of rights at home and abroad, they regularly but judiciously utilized all of these strategies.[49]

If the patrician American Jewish Committee strived to act as the political voice of American Jewry, its actual role as such was never fully realized.[50] For instance, the National Council of Jewish Women (NCJW), founded in 1893 and with an active leadership of middle-class, college-educated women in chapters across America, was also at the forefront of American Jewish social projects before the start of the war, including meeting unaccompanied young women in harbors and running Americanization and other settlement house–like programs for immigrants.[51] The Hebrew Sheltering and Immigration Aid Society (Hias), on the other hand, was an organization designed around the turn of the century to assist incoming Jewish immigrants to America, founded by Russian Jewish immigrants, whose leadership remained filled out by immigrants themselves.[52] Then there were Zionist organizations, which attracted a cross section of American Jews: the Federation of American Zionists and the new women's Zionist organization of America, Hadassah.[53] There was also the New York Kehillah, a conscious attempt to recreate in America a version of the traditional Eastern European Jewish *kehile*, the organized, autonomous, corporate Jewish community in a given locality. Mixing mass Jewish democratization politics and elite leadership, it pulled its elite founders, notably Rabbi Judah Magnes, into mass Jewish politics.[54] Finally, the American Jewish Congress came into existence during the war itself in order to send a representative from the

American Jewish delegation to the Versailles peace negotiations; it was designed to undertake the same kind of work as the American Jewish Committee, but "downtown" style – through strident mass democracy and public visibility.[55]

American Jews built their distinct social infrastructure to take care of vulnerable American Jews amid rich and growing associational life in America. This included the aforementioned national organizations and a large network of local societies focused on the provision of services, which became larger, more professionalized, and undertook consolidated fundraising following the onset of large-scale immigration in the 1880s. Until the nineteenth century, sectarian forms, religious or ethnic, of philanthropy and charity were the framework for this kind of activity in the United States. American Jewish charity, however, was not connected to the synagogue and the kehile, as it had been in Eastern Europe, but was organized in response to Protestant American charities. Late nineteenth-century Protestant churches supported secular and sectarian causes.[56] Meanwhile, from the Gilded Age and into the Progressive Era, an organizational revolution powered reforms that were national in scope but stopped short of merging into a powerful central state. Progressive Era federal governance seemed inconspicuous by relying on cooperation with nongovernmental associations.[57] By the early twentieth century, then, there was an active field of philanthropic and social reform agencies, local and national, small and large, of which Jewish agencies were in some ways a part. Yet, continual overlapping of secular and religious spheres in social welfare work, barriers to Jewish entry within mainstream institutions, and a Jewish desire to maintain distinctive Jewish institutions and values meant that Jewish social services in America grew as a parallel entity in the early twentieth century, even as some Jews contributed to and utilized more secularized services.

Sitting between the uptown and downtown Jews of Progressive America were middle-class, acculturated, professional Jews. Some felt a real sense of kinship and responsibility for newcomers and made an effort to listen to immigrants and make space for their concerns. Further, in the decades leading up to the war, social work had become a well-respected, transatlantic occupation as it moved away from charity and attached itself to the new social sciences.[58] Jewish social workers had been key to establishing professional training programs in the United States. Through professionalization of social work in New York, idealistic uptown Jews, including women, and upwardly mobile downtown Jews, usually men, came together toward common causes. Both the elite bankers and middle-class social workers of American Jewish social institutions imbibed the values of Progressive America, especially its gradualist and pro-capitalist assumptions, and thus could work together and avoid grappling with the structural critiques leveled by immigrants and the democratization movement.

More intent on fighting small battles and creating an American Jewish community at home, American Jews only episodically paid attention to the Jewish Question abroad. Meanwhile there were American business-men seeking a predictable foreign policy, immigrants wishing to maintain connections, and missionaries undertaking organized "humanitarian" campaigns abroad by the 1890s. Yet, the US state and military likewise were mainly uninterested in expanding their role outside the Americas and the Pacific.[59] While Zionists were the most consistently outward-looking of the various strands of American Jewry, their activities stayed mostly in the realm of thought before the war, though Hadassah had begun to sponsor a maternal health mission to Palestine when the war broke out.[60] The AJC had some experience of diplomacy and relief, when it had aided Jews caught in the Balkan Wars in 1912–13 and lobbied the US government to abrogate a commercial treaty with Russia in 1911 on the basis of Russia discriminating against certain US passport holders (namely, Jews). Long before that, in 1878, American Jews helped put pressure on the Congress of Berlin, alongside their European Jewish peers, in favor of Jewish rights in Romania; mobilized to collect relief for victims of the Kishinev pogroms in 1903; and lent money to the Japanese government in 1904–5 in an effort to weaken the Russian government. American Jews also attempted to tame immigration by cooperating with Jewish organizations abroad, while meeting immigrants at ports and advocating for them in court since the 1890s.[61] When they undertook these diplomatic activities on behalf of Jews abroad, American Jews argued that they were already acting within the scope of America's attempt to safeguard rights internationally and were thus applying reli-gious and civil liberties fundamental to the United States.[62] American Jews still largely defaulted to Western and Central European Jewish leadership to build Jewish solidarity and guide Jewish life into modernity.

Thus, by the Great War, American Jews were no strangers to mobiliza-tion in the name of Jewish solidarity and rights abroad, but neither were they established leaders who had founded time-tested international insti-tutions. The exigencies of the war itself propelled tendencies that had been developing at home in America into the world, and quickly, fusing them with preexisting international networks of businessmen, missionar-ies, and immigrants. The war was the catalyst that rapidly set into motion the creation of a humanitarian architecture, congealing the American Jewish community around the specific aim of saving suffering Jews abroad.

American Jews Become International Humanitarians

As European destruction raged, US neutrality during most of the war provided an opportunity for Americans to play a key wartime role as humanitarians. Quasi-governmental humanitarian organizations, such as Herbert Hoover's American Relief Administration and the American Red Cross, and a plethora of civil society organizations, from the Quakers to Smith College to the Rockefeller Foundation to the Near East Relief, became involved. Within weeks of the war's outbreak, American Jews rushed to send relief for Jews caught in the crossfire of crumbling empires. To aid Jewish war sufferers specifically, American Jews founded the Joint Distribution Committee. To move aid in wartime, the subject of Chapter 1, American Jews worked with the US government, the largest neutral power. Cash aid traveled to Jews in war zones through the US diplomatic pouch and family connections. Preexisting Jewish organizations in Europe delivered the monies. The war promoted the growth of new American charitable organizations, and these organizations took their American visions abroad to help others, with the support of the US government, which had no programs like USAID in place at the time. American Jews joined America's expanding state at the critical juncture of the war, as they wandered into the center of American foreign policy and less-official humanitarian relief initiatives to carry out basic relief to Jews abroad. They became more "American," while simultaneously relying on the Jewish diasporic network and immigrant practices.

After the armistice on the Western Front in 1918, the United States provided major food aid programs across Central and Eastern Europe. The American Relief Administration (ARA) and the American Red Cross (ARC) rushed into these fragile new nation-states where violence was ongoing with programs aimed largely at children. They had several political goals beyond altruism, such as: getting rid of American corn that was stockpiled during the war; stabilizing Europe, especially in the face of Bolshevism; establishing American scientific practices as the international standard; opening Europe and the Middle East to US business; and keeping America engaged in the world as the US Congress rejected the League of Nations. As detailed in Chapter 2, the JDC jumped aboard other American emergency relief efforts, which helped it reach Poland and later Russia, where Jews were in greatest need. Deployed around Europe, American Jews distributed emergency food relief, medicines, sanitary supplies, and clothing during harsh winters.

The Great War precipitated America's expanding role in the world. While there was no Marshall Plan, this semi-official humanitarian effort was in some ways its first deployment. Much like American postwar diplomacy carried out by the ARA and through private loans with tacit and direct support from the US government, Jewish "diplomacy" was carried out by the JDC, a private humanitarian association. The JDC had to build partnerships with other American relief workers in order to gain access to territories still in violent flux, though these were always fragile. American Jews thereby led the way for American humanitarians of all kinds: as food remitters and as the first American organization in Soviet Russia. Yet, American Jewish relief paradoxically appeared at once as a peripheral humanitarian undertaking and as a central partner in the main humanitarian projects of the day.

By 1921, peace was returning to Europe and the League of Nations was formed in Geneva. The catastrophe seemed to have passed, and the JDC was ready to rehabilitate Europe's Jews before making a quick exit. That same year, however, would bring new crises, pushing Jewish security into the ever-receding distance. The other American organizations left Europe in the early 1920s, but the JDC stayed. The goals of these other organizations – to prevent revolution and feed children – were too short term and narrow for the JDC. More investment was needed to reach the goal of reconstructing Jewish life. While American Jews hoped that the situation for Jews elsewhere would improve, the economic boycott of Jews in Poland, the absence of treatment for Jews who contracted typhus, refugee expulsions, *numerus clausus* restrictions on Jews attending universities, and pogroms made it clear that it wouldn't. Unlike other organized Americans, American Jews could not ignore their duty to help their still-suffering Jewish kin.

There were four prongs to this longer-term, rehabilitative social welfare work, which began in earnest in 1921: refugee, medical, child, and economic work. In these arenas especially, Hias and Hadassah were active alongside the JDC. Immigrants in the United States continued to help their hometowns through landsmanshaftn. European Jewish organizations were starting to regain their footing in the postwar world as well, some rehabilitated through JDC support itself. The JDC continued to finance its own projects and those of other organizations, though gradually, Jewish American workers left Europe and turned over work to European Jewish organizations and local Jews, who typically had very different ideas about how to use and divide the money. Through these various social welfare projects, the international Jewish humanitarian effort became a permanent fixture of interwar Jewish life.

Chapter 3 is thus about refugee relief. Hias, the JDC, and a loose network of European organizations were invested in the cause. With Fridtjof Nansen at the center of the intergovernmental interwar refugee regime, and the United States closing its borders in an antisemitic campaign, Jewish organizations argued over the definitions of refugees and other migrants and devised solutions accordingly. Ultimately, the refugee crisis that had its origins in mass expulsions along the Eastern Front could not be solved and remained a stubborn human crisis across Europe that persisted into the 1930s.

Meanwhile, the JDC failed to coordinate effectively among the reactive, incoherent international health campaigns undertaken to prevent the spread of typhus. As explored in Chapter 4, reactions to this failure to make public health more sensitive to Jewish needs resulted in the establishment of autonomous Jewish health programs. Jewish social medicine thus flourished, with American Jews, including Hadassah, acting as the bridge from prewar years. These programs allowed Jews to reconstruct and even seek to improve their local status through incremental change, without state sanction. Furthermore, medicine was uncontroversial within Jewish communities and Jewish health professionals were relatively abundant. Unlike battling disease, which required governmental collaboration that was difficult to achieve, social medicine could work as a form of apolitical resistance to oppression.

The JDC cooperated with other American organizations to feed Jewish children after the armistice, more successfully than what was achieved in public health. But Jews were always concerned about the Jewish future, and these worries manifested in heated Eastern European Jewish debates over the right way to bring up Jewish children in the postwar economy. As explained in Chapter 5, American Jewish organizations could only achieve so much in terms of exporting Progressive child welfare schemes to Poland. Their vision of child welfare and self-help depended on an improving economy and the related ability of local Jews to absorb the initiatives begun by American Jews. When such improvements failed to materialize outside Palestine, the JDC felt morally obliged to continue its work, constructing a collective welfare system that in many ways aspired to that of a social welfare state.

The culmination of an ambitious and unique campaign to make humanitarianism self-sufficient, comprehensive reconstruction work became the focus of and heir to all the previous international Jewish social welfare work. Lastly, Chapter 6 considers this humanitarian response to Jewish impoverishment as a result of war. Superimposing American wealth and Progressivism onto longstanding Jewish self-help ideology, prewar vocational training, housing construction, and agricultural colonization were revived and expanded, especially in the Soviet Union. Crucially, this involved the creation of two American–Western European foundations to foster Jewish microlending and cooperative systems in Eastern Europe and Palestine. Jewish reconstruction sat somewhere between state social welfare and international development.

The dispersed Jewish people, who might have placed trust and hope in their new states and the League of Nations, turned to other options in the 1920s to bolster their security and survival. For the Jews, then, the Great War did not stop with the armistice, and the humanitarian response of American Jews, unlike other humanitarians who left Europe much earlier, continued in an unbroken chain far into "peacetime" and then back into war.[63] Jewish humanitarians looked inward and outward, backward and forward, locally and internationally. Jewish international humanitarianism would redefine many aspects of modern Jewish life across Europe and the Eastern Mediterranean, particularly those related to social and economic welfare, by replacing rights with food, education, healthcare, and loans. Over time, Jewish humanitarianism became rehabilitative in character, extending far beyond palliative relief. But it remained communally, not individually, oriented. It was not obvious to American Jews that the Minorities Treaties would fail to improve Jewish lives, or that the JDC, Hias, or Zionist organizations, despite their creativity, would be unable to resolve major crises, like refugee status and poverty. What they built used the resources of American empire and might have looked like pluralist Progressivism internationalized, but it was also defenseless and unable to transcend the nineteenth-century Jewish enlightenment "solutions" of self-help and intercession.

A worldwide financial depression and the rise of fascism radically reshaped the means and the priorities of Jewish philanthropy after 1929, where this narrative ends, and in short order would tragically expose its vulnerability. The crises that began in the Great War and upended Jewish life continued straight into the 1930s and into the Holocaust. Abraham Duker clearly understood that for Jews, the Great War had set in motion terrible trends that began to reveal their full horror in 1939.

International Jewish humanitarians only defined the work they did as "humanitarian" when it was carried out for non-Jews, or when it had to be explained to a non-Jewish audience. Viewing their work in terms of Jewish solidarity,[64] they were motivated by a sense of responsibility and duty toward Jews in need and by a sense of common fate. They would more likely have defined themselves as doing "Jewish philanthropy," which is itself a carefully chosen label, meant to evoke humanitarian principles through philanthropy and Jewish national solidarity without explicitly stating it. Jews did not imagine themselves crossing borders because they were Jews helping Jews. In reality, even though they were Jewish actors targeting Jewish populations, there were still many difficult borders to cross, and they shared the practices and activities of other supposedly "humanitarian" organizations, helping far-away people who were truly suffering. Like other forms of humanitarianism, Jewish humanitarianism was political. As Derek Penslar explains about what he calls "Jewish social policy": "Diplomacy and systematic social work were inseparable; the former sought to improve the political and economic environment in which ... Jews lived, but the latter aimed at improving the Jews themselves."[65] It was convenient for Jewish international social work to divorce itself from politics to act as a "neutral," benevolent force in modern Western society. However, Jewish humanitarianism was a coherent political and social system that was as impressive as it was vulnerable. Nationalism was not the motivating factor, Jewish solidarity was, but it served broadly nationalist ends. International Jewish humanitarianism was, in short, a project of collectivist Jewish welfarism.

The work of American Jewish international humanitarianism was deeply indebted to growing American influence in the world and to domestic developments in science and social work, but it was qualitatively different. While the JDC tried to be seen by outsiders as nonsectarian and very American, it was resolutely focused on assisting Jews. Furthermore, international Jewish humanitarianism involved active donor, humanitarian, and recipient participation in a responsive loop quite unlike other humanitarian arrangements, which were usually far more entwined in highly imbalanced imperial practices. Also, any general humanitarian work undertaken by the JDC was typically a bargain with other American humanitarians and the US government, struck to gain access to a particular Jewish population in need. The JDC exported American models of Progressive and business-oriented philanthropy to its target regions, because it was the American thing to do, and most of its leaders deeply believed in the correctness of this rationalized philanthropy. Yet these Jewish organizations struggled, worrying about antisemitism and the related fear that Jews would be left out of new state-building processes. Attempts to prevent and dispel antisemitism quietly underpinned nearly everything about Jewish relief and organizational practice. The entire Jewish humanitarian project worked to lower its own visibility, and this self-effacement has been carried forward in the historical literature, erroneously.

More concretely, American Jews made ample use of immigrant networks when it came to relief, through hometown societies, remittances, food packages, child sponsorship, and cooperatives. Innovation in remittance and food draft delivery were key to the JDC's operations, and convincing other American organizations to take up this model belonged to that emerging strategy. The ARA came to look like the JDC in its operational form, not just because it influenced the JDC but also because it was influenced by the JDC. American Jews were enthusiastic about their relief work, raising large sums of money and staffing an impressive organization. They were also noticeable in the field despite their American uniforms, attending always to local Jews. Compared to other American organizations, except for missionary associations, Jewish groups had far more experience in international philanthropy. Furthermore, Jewish individuals in America retained close ties to families and friends back in Europe, which gave Jewish organizations cultural expertise and firsthand knowledge of chaotic events, especially when compared to the many American organizations staffed by monolingual elites and demobilized soldiers.

The entire American philanthropic enterprise was steeped in the philosophy of pluralism, an organizing principle that could seemingly bridge the chasms within Jews and between Jews and their neighbors.[66] This American liberal vision could intersect with and make room for the idea of minority rights and Zionist nationalism centered around Palestine in a way that was palatable to liberal American Jews raised on guarantees of full civil rights. The JDC's unnamed operating principle, then, which it imposed on other organizations in New York and overseas, Jewish as well as non-Jewish, was to create democracy and a foundation of social good through pluralism. The JDC effectively deployed this strategy to maintain its monopoly on American Jewish relief while remaining somewhat open to contradictory voices: Every committee and organization was to have representatives in proportion to the population it represented. This representation called for defining people through collectivities to attain their representation, and definitions were typically made by an educated, objective leader. This vision of democracy contrasted, for example, with the American Jewish Congress, where mass meetings of Eastern European Jewish immigrants, mass membership, and direct referendum guided decision-making. JDC social workers traveled around Poland and elsewhere forming local committees of bourgeois, socialists, Zionists, Orthodox, and charitable leaders, often with apolitical local doctors directed to facilitate. This method was frequently met with resistance and protests of unfair treatment on the ground, which flabbergasted JDC leaders, because to them, this pluralistic inclusion signaled a healthy democracy. The ARA, too, strove for non-duplication of its own work by integrating representatives from various American international private associations and appointed representatives of local constituencies to its overseas committees, having also absorbed the idea that democracy, pluralism, and efficiency were intertwined. It was a philosophy that worked for Jews as they organized among themselves *and* it worked for relations with non-Jews. It allowed the JDC to take a seat at the proverbial ARA table, expecting parity alongside representatives of the ARC and YMCA, to ask for kosher packages and soup kitchens to be included in American relief, and to advocate for Jewish representatives on Polish food distribution committees.

American Jews were not the only humanitarians whose organizations acted "state-like." Great War–era humanitarian organizations routinely negotiated their own treaties, dispatched military officers, wore military uniforms, carried their own flags, received state funding, and rode on the coattails of their actual states. States sanctioned and relied on this assistance. Other organizations and colonized peoples tried to prove that they were capable of statehood by establishing that they could, in fact, successfully take on state-type projects requiring expertise, like creating social welfare and banking systems, dispatching medical missions, or, alternatively, by functioning as intermediaries among states, a space especially inhabited by American philanthropies whose social welfare knowledge was greater than that of government bureaucracies.[67] American Jewish organizations both drew on American state resources and amplified them while presenting themselves as quasi-representatives of America. They also acted aspirationally, demonstrating the successes and modernity of Jewish relief. Over the course of the 1920s, they moved from the first model toward the second, and from relief to rehabilitation. Intended first to provide palliative relief until the Minorities Treaties kicked in and Jews in the East could reestablish themselves as full citizens, American Jewish organizations responded to the continued precariousness of Jewish life by hesitatingly building a more extensive welfare program, drawing on models from American Progressivism and long-standing Jewish self-help ideologies. Jewish Americans would serve as a united "tax" base to make this all possible. In effect, this statist humanitarianism had to act as a substitute for the rights Jews hoped to receive. Although the Minorities Treaties faltered, their communitarian logic remained that of governments and humanitarian workers, including Jewish organizations that created a network of Jewish-only social services, but also organizations that claimed to be nonsectarian (meaning, they defaulted to serving the majority or the elite).

American Jewish humanitarian work abroad was one part of a broader network of Jewish self-government-like initiatives started by elites but involving ordinary Jewish people. In various ways and places, Jewish social organizations took on aspects of what was otherwise increasingly turned over to the purview of states in that era. The JDC and its offshoots resembled an American version of European Jewish organizations, which continued to express statist tendencies in a variety of ways. Supporters of YIVO (the Yiddish Scientific Institute in Vilna) from Jewish communities around the globe described how YIVO itself, rather than a government, served the Jews. Founded in 1925, YIVO used scholarship to construct a modern, national Jewish identity, not just to document Jewish culture.[68] In Weimar Germany, Jewish social work allowed Jews to expand the scope and authority of the Jewish community, just as social work became an instrument of the state, institutionalized in a new national German Jewish welfare organization.[69] In Palestine, Jews, partly in coordination with humanitarian organizations, formed their own government and concentrated on building a state. Here, Zionism was the engine on which the proto-Jewish state ran.[70] In wartime and post-1917 Russia, the main objective of Jewish health and other Jewish welfare organizations was to pursue Jewish autonomy and social reform through public welfare. They thereby became contenders for political power either in competition with or in an attempt to unite the parties of Jewish mass politics.[71]

During and after the Great War, American Jewish overseas philanthropy was a form of political internationalism connected to American soft diplomacy, which avoided the League of Nations, entangling alliances, or explicit articulations of a Jewish internationalism or nationalism. Yet, Jewish humanitarianism wandered into American foreign policy and empire building accidentally, due to contingencies and opportunities that appeared while navigating a wartime political landscape. Over the next fifteen years, American Jews built an unprecedented humanitarian infrastructure, in a long-term project to protect, rebuild, and remake Jewish life abroad. Trying to reconstruct Jewish life when nation-states became the new organizing principle of international society and Progressive reformers in the West focused on the creation of domestic social welfare programs, American Jewish organizations reluctantly built something resembling a private, non-territorial, diaspora social welfare state through a vast network of international development programs they installed abroad. To do this, they drew on models of Western European Jewish philanthropy and joined American humanitarian initiatives of the early interwar years. This statist, systematic international social work was suffused with American principles of pluralism, intended to promote democracy and Jewish rights through technocracy rather than diplomacy. American Jews went into the world as a humanitarian response to war, but ended up changing their own place in the world, forging a new American Jewish international leadership and tipping the Jewish future into an uneasy American embrace.

Sources and Methods

This study is grounded in empirical, multi-archival findings. While the archival research covers a range of organizations and individuals who acted across the United States, Europe, Russia, and the Eastern Mediterranean over a fifteen-year time frame, the records of the Joint Distribution Committee from 1914–32 form the core source base. Given their careful organization, detail, abundance, and pristine condition, these archives have been used in myriad projects; such richness reflects the ways that the JDC touched Jews the world over and linked them. I use the archives to turn an investigative lens on the practices, tropes, and motivations behind the humanitarian work itself. I have used many other archives to verify my findings, provide narrative perspectives absent from the bureaucratic organization of the JDC archives, explore relationships and trajectories, and understand the relationships of the JDC with its collaborators and competitors. Many organizational documents were mimeographed and can be found in duplicate in multiple collections, and I have defaulted to the JDC citation in these cases when possible.

This book is organized thematically and chronologically. Beyond the literatures on Jewish politics and philanthropy, humanitarianism, US foreign relations, international diplomacy, and European crisis, this study is immersed in new historiographical debates. These range from Progressivism, to histories of war and macroeconomics, the history of nutrition science and home economics, refugee and immigration studies, the history of medicine and science, the history of childhood and child welfare, and to the study of cooperative movements and international development practices. In each chapter, I draw mainly on Jewish perspectives, framing them within their broader thematic and multiple national and international contexts. Along the way, these chapters demonstrate the way in which all these organizations were only the sum of their ever-changing parts; how ideas, practices, and prejudices were disarticulated and rearticulated as they were exported and transplanted into different contexts; and how these actors tried to prevent and cope with antisemitism. They also show the adaptation of international Jewish humanitarianism against a backdrop of war, revolution, and reconstruction – rapid and violent social, economic, and political change. As such, Jewish humanitarianism evolved from fact-finding and channeling funds across lines in wartime, to emergency relief on European soil after the armistice, to a long-term rehabilitative program through the 1920s.

From New York, this study extends to three main theaters of relief: East Central Europe, Russia, and the Eastern Mediterranean. The war experience and aftermath of empire explain how this trio of regions dominated the operation of American Jewish humanitarianism over an extended period. Although the borders of these three theaters changed, it was within each region that the JDC developed programs and attempted to scale them up – it could never find a way to integrate these regions; there always had to be three approaches, including three political networks, three logistics networks, and three sets of workers. Within each region, there was always a hub: Poland (Warsaw) was always at the center of East Central Europe, Ukraine in Russia, and Palestine (Jerusalem) in the Eastern Mediterranean. After 1918, American Jewish institutions also maintained a presence in key Western and Central European cities (Paris, Vienna, and Berlin), which in the JDC's case could stand in for New York or act as a relay station. This book as a whole thus shifts back and forth between America (New York), Western Europe, and the three theaters of relief. This research, which illumines organizations and individuals crisscrossing the Jewish world, from Paris to Poland to Ukraine to Palestine, allows for comparisons across Western Europe, Eastern Europe, and the Eastern Mediterranean, putting Palestine and philanthropic exertions in that land into the context of philanthropic patterns elsewhere.

This history is *both* a *Jewish* intervention into the field of humanitarian history *and* a rethinking of the master narrative of humanitarianism *via* the Jews. This monograph centers Jews as humanitarian actors, showing Jews acting as Jews, confronting and reshaping state power. Though my narrative starts to rub up against antisemitic tropes regarding Jews and money, Jews as an international cabal, Jews holding multiple loyalties, and Jews as rootless cosmopolitans, it of course shows them to be just that: antisemitic tropes. If the prototype for studying Jews and humanitarianism has been that of refugees (acted on) and advocates (acting on from afar), I am pushing well past that dichotomy to demonstrate the real experience of Jewish aid delivery and humanitarian–victim relations. My refusal to universalize this story beyond comparison and context is a crucial feature. I hope my book will act as a model from which other scholars can on their own unsettle white, ecumenical Christonormative humanitarianism from its supposed peripheries, using a completely different approach than a global, postcolonial history would, but with a similar result.[72] Forms of humanitarianism in history were a primary political tool of diaspora and non-state transnational politics, both within Europe, and beyond it. Issues of refugees, human rights, relief and advocacy work, global inequality, and interethnic violence are central to the new international history. In this formative era, the Jewish experience was both exceptional and paradigmatic.

1 War Sufferers
Moving Money in War

The creation of the Joint Distribution Committee for relief to Jews overseas in 1914 marked not just the opening of transnational, institutionalized American Jewish philanthropy, but also a new and unprecedented form of American Jewish politics and diplomacy involving the State Department and the US military. Sending funds and individuals into war zones required diplomatic sophistication, especially after the United States entered the war in 1917. American Jewish aid was delivered before and after the United States became a belligerent, even though many recipients remained behind enemy lines and despite the British blockade. While states at war permitted international aid for desperate civilian populations, private organizations and neutral states had to navigate these treacherous waters and faced criticism at home and abroad.[1] The JDC and the Hebrew Sheltering and Immigrant Aid Society (Hias) carried out their overseas actions by maintaining a dual identity: civilian neutrality rooted in a Jewish philanthropic tradition and an increasing connectedness to US war operations. The story of American Jewish relief illuminates the complexity and limits of building and maintaining international networks of private actors in wartime to sustain beleaguered populations. Jewish relief organizations operated within a highly charged political environment characterized by the United States' march toward war, by state-sanctioned anti-Jewish violence along the Eastern Front and in the Eastern Mediterranean, and by internal dissent among Jews over the control of relief funds. Still, they struggled to carry on their tasks as advocates and relievers of Jews in Central and Eastern Europe and the Eastern Mediterranean. This story ties the rise of American Jewry within international Jewish politics to the rise of America as a global power during the Great War. It explains how the bitterly contested nature of American Jewish relief among Jews was connected to these shifting dynamics.

From the start, the war changed America, and it changed American Jews. This chapter first explains how American Jews mobilized a humanitarian response in reaction to the war. Gathering together under the banner of war relief, American Jews threw together "not a carefully planned organization, but ... what may be termed a fortuitous organization":[2] the JDC.

The second part of this chapter shows how, during the war years in which America remained a neutral power, the JDC established three "theaters" of relief. These were to form a foundational organizing principle of relief at least until 1929. At the start of the war, these theaters were the German and Austro-Hungarian Empires and their occupied lands, the Russian Empire and its occupied territories, and the Ottoman Empire. Making the most of American neutrality, the JDC reached Jews across Europe and the Eastern Mediterranean by transferring funds to Jewish organizations located in the major cities of the various empires at war. These groups then distributed cash to Jews behind their respective war fronts. Navigating the war overseas brought American Jewish leaders into contact with the US state apparatus and the growing array of private American overseas philanthropy. The geography of Jewish relief was intimately connected to empire, war, and the war's operational theaters. This explains some of the patterns and assumptions that undergirded Jewish international philanthropy throughout the twentieth century.

American Jewish relief efforts built upon preexisting and sophisticated, yet deeply threatened, philanthropic networks spanning Western and Central Europe and East Central Europe, Russia, and the Eastern Mediterranean. The wartime reordering of and reliance on a preexisting diaspora network was quite unlike the American Red Cross's organization of relief, which employed American medics to provide direct medical aid to soldiers on the ground, and only in the Western war zones. The JDC was instead in the company of other American associations that provided relief to civilians.[3] In scale, ambition, modern sophistication, and institutional endurance, however, the JDC outpaced other American organizations responding to the civilian crisis of war. The JDC straddled and embraced this inherent ambiguity of being one of the most prominent mainstream American philanthropic organizations, even as its non-state, diaspora-defined, Eastern-facing characteristics resembled a particularist interest group.

The third part of this chapter delves more deeply into the distinctive features of American Jewish relief, especially the aggregation of the individual input of many Jews, allowing for wide participation, if not leadership, in the project. Since American Jewish organizations focused on keeping Jewish communities and relatives connected across the Atlantic, American Jewish relief was more than the addition of an American component onto existing modern philanthropic institutions and networks. The connecting project sought to restore, en masse, the fragile, individual links between American immigrants and their loved ones in the old country and to channel financial remittances through a central organization during the war. The difficult work of relief, in an environment where the rules were always changing, made the engagement of a broad base of Jews essential to the effective distribution of aid. The JDC's entanglement with Jewish politics and the constant attacks it experienced from donors and recipients pushed it to a pluralist, carefully circumscribed receptivity to a broad range of Jewish political ideologies and movements.

The last part of the chapter shows that US entry into the war solidified the new American Jewish international leadership, ensuring a future for Jewish overseas relief with enduring ties to the US government. The theaters of relief had already congealed. The primary task of American Jewish relief efforts was now to find ways of working around the existing relief system once the United States was at war. Ad hoc methods and familial networks from the period of US neutrality gave way to close cooperation with the US State Department. Superficially, remarkably little changed for Jews when the United States joined the conflict, but the shift that American Jews made toward cooperation with the US state apparatus was not insignificant. Rather, this Americanization of Jewish relief that occurred as America declared war signaled the start of a sustained closeness between American Jewish institutions, the US government, and international affairs.

During the war, the JDC dispersed about $13.75 million across Europe and the Eastern Mediterranean to Jewish war sufferers.[4] American Jewish war relief organizations branded their aid as "American" to deflect antisemitism. They also sought to keep Jewish dissent at bay by appearing neutral and benevolent, while maintaining American support for their efforts. They did so at the risk of refusal or confiscation of aid by belligerents. The relative success of the JDC's relief efforts in Palestine, compared to Eastern Europe, confirms that it was able to carry out its actions further in places where the United States had the greatest interests and diplomatic presence. This demonstrates both the advantage of acting in concert with the US government and the limits that American Jewish relief encountered when attempting to undertake relief where the American state was not willing to venture. Furthermore, wartime offered the JDC the opportunity to develop ways of managing and responding to Jewish dissent both at home and abroad while appearing externally American. The work of sending individual relief and general relief, along with multiple constituent fundraising agencies, made the JDC a powerful, hybrid organization that blended typical models of diaspora charity, traditional Jewish charity, and Progressive American humanitarian relief.

Humanitarian Mobilization

The Great War changed America long before America officially entered it. The conflict transformed America's relations with the world and upgraded its position in the international hierarchy. It contributed to the growth of the American state in American society and provided new opportunities for individuals and organizations. America's businessmen, immigrants, engineers, the faithful, and social workers were suddenly called upon to address escalating misery across Europe. Coalescing under Wilson, many Progressive leaders turned their reformist habits outward in response to war. Uniting amid crisis overseas, compassionate Americans put to use abroad the latest developments at home. Humanitarianism became more secular and state oriented as American Progressivism became more international. American neutrality presented an occasion to spread the best elements of Progressive America to the world.

At the beginning of the war, debate simmered in the American Jewish community over the meaning of Germany's and Russia's involvement. The response of American Jews, who formed the largest and wealthiest Jewish community in a neutral country, suddenly mattered for Jews everywhere. Some Jewish leaders publicly declared pacifism or neutrality. While Judah Magnes never strayed from this position, most maintained it only when America officially remained neutral. For uptown German Jewish bankers accustomed to running and financing American Jewish affairs, this was a time of uncertainty and personal crisis. European associates needed their American capital. Jacob Schiff and others could not hide their pro-German, anti-Russian sentiments, and Kuhn Loeb would not underwrite the Allied cause. America's entry into the war against Germany became a liability for German Jewish banks in America, which were suddenly seen as potential internal enemies. Kuhn Loeb threw itself behind the American war effort; at least the United States was not a partner of Tsarist Russia after the revolution.[5] For the first time, American Jews called for the creation of a broad-based institution to provide relief abroad. This was in part because sustaining the coordination that had become standard among major Jewish communities in Europe and the United States was impossible.[6]

The American Jewish Committee immediately responded to appeals by appropriating $100,000, and in late October 1914, at the Conference of National Jewish Organizations, it called for unity "given the serious exigencies confronting the Jewish people" due to the war in Europe. "We have the opportunity now for the first time of having an organization of American Jewry—an American Jewish community," said Judah Magnes.[7] Working hard at making "an American Jewish community" via the New York Kehillah, Magnes instantly saw the potential in a new overseas relief organization, not only for what it could do for suffering Jews abroad but also for how it would rally American Jews around the concept of Jewish solidarity in a time of need. But the Central Relief Committee, created by the Union of Orthodox Congregations, pre-empted the American Jewish Committee on October 4, 1914, as the first to formally organize in response to calls for relief. Central Relief planned to organize and fundraise among Orthodox Jews, building on a tradition of charity. The American Jewish Relief Committee (AJRC), which was formed in November 1914, functioned as a relief–fundraising offshoot of the American Jewish Committee. It was populated by the same individuals and attracted the same uptown donors. After several meetings that spawned many emergency organizations, the JDC was established. Later, labor unions and Jewish socialists formed the People's Relief Committee, which became affiliated with the JDC in autumn 1915. Although American Jewish women had expertise and leadership that was at least equal to men at the local and national level in social work, immigrant welfare, and nursing – the main requirements for international humanitarian work – Jewish men blocked the qualified leaders of the National Council of Jewish Women from joining.[8] The Joint Distribution Committee of American Funds for the Relief of Jewish War Sufferers was to act as its name suggested: as the joint distributing agent of these three constituent American fundraising committees to Jewish victims of the war. It did not take long before this tripartite organization became known as the American Jewish Joint Distribution Committee, or "the JDC" in America and "the Joint" abroad.[9]

It was not inevitable that a distinctly Jewish organization would arise from the expanding ranks of American international humanitarian organizations. Alongside the American Jewish Joint Distribution Committee, the Great War called into being the American Relief Administration, the Near East Relief, and the American Friends Service Committee, and allowed other organizations to expand their reach, like the American Red Cross, the YMCA, and Hias.[10] World War I put sectarian fundraising organizations in second place, as hyper-patriotism emphasized the importance of a single "American" identity.[11] Scientific rationalization and greater state involvement shifted American associational life away from separate organizations for different religions or ethnic groups. In a telling conversation, echoed by many others, JDC leaders Felix Warburg and Louis Marshall debated whether there ought to be an independent Jewish sectarian organization. Warburg worried that the American Red Cross might see a separate organization as an excuse to exclude Jewish sufferers in its own plans and felt it would not be wise for Jews to be the first religious denomination to start a relief fund. Marshall countered: "All these non-sectarian, non-partisan dispensations of charity sound very well, but it only means that we receive nothing from the other altruists, but are giving up the money which of right belongs to those who have a distinct right to appeal to us, namely, our own co-religionists."[12] Even if there was minimal threat of anti-Jewish violence at home, American Jews saw antisemitism's dangerous reality overseas and called for a separate approach. Though other "sectarian" (defined along religious lines) and otherwise community-oriented associations of all stripes did arise,[13] the Joint remained uniquely active and well funded, and continued its work for much longer. American Jews contributed to general relief campaigns as well as Jewish ones and made the case for an overseas American philanthropy that was diverse and yet united: pluralistic, in other words.

The New York leadership of the American Jewish Joint Distribution Committee was mostly comprised of the uptown crowd. The men at its decision-making core in New York City were simultaneously associated with the patrician American Jewish Committee. Several leaders within the JDC, or those closely connected to them, were longtime friends and supporters of President Wilson who had campaigned for him as early as his run for New Jersey governor, which made possible close cooperation with the Wilson administration.[14] These prominent men, including Felix Warburg, Louis Marshall, Jacob Schiff, Cyrus Adler, Judah Magnes, Stephen Wise, and Herbert Lehman, appointed themselves the new stewards of Jewish philanthropy in a time of war. The Joint pulled in other wealthy, well-connected, or rising Jews, like Ambassadors Henry Morgenthau and Abram Elkus, some of whom had not been especially involved in Jewish life.

Among the key individuals comprising this leadership was Louis Marshall, a renowned lawyer and the man behind the American Jewish Relief Committee, respected for his diplomacy but perceived as an autocrat who refused to relinquish personal control over American Jewish affairs.[15] There was also the esteemed but aging Jacob Schiff, a leading banker at Kuhn, Loeb & Company and a philanthropist, committed to using his ample wealth to secure the safety of Jews around the world. Fiercely anti-Russian, he bankrolled war loans to Japan during the Russo–Japanese war.[16] He sat prominently on the advisory board of Hias as a longtime champion of controlled immigration.[17] Young Herbert and

Figure 1.1 Painting of the JDC founders. This 1929 painting by Geza
Fischer depicts the JDC's founders meeting in 1918 in Felix Warburg's
office in New York's Financial District. Louis Marshall and Felix
Warburg (left), and Jacob Schiff (right) are closest to the viewer.
Herbert Lehman, Albert Lucas, Boris Bogen, Sholem Asch, Harriet
Lowenstein, Isidore Hershfield, Aaron Teitelbaum, Israel Friedlaender,
and Cyrus Adler are included (left to right).
(JDC, Artifact_00397)

Arthur Lehman, successive treasurers of the JDC, also from a banking
family, would go on to become noteworthy figures in US government
and at the United Nations. At the helm of the JDC sat Felix Warburg.
Felix, the brother of the great German Jewish Hamburg–based banker,
Maximilian Warburg, married Jacob Schiff's daughter and into the Kuhn
Loeb bank. Warburg should be given "chief credit for building a strong
and lasting machine out of such unlikely material," for his ability to
persuade people to work together, famously making them ashamed to
quarrel when there was important work to be done.[18] He devoted more
time to his philanthropic endeavors than to working in the bank, and the
JDC became his "all-consuming passion."[19] Warburg kept a low profile
by staying far from controversy, and has barely been recognized

historically, despite his deep involvement in many Jewish and main-stream philanthropies of his time.

Headquartered in New York, the uptown leadership of the JDC did not represent the entire organization. The JDC had professional leaders in the field – Boris Bogen, Bernard Kahn, Frank Rosenblatt, Harriet Lowenstein, James Rosenberg, and Joseph Rosen – who made recommendations on how to allocate money. The JDC employed young social workers, engineers, doctors, nurses, rabbis, labor leaders, and military officers who spread out across East Central Europe and Ukraine, each having enormous responsibility in supervising relief over vast tracts of land in volatile places. Under them were local committees organizing the distribution of aid, and the New York relatives of members of those local committees, who weighed in on the pages of the Yiddish press and through numerous small donations. In America, a largely volunteer and women-driven fundraising organization developed across the country's Jewish communities. Its stable of young clerks were overseen by fundraising directors in New York. At the helm of New York fundraising sat yet another professional social worker, an immigrant from Lithuania who soon married Louis Marshall's daughter: Jacob Billikopf.[20] Women occasionally played a larger role in overseas activities, usually due to close ties with JDC men or professional experience that could not be overlooked; women served as accountants, social workers, nurses, and child welfare advocates.

The JDC formed a larger umbrella in that it consistently worked to pull *landsmanshaftn* (hometown associations) into the organization rather than allowing them to operate independently, which they still did, even after the JDC set up a special department for channelling *landsmanshaft* efforts.[21] Still, the JDC was adept at facilitating limited Jewish pluralism within its own organization while running an operation with just a handful of primary decision-makers. Usually described as oligarchic and plutocratic, despite its complex organizational structure that reached into local communities, JDC leadership was responsive to outside pressures and to its own professionals' advice. During the war and in the years that followed, the relationship between the central distributing organization and its constituent fundraising organizations in the United States changed, becoming more centralized and similar to the leadership and decision-making norms of just one of its constituent organizations, the American Jewish Relief Committee, which also happened to contribute the largest dollar amount to the JDC.

The three JDC constituent organizations began raising funds, using methods familiar to other American relief organizations. In fact, separate fundraising networks remained what distinguished the constituent organizations from one another. By the end of 1915, over $1.5 million had been collected to relieve war sufferers, and a series of mass meetings raised even more funds. Wealthy American Jews set examples by publicly announcing donations and matching those of others. Local committees in cities with Jewish communities held their own fundraisers and strove to meet quotas under the guidance of the JDC, eventually contributing far more than New York Jews.[22] These local efforts were often driven by networks of women and had a major impact toward institutionally and locally organizing Jews via philanthropy. The constituent organizations of the JDC also appealed to their own membership base; the AJRC received money from a few large donors on its own committee, while Central Relief collected in synagogues and People's Relief worked via door-to-door campaigns and button sales. President Wilson and the US Senate designated January 27, 1916 Jewish Relief Day.[23] Fundraising campaigns were designed to raise the largest possible amounts but also to ensure that tensions among local relief committees or the three constituents of the JDC would not be inflamed.[24] On behalf of the AJRC, Jacob Billikopf designed a remarkable fundraising strategy that guided the JDC through its first fifteen years.[25] In this way, the JDC brought unprecedented donations from Jews living across the United States, including philanthropists, professionals, immigrants, Orthodox Jews, laborers, women, and small business owners.

Like other American organizations, American Jews, following the State Department's lead, tried to separate relief from politics. While the distinction was superficial it made relief work easier to undertake. The stark gendering that occurred when Jewish women's organizations were sidelined, told to defer to the principle of unity and to put the community's interests ahead of women, was a clear indicator that Jewish humanitarianism was about political power within the Jewish world and its representation to the rest of the world.[26] The relationship between the American Jewish Committee and the JDC was quite unlike peer European organizations, which had long mixed diplomatic and philanthropic functions. The difference was more a question of membership composition than anything else. If the relief effort was going to bring in a wide variety of Jews, which was crucial for success, and if it was going to finally organize the American Jewish community behind a common goal, as Magnes and other Jewish leaders dreamed, it could not simply reproduce the patrician structure of the American Jewish Committee. American Jewish Committee men knew this from the start, and by acknowledging the need for a separate, "joint" institution, they more or less maintained their grip on the institution. They called for unity and centralization, much like other American groups that sought to avoid duplication and waste.

As much as the JDC sought to act as American Jewry's only humanitarian organization, it lacked the authority to enforce this. That left other organizations and individuals to seek alternatives when dissatisfied. They presented the JDC with the choice to absorb them, change its ways, or allow them to compete. The American Jewish Relief Committee retained a central position and became indistinguishable from the JDC, yet People's Relief and Central Relief remained an active part and consistently pushed the JDC to include their representatives on committees and as overseas delegates, and to give traditional Jews and workers a fair deal abroad. Furthermore, other American Jewish organizations continued to operate outside the realm of the JDC, pushing it to react. Despite organizational factionalization along many lines, including by geographical origin, political ideology, gender, cultural and religious values, and mission, individuals who engaged in the conversation around Jewish relief, at times acrimoniously, frequently crossed these divisions. It was often social welfare for the good of Jews abroad that induced individuals to step out of their rigid camps and cross into the orbit of the JDC, bringing their ideological position to a discussion of social welfare, or minimizing their own jockeying for power within the world of Jewish politics in favor of the common good. The JDC was a mirror of American Jewish politics, reflecting mostly the prettiest parts.

The war also propelled nascent movements within American Jewry that looked to open up politics and philanthropy to recent immigrants, arguing that business elites should not be the sole representatives of American Jews. The rival American Jewish Congress, seeking to democratize Jewish representation to the non-Jewish world and internal Jewish communal decision-making, also arrived on the scene thanks to opportunities presented by the Great War. A seemingly innocuous word, "congress," indicated a radical commitment to broadening the scope of participants in American Jewish politics, mainly to include immigrant voices. The American Jewish Congress elected American Jewish delegates to join an unrecognized Jewish delegation at the Paris Peace Conference, led by the same patrician leaders at the head of the American Jewish Committee and the JDC. Yet, the Congress Movement did not disappear after Paris and, with Rabbi Stephen Wise as its staunch leader, called upon the JDC to provide solutions beyond short-term, palliative relief to Jewish war sufferers.[27]

American Zionists, while not part of the structure of the JDC, were a major part of the relief effort, especially when it came to Palestine. There were Zionists in all three of the JDC's constituent organizations, making them an integral part of the JDC, which put Palestine high on the JDC's agenda. Shape-shifting Zionist organizations also sat outside the JDC, including the Provisional Executive Committee for General Zionist Affairs, the Federation of American Zionists (which became the Zionist Organization of America after the war), the Palestine Economic Corporation, and Hadassah, the Women's Zionist Organization. The war, the Balfour Declaration, and the British Mandate in Palestine transformed the Zionist Movement. Just as it was difficult for European Jewish organizations to manage relief efforts in Eastern Europe during or right after the war, the Zionist Movement experienced a shift toward American leadership once the war broke out. Hadassah, and later, the Palestine Economic Corporation, concentrated on practical social and economic interventions rather than high politics in their effort to build a Jewish homeland in Palestine, much like the Joint Distribution Committee.[28] Thus, the JDC not only funded projects in Palestine, but after the war, it directly funded Hadassah to carry out projects autonomously, rather than sending its own duplicate relief workers. An enduring need to cooperate, despite ongoing tensions over the relative needs of Jews in Palestine versus Eastern Europe, led to experiments in united fundraising for overseas needs throughout the 1920s, including the successful 1929 Allied Jewish Campaign.[29]

Thanks to the Great War, Hias found itself operating independently and internationally. Its leadership overlapped with that of the People's Relief and Central Relief, but it filled a niche in the controversial area of migration, where the JDC had no desire to act. No longer content to wait for immigrants at Ellis Island, it set up bureaus along the West Coast to receive incoming immigrants who had crossed Siberia, and moved operations to Poland, the source of emigration after the war.[30] While independent and drawing on a large membership pool for funding, it operated in the shadow of the more powerful JDC and was subject to the whims and financial hardships of its members. Still, Hias and landsmanshaft leaders found that their immigrant ethnicity was just that – immigrant-based, and thus, situational. The delegates they sent to the old world, often poor and struggling in New York, were received as celebrities and rich American philanthropists when they came "home" with aid.[31] They could command power "at home" while abroad, and had the advantage of seeming less aloof, bureaucratic, and clinical in their humanitarian efforts than the larger, more centralized JDC.

These organizations drew on coexisting and sometimes overlapping strains in nineteenth- and early twentieth-century American society and foreign policy. They were also inspired by Western social trends originating outside the United States to build their international organizations. American Progressivism and domestic social welfare concerns, in particular, found their way into humanitarian impulses abroad. They all benefited greatly from the 1917 tax law amendment increasing incentives for rich people to donate to philanthropy, a breakthrough that allowed them to collect unprecedented sums in the millions of dollars with comparative ease.[32] The rapid development of various branches of science, technology, and management, in lockstep with Progressive activity, meant that American organizations were keen to incorporate and experiment with new rational methods in their work overseas as well as at home.[33]

By focusing on a crisis beyond America's domestic space, American Jews discovered a coherent Jewish solidarity. American Jewish institutions went global, and entirely new ones emerged. These institutions are all still around today, showing remarkable resilience and representing some of America's oldest organizations in their fields. Coordinated American Jewish foreign relations represented a major break with the prewar American Jewish past, where facing the world was ephemeral. Furthermore, not unlike Jews who had built great Jewish–French, Jewish–British, Jewish–German, and Jewish–Austrian organizations and who now signed up for military service in France, England, German, and Austria, American Jews were anxious to prove themselves in mainstream society and to promote the American way outside America.[34] This was also the moment when American Jewish leadership turned its efforts away from Americanizing the Jewish immigrant to Americanizing the Jew, wherever that Jew could be reached.[35] American Jews joined America's expanding state at the critical juncture of World War I, participating in the soft diplomacy of humanitarian relief before American officially entered the war. They became part of American foreign relations and American empire, and in so doing, they became more American. But they were also still distinctively Jews, more tightly knit and organized than ever before.

Theaters and Operational Realities

In the years of American neutrality, Jewish Americans largely drew on existing, largely informal Jewish networks that stretched across the old country through family, professional, and philanthropic ties. The JDC entrusted money it raised from Jews across America to partners in Europe and the Eastern Mediterranean, despite ever-shifting territorial divisions and waves of population displacement. As these transatlantic pathways materialized to send money to Jews in the war zones along the fronts, from behind the lines rather than across them, three distinct, stable theaters of relief developed: in German-occupied Poland and the Baltic, an offshoot of the Hilfsverein der Deutschen Juden in Berlin, called the Jüdische Hilfskomite für Polen; in Russia, the Central Jewish Committee for the Relief of Sufferers of War (EKOPO) based in Petrograd; and in Palestine, which was still part of the Ottoman Empire, the American Relief Fund for Palestine.

I extend the word "theater," used in connection with logistical operations and violent drama in combat zones, to its humanitarian corollary. The drama of the humanitarian theater persisted long after peace treaties were signed, as humanitarians sought to combat remaining human, infrastructural, and political damage. The Great War and the Jewish humanitarian response to it thus created a new Jewish geography with a new internal, international hierarchy not just for the war era itself, but also for the remainder of the twentieth century.

Sending American Jewish aid to Berlin, Petrograd, and Palestine required carefully navigating war alliances and blockades. Developing a good working relationship with the US State Department became crucial to American Jews. On their own, Jewish overseas networks could not cross the hurdles created by war. Fortunately for them, the US government freely cooperated with the JDC and its partner organizations in facilitating the international transfer of funds and accompanying instructions. Almost all correspondence between American Jews and their European recipients moved through the diplomatic pouch of the US State Department – in particular, instructions for how the relief committees on the ground should use the money they were receiving.

Cooperation with the US government had its limits, which had to do with America's own geopolitical considerations as a neutral power in the war. In particular, the US government deferred to the British government's embargo on the importation of foodstuffs into the Central Powers, despite sustained lobbying by the JDC and Polish Americans.[36] In contrast, when it came to getting aid to Jews in Palestine, the JDC established a strong relationship with the US State Department and its consular officials in Constantinople, Jerusalem, and Alexandria, and were able to send material goods there. It probably helped that before and during the war, the Ottoman Empire was the only state to host an American ambassador who was Jewish; that American religious and business interests were growing in the Middle East; that Palestine had accessible port cities on a navigable sea; and that the Armenian genocide haunted the American conscience. Still, the JDC remained hopeful that it could do more for Jews in Eastern Europe. Although American Jews may have organized themselves in response to appeals from Jews in Palestine, really, the "first purpose for which [the JDC] was created [was] Poland and Russia."[37] Basing its efforts on the example of close ties between the State Department, its European embassies and consulates, and Herbert C. Hoover's privately managed Commission for Relief in Belgium (CRB), the JDC regularly sought greater American governmental support to enable it to send material goods, especially food, directly to Polish Jews.[38] In fact, the JDC made every exertion to cooperate with and push the Rockefeller Foundation, Polish relief societies, and the Red Cross to replicate the CRB's successes in Poland, but the US government was only willing to provide limited support, and these efforts never came to fruition.

Tolerant as the American state was of American Jewish humanitarian initiative, it was not prepared to take risks or invest major resources in Jewish relief. The historical record clearly indicates that political expediency has always been a major factor in determining when states take, or fail to take, humanitarian action. A combination of the following reasons explains why the US government gave comparatively little support to Polish relief: The need for Polish relief was publicly established later than Belgian relief and thus from the outset faced more wartime restrictions; other American organizations did not want to involve themselves in the sectarian and nationalist complexities of the Eastern Front; the US government could not persuade the British government that it was logistically possible for material goods or large sums of money to reach Poland without confiscation by Britain's enemies; the Western Allies did not want to attract attention to Allied Russian atrocities in Poland by pointing out similar German outrages; and the US diplomatic presence in Eastern Europe was much weaker than in the Ottoman Empire and did not include officials who forcefully advocated for humanitarian relief.[39] Seen in this light, it is not surprising that the JDC's efforts to send food or American relief workers were largely unsuccessful outside Palestine. It was easier and of obvious political benefit in America to assist Belgians in Belgium or needy populations in Palestine.

Limited to sending money, the JDC utilized preexisting Jewish philanthropic networks in Europe, rather than depending on US consulates or sending their own American Jewish representatives for distribution. Since relief work exacerbated ideological ferment among Ashkenazi Jews, the JDC and Hias never fully trusted their Jewish organizational partners in Europe to distribute aid effectively and fairly, yet had no choice but to rely on them in the moment. Meanwhile, Jews on the ground were asked to tolerate not only the depravities of war, but also a new dependence on their American brethren and their interlocutors, on American terms, despite the limited nature of this relief.

Map 1.1 Map of Jewish homelands in peril in the First World War

To the Central Powers

Soon after the war began in Europe, Germany occupied territory that had been part of the Russian Empire, including Poland as well as the Baltics. Austria-Hungary also pushed eastward, occupying more of Poland and Galicia. The Central Powers failed to provide sufficient food in their occupied war zones. German occupiers in Poland inflamed the local situation by trying to win Jews to their side, providing them with immediate freedoms, but also turning Christian Poles against Polish Jews. Germany forcibly deported laborers to Germany, including Polish and Lithuanian Jews. In Germany and Austria, the presence of Eastern European Jewish refugees and laborers in major cities, the contact German soldiers had with Jews in their Eastern borderlands, and competition over scarce resources that were perceived as controlled by Jewish middlemen stoked antisemitic sentiments.[40]

The suffering of civilians in Poland and Austrian Galicia presented an obstacle for outside relief. Hypothetically, the United States' neutrality allowed for pumping aid to civilians in Poland. However, early into the war, the US State Department made clear that it would only passively support relief to the Eastern Front, citing its "very strict rule that the Government of the United States could not act as the medium for the transfer of money from the United States to the subjects or citizens of the nations now at war; nor could it undertake the task of distributing relief among the civil population." Instead, the State Department encouraged transfers through private banks.[41]

The Joint Distribution Committee quickly found a way to effect such private transfers: It would send funds to Jews living in Berlin, who could then distribute the money where it was needed in now-German territory in Warsaw and the Ober Ost further north. Those same German Jews would also forward part of that money to Vienna for the Israelitische Allianz zu Wien (hereafter, the Allianz) to use throughout Austria-Hungary. From Berlin, and then Vienna and Warsaw, money could reach the majority of Jews living in the zones occupied by the Central Powers. At the peak of German occupation, American Jewish funds reached 252 cities and towns in Poland and Lithuania.[42] The JDC sent nearly $1.6 million to Jews in Austria-Hungary and over $2.5 million to Polish Jews from January 1915 to July 1917. On the other hand, the American Jewish Committee calculated that the many American dollars being transferred to Poland represented "less than one cent a day per needy Jew."[43] Aware that they were far from meeting the need created by the humanitarian disaster, JDC leadership sought at least to ensure accountability of the Jewish representatives charged with distribution, to make the process as "American" as possible, and to expand the nature of relief in Poland to include foodstuffs and medical supplies.

The Hilfsverein der Deutschen Juden (hereafter, Hilfsverein) was the obvious, reliable choice for the JDC to seek out in Germany. An organization of well-to-do, acculturated Jews in Berlin, the Hilfsverein was a model for the American Jewish Committee. Maximilian Warburg, Felix Warburg's brother and owner of the M. M. Warburg & Co. Bank based in Hamburg, was part of the Hilfsverein.[44] Even while living in America and chairing the JDC, Felix remained a partner in M. M. Warburg until 1917.[45]

On January 1, 1915, Max appealed to Felix from Berlin, informing him that 2.5 million Jews in Poland needed relief, that the Hilfsverein was considering a special mission to Poland, and that "we need above all funds for distribution and foodstuffs," and urging Felix to respond quickly.[46] The AJRC sent $45,000 on January 9 to the Hilfsverein, and on January 19, cabled Max to release the funds for German-occupied Poland.[47] To effect this international transfer, the bank Felix had married into, Kuhn Loeb, New York, credited funds raised by the American Jewish relief organizations on behalf of the JDC directly to M. M. Warburg & Co. Max then turned over the funds to the Hilfsverein. Felix not only leveraged his personal financial connections to facilitate the distribution of JDC funds, but also sent notes through the diplomatic pouch of the US State Department to Max explaining how the money was to be used and forwarded. Besides taking care of the banking end, Max Warburg regularly sent back information and requests to the JDC concerning what was needed in Poland. This relationship remained essentially unchanged during the entire period of American neutrality.[48]

The arrangement between the JDC and the State Department to safeguard and expedite transatlantic communications reflected the special connections that leading American humanitarian organizations often enjoyed with the US government. Close cooperation also signified a quasi-official status for the particular form of relief work and solidified the JDC's claim to authority among American Jews. This was true even though the State Department rejected the idea of undertaking money transfers directly to Germany's occupied territories.[49]

The JDC seemed to think the best way to create a positive image of its work was to be associated with American humanitarian initiatives during the war. The JDC highlighted Americanness as routine procedure without its leaders reflecting on why they were doing it; yet, something about being marked as American did seem universally well suited to the circumstances. The JDC was American, and this aspect of its institutional and operational identity seemed better to foreground than Jewishness.

Shortly after Germany occupied Poland, the Hilfsverein founded a committee, the Jüdische Hilfskomite für Polen (hereafter, Hilfskomite), with the explicit mission of providing relief to Polish Jews and to make clear that American funds, not German Jewish funds, were being distributed. The JDC linked its status to that of America's, and at a March 1915 meeting of its executive committee, was already hoping that, in order to prevent reprisals, Max Warburg could make it clear that the funds distributed by him were American.[50] In the summer of 1916, the JDC executive committee interrogated a representative of Hias, Isidore Hershfield, who had recently returned from Poland, inquiring if the money had been distributed "as from the German Jews or America." After Hershfield replied that he was unsure,[51] the executive committee argued over whether having the Hilfsverein, the Hilfskomite, or the Allianz distribute the JDC's money hurt the Jews in the territories. They proposed setting up separate American committees so it could be clear the aid was American.[52]

The JDC assumed this "American" label would prevent reprisals in the form of anti-Jewish violence or the confiscation of funds. Perhaps the JDC figured that American aid would seem less suspicious to Poles or Russians or Germans than Jewish aid of any kind, given antisemitic tropes about Jews and money and heightened prejudice against Jews brought out by the war. The JDC may have recognized that American aid to Belgium, conspicuous and successful, had enhanced the legitimacy of relief delivered under "American" auspices. On the other hand, if the aid was obviously Jewish, and not in fact delivered by Americans, but by the German Jews of the Hilfsverein, then the aid could appear as something originating with their occupiers: the Germans. The fact that Yiddish resembled German, and that Jews were routinely suspected of German sympathies, was perhaps a good reason for the JDC to portray its aid as originating from a neutral source. Establishing the Americanness of the JDC's aid also minimized potential harm to its relief offerings in the event of the reconquest of the region by an avowedly antisemitic Russian army.

Meanwhile, the war's ongoing disruption to traditional Jewish leadership structures, combined with this new American Jewish interference, accelerated the Jewish political ferment that would characterize the interwar period. Jews in Germany and Poland did not agree that funds from American Jews should be controlled by American Jews. German Zionists and Polish Jews complained about their lack of control over funds and unfair distribution, blaming the Hilfsverein. German Jews disagreed over which German Jewish faction should direct American relief money. The German Zionist organization seeking to distribute relief, the Komitee für den Osten, protested its lack of involvement. Some German Jews had their own strategy until early 1917 of helping Polish Jews by convincing the Reich that Polish Jews could act as a "vanguard of Germandom" in a German Mitteleuropa, which of course fed directly into Polish and Russian concerns about Jews embracing German occupation.[53] In the Warsaw region and other Polish areas under civil German administration, Polish Jews of various ideological stripes accused one another and the feuding German Jewish organizations of various misdeeds and complained of unfair treatment.[54]

In response, the JDC floated various proposals to have aid directed entirely by Polish Jews from a relief committee in Warsaw, which had been established at the beginning of the war by the Warsaw Jewish Community Council. This Polish Jewish-run relief committee would receive money via Max Warburg, who transferred money to the US Consul in Warsaw.[55] Elie Lewin-Epstein, a Zionist leader in America, went to Poland in the winter of 1915–16, reporting dissatisfaction with the Hilfsverein as an intermediary. He suggested that the American Consul in Warsaw direct money to Polish Jews via the Jewish relief committee in Warsaw. Lewin-Epstein thought the US Consul would be more capable of insisting on the rights of suffering civilians than German citizens.[56] But in May 1916, the Hilfsverein protested the JDC's micromanagement: "the spread of our organization threatens to be checked by the new demands, which, as you must know, are coming from America. We shall not permit these demands upon the organization to hinder us very much in the future. Meanwhile, we shall try to spread the net of our organization farther and farther."[57]

Controversy surrounding the methods of distributing American Jewish relief in German-occupied Poland continued. In the summer of 1916, Judah Magnes went to Poland and other centers of East European Jewish life to investigate on behalf of the JDC.[58] What Magnes found on the ground was depressing. Known for his leadership of the New York Kehillah, the organization that successfully brought together "uptown" and "downtown" Jews, Magnes was respected by many Jewish groups.[59] Magnes wrote back to New York that it was "sickening to think of petty quarrels and intrigues in the face of this fearful calamity." There was no food, no work, no clothes, no heat, and no medical care. Magnes concluded, "Jewish relief work in the occupied districts is altogether impossible without a strong Jewish German Committee in Berlin," noting that the "transmission work of the Hilfsverein is really remarkable." He recognized that it was "of the utmost importance to have all sections of Jewry working together in the relief cause. But it is, for the present at least, of more importance that the Jews of Poland and Lithuania be helped."[60] He dismissed fears that Russian Jews might get punished for receiving aid from Germans in case of Poland's return to Russian rule to be "of no real concern."[61] Moreover, the US Consul, he noted, was far from influential. Concluding that the Hilfskomite was the best option, Magnes prioritized the effective distribution of relief over the means of distribution, even though the JDC sought broad support at both the donor and recipient ends. He encouraged the Hilfskomite to broaden its membership to include Zionists and Orthodox Jews. In New York, the JDC, after studying Magnes's report, made some recommendations in that direction, expressing the hope that the Warsaw relief committee could continue to provide relief independently after German occupation and demanding a separation of the Hilfsverein and the Hilfskomite so that the Hilfskomite's source of funding in America would become clearer.[62] Accusations of the JDC's favoritism were not, however, put to rest. Instead, Magnes's investigation led to accusations that both he and the JDC were pro-German and favored philanthropies directed by assimilated German Jews.[63]

Not every part of the Central Powers' occupation was steeped in such internal dissent that it flowed to New York. The Ober-Ost region, east and north of Central Poland (Lithuania, Latvia, and Belarus) remained under direct German military administration and experienced less Jewish tension. The influence of German Jews ensured that sectarian relief could take place in this German militarized zone and the military administration made internal communications so difficult that direct reliance on the Hilfskomite was the only plausible option.[64] And from Vienna, the Allianz provided relief for Jews in once-Russian, now-Austrian-occupied parts of Galicia and Poland. Max Warburg forwarded earmarked funds to the Allianz, which worked effectively and peaceably enough through cooperating committees in Budapest, Lemberg (Lviv), and Krakow.[65] Still, the JDC longed to remove troublesome intermediaries and capitalize on its American privileges by sending its own American Jewish social workers to German and Austrian territory to conduct relief work on the spot.[66]

The JDC clung to the hope that more work could be done through American networks. It wanted the US State Department to push Britain to lift its blockade to allow for relief supplies.[67] The Commission for Relief in Belgium (CRB), the private association led by Herbert Hoover and Progressive professionals, had succeeded in getting food into German-occupied Belgium and feeding millions of people daily, and

Figure 1.2 Jewish refugees in Galicia, 1916. A rare photograph of Jewish refugees traveling away from their homes along a deserted dirt road in Galicia during the Great War, October 1916. The JDC used this photograph in America to fundraise by appealing to Jewish solidarity, making what was distant seem close: "Merely because they are in Galicia, in Lithuania, in Poland, in Palestine, does not lessen your responsibility ... You are asked to give your aid for your very own, for the Jewish women and children and the aged such as are pictured here." (JDC, NY_54912)

was a source of inspiration and frustration for the JDC.[68] As early as July 1915, Max Warburg requested sanitation supplies from the JDC for occupied Poland, not just money.[69] But these were not forthcoming because of the blockade. The State Department explained that the CRB was a partial exception to its rule of abstaining from relief.[70] The JDC looked to cooperate with other American organizations to make its case. In January 1916, the CRB and the Rockefeller Foundation (RF) asked the JDC to join them in a conference on sending foodstuffs to Poland.[71] The RF and the CRB had already cooperated in getting food to Belgium, with the Rockefeller–owned Standard Oil chartering ships, but nothing similar emerged from the conference on Poland.[72] Soon after, Magnes's report urged, "serious efforts must be made to have our government take up again the question of bringing food-stuffs, clothing, shoes, medicines, into the occupied territories," suggesting again that the JDC seek partnerships with the RF, the American Red Cross (ARC), and Polish American relief societies.[73] The State Department claimed it was working on a solution to allow relief supplies into Poland, "by appealing to the sense of humanity of the principal belligerent powers of Europe."[74] Yet, nothing changed, and American private associations were shut out of sending relief to Poland.

Still, American Jewish aid to Polish and Habsburg Jews benefited greatly from official neutrality, which enabled aid dollars to enter war zones with striking ease. Of course, US neutrality had its limitations, and was insufficient without explicit State Department support for the cause of getting goods to Poland, not just Belgium. Preestablished connections on the ground, particularly in Berlin, turned out also to be of enormous use for American Jews, despite the ascerbic nature of the relief effort in the eastern reaches of the Central Powers. This combination of diaspora ties to civilian Jewish networks in Germany, Austria-Hungary, and Poland, plus the tacit support of the neutral US government meant that, at the very least, American Jews were able to effectively get funds where they were urgently needed and partially avert the civilian suffering caused by war. On the other side of the Eastern Front, in Russian territory, things played out differently.

To Russia

In Russian territory along the Eastern Front, Jews were on the move, abandoning their small villages by force or in fear and heading in desperation toward the relative safety of nearby cities or remote destinations further east. Although the Pale of Settlement was abolished in August 1915, this did not in practice remove restrictions on Jews in Russia, and Jewish leaders suspected it was done only to court Western public opinion. Instead, some 30 percent of Jews in the Russian Empire faced expulsion. In March 1915, Russian military authorities began systematically deporting Jews from the Polish provinces still under Russian control, even if German troops remained far away, first by clearing small towns.[75] Whole Jewish communities were forced onto heated freight trains headed to unknown, unplanned destinations, while others were forced to leave on foot with whatever they could gather in a few hours' time.[76] The forced dispersal of Jews into Russia's interior continued after the Russian civil war, which, by 1923, increased the number of Jews living east of the Pale fivefold.[77] Jews in Galicia, at the eastern reaches of the Habsburg empire, who were captured by the invading Russian army were treated as enemies of state, even though they were civilians.[78]

From the comparative safety of St. Petersburg (Petrograd), the established Jewish lay leadership quickly responded to the urgent humanitarian needs created by the war. American Jews found a ready partner in this relief committee, EKOPO; the JDC transferred to it some $2.2 million over the course of the war.[79] The JDC had no choice but to trust the relief committee in Petrograd and its associated committees, along with the sympathetic American ambassador in Petrograd as of 1916, David R. Francis. No JDC representatives were able to obtain Russian visas, the US State Department was weakly represented in Russia, and scarce information was available as to the situation on the ground. Although Russian Jews raised a significant part of their funds internally, American Jewish aid turned out to be particularly useful for assisting Jewish refugees who entered Russia from enemy territory, and who were considered enemy citizens. In Russia especially, activating the homegrown, preexisting tradition of empire–wide Jewish charity proved crucial to the war relief effort.

When the war broke out, Russian Jewish leaders immediately recognized the need to invigorate their developing philanthropic infrastructure and that they could use support from American Jews. Underestimating the war, as most did early on, the Jewish Colonisation Association's (hereafter, Ica) St. Petersburg office proposed to French headquarters in July 1914 a Russian-wide, independent network to concentrate remittances from American Jews and deliver them to Jews across the empire.[80] Ica was at the time the wealthiest Jewish philanthropy in existence, drawing funds from the estate of railway magnate Baron Maurice de Hirsch.[81] But the war proved insurmountable for this transnational European Jewish migration organization. Instead, as remittances became insufficient and delivery untenable from August to September 1914, the Russian Jewish charitable elite based in St. Petersburg established a new organization, EKOPO (acronym for Evreiskii komitet pomoshchi zhertvam voiny, meaning Central Jewish Committee for the Relief of War Sufferers) as the main, centralized body in Russia for Jewish war relief. Although imperial rule typically emphasized political restraint, wartime conditions encouraged Russian society to mobilize around philanthropy and relief, spawning groups like the Union of Zemstvos and the Union of Towns.[82] EKOPO was granted permission in September 1914 to exist in the newly renamed Petrograd, but not to create branches, so EKOPO linked itself informally with independent local relief associations in Moscow, Kiev, Minsk, Vilna, and Odessa.[83] The war created the conditions for an overarching Jewish communal body in Russia for the first time since the late eighteenth century.[84]

The leaders of EKOPO were the established leaders of Russian Jewry in Petrograd, who had made their fortunes in industry and finance. EKOPO had close ties to Baron Alexander Gunzburg of the Gunzburg family, the most prominent Jewish family in Imperial Russia, whose members had long provided philanthropy and intercession on behalf of Russian Jews. Its first chair was Marc A. Varshavsky, banker, president of the St. Petersburg Jewish community, and president of the Russian Ica. EKOPO superficially resembled prewar Jewish philanthropic institutions in Russia, which were small, oligarchical, elitist, apolitical, familiar with the Russian elite, discreet, and modest in ambition.[85] Sitting and former Jewish members of the Duma, rabbinical leaders, and leaders of most other Jewish projects in St. Petersburg composed its membership.[86] These prewar organizations, including the ORT (occupational training), Ica (emigration, a branch of the French–British Jewish organization), OPE (education), and OZE (health), came to be affiliated with EKOPO.[87] Yet EKOPO's ambitions had to be much greater, its financial resources vaster, and its workforce more professional to deal with the unprecedented scale of the crisis.[88] Its backbone was a corps of traveling emissaries of young progressives who worked to establish new communities in the Russian interior and to rehabilitate communities in the Pale of Settlement.[89]

For American Jews hoping to provide relief to brethren in Russia, EKOPO presented an ideal scenario; all that was needed from Jews outside Russia was money, not organizational support.[90] Any controversy surrounding EKOPO was not perceived as a problem that American Jews had to address as they did in occupied Poland. Nor was it up to American Jews to set up a mechanism for distribution, as will be seen in the case of Palestine. December 1914 marked the first delivery of general relief moneys from the JDC to EKOPO.[91] The National City Bank in New York transferred AJRC dollars to the Ica account at the Azov Don Commercial Bank of St. Petersburg.[92] Ica acted as the JDC's "agent in Russia."[93] EKOPO used preexisting, empire-wide networks formed by its affiliated prewar organizations to distribute money, or American money came through the Azov Don bank's Ica account, to be handled by EKOPO and prewar charities.[94]

To aid refugees, EKOPO raised money through a Russian Jewish self-taxation scheme. It also received government funds, which made it a quasi-governmental agency, and derived prestige there from an arrangement to which the JDC might have itself aspired.[95] EKOPO secured food and clothing expenditures covered by the Russian government and solicited contributions from abroad, particularly from American, British, and South African Jews.[96] EKOPO organized "means of transportation for [displaced Jews], met them at way-stations with food and other necessaries, and did everything possible to help them to become self-supporting in their new environments."[97] EKOPO held joint meetings of its local committees and prewar organizations and set up relief in war-torn provinces by sending delegates from Petrograd to look for people who could be trusted to distribute relief moneys.[98] EKOPO's reports noted a substantial relief infrastructure, including doctors organizing dispensaries to welcome patients, feeding stations and food storehouses, the provision of clothing and footwear, the provision of shelter in communal buildings and private quarters, occupational training, and cooperation with the Union of Towns. The reports also lamented the inadequacy of relief on behalf of children, especially schooling, even with the OPE providing education to refugee children.[99] By the summer of 1916, EKOPO was helping Jewish communities along the front, not just refugees.[100] Alexander Gunzburg, now chairman, wrote in early 1917 that EKOPO was providing relief to 238,000 people, describing more than half as children or elderly, and thus unemployable.[101] This statistic indicated the extent to which recipients depended on relief and discouraged donors from believing that rehabilitation projects could replace charity. By summer, EKOPO refocused its work on economic crisis, refugees, relief in Poland (the part still in Russia), medical aid, the Jews of Galicia, Romanian Jews, and Jewish prisoners of war from Germany and Austria.[102] This Jewish self-government through relief work generated a de facto Jewish autonomism, which extended even to Jews in Romania, Russia's war ally.[103]

Meanwhile, the US State Department readily admitted that its endeavors to help Jewish relief in Russia were limited. Jewish relief in Russia could make do regardless; neutral American money was already traveling from the JDC to EKOPO in St. Petersburg. Diplomats in the Russian Empire had limited power, and American consular officials focused on "general" rather than sectarian aid where it existed.[104] This was especially true until the spring of 1916, when a American ambassador, David R. Francis, friend of Paul Warburg, another of Felix's brothers, was appointed to Petrograd.[105] Francis proved friendly to the cause of Jewish relief, communicating regularly with the JDC, EKOPO, and Ica Petrograd, handling messages sent through the US diplomatic pouch and sometimes working on transferring funds. In particular, the JDC found it useful to send Francis money earmarked for the American envoy in Jassy (Iași), Romania, Charles Vopicka, on behalf of Jews in Romania. David Francis also assisted Judah Magnes arrange a visit to Russia during his summer 1916 JDC fact-finding trip to Eastern Europe, but visas were not forthcoming.[106]

The greatest benefit to EKOPO and Russian Jews from the infusion of American Jewish dollars was neither infrastructural nor diplomatic support; instead, American money provided a way for Russian Jews to succor so-called enemy Jews who had formerly lived in non-Russian territory, namely, in the Galicia region of Austria-Hungary. EKOPO experienced difficulties helping Jews from Galicia due to continuing restrictions on Russian Jewish movement and to the Russian government's categorical insistence on treating Galician Jewish non-combatants as enemies because they were from Austria-Hungary. The JDC's oft-repeated refrain that EKOPO (and its European partners) should "make public this is American money"[107] was put to work when it came to helping Jews in Galicia, "the most miserable country of all."[108] Jews in Galicia, fleeing their homes "voluntarily" under Austro–Hungarian military rule and then under Russian military authority, suffered acute distress: dislocation, poverty, and violence. At first, Russian Jewish relief workers were not allowed to enter Russian-occupied Galicia and had to rely on general Russian relief organizations. EKOPO/Ica's David Feinberg managed to convince the Russian government to let in Jewish aid workers and allow a relief committee to form there in early 1915 to distribute American, rather than Russian, relief money.[109] In January 1916, when the JDC realized that EKOPO was not altogether capable of getting help to Galician refugees who were deported into the interior of Russia, the American consul in Moscow sidestepped these obstacles and sent help with American Jewish funds.[110]

EKOPO was something of a Jewish proto-government or a "para-statal complex," which made unimportant the American provenance of its funds.[111] Its well-connected St. Petersburg Jewish leaders had little difficulty finding ways to receive aid from abroad, raise money at home, and put it all to use across the empire. The JDC acted as just one (albeit crucial) fundraising entity for an autonomous Russian Jewish charity.[112] Although American support would become more critical to the ability of the JDC to help Jews in Soviet Russia, before the revolution, it was nearly inconsequential for the highly organized Russian Jewish community. To the south, in the Ottoman Empire, and in Palestine especially, there was yet a third situation requiring attention from abroad.

To Palestine

Jewish residents of Palestine were the first Jewish war sufferers whose pleas were heard by American Jews. Although war had not yet come to Palestine, the *chalukah* support they relied upon from European Jewish communities suddenly vanished in the summer of 1914.[113] Due to the confluence of war and natural disaster, the entire population of the Ottoman Empire was going hungry, and Jews were dying of hunger and disease alongside everyone else.[114] The terrible fate of the Armenians haunted the Jews of the Yishuv. Russian Jews numbered about half of Palestine's 100,000 Jews, and were expelled in 1914, mostly ending up in Alexandria, Egypt, which harbored more than 11,000 deportees.[115] Jews in the Ottoman Empire called for emergency relief from a new source: America. Growing Zionist support in America bolstered their appeals.

Since Jewish welfare in Palestine was decentralized and highly dependent on outsiders before the war, American Jews could not simply channel money to existing or newly formed groups. But unlike Europe, where the JDC was never able to send supplies or food, the US State Department was able to negotiate multiple relief shipments to Palestine. There was also significant energy dedicated to the cause, as American Zionists were intent on using the cause of relief toward building the Jewish nationalist program. This was helped by the US State Department's privileged status in the Ottoman Empire, whose officials were sympathetic both to the Jewish presence in Palestine and humanitarian relief work in general. The JDC sent nearly $800,000 to Palestine from the United States from the beginning of war until March 1917, a figure that does not include additional moneys from the Provisional Zionist Committee.[116]

In the early days of the war, in September 1914, Henry Morgenthau, the US ambassador to the Ottoman Empire in Constantinople and an American Jew, sent urgent telegrams to the American Jewish Committee. Via the State Department, he requested $50,000 for the 60,000 or so Jews in Palestine who were cut off from their European lifeline. Both the JDC and the Provisional Zionist Committee (formally, the Provisional Executive Committee for General Zionist Affairs, PZC for short) coalesced institutionally in response to these same early appeals coming from Palestine.[117] Henry Morgenthau's nephew, Maurice Wertheim, landed in Jaffa later that month with money he had brought at his uncle's request. He instructed that funds be distributed according to the American Jewish Committee's directives: to give money where it would afford greatest relief and to give preference to "productive" uses rather than handouts.[118] Wertheim established a small committee in Jerusalem to oversee future distributions: the American Relief Fund for Palestine. The fund divided relief, destined for Jaffa and Jerusalem, for "Humanitarian Institutions," especially soup kitchens, loans for mechanics and laborers, and to establish shops and a provision store.[119] Difficulties inexorably arose in distribution, but never reached the level of conflict that marked the relief effort in the Central Powers. The preeminent Jacob Schiff of the American Jewish Committee insisted for a time that a non-Zionist serve on the otherwise Zionist distributing committee, but disagreements abated when he eventually withdrew this demand.[120]

The American Relief Fund was headed by Dr. Arthur Ruppin, who trumpeted the way in which relief created close connections between Palestine and America. Ruppin was a German Jewish sociologist and demographer who moved to Israel to direct Zionist settlement, acting as the Zionist Organization's "chief technocrat" in Palestine.[121] Unlike his counterparts in Europe, he predicted the prestige and security this relief connection would bring the Jews of Palestine, who would thereby demonstrate that they had the most powerful neutral country, America, to support them.[122] He told Judah Magnes, "The establishment of this Fund has been regarded in this country as the first step towards a close and permanent connection between America and Palestine."[123] Ruppin sought to associate private American Jewish relief with the full power of the United States, a view helped along by its official-seeming arrival via a US ambassador.

But American state support required elaborate negotiations at the highest levels. Given the nature of the blockade, which ostensibly blocked supplies from entering Poland, it is in some sense surprising that aid made it to Palestine, since the blockade applied there, too. Only a few consulates remained open in Jerusalem to help with any aid coming in – the American and Spanish were among them. The US Navy had to employ its own ships, the British and French governments had to lift their naval blockade, and the Ottoman authorities had to cooperate.[124] Illustrating this point, US Consul Otis Glazebrook in Jerusalem sent notice in November 1914 that the precarious wartime humanitarian situation continued after Wertheim's visit. The State Department contacted Louis Marshall once again, who then asked if protection from belligerent states could be assured if the American Jewish Relief Committee sent a food ship. The State Department checked with Ambassador Morgenthau in Constantinople and the American ambassadors in London and Paris to ascertain if Turkey, Britain, and France would consent, and after some negotiation, they did. Secretary of the Navy Josephus Daniels was then persuaded by his friend, Jewish journalist Herman Bernstein, to support the cause of relief, and Daniels accordingly facilitated the Navy's cooperation, beginning by offering shipping space on the USS *Vulcan*.[125] Finally, Judah Magnes, as the chairman of the Palestine Relief Ship subcommittee of the JDC, purchased flour through Hoover's CRB at a low price and bought other supplies to send to Palestine.[126] The *Vulcan* set sail in March 1915 carrying 900 tons of food and medicine, with Louis Levin accompanying the ship on behalf of the AJRC to help with the distribution. Jews received 55 percent and the rest was distributed on a nonsectarian basis by Consul Glazebrook.[127]

The *Vulcan* was not the last relief to make it from American Jews to Palestine during the war. Over the course of 1915, US naval ships brought medical and agricultural supplies for Jews, Muslims, and Christians, supplied by the JDC, the RF, and the ARC.[128] In addition, the same US naval ships transported people, namely American citizens and Russian Jewish refugees who were expelled by the Ottomans, which was yet another tricky diplomatic question requiring extensive negotiations between the US government and Ottoman authorities. Meanwhile, for American Zionists, war opened new possibilities to demonstrate Jewish national solidarity through humanitarian relief and have it tacitly endorsed by mainstream, non-Zionist Jewish leaders. Zionists in each of the three constituent organizations of the JDC ensured that Palestine remained high on the JDC agenda despite a lack of official representation. While the PZC and JDC split costs and negotiation efforts with the State Department, the PZC sent additional money to sustain Jewish institutions, Jewish agricultural colonies, and the Palestine Office and the Jewish Agency in Constantinople.[129] The funds moved by several means, including via the State Department to Consul Glazebrook in Jerusalem or to Morgenthau in Constantinople, via the Standard Oil Company, or even on ships.[130] In late 1916, however, with war escalating in the region, the movement of goods and people became impossible, and supplies in transit languished until the end of the war.[131]

Relief funds in Palestine betrayed obvious American governmental involvement. The conspicuous arrivals of US warships, resulting nonsectarian distribution, the Americans who sometimes accompanied the relief, and the noticeable involvement of one of the only consuls of any country left in town surely made an impact on the local population. Jaffa and Jerusalem were simply too small, the economy was in such distress, and very little other outside aid of any kind was provided to the Ottoman Empire, even during wartime famine, for that kind of presence to go unnoticed. It must have seemed that the American government was highly dedicated to the Jews, particularly in comparison with the lesser aid provided by Americans to suffering minority Armenian and Syrian populations also under Ottoman rule. While the JDC "negotiated constantly with [the State Department] to secure the transport of relief supplies for Palestine," it also did so even more strenuously for Poland, but to less effect.[132]

What explains the relative success of American Jewish relief in Palestine, compared to other wartime humanitarian initiatives aimed at the Ottoman Empire and to American Jewish relief in Europe? US support for American missionaries, for American business, and for relief to Jews in Palestine dovetailed in the war years, blending the articulation of US foreign policy with the private, sectarian interests of the JDC and PZC. US leaders saw several reasons to make use of the war to attach America to the Eastern Mediterranean more deeply, building on an array of prewar American initiatives and ideologies.[133] The political situation could not be described as easier than in Europe, but the diplomacy and logistics played to America's favor. The US State Department credited its own influence in the region to "the existence of extraterritorial rights in Turkey [that] give the American Consuls a very different status and the United States Government much greater rights than is the case in Russia,"[134] which had to do with the capitulations. America maintained long-standing cultural interests in the Middle East, enhanced by President Wilson's and Consul Glazebrook's special religious attention to the region.[135] American business interests had been developing in the Ottoman Empire since the turn of the century, and it was Standard Oil, already installed there, that enabled the transfer of philanthropic funds. Missionary and philanthropic work was an established, primary American interest in the region.[136]

Jews appeared as the logical, instrumental connection between the Middle East and America. The appointment of Jewish American diplomats in the region, when American ambassadors elsewhere were never Jews, was due to the long-held assumption that "the Jews represented a natural bridge between Muslim Turks and Christian Americans."[137] The exertions of US ambassadors in the Ottoman Empire, Henry Morgenthau, and later, Abram Elkus, both American Jews, turned out to be critical for the war relief effort.[138] American Jewish relief was able to make the furthest inroads in the places where the US State Department supported them best and the American name could take them farthest. Before the United States entered the war, Palestine was that place.

The Jewishness of Jewish Relief

So far, we have looked at what the JDC called "general relief": the centrally organized collection of money in the United States and its rationalized distribution in the Central Powers, Russia, and Palestine. "Individual relief" constituted another critically important dimension of the relief apparatus conceived to aid Jewish war victims. Individual relief mobilized a feature of American immigrant life: financial remittances from immigrants, sent from America to families and friends in the old country. The neutrality of the United States and its tolerant attitude toward private initiatives for humanitarian purposes at the start of the war allowed creative solutions to flourish, such as the creation of a postal route from Poland to Hias offices in New York and the merging of remittances into institutionalized humanitarian relief. Mainstream organizations like the ARC or the CRB utilized only "general relief," while "individual relief" was replicated by other organizations that drew on immigrant ties, like the Near East Relief. Although Jewish organizations hardly had a monopoly on individual relief, Jewish individual relief was, by definition, particularly Jewish in its reliance on intimate Jewish networks and Jewish knowledge.

Individual relief helped the JDC augment and retain the support of immigrants; use the knowledge and networks of immigrants who were more closely connected to suffering Jews than most of JDC leadership; send relief in excess of the War Trade Board's restrictions on general relief; and channel aid efficiently where it was urgently needed without bureaucratic decision-making. The institutionalization of individual relief took several forms. The JDC built a transmission bureau, which accepted and delivered individual remittances, developing a tracing service in the process. Hias set up a postal route to reconnect individuals. Landsmanshaftn were drawn in to provide information and activism clustered around certain geographical locations. Information was gathered from individuals to inform organizational decisions.

Less centralized, less public, and thus harder for the historian to study, individual relief efforts linking Jewish immigrants, Jewish banks, the Jewish press, landsmanshaftn, Hias, synagogues, the JDC, Zionist organizations, European Jewish organizations, and Jewish war sufferers marked a sphere of distinctly Jewish collective humanitarianism. This section will loop back over the three operational theaters to focus on individual relief that was bundled into the general Jewish humanitarian effort in each region, reflecting on the nature of this unprecedented merger between private relationships and modern humanitarian relief.

Long before 1914, American Jewish immigrants were already sending remittances in the millions of dollars to the East European old country and Palestine.[139] The war meant that immigrants seeking to send remittances faced censored postal services, banks that could not guarantee transfers abroad, and no way of keeping track of the location of fleeing relatives and friends. Among American Jews, it became clear that the relief effort would have to reconnect broken threads across individuals and hometowns so that relief could travel within kinship networks. "It was felt that aiding in the transmission of moneys on the part of people in this country to their needy relatives and friends abroad was as much a work of charity as giving from general funds to needy people in the war zone," stated Harriet Lowenstein, the JDC's comptroller and Felix Warburg's philanthropic adviser.[140] The benefit of remittances was that they made practitioners and recipients feel independent of charity, and sometimes more willing to give and accept them than to partake in general relief.[141] The question organizations faced was how to reenable this traditional practice and make efficient use of it alongside top-down, rationally planned general relief.

The JDC established a remittances bureau to accept small sums designated for individual recipients and bundle it with general relief appropriations. A month into the war, Harriet Lowenstein had the idea to set up a station to transmit individual remittances at market rate on behalf of the AJRC. The resulting Transmission Bureau began as a cramped office staffed by young women, volunteers, and inexperienced clerks. As demand increased, the AJRC began transmissions to Russia, Austria, the Ottoman Empire, and German-occupied Poland.[142] When an interruption in operations in 1916 elicited a stream of complaints, Herbert Lehman, treasurer of the JDC, took over the Transmission Bureau with a full staff of clerks; it was clear that the JDC needed to continue and expand remittance work, if only to keep immigrants supportive of the JDC as a whole.[143] By November 1916, the JDC was working on a plan to make remittances more accessible by setting up branches of the Transmission Bureau in Jewish institutions across New York City and in communities across the country.[144] Branches with after-work hours opened on the Lower East Side, in the Bronx, and in Brownsville.[145] By January 1917, the JDC had sent 90,000 individual remittances to Russia, Poland, Galicia, Lithuania, Palestine, Turkey, and Romania.[146] A sum of $500,000 amassed in small denominations remitted by thousands of concerned family members were sent this way by summer 1917.[147]

The Transmission Bureau, beloved by immigrants desperate to reach loved ones, handled extraordinarily challenging logistics for a private philanthropy. It had to be both flexible enough to accommodate changing conditions and simple enough for untrained persons to use it and act as paying agents. It also had to be compatible with the JDC's system of general relief without creating significant overhead costs. Given these constraints, the JDC designed the Transmission Bureau as a tracing and distribution service, recorded and tracked through a standardized system of receipts. The dual function of the Transmission Bureau, which delivered otherwise undeliverable cash relief and traced missing people, proved its value. Information on recipient whereabouts was critical to the relief operation as a whole, demonstrating how remittance work had its own efficiency apart from general relief.

The process began when an individual in the United States formally requested a search for a relative or friend by remitting any sum of money through the JDC Transmission Bureau. Remittances and their receipts, drawn up in New York, were bundled into the general relief money

transfers of the JDC. Then the already engaged JDC distributing organizations in Europe and the Eastern Mediterranean had to find and deliver
these remittances to their designated recipients. The Hilfskomite for
Poland and the Russian Ica labored to track down the addresses of the
intended recipients and deliver the money, collecting a signature from
the recipient in any language. The remarkable success rate of German
Jewish remittance delivery in occupied Poland was a good reason for
JDC leaders to keep the Hilfskomite in place. Ica also worked assidu-
ously, reporting to its Paris office in July 1915 that it had processed over
1,000 individual inquiries that had come in from abroad, from Hias, the
Industrial Removal Office, the AJRC, Canada, Argentina, and beyond.
The US State Department also assisted directly in this transmission of
funds and tracing recipients, finding that this was within its
capabilities.[148] Upon payment, local organizations would return receipts
with recipient signatures, sometimes including letters and appeals for
help directed at relatives in the United States, to the Transmission
Bureau. Once received in the United States, the Transmission Bureau
would summon the original sender to inspect the signature, offering an
updated account of the livelihood and recent location of the recipient.[149]

Although Jewish institutions besides the JDC, including the PZC,
Hias, and private banks, sent remittances at times, the JDC
Transmission Bureau was uniquely and dependably successful at
covering a vast geography despite wartime disruption at the lowest possible rates. The Transatlantic Trust Company and immigrant banks also
remitted money, but at a higher rate and with less reliability. When the
Transatlantic Trust announced it could no longer make payments to
individuals in Galicia, the JDC picked up the slack; Lowenstein engaged
Ica's representative in Lemberg to distribute remittances in Russian-
occupied Galicia after early 1915.[150] When Hias debated whether it
should have its own agreement with a bank, it eventually decided to stick
with suggesting that members transfer through the JDC. The JDC's
singularly impressive remittance services were sometimes even utilized
by non-Jewish organizations, like the ARC and the Polish Fund, fore-
shadowing the humble remittance's entry into mainstream relief work
after the war.[151]

Beyond the cash-only JDC Transmission Bureau, a major feature of
wartime relief became the act of reconnecting families and friends. This
took on many forms, during the war and for decades after. With the JDC
taking care of remittances, Hias, for example, investigated alternative
ways of connecting relatives.[152] In this pursuit, it sent Isidore
Hershfield, an American-born lawyer, to German-occupied territories
in 1915.[153] Seeing the effective relief work of the Hilfsverein,

Hershfield focused on a complementary mechanism for tracing.[154] In February 1916, Hershfield cabled that he had obtained special permission from German and Austrian officials for individuals living in occupied territories to send mail to the United States. He distributed postcards pre-addressed to Hias New York and published announcements in the local press explaining that these cards could go directly to America, if they were written in Polish or German, with only the desired relative's name and address, a prefabricated sentence (translated to "We are well, but need financial assistance. Please help us. We send heartfelt greetings."), and the sender's name and address on it.[155] These special postcards, mailed by Europeans living under German and Austrian occupation, bypassed censors and arrived swiftly at Hias offices in New York. While designed for Jewish use, these Hias postcards were not restricted to it. The Polish National Society and Lithuanian National Society also made use of this special mail route.[156] Meanwhile, Russian Jewish families passed unaddressed letters to Ica to forward via the JDC to American Jewish societies, asking their own relatives in the United States to send money to relieve their distress.[157] Hias and the National Council of Jewish Women traced the intended American Jewish recipients of these appeals, as Hias did with its postcards, via name-reading ceremonies, publishing lists in Jewish newspapers, through organizational literature, and posting lists at remittance bureaus.

Hias and the JDC complemented each other when it came to individual relief. They were also able to incorporate the institutional force of American Jewish women on the home front, allowing women's roles to expand slightly from fundraising to include tracing work within America. The JDC, never relishing remittance and tracing work, did not mind that Hias enhanced connections by other means, while Hias could maintain its raison d'être during a time of severely restricted immigration. This postcard project in fact marked the moment when Hias became an international organization. Instead of reacting to events abroad, helping immigrants on American soil, and lobbying the US government on immigration, Hias took action abroad. By war's end, Hias had processed 300,000 communications and even helped facilitate the immigration of 7,000 women and children by connecting them to male relatives in the United States.[158]

Meanwhile, landsmanshaftn were also interested in undertaking relief work. The JDC had two main reasons to seek their cooperation: to add more funds to the JDC's general pool, and to find valuable, hyper-local information regarding the volatile situation in Eastern Europe. Landsmanshaft members were personally touched by the war's horrors as they heard about the decimation of their former hometowns, and as a result, had a personal stake in providing relief to their hometowns. Just two weeks after war was declared, one landsmanshaft had already begun to raise money on its own. Landsmanshaftn solicited donations from their US members and tried to send money to their hometowns in the old country in a number of ways. Previously competitors, landsmanshaftn began banding together for the purposes of relief, forming regional federations. Intent on maintaining links to their hometowns, they called mass meetings to share information that was gathered from new arrivals from the old country.[159]

Still, these federations were no match for wartime conditions. They typically ended up hoarding money to use postwar or relinquished it to the JDC, the only American Jewish institution with the administrative capacity to deliver funds abroad in war. Landsmanshaftn reluctantly participated in all three of the JDC constituent groups, particularly through the Central Relief and People's Relief. Landsmanshaftn made extensive use of the JDC's transmission services, sending remittances to locations rather than individuals. They also contributed to Hias' work, since it was, after all, partially an outgrowth of a landsmanshaft and run by immigrants. But their combined distrust for these institutions and deep concern for their specific hometowns, which the JDC could not always reach, led to erratic evasion of the JDC. The Federation of Galician and Bucovinean Jews of America, for example, attempted a side project, encouraging its affiliates to send money via the Austrian embassy to the Israelitische Allianz zu Wien. They then abandoned that project in favor of trying to connect refugees in Austria to relatives in America by transmitting letters and publishing the names of recipients. They mimicked the strategies of the JDC and Hias, but attempted, with mixed to poor results, to go it alone.[160]

There was mistrust between the JDC and landsmanshaftn. For some immigrants, the JDC seemed too bureaucratic, assimilated, and not necessarily invested in the towns they represented. To the JDC, the landsmanshaftn appeared amateurish and wasteful.[161] Like with remittances sent by individuals, the ethnic, seemingly non-American nature of landsmanshaftn frustrated the JDC, which sought to absorb them into an American way of operating, meaning cooperation and non-duplication. The landsmanshaft practice of providing their own funds and, once the intense danger of war passed, sending their own delegates, continued well after the war, along with the JDC's and Hias' continued attempts to harness and corral them.

The search for credible information was so crucial that the JDC always hoped to send its own representatives to act in the most professional and expert way possible, instead of relying on landsmanshaftn. Yet Judah

Magnes was the only official JDC visitor to the war zones, and he alone could hardly provide a complete account, especially since he never made it into Russia. Given the inadequacy and datedness of many reports, the JDC decided that the best way to obtain correct information was to cross-reference a wide variety of reports from various sources to make informed decisions about where and how to send money. Although firsthand accounts were episodic and lacked the coherency the JDC may have desired, they filled the innumerable gaps in knowledge created by evolving war operations and censorship. Intimate, relatively recent information and local contacts culled from the diaspora network gave Hias and the JDC legitimacy to act separately from other, mainstream humanitarian associations on behalf of Jews since no other organizations could make a claim to their specific knowledge.

The JDC responded to appeals from abroad or reports of violence and destitution by trying to ascertain correct information. It required recipients to provide detailed reports on how their funds were distributed and used to make rational decisions for general relief. Continued funding was contingent on regular information provided by the main distributing agents.[162] The JDC drew on Jewish networks abroad for information, particularly British Jews, who had organized their own relief committees. JDC clerks read the Jewish press, keeping relevant clippings and writing summaries. The JDC made requests of the State Department to investigate an issue through its officials overseas. The State Department almost always complied, even if it kept plenty of its findings classified and reported only half-truths. Finally, the JDC interrogated commissioners that other organizations managed to send abroad, American Jewish foreign correspondents, and American Jews sent abroad to serve in non-Jewish capacities.[163]

While the American Jewish war relief effort seemed centralized, it was actually a hybrid operation, combining traditional Jewish charity, diaspora remittances, information gathering both anecdotal and statistical, and planned philanthropy. Although JDC leaders were inclined to operate in a progressive, institutional, corporate, American style befitting their own professional status and the success they wished to achieve, they also realized the multifaceted potential of harnessing the collective will and knowledge of individuals for their own relief purposes. Ordinary Jews, not just the leaders of the JDC or Hias, had roles to play in wartime relief. Most individuals were not decision-makers themselves, but informants and donors who relied on the US government and established American Jewish organizations to make use of these contributions. By coordinating individual remittances, cooperating with landsmanshaftn, and seeking knowledge, the JDC brought together various diasporic links to make them work for general, American-style relief. The JDC's extension into the arena of individual relief is what allowed it to nearly corner the market in American Jewish relief. The Jewish overseas humanitarian project was itself galvanizing American Jews into constituting a cohesive Jewish community. On the home front, the JDC appealed to large donors, small donors, American organizations, and the US government, as well as a wide range of Jewish organizations. Acting abroad, it had the support of these organizations behind it and the collective knowledge of immigrants, distributing organizations, and high-level US officials to act effectively. Once the United States entered the war, sending representatives became impossible and funds were more restricted, but individual remittances and connecting relatives continued.

America Enters the War

In April 1917, the United States declared war; for most Americans, this signaled the beginning of war. For Jewish relief agencies, by contrast, the war had been ongoing for years. For Jewish life overall, America's entry into the war was far less significant than the Russian Revolution or the Balfour Declaration. Though America's entry into the war marked the beginning of the end of the war, this too was not particularly significant for Jews, since paramilitary violence, interstate war, and civil war persisted for years along the Eastern Front. So while the totality of the war upended Jewish life, American belligerency mostly meant that American Jewish relief efforts had to navigate even more obstacles. American Jewish humanitarian leaders moved closer to the US war government to find ways of continuing their relief efforts and relied more heavily on Jewish individual relief.

While procedures became more bureaucratic and limits stricter in April 1917, the Wilson administration began to rely on relief from private organizations and to think of aid to civilians as having essential strategic and ideological importance. American relief signified US commitment to Allied Europe and toward a European future premised on international community and stability. The American Red Cross was deployed across Europe for civilian relief in June 1917.[164] This was a good time for private associations to do their work with the full backing of the US government. On the other hand, Jewish associations in America faced a conundrum: They still wanted to get aid to civilians in what was now enemy territory without aiding the enemy. In other words, they wanted to continue relief to Polish Jews even though America was now officially at war with Poland's German occupiers. This situation was resolved when the US State Department and the JDC worked together to negotiate a solution with the still-neutral Netherlands, whereby money would pass through the Netherlands on its way to Berlin and Jerusalem, which turned it into neutral, humanitarian money. The revolution in Russia, however, meant a breakdown in relief transmission to Jews within Russia, which was then cobbled together on the promise of future peaceful relations between America and Russia.

Over the spring and summer 1917, the JDC faced its biggest diplomatic challenge yet: finding a way, with the State Department's approval, to send aid to still-desperate Jews in places occupied by the enemy. Negotiations centered on still-neutral Spain, which the JDC hoped could distribute relief through its embassies in enemy territory.[165] Dr. Stephen S. Wise, a rabbi who frequently spoke out on Jewish nationalism and rights and who was close to President Wilson, allegedly negotiated on behalf of the JDC executive committee with William G. Phillips, the assistant secretary of state. Wise, with Louis Brandeis' backing, suggested to Phillips that the JDC organize a committee of Jews in a neutral country such as Holland rather than having Spanish embassies distribute relief, arguing that the Commission for Relief in Belgium already operated in a similar way. Wise thus shifted the distribution logistics away from Spanish consulates and from the Hilfskomite and instead toward Zionists in a neutral country – a pro-Zionist move that was not what the JDC executive committee had intended. But the damage to the Spanish option was done, with the Spanish ambassador refusing his good offices. Henry Morgenthau, Oscar Straus, Louis Marshall, and JDC executive secretary Albert Lucas went to Washington to meet with Phillips and discuss a change of plans. The State Department sent out a few inquiries and in May, entered negotiations with the Dutch government. After intense diplomatic negotiations through April and May, the JDC and the State Department settled on Holland.[166]

There were still some problems with the German government accepting these terms, but no way to resolve German hesitations from America. The JDC sent a capable social worker, Boris Bogen, to the Hague to investigate the situation and try to make a Holland route work. Bogen's trip to Holland was to launch him into many field projects on behalf of the JDC, which transformed him into a key early figure of the Joint. Originally from an educated Jewish merchant family living in Moscow, he moved as an adult to the United States and became a social worker. While providing social services to Jews in Cincinnati, Ohio, he earned an outstanding reputation. He spoke many languages – Russian, English, Yiddish, Polish, German – and took a particular interest in war relief work. He had already been considered a candidate to accompany

Judah Magnes to Europe. For this mission to Holland, Bogen was accompanied by his colleague from Cincinnati, Max Senior. After a long and uncertain journey across the Atlantic, the pair arrived in London in mid-September 1917. In Bogen's recounting, he described how after their treacherous trip across the Atlantic, they discovered that the US representative in Holland had not been alerted to their arrival, nor had he heard of the JDC.[167] When the relevant paperwork finally arrived several days later from the United States, Bogen and Senior organized a committee of Dutch Jews to forward money, under the rationale that "[w]ith money the beneficiaries could buy what they needed within the occupied territories. And it satisfied the current patriotism to believe that, buying foodstuffs within the occupied territory, our people would diminish the resources of the enemy to an extent." Once this was completed, the Dutch Jewish committee negotiated with the German government without letting on that there were Americans involved.[168] The German government accepted that a Dutch committee could forward funds, but not distribute aid directly, and appointed a German Jew in the Hague as facilitator. Bogen and Senior tested the plan by sending money to Warsaw and waiting for a receipt: it came. By the time they left Holland in January 1918, they had already sent $500,000 to Poland and Lithuania.[169]

Accordingly, a committee of Dutch Zionists received money and sent it to Dutch diplomatic officers posted in war zones. It was distributed according to guidelines sent from New York to Holland. General and individual relief thus continued through America's belligerency, passing in this way not only to Jews in German territory in Warsaw and Lithuania, but also still to Jews in Austria-Hungary. Since enemy subjects could not touch this money under US law (i.e., the German Jews of the Hilfsverein or the Austrian Jews of the Allianz), Dutch consuls handed relief funds to local committees of Jews under occupation by the Central Powers that had previously distributed for the Hilfsverein and Allianz.[170]

In creating this Netherlands route, the JDC had to carefully negotiate a delicate but far from impossible situation. Germany was willing to accept humanitarian relief, since it was facing severe shortages due to the blockade, and outside support would ease its own burden.[171] As American Consul in Warsaw Hernando de Soto noted, "the Germans distinctly favor foreign relief measures in Poland."[172] The US government allowed limited American relief to travel to Poland, as Assistant Secretary of State William Phillips wrote, to maintain Polish-American support for the war and to prevent Poles from turning against the Allies.[173] Phillips was well aware that this would aid Germany, but in contrast to British policy, he thought the benefits of relief outweighed the disadvantages. De Soto agreed: "Without American aid the Poles will be taught to look upon Germany as their only savior and friend. In fact, direct American relief would serve to increase the enthusiasm already prevailing among the Poles ... over the utterances of President Wilson."[174]

Regarding Palestine, the JDC maintained its relief link through Western/Central Europe. Since relief traveled so similarly through the Central Powers, the JDC kept hoping that East Central Europe and Palestine could merge into one humanitarian theater. Upon declaring war on Germany, the United States recalled its American diplomats, including Ambassador Elkus and Consul Glazebrook, from the Ottoman Empire. For a brief period, relief funds went to the Spanish Consul in Jerusalem.[175] Once the Netherlands route was established, however, a Dutchman in Palestine, Siegfried Hoofien, began to receive moneys from the Dutch committee in Amsterdam. Assistant director of the covertly operating Anglo-Palestine Bank that held the American Relief Fund's account, Hoofien acted in the same way Glazebrook had, transferring money to local relief committees. Approximately $500,000 reached Palestine during US involvement in the war.[176] Concurrently, the Jewish National Fund had relocated to neutral Holland, and this Zionist organization also sent money to Palestine to sustain its agricultural colonies there.[177] Despite British occupation of Palestine in December 1917, ports were not yet active, and Palestine remained isolated from food supplies. The British military governor of Jerusalem, Ronald Storrs, ordered food from Egypt, but it was not forthcoming from America until after the war.[178]

Meanwhile, the Russian Revolution began in March 1917. Since America entered the war during this Russian upheaval, relations with this Allied Power were uncertain. The United States took a noninterventionist stance, and American Jews let their Russian brethren guide their efforts. In April 1917, the American Consul in Petrograd announced the abolishment of restrictions on Russian citizens based on race and religion; the emancipation of Russian Jews had come at last.[179] Displaced Jews in the Russian interior could return to the former Pale of Settlement. Although Russia was not a US war enemy, the confusion created by the revolution and the US government's ambivalence toward it challenged continued relief efforts. Meanwhile, the Russian revolutionary government diminished its support for Jewish relief; the autonomy of EKOPO and associated local relief groups was falling apart amid a mounting humanitarian crisis. With refugees returning and pogroms becoming increasingly violent and widespread across Ukraine, and no way to address these issues, Russian Jewish life was headed toward catastrophe.[180] After the fall of the tsar, the American ambassador remaining in Petrograd, David R. Francis, told the State Department on March 26, 1917, that financial help by American Jews would be welcome but would have to be done with discretion. It was not clear to all American Jews that relief was necessary after emancipation. There were the usual worries about helping the Russian government or inflaming antisemitism, too.[181] Yet when EKOPO cabled for assistance, the JDC responded. From March 1917 to December 1917, it sent a total $450,300.[182]

But the October Revolution brought trouble. Informed that funds sent in September were the last to reach their intended destination, the JDC set up a committee to find a way for money to reach Russia. The Committee on Russia tried several different paths and, in their exertions over the course of 1918, corresponded with other private associations and the State Department. The JDC's main source of information and line of communication with EKOPO was the journalist Herman Bernstein, the same man who had mustered US Naval support for Jewish relief in Palestine and who would soon write the pioneering study (*The History of a Lie*, 1921) of the infamous Russian antisemitic text, *The Protocols of the Elders of Zion*. Bernstein happened to be on a reporting trip to Russia during the winter of 1917–18 and became the de facto representative of the JDC. It was Herman Bernstein who, in April, cabled the JDC that EKOPO had received nothing since September. He wrote that the Petrograd EKOPO requested $1 million and said that after the JDC made a decision regarding an appropriation, they would send recommendations on how to transfer the funds.[183] As Jewish relief and remittances stopped amid revolutionary turmoil and the ongoing chaos, restrictions, and deprivation of the Great War, conditions in Russia deteriorated.

Albert Lucas, JDC secretary, hoped to push the United States toward establishing a postrevolutionary relationship with the Soviets through civilian relief. Writing to Secretary of State Lansing in summer 1918, he explained:

The interest of the President of the United States in the future prosperity of the Russian people is a matter of public knowledge. The Department of State has during all the time that the Joint Distribution Committee has been in existence given its unqualified support to all the efforts of that Committee to enable the Jews of America to relieve their brethren in Russia and elsewhere. The present moment seems to be opportune for an effort to be made to re-establish the means of assistance which have hitherto existed between the people of the United States and the people of Russia.[184]

In August, Warburg, Lucas, Bogen, and Jacob Billikopf traveled to Washington, DC, to look into getting Boris Bogen permission to travel to Russia to recreate the Netherlands success, enlisting the help of Major Samuel Rosenson of the War Department to speak with State Department officials on behalf of the JDC.[185] However, this effort to deploy Bogen was doomed – the Soviet government would not allow a former Russian subject to return for the purposes of relief.[186] Ambivalence on the part of the State Department meant no funds were transferred and no relief could be undertaken in Russia. As government routes floundered, the JDC sought possibilities and information through the ARC, the YMCA, and the Russian Information Bureau in New York in spring and summer 1918. The ARC and the YMCA had both been able to undertake limited relief in Russia, but the JDC's overtures to follow in their stead led nowhere.[187]

Herman Bernstein cabled the JDC in spring 1918 with good news: He had ensured that relief could still take place without Bolshevik interference if distributed by EKOPO.[188] He added that the JDC could wait to send money until after the war as long as it informed EKOPO how much it was setting aside for that purpose; EKOPO could secure borrowed funds immediately.[189] Sending relief to Russia remained difficult for years to come, largely because cooperation with other American associations or the government was not possible for what had become Soviet Russia. The JDC's fundamental reliance on US foreign relations was becoming clear in a way that the period of US neutrality had not made visible.

US belligerency created a closer relationship between Jewish relief and the US State Department. According to the US Trade with the Enemy Act of 6 October 1917, the War Trade Board had to approve and license money and supply transfers in advance. Once the war transfer routes were in place, the State Department still restricted the relief funds destined for enemy countries.[190] Interestingly, the State Department became further involved in Jewish relief, as it, rather than private banks, became responsible for the transmission of funds. New bureaucratic matters necessitated by the US declaration of war meant the State Department read years of overseas Jewish correspondence, while affording Jewish organizations the opportunity to learn the State Department system and network. Meanwhile, the JDC was undertaking multimillion-dollar fundraising campaigns, setting aside "chests" of money for postwar reconstruction. It became dependent on the US government and an ambassador of American goodwill to occupied populations in wartime. To assure the continued, critical cooperation of the US government, the JDC chose to align itself with the US war effort, making arguments that appealed to a sense of humanitarianism and to desires to win the war. Complying with caps created by the War Trade Board, the JDC still sent more than $5 million in general relief abroad in 1918, not including remittances.[191]

The Washington-based lawyer, Fulton Brylawski, usually communicated with the State Department pro bono on behalf of the JDC. When the JDC needed to send a message to a Jewish relief committee in Germany, Russia, or elsewhere, he received the message from JDC New York and took it to the State Department where it would travel through the department's diplomatic pouch to an American consular official in Berlin, Petrograd, Vienna, Bucharest, Constantinople, or Jerusalem. That American official would then pass the letter to the relevant local Jewish relief committee. These messages usually carried instructions for using the money. Brylawski received replies sent through the diplomatic pouch and forwarded them accordingly. After May and June 1917, when Brylawski hashed out plans to transfer the relief route through Holland, he had to run back and forth to get licenses from the War Trade Board for every financial transaction and communication to enemy countries. He also deposited checks at the State Department for transfer to the American Minister at Holland. Hias' representatives in Washington, Simon Wolf and then Louis Gottlieb, also facilitated communications via the State Department, and of course, discussed cases of potential immigrants who were having difficulty entering the United States.

On occasion, the JDC approached the State Department with potentially difficult requests. As has been seen, well-known and well-connected Jewish leaders would travel from New York and elsewhere to direct Jewish initiatives with the State Department, President Wilson, or Congress. Brylawski and other JDC representatives mostly discussed matters with William Phillips, assistant secretary of state. Alvey Adee, also assistant secretary of state, and Secretary of State Robert Lansing were also part of the conversation. But the JDC's reliance on sending Jewish leaders from New York as well as recruiting Jews in American government to its cause meant that clusters of leading Jews could also go to Washington without the sanction of the JDC and have the US government's ear, as did Stephen Wise and Louis Brandeis. There was no authorized Jewish body, just personal networks and reputation. Relief negotiations thus provided the State Department with an opportunity to glimpse inside the world of American Jewish politics and provided Zionists a way to build their own relationship with the US government.

The burgeoning American Jewish–State Department relationship did not bear immediate results; the US government actually reduced the amount of money the JDC could send.[192] After March 1918, the State

Department permitted the JDC to send only $300,000 monthly to Poland ($100,000 of it individual remittances), far lower than the JDC's intended $700,000. The State Department controlled where it was sent, announcing that nothing could go to Lithuania as of April 1, 1918, due to fears that Lithuania supported Germany and that Lithuanian Jews might work against Allied interests.[193] Although the State Department was reluctant to allow too much relief, permitted amounts were much more generous than, say, what London, having blocked aid before US entry and now opposing it as aid to Germany, allowed.[194] Despite comparative US benevolence, the JDC relentlessly pursued the challenge of getting food and clothing into Poland. While cutting the amounts it would let humanitarian organizations send to Poland, the State Department continued to negotiate with the JDC. In November 1917, Albert Lucas proposed adapting the model of the CRB to Poland. Warburg explained that it would take convincing President Wilson to make this Hoover plan a reality, and that despite some remaining optimism and Morgenthau requesting a conference, the frustrations of dealing with the government resembled "a very beautiful game of going around a circle."[195] The circle game persisted until war's end, but it positioned the JDC to demand inclusion in immediate postwar relief in Poland. Meanwhile, the Balfour Declaration of 1917 bolstered Zionist claims and supported what had already been an intense American effort to provide relief in Palestine.

Naturally, the US government did not protest that funds sent by Jews abroad were called "American." Humanitarian relief in war-torn regions put America in a positive light, such that when the United States declared war, the War Trade Board notified the JDC that "all receipts [for individual remittances of any character destined for Poland or Turkey] should indicate that these funds are of American origin."[196] The US government stated that it wanted even private funds coming from America through its official diplomatic channels to be perceived as unambiguously American. Given that these funds were going to populations that were not all well disposed toward their current rulers, the US government was strategically self-interested in informing these unfortunate civilians that American goodwill was helping them, and that Germany, Austria-Hungary, and the Ottomans were their oppressors. The War Trade Board's diktat was a central part of a clearly designed foreign policy strategy to turn the Jewish population in Eastern Europe and the Eastern Mediterranean against America's enemies and to inculcate support for the Allies as liberating humanitarians.[197] It just so happened that this evolution in US policy coincided perfectly with the JDC's long-standing policy to emphasize the Americanness of its aid.

The JDC was happy to oblige the US government and play the patriot, even if its own reasons for deploying Americanness might have differed. Throughout the war, the JDC made its requests to the US government politely and never put the State Department in a position where it would have to formally refuse the JDC. The JDC was careful to pick its battles and make sure it would never be met with outright government rejection, no matter how much American Jews resented wartime decrees and ambiguous responses from the government.[198] JDC leaders knew well that getting any relief whatsoever to their brethren was entirely dependent on the goodwill of the State Department. This was the case even as the JDC used its neutrality, as an organization of civilians and servers of humanity, to encourage Germany and the Ottomans to accept aid. Balancing these seemingly irreconcilable positions was essential to the JDC's continued campaign to aid Jews.

Accordingly, William Phillips wrote in late 1918, "I have always found the officers of the [Joint Distribution] Committee anxious to cooperate with the Department [of State], to be guided by its advice and to take no step which did not have the cordial approval of the Government." His words of praise did not end with JDC compliance. Overall, Phillips, the State Department official in closest contact with the JDC, had a favorable impression of American Jewish relief efforts toward the end of the war: "I should have liked to express in person my intense admiration for the vast humanitarian work of the Jews in this country and of their untiring efforts to ameliorate the suffering of whole populations in Europe and the Near East. It has been my good fortune to occupy a position where I could watch and sometimes help this great task of relief."[199] Given the chaos and restrictions of war, American Jews fared well when it came to their relationship with the US government and resulting ability to work abroad. After all, American Jewish relief was close to the only relief to reach Poland and Palestine throughout the war. This solidifying relationship with the highest levels of the US government continued to pay dividends in the years to come. American Jews were set to take the lead in postwar Jewish international affairs.

The Americanness of Jewish Relief

American humanitarian organizations extracted major concessions from the belligerents and overcame formidable obstacles. Carrying out relief work and navigating the diplomatic perils of wartime involved great skill. For the JDC, Hias, and PZC, credible information to make decisions was difficult to obtain. These organizations worried constantly about inciting antisemitic sentiment in places where they were supposed to be providing relief, and they had to contend with internal debates in every Jewish community they touched. They did not accomplish everything they hoped to do in the manner they intended in sending Americans to conduct relief on the ground, making more use of US diplomats in Europe, and sending food, medicine, and clothing anywhere but Palestine. Yet they provided critical support to Jews across a vast geographic space.

Although these organizations provided relief intended for other Jews, the war provided them with a way to become more American. American Jews discovered that they could operate freely on behalf of Jews directly affected by the war within a broader American humanitarian movement that embraced aid to distressed populations. A cartoon designed by JDC secretary, Albert Lucas, appealing for funds, illustrates this duality: An imposing arch on US soil facing an impoverished population on the shores of Europe reads both "Jewish Mutual Responsibility" and "American Jewish Opportunity."[200] Jewish organizations, moreover, realized that they could appropriate an American identity rather than an ethnic immigrant identity by labeling their aid "American." This maneuver gained credence with the State Department's initially informal and then more expansive association with Jewish relief.

The relatively harmonious and unrestricted situation in which the JDC and the PZC operated in Palestine was an excellent example of what was possible when American state interests and the interests of Jewish Americans aligned. Since relief figures went down once the United States declared war, it might seem as if these organizations became incapacitated or lost their credibility with the State Department, when in fact, organizing the relief route via the Netherlands, continuing regular relief payments in enemy and revolutionary states, and doing it under an "American" brand were remarkable feats.

Yet the distinction between private and state organizations was stronger between the Jewish organizations and the state than, say, for the American Red Cross, the Commission for Relief in Belgium, or even the Rockefeller Foundation. As Jewish associations, a particular identity defined everything from their fundraising pool, committee members, solidarity with strangers, fears, and overseas networks. In a way, these American Jewish organizations were inherently international and neutral from the outset: concerned with Jewish survival everywhere.

The American Jewish response to Jewish war sufferers sets the scene for the rest of this book. The Joint Distribution Committee and Hias aided war sufferers for the next decade. It was only after the end of the war that the Joint Distribution Committee and other organizations were able to spend their amassed funds and physically enter previously war-

torn territories to administer relief, distribute aid, and rebuild infrastructure. Based on wartime collaborations, these organizations took decisive
steps to continue working hand in hand with other Americans, most
especially, the American Relief Administration, and move to the field
to carry out a vast plan for the relief and eventual reconstruction of Jewish
life in Europe for the next ten years. They brought aspects of their relief
with them to the greater field of American humanitarian relief – namely,
institutionalized remittance delivery – and tied themselves closer to
America, increasing the distance with their immigrant past even while
continuing to aid relatives from the old world.

2 The Hungry
Establishing In-Kind Relief in the Field

"Dear Brother Max: After not communicating with you for nearly two years, it is not without emotion that I dictate these lines, which naturally bring to you, to Mother and the whole family the fondest love, and the hope that you are all well." Felix Warburg penned this note to his brother in Germany, Max Warburg, on November 15, 1918, just four days after the armistice between the Allies and Germany. He continued, "I cannot let this opportunity pass without telling you how happy we are that this horrible nightmare is over and by the time this reaches you, I hope that conditions surrounding you have quieted down."[1] This formal yet touching letter reminds us that even the wealthiest men at the head of Jewish relief were personally affected by the war. However, Felix did not write the letter only to greet his family, which would likely have been impossible just after the armistice – the letter traveled to Europe with the American Relief Administration.

Felix explained: "Herbert Hoover is going to Europe on a flying trip to study the food conditions and to map out a program for reconstruction work on behalf of the United States."[2] Hoover's personal secretary was a young Lewis L. Strauss, an American Jew who had worked since June 1917 for Hoover, then head of the US Food Administration.[3] Before leaving for the flying trip, Strauss discussed the question of Jewish relief with Felix Warburg, agreeing to help collect information on the status of Jews in war-torn regions of Europe.[4]

Hoover and Strauss headed to Paris along with other delegates of the American Relief Administration. The JDC and the American Jewish Congress were making plans to send their own representatives as quickly as possible. Paris would soon be the epicenter of not only postwar diplomacy but also humanitarian relief. In Paris, American Jews would meet Jewish delegates from Eastern Europe and send the first relief operations to Warsaw, and then Prague and Bucharest.

The armistice meant that it was now possible for American relief workers and emergency provisions, especially food, clothing, and basic medical supplies, to travel safely and often to Western and Central

Europe. But along the Eastern Front, the war was not over.[5] For millions of Jews living in this shatterzone, the "horrible nightmare" of war was to last several more years. Relief workers in East Central Europe contended with unpredictable violence and disruption as they tried to carry out planned relief activities and could not travel further east, into the new Soviet Russia, at all. It was only in 1922 that the American Relief Administration, with the JDC as an integral part, entered Ukraine to provide famine relief and emergency operations based on their earlier efforts in Poland.

This chapter examines how Americans organized to feed the hungry civilian victims of the continuing war in East Central Europe and then in Soviet Russia. JDC representatives spent far less energy worrying about the contents of food or the meaning and politics of food than figuring out how to operate a truly transnational organization; how to build necessary alliances and navigate politics; how to remain functional amid continued insecurity in Eastern Europe; and how to reach the most needy Jews. While food relief was a major feature of post–armistice urgent relief, there was also clothing distribution, remittance deliveries, the provision of basic sanitary supplies and shelter, and general social reconstruction. Since the JDC worked toward all of these goals simultaneously, this chapter will use "hungry," "naked," and "food" as metonyms for emergency relief writ large and is mainly concerned with understanding the mechanism and politics by which the JDC reached the hungry. Hungry and naked Jews, and the food and clothing needed to sustain these people, were the first metrics used by the JDC to confront the humanitarian crisis.

American food relief to Europe, which began on an unprecedented scale during the war, was always strategic – a way of winning the conflict, boosting America's standing in Europe, and then stabilizing Europe after the war.[6] The story of emergency food relief to Europe from 1918 to 1922 is a story about American engagement with the world. This story becomes more important when juxtaposed with the US Congress' simultaneous rejection of membership in the League of Nations. Food relief was America's answer, both humanitarian and political, to social chaos and revolution. Its face was Herbert Hoover: engineer, humanitarian, and future president. Hoover stated, "there is a strong tendency on the part of the American people to return to their instinctive desire for separation from European entanglements ... There is no way through which the national conscience can be so awakened as ... they should be providing food stuffs for millions of people in Europe."[7]

Emergency relief undertaken by Jews and for Jews was American in a way it had only been rhetorically during war. With the ARA, the JDC moved into political vacuums, and the two organizations mimicked each other and cooperated in their self-perceived modern logistics and problem-solving behaviors. Their motives and goals overlapped, but only partially. The ARA set out to contain revolution, stabilize Europe through private initiatives, and prove America's progressive and business value to the world. The JDC also sought stability in Europe for the benefit of Europe's Jews, but the urgency of relief at this point demanded a more limited goal of feeding and clothing as many suffering Jews as possible, by using its relationships with other American organizations and the US State Department. The JDC provided one answer to the Jewish Question that was then being hashed out in Paris: Bring Jews productively into modernity through rehabilitative projects and the support of Jewish institutions, helping them as Jews, but also as a crucial part of the new states in which they lived. This functionalist answer, carried out through relief work, echoed the hopes American Jewish organizations placed in the Minorities Treaties and their promise of collective rights for Jews within modern nation-states. From the beginning of the negotiations that would result in these Minorities Treaties, humanitarian field work served in some ways as a testing ground for diplomacy going on in Paris, London, and Washington, by providing instant feedback for what kind of postwar settlement was required to create stability and a durable peace. And it cemented the process of recalibrating the American Jewish role in global Jewish life that began in 1914, as American Jews spread out through the old country and began to shape the terms of their Jewish brethren's postwar conditions.

The chapter will make its own European "flying trip," beginning in Paris, and following relief workers from there to Poland and other Central and Eastern European countries, and years later, to Ukraine. The provision of emergency relief transformed the JDC from an organization of New York bankers and lawyers who sent money overseas to an entrenched organization on the ground across Europe and the Eastern Mediterranean, represented by American Jewish social service professionals. The first section will explore how, in the immediate aftermath of the armistice, Paris became the staging ground for international socioeconomic welfare diplomacy, not just political diplomacy. Humanitarians and diplomats who gathered in Paris, the headquarters for relief operations, connected the field and the negotiating room. Second, once JDC social worker Boris Bogen reached Poland, he and other JDC delegates worked to establish relief, drawing deeply on the JDC's relationship with the ARA and State Department and relying once again on remittances to fill out relief provisions and provide information as to where general relief should be directed. Incidents like a pogrom in

Pinsk just after a visit from a JDC delegate and an incursion into Poland by the Red Cavalry threatened to shatter this delicate system of relief and rewrite the negotiations in Paris. Third and finally, this chapter investigates the JDC's long-standing efforts to find a way to help Jews in Ukraine, which only became possible on a large scale when the ARA decided to conduct famine relief in Russia. As it turned out, trying to provide humanitarian relief to a minority within recently post-revolutionary, communist Russia was far more politically fraught than entering a politically fragile new Poland with a ship full of American food. As the chapter progresses eastward, it will consider how the JDC evolved into an international organization by delivering food relief during political instability and violence, and what kind of cooperation and networks this involved, from the American state to immigrant groups.

The Humanitarian Periphery at Paris

In the months after the armistice, diplomats, heads of state, heads of private associations, journalists, and groups of political hopefuls descended on Paris. State officials negotiated against a backdrop of interest group politicking, intense relief organization, and extensive press coverage. While historians have treated postwar state diplomacy, private associations, business ventures, and philanthropy as separate spheres of activity, in this moment in Paris, they were closely interconnected. Allied heads of state and their diplomatic corps led the negotiations. There were also private citizens in town for the conference – leaders of aspiring nationalities, colonized peoples seeking self-determination, women, and other entities seeking recognition, as well as businessmen and former diplomats. Furthermore, representatives of American relief organizations were present – including the American Red Cross, the budding American Relief Administration under Herbert Hoover, and the Joint Distribution Committee. Demobilizing soldiers in Paris also formed a vast, potential source of relief workers.

Food relief and the blockade were on the Allied agenda, even if they were of secondary importance. American leaders in Paris, including President Wilson, Colonel House, Hoover, Secretary of State Lansing, the heads of the ARC, the US War Department, and the military coordinated their relief plans. Hoover pushed for the creation of the ARA to provide humanitarian food aid in East Central Europe and use up the US Food Administration's surpluses, over the protests of Britain and France, which sought to maintain their blockade.[8] Hoover argued that relief required a $100 million appropriation from Congress, since it was of crucial political importance and would increase America's "statesmanlike influence." He claimed, "In [Austria, Turkey, Poland, and Western Russia] freedom and government will slowly emerge from chaos and require our every assistance."[9]

Meanwhile, American and European Jewish leaders traveled to Paris to try to work out a coherent Jewish political platform to present to the peacemakers. Americans Louis Marshall, Julian Mack, and Cyrus Adler represented the nascent American Jewish Congress, which was formed for the occasion. Jewish delegates trickled in from the east, forming the Committee of Jewish Delegations. Within this early prototype of a world Jewish congress, delegates were embroiled in arguments about the correct Jewish answer to the Jewish Question and the practical reality of interceding in the diplomacy of the Allied Powers, especially Great Britain and the United States, to get results. The sudden importance of American Jewish leaders in international Jewish intercession was, of course, predicated on the newfound American Jewish prominence created by the JDC during the war, and on the heightened global role of Wilson and the American state. While the Committee of Jewish Delegations sought political recognition for national minorities but had no access to power, Louis Marshall and Lucien Wolf of Great Britain lobbied their respective diplomatic delegations for a minority rights guarantee within the peace treaty. The end result of these exertions was a collection of ad hoc treaties with small eastern states, collectively termed the Minorities Treaties.[10] The Minorities Treaties seemed to promise collective rights to Jews and other minorities within their respective nation-states, a suitable compromise between the Western Jewish vision of full emancipation and civil rights within a nation-state and the Eastern European Jewish vision of Jewish autonomy or nationalism.

Among the many American Jews in Paris during the Peace Conference were JDC representatives. Lewis Strauss arranged for JDC social worker Boris Bogen, who set up the Netherlands route for wartime fund transfers, to come to Paris and speak with Hoover in January 1919. On Bogen's recommendation, the JDC's eminently capable Harriet Lowenstein arrived soon afterward to coordinate relief in Paris with Hoover and set up a permanent headquarters.[11] As Bogen departed Paris to join Hoover's mission to Poland, Lowenstein was quickly surrounded by elite American Jews who were in Paris for reasons related to the peace and who had connections to high-ranking philanthropic and government leaders outside the Jewish world. By late March 1919, Louis Marshall and Cyrus Adler arrived for the peace conference as delegates of the American Jewish Congress. As executive committee members of the JDC, as well, they conferred frequently to make decisions about relief that could be quickly relayed to Bogen in Poland, instead of routing urgent questions through New York.[12] Adler, Marshall, and other prominent American Jewish men who found themselves in Paris in 1919 formed an advisory committee that shifted as men moved to and from Paris.[13]

The Paris "office" of the JDC opened in March 1919, with Harriet Lowenstein as executive secretary in a two-room suite in the Hotel Brighton, across from the Tuileries. Fortunately for the JDC, she had clerical and managerial skills and worked from morning until midnight with just one or two assistants.[14] Lowenstein's office connected the field and New York. She received and sent telegrams routed through the ARA's cable address via Lewis Strauss.[15] All cables, mail, and parcels went through the ARA's courier services to JDC delegates in Europe. She received money and forwarded it on to designated recipients, mainly through the French-Jewish Lazard Frères bank. She made recommendations to delegates and New York with the assistance of the shifting advisory committee and Lewis Strauss. As JDC delegates arrived in Europe, traveled around, and returned to the United States, she facilitated their movements and kept them updated with important news. She also built relationships with the Paris offices of the ARA and the ARC, stronger with the former than the latter, and with the American Expeditionary Forces (AEF) and Jewish Welfare Board (the new US Jewish soldiers' welfare program, JWB) to recruit demobilized officers as workers, obtain uniforms, and buy surplus supplies. The supplies she secured through intrepid business negotiations in France, mainly surplus military goods, additional clothing, and some sanitary supplies, she personally sent to relief sites.[16] Bogen's incoming cables directed these acquisitions, which reached Poland faster than if they had been shipped from America. America had abundant food at the ready, courtesy of Hoover's Food Administration, but clothing was available at low prices in Western Europe from the Army Liquidation Board.[17]

JDC Secretary Albert Lucas in New York told Lowenstein, "Paris is the hub of the world and you are the center of the Jewish maelstrom."[18] The decision to put the JDC European office in Paris, rather than the Hague, which served as the Western European link during the war, meant the JDC could be close to the ARA.[19] Beyond this convenience, this small hotel suite became a discreet hub of simultaneous international Jewish and relief activity on the periphery of the Peace Conference. As Cyrus Adler explained to JDC leadership in New York in August 1919: "This office, as the members of the delegation will tell you, was headquarters for the interchanging of views, and when they were in Paris they came there ... Gradually this place became known to many of our brethren from eastern Europe and they frequently came there with statements, with news, and with reports."[20] Adler and Marshall made use of the information from eastern Jewish delegates to Paris and reports conveyed by JDC delegates to inform their strategy and tactics in the Paris peace negotiations. Although Adler and Marshall publicly kept politics and philanthropy in the respective separate arenas of the American Jewish Congress and the JDC, this did not happen in reality. In a telling personal note from Adler to Lowenstein in April, after one of the first meetings of the advisory committee in Paris, he wrote, "I wish to take the responsibility of strongly advising you not to send these minutes through the mail. I know as a matter of fact that letters are still subject to some kind of censorship ... There is material in these minutes of a political nature which might cause our relief work trouble."[21]

The JDC reacted haphazardly to the various reports and requests it received, since it was so difficult to collect data that might have prompted "rational" decision-making, and decided it could not wait. The JDC New York and its relief workers aspired to a Progressive-era, business-like, data-driven relief method that also resembled the ARA's. Since the beginning of the war, other strategies for Jewish philanthropy competed: Orthodox Jews collected charity by congregation to respond to appeals on a first-come, first-serve basis; left-leaning Jews sought radical solutions that required restructuring and collective bargaining; Zionists thought most money should go toward building Palestine; nationalists wanted political recognition and economic independence for the Jews; and immigrants sought to direct relief straight to their hometowns. Yet the JDC had pushed American Jews toward a collective, professionally managed effort that sought to spread thin resources in the most efficient and productive manner possible. Since the JDC knew its information about conditions on the ground to be patchy, most of this science-driven effort was directed to purchasing food and clothing. Rather than accepting donated used clothing, the JDC almost always bought clothing in bulk to be able to standardize it, make it appropriate for the weather its wearers faced, provide a range of sizes, and control quality. It was true of the ARA, too, that it emphasized the rational management of relief logistics rather than putting cutting-edge nutritional or other sciences to use, given that urgency left no time for scientific study. For the ARA, ARC, JDC, and other organizations, rational management often veered toward eugenics as each organization sought rational ways to prioritize and standardize distribution.[22]

When it came to food, the JDC assembled relief according to what could be shipped, Jewish dietary laws, and prevailing nutritional wisdom. For example, one JDC delegate based his calculations on "the minimum food requirements worked out by a group of social agencies in Massachusetts and used as a form in relief work in many centers of the United States."[23] During the war, Hoover's Food Administration selected nutrients in their most concentrated form that could keep during the transatlantic voyage. In keeping with these priorities, the first ships, post-armistice, traveled with flour, oil, and condensed milk, while later shipments brought salted kosher meat, cocoa, rice, sugar, and beans. Vegetables of any sort were absent from food relief – no one considered them essential for health. Nutritional science was still relatively new and in flux, and the experience the ARA and other humanitarian agencies brought home affected food policy in the United States, increasing the state's reach in this arena. The JDC calibrated food relief in terms of calories, in order to maximize value. But unlike the ARA, it knew that satisfying donors and recipients meant it could not erase the cultural component of food entirely – some food would have to be kosher.[24]

Although Lowenstein returned to New York in August 1919, her legacy endured. By the time peace negotiations in Paris came to a close, she had single-handedly established the JDC on European soil, creating a permanent European headquarters that mediated between the JDC's humanitarian theaters and New York, and between mainstream relief and Jewish relief. In January 1920, the JDC launched a more ambitious, rationalized plan for relief, in which this European anchor played a key role. Meanwhile, Hias also set down roots in Paris in early 1920 to launch its European migration operations centered in Warsaw. Seventy-six-year-old Julius Goldman then arrived in Paris in February 1920 as JDC European Director General, coordinating work among various points in the field and New York.[25] Goldman was Felix Warburg's lawyer, and his father had founded the bank Goldman Sachs. The whole Goldman family was involved in the Jewish relief effort: His daughter, Hetty Goldman, a recent PhD in archaeology from Radcliffe College, worked on behalf of the JDC in the Balkans in late 1918 and early 1919 and helped her father in Paris, before returning to excavation. Sarah Adler Goldman, Julius' wife, worked alongside Julius in an informal capacity, paying special attention to women's concerns when local men typically were the ones to interact with JDC workers – though such gender-aware relief was never institutionalized.[26]

By then, the JDC's communications passed through the diplomatic pouch of the network of US Embassies in Europe following the closure of the ARA's Paris office.[27] When Goldman burned out, young Lieutenant James Becker took over in October 1920.[28] He had moved from wartime service in the AEF to working for the ARA in Poland and then for the JDC in Romania before leading from Paris. At just twenty-five years old, he argued that the JDC should cede more control to its own professionals within Europe and curtail its micromanagement from New York.[29] Frank Rosenblatt and then James N. Rosenberg took over from Becker in 1921 to deal with the remaining emergency: Russian Jews. They moved the JDC European headquarters from Paris to Vienna. Eventually, Dr. Bernard Kahn, formerly of the Hilfsverein, took over as the JDC European director in 1922, moving the European headquarters to Berlin.

Instead of moving to Vienna or Berlin, however, this chapter will abide by Becker's exhortations to pay attention to relief workers. It follows Boris Bogen from the City of Light to Poland in early 1919 and then to Russia in 1922 as he set up emergency relief in each country, always with an eye on his organization's European and New York headquarters.

Feeding Poland at War

As Britain, France, and the United States prepared the peace settlement, violence continued along the Eastern Front. Facts on the ground changed as the Great Powers sat in Paris, but the Allies had not fought to free Eastern Europe. Poland and other contested land in the shatterzone were seen through the prism of conflicting diplomacy with Germany and Russia. Hoover quickly organized emergency relief after the armistice and sent American relief workers to survey Polish and other Eastern European cities. Yet no clarity could be discerned through brief observation. In the volatile, chaotic, and violent conditions prevailing in the east, humanitarians thrived – and were quickly overwhelmed. Eastern Europe was not even formally liberated.

In summer 1918, Hoover was planning to ensure the Allies had enough food for the coming winter. In November 1918, he founded the American Relief Administration, redefining the food problem as the critical shortage of food in Central and Eastern Europe. Poland was the main target for relief, and by early January 1919, Americans Vernon Kellogg and Col. William Grove were in the region, well before political stability or defined borders were achieved there, investigating relief requirements on behalf of the US Food Administration. They determined that some ten million people needed at least partial food relief.[30] By March 1919, the Allies granted Hoover, US Congressional appropriation in hand, permission to sell US surpluses to their former enemies in Central and East Central Europe.[31] With the $100 million Congressional appropriation, Hoover kept the ARA out of politics. Due to the relative abundance of American resources and Hoover's imposing will, American humanitarian assistance dominated the relief field.[32]

The JDC, sensing that American sympathy was coalescing around Poland's political aspirations and its urgent basic needs, looked hopefully toward it once again.[33] Poland had millions of Jewish residents (the JDC estimated four million in 1920)[34] and a long history of tolerance toward Jews but, more recently, outbursts of antisemitic violence and a Polish boycott of Jewish business.[35] Yiddish-speaking Jews lived throughout the region and had thrived, religiously and culturally, for hundreds of years. Russian Poland was viewed as the center of Jewish life before the war. American Jews felt great urgency to save their relatives and their Ashkenazi Jewish culture. For them it was not a matter of helping strangers but of helping themselves. The JDC spent the war searching for opportunities to augment their relief to Jews in Poland, with only limited success. While the negotiations on minorities in Paris, the Balfour Declaration, and the Bolshevik Revolution provided many possible routes for the future of Jewish life, it was clear to the JDC and its donors that Jews in Poland needed more than steamer tickets and promises enshrined in treaties. First, Polish Jews urgently needed the basic necessities of life. Now was the time to act.

So, at last, as Hoover retrained his eye on Poland in 1918 and pushed past the resistance of British and French leaders, the JDC was quick to follow. This was its long-awaited opportunity. Fortunately, the JDC and Hoover were already closely connected, not least, through Lewis Strauss. While Lewis Strauss was sent off with letters and general guidelines from the JDC, Boris Bogen traveled back to Europe, this time to organize JDC relief in Poland. Although Felix Warburg went to Washington in the days following the armistice to request the State Department's consent to Bogen's commission, the State Department demurred, saying that Hoover was in charge of all American relief operations.[36] Bogen went just the same, and once again, with only loose plans.

This time, when Bogen landed in England (around the same time Kellogg and Grove ventured into Poland), he reconnected with familiar faces from his journey a year and a half earlier, many of them prominent Zionists who had helped bring about the Balfour Declaration, and Lucien Wolf, who was headed to Paris to work on what would become the Minorities Treaties. Bogen soon heard rumors that Hoover was organizing a relief commission to Poland. Immediately, he sought contact with Strauss to see if he could join.[37] He knew Hoover was not eager to allow sectarian relief as part of the American relief commission. But Strauss managed to organize an interview for Bogen with Hoover, and Bogen headed straight to Paris to meet him.[38]

Improvising Relief against the Threat of Violence

An ARA party, filled with AEF personnel and Boris Bogen, arrived in Warsaw in early February 1919. Mortimer Schiff, the JWB's representative in Paris and part of the JDC's advisory committee there, had pushed Hoover to include Bogen as an unofficial observer. He outfitted Bogen with the military uniform of the JWB.[39] Hoover's acquiescence to cooperation with the JDC was mainly a "functional union to bring relief."[40] Bogen's presence was arranged, despite Hoover's discomfort with a private, sectarian organization, only by the JDC's agreement to fund a $1.3 million Food Administration cargo on Hoover's terms – that is, for general distribution.[41] Before he left Paris, Bogen cabled the JDC New York to send him a "substantial amount" he could draw in cash from Lazard Frères before leaving, realizing money transfers to Poland would be impossible and that more than shipments of food would be required.[42] Also in the ARA party was Lieutenant James Becker, a twenty-four-year-old Jew from Chicago. Lewis Strauss sent Becker along with the ARA Commission to make sure that minorities were treated equitably.[43] On the train ride to Warsaw, the military men coached Bogen on how to "present a rather impressive military appearance," while he and Becker "dared not to acknowledge our acquaintance lest we arouse ... suspicion ... that we, as Jews, were in some secret understanding."[44]

Bogen struggled to find his place on the commission, promising Col. Grove that information on him would arrive in the mail pouch. He pondered joining the ARC Commission to Poland in addition to or instead of the ARA.[45] Regardless, Bogen was establishing Poland, and Warsaw in particular, as the center of the East Central European Jewish humanitarian theater. Without directions or official sanction, he started to investigate the Jewish situation, which he found overwhelmingly contradictory and frightening. He wrote later, "The livelong day the procession of Jewry passed through my [reception] room, some with appeals for their own poverty and others to speak for their people; some with no message at all but only to shake the hand of the American emissary whom their tired eyes persisted in regarding as a messenger bringing good hope ... I felt humble and unworthy in the presence of their pathetic faith."[46] Meanwhile, Becker boasted to his parents in Chicago, "Everywhere, in Italy, Austria, Czecho-Slovakia and Poland we are treated as great curiosities: people turn around and stare at us, ask us what troops we are and a million other questions. Everywhere the Americans are liked ... [T]he crowds immediately collect about us and the chances are that not one person in a thousand had seen any other Americans up to this time."[47]

Far away from East Central Europe, most Americans shared little of Bogen's familiarity with the local community. Bogen straddled the new and old world, and was seen by local Jews as a friendly American emissary, and by other American relief leaders as mainly a Jew. On the other hand, Becker wrote about the famous people he met and places he stayed from the privileged perspective of someone who passed as an American, and who was not read as an American Jew. But he, too, straddled cultures and worlds, if less obviously so, frequently mentioning Bogen's work, the plight of local Jews, and his unofficial work with Bogen. The acculturated, Cornell-educated, American-born son of a businessman, Becker determined that Bogen needed military men who looked like Americans and could "talk turkey" to the Polish government.[48]

As American food arrived in Poland, Bogen busied himself assisting the ARA to organize the unloading of shipments in February, and was immediately faced with having to navigate the gulf between Jewish and American priorities. A more than $2 million shipment of the *Westward Ho*, half consisting of supplies paid for by the JDC, arrived in the port of Danzig on February 25.[49] It was "one of the first large pieces of actual relief work" after the war.[50] Bogen was impressed at the ARA mission's efficiency and "just attitude to all classes of the people."[51] Cooperation with the ARA allowed the JDC to use its money in Poland, since the new Polish government had placed restrictions on how Jewish funds could be used.[52] Bogen wrote Strauss in Paris that he would distribute the shipment without regard to religious or other differences, since this was the arrangement Hoover had negotiated with the JDC. However, there was pressure on the ground to take half of it for the Jews. Bogen worried over the bad feelings he might create either way.[53] Also, as Lewis Strauss reminded Felix Warburg, the nearly 7,000 tons of food carried on the *Westward Ho* would feed just 75,000 Jews in the Warsaw area, and only for a short time, "as one cargo is but a drop of water on a hot iron."[54] The British blockade was still not sufficiently relaxed to allow in all the food that Hoover hoped to send.

Other JDC American delegates were also crossing the Atlantic, passing through Paris and spreading across Europe and Palestine to investigate local conditions. These included Baruch/Barnet Zuckerman, Isidore Hershfield, and Bernard Horwich first, in January. Then came Sholem Asch, Jacob Billikopf, Max Pine, Harriet Lowenstein, Meyer Gilles, Morris Engelman, Frank Rosenblatt (straight to Siberia across the Pacific), and Aaron Teitelbaum (straight to Palestine in cooperation with the American Committee for Armenian and Syrian Relief) in March. Henry Alsberg, Hetty Goldman, and Solomon Lowenstein were already in Europe, in Czechslovakia, the Balkans, and Romania, respectively, and entering the orbit of the JDC. By the end of March, Harriet Lowenstein reached Paris and, along with the other Jewish leaders there, provided Bogen with long-sought feedback and the clothing supplies he requested. James Becker's increasing interest in Jewish relief landed him in the homes of American Jewish leaders in Paris when he was recalled by the ARA in April 1919, and there he formally transferred his allegiance to the JDC. Becker was dispatched to Romania to organize emergency JDC relief work there.[55]

These JDC delegates were chosen through a process in New York that was based on seniority and satisfying the ideological interests of the three constituent committees. Labor leaders and respected Orthodox Jews, not just acculturated professionals, had to be part of the mix. Delegates were also chosen to visit places they knew, most often because they had emigrated from them before the war – but they did not necessarily know much about war, data collection, or relief work.[56] The JDC had mixed results with its commissioners, since it appeared that each delegate followed his own plan and ideological orientation rather than objectively representing the JDC. The next time, the JDC opted only for professionals and technocrats, rather than established leaders of various American Jewish factions.

On April 3, Bogen set out on a two-week ARC expedition to organize relief to the east of the Bug River, "the most desperate problem of Poland."[57] From Vilna to Lemberg, the front between Poland, Russia, and Ukraine shifted even as refugees tried to return to their prewar homes, making relief work treacherous, poverty rampant, and the atmosphere tense in what was still a combat zone. JDC Delegates Horwich and Hershfield covered for Bogen in Galicia, Lublin, and Warsaw. Barnet Zuckerman was bound for the same eastern territory as Bogen, to organize local Jewish committees as a JDC delegate. Two days later, an incident in Pinsk on April 5 raised alarms across the Jewish world and set back Poland's national aspirations, prompting a flurry of philanthropic and diplomatic activity in Paris.

In Pinsk, a city in the combat zone between Poland and Russia, Polish soldiers stormed a gathering of Jews who were organizing the distribution of Passover food provided by JDC delegate Barnet Zuckerman. The soldiers, assuming they had encountered a meeting for subversive, Bolshevist purposes, marched out the Jews, shooting thirty-five and imprisoning more.

Bogen was with the ARC, not too far away, when the shootings happened, and he penned Lowenstein several letters as he journeyed to Warsaw, writing on April 11, "there is no question in my mind that this incident marks a crucial point in our endeavors and I am still at a loss to know how to proceed." He wondered if the JDC could even continue its program.[58] "Bogen[']s description of general conditions other than those [of the] Pinsk disaster," wrote Lowenstein, "are sad in extreme."[59] The relief effort was momentarily paralyzed, and conflicting news and reactions from relief workers in the field, including from Zuckerman and the ARC, redefined Jewish and Polish strategy in Paris – particularly since it happened just days after Louis Marshall and Cyrus Adler arrived in the city. President Wilson and Secretary Lansing sent Henry Morgenthau and Edgar Jadwin to investigate Polish–Jewish relations in the fall of 1919, after the Pinsk situation had already changed the relief and diplomatic landscape; demonstrated the vulnerability of Jews and relief work; aroused the American Minister in Warsaw's distaste for the American Jewish presence in Poland; and deflated American sympathy for the Polish national cause.[60]

One result of Pinsk was to strengthen the JDC's resolve to seem official and American. "Americanness" was no longer just a matter of access; embodying it was conceived of as a form of protection against anti-Jewish violence. JDC workers were to wear surplus military uniforms, deemed necessary to their safety. The JDC was not the only relief organization to wear these uniforms – at least the ARC and the Quakers did too. Since JDC relief workers were able to maintain the letters "U.S." on their lapel insignia pins, these uniforms labeled all JDC workers as American – as former soldiers or relief workers (or both), and only upon closer inspection, as Jewish.[61] Uniforms brought all the privilege and prestige of representing America, granting workers deference, personal security and access, and helping them maintain a degree of detached neutrality. This was particularly important for the JDC while traveling east of the Bug River, where everything was under military control and, for all the JDC knew, another Pinsk was on the horizon.[62] In the spring of 1920, the US government banned the use of the letters "U.S." on these uniforms, divorcing relief workers from their protection – a move that generated vast paperwork in the JDC. After obeying, grudgingly, the JDC made its uniforms resemble those of the ARC.[63]

After the situation in Poland cleared somewhat, Bogen and Henry Alsberg, a young, uniformed, Harvard-educated journalist and former assistant to Abram Elkus in the US Embassay in Constantinople, worked to set up relief in Poland while the JDC's other delegates began relief efforts elsewhere or returned to New York. Pinsk convinced Bogen of the wisdom of full, nonsectarian cooperation with the ARA in order to best be able to relieve Polish Jews, of joining Hoover's developing plan to feed 800,000 children. Bogen was determined to work past Pinsk, writing,

"Things are naturally bad (putting it mildly) but I think it would be a calamity to withdraw our work."[64] Bogen functioned as the lone American Jewish social worker among millions of Polish Jews, albeit with the assistance of Alsberg, a small staff, and the cooperation of the ARA and ARC. Bogen "organized" the work of the JDC, investigating conditions; meeting individuals; deciding how much was needed and where; directing and sometimes delivering supplies sent from Paris and the US on railway cars to small towns; setting up and supervising food kitchens; negotiating with governmental officials and other American organizations; and ultimately organizing and supporting local committees and local leaders to do the actual distribution. Bogen also decided, as the Polish Army advanced, that he would tail it, hoping his presence and uniform might keep violence directed toward Jews at bay.[65]

The food kitchens Bogen supervised included milk stations set up for children, in the style of the Progressive-era milk depots Nathan Straus had promoted and funded in New York City to provide pasteurized milk to poor city children. Canned milk arrived pasteurized, sweetened, and condensed and was thinned with hot water and served on site.[66] Kosher meat made its arrival in Poland in summer 1919, shipped independently by the JDC rather than the usual protocol as part of an ARA shipment. It was heavily salted to prevent spoilage since it traveled from the United States.[67] The issue of kosher food was a distinct aspect of the JDC's work that substantiated the organization's claim to the need for distinctly Jewish aid. Concerns regarding kosher certification, the type of fat provided, availability of kosher meat, and flour for Passover matzos, were regularly considered by the JDC, which knew that many hungry Jews cared deeply about the kosher preparation of their food, even in an emergency situation. In the beginning, it meant that hungry Jews simply forwent the pork that was offered to Poles. The ARA distributed an all-American, Crisco-like vegetable oil alternative to lard, which Jewish recipients refused to believe was truly vegetal in origin.[68]

In a sense, little had changed from the war years when the JDC sent money and local committees distributed. Only now, the JDC added American middlemen in Paris and Poland. Individual remittances and the work of connecting relatives continued after the war. Remittances were handled mainly by Bogen's small staff and hired local couriers. Lists of names and addresses were traded between Poland and New York, with clerks seeking matches so money could be transferred to individuals. Hias and the National Council of Jewish Women also busily worked in their New York offices to find these connections. Albert Lucas complained of the difficulty facing the New York JDC Transmission Bureau's clerks who had to read illegible handwriting from Poland with

Figure 2.1 A JDC Transmission Office. New York Jews queue at a JDC
Transmission Office on Second Avenue between 5th and 6th Streets to
send individual relief remittances or other forms of individual relief
home to their friends and family in the war zones. When they receive a
confirmation of delivery, they will also learn the current location of their
loved ones. This particular Branch B office and scene likely takes place a
couple of years after the armistice.
(JDC, NY_03488)

outdated addresses.[69] To alleviate this burden, the JDC tried in May to
use the ARA's new postcard system, which was not unlike Hias's wartime
postcards, but the ARA experienced a major backlog.[70]

Bogen regularly reported back to the JDC on conditions and his
activities. His long letters described where he had been, whom he met,
what he organized, how many Jews he counted, what he saw, and the like.
Alone, he covered a vast space, and his reports captured the overwhelming nature of the situation on the ground in a way that statistical reports
could not.

Although relief carried on, the post-Pinsk summer was a time of
cautious waiting in Poland. The JDC waited to see what would happen
in Paris with the June signature of the peace treaty and the minorities

treaty with Poland. Serious relief work began in Romania and the former Austro–Hungarian Empire in summer 1919, as post–Pinsk JDC delegates and Becker moved on to those regions and made requests for supplies. From Paris, leaders of the Committee of Jewish Delegations wrote optimistically to Bogen: "Let our eyes be turned toward a better future and let us rejoice that the Jews of Poland are now, in law and in fact, members of the Polish State."[71] Bogen followed Morgenthau on his commission to Poland to provide advice, met with Hoover as he toured Poland, met with Felix Warburg on his trip, and then traveled to the JDC New York to train his new recruits. Isidore Hershfield, the former Hias delegate and JDC (Central Relief) delegate to Poland substituted for Bogen in Warsaw.

Standardizing Relief in Hopes of Peace

By August 1919, JDC delegates had returned to New York. A conference was convened in August 1919 at the city's Astor Hotel to pool information and decide on next steps. New committees were created to address the need for expert medical work, and a new fundraising campaign was launched.[72] Following the conference, JDC committees, new and old, hammered out plans, and Warburg went to Western Europe for a month to conduct his own survey of Jewish leaders from Eastern Europe.[73] The idea was to transform relief from improvisation toward standardization, from investigation to decision-making, and from management by elites to joint operation by professionals. JDC leaders and committees worked against the clock, knowing that in the field even maintenance-level relief had not been reached. In fact, ongoing crises demanded attention, like the following cable, which arrived from Hershfield in Poland, just after the Jewish new year:

> The large section of Ukrainia just taken by Poland brings an additional two hundred thousand people under our care ... Our special New Years present, the subvention of one million two hundred ninety thousand marks, appears a mockery in the face of the overwhelming magnitude of general need.[74]

In January 1920, twenty-six JDC professionals crossed the Atlantic on the *Nieuw Amsterdam* with representatives of the Polish government and the Polish Relief Committee on board.[75] From France, they traveled on trains eastward across Europe.[76] Bogen, now director general of the JDC, led a unit that included military men, an engineer, social workers (one was Jessie Bogen, Boris' daughter), stenographers, teachers, a medical doctor, a pharmacist, two rabbis (one was AEF/JWB chaplain Elkan Voorsanger, also known as "the fighting rabbi"), businessmen, a journalist, and an accountant. Here were Becker and Alsberg's peers, now carefully selected – born American Jews, young professionals, or military men. They were, according to the JDC, "a well-balanced and effectively-coordinated working machine." The unit prepared for departure with an intensive course, including Polish language instruction, classes in Polish and European history and culture, and lectures by Boris Bogen on practical matters.[77] Many of these professionals would remain in Eastern Europe for years.

Warburg defined the purposes of the Overseas Unit: to establish the safe and speedy delivery of packages and individual remittances; to "stimulate the people in the local communities to the support of the work towards which the [JDC] directs its efforts"; and to "[establish] a distributing and apportioning organization, through which the local people themselves may determine upon the best manner of utilizing the funds contributed for the relief."[78] Given the need for urgent relief, staff quickly set about organizing geographical districts for supervision. "Permanent Assignments" included Galicia, Ukraine (a and b), Bialystok, Vilna, Austria, and Warsaw. Each of these immense districts was assigned to a couple of American staff, except for Austria and Warsaw, which were assigned more Americans who had specialized roles.[79] The JDC worked to set up a distributing agency, complete with automobiles and district offices, that would reach almost everywhere that was accessible from Warsaw. A few workers moved to provide relief to parts of Ukraine held by Poland and to find a way to cross the front lines into Soviet Russia. Bogen thought that having so many uniformed Americans always moving throughout this vast territory meant that local Jews would benefit from the protection American uniforms carried.[80]

Cyrus Adler and Louis Marshall had extolled that Jews would be members of the Polish State under the Minorities Treaties. Meanwhile, the Overseas Unit busied itself with stimulating Jewish institutions and communities. The idea of the Minorities Treaties, at least according to Louis Marshall and other Jewish intellectuals, was that Jews would be members of the Polish state but as Jews, not Poles. Thus, institutions that represented Jews as a collective were to be supported, and the JDC provided aid through Jewish organizations rather than directly to individuals. If no organization was poised to undertake distribution of aid in a given locality, a JDC district worker would help create that organization. The JDC typically pursued this strategy with the goal of eventually withdrawing from Jewish communities that would become self-sufficient. It was always with an eye toward modernizing Jewish, and not Polish, institutions. Relief was guided by the principles Louis Marshall had pushed for in Paris, somewhere at the interface between national minority rights and civil rights. It looked remarkably like the contemporaneous American idea, promoted by many acculturated Jews and other white ethnic/immigrant groups: pluralism.

Yet the ARA and the State Department did not so easily integrate new JDC delegates organizing Jewish relief across East Central Europe. In early 1920, the JDC and the State Department argued over the question of whether the American minister in Warsaw, Hugh Gibson, could continue to offer certificates of endorsement for the JDC.[81] The ARA chief in Warsaw, W. P. Fuller, felt that the JDC was taking undue advantage of its own good offices. "The fact that they showed no papers indicates that the wording or even possession of credentials is only a side-issue of the general problem of keeping these birds [the JDC representatives] in hand," he wrote to ARA London.[82] The State Department did not want to give the JDC preferential treatment, but the JDC, with the backing of former Ambassador Elkus, argued that it was not just *any* relief organization that might misuse the good name of the American government. It deserved special treatment.[83] Eventually, the State Department issued a certificate.[84]

The JDC was able to deliver cash remittances to places that no private companies could guarantee, and even agreed to take on remittance cases referred by the State Department.[85] Since the JDC provided this service as a form of relief work, it did not charge remitters. The New York Transmission Bureau continued to send weekly lists of accounts to Warsaw. Marks were then purchased in aggregate amounts to take advantage of the exchange rate, and then JDC Warsaw staff divided the funds for distribution. Sometimes a remittance would go to individual payees by way of an Overseas Unit district supervisor, sometimes as a lump sum to a community for distribution, or sometimes directly by Polish post.[86]

Alongside cash remittances, the JDC extended the concept of individual relief into new realms. Harriet Lowenstein and Bernard Horwich created a package system that allowed individuals in the United States to send food, clothing, and linens directly to loved ones in what JDC hoped was an efficient, reliable way that was vastly superior to throwing food-stuffs into a box and mailing it to someone in Poland.[87] Around the same time, the ARA had the idea to create a food remittance system.[88] Although it is not clear where the ARA got this idea, it likely grew out of ARA observation of the JDC's commitment to remittance delivery as humanitarian relief work in Poland. The ARA further conceived of these packages as an alternative to cash remittances at a moment when cash remittances were still hard to send and food was not widely available, even if money arrived. Needy individuals rather than banks, would profit from remittances under this system.[89] The ARA and JDC both instituted food drafts in early 1920, and after its first independent shipment of 10,000 packages, the JDC joined the ARA effort.[90] As the ARA filled a growing network of warehouses in East Central Europe with food, it also made bulk foodstuffs available for purchase by other American humanitarian organizations.[91]

Under the ARA, food for packages was purchased in bulk, shipped internally along with general relief, and stored at warehouses in Poland, Austria, Germany, Hungary, and Czechoslovakia. Jewish Americans bought a $10 or $50 package draft at the JDC Transmission Bureau, which meant that local Jewish organizations sold ARA food drafts across the United States. Recipients received this draft like a remittance, but then had to present the draft at a nearby warehouse to claim the food package. The JDC and ARA coordinated their work in some outlying areas with the ARA's European Children's Fund: The JDC distributed the ARA's packages at JDC's expense, with the ARA making the profit, which it then invested in general relief.[92] This allowed the JDC to reach Jews in remote areas that the ARA might not otherwise cover, and to do so under the banner of the ARA. In addition to "ordinary" packages, the ARA began carrying more expensive kosher packages that substituted cans of milk for bacon and oil for lard.[93] For the ARA, converting American Jewish cash remittance loyalty into purchases of ARA food drafts meant integrating its "biggest competitor," and ensuring success.[94] By October 1920, the ARA announced that more than $4.1 million in food drafts had been purchased by Americans – about 18 percent was for the kosher option.[95] Because the process was driven by demand for food packages, cooperation between the ARA and JDC met the JDC's expectations; it did not rely on the judgment of ARA workers to know how many Jews needed assistance or how to get it to them.

By December 1920, work in Poland and elsewhere in Central and Eastern Europe was far more organized than before. Bogen spent about $6 million in Poland alone,[96] and the JDC had more or less normalized its operations amid continuing violence. But as the Red Army marched on Warsaw in July 1920, the American embassy, the JDC, ARA, ARC, and other American relief organizations planned for an evacuation as retreating Polish soldiers and refugees fleeing the Bolsheviks flooded the city.[97] Warsaw JDC headquarters evacuated some district posts in July, and left the city in August for Danzig, leaving local committees in charge of relief and supplies. Bogen was on leave in the United States at the time, receiving updates and pleas for his return via Goldman in Paris. When he and other Overseas Unit members arrived in Warsaw in

September, they found the eastern districts they had worked hard to relieve in a terrible situation; emergency relief had to begin all over again.[98] Two JDC workers and a local Jew accompanying them were murdered by Red Cavalry soldiers who had broken through the front line. Professor Israel Friedlaender and Rabbi Bernard Cantor died in their American uniforms as they sought to provide relief to Jews in the shrinking piece of Ukraine occupied by Poland.[99]

While stability remained on the horizon, wholesale death by starvation no longer seemed imminent after a year of planned relief work. The JDC looked to a future of more targeted forms of relief and eventual rehabilitation. Becker estimated that there were nearly 4,000 local JDC committees in Europe, half in Poland.[100] Jews had also received food relief through JDC delegates in Lithuania, Romania, Austria, Hungary, Czechoslovakia, and Palestine. The top of the distribution effort was run by Americans, but the bottom was cobbled together from both preexisting and new forces in European Jewish life. Some basic revitalization of Jewish civil society had thus begun through the distribution of food. Yet, another story was unfolding in Ukraine. The murders of Friedlaender and Cantor were a hint of what might await the JDC – if it could ever get inside.

Famine As Pretext in Ukraine

Along the southwestern edge of Russia, where the imperial Pale of Settlement had been and where the Great War, Polish–Soviet War, and Russian Civil War raged, the civilian population was devastated. Given the instability and military occupations, including by paramilitary forces, hunger and disease were rampant. The local population suffered from cold and lack of shelter. Moreover, the economy was in shambles, and civil society and government were weak. For Ukraine and Belorussia's three to four million Jews, conditions were particularly difficult.[101] While Jews had frequently been the victims of violent outbursts directed by lawless troops, "the scale of the pogroms of 1919 dwarfed previous violence"[102] in the region, in terms of geographical range, number of pogroms, number of fatalities, prevalence of mass rape, large-scale torture, and loss of property. There were patterns to the violence – it was systematic and officially sanctioned – and from 1917 to 1920, pogroms began to look less like archetypal Imperial Russian pogroms and more like the mass interethnic violence that characterized the twentieth century.[103] There were approximately 200,000 Jewish deaths.[104] It was an astounding, unprecedented figure, such that one JDC physician considered Jewish deaths in Russia since 1914 "race suicide to a degree that threatens national annihilation."[105] Others spoke in terms of "extermination";[106] the word genocide did not yet exist. The JDC remained more or less helpless, busily shipping relief to Poland, Romania, Vienna, and Prague. Two JDC delegates in Ukraine wrote in astonishment in 1920: "Everybody stands bewildered at the magnitude of the necessary undertaking, and does little."[107]

The JDC was aware of the unfolding tragedy and relentlessly pursued its options in Ukraine. It took a famine elsewhere in Russia to spark ARA action in 1921, and only then could American Jews bring greater American attention to Ukraine. Existing histories deeply misunderstand how the JDC and ARA relief in Soviet Russia were uneasily connected.[108] Admittedly, it is an uncomfortable task to face the long history of antisemitism and anti-Jewish violence in Russia, its "softer" American counterpart of complicity and feigned ignorance, and the "globalist" strain of antisemitic conspiracy theory when looking at international humanitarianism. The story is fraught with political difficulties and the history of Stalin's cynical manipulation of the JDC's work in the Soviet Union to persecute Soviet Jews after World War II.[109] Famine in Ukraine was not news to American Jews – since the start of the war, the JDC actively sought an opening to enter Ukraine to conduct relief. Famine was just one aspect of the shocking horrors occurring there. As Polish troops advanced into Ukraine, JDC delegates managed to begin limited work inside Soviet Russia in 1920 on its own. US State Department and ARA leaders had heard from the JDC about the urgent need for relief in Ukraine for years; yet there was no will to do anything. If mainstream relief was idealized as "nonsectarian," this meant not bothering to help Jews if they were singled out as targets of unfathomable violence. Only by positioning Jewish need within the framework of famine relief was it possible for the JDC to combine forces with other Americans. But it was far too late to save thousands of Jewish lives.

Max Pine and Harry M. Fisher entered Russia without US State Department approval. They signed an agreement in Moscow that created a Party-controlled Jewish body to oversee relief in Soviet territory, where once great Jewish philanthropic organizations had nearly disappeared. They were desperate to succor Jews suffering from the continuous hardships of war, revolution, and pogroms. Yet it was impossible to be neutral, or liberal pluralists, in Soviet Russia, where all differences were reduced to one sharp line between communist and counter-revolutionary. The JDC watched as the Fisher–Pine initiative nearly derailed the organization, igniting something of an internal communist revolution. As the situation grew out of control, the JDC sought a third way that would not risk intimating that Jewish relief and Bolshevism were connected. In the summer of 1921, the JDC worked out an agreement with the American Friends Service Committee to fund the Quakers to work in Ukraine.

When the ARA answered Soviet Russia's call to assist with a famine emergency in the Volga region, the JDC hooked itself onto the ARA's famine relief effort in order to enter Ukraine – this was the state-sanctioned entrance to Soviet Russia the JDC had been seeking for years. The JDC even had a famed agronomist to send as an ARA delegate with the dual purpose of helping the ARA develop technical answers to famine, while scouting out the Jewish situation in Ukraine. By the time official American relief in Russia got underway in late 1921, the JDC had already begun reconstructive work elsewhere in Europe. Emergency food relief had to begin anew. While the JDC's organizational infrastructure had been expanded and refined since the Great War, working in the Soviet Union made undertaking relief uncertain once again. Who better for the task than Boris Bogen, who returned to Moscow, the city of his birth, with the ARA. Lewis Strauss directed JDC work in Russia from New York, as an official JDC leader and banker at Kuhn Loeb. First, the JDC had to turn the ARA's famine relief gaze toward Ukraine.

Creating a Communist Golem

While the JDC organized its first Overseas Unit in late 1919, it began investigating the possibility of further operations in Ukraine.[110] Accordingly, Harry Fisher, Max Pine, and Israel Friedlaender traveled with the JDC Overseas Unit for Poland, launching their attempts to enter Ukraine from Warsaw.[111] For months, this JDC Ukraine Commission, Goldman in Paris, and JDC New York tried a variety of ways, all of which resulted only in bringing relief to Polish-occupied or White Army–controlled parts of Ukraine.[112] This work was significant in its own right – in late spring 1920, JDC workers were distributing relief supplies and organizing locals into committees in Kiev, Rovno (Rivne), Zhitomir, Tarnopol, and surrounding areas – but it was short-lived, dangerous, and geographically limited. These JDC delegates proclaimed the Jewish situation in Ukraine "hopeless" as compared to "desperate" in Poland.[113] Yet the JDC set aside a large sum of money for Jews in Ukraine and made unilateral plans, such that supplies and funds would be ready to go just as soon as the JDC found a way to send them.[114]

At this time, Soviet Russia maintained an information blockade, and rumors circulated instead.[115] But the JDC heard from Jews familiar with Soviet Russia as Polish troops and Symon Petliura's White Army advanced into Soviet lands.[116] As JDC delegates seeking to enter

Russia often pointed out, whatever information could be gleaned tended to be outdated – not only did circumstances change rapidly, but also because sources were no longer within Soviet borders, and thus instantly out of touch with internal Soviet reality.[117] In general, however, the JDC did know that its help was needed primarily in Ukraine and Belorussia. There was no discussion of famine per se, but JDC leaders worried that they were already too late.[118] Typhus and other diseases raged across the land; refugees and orphans crowded Kiev and Odessa. Once in a while, news would come directly from someone in Soviet Russia, often a member of EKOPO, like Henry Sliosberg, who cabled in March that he escaped Petrograd just to communicate with the JDC, to say that its funds were exhausted, that the Zionists expected repayment of their loan, and that hundreds of thousands of people in Ukraine were without assistance.[119] Henry Alsberg managed to travel through Soviet Russia for four months in 1920. While he spoke of great tragedy in Ukraine, he noted that food could be purchased cheaply where Jews lived in Russia. They mostly needed funds to buy food and clothing, and help with the refugee crisis.[120]

Obtaining permission from the Soviets and the US State Department to enter proved difficult. American Jewish leaders sent protest letters to the State Department through 1919, pleading for information and for the United States to undertake relief in Soviet Russia.[121] An American Jewish Congress committee came to Washington for a meeting with Secretary Lansing in December 1919, after the group returned from negotiations in Paris.[122] That month, the Senate passed a resolution demanding information from the State Department on massacres of Jews in Ukraine, which led to an investigative report undertaken by General Edgar Jadwin, the same person who led investigations in Poland after Pinsk.[123] The Allies, however, maintained an informal blockade on Soviet Russia, which was finally lifted in January of 1920. While Hoover had made some efforts to direct the Allies toward a relief plan for Soviet Russia, they were not working out. In the spring of 1920, the JDC still could not obtain the support it needed to enter Russia, nor was it able to convince the ARA to match its effort.[124] The ARC, the American Friends Service Committee, and the JDC all wanted to do relief work in Soviet Russia, and mounted a semi-coordinated campaign to convince the State Department and the ARA.[125]

In March 1920, the US State Department consented to JDC delegates entering Soviet Ukraine without any support or protection.[126] Finding a way into Russia was not easy. Goldman held meetings with Russian representatives in Paris, Berlin (Vigdor Kopp), and Denmark (Maxim Litvinov). The Ukraine Commission of the JDC Overseas Unit took exploratory trips along Soviet borders, to little effect.[127] But once the US State Department did not object, JDC delegates Max Pine, a labor leader, and Harry M. Fisher, a judge from Chicago, went to Reval to apply for Soviet visas and to arrange for JDC supplies to come through the port of Reval, since entering Ukraine directly did not seem possible.[128] Reval (Tallinn, Estonia) was a Baltic port near the Soviet border, on the other side of which lay Petrograd. Max Pine reached Moscow in late May and Fisher joined soon after.[129] Probably, Litvinov's intercession after his meeting with Goldman helped with the authorization of their visas. The pair was the first American organization in Soviet Russia, opening the Kremlin's first window to the West.

On June 15, Goldman cabled JDC New York. The pair was "delighted" with their achievements in Soviet Russia. They had organized the "All Russian and Ukrainian Committee of All Jewish Elements for Aid of Pogrom Sufferers" and the Ukrainian government sanctioned it,[130] promising transportation and the safety of shipments. Fisher and Pine requested that the JDC send clothing, milk, grains, medicine, and tools.[131] As the JDC awaited their return, Goldman organized to send supplies through Reval, and the JDC instructed Frank Rosenblatt to head to Russia.[132]

Fisher and Pine signed an agreement with the Bolshevik government in Moscow, creating a new organization, the Jewish Social Committee for Relief among the Victims of Pogroms and Counterrevolution (Evobshchestkom).[133] These JDC representatives were desperate to do almost anything if it could help Jews in Ukraine and Belorussia, and the terms of the agreement swung toward the benefit of the Bolsheviks. They had no less than indirectly suggested United States recognition of the Soviet government.[134] Fisher and Pine acknowledged shortcomings but wrote, "this contract is justified on the basis that an extreme emergency exists in the matter of pogrom sufferers which requires extraordinary measures to be applied to it."[135] As Fisher and Pine left Eastern Europe, the first shipment of six carloads of relief supplies went via Reval into Soviet Russia.[136] Two JDC workers hired from local Jewish populations, Abram Pumpiansky in Reval and Semion Ilya Koldowsky in Moscow, coordinated these small shipments of JDC goods into Russia via Reval toward Ukraine, kept up correspondence, and managed relations with the Soviets.[137]

Soviet authorities, unwilling to condone sectarian relief, granted permission for the JDC to assist those who had suffered in the pogroms. The Bolsheviks were willing to fund the victims of counter-revolution, and classified the pogroms as part of the counter-revolution. In reality, not *all* Jews were pogrom victims – but all suffered the effects of war and revolution, which were bad enough. Furthermore, plenty of anti-Jewish violence was carried out within the ranks of the Red Army.[138] This formulation, however, provided the JDC with a highly correlated proxy for Jewish relief that was acceptable to the authorities.

The unlikely creation of an American pluralist Jewish space in early Soviet Ukraine was described in Fisher and Pine's report. The men spent two weeks listening, holding meetings daily with spokesmen from social service organizations – parties of the right, center, and left, and other factions of Jewish life – whose advice threatened to become "bewildering and confusing." Fisher and Pine explained that they "suddenly surprise[d] them with a plan which takes into account all their differences and gives them a certain and practicable basis for joint action." Two representatives from each Jewish social organization and each Jewish political party would serve on a committee. Although it first "arouse[d] violent protest on the part of all factions," no one had an alternative proposal. In fact, Ukrainian Jews created a remarkable, unified, independent Central Aid Committee just the previous year. Working together was not a new idea, as Fisher and Pine assumed, just one that had imploded. Still, Ukrainian Jews needed American Jews, and eventually the group took the JDC's suggestion.[139]

Unlike EKOPO at the start of the Great War, or the Central Aid Committee in Ukraine, Evobshchestkom was not an independent organization. Rather, it was part of the Bolshevik government under the Central Commissariat for Jewish Affairs in Soviet Russia. Government and society were synonymous, as Fisher and Pine noted. The case for Jewish national autonomy would not work. While Evobshchestkom's organizational structure contained remnants of the old philanthropic Russian Jewish organizations on the JDC's insistence – EKOPO, ORT, and OZE – they were overwhelmed by leftist and communist Jewish parties. The JDC was given one representative on Evobshchestkom. Fisher and Pine appointed an American from Bogen's Polish Overseas Unit and hired a local professor to assist him. The agreement called for local Jewish social service commissions, built upon a union of existing political and civic organizations and in cooperation with general relief work, and entailed using the Russian Red Cross Society to store and move commodities. The JDC was to turn over its relief supplies to Evobshchestkom, and the Soviet government was supposed to provide funds, although the exchange rate remained a sticking point.[140] In short, the committee turned the JDC's usual practice on its head, moving control over relief out of the hands of American Jewish leadership and into those of the receiving government. It also traded American Jewish support for the last shreds of Russian Jewish autonomy. It was an unusual humanitarian arrangement, to say the least.

Dr. Frank F. Rosenblatt supervised the Fisher–Pine agreement in Soviet Russia from September 1920 to February 1921. As he tried to lay the groundwork for relief in Russia, he discovered many misunderstandings, including the amount of money the JDC had committed.[141] The JDC decided it would adhere to the Fisher–Pine agreement, but test out sending small sums, even though it suspected the only reason the Soviets had signed an agreement was to bring in badly needed funds.[142] This resembled the procedure that Bogen had arranged from the Hague in 1917, when he sent a test sum of JDC money through the Hague to German Jews for distribution. Meanwhile, in New York, the JDC Committee on Russia was busy seeking State Department approval for the Fisher–Pine agreement, without success.[143] Rosenblatt entered Soviet Russia via Reval, without explicit State Department approval and without an American passport to travel there.

The JDC never sent larger sums or shipments of goods under the Fisher–Pine Agreement. After months of frustrating negotiations with Evobshchestkom, Rosenblatt came to agree with Fisher and Pine: Getting any aid to Jews in Soviet Russia would require deference to the Bolshevik government at exploitative exchange rates. Moreover, without a visible relief organization at the local level or opening Odessa as a closer port, it was hard to imagine how appropriations of money or goods would ever reach those in need. When Rosenblatt refused to play Soviet politics, OZE, EKOPO, and ORT – the last vestiges of non-Party participation in Jewish relief – were officially dismantled (unofficially, though, the OZE and the ORT in fact limped on).[144]

Evobshchestkom took on a life of its own that shocked and dismayed the JDC, as the Soviets seemed to use it as a wedge to force open a window to America. It sent a representative, David H. Dubrowksy, to New York as its agent in September 1920.[145] He set up an office and began soliciting funds, goods, and remittances from American Jews, competing with the JDC, even as the JDC continued to operate cautiously through it via Rosenblatt in Russia. By late 1921, Dubrowsky also represented the Russian Red Cross Society as a quasi-diplomat in New York, selling remittance food packages under the name of Fridtjof Nansen's International Committee for Russian Relief, the Russian famine relief organized through the League of Nations.[146] Dubrowsky had a penchant for writing scathing remarks and publishing private letters in the Yiddish press. He publicly shamed the JDC, which refused to cooperate with him. Meanwhile, landsmanshaftn that the JDC had carefully cultivated and the People's Relief Committee, the left-wing constituent organization of the JDC, began to use Dubrowksy's services to send relief to Russia. Within People's Relief, there arose calls to secede from the JDC, which nearly happened on several occasions.

It was obvious that Evobshchestkom charged exorbitant exchange rates, was willing to send unsorted and used clothing, did not have the infrastructure to deliver remittances or food packages, and had no way to guarantee its accountability to donors. The Bolshevik government was happy to exploit Jewish relief to take American dollars and stake out a presence in New York. Yet, some prominent JDC figures, such as Judah Magnes, decided that Dubrowsky was the only way to reach Russian Jews.[147] Meanwhile, the Red Scare was ascendant in America, with its canard of "Jewish Bolshevism" threatening Jewish security.[148] Difficulties with Dubrowsky, in the context of the Red Scare, prompted the JDC to limit all its cooperation with Evobshchestkom. As a result, the JDC was incapacitated when it came to Russian relief.[149]

Later, Boris Bogen reflected that the JDC was too timid and could have done more to cooperate with Evobshchestkom, despite its drawbacks.[150] Perhaps this was true, but the JDC had successfully relied on the goodwill and protection of the State Department and the ARA during the war and in Poland, and it was unable to make a firm decision to cut off these relationships in favor of cooperation with the Bolsheviks, even for humanitarian purposes. Like other American humanitarian organizations, one of the JDC's core operating principles was organizational neutrality.

The JDC eventually found a way to make some of its funds available to Jews in Ukraine, by asking the American Friends Service Committee (AFSC) to extend its operations on the JDC's behalf. The Quakers had experienced similar political problems working in Soviet Russia, including resistance from the US State Department. But the Friends, unlike the JDC, did not have to cope with the baggage of antisemitism. The British Friends sorted out matters, and the AFSC joined the British Friends' relief work in Russia in September 1920, as Rosenblatt entered the country.[151] The AFSC distributed relief for many organizations in Russia and acted as a clearinghouse for information regarding wider relief efforts there. Rosenblatt came home in the spring of 1921, pleading for the JDC to continue working with Evobshchestkom in Russia; he must have seen some promise there, but had not experienced Dubrowsky's campaign. He asked the JDC to spend $3–4 million on land and farm equipment for Jewish farmers and supplies for hospitals and schools in Ukraine's big cities.[152] Instead, the JDC began to work toward sending small sums for distribution by the Quakers.[153] Warburg wrote Bogen that he felt Rosenblatt's agreement with the Soviet government was worse than the Fisher–Pine terms and would not satisfy the "many shades of contributors," especially in light of the possibility of working with the Friends.[154]

In April, leaders of the JDC and the AFSC met twice, and the JDC expressed its hope to send along its own representatives as AFSC representatives.[155] Rosenblatt felt that "only a Jew would be able to know what was necessary to alleviate the misery of the Jews, and where it should be sent." He also worried that the Friends already in Russia were afraid of adding a JDC representative, "because of the theory that Jews are not cooperative and cannot work in harmony with non-Jewish members of their Unit." The AFSC did agree to distribute the $100,000 appropriation of JDC money, but without publicity. The JDC was made to understand that "the inclusion of Jewish workers would menace their [Friends'] influence and lead to misunderstanding their work and thus defeat our purposes as well as theirs."[156] Still, the AFSC agreed to send money to Jewish-dominated areas in Ukraine and Belorussia. This challenged the AFSC's appearance of equal treatment regardless of religious or ethnic affiliation.[157]

The JDC planned to send millions of dollars to Russia but was unable to take action in a way that could bridge America and Soviet Russia. Thus, after a year and a half of actively struggling to support Jews in Ukraine, it only sent some carloads of rice, condensed milk, and oil.[158] Although JDC delegates worked out bold agreements in Moscow, once they returned to New York, they could not convince the JDC to bet millions on Jewish communists in Russia on the chance that some relief could be distributed. Evobshchestkom was a golem of the JDC's own creation, a Jewish arm of the Party that was unreliable at best and sometimes downright hostile, but which now had a full monopoly on Jewish relief in Russia. Fortunately for the JDC and Jewish sufferers in Ukraine, in the summer of 1921, the ARA and the State Department finally came around to the idea of a Russian mission. The JDC had waited a whole Great War to go with the ARA to Poland; for Russia, it would take a Great War, a revolution, a civil war, an interstate war, and a famine.

The Elusive Politics of Relief

Speaking to the JDC executive committee in March 1921, Frank Rosenblatt expressed despair at the overwhelming needs of Jews in Ukraine and at the JDC's inability to help. Yet, he insisted that any effort was better than doing nothing: "No physician will kill a patient even if he knows that he is going to die. The situation is so terrible that we cannot— because we cannot save them all—refuse to save some. We must do what we can."[159] By the summer of 1921, various left-wing Jewish groups and landsmanshaftn in the United States were sending money and packages through the New York office of Evobshchestkom, while the JDC provided about $100,000 to the AFSC for relief in Ukraine. Following the famine appeal of Maxim Gorky for the Volga region, the ARA entered Russia at last, opening an official American door to Soviet Russia just as that country was transitioning to the New Economic Policy (NEP).[160] While the JDC's relief work in Soviet Russia might be just a subplot within the story of the ARA, it was a serious dimension of the JDC's overall relief work, and it had the potential to change the lives of the millions of Jews within Soviet borders. The JDC slowly transitioned into a relief role with the ARA in Russia, not committing itself fully until March 1922. But first, the ARA had to be convinced there was a famine in Ukraine, and only then could the JDC even hope to relieve the Jews who were concentrated there.

The ARA signed an agreement in Riga with the Soviet government at the end of August 1921.[161] The JDC did not immediately join the ARA or abandon its partnership with the AFSC. Days after the Riga agreement of the ARA had been signed, Herbert Hoover held a meeting with representatives of the European Relief Council, including the ARA, AFSC, ARC, and JDC.[162] Following the meeting, the JDC began to cooperate with the ARA Mission to Russia insofar as it provided $750,000 for the Volga region and one representative on ARA staff.[163] Even though the ARA's original plan was to employ no Jews because it worried about pogroms, the JDC sent the agronomist Dr. Joseph Rosen for his technical expertise. Rosen was born to an elite family in Moscow and fled from exile in Siberia to America, receiving his PhD at the University of Michigan.[164] Rosen's main contribution to the ARA mission was that he paved the way for corn to be planted instead of rye. Corn could be planted two months later in the season than rye, by which time grain seed could actually reach farmers through the transportation bottleneck on the Russian railroads that plagued the ARA's relief efforts, and at a lower cost.[165] He simultaneously began organizing the distribution of seeds funded by the JDC and intended for Jews in Ukraine in December 1921, ensuring Jewish farmers could take part in the agricultural initiatives of the ARA in Russia and opening the door to a Jewish philanthropic focus on farming there.[166] He also took part in organizing ARA relief distribution to Belorussia, particularly in Minsk, with its significant Jewish population.[167]

ARA food remittance package delivery began in Russia with the intention that food would be sent to the Volga region. Food remittances as relief continued to appeal to American Jews, who maintained a strong desire to help their families and friends still living in Russia.[168] This program was roughly double the size of the ARA food remittance program in East Central Europe, with bigger packages meant to sustain more people for longer.[169] The JDC sold ARA food remittance coupons alongside their other remittance offerings at their landsmanshaft department and transmission offices across the United States. As soon as the ARA announced that it would be delivering food remittances in Russia, it started receiving personal inquiries from American Jews as to whether it would now deliver to Ukraine. This reaction caused the ARA to wonder if there might be a serious famine in Ukraine, too.[170] Yet the ARA was well aware that American Jews, and their landsmanshaftn especially, had "for seven years tried to send aid." Since the Evobshchestkom effort had not gone well, American Jews "hailed ARA work as finally accomplishing their desire."[171]

American Jews wished to feed mainly Jews, and the JDC liked the idea of working with the ARA again. But based in the Volga region, the ARA was not anywhere near the Jews most needing relief. To remedy the situation, James N. Rosenberg, the new JDC director in Europe, and Walter Lyman Brown of the ARA met in London in October 1921. Rosenberg pointed out the suffering of the Jews in Ukraine and Belorussia, but Brown answered that the ARA had to confine its necessarily limited operations to the Volga valley, "where extreme famine exists," and not Ukraine, where the ARA was unaware of similar difficulties. Nevertheless, they agreed to carry out a full investigation of conditions in southwest Russia, and the ARA agreed to extend its food remittance work to Ukraine if it received enough remittances aimed there.[172] As a result of Rosenberg's October negotiations with Brown and the flood of inquiries about remittance deliveries in Ukraine, Col. William Haskell, head of the ARA Russian mission, sent two men to investigate Ukraine in January 1922.[173] The pair found evidence of a severe famine they had not expected, estimating there were 1.1 million adults in need of food, but also found that famine was not taking place in regions of Ukraine that had a dense Jewish population.[174] Following the discovery of famine in Ukraine, the ARA renegotiated the Riga contract.[175] The ARA's investigation and resulting negotiations to conduct famine relief in Ukraine were both fortuitous and devastating for the JDC; on the one hand, the ARA had at last opened the possibility of doing relief work in Ukraine, but on the other, the Jews had for once been spared a misfortune, and as a result, they might still see no relief.

Following the ARA's new agreement for Ukraine, JDC New York decided in March 1922 to cooperate fully with it.[176] By this point, the ARA was already contemplating its departure, so the plan under the

"London Agreement" was to allow the JDC to fully take over relief operations in Ukraine, including famine and non-famine areas, under the identity of the ARA.[177] Col. William Grove of the ARA took charge, reuniting with his friend, Boris Bogen, as his Jewish assistant on their visit to Odessa and Ukraine in April and May 1922.[178] Additional JDC workers would join Bogen after the JDC selected appropriate personnel – many came from the JDC Overseas Unit to Poland, just as ARA workers in Russia had come from ARA missions elsewhere. Meanwhile, in February 1922, the JDC embarked on a $14 million fundraising campaign in America, in the hopes that much of this money would go to the budding initiative in Russia.[179]

The ARA insisted that all other American agencies work under it. This was especially true for the JDC, which had to pretend to *be* the ARA in districts of Ukraine under its purview and follow the orders of Col. Grove, the ARA's Ukrainian supervisor.[180] In fact, by some measures, such as child feeding, the JDC distributed as much relief in Ukraine – acting as the ARA – as the ARA itself.[181] This arrangement was worrisome for JDC leaders. Rosenberg fretted that the JDC acting as a nonsectarian agency to alleviate famine was a major problem, because Jews were not in officially designated famine areas.[182] He felt it was inadequate for donors who contributed to a Jewish cause and to Jews who needed relief in Ukraine that no more than 20 percent of supplies would go to Jews through the ARA.[183] Bogen felt that directing supplies to the Jews' recent enemies was unfair, when no other organizations were being asked to do such a thing.[184] Rosenberg hoped that JDC efforts would diminish local antisemitism, if the ARA would permit placards and notes on packages stating that relief was funded by Jews.[185] The ARA, however, determined that the JDC had to contribute substantial funding for all of Ukraine and work in the famine zones to justify being part of the ARA mission.[186]

Despite its reservations, the JDC agreed to provide a first donation of $1.5 million in foodstuffs for ARA work across Ukraine in the summer of 1921. Of that, 50 percent would be geared toward relief in Jewish areas.[187] This made the JDC the largest private donor to the ARA, larger than what the British or French governments gave to Russian famine relief through the International Committee of the Red Cross and League of Nations.[188] JDC–ARA relations were marked by ongoing tensions over control, the nonsectarian versus Jewish missions of the organizations, personality clashes, and differing views of how to combat antisemitism.[189] Significantly, the JDC did not want to focus only on feeding, since rehabilitating Jewish civil society was a fundamental goal that could not be achieved through food alone. As in Poland, the JDC insisted on the need for Jewish-specific relief and on reviving Jewish institutions and civil society. Although the Minorities Treaties did not extend to Soviet Russia, JDC leaders planned relief in accordance with that vision, in the hopes of helping local Jews establish Jewish life within Soviet Russia. This idea was consistently at odds with the ARA, which eschewed the idea of making overt distinctions among suffering people.

Bogen recommended that the JDC (and, thus, the ARA) focus on supporting Jewish social institutions, like orphanages, old people's homes, and hospitals, none of which were reached by Evobshchestkom, which was intent on relieving victims of pogroms. He further proposed that the ARA concentrate on refugees as a category that included non-Jewish famine refugees and Jews. This would achieve the goal of reaching many Jews while appearing nonsectarian.[190] Rosenberg looked at the model of the Friends' cooperation with the ARA, which allowed the Friends to operate autonomously without being subsumed by the ARA, although Lewis Strauss in New York advised that the JDC would do better to simply free itself of the ARA once it had established relief in Ukraine.[191]

According to the ARA–JDC arrangement, feeding programs to prevent starvation had to be the JDC's main priority. Beginning on April 30, 1922, in Ukraine, adults could eat in soup kitchens paid for by the JDC, children ate in schools and orphanages, and students could go to specially organized kitchens.[192] The JDC supplied food for adults and children in Ukraine on behalf of the ARA, although the JDC, especially Rosenberg, remained reluctant to carry out the extensive non-Jewish adult feeding that was central to the ARA's famine relief program.[193] The JDC and the ARA finally reached a formal compromise in June wherein half of JDC adult feeding would go to famine areas where there were few Jews, and the other half would go to refugees in cities outside official famine areas.[194] In the summer of 1922, the JDC–ARA in Ukraine fed 800,000 children and 800,000 adults in some fashion.[195] In addition, the Friends in Minsk continued to quietly feed and clothe Jewish and non-Jewish children in Belorussia with money the JDC had appropriated for it.[196]

Once the JDC concluded its agreement with the ARA, the ARA began delivering remittances to Ukraine. Since American Jews came out in force to buy food remittances, and because the ARA restricted aid that JDC could otherwise provide to Jews, these food remittances were even more important to relief efforts in Ukraine than they were in other regions.[197] For the ARA, however, food remittances were already a sensitive issue, because they benefited the bourgeoisie and intelligentsia, who had connections abroad.[198] In 1922 and 1923, the JDC and ARA delivered over 40,000 food packages to Jews in Russia.[199] By consciously mobilizing immigrants in the United States to send food remittances and ensuring the free delivery of these remittances in the ARA–JDC agreement, the JDC ensured that a significant amount of food went to hungry Jews in Ukraine.[200]

Meanwhile, the JDC's Landsmanshaft Department attempted to create a town-based, rather than individualized, food remittance program in 1922, wherein landsmanshaftn could purchase food deliveries in bulk for their hometowns through JDC–ARA Russian units in Ukraine. They called these "bulk food deliveries." Landsmanshaftn hoped to delegate local committees in their hometowns to undertake distribution,

Figure 2.2 Food draft recipients in Ukraine. Food draft recipients queue to receive their standardized packages in a JDC warehouse in Kremenchug, Ukraine, 1921. These were sent directly to them by loved ones and the Kremenchug landsmanshaft in America. Dependent on JDC and ARA relief, Kremenchug's populace showed signs of extreme starvation and had numerous homeless children. It was half populated by 37,633 Jews who had fled from destroyed surrounding towns; the prewar Jewish population had themselves fled or perished. (JDC, NY_00446; Report on Krementchug by Dr. Kaplan. 27 April 1923. Folder 497. item=356318. JDC, NY:21-32)

but the JDC, Evobshchestkom, and ARA insisted that distribution committees would have to be organized by a recognized organization. Probably, the Soviets were suspicious of these bulk remittances because they associated them with the special relief packages the ARA provided to intelligentsia through professional groups.[201] JDC New York, trying to win landsmanshaftn support from Dubrowsky and recognizing that immigrants were essential to effective Jewish relief in Ukraine, insisted that Bogen and his staff try variations on the landsmanshaft bulk relief. Bogen found it impossible to distribute bulk relief in a way that pleased everyone.[202] So while the JDC could encourage American Jewish immigrants' desire to buy as many remittances as possible, which helped route Jewish relief dollars directly to Jews, those immigrants could also be destabilizing. The JDC strove to harness the collective will of Jewish immigrants; it understood that sometimes, the collectivity could be more effective than any planned action the JDC undertook as a private, sectarian organization. But the JDC was just as likely to have its plans backfire. Even though it downplayed this bulk food possibility once it proved to provoke endless griping, the JDC handled about $1.5 million of these bulk packages.[203]

JDC men working under the auspices of the ARA still found ways to push their work toward Jewish relief despite ARA and Soviet resistance. Although the JDC was subject to the supervision of Col. Grove, who was in charge of the ARA in Ukraine, Bogen's friendly relationship with him paid off.[204] Within months of his arrival, Bogen remarked on how Jewish institutions, such as trade schools and hospitals, seemed to be reviving.[205] Materials now entered through Odessa and could bypass the long journey via Reval and through Russia. The ARA ran a medical operation in the cities of Ukraine, distributing medical supplies. Bogen was optimistic and felt that Jews were not discriminated against in relief, despite some evidence to the contrary. Of course, terrible pogroms in Ukraine had not yet receded into the distant past; the New Economic Policy encouraged locals and authorities to conflate Bolsheviks and Jews and to accuse Jews of acting as speculators; and Ukrainians remained suspicious of the ARA and its ties to Jews and capitalism.[206] Still, Bogen credited the New Economic Policy for a remarkable turnaround, though he was also convinced that the JDC had saved thousands from starvation.[207]

As the ARA made plans to leave Russia, the JDC sought to remain and work on projects that went toward providing a future for an estimated 2.45 million Jews in Russia.[208] The JDC began negotiating a new contract with the ARA in August 1922.[209] Negotiations started poorly with the ARA trying to dump its entire Ukraine activity, nonsectarian principles and all, on JDC. But a new agreement, finalized in September, gave the JDC more latitude. It turned the JDC into an ARA affiliate directed by Bogen for the purposes of continued child feeding; put a JDC medical representative on the ARA medical team; and permitted Joseph Rosen to start JDC reconstruction efforts.[210] This newfound semi-autonomy, combined with sudden favor from the Soviet government, suggested that the JDC might finally be able to sign an independent agreement with the Soviets similar to what the Quakers, YMCA, and the Mennonites had established.[211] Bogen and the Soviets negotiated a provisional agreement in September 1922, and in December, Joseph Rosen concluded it on behalf of the JDC.[212] To be sure, there were problems; Bernard Kahn worried about the ramifications of an American Jewish organization recognizing the Soviet government.[213] Under the new agreement, the JDC could support Russian Jews, as long as its efforts had no whiff of religion – like the provision of matzos on Passover.[214] There were additional downsides: The JDC often had to work through government agencies and Evobshchestkom.[215] Its primary strategy was to subsidize institutions and make them self-supporting, but the Soviets did not always cooperate.[216]

Yet in 1923, the JDC operated mostly independently in Ukraine, with Bogen still cooperating with a shrinking ARA that was pulling out of Russia. Now revealing itself as the JDC instead of acting under ARA's name and nonsectarian programs, the JDC name was emblazoned on its offices, warehouses, and automobiles.[217] The JDC launched a long-awaited clothing remittance program, bought food locally in cooperation with the Soviet government instead of shipping it from the United States, and worked on its own in Belorussia alongside the Friends.[218] But most importantly, JDC activities could now concentrate on "one ultimate aim, namely, the revival of Jewish social agencies which existed prior to the war, and adjustment of the Jews to the new conditions of social and political equality in Russia."[219] Joseph Rosen was on hand to help start a new reconstructive effort, unique to Russia. After his recent successes with the ARA's agricultural efforts, he turned his attention to helping Russia's Jews.[220] Under Rosen's guidance, the JDC began planning to distribute grain, straw, vegetable seeds, and farm tools to the tune of $100,000 to existing Jewish farm colonies in Ukraine to ensure their survival.[221] Rosen obtained the consent of President Rakowsky of the Ukrainian Republic allowing the JDC to continue working in Ukraine, with or without the ARA.[222] A ship carrying seeds, oil, and machinery (including tractors), per Rosen's specifications, sailed from New York to Odessa in December 1922, and a team of workers traveled to Russia to prepare for the 1923 spring sowing.[223] The seeds of an effort to create Jewish agricultural colonies in Crimea in cooperation with Russian Jewish organizations were planted and would become the focus of the JDC in Russia in the coming years.[224]

The perils of working in the new Soviet state had become abundantly clear as the JDC tried to reach Ukraine. As difficult as it was for the ARA to function in Russia, the JDC had the additional hardships of being a private, Jewish organization with a deep personal investment in the outcome of their negotiations. It also had some advantages, like Bogen and Rosen's familiarity with the languages, history, and geography of Russia and a community of immigrants ready to send remittances. Bogen, the JDC's prized social worker, was pleased with the results of the effort invested in American Jewish relief to Soviet Russia. Although the JDC never intended to conduct famine relief, its successful history working with the ARA in Poland, experience providing emergency food relief, and impressive fundraising back home meant that it could feed Jews in Kiev, Odessa, Kharkov, and Ekaterinoslav, largely through remittances, by agreeing to assist the ARA with famine relief. Under the ARA in Russia, the JDC provided about $8 million – almost a third of the total ARA budget of $26 million. Over $3.5 million went directly to the ARA's nonsectarian feeding and clothing programs, some went to the Quakers, and over $4 million was distributed through JDC representatives as the ARA.[225]

The real troubles of dealing with Soviet Russia had not yet revealed themselves in 1919, when the JDC first headed to Europe to save Jewish life. Still, during the stages of emergency relief, the JDC systematized its operations, defined specific needs, and began to address problems, relying on coordination with the ARA. In Europe, and, eventually Russia, the JDC began to reach toward reconstruction and rehabilitation, tackling relief thematically, rather than geographically, and in cooperation with other Jewish organizations. Whereas emergency relief was mostly an improvised response, the JDC now used its experience in the field to design durable solutions for the problems it observed. One of the first issues to confront it was the Jewish refugee crisis that gnawed at the postwar nation-state system.

3 Refugee

Solutions without Resolution

The collapse of the Ottoman, Romanov, Hapsburg, and Hohenzollern empires in the Great War left a vacuum. The principle of national self-determination, enshrined in Woodrow Wilson's Fourteen Points, came to define the terms of the peace. However, it proved impossible in Paris to carve up these former imperial lands into perfect ethnogeographic units, as the Allied Powers intended. The nation-state system created by the peace treaty, with a League of Nations in Geneva, to collectively ensure peace and enforce a series of ad hoc Minorities Treaties, left millions of people in Central, Eastern, and Southern Europe and the Eastern Mediterranean without the protection of the basic unit of the new world order: the nation-state. From the shatterzones came a "flood of refugees released by the crumbling of empires."[1] A recent estimate suggests there were fourteen or fifteen million refugees from these regions in the Great War era.[2] The issue of refugees became not just a humanitarian concern but also a political question.

Refugees embodied and displayed the deep fault lines of the postwar peace. Yet there was no ready-made solution to stem the tide; the new phenomenon of mass refugees proved difficult to define, count, and categorize, let alone address in real time – indeed, historians are still counting. What to do about the more than a million Jewish refugees, when Jews were a category that straddled boundaries in this new world of reified nation-states?

Refugees were already in the making during the Great War, an amorphous part of the vast destruction and chaos wrought by the conflict. Food provision developed for militaries and delivered from the home front meant that armies that depended on local populations for sustenance and shelter in past wars could afford to turn against "enemy" civilians in the war zones. Militaries were not reluctant to ruin their enemies' war-making abilities by destroying industry, agriculture, and cities near the front; to expel civilians from the front; and to refuse the responsibility of assisting these uprooted civilians.[3] Without any inter-governmental organization to coordinate international aid and promote

Map 3.1 Map of Jewish flight and antisemitism, 1914–1929

broad planning, as UNRRA would in the next war, private relief organizations aided war refugees as states abdicated responsibility.[4] There was
no authoritative entity charged with postwar planning for refugees or
asked to represent their interests at the peace conference. Private

organizations that fancied themselves modern, rational, and technically expert, were relatively new to this job, especially on this scale, and had limited resources at their disposal. Acting from the Paris periphery, they could not extend the jurisdiction of states, alter the trend toward ethnic violence, negotiate an alternative geopolitical world order, or reverse citizenship decisions en masse. Rather, the interwar refugee regime eventually coalesced around the chronically understaffed and underfunded office of the High Commissioner for Refugees, nominally attached to the League of Nations and the International Labour Organization in Geneva, with Fridtjof Nansen as its charismatic leader. The goal was repatriation for refugees, as if that was a simple solution that could work on this new map of ethno-national states in the shatterzones.

Jews were the war's paradigmatic refugee. They experienced upheaval and displacement as a group, plus anti-Jewish persecution.[5] Yet of all the refugee issues created by the war and in its wake, the Jewish one could not be solved by repatriation or population exchanges. Nowhere did a "home" ethno-national state even exist, except for a distant glimmer of a national home in Palestine after the 1917 Balfour Declaration. Meanwhile, Jewish geographical groupings of the imperial past – Jewish "Lithuania," "Poland," "Galicia," and "Ottomania" for example – were split and parceled into new nation-states, fracturing Jewish societal continuity. The Jewish Question in interwar Europe and the political issues raised by Jewish refugees were two parts of the same question – and neither had an easy answer. Indeed, the "answers" devised by diplomats in Paris, and later Geneva, exacerbated the Jewish Question and the Jewish refugee problem, by marking Jews as the exception, the uncategorizable, and the eternal other, even as they languished, quite visibly, in cities across Europe and the Eastern Mediterranean, where they found precarious shelter. The interwar refugee regime formally identified refugees according to country of origin, putting Jewish refugees, who were defined by their Jewishness, in a singular situation.

The refugee problem became a Jewish problem. Jewish refugees expected fellow Jews to help them, and governments neglected to help "foreign" Jewish refugees. Jewish organizations had to rise to the occasion. Prewar Jewish organizations had an accomplished record, namely dealing with the exodus of 2.5 million Jews from Imperial Russia, Austria-Hungary, and the Balkans starting in the late nineteenth century. These organizations were adept at housing and feeding Jewish migrants on their journeys, negotiating with steamship companies and government authorities, preventing abuse, helping them move toward America or Palestine, or encouraging them to stay put in the land of their birth.[6]

Jewish organizations like the Jewish Colonization Association (Ica),[7] the Hilfsverein, and the new World Jewish Relief Conference (Werelief)[8] had to (re)constitute themselves after the war. They had to adapt to new postwar circumstances by restructuring Jewish political and philanthropic networks to accommodate the new map and a new international and multinational legal framework. They had to deal with the sheer magnitude and abruptness of the refugee crisis.[9] Then there was the question of how to integrate American Jewish organizations, newly internationalized, when America was legalizing restrictions on immigration and refusing to accede to the League of Nations, including its tiny High Commissioner for Refugees.

The war was a major turning point in American nativism. It created a new strident, conformist US national solidarity that persisted into the 1920s.[10] Many American humanitarian organizations steered clear of politically treacherous waters as the Klu Klux Klan mobilized around antisemitic nativism and Congress raised migration quotas.[11] Only the Americans involved in the Near East Relief, mobilizing for Armenians based on diaspora affinity, resembled American Jewish interest in refugees.[12] The cause of liberal immigration and refugee assistance was thus advanced by American Jewish Progressives abroad, even as it was abandoned in America.

Out of necessity, American Jewish organizations found themselves working in primarily European networks: Western European Jewish migration and refugee assistance associations, and the High Commissioner for Refugees' initiatives to coordinate the efforts of all European private associations working on refugee relief. The Jewish refugee relief network was informal, patchy, and internally competitive – all told, forming an articulate but contradictory leadership on refugee issues, without any state backing. The JDC was always uncomfortable in this arena, wishing to help European Jews without contradicting US policy or practice and while minimizing political controversy as much as possible. Hias, a migration assistance organization at its core, was ready to take on political challenges the JDC avoided, and so Hias stepped into postwar international Jewish relief, too, through the refugee issue.

All the Jewish organizations seemed to agree with the sentiments expressed by John L. Bernstein of Hias:

The question of Jewish migration is one which must give American Jewry and world Jewry great concern. In view of the widespread antisemitism in Europe and the difficulties of finding new centers for immigrants, the matter must engage our attention. It no doubt will take a long time before European conditions will become stabilized. Meanwhile thousands of Jews are at the mercy of anyone who desires to take advantage of them. This is not a problem for the Jews of any one country to solve. It is a problem for entire world Jewry.[13]

They all wanted to help Jewish refugees but had limited resources to tackle a seemingly boundless problem. They knew they needed Jewish associational allies but were unsure how to form a coalition when each was ultimately afraid of sparking an antisemitic backlash to Jewish international organizing and when each distrusted the others' ability to keep antisemitism in check. All these Jewish organizations were highly aware of what the others were doing, yet they remained profoundly wary. And so, despite common goals and worries, they carried out barely disguised ideological warfare, similar to the Congress Movement and Zionism. Jewish organizations expended their energies trying to make themselves and the Jewish refugee problem fit into internationally acceptable paradigms. Yet despite accusations that they were undermining one another's work, the evidence mostly shows that these organizations found their niches or worked in tandem on complementary tasks.

All organizations that dealt with Jewish refugees, at all stages and places, had to confront the issue of how to deal with a border-crossing category that confounded the contours of the international refugee regime's nation-state model. There were three possible solutions to the refugee problem, beyond keeping refugees alive: repatriation; finding a country willing to accept refugees long term; or integrating refugees indefinitely into countries providing temporary asylum.[14] While Nansen and states seemed to gravitate toward the first option, Jewish organizations pursued all of these options, unofficially dividing them along organizational lines. Each private Jewish organization defined "refugee" differently to match its own ideological orientation and vision for how Jews were to fit in the modern postwar world. Still, they based their responses to Jewish refugees on political expediency and on their divergent experiences of migration assistance. They had to make compromises between ideal solutions and practical limits, including how to deal with antisemitism.

The JDC's rationalized, Progressive approach was to work on sheltering and feeding refugees in the short term, and then to try to find solutions to integrate refugees into their lands of asylum (or even repatriation) by providing education and training. Meanwhile, Hias's goal was to remove as many refugees as possible from Europe via emigration, which they did by filling US quotas and finding immigration opportunities elsewhere. For European Jewish organizations especially, dealing with refugees postwar seemed a continuation of earlier work, and they saw the strategies of emigration facilitation, maintaining stranded refugees, and negotiating with authorities as valid ways of dealing with the issue. Ica, particularly its League of Nations representative, Lucien Wolf, was busy negotiating diplomatic solutions, both at the League of Nation's with Fridtjof Nansen and directly with national governments. Diplomatic solutions included organized repatriation, as well as population exchanges, or converting asylum states into receiving states.

This chapter examines the ways in which the JDC, Hias, Ica, and Werelief attempted to aid Jewish refugees and find long-term solutions for them as they engaged in collective self-criticism provoked by the unreasonable demands of the international refugee regime. Focusing on the Jewish refugee issue, this chapter bridges turn-of-the-century and World War II–era wisdom on Jewish mass migration and refugee-dom, and, in the process, sheds new light on the limits of American humanitarian relief and the underside of Europe's interwar refugee regime. It reveals how private humanitarians, especially Jewish ones, were ill-equipped to fix underlying geopolitical issues that centered the primacy of the state over all else. Even so, this very Jewish and deeply political story demonstrates the extraordinary initiative, cre-ativity, and humanity of Jewish humanitarians who attempted to keep their activities buried in the background. Despite these intentions, Jewish organizations became the face of American foreign policy in Europe in the 1920s.

On the Ground: Sheltering Refugees

During his flying trip to Europe in autumn 1919, Felix Warburg remarked of Galician refugees crowded into Vienna, "How soon this situation will be relieved and how these people can be taken back to their homes, if such one can call the remains of their former abodes, is entirely an unsolved problem, and I am quite sure that we will have to take a hand in it if it is to be solved before long."[15]

The JDC responded in the way it knew best: a care and maintenance program on behalf of refugees, alongside relief for other Jewish war sufferers in need.[16] But in the two years following the armistice, the JDC's refugee program had a distinct difference: The JDC treated refu-gees as a special class dependent directly on JDC. Jewish refugees did not "belong" to the Jewish communities in which they sheltered, but to the JDC, which stepped in to help them. Meanwhile, the JDC attempted to rehabilitate Jewish communities sheltering Jewish refugees. The goal was for Jewish communities to eventually "own" these Jewish refugees, taking over the work of caring for and integrating them.

As states devolved responsibility for refugees at both the domestic and international levels, non-state humanitarian agencies stepped into the void. The obvious insufficiency of non-state actors to solve the issue and the creation of a new international organization, the League of Nations, did result in the appointment of the High Commissioner for Refugees, but its main currency was Nansen's charisma. By and large, American humanitarians, private and state, remained detached from the League of Nations and showed no direct interest in relieving the refugee crisis. But for American Jews, no Jewish war relief program made sense without addressing it.

The JDC hardly wished to dive into this politically fraught issue on its own. It let Hias step into the political limelight and absorb the resulting fallout, as will be explored in the next section. Instead, the JDC pursued a depoliticized middle path of assisting refugees and trying to find ways to settle them, without creating systemic changes or challenging the nation-state system that had emerged postwar. This was an effort to maintain a benign, humanitarian presence and authority to sustain organizational solvency and continue its work. This path was forged by a new JDC professional, Bernard Kahn, who was appointed in 1921 to direct the JDC's new Refugee Department, rising to a level of prominence set only by Boris Bogen and perhaps Harriet Lowenstein.

Like in Soviet Ukraine, the JDC acted as a non-state actor in the fullest sense of "non-state": without the backing of a state on an issue where it desperately needed this backing. The JDC informally relied on the only allies it had: a handful of non-state European Jewish organizations. The JDC categorized and defined refugees to make the issue of indefinite refugee maintenance more manageable and to stretch limited resources to the maximum. Yet, there were inherent contradictions and limits of this calculated approach, due to larger forces beyond the control of any private association.

Defining Away the Refugee

In the immediate post-armistice years, the JDC planned to send professional Jewish Americans in their overseas units to organize refugee programs and to bring together and train local Jews, as needed, to take over the work. Doing this, they hoped to convert refugees from direct dependents of the JDC to dependents of the locally organized or reorganized Jewish philanthropic system. It was up to each JDC country director to deal with refugees in that country. Since general palliative relief was provided to all who needed it in these initial postwar years, dealing with refugees did not present a significantly larger burden. Refugees received shelter, food, clothing, medical aid, child assistance, relative tracing services to receive remittances, and sometimes landsmanshaft support.

The JDC was adept at keeping refugees alive in a marginal state, the way refugee relief organizations had learned to do with the help of modern technology and infrastructure by the late nineteenth century.

Since no international organizations, including the JDC, had agreed on a lexicon of displacement, it was not clear who exactly counted as a refugee. European Jewish organizations often referred to refugees as "homeless" or "wanderers," although the JDC stuck with "refugee." Many refugees were, literally, homeless and wandering; some were also stateless due to the circumstances. Meanwhile, governments described refugees as "evacuees," "internees" (Austria), or "forced migrants" (Russia), and more. Such terms were rarely politically neutral. Although states tried to draw these kinds of distinctions to shed responsibility, distinctions soon became irrelevant.[17] Refugees awaited "discovery," or rather, holistic attention by authorities who might be in a position to help. The term "refugee" acquired new resonance in this era of so many refugees. Meanwhile, relief was an immense drain on resources without any seeming rehabilitative future, since underlying causes went unaddressed.

The JDC did not create targeted refugee programs from 1918 to 1920, but the particular issues presented by refugees were a constant feature of JDC workers' reports. As American JDC delegates fanned out across East Central Europe and the Eastern Mediterranean to assess and address the multiple issues facing Jews in 1919, it dawned upon them that refugees were a significant issue everywhere they worked. When they gathered in New York at the Astor Conference in late summer to plan future JDC work, it was noted that there were hundreds of thousands of Jewish refugees.

Specifically, Poland was experiencing a massive, unsteady refugee inflow as its borders expanded and shrank – Bogen contended with it daily. Palestine experienced a return of Jewish refugees who were expelled to Egypt by Ottoman authorities during the war, followed by waves of over 1,000 penniless Russian Jews per month, mostly young men ready to work as Zionist pioneers (*chalutzim*). The JDC and the Zionist Commission covered the costs of these refugees qua chalutzim, putting them to work as laborers on British Mandate government projects, like roads. Latvia had refugees returning to their homelands from Russia at the rate of almost 8,000 per month by 1920, at first mostly Jews, then mostly Christians. At the Russian/Latvian border, they were put into refugee camps by Latvian authorities, and since Latvian Jewish associations focused on emigration, the JDC did relief work at the main camp. In Vienna, refugees were the main responsibility of the JDC in that city. Approximately 35,000 refugees fled within the Austro–Hungarian Empire during the war, especially from Galicia, and they were still arriving. Neither the Austrian government nor the JDC wished to support them in the long term. Constantinople (Istanbul) and other places in Turkey were awash in about 10,000 Jewish refugees from Russia and elsewhere. The American Red Cross worked to relieve and evacuate these refugees from such an expensive city. Refugees from Galicia, Ukraine, and Poland lingered in Hungary, and Hungarian Jews endeavored to clothe, shelter, and protect them as the Hungarian government enacted antisemitic policies. And within Soviet Russia, Jews fled famine, Bolshevism, civil war, and pogroms, moving east, south, and west to be attended to by Russian Jewish organizations.[18] There were also cities across Central and Western Europe that received Jewish refugees in unprecedented numbers, but the JDC simply expected German, French, and British Jews to take care of refugees in their midst.

Figure 3.1 Refugees in Brest-Litovsk synagogue. Ten families taking shelter in the women's gallery of a synagogue in Brest-Litovsk, then Poland, 1922. This was one of a dozen such insufficient, makeshift barracks set up in the city as the JDC worked to provide long-term housing. Brest's population was hastily evacuated in August 1915 and permitted to return in May 1918, but more than 50 percent of the city's buildings were demolished. Synagogues and other Jewish communal spaces often became de facto shelters for Jewish refugees.
(JDC, NY_01678; Hortense Breckler on Brest-Litowsk. July 27, 1922. Folder 407. item=350001. JDC, NY:21–32)

It had become apparent that refugees were a significant issue that defied borders – both the borders of new states and those of the JDC's humanitarian theaters. The unwieldiness and extent of refugee issues was now obvious, abounding in every JDC delegate report. Though there appeared to be patterns to the causes of refugee flight and the problems refugees faced, they were unpredictable. For the JDC, it did not make sense to think of the refugee problem in terms of where refugees found themselves, nor according to their countries of origin.

After a year of piecemeal efforts to grapple with refugees, leading JDC practitioners gathered to discuss the major issues they faced. James Becker presided over a weeklong meeting of the European regional directors of the JDC in Russia, Poland, Germany, Lithuania, Latvia, Hungary, Czechoslovakia, Austria, Romania, Bulgaria, Palestine, and Turkey in Vienna in November 1920. The unhappy prospect of a severe budget cut focused the otherwise wide-ranging, intense discussion. The budget of $3 million, set by JDC New York for the following year, was based on donations that seemed pitifully small to regional directors. Looming over the discussion was Russia, an urgent but shadowy issue. As each director despairingly pleaded his region's case for a greater portion of funds, it became increasingly apparent that refugees posed a fundamental, vexing issue that pervaded the struggle to stabilize the Jewish community in each place.

By the end of the meeting, the JDC resolved to end "non-co-ordinated treatment of this [refugee] problem" by centralizing refugee work across its operations. While they proposed to set aside 10 percent of each country's budget for refugees, the directors simply could not stand to further reduce their local budgets, where each felt that they could envision a way to do some kind of concrete, long-term, local good. Thus the Vienna Conference reported back to New York that the existing funds were totally inadequate, and that refugees would have to be addressed separately and additionally to the general funding pool of $3 million.[19]

Consequently, in early 1921, the directors formed the JDC European Executive Council (Eurexco), which shifted the JDC's focus from addressing issues on a geographical basis to addressing them thematically, starting with refugees.[20] Leadership by European regional directors thus evolved into leadership by directors of "Functional Departments," each specializing in an issue rather than a place, including refugees, medicine, child welfare, and reconstruction. This new thematic logic would be applied everywhere besides the Russian humanitarian theater, where Boris Bogen was just getting relief underway with the ARA. By 1921, refugees had been identified and named as a crucial, enduring issue, awaiting its own department and directorship.

Newly appointed Dr. Bernard Kahn directed the new Refugee Department. In this new pan-European position, Kahn quickly transitioned to becoming "the most prominent administrator of philanthropic services in Europe," where he remained for several decades.[21] While Bogen focused on the tricky question of Russian relief, Kahn stepped into his shoes and took on many roles that were previously overseen from Paris. Soon, Kahn became director of the JDC in Europe.

Kahn brought the particular experience of German Jewish leadership. Before the war, he sped Jewish transmigrants through Germany, dealing with an overwhelming situation by finding ways to artificially reduce numbers; making sure Jewish transmigrants would not become public charges; and retraining 70,000 Jewish migrants who had settled in Germany by the eve of the Great War.[22] Kahn's refugee aid experience was apparent in Vienna; it was Kahn who presented the overall refugee issue to the assembled directors.[23] He was well-qualified, though not American; he was versed in Jewish tradition, spoke Jewish and European languages, and held an LLD in law and economics from the University of Würzburg.[24] He was also a longtime Zionist but did not favor mass immigration to Palestine.[25] Kahn generally took a conservative view of relief, believing it should be used sparingly; he had handed back to the JDC some of the money apportioned for his use in Germany.[26] His rational, logical approach complemented the JDC's Progressive orientation. While Kahn was clearly suited to designing and implementing the largest ever Jewish refugee program, his rise in connection with it was a testament to the importance of the Jewish refugee issue.

Kahn guided the JDC refugee program through the 1920s by narrowly defining its mandate. This represented his clear vision of how to tackle the Jewish refugee problem. At the directors' conference in Vienna in 1920, he proposed thinking of refugees in two broad categories, each having two subcategories: first, refugees already living in cities with many refugees, either (a) those who made the new city their home or (b) those for whom the new city was a temporary holdover. Second, those still wandering, either (a) leaving their homes with plans to emigrate or (b) those trying to return to their homes in East Central Europe. Even as he laid out this framework, he could not explain it in these simple terms.[27] Refugees were only to be treated as refugees if they were in transit but not legal migrants, so just a fraction of the second category, argued Kahn.[28] After a while, even these illegal transmigrants would no longer be refugees: "where a man remains domiciled in one place for a considerable period, we are compelled to assume that he has found some means of becoming self-supporting, or that the local community has been approached and is rendering him some assistance ... he ceases ... to be a 'refugee.'"[29] War refugees living in Vienna, Budapest, Danzig, the Hague, Amsterdam, Antwerp, Hamberg, Berlin, or Paris did not come under his jurisdiction – he had only the resources to focus on those in flight and not residing in communities that should have the means to care for them on their own. Kahn mainly aimed for settlement, to establish a durable solution on the ground even if the legal situation was still hazy. He recognized the limits and moral failings of this approach but emphasized maintaining JDC organizational solvency by compelling refugees and the communities sheltering them to self or local sufficiency. All this meant, for example, that Kahn estimated in late 1921 that there were just 26,500 Jewish refugees between the Baltic and Black Seas.[30] One must keep in mind that the JDC's refugee figures from 1920 onward were a conservative estimate of what could otherwise be reasonably counted as hundreds of thousands of refugees.

Kahn was not alone in his pragmatic belief that "refugees" had to be a carefully circumscribed term and that care for them had to have an end in sight. Other European directors at the Vienna Conference agreed with Kahn's perspective. By contrast, James Becker dissented, believing that each refugee should be given options: going to America, being put in contact with relatives, returning home, or becoming self-supporting where they currently resided.[31] Yet to offer settlement anywhere was not practicable for a private association, even one with local partners and a claim to Americanness. While JDC delegates in Ukraine wished for "immigration en masse" for the Jews, they still understood it to be "apparently impossible."[32]

The Vienna Conference made perfectly clear that although the JDC wanted to help refugees, it did not know how without undermining itself. The whole point of the JDC Refugee Department as conceived in Vienna was to make sure relief would still be provided to refugees across borders and independent of other forms of relief. Still, over time, the JDC allotted its resources to more clearly defined, stable projects. The privileging of "scientific giving" resembled other large American philanthropic agencies, like the Rockefeller Foundation, which provided appropriations for clear projects rather than lump sums for bottomless undertakings.

Even as refugee emergencies continued throughout the 1920s, the budget for refugees shrank. The Refugee Department was born out of a contradiction: that responding to Jewish refugees was the most important issue that only JDC could address, but also that refugees posed such an immense, incognizable issue that there would be no funding. In this way, the refugee situation was not unlike the bewildering, disastrous problem of succoring Jews in Soviet Ukraine. Bogen declared with unnerving foresight at Vienna: "I think that the great task before us, or the problem that will loom up all over the world, will be the problem of refugees."[33]

The Emergency Department

It was one thing to define away refugees as an abstract or monetary issue. But how exactly Kahn and the JDC under his guidance tried to manage the Jewish refugee situation given the inherent contradictions that became apparent beginning in late 1920 is the subject of this section. The JDC Refugee Department evolved into having two primary, inter-related functions. The first was to conduct short-term emergency relief to keep desperate refugees alive in crisis situations, responding to the crisis moment of displacement wherever it occurred. The second was to "enroot"[34] refugees as quickly as possible – to convert desperate refugees into local residents wherever they were, or at least to give them the trappings, appearance, and relationships of a local resident. Still, taken as a whole, despite efforts to make refugee relief temporary, crises kept appearing in new places and new violence erupted: Jewish refugee relief was interminable and unrelenting. The Refugee Department developed into an emergency department, an arena where emergency was routin-ized and accepted as a long-term phenomenon, while other aspects of the refugee problem were left to other organizations.

Kahn immediately got to work from Berlin, where he lived, narrowing the scope of the refugee issue and trying to plan a budget. In New York, the JDC scraped together a $500,000 refugee budget, a third of what had been requested.[35] Kahn wrote that such a budget would be acceptable, "provided new catastrophes did not arise."[36] He broke down work according to where refugees were concentrated. With remittances by now a long-established form of JDC relief, Kahn spoke to the continued importance of maintaining a connection and remittance service, now on behalf of refugees. His conservative budget allowed for the same kind of maintenance relief as had been carried out prior to the creation of the Refugee Department but now under a strict time delimitation of six to ten weeks of palliative relief for each refugee.[37] The goal was to transfer the work to local committees as before, or to Alexander Landesco's new Reconstruction Department of the JDC, so that the JDC Refugee Department would not be responsible for refugees sheltering in place for more than ten weeks.

Kahn, more than other JDC leaders, pushed to make refugees a local responsibility rather than an international one. Perhaps he imagined a return to prewar times, when countries and cities absorbed refugees instead of leaving this task to international organizations. Or, perhaps he was rather astutely crafting the Refugee Department into what might as well have been called the Emergency Department, designing it to mobilize and concentrate emergency resources effectively around unpredictably recurring crises. Kahn had to function more like a one-man wartime military emergency medical corps than a stable hospital emergency room, constantly traveling and looping from one refugee center to the next with stops in Berlin, and by 1922 in Vienna, the new headquarters of JDC Europe.

It would have been better for Kahn to have other organizations willing to shoulder some of the burden of dealing with Jewish refugees. Ica and the Alliance Israélite Universelle both had the experience to undertake reconstructive and training work, and Hias could potentially help with migration.[38] Kahn and James Rosenberg were hoping by late 1921 to create a general Refugee Committee in Europe, composed of representatives of European Jewish organizations with the JDC in charge.[39] However, other Jewish organizations simultaneously imagined organizing collaboration and assisting refugees, and their imaginations led them elsewhere. Instead, Ica, Hias, and Werelief together formed Emigdirect, an organization focused on emigration, and independent of the JDC. Whereas Kahn had been aiming for a general refugee coordination organization in which the JDC would take an active part, he decided that the JDC should just amicably coordinate with Ica, Hias, and ORT in the field.[40] It was when the plan for a shared central committee fell through that Kahn committed to shifting responsibility for maintaining refugees from the JDC toward locals. He tried to get homegrown committees to carry out the JDC's work.

Kahn saw repatriation as falling within the scope of the JDC's refugee work and as the most desirable outcome for refugees. In the JDC ethos, repatriation seemed to mean assisting Jews to return home to places in Poland, Lithuania, and Latvia, after having fled eastward into Russia during the war. This was consistent with Kahn's understanding of what would prevent further refugee crises: swiftly enrooting refugees in any way he could. Returning them home was a clear path to their reclamation of localness. However, the JDC was neither in the business of moving people around, nor trying to deport them into Russia if they had fled westward. By contrast, the governments of Russia, Poland, and Lithuania actively undertook population transfers. Kahn did see it as the JDC's duty to make sure these governments included Jewish refugees in repatriation transfers from Russia into the new countries of East Central Europe once peace was established.[41]

The problem was often that "home" was by then an imagined destination, a place wiped off the map in the war. At a refugee's point of entry into Poland or elsewhere, the JDC provided food and clothing, and once repatriated refugees reached their "destination," the JDC tried to assist with lodging and loans. But it was not easy to help these tens of thousands of returning refugees to rebuild their destroyed homes and towns and find work. In practice, the JDC and local committees housed returned refugees in temporary barracks, synagogues, and homes in crowded, dirty, unheated conditions, as Alexander Landesco made plans for reconstruction.[42] Sometimes, these returnees did not even survive – in Baranowicze, the Jewish press reported an astoundingly high death rate of about thirty returned refugees per day.[43] Once again, Kahn made it clear that it was not the responsibility of private international organizations to care for refugees indefinitely, but that refugees had to be absorbed into their surroundings as soon as possible for their own long-term good and stability's sake, even if that meant some might die.

Despite efforts at collaboration and then, in lieu of collaboration, to respond to emergencies and enroot or return refugees, evidence on the ground made clear that the refugee problem could not simply be defined away. First, there was the mortality and wretched conditions of returnees. Then, war refugees were trapped in big cities, initially having been herded there in a hyper-accelerated urbanization of European Jewish life in wartime. They had none of the legal protection required to leave by choice or remain in safety, and these sometimes hopeful "transmigrants" were unable to successfully immigrate anywhere else.[44] The sheer visibility of concentrated Jewish refugees precariously sheltering in cities fueled antisemitism in those places; Jews were threatened with expulsions or forced internment in camps.

Dead bodies and desperation did not compel Kahn to loosen his definitions – on the contrary. Kahn worried that the JDC unwittingly *caused* refugee crises when it tried to assist refugees. In his understanding of anti-Jewish violence, the JDC could accidentally set off refugee crises simply by treating Jews as refugees rather than locals, thereby openly demonstrating to hostile governments the extent of the refugee problem. The JDC was quite certain, for example, that deportations of Jewish refugees in Hungary undertaken by the Hungarian government had to do with the fact that the JDC had unintentionally indicated to the government that some Jews living there for over three years were actually refugees.[45] In Romania, hanging over the relief of Jewish refugees from Ukraine were Romanian authorities' antisemitic suspicions, widespread at the time, that Jews from Ukraine brought Bolshevism into the country (despite the Jews fleeing Bolshevism).[46] The JDC and others had to pretend that there were almost no refugees and play down the issue, if Jewish refugees stood any chance of long-term survival.

As Kahn clung to his enrooting project, and downplayed the refugee issue, he focused on crises that created new refugees, or recreated refugees anew. Such anti-Jewish crises occurred in Poland, Czechoslovakia, Hungary, and the Baltics.[47] Besides the expulsions of war refugees from places of precarious settlement, he was eyeing the massive crisis of refugees along the Russian border, especially Jews fleeing Ukraine. At the Polish–Soviet border clash and as the Russian Civil War escalated in Ukraine in the summer of 1920, as discussed in the previous chapter, Jews fled wherever they could – mainly, west and south. To the southwest lay Romania, in particular Bessarabia, a recent province of the Russian Empire (now Moldova), located along the western bank of the Dniester River bordering Ukraine. To the south, across the Black Sea port of Odessa, was Turkey – Constantinople in particular. The situation in Romania created a series of crises not just for the JDC, but also for Romanian Jewish organizations and other transnational Jewish groups, like Ica. Kahn accepted that crisis was unavoidable and dealt with its ramifications, by assuaging the refugees' difficulties in the least financially burdensome way he could find. If the JDC intervened with government authorities, it was mainly to push them to be slightly more humanitarian and reasonable, but the JDC never fundamentally questioned or addressed the causes of these crises. Rather, Kahn hoped to systematize emergency care for refugees, instituting the practice that JDC offices remain in touch with nearby frontiers and that these JDC offices all kept in close communication with one another.[48]

In June 1920, Romanian authorities noticed an influx of Ukrainian Jewish refugees and ordered that they be sent back and the border closed. As JDC director for Romania, Alexander Landesco, reported sarcastically, "We then had the wonderful sight of Jewish refugees swimming back and forth ... across the Nestor [sic], being shot at from that side for running away, and from this side for trying to land." Landesco intervened with Romanian authorities on behalf of these estimated 12,000 refugees and got permission for those already in Romania to stay, using JDC funds allotted for Romania to care for them.[49] But this was hardly the end of the situation – the river border was still the most porous option for fleeing Ukrainian Jews. Romanian authorities wavered between exclusion and inclusion, ultimately transferring responsibility to established Romanian Jews.[50] Late in the following year, Kahn received a cable that the Romanian Ministry had ordered the evacuation of an estimated 40,000 refugees in Bessarabia to towns near Bucharest. It was up to local Romanian Jewish organizations to organize and pay for the evacuation, under threat of the government interning refugees in concentration camps at the Jewish organizations' expense.[51]

Kahn went to Romania to make sure local organizations used JDC funds efficiently and to bring local Jewish committees in Bessarabia (led by Dr. Jacob Bernstein-Kohan of Kishinev) and Bucharest (led by Wilhelm Filderman, seen as the leader of Romanian Jews) into cooperation. This was not an easy task, explained Hias' Adolph Held, because Bessarabian Jews felt there was no way the government had the capacity to carry out the expulsion and should therefore intentionally ignore the order. But Jews from Bucharest thought, as did various international organizations, that the best way to respond was to carry out the evacuations but in an orderly way that reduced suffering.[52] Neither Kahn nor Held seemed to consider what would happen if they did not manage to effect the evacuation; they just took the Romanian authorities at their word. By assisting the Romanian authorities to complete a task that was far from fait accompli, the JDC may have unwittingly contributed to anti-Jewish violence in a way that Kahn did not seriously consider. It was, on the other hand, this same assistance to Romanian authorities that guaranteed the JDC's welcome in a Romania focused on nation building and suspicious of transnational Jewish networks. One could envision the JDC's role in Romania as dual: helping Romanian authorities manage the crisis while helping Jewish refugees survive the crisis.[53]

Bernstein-Kohan's and Filderman's Jewish committees received JDC subsidies to look after refugees for brief periods and help them find work and relatives abroad under Kahn's careful eye. The JDC housed 4,500 refugees in synagogues and shelters (about a tenth of Jewish refugees in Bessarabia), fed refugees, and ran a school, an orphanage, a maternity home, one workshop, and some emergency clinics.[54] The JDC asked for Hias' help to search for American relatives.[55] If Kahn presumably wished to enroot refugees somewhere within Romania, he did not contradict the Romanian authorities' investment in the tracing service-type activities that would facilitate the refugees' westward movement as transmigrants.[56] Werelief, represented by Vladimir Tiomkin, also oversaw relief of basic needs.[57]

For Bogen, Kahn's strict adherence to a narrow definition of refugee, extreme fiscal conservatism, and push to divest the JDC of responsibility for refugees were too extreme. He believed the JDC could afford to be doing more for refugees with a new fundraising campaign. Furthermore, he fretted with the JDC Refugee Committee in New York that if the organization did not raise or allocate more funds for refugees and do a better job of relieving them, alternate organizations like Emigdirect or

Polish Jewish organizations would launch competing refugee relief campaigns.[58] Bogen reflected, "Is it or is it not true that there are many refugees freezing to death because of lack of shelter? Is it or is it not true that sickness is rampant among refugees? Is it or is it not true that thousands of refugees are unattended at the border lines of Poland, Romania, etc. If this is true, I believe that the withdrawing of assistance is not in accordance with our policy."[59] But the future of the JDC in Europe was Kahn's tough love; Bogen's energies were directed elsewhere, to finding a way to help Jews in Soviet Russia, including hundreds of thousands of displaced persons, and to stemming the tide of refugees at the source.

Kahn persisted according to his core principles and was extremely reluctant to ever again direct refugee work toward palliative relief. Consistently, he argued that refugees needed constructive work to pull themselves out of misery.[60] In 1923, he set about dissolving the Refugee Department across most of East Central Europe. It had helped 185,000 refugees in Poland and Romania alone since its creation.[61] Kahn felt satisfied with the new housing and community buildings the JDC had left behind for repatriates and its extensive work, generally, in Poland. But yet another crisis – Argentina's closing its doors to immigration and the resulting evaporation of Ica's plan for resettling the last of the Jewish refugees there – made it difficult, though not impossible, for him to part with the situation in Romania. He could see only that these refugees would have to return to Russia via a circuitous route under the care of European Jewish organizations, and he blamed Jewish emigration organizations for "indiscriminate migration that has been encouraged to Argentine."[62] Of course, there were still many other refugees remaining in Europe besides this group – but Kahn defined them as mostly deliberate emigrants, and therefore, not his problem. The "problem of the movement of large masses of people—has been solved," he wrote. The department dissolved January 1, 1924, except for work in Romania, which continued through June.[63]

For all of Kahn's commitment to the limited nature of the Refugee Department, he surmised that the refugee problem in Europe was probably not over. Rather than creating a central refugee committee under the JDC Europe or shifting refugee work to locals in 1921 as had been the original plan, Kahn allowed the Refugee Department to persist and develop into an emergency department for refugees. He pointed out that the refugee situation was, in fact, still "quite serious," and that "it must be clear, if new catastrophes arise and a new refugee problem is created, the Joint can never consider its activities for the refugees as closed so long as any remnant of the JDC remains in Europe." He recommended establishing an emergency fund for refugees so that the JDC would not totally lose its capacity to help them.[64] This was prescient, because almost immediately, pressure from other American Jewish organizations following an even tighter US immigration law in 1924 compelled the JDC to revive the refugee committee under a different name: the United Evacuation Committee. Kahn realized that trying to define away the problem or prevent problems through careful planning could not solve recurrent crises. The United Evacuation Committee dissolved by 1927. Since most of its refugees stayed in place long enough to become the responsibility of a locality, the JDC declared the problem fixed.[65] Still, it retained latent knowledge about how to deal with refugees, not least by retaining and promoting the indefatigable Kahn.

As his temporary Refugee Department evolved into a semi-permanent emergency department, Kahn fashioned the JDC into an organization for Jewish refugees. He unintentionally built into twentieth-century Jewish humanitarianism infrastructure and expertise that would carry into a darker chapter of Jewish refugeedom under the Nazis.

Crossings: Hias and Migration Support

Before the Great War, Jewish emigration from Eastern Europe had a preferred destination: America. Millions of Jews poured into American cities, especially New York, changing the character of American Jewish life and American life in general. The arrival of so many immigrant Jews provoked anxiety regarding the continued ability of Jews to enter the United States. While "uptown" Jewish Americans, especially Jacob Schiff and Louis Marshall, might have had some distaste for Eastern European Jewish immigrants, they firmly believed in the responsibility of keeping the American door open.[66] They spent years battling calls for a stringent federal policy on immigration, rooted in racist, antisemitic nationalism. Immigration quotas enacted by Congress in 1921 and 1924, helped significantly by State Department officials overzealously restricting Jewish migration, brought migration to a near standstill. Historians of the Jewish refugee crisis of the 1930s have tried to make sense of America's pitiless response without recognizing how the First World War set the conditions for the 1930s, through migration restrictions and the State Department's cold-blooded response to Jewish refugees in the war's immediate aftermath.

Jewish refugees were largely emigrant hopefuls in these postwar years, often stuck in transit. Hias, the organization of and for Jewish immigrants to America, struggled into the 1920s to help Jews who wished to leave East Central Europe. "Hias understood," wrote historian Aryeh

Tartakower, a former worker of the Jewish Emigrant Aid Society of Poland (JEAS), "that it was not sufficient to care for the immigrants, but that the great Jewish mass immigration needed direction and planning."[67] Refugees and immigrants, of course, are different, but related, concepts.[68] While before 1914, refugees were viewed in the West as small groups or individuals who were victims of political persecution, migration had more to do with economically motivated population movement. In the interwar years, the international community was just figuring out how to define a refugee. What were East European Jews to do? They were stripped of citizenship by the successor states to the empires where they once lived, or took flight as invading armies pushed them to the wrong side of the border. Hias referred to the East European Jews it helped as refugees, emigrants, and immigrants. To Hias, the best way to approach them was as potential immigrants, and to keep doing the work the organization was founded to do: assist Jewish immigrants to the United States. As the United States erected "paper walls" around its borders and relocated border patrol offshore, from border officials to consular officials, Hias simply followed.[69]

This section offers the first account of how Hias and European organizations assisted Jewish migration in the early interwar period. It explores the evolution of Hias' work on behalf of Jewish migrants from 1918 to 1927 as a counterpart to the offshore relocation of immigration processing, and how Hias unwittingly legitimized paper walls by helping immigrants scale them. Hias evolved from a domestic American Jewish immigrant association in the prewar period to an American international organization for Jewish immigrants to America after the war and, finally, to an international organization for Jewish emigrants in the mid-1920s. As America moved away from open immigration, Hias was increasingly marginalized from American relief work, including the JDC's. Immigration to America was once a panacea for economically disenfranchised Eastern Jews, but in the interwar world of surveillance and citizenship, Hias could not provide for an overwhelming number of refugees, let alone remain relevant, because its prewar solution had been taken off the political table.

Hias Goes East

By the end of the Great War, Hias was expanding its work abroad. In response to the evaporation of nearly unrestricted immigration of Jews and the concurrent offshoring of border control to American consulates rather than Ellis Island, Hias moved to facilitate Jewish migration within this new "remote control" system.[70] This meant that within just a few years, Hias became an international organization and a key player in the emerging interwar Jewish migration assistance network. Since Hias saw itself as remaining within the law and spirit of American legal norms, it worked to gain the support and cooperation of American consuls as it helped Jewish emigrants become US immigrants. Meanwhile, new archival evidence demonstrates that the US State Department began to track Hias, discreetly making targeted, antisemitic efforts to block its success by erecting bureaucratic obstacles. Without realizing it, Hias was training State Department officials in how to create effective paper walls around US borders, far before formal quotas had even become law.

During the war, Hias looked for ways to help immigrants and maintain organizational purpose as new restrictions were put in place. It sent a commissioner, Isidore Hershfield, abroad in 1915 to connect relatives and opened or affiliated with standing Jewish migration offices in Europe.[71] From 1915 to mid-1917, Jewish refugees fleeing east from the war zones traveled across Siberia and into the Far East, gathering in Irkutsk, Vladivostock, Harbin, and Yokohama. Some crossed the Pacific to arrive in Seattle or San Francisco, and Hias hastily set up new branches on the West Coast to assist these incoming immigrants. European Jews with origins in the Pale of Settlement were now encircling the globe as war refugees, washing up on both American coasts. Still, Hias' leaders assumed that following the war, immigration would resume as before. Given that imagined future, it seemed best to prepare at home for an onslaught of postwar immigrants on both coasts.[72] Hias thus focused on shoring up its work at home, such as paying off its new building. It formed a committee for work in foreign countries, but this remained a small part of its wartime operations.[73]

With the onset of the Russian Revolution, however, and the corollary ending of Russian participation in the Great War, Hias began shifting gears. In late 1917, Hias received hundreds of letters pointing to the terrible plight of those refugees in the Far East, filled with appeals from Jews wishing to immigrate.[74] In response, Hias planned to continue its task of facilitating the passage of immigrants and improving the conditions of their migration. In a climate of wartime restrictions on immigration and travel, Hias would have to do this from abroad; waiting for immigrants to arrive was simply no longer an option. During the war, immigration bureaucracy moved from Ellis Island to American embassies abroad.

As an American organization, Hias could conceivably reach part of the Far East in Allied territory outside Soviet Russia: eastern Siberia, China (Manchuria), and Japan. With the assistance of Jacob Schiff[75] and the US State Department, Hias sent Samuel Mason as its representative to the

Far East in the winter of 1918 to improve shelter there, connect refugees to American relatives, and improve Pacific steamship routes.[76] Mason was a Russian Jewish immigrant, a journalist, trained accountant, and recent executive director of Hias.[77] He busied himself smoothing out the bureaucracy of international communications and money wiring, mediating among local Jewish factions, cleaning up refugee housing, and setting up a new Central Information Bureau for Jewish War Sufferers in Yokohama with an associated network of branch offices and correspondents. American, Japanese, British, and Russian government officials provided him with assistance at various points.[78]

Hias hewed closely to all relevant laws, including making sure to never actively encourage immigration. Like the JDC, it was inclined to scrupulously follow US law and international legal norms, assuming that its continued existence was contingent on compliance. Mason remarked after his January to June 1918 trip to the Far East, "It is but natural that among the thousands of refugees eager to escape from intolerable conditions there should be those who cannot possibly be admitted into the United States … It is the function of the Bureaus at Harbin, Vladivostock and Yokohama to prevent such making even the attempt to sail for America. The Bureaus are strictly guided by the United States Immigration Laws."[79] Here was Hias, run by immigrants, insisting on Americanness and encouraging adherents to follow the American playbook. Although this positioning might have seemed contradictory to its mission and the lived experience of its leaders, this proximity to immigration meant precarity for the organization. Hias worked toward an America that was welcoming to immigrants. It frequently engaged in protecting immigrants at home in America and lobbying for open migration policies – these were exactly the issues from which the JDC steered clear. In fact, it was not the case that Hias always refrained from encouraging immigration, as will be seen. Still, as US immigration control moved overseas, Hias went right along with it, creating its own information services abroad. There seemed no way to fight emergency war restrictions, and Hias could, after all, assume that the postwar world would be friendlier toward migration.

By early 1919, Hias' Committee on US Immigration Stations and its Committee on Foreign Relations had merged into its largest committee.[80] Contrary to the organization's expectations, wartime migration restrictions remained in place, even after Mason's mission to the Far East, the armistice between the Western Allies and the Central Powers, and the Russian Revolution.[81] As the United States and Britain undertook a military campaign in eastern Siberia to topple the Bolsheviks, Mason returned to the Far East. He set about fixing buildings and providing emergency relief.[82] He developed a collaboration with the ARC Siberian Commission, which supported the military intervention by treating typhus in mobile train medical units. Hias took charge of one ARC relief train and gained official standing as a member of the ARC Siberian Commission.[83] Hias even compared itself to the ARC: "our Society performs among our people all the functions of the Red Cross Society" in wartime.[84] Hias carried out extensive sheltering and relief activities (Mason referred to this as assisting "non-emigrant refugees"), much like the JDC, though in Siberia. Mason further tried to convince the ARC, with which Hias was eager to work, to set up loan societies for refugees, rather than just providing charity, but the ARC politely declined.[85] At Mason's urging, a JDC delegate and a Jewish journalist arrived in Siberia, too.[86] Together, the JDC and Hias tried to assist Jewish prisoners of war and political prisoners, tasks Hias readily transferred to the JDC as soon as it could.[87]

While Mason was in the Far East in 1919, Hias planned its official launch of relief work in Europe. Working in Warsaw for the JDC under Bogen, Isidore Hershfield confirmed that families clamored to join their relatives in America.[88] Hias president John Bernstein wrote that although Hias had not been created as a relief organization, the war made relief necessary. The need to reconstruct Jewish life propelled Hias: "The finger of destiny is pointing to the Jews of the United States as that part of Jewry which at this time can be of greatest service to world Jewry."[89] Hias prepared to continue connecting relatives and to guide a restored flow of immigrants into the United States.[90] Accordingly, it planned a survey of Jews in America to see who wished for relatives to join them. It began to search for housing for these anticipated new immigrants.[91] Hias thus built its capacity to foster chain migration, the easiest way to move Jews from Europe to America; and hopefully resistant to shifting political winds.

In the spring of 1920, Leon Kamaiky and Jacob Massel went to Warsaw to set up a Hias office. Massel, known for his public speaking skills, was a Russian immigrant who worked for the Zionist movement, Jewish fraternal orders, and the New York Kehillah. Kamaiky was an editor in the Jewish press, vice president of Hias, a leader in the Orthodox Jewish community in America – and also the chairman of the Central Relief Committee and therefore involved with the JDC.[92] Kamaiky and Massel stopped in Paris and various port cities, providing relief for transmigrants and arranging for a ship to take migrants from Danzig to London, where they could transfer to an America-bound vessel. Arriving in Warsaw a week before Passover in 1920, Kamaiky and Massel set up an office in the Jewish quarter, taking out a three-year lease. "Besieged by persons who were most anxious to join their relatives in America," they quickly engaged a support staff of fifty-four English, Polish, and Yiddish-speaking locals, following JDC salary practices.[93] Thus began the European Hias, where it was known as "Hias of America."

Hias' optimistic plans were no match for what it discovered when its delegates landed in Europe: It would have to contend with overwhelming numbers of uprooted Jews who desperately sought a way out of East Central Europe, just as the United States closed its doors. Already in its April 1920 bulletin, Hias lamented the bureaucratic challenges of navigating paperwork and travel. One perplexing issue among many was that visas had to be procured at the American Consul in the prospective immigrant's country of origin. Many wishing to migrate found themselves far from their country of origin, and not every new East Central European state had an American Consul.[94] The US State Department was entirely unprepared to face the burden of remote border control, or had already decided to avoid this burden by stalling and deflecting would-be immigrants. Groundwork was already being laid to organize and restrict immigrants by their country of origin, a process that did not require Congress to pass new laws.

Hias worked to build rapport with the State Department to continue preparing immigration applications and to make judgments about who was fit to enter the United States. Its representatives visited the State Department to appeal for the broad admission of relatives of American Jewish immigrants who planned to reunite with their families and to request the removal of red tape. Due to a shortage of office space in Warsaw, American Consul Harry McBride was unable to take out a suitable lease under State Department policy; Hias jumped at the opportunity and provided a no-interest loan, knowing that McBride's office was essential to immigrants and that it would establish a reciprocal, mutually beneficial relationship between the consulate and Hias of America. Kamaiky and Massel made it a top priority to "establish [a] relationship with the American representatives in Warsaw," including Hugh Gibson and McBride. McBride introduced the Hias men to Polish government officials as well, who eased the way for Polish Jews to obtain Polish passports on Hias' request.[95]

But behind Hias' back, State Department officials were keeping tabs on Hias' activities, looking to see where it could limit the organization's influence and create new difficulties for immigrants. Before the Rogers Act of 1924 professionalized the State Department to some extent, it represented a club of America's elite, white, Christian men, many of whom harbored anti-Jewish feelings.[96] Reporting on Hias, the American charge d'affaires in Warsaw, John C. White, wrote that "all the immigrants who passed through Danzig are decidedly inferior types physically, mentally, and morally, and because of their unsanitary habits, constitute a menace," couching in diplomatic language antisemitic tropes linking Jews and disease. The third assistant secretary of state suggested that the secretary of labor authorize "the consuls in their discretion to refuse visas to any immigrants coming from a region where typhus or other infectious diseases are epidemic and also authorizing them to revuse [sic.] visas in any cases where they are convinced that the immigrants are being financially assisted by the Hebrew Sheltering and Aid Society."[97] In separate conversations, State Department officials claimed that Hias actively encouraged immigration against US policy and moved to shut it down.[98]

Restrictionists marshaled the same facts that Hias proudly publicized as humanitarian accomplishments, using them to incite nativist feelings. A confidential letter to the secretary of state quoted with alarm, "Mr. Jacob Massel ... told me that nine out of every ten of the emigrants who had been granted visas at this Consul General during that period, went to the United States under the auspices of their organization," warning that if quotas were put in place the State Department would have to figure out how to keep Jews from crowding out the "preferential classes."[99] A report prepared by the Bureau of Immigration for the Department of Labor and State Department calculated that 95 percent of the immigrants on their way to the United States were Jews, mostly young and "ready to breed." The author, Robe Carl White, suggested that extra scrutiny should be reserved for Jews hoping to immigrate, so that Jews would be subject to secret, "additional searching examination."[100]

At least some of the State Department was using Hias to figure out the architecture of remote control and how to push an anti-immigrant agenda into reality. Archival documents implicate the US Labor Department and the Bureau of Immigration in these conversations, as well. It is clear that the State Department and officials at other US government agencies monitored Jewish immigration. In the State Department, the Department of Labor, the Department of Commerce, US Public Health Service, and in Congressional hearings, Jews were identified as threats to public health as well as to social, political, and economic life.[101] Reports and letters scrutinized Hias and often mentioned the JDC; intelligence agents even attended Hias meetings.[102] Individuals and consulates trying to prevent Jews from immigrating met no internal objection. Instead, these actors enjoyed discretion and power over policy-making. Antisemitic is the right word here, since the aforementioned language indicates an obsession with documenting and singling out Jewish immigration. This corroborates the extent of antisemitism in the ranks of the US State Department, beyond what has emerged in other histories of the institution. Antisemitism directly contributed to the creation of US remote control border protection in the wake of the Great War; it was not a product of the US Quota Acts, but a progenitor.

In Warsaw, Hias grew into a paperwork-crunching operation, despite its best efforts to manage bureaucratic inflation. Deeply legalistic in orientation, Hias slowly absorbed reality: The immigration process had changed, becoming far less predictable now that it was offshore and at the consul's discretion. Massel realized, "the American Consulate was not a court and that to be guided in our appeals by precedent, rule, or set of rules, was entirely out of the question. All we could do was ... namely beg, supplicate and ask for mercy ... We were not in a position to protect or demand our rights."[103] Hias attempted to streamline application paperwork in an effort to make it more humane, and won permission to process immigration applications and take posted-in applications at a much faster pace than McBride's US Consulate. Of course, Hias was more motivated than the consul to pursue these activities. As Massel manned the office in Warsaw, Kamaiky traveled around Jewish centers and small nearby villages to work on visas and support the work of the one American Consul of Lithuania and Latvia.[104] In some places, Hias organized committees of locals to do the work.[105]

Hias also engaged in rudimentary banking activity, providing dollars to immigrants, sent by American relatives, to pay the recommended $200 for passage. This fare-for-migrants banking was a postwar restoration of long-standing US Jewish immigrant banking practices, which were intimately tied to the steam shipping industry and the mass migration of Eastern European Jews to America in the late nineteen century.[106] Hias New York did not like the idea of doing this banking, or the appearance that they might be profiting from it, knowing well that anti-semitic rhetoric often targeted financial assistance to immigrants. In 1909, for example, the commissioner of immigration on Ellis Island fought to make it illegal for Hias and other immigrant aid organizations to give poor immigrants money for the purpose of securing their admission.[107] But Hias was still unable to convince the JDC to take on payments to waiting emigrants as part of its remittance work. Anyway, Kamaiky felt that internal Hias transfers most benefited the emigrant.[108] This banking activity was also targeted by various State Department and Labor Department officials who insisted that visas should be refused to those whose passage was paid by Hias, though the State Department ultimately ruled that this could not be the sole reason for refusal.[109]

Besides simplifying and churning out the mass of paperwork now required for immigration, Hias workers rebuilt a physical path for immigrants to reach the United States. They started by approaching steam-ship lines in Western Europe, which also became targets of State Department officials intent on finding something illegal.[110] They set up Danzig as the primary exit port for Jewish immigrants to America, and from 1920–25, about 60,000 Jews passed through this port.[111] Hias repurposed a camp built for war prisoners, the Troyl Camp, as a sheltering house for up to 2,500 emigrants who waited in Danzig – and thus, Hias began to perform the sheltering activity that usually lay in the JDC's domain. The US govern-ment insisted on a quarantine and sanitizing emigrants. Hias complied, although Kamaiky admitted that the practice was cruel.[112]

On Kamaiky and Massel's recommendations, Hias scrambled to find American Jews to head to Europe in the summer of 1920 to fill its offices there. John Bernstein, Hias president, an immigrant, and prominent immigration lawyer, paid for his travel and ended up managing a refugee crisis in Danzig as the Red Army took Warsaw.[113] Another shift in Hias staff occurred in early 1921, when immigrant American Jews with strong profiles in Jewish service and multilingual abilities transferred to Europe. Among them was Adolph Held, who arrived to take over in Warsaw, and who became the leader of Hias in Europe until 1925 and then its director through World War II.[114] One American Hias worker in Warsaw remarked that shortly after arriving in 1921, "we felt that we were being literally swamped, over-whelmed by an ever-rising tide of misery and horror. Before we knew it, we were in the midst of a bleak vastness, thick with groans and tears. It seemed that each one of us felt unequal to the immensity of the task."[115] By summer 1921, Hias had a network of city offices across East Central Europe: in Poland (including Warsaw and Danzig), Latvia, Lithuania, and Romania.[116] In its first two years of European operations, Hias spent about half a million dollars.[117]

As Hias expanded its work on behalf of Jewish refugees in Europe, the JDC scrupulously avoided this hot-button issue as much as possible. The JDC let Hias fill a niche at the crossroads of philanthropy and politics, seeing Hias' work as fundamentally different from that of the JDC's: Hias dealt with transmigrants, and not with the JDC's time-limited version of a refugee.[118] Hias' half a million also paled in comparison to the JDC's budget. To Kahn's mind, it was as if Hias was the JDC's independent "travel bureau."[119] By emphasizing remittances, connections, and fun-draising for Europe, the JDC knew it had enhanced the interest of American Jews in their European families left behind and the desire to help them by bringing them to the United States. But the JDC con-sidered emigration beyond the scope of its work.[120]

Louis Marshall said that the JDC had no interest in taking up "assisted immigration" because doing so could be "misinterpreted by the various

Governments."[121] Although many JDC leaders sat on Hias' Board of Advisers and agreed with Hias on the importance of allowing immigrants freely into the United States, the JDC prioritized the maintenance of government support and humanitarian neutrality. And so the JDC saw Hias not as a competitor, as it might have seen landsmanshaftn, the National Council of Jewish Women, Zionist organizations, or various Eastern European Jewish organizations that went on independent fundraising tours in America. Instead, Hias appeared as a bolder, necessary extension of work that was too risky for the JDC to undertake. Relations between the two organizations were positive and collaborative in the first years after the war. In an October 1918 Hias public meeting, Louis Marshall expressed that the organization had the full support of the JDC.[122] While Hershfield was in Poland representing the JDC, Warburg allowed him to privately work on behalf of Hias. And at a conference Hias held with the JDC in October 1919 to discuss questions of duplicating each other's work in the Far East, Marshall suggested that all work reuniting families should be turned over to Hias.[123] Yet, Hias was not as well connected or as strong as the JDC, and in dealing with migration, a touchy issue, it had far less weight than the JDC to garner political support and large donations. Hias relied on its large network of small immigrant members across the United States for its operating budget and support, and soon became overextended, running up a deficit as it struggled to attend to the millions of Jews who wished to leave Europe.

Migration without America

The Emergency Quota Act, passed in May 1921, cut Jewish arrivals to America by more than half by 1922.[124] Even after the Act came into force, there were many more visas issued abroad than the United States had legislated to admit; enforcing such restrictive measures was beyond the means of the US government.[125] One immediate effect of the quota was that many Jewish refugees, already outside their country of origin, got stuck in transit ports along the way. Hias was suddenly incapacitated, and its attempts to find lenience failed. Only a small number of exceptions and waivers were granted.[126]

Hias found itself coping with disaster on many fronts. Besides the overwhelming needs of refugees who flooded port cities in Europe, it was experiencing crisis at home. Its immigrant base felt that its professional directors were losing touch with its constituency, it was running a deficit due to European work and a new building in preparation for immigrants who could never come, it paid too much overhead to collect money from many small donors to stay afloat, and it clashed with other Jewish organizations.[127] Hias eventually abandoned the JDC and joined with Werelief to run Emigdirect, a new interwar Jewish migration organization, to help Jewish refugees despite American restrictions.

With remote border control still in its infancy in 1921, Hias continued, unknowingly, to assist in its expansion. Hias made a point of continuing to help immigrants climb growing paper walls, advocating for bureaucratic lenience and training its staff to navigate red tape. As it helped Jews scale these walls, it filled quotas with Jews, giving them a perceived advantage – which the State Department noticed and attempted to curtail.[128] Facilitating migration thus had the effect of strengthening the movement within the United States to restrict immigration. In 1920, Kamaiky publicly declared that "If there were in existence a ship that could hold three million human beings, the three million Jews of Poland would board it and escape to America."[129] Hias appeared to be trying to help bring all three million of them to the United States. This statement was repeated by gleeful antisemites who marshaled evidence against open immigration, which reverberated in Congress.[130] Decades later, Adolph Held described Kamaiky's pronouncement as having "made an unfavorable impression in the U.S."[131]

Although American Jews and Eastern European Jews were not one and the same, immigration restriction highlighted interdependence and that American fears of Eastern European Jewish immigrants affected all American Jews.[132] The issue of migration and the campaign to exclude immigrant Jews seemed to be increasing antisemitism in the United States and therefore posed a threat to established American Jews. Henry Ford backed the circulation of antisemitic canards, and restrictions on Jews proliferated in America.[133] White's Bureau of Immigration report concluded that while there was no Jewish conspiracy, Hias and other Jewish organizations profiteered and facilitated fraud. Alongside Hias, the JDC was implicated in fraud and illegal activity – so much for the JDC's attempts to distinguish itself.[134] Even as this report dismissed some antisemitic conspiracy theories, it reproduced others. The JDC and Hias were left to guess who might be friendly or antisemitic and to censor themselves to overcome impenetrable obstacles. Yet Hias knew itself to be a humanitarian agency conducting activities that "in no way differed from the activities of other organizations such as the American Relief Administration, the America Red Cross, and others."[135] After the Quota Act, Hias beefed up its presence in Washington – Isidore Hershfield soon became the Washington delegate – and fought to repeal or soften the laws, represent immigrant cases, and understand the nuances of ever-mounting regulations.

As Jews continued to enter the United States with Hias' help, Congress passed the National Origins Act of 1924. Immediately, 6,000 Jews were stranded in European ports, and thousands more were stuck in Cuba, Mexico, and Canada on their way to the United States.[136] Only 10,000–12,000 Jewish immigrants could enter the United States per year thereafter.[137] With the passing of the National Origins Act, it became clear to American Jews that immigration truly could no longer be the solution. The paper walls were simply too high, and immigrants already within the United States did not have the political clout to roll them back. Yet, Hias was at this point committed to its overseas work. "Practically all the activities [of Hias] radiate around the Foreign Relations Department," read a 1921 report.[138] The Foreign Relations Department in New York carried out work for the European Commission of Hias. By summer 1922, Hias was questioning whether it should still work in Europe – but continued to.[139] There were still Jewish refugees, and a reversion to prewar Hias was impossible. By 1925, despite its best attempts to liquidate its European work and turn it over to European partners, Hias remained, just trying to alleviate misery, not solve or prevent it, primarily through cash infusions to its European partners.[140]

Relations between Hias and the JDC deteriorated in the wake of postwar immigration restrictions, as Hias' European work and budgetary shortcomings began to rub up against the work of Kahn's newly established Refugee Department and the JDC's faltering fundraising efforts. The JDC and Hias differed, increasingly, on who constituted a refugee and on the nature of the refugee problem. The JDC did not approve of the "serious commotion" created by Kamaiky's three million pronouncement.[141] Furthermore, in Kahn's assessment, Hias' limited resources meant it was not equipped to help those who most *needed* to emigrate, especially refugees, but facilitated paperwork and travel plans for more fortunate hopefuls who probably could have managed to emigrate on their own. According to Kahn, Hias aspired to, but did not actually do, emigration work for refugees.[142] On the other hand, it veered into other refugee work, such as accompanying the evacuations of Jews from Bessarabia and building barracks.[143]

To deal with the fallout, the two organizations tried to set formal terms of agreement in autumn 1921. The terms mirrored what was already happening; the need for codification pointed to rising tensions exacerbated by the Quota Act.[144] Hias then pleaded for a loan from the JDC to cover its deficit.[145] In response, the JDC tried to require that Hias leave Europe; the JDC viewed Hias as impinging on Kahn's territory by handling refugees and acting financially irresponsible. The JDC refused a loan, Warburg penned threatening letters to Adolph Held, and Boris

Bogen pronounced that the handling of the refugee problem belonged to Kahn and not Hias, even though the JDC was far from meeting refugee needs.[146] Hias protested and ultimately did not follow the terms of agreement.[147] It started a new, successful fundraising campaign, and Louis Marshall resigned from its Board of Advisers.[148] The relationship was over.[149]

Hias decided in 1922 that remittances and banking would have to be a major part of its operations, because it saw remittances as a way to protect migrants. In 1923, Hias set up a new bank in America, in defiance of the JDC, to undertake these transactions.[150] It reckoned that banking connections between the United States and Poland and Romania would support Jews who could no longer emigrate, particularly after the JDC dissolved much of its remittance delivery work.[151] In 1927, the Hias Emigrant Bank was still sending remittances, with its small staff to distribute them.[152] Hias transferred nearly $29.1 million over 1920–28 in hundreds of thousands of unique payments, a sum well over what Hias could spend on general relief abroad.[153]

Given Hias' difficulties with the JDC and the State Department, and its conviction that it had a role to play in helping Eastern Jewish refugees, it turned away from American networks and toward Jewish organizations in Europe. Whereas the JDC had established its European partners in the form of local welfare societies (often newly created, pluralist groups), alongside larger Eastern European philanthropic agencies it helped to rehabilitate, Hias formed partnerships where the JDC had decided that collaboration would appear unpatriotic, or where the JDC felt it would not have control. Hias therefore sought collaboration from Ica and Werelief. The search for European partners began soon after Hias started working in Europe, as Hias began to experience donor pushback at home and felt unequipped to remain in Europe long term, and well before the United Evacuation Committee became necessary. Hias had to negotiate its position not just with the JDC but it also had to navigate how an organization of American immigrants fit into the network of Western and Central European Jewish relief organizations.

Emigdirect emerged at the end of 1921, following a year of meetings of various Jewish relief agencies, all of which Hias' Adolph Held attended.[154] Emigdirect's descendent, Hicem, is better known for its role in Nazi-era relief than for its Great War–era early history, told here.[155] John Bernstein described Emigdirect as "a federation of emigration committees in Poland, Latvia, Lithuania, Romania and Danzig. [It] has been receiving its sole financial support from Hias."[156] This federation of emigration committees was brought together by Werelief, and the JDC declined to join.[157] Despite initial agreements to collaborate, Ica did not become actively involved. As the American outsider in this otherwise-European federation, Hias deferred to European Jewish expertise and, despite its financial troubles, bankrolled the organization. Emigdirect tried to find outlets for immigration and to improve conditions in Cuba, Palestine, and South America and secured permission for Russian refugees to travel through states bordering the Soviet Union, reaching an agreement on emigration with the Soviet government.[158]

Although the JDC was not a partner in Emigdirect, noncooperation did not last indefinitely. When Quota Act refugees became stranded in ports in 1924, Hias joined with landsmanshaftn and the remains of the American Jewish Congress to demand a meeting with the JDC to convince it to take action.[159] Kahn then pleaded with David Bressler, chair of the JDC Refugee Committee in New York, regarding the "utter absence of funds" preventing him from alleviating the distress of refugees.[160] Despite JDC administrative reluctance, these organizations collectively created the Emergency Committee for the Relief of Jewish Refugees, spearheaded by the JDC, to deal with the particular problem of migrants stranded mid-route and raised half a million dollars for that purpose.[161] Louis Marshall and Stephen Wise went abroad to investigate the situation under the auspices of the JDC. From this visit, they created the United Evacuation Committee in 1924 – with representatives from the Emergency Committee on Jewish Refugees, Emigdirect, and Ica – to help stranded emigrants return to their old homes or find new ones outside the United States. Together, Ica's Louis Oungre, Bernard Kahn of the Emergency Committee, and Yisroel Efroikin of Emigdirect negotiated the removal of stranded emigrants, using about $500,000 primarily from the JDC.[162] There were signs that collaboration between the largest Jewish international organizations could achieve real results, though this only seemed possible in the face of a narrowly defined and urgent crisis. The United Evacuation Committee did not last long or expand its goals. Yet even if Hias and the JDC did not cooperate again for several years, they remained entangled in the same complex, transnational web of organizational and personal relationships of Jewish diplomacy and philanthropy; regular, indirect contact was simply unavoidable.

The persistence of Jewish refugees in Europe and the successes of the United Evacuation Committee, followed by its dissolution, moved Ica to collaborate with Hias. By then, Hias had proved to be remarkably resilient (unlike Werelief, which had faded as an independent entity). Together, Hias and Ica created Hicem in April 1927, merging Emigdirect into this new organization – its name reflects the three parent organizations. At least at first, Hicem retained two offices, one in Paris for Ica, and one in Berlin as a successor to Emigdirect; despite the ensuing confusion, the main Jewish migration organizations were finally cooperating. The Central Jewish Emigration Society (JEAS), which was previously Ica in Poland and then worked on behalf of the United Evacuation Committee, acted as Hicem's agent on the ground in Poland, with headquarters in Warsaw and offices in other cities. In Bucharest, a Hias office served Romania. Hias hoped, with Ica, to take charge of refugees in Europe and relocate them to some better place, from Poland to Argentina, Brazil, Uruguay, Cuba, Mexico, Australia, South Africa, and Palestine. Tens of thousands of Jews moved to these new lands – the tradition of chain migration had broken, and a global restructuring of Jewish migration had begun. Ica and Hias contributed funds to Hicem projects. Yet, as time went on, more doors closed, paperwork increased, and it became ever more expensive to resettle emigrants and refugees.[163]

By 1927, Kahn once again was working to liquidate the JDC's Refugee Department and the United Evacuation Committee, telling Abraham Herman, then-president of Hias, that the stranded emigrant situation was no longer serious. When Herman visited, however, he ascertained that it was still serious and that many emigrants, fearing their illegal status, avoided registering. Herman surmised that Kahn relied too heavily on reports rather than firsthand information.[164] Kahn divested the JDC of responsibility for working with Emigdirect, as the JDC proclaimed unilaterally that the refugee issue was solved.[165] Clearly, the JDC preferred that Hicem also accept the JDC conclusion that refugees no longer existed. Of course, this all depended on the definition of refugee and willingness to see refugees. Hias and Hicem maintained that as long as European Jews still wished to leave Europe but were stranded or illegal residents somewhere, they remained refugees. Even settled Jews hoping to emigrate deserved that opportunity.

Hias' struggles to remain relevant even as the refugee situation was far from over in Europe raises multiple questions: What is an American Jewish organization, or, any hyphenated organization, if it loses its American moorings? If American politics evolve to contradict its core existence? Quotas forced a readjustment in American Jewish immigrant foreign relations,[166] as the long-standing alignment between a globally oriented US government with globally oriented, chain-migration-seeking ethnic and immigrant groups in America fell apart. Hias and other Jewish immigration advocates could no longer assume that liberal immigration was an *American* value. John Bernstein despaired: "If America is to repeat here the mistakes of the Old World, if the racial and religious antipathies of Europe are to find fertile soil here, then all the struggles of past generations and of the present generation for real democracy have been in vain."[167]

The Great War transformed Hias into an American international organization on the one hand, but on the other, postwar immigration culture and policy pushed Hias to become more ethnic and more Jewish. Hias was stripped of its claims to Americanness. The organization began to rely on non-American, European Jewish partners – not even the JDC – for its institutional survival and a continued chance to help as many refugees as possible. It felt duty bound to continue its work, rejecting the JDC's idea that the Jewish Question had to be solved within the countries of Jewish residence and pushing to facilitate emigration as much as possible. Abraham Herman wrote miserably at the end of 1929, as the Great Depression crashed markets and German Jews worried for their futures, "It cannot be expected that a people wait for the grace and favors of others till it please these to offer the benefits which come from recognition of elementary human rights. It is tantamount to asking thousands of our people quietly to submit to what may be ultimate extermination ... Jews are therefore compelled to wander."[168]

And yet, Hias was inadvertently complicit in its troubles, as it failed to win the battle over open immigration but unintentionally assisted the US government by legitimizing its remote control project. Hias' story testifies to what happened when American Jewish organizations stepped beyond their circumscribed role in American politics, illuminating the limits of American Jewish power.

On High: Repatriation and Citizenship

While the JDC and Hias pursued their respective refugee strategies of caring for the basic needs of refugees and helping some of them emigrate, European Jewish organizations, namely Ica and Werelief, were busy pursuing a third: diplomacy. They drew on a tradition more than a half century old of Western European Jewish organizations focusing on a wide array of international philanthropic projects and political goals to improve Jewish life. The "Jewish diplomacy" aspect of their work sought to influence international and state actors on behalf of Jewish issues. It was undertaken by Jewish individuals or associations, sometimes in a loosely coordinated fashion, sometimes in ways that resembled competitive politicking.[169] After the war, Jewish diplomatic efforts were targeted first at the peace conference and resulted in the Minorities Treaties, and then aimed at the new League of Nations in Geneva. The shift from Great Power politics to a collective security arrangement marked a decisive shift in how Jewish diplomacy had to function. Lucien Wolf frequented Geneva on behalf of Jewish interests, as did Zevi Aberson. Both men represented a cluster of Jewish organizations: Wolf saw himself as a liberal Jewish diplomat carrying on the traditions of the Alliance Israélite, while Aberson styled himself as a Jewish populist, representing Jewish nationalist organizations filled out by Eastern European Jewish immigrants newly demanding access to Jewish diplomacy. Their attention was concentrated largely on the Minorities Section of the League Secretariat and on pressuring League member states to act on the League's commitments in the Minorities Treaties.[170] The appointment of a High Commissioner for Russian Refugees (the HC), Fridtjof Nansen, redirected some of their energies to the politics of refugee work, the subject of this section.

Jews in Geneva

The year 1921 was a turning point not just for humanitarian relief work and new migration laws but also for the League of Nations system. As the JDC was reorganizing itself thematically to address a world order that was finally settling into place, the fledgling League of Nations finally put into action its Covenant and technical functions, and Fridtjof Nansen began as the High Commissioner for Refugees. The appointments of the High Commissioner (the HC) and Kahn as refugee director for the JDC were separate but similar responses to states not wanting or not knowing how to divert resources to foreigners rather than their own people. Nansen's appointment at the margins of the League of Nations allowed him to coordinate but not actually provide relief. He had a limited political mandate, ad hoc funding, and independently appointed employees rather than a mandated commission. The League's member states did not agree that refugees were a pressing security issue requiring international commitment and extensive funding. Remarkably, it mirrored Kahn's JDC Refugee Department with its limited capacity and plan to liquidate itself as soon as possible. The parallels between the weakness of the JDC's refugee relief and the HC did not end there. In 1923, the League decided that the refugee issue was solved just as Kahn did, but other private associations convinced each organization to keep doing refugee work.[171]

The international refugee regime, embodied by the HC, defined refugee anew through legal mandates and humanitarian practice. The HC had the mandate to assist only certain groups of refugees, and only on an ad hoc basis. These groups were defined by places of origin – such that most Jews were folded into the case of Russian refugees. While Kahn categorized refugees by their present location and cause and length of flight, the international refugee regime imposed a nationality to which a refugee supposedly belonged, guided by the new nation-state system. Diplomatic procedures such as population exchanges seemed to offer solutions for Armenian, Turkish, and Greek refugees, but there was no obvious solution for the Jews, who formed minority populations in many states. Furthermore, most Jews had no desire to be repatriated to the Russia they had fled. In addition, there was no space in the refugee regime for Jewish refugees who were born not in Russia but in formerly Austrian Galicia and now languished in Warsaw, Vienna, Budapest, and elsewhere. Nor did it have a way of conceiving of Jews who were internally displaced within Russia's vast territory, even though some were in the Far East, a continent away from their homes in the former Pale of Settlement. Thus, the refugee regime in no way explicitly or implicitly recognized the extensive Jewish dimension of the interwar refugee problem, although an ongoing Jewish refugee crisis would have been obvious to any Central or Eastern Europeans at the time.

As one of his first activities in office, Nansen institutionalized an Advisory Committee of Private Organizations to provide a forum. Lucien Wolf of Ica and Zevi Aberson of Werelief sat on this committee. American Jewish organizations avoided the League and international bodies in its orbit, though the JDC and Hias were, of course, in close contact with Ica and Werelief. Like the technical and social sections of the League, which were considered the domain of experts rather than politicians, many experts on the Advisory Committee derived their expertise from nongovernmental experience. State representatives were not allowed at Advisory Committee meetings, which were intended to foster cooperation and information sharing and to solicit advice and support for Nansen's projects. This informal arrangement proved beneficial to both the private organizations and Nansen.[172] The committee legitimized the presence of non-state organizational actors in the international system for the first time, even though the HC was peripheral to the League framework. And since governments were mainly concerned with state interests and not refugees, private organizations could take the lead addressing the issue. They contributed expertise and funding to Nansen, while carrying out the relief work on the ground on behalf of refugees. Meanwhile, Nansen provided these organizations with a framework for coordination and took care of administrative work, and his position as HC gave him the authority to intercede with governments, cross political borders in a way that neither refugees nor private citizens could, and create the transit pass for undocumented refugees for which he is best known: the Nansen passport.

Wolf worked to ensure that Jewish refugees were included in whatever assistance Nansen or the HC's associated organizations might provide through their specific mandates. Jewish refugees would only benefit from the HC's assistance if Wolf or Aberson could find a way to frame Jewish problems within the problem of Russian refugees. Before the establishment of the Advisory Committee, Wolf sat in on the second conference on Russian refugees alongside government representatives and other private associations. He suggested that the problem with current Russian refugee relief was that only a few states and organizations were dealing with a problem that was larger than them. Plus, the financial burden should be shared across the world.[173] This appeal to interstate cooperation was obviously at odds with the way that diplomatic representatives guarded their national interest, using cooperation as an excuse to *divest* themselves of responsibility.[174] Wolf sent Nansen minutes from a spontaneous meeting of voluntary associations that occurred alongside the formal conference, suggesting names of delegates from non-Jewish and Jewish organizations alike for Nansen to consider nominating to Nansen's proposed advisory committee. Wolf suggested that he represent Ica.[175] Fortunately for Wolf, in the Advisory Committee's relatively welcoming, supposedly apolitical atmosphere, he was able to build relationships and sometimes leverage them on behalf of Jewish refugees.

Within the world of Jewish organizations, Wolf's position as the singular Jewish diplomat was contested. As described earlier in the chapter, American and European Jewish humanitarian organizations gathered several times in 1921 to try to unify refugee relief work and the role each organization should play, but these negotiations were never conclusive. Competition over leadership and visions for the Jewish future emerged outside the Jewish organizational world in the realms of the Advisory Committee, other sections of the League of Nations, and the International Labour Organization (ILO). (Other clusters of private associations had their own clashes, too, such as women's organizations around the ILO surrounding the issue of women's working hours.[176]) Werelief insisted on representation vis-à-vis the HC. In one Advisory Committee meeting, Aberson pointed out that the question of evacuating Jewish refugees from Constantinople ought to involve considerations of emigration to Palestine, which was not true for other Russian refugees in Constantinople – and conveniently aligned with Werelief's Zionist orientation.[177]

The JDC declined to participate in the HC. It reasoned that if America had rejected the League, so must the JDC as a resolutely American organization.[178] In one stroke, the JDC, the strongest of Jewish international organizations, eliminated itself from any official supranational negotiations. It pursued the middle ground of humanitarianism and left domestic political negotiations to the American Jewish Committee and Hias.

Still, Wolf positioned himself as the Jewish representative in International Geneva, and he was typically understood as such by civil servants, diplomats, and other private associations. Wolf was a journalist and a diplomat without a state; his cultivated connections in both the worlds of high diplomacy and Jewish political and philanthropic life were unparalleled, and his expert knowledge was unsurpassed on everything connected to the Jewish Question, from statistical facts to breaking news to an ability to argue in international legal jargon. That he was a British subject assisted Wolf in his mission to represent Jews at the League of Nations – British civil servants and diplomats were overrepresented at the League, and the British government was particularly influential on the question of refugees in the interwar period.[179] Though Wolf maintained no permanent residence in Geneva, he represented the Joint Foreign Committee of British Jews, the Alliance Israélite, the Jewish Association for the Protection of Girls and Women, and Ica.[180] The Joint Foreign Committee distributed his carefully documented and researched yearly reports on questions of Jewish interest at the League and on refugee questions.

Wolf's presence was felt in multiple sections of the League of Nations and its connected bodies, including the Minorities Section, the Social Section, which dealt with the traffic of women, the emigration committee of the ILO, and the Advisory Committee to the High Commissioner for Refugees. He covered the complete range of Jewish concerns in Geneva, working tirelessly on Minorities Treaties issues as well as refugee issues, which went hand in hand. Relentlessly, he struggled to push the League and the ILO toward pushing non-European countries to loosen their immigration restrictions, in one instance requesting the ILO undertake negotiations on migration to the United States and Palestine for Jewish refugees.[181] He attempted to negotiate the repatriation of refugees with Soviet Russia, working at both state and international levels.[182] He tackled the evacuation of Russian refugees from Constantinople, a thorny issue.[183] And he led the campaign in Geneva to develop a legal concept of statelessness, which derived from his concurrent analyses of minority and refugee issues. The Alliance Israélite and the Joint Foreign Committee worked together on the statelessness campaign, via Wolf, backed by initiatives from the International Committee of the Red Cross.[184] Yet, despite Wolf's long-term and crucial involvement with the HC and especially the Advisory Committee, his presence was summarily rejected at the Conference of Government Experts for Staatenlose Passports in 1926; he received only an agenda.[185] If civil servants and governments complained about what they saw as Wolf's persistent meddling and diplomatic pretensions, this shutdown was a blatant reminder that Wolf's Jewish diplomacy was not always welcome.[186]

Despite Wolf's facility, he represented no state in this organization of states, and was easy to ignore, especially after 1924–25, when cooperation with private associations was rebuked by the League. In 1925, the HC stopped including private associations when it transferred its affiliation to the ILO.[187] Thus, regardless of major problems of Jewish statelessness in Poland, Romania, and Austria, and Wolf's unmatched expertise, there was little he or other Jewish voices could do. The limits of an international route to Jewish rehabilitation became increasingly apparent.

Nansen in the Field

Although Wolf was the standout Jewish diplomat in International Geneva, American Jewish rejection of the League was not as simple as it seemed. The American Jewish Congress and its leader Stephen Wise maintained correspondence with the Committee of Jewish Delegations/ Werelief and from 1925–28, even had an American Jewish representative in Geneva, historian Marvin Lowenthal.[188] On refugees, the JDC did collaborate informally with the HC. It maintained a good relationship with Ica and together, the two undertook various projects, so that Wolf likely felt himself to be the unofficial representative of the JDC on the Advisory Committee. Kahn wrote, "We, as an American organization cannot act against the intentions of the American government and we must hold ourselves absolutely free from the Nansen Committee," but continued, "On the other hand we cannot ignore the work of the Nansen Committee. If we Jews hold ourselves aloof from the Nansen Committee the consequence would be that the Nansen Committee would only look after the Christian refugees."[189] This was a clue that the JDC saw itself as the representative of Jewish refugees – not Wolf, whose extraordinary efforts Kahn did not even credit. Accordingly, Kahn occasionally met with representatives of the HC outside Geneva. For example, in Berlin, as Kahn set up the JDC Refugee Department and Nansen set up the HC, Kahn and Eduard Frick of the HC/ICRC discussed the evolving refugee situation in Romania and how Jewish organizations might form a united refugee committee.[190] More often, however, Kahn cooperated closely with Nansen's/the ICRC's representatives in the field.

Returning to the Ukrainian Jewish refugee crisis in Romania reveals the competitive and collaborative nature of organized Jewish refugee relief work from the perspective of the HC and Wolf, rather than the JDC.[191] Kahn relied heavily on the Nansen Committee in Romania and on Lucien Wolf (as Ica) for negotiations with the government to stall evacuation and smooth its own work there. Dr. Wilhelm Bacilieri was already in Bucharest as part of the Swiss Legation and for the

International Committee of the Red Cross (ICRC) when Nansen requested his services in September 1921; he then jointly represented the ICRC and the HC for two years. Bacilieri took charge of transporting refugees safely across the Dniester. Bacilieri also spoke with Romanian officials on behalf of refugee assistance organizations in Romania, including those helping Christian refugees, all of which could never seem to agree on a unified plan, leaving him as their spokesman by default. Bacilieri successfully postponed refugee internment multiple times by promising Romanian authorities that Ica would eventually undertake organized evacuations. Ica assured the HC that it would assume all financial responsibility for Jewish refugees in return for the HC's diplomatic assistance. Romanian military authorities tried twice to expel remaining refugees, but again the HC intervened. The expulsion was then postponed until the summer of 1924, largely as a result of the intercession of Dr. Wilhelm Filderman, Jewish leader in Bucharest and JDC representative, on behalf of all Russian refugees in Romania. Meanwhile, Ica helped local Jewish committees in Romania gradually evacuate Jewish refugees in Bessarabia, focusing on finding countries to which refugees could immigrate. Romanian authorities acknowledged Ica and Bacilieri for alleviating the crisis – it is thus clear that Ica/Wolf and the HC/Bacilieri were the most visible "Jewish diplomats" to the Romanian government and international authorities.[192]

The Jewish debate over which organizations should and should not be allowed to participate in relief work and how much control each should have played out in invitation-only conferences, the Jewish press, and furious exchanges of letters. When it spilled beyond its Jewish contexts, rearticulated in the context of the League, the debate was missing core American Jewish organizations. HC staff was irritated by the multiplicity of Jewish voices and pushed Wolf and Aberson to resolve their differences, which the men were unable to do despite their strenuous efforts.[193] These international Jewish organizations were expected to navigate the boundaries of their own states and reach across these borders to collaborate with Jewish representatives in other nation-states. The League of Nations system, while refusing to recognize Jews as a cohesive minority or political polity, expected that when Jews did approach international bodies, they would do so with the cohesion of a state. The Jewish response to this demand was to argue endlessly about how to achieve that cohesion, and thus, when League of Nations employees and diplomats insisted on having a unified Jewish voice on technical committees, they effectively derailed Jewish actors' work. International organizations and governments also gave themselves ready-made justifications to ignore Jewish voices because of intense competition among Jewish groups to be heard.[194]

Political diplomacy undertaken by Jewish actors and organizations was a fraught undertaking. It held the promise to resolve fundamental problems, yet it also contributed to the fragmentation of Jewish relief work and absorbed energy that might have better gone to relief. The League's ability to accomplish anything depended on the goodwill of its member states, and they did not want to take responsibility for the crisis of refugees and statelessness, despite obvious political causes and potential solutions. Jewish organizations worked together for common action, but doing so within the structure of the League of Nations system was nearly impossible, which became increasingly conspicuous. Wolf grew more and more frustrated with the HC on refugee work, as it seemed to expect Jewish organizations to serve as bankrollers despite their weary donors, even as the HC closed itself off from Jewish expertise. His efforts achieved no long-lasting or structural change, and diplomacy did not achieve more for refugees than emigration assistance or basic relief.

American, European, and Jewish (American and European) organizations pursued their own paths toward a resolution of the Jewish refugee crisis, slowly chipping away at the mass of refugees. While struggling against one another and grappling with the limits of their own power, they struggled with the most basic questions regarding refugees. Refugee relief in particular brought out Jewishness as it highlighted Jewish solidarity and vulnerability across borders in contrast to states closing down and acting against perceived refugee "threats." Although each Jewish organization could barely tolerate the others' presence in the same room, when they came together and with other international organizations, they could defuse a refugee crisis. As violence waned, the League of Nations took root, and humanitarian organizations fanned out across Europe, many thousands of refugees assimilated into the new postwar order. Yet, the JDC estimated that there were 500,000 "nomadic" Jews in Ukraine in 1922.[195] In 1926, there remained an estimated 9.5 million European refugees, including Jews.[196] Russia and refugees were the most uncontainable Jewish tragedies of the period, with ramifications that shook Jewish life to the core across the twentieth century. There simply could not be a private, humanitarian solution to an interstate political issue, particularly when antisemitic and racist fears underpinned European and American politics.

4   The Sick
Jewish Fitness through Jewish Health

At an August 1919 gathering, Major Haim Davis entreated the JDC to get on with medical relief, accusing it of failing Polish Jews and forsaking Boris Bogen with its lack of health provisions. Davis, a Jewish psychiatrist from Chicago and a physician for the American Expeditionary Forces, had been in Warsaw earlier that year. While Bogen did the work of a dozen men, he said, the JDC neglected to provide a single medical doctor and instead sent scouts, engineers, Red Cross–like social workers, and even women! On the other hand, Solomon Lowenstein, a well-known social worker, had just returned from an American Red Cross commission to Palestine, where Hadassah's American Zionist Medical Unit had begun postwar medical work. Lowenstein deemed the situation in that land as comparatively "very fortunate."[1]

The war was terrible in Palestine, but along Europe's still-violent Eastern Front, typhus spread quickly with deadly results. Whereas in Palestine, the British Mandate opened up opportunities for Jewish autonomy, in Poland and Russia, where the situation was urgent, Jews found it difficult to start their own initiatives. In 1918, Hadassah, the Women's Zionist Organization of America went to Palestine, bringing American public health practices with a focus on long-term goals of Jewish health and Jewish nation building. In 1920, a second program under the Joint Distribution Committee headed for Poland to fight an epidemic in collaboration with the AEF's typhus group, European governments, and the new League of Nations Heath Committee, while trying to improve general Jewish hygiene. Eventually, as typhus epidemics subsided, Jewish health care in East Central Europe turned to social medicine to increase the health of Jews as a people, especially as the JDC handed over the reins to its Eastern European Jewish partners. As the 1920s ticked along, Jewish health preoccupied Jewish groups from Palestine to Poland and became a means of asserting Jewish autonomy and expertise.

The emergence of Jewish health as a way for Americans to facilitate Jewish self-help in Europe was unintentional. But it quickly became a non-divisive, widely supported way to assist Eastern Jews in gaining autonomy. Following a catastrophic war, the interwar period was defined by national and international concerns over public health and the fitness of populations.[2] Yet even before the war, European Jews actively resisted intra-European colonialism and its exclusion of Jewish bodies by constructing their own variant of biopolitics.[3] Jewish health in modernity was about finding answers to the Jewish Question from within, rather than applying the latest laboratory findings. It prioritized the health of society over the sickness of individuals. The JDC did not wield science beyond trying to prove equality and seek collaboration with contemporary humanitarian organizations, yet its medical work tapped into a profound biopolitical, nationalist strain in Eastern European Jewish life. The JDC gave money, tools, and a veneer of US backing to this enterprise as it handed over responsibility to local medical organizations that carried out this work until the Holocaust. Hadassah actively promoted a Zionism centered in Palestine, bringing even more expertise and maintaining American Jewish control over medical matters into the creation of the state of Israel.

American Jews began an international health program akin to what would be called, in the age of decolonization and postcolonial medicine after another world war, global health development. Public health initiatives undertaken by Jewish organizations after the Great War ranged from epidemic control and disease eradication to maternal and child health to sanitary facilities and medical training. While they ought to be seen as central international public health initiatives in the interwar period, typically they are not; originating as civil initiatives trying to promote minority health, they were a system apart from but entangled with the formal national and international order.[4] America was extracting itself from Europe and turning inward during these years; America's Jews, by contrast, took American Progressive social medicine out into the world to meet Jews who would never be able to immigrate to America. Even if the JDC wished to retreat to America, its empathy with Jews abroad made it more committed to the cause of relief than its non-Jewish counterparts. Linked transnationally to more widely recognized health organizations and practices, international Jewish social medicine in the 1920s resembled domestic social medicine, colonial medicine, and proto-global health development.

American Jews prioritized relief and the rehabilitation of Jews in interwar Poland, Soviet Ukraine, and Palestine, centers of Jewish life within their respective humanitarian theaters. Though refugee relief demanded that the JDC follow crises wherever they appeared, other forms of humanitarianism became rooted in these three hubs. The JDC reached a broader geography with funds and general representatives, into the Baltics, south and west to Austria, Czechoslovakia, Romania, Greece, Hungary, and Turkey, but only in rare instances did it begin large-scale, innovative programs in what was considered the Jewish periphery. Initially, health was subsumed within regional relief efforts. Then, like refugee relief, it was organized as a cross-cutting, international issue at the JDC's 1920 Vienna Conference.

This chapter includes two parts. The first follows JDC engagement in a disorderly international campaign to fight a border–defying wartime epidemic that threatened to further stigmatize Jews. Second, it examines the long-term effort to improve Jewish health and, thereby, improve Jewish society. Three tensions become visible in all these responses. The first was between short-term medical care (exemplified by the typhus response) and long-term, public health "uplift" (exemplified by a favus eradication campaign). The second was between JDC attempts to reproduce American Progressivism and the need to adjust this frame-work to respond to local needs and capacities, which produced different outcomes in Poland, the Soviet Union, and Palestine. Compounding both of these was a third tension: the JDC's constant consideration of self-liquidation while it searched for effectiveness and staying power in its work.

A Failed Battle against Typhus

As the armistice took effect along the Western Front, an awareness dawned that typhus, an epidemic disease spreading along the Eastern Front, could present a threat more dangerous than violence. Transmitted by body lice, typhus was not too difficult to control in times of peace, but along the wartime vectors of mobility, hunger, and dirt the disease easily spread, causing a rash and often-deadly fever (with a mortality rate of 5–40 percent). Typhus was endemic to nineteenth- and early twentieth-century Russia and its Pale of Settlement, but the worst epidemics took place during the Great War and years following it, taking millions of lives from 1918 to 1922. Typhus claimed Jewish lives all over Eastern Europe during and after the war and was likely a primary contributor to the surge in war–era Jewish mortality rates not directly resulting from violence, although reliable data is not available.

German occupying authorities in Poland kept typhus under control during the war. A continuously functioning local government and steady food and relief supply, plus systematic delousing of troops, prevented its westward spread.[5] After the armistice, organizations and governments, including the JDC, sprang into inchoate action against typhus. Yet the same disruptive social forces contributing to the lice's flourishing made combatting the disease through louse control and supportive care of the infected nearly impossible along the former Eastern Front, the site of the Polish–Soviet War and Russian Civil War. Furthermore, the prejudices and differing priorities of health activists led to piecemeal and insensitive epidemic control. The JDC found itself waging a campaign for care and health of the Jews, while other organizations tended to see Jews as carriers of contagion who should be isolated rather than restored to health.

The war's abrupt intrusion into Eastern European Jewish life and the destruction of its communities primed Jewish resistance to outside interference, even when it came to life-threatening diseases. Without an available vaccination or cure for typhus, treatments were by definition invasive, involving quarantine and the forced cleansing of bodies, clothes, belongings, and homes, alongside the shuttering of businesses and institutions. Just how invasive and coercive was a matter of scale; in general, the Western Allies instituted less coercive measures such as regular laundering and bathing, while Germany was especially coercive, insisting on shaving and chemical fumigation. German occupying authorities incorporated colonial–style sanitary regimentation in Eastern Europe for civilians, soldiers, and prisoners of war. Stringent separation, total nudity, and shaving of all hair was enforced, and civilians or prisoners were sometimes used in experimental medical trials. Under German wartime occupation, Jews were the target of propaganda in Yiddish, Polish, and German that warned of the dangers of lice, and German officials worked to gain the support of Jewish leaders. In Warsaw and Łódź, Jewish quarters were singled out as unsanitary; Jews became synonymous with contagion in the antisemitic mindset. Only sporadic efforts were made to respect Jewish customs. The Russian administration's irregular and heavy-handed disinfection procedures provoked popular resistance as Russia quickly developed similarly invasive delousing procedures for civilians and soldiers headed into the Russian interior. Perceiving delousing and quarantine as collective punishment, Jews evaded treatment; besides, these procedures were no guarantee against infection.[6]

Both the antisemitic link between Jews and contagion, and an apologetic Jewish organizational response of trying to control contagion among Jews in order to make Jews more acceptable, had antecedents. For decades before the war, European Jewish migration assistance organizations had swept Jewish migrants westward due to European fears of the diseases they carried. Upon entry to the United States, Jewish immigrants were screened for disease. In 1916, 69 percent of hopeful immigrants excluded from the United States were barred due to medical reasons, a rate that rose steadily from 1890. In America, these anti-immigrant sentiments were not exclusively directed at Jews, but Jews were a substantial portion of those immigrants blamed for epidemics.[7] To counteract blame and restrain the growth of antisemitism at home, American Jewish benevolent societies subjected immigrants to medical interventions as part of their broader assistance.[8] American Jewish organizations obligated their European Jewish partners to screen or treat emigrants for physical fitness before they departed for the United States.[9] As discussed in the last chapter, the US immigration quotas of 1921 and 1924 were in line with anti-immigrant and anti-Jewish prejudice that viewed immigrants as dangerous and unfit. Jewish organizations, including Hias and Emigdirect, did not challenge but cooperated with these paper walls, for example, by forcibly quarantining prospective immigrants before they departed Europe's shores at Hias' repurposed barracks near Danzig.[10]

The postwar typhus outbreak compelled the JDC into active medical work. The JDC wished to save the Jews in Eastern Europe from succumbing to the disease but also sought to stamp out contagion for the sake of Jews who primarily risked the effects of its corollary: rising antisemitism. Such a campaign would require involving governments in the battle against typhus in Europe and Russia, as well as coordinating with Bernard Kahn and his Refugee Department to make sure that Jewish refugees could not in fact be blamed for carrying contagion.[11]

Westerners in Poland

A few months after the November 1918 armistice, the Bolsheviks invaded Poland. Without a strong government in place, typhus spread unchecked along the unstable Polish–Soviet border and throughout Bolshevik Russia. As the Polish–Soviet War was being fought, refugees, returning prisoners of war, and repatriates flowed into Poland's east and south. Several incongruous attempts to fight typhus began in 1919. Ludwik Rajchman, an assimilated Polish Jewish physician specializing in bacteriology who lived in London during the war, rushed back to Warsaw in 1918 as the armistice was declared. He spearheaded epidemic control as the new Polish Minister of Public Health, founding the National Institute of Hygiene in Poland (Państwowy Zakład Higieny) and a network of laboratories. He bought sanitary materials from departing German troops, purchased goods liquidated by the AEF, and deployed doctors eastward. The AEF sent a group of soldiers, the American-Polish Typhus Relief Expedition, to accompany their state-of-the-art delousing machines and baths to Poland, in cooperation with the ARA and the Polish government, from August 1919 through 1920. Another attempt to control epidemics was directed by the ARC in cooperation with the national Red Cross Societies of other Allied states, or, collectively, the new League of Red Cross Societies, which sent an investigatory commission to Poland in June 1919. The AFSC and British Friends also set up a typhus unit in Poland in August 1919. Shipments of food from the ARA, JDC, and others also contained crucial sanitary supplies for fighting typhus starting in the spring of 1919. The League of Nations then created a special Epidemic Commission in May 1920, headed by Rajchman, in conjunction with the International Committee of the Red Cross. From 1920 to 1921, the commission studied the spread of the disease, partially took over coordinating humanitarian aid, and reinforced the nascent Polish hygiene system.[12]

Clearly, many organizations were interested in confronting the epidemic, while the JDC in 1919 was limited in its ability to undertake medical work. It began to actively court other American organizations working in the medical field in East Central Europe, with Bogen figuring that the JDC could extend its medical reach in Poland through cooperation. The JDC connected with the ARC early in 1919, as Bogen reached Poland with the ARA, hoping to send along American Jewish nurses. At that point, the ARC agreed that it would allow the JDC to contribute to the ARC's work in Poland so that the ARC could reach further, but it would not let in sectarian nurses running a separate operation.[13] The JDC found it difficult to move the ARC in Europe to joint work, despite good relations in Washington. The ARC promised collaborations but never followed through, or resisted them outright, explaining that it did not undertake sectarian work. Yet, newspapers reporting that 65 percent of the 5,000 deaths in Odessa were Jews spurred the JDC into action, even as Judah Magnes noted, "Of course we realize that by ourselves we cannot in any way cope with this plague."[14]

After Maj. Davis excoriated the JDC at the Astor Conference in the autumn of 1919, the JDC arranged to send to Poland a medical doctor who was an authority on typhus. Dr. Harry Plotz would investigate typhus and suggest how to combat it. Just one man could not delouse all the Jews in Poland, but Plotz hoped to test his experimental serum and, if it was successful, provide a cure. The plan was to appoint him under the ARC in Poland, but when that failed, New York's Mount Sinai Hospital contributed the necessary funds.[15] In February 1920, Magnes and Felix Warburg held a long conference with Frederick P. Keppel of the ARC to discuss several issues: exchanging information, war prisoners, how the ARC might enter Soviet Russia, the question of Jews on commissions of the ARC in countries with large Jewish populations, and the Polish Red Cross. The JDC inquired if Keppel knew the details of the Typhus Expedition, and Keppel confirmed that President Wilson had established it under Hoover's direction. Hoover, said Keppel, thought he might make use of the typhus equipment of the AEF, but from what fund Keppel did not know.[16] In pursuit of further information, Albert Lucas traveled to Washington in April to see if the JDC could join the American Typhus Mission. There, he met the American Minister to Poland Hugh Gibson and Secretary of War Newton Diehl Baker. Tellingly, Lucas said, "Nobody seems to know who owns the [typhus] mission." Still, the JDC was willing to contribute up to half a million dollars, though Lucas had yet to mention it to any government officials. Lucas understood that the US government's priority was to bring Typhus Expedition troops home as soon as possible, whereas the JDC desperately wanted the men and equipment to stay longer in Poland.[17]

Simultaneously, Julius Goldman, who had just arrived at the JDC's European headquarters in Paris, reported to JDC New York that he had met with Col. Robert E. Olds of the ARC to discuss future cooperation. Although Goldman described Olds as having "a true friendly feeling for me," Olds saw fit to explain to Goldman that doing work just for Jews aggravates antisemitism.[18] This kind of argument indicated a fundamental misunderstanding of the Jewish condition and suggested an antisemitic outlook. Nevertheless, Goldman was serious about cooperating with the ARC regarding typhus work. He reminded Olds that the JDC had in fact just sent $500,000 to the ARA and spent substantial sums on nonsectarian relief.[19] Boris Bogen had told Goldman about the raging epidemic east of the Bug River, and the words Dr. Plotz had heard from the Polish minister in Washington, DC echoed in his head: "What is the use of feeding and clothing people today if they die of typhus tomorrow?" Goldman saw clearly that the only way to beat an epidemic would be through international relief cooperation and plenty of money. Goldman was operating on information that nearly 50 percent of typhus cases in Poland were Jewish; this was a Jewish problem.[20] The JDC could not save Jewish lives by fighting a contagious epidemic alone. Nor could it rely on Jewish doctors from the affected regions – they were themselves "dying off like flies."[21] Meetings with other American medical professionals in Paris associated with the AEF and the ARC made him suspect that tensions between the two were delaying work.[22] A few days later, he secured an agreement with the American Typhus Expedition headed by Lt. Col. Harry Gilchrist, an AEF physician, with his "most complete equipment in the world to combat typhus," including 30 AEF officers and 500 soldiers. The American Typhus Expedition was given $100,000 from the JDC, via Boris Bogen, for field work combating typhus in

Poland, including Galicia and east of the Bug River. Primarily, this money was to be spent on coal to power the delousing machinery. Goldman felt that this strategy of furnishing medical supplies might get other organizations to cooperate, too.[23]

Dr. Harry Plotz arrived in Warsaw in early May 1920. He was a young army doctor who had served with the ARC in Serbia during the war and a bacteriologist who discovered the typhus "germ."[24] In his first days in Warsaw, he sought out Col. Gilchrist of the American Typhus Expedition, Col. Shaw of the League of Red Cross Societies, and, Col. Emil Godlewski, the "typhus dictator in Poland." As Plotz inspected refugee camps and the typhus situation in his AEF uniform, he remained in close contact with American health agencies, emphasizing that these connections opened doors and put him in touch with key Polish authorities. He returned to the United States in August to write his recommendations, describing a demoralizing "vicious circle" in which poor conditions, lack of infrastructure, high mobility of louse-infested refugees and repatriates, and low morale meant people continued to die. He was horrified that persons already infected with typhus or other diseases often received no attention whatsoever and were simply left to their fate. Plotz worried that the coming winter would bring an even worse epidemic than the previous one, when Kiev cemetery records indicated that 25,000 Jews, nearly a quarter of the Jewish population there, had died of typhus within six weeks. He, too, urged urgent and collaborative medical care to combat the catastrophic effects of the war on the health of the Jewish population; the Polish government's effort was far too underfunded and ineffectual.[25]

Plotz recommended that the JDC become deeply involved in battling typhus, working in prevention, control, and care, and not simply because so many Jews were affected by typhus. He saw that the JDC had a specific role to play in an international collaboration. He knew that Jews did not trust health advice from the Polish government, since "under the guise of health propaganda, anti-semitic literature is distributed, and, in the zeal for cleanliness, beards are violently shaved and pogroms occur." He reported that in Kiev, victims of pogroms were neglected in general clinics, and he ended up relocating 250 of them to Jewish hospitals, where they were treated. Only a Jewish organization like the JDC would have any hope of reaching and gaining the trust of Jews, and therefore Plotz prescribed that the JDC in Poland, in cooperation with other organizations, distribute literature, construct bath houses, distribute soap, and provide hospital facilities for the sick.[26] In Poland, locals associated sanitary measures with coercive foreign intervention, and US sanitary measures were based on coercive hair clipping and cold baths.

And like their occupying predecessors, US officers showed considerable antisemitic bias. The cutting of hair and beards, part of the standard regimen, became associated with pogroms in Poland and Ukraine when Jews were assaulted as "vermin."[27] One American officer complained that he had to help Jews "overcome" their belief that they would not be able to keep kosher or be buried according to Jewish custom if they sought help at the local hospital, while another charged that Jews forged and sold tickets provided after bathing to purchase food staples. Others spoke of Jewish idleness and indifference to bathing while the Jews instead tried to observe the holiest days of the Jewish calendar.[28]

Plotz estimated that this medical work would require $2 million. The JDC New York did not have the funds on hand and decided to attempt to secure funding while tentatively beginning the first steps of his plan.[29] In February 1921, a JDC Medical Commission of eighteen men arrived in Poland – thirteen physicians, two sanitarians, a dentist, a pharmacist, and a secretary.[30] They were all expected to know "European languages including that of Yiddish," and those with experience in public health work were preferred.[31] A corresponding medical committee in New York oversaw the medical commission in Poland, in line with JDC protocol for all commissions and initiatives abroad. The men of the commission dispersed throughout Poland.

Dr. Irvin Michlin, who was in charge of the West Galicia district, wrote about how the JDC suppressed a typhus epidemic in a little town in Eastern Galicia, west of Lemberg, called Mosciska, with 2,800 Jews among its 7,000 inhabitants. Receiving information of an epidemic there, Michlin set off toward the town, requesting the JDC's medical commissioner in Lemberg and the Polish government's health commissioner (the "typhus dictator") for East Galicia to join him. Typhus had been carried to Mosciska by four Jewish refugees from Ukraine seeking shelter in the local synagogue. The outbreak in the town was unusually virulent. With 120 confirmed cases and another estimated 40–50 ("which no doubt have succeeded to conceal themselves in order to evade the drastic rules of isolation and the many other quarantine regulations"), local physicians cared for the ill and both the JDC and the Polish government sent medicine and cash. On May 6, 1921, local, JDC, and typhus dictator physicians assembled to enforce sanitary measures. A strict quarantine surrounded the city, and buildings open to the public were closed. Residents who housed ill persons were ordered to disinfect all textiles in mobile delousing ovens, and a school was requisitioned by the typhus dictator to serve as an isolation hospital.[32]

Figure 4.1 Anti-typhus staff in Volhynia. Three physicians, four public health nurses, and two sanitary inspectors stand in front of a mobile delousing unit for clothes in Rovno, Volhynia (then Poland), rendering medical aid in the JDC's 1921–1922 campaign against the deadly typhus epidemic.
(JDC, NY_04155)

Western Europe was concerned about the typhus epidemic not only because it could possibly infect the West, but also the specter of contagion was embedded in fears of Bolshevism's spread. Western governments sought typhus relief primarily for political reasons, not altruistic ones, and there was no reason to expect typhus to arrive in Western Europe if it had not already. It was impossible to control infested refugees and evasive locals, but still, the disease had not traveled far west. Increasing immigration restrictions alone solved that issue. Since the war, the German government instrumentalized typhus control as an excuse to close the border to Jews.[33] For the British and French governments, supporting the Poles' typhus efforts and the sanitary cordon encouraged Poland to consolidate its hold over its conquests and propped up the post–Versailles European order behind a humanitarian facade. The experts from the League's Epidemic Commission were more concerned with constructing a permanent organization and long-term sanitary defense to consolidate the post-Versailles system. Even though by 1921, typhus was already declining in Poland, the threat was enough to justify foreign aid to Poland.[34] From the Western perspective, it was beside the point that the American-Polish Typhus Expedition and Red Cross efforts accomplished very little and collaboration was impossible.

As one of the primary populations moving west, and already linked with Bolshevism in the antisemitic imagination, Jews were seen as both carriers of contagion and Bolshevism. An impulse to keep Europe safe from Bolshevism and disease meant, therefore, that Jews were to bear the brunt of a quarantine against both. Despite the JDC's hopes to organize an international battle against typhus in Eastern Europe, such coordinated action never materialized. By the time the JDC got medical relief to Poland in early 1921, the American-Polish Typhus Expedition was stepping out and typhus had become more of a political concern than an epidemic threat. Yet, Jews and other locals still suffered from typhus and other diseases. Organizations and commissions just went about their general relief with some ad hoc cooperation with each other and the Polish government. As one JDC physician described it, the government response to outbreaks of typhus was "slow and unwieldy and as experience has shown it takes from three till four weeks before the machinery is in operation, or in other words the epidemic is in full swing with sometimes hundreds of lives lost and the problem of suppressing the epidemic has become of appalling magnitude."[35]

Like in Mosciska, the JDC cooperated most with Polish officials in epidemic flare-ups. That was not the plan, but Polish authorities such as Rajchman, Godlewski, and others at the Polish Ministry of Public Health were receptive, willing to cooperate on repairing Jewish bathhouses and hoping to learn from Plotz.[36] Still, the JDC's Medical Commission did not have the manpower or the equipment to battle typhus nearly alone. It lacked authority to bring about the necessary international cooperation. Beholden to governments whose work was never coherent or particularly sympathetic to Jews, the JDC discovered that even when it took part in epidemic control, as in Mosciska, Jews were not ready to trust the JDC any more than they trusted the Russians, Germans, Austrians, Poles, or other Americans. Plotz's fears were confirmed, and Jews were mostly left to suffer and wait for general stabilization.

Bolshevism and Epidemic Response

The border-defying typhus epidemic has been understood either as a quarantine issue to protect Western Europe or as a domestic issue facing revolutionary Russia. While Western Jews did not encourage vast numbers of Eastern Jews to make their way westward, they were not inclined to seal off Jews in Ukraine from the West in a quarantine of Soviet Russia. The JDC assumed that the only possible, large-scale way to address Jewish suffering was to rejuvenate Jewish life wherever Jews were suffering. Controlling typhus both in Ukraine and Poland went hand in hand with Jewish health and, it was hoped, with lowering the stigma of Eastern Jewishness to improve the integration of Jewish refugees into Europe. Yet, the JDC continued to face challenges reaching Jews in Ukraine, except for a brief period in 1920.

During the war, the Russian Jewish health organization, OZE, was involved in the EKOPO operation funded in part by the JDC. Having already acquired information on the epidemiology of typhus, physicians from the *zemstvos* (self-governing districts) public health departments and from the Red Cross undertook preventive measures, which at first seemed to have typhus under control, especially among civilians.[37] As the war progressed, OZE expanded from aiding Jewish soldiers to assisting civilian war sufferers, sending four mobile detachments to combat epidemic diseases. OZE had privileges, like the Red Cross, to help Jewish refugees with army supplies. When Jews were deported into the Russian interior from the front, OZE responded by sending more mobile units in train cars to accompany these refugees. OZE managed Jewish health care in the war zones nearly alone, with JDC funding filtered through EKOPO.[38] But the Russian Revolution set off a crisis; funding from Jews outside Russia no longer arrived. The revolution and the harsh winter that followed begot the great typhus epidemic, "unprecedented in the history of the disease," flaring during the civil war and then again during the famine. According to the physician who would represent the JDC to the Narkomzdrav, the Soviet health authority, the epidemic infected six million in Russia from 1918 to 1920, with cases concentrated in Ukraine, in other words, among Jews. The act of trying to flee meant that Jews, headed toward cities or trying to leave Russia, caught the illness along louse-infested rail lines. From autumn 1918 to the following one, the Narkomzdrav mounted an anti-typhus campaign, providing 200 million rubles, adding beds to hospitals, establishing baths and delousing stations, and creating special laboratories. The Narkomzdrav was constructing a new, centralized, professionalized, free Soviet medical system that would combat epidemics. In the process, a few thousand medical professionals died from the epidemic, which was significant because now Russia had just 15,000 physicians.[39]

The embryonic international health system was entirely focused on protecting Europe from the menace of westward-traveling lice. Allied leadership, in fact, hoped that epidemics would destabilize fragile

Bolshevik structures. There was no reason to try to quell epidemics at their source and help suffering civilians; the goal was just to keep them contained to Russia. Similar sentiments fueled Anglo-American intervention in Siberia on behalf of White Russian Armies in Russia's Civil War and general Allied support for Poland.[40] Under the Whites, sporadic delousing measures could not overcome chronic shortages of medical supplies and institutions overtaxed by refugees and war prisoners. In Siberia, the ARC relieved civilians to demonstrate American benevolence and curry local favor in what was, at heart, a military intervention.[41] Judah Magnes decried these politics, denouncing America's foreign policy as hypocritical, and asking why, if America was not at war with Russia, it was furnishing munitions to Russia's enemies while allowing civilians to suffer. Of the sanitary cordon in Poland, he concluded hopefully: "We shall make it into a cordon of health and not of death. We shall make of it a cordon of hope and of life through the bonds of human brotherhood."[42]

In the part of Ukraine not under Bolshevik control for the first half of 1920, JDC representatives hovered behind Polish and White Army forces at the front, bringing relief, including medical aid, to communities in distress. After Harry Fisher, who would shortly enter Soviet Russia with Max Pine to negotiate an agreement on behalf of the JDC, took his first trip to these parts of Ukraine, he cabled back only: "Typhus is taking a large toll of victims leaving many orphans."[43] When Plotz first arrived in Poland, he was also able to visit some of Ukraine, including Kiev, to see the damage firsthand.[44] He visited a "concentration camp" of 6,000 Jewish refugees outside Kiev, where refugees died of starvation, and counted 8,000 Jewish orphans in Kiev. Bolsheviks entered Kiev while Plotz was there. He stayed with despairing Jews, only evacuating the city with the ARC following orders.[45] He quickly compiled a list of needed sanitary supplies and medications, and in the summer of 1920, the JDC shipped $50,000 of supplies via Reval, hoping to reach Ukraine under the new Fisher-Pine agreement, through Evobshchestkom.[46]

By the time the JDC sent reinforcements in the form of the Medical Commission in the winter of 1921, Ukraine was firmly part of Soviet Russia, sealed off from American activities. Yet, there were signs of hope; under Frank Rosenblatt's supervision of the JDC's first attempt to work in Soviet Russia through cooperation with Evobshchestkom, William Wovschin, a physician trained in the United States, went to Russia to study sanitary and epidemiological conditions. In reports to Rosenblatt in December 1920 and March 1921, Wovschin offered reflections gleaned from the conferences of social and professional committees he attended. In his account, epidemic diseases still claimed far too many lives though they had abated somewhat. He focused on the need to improve child welfare, the dearth of medications and dispensaries, and listed the comorbidities associated with chronic hunger – weakness, amenorrhea, nutritional disorders like Beri-Beri and scurvy, chronic gastric distress, and a low prevalence of diabetes. More unusually, he pointed out the absence of light sources after dark, the need for medical relief directed toward women, and a lack of heating material.[47] Disappointed, Rosenblatt cabled Plotz in June 1921 that despite Wovschin's recommendations, "conditions are such that it will be impossible for us to undertake any relief program in the name of the JDC."[48] The JDC was giving up on Evobshchestkom and transferring its funds to the AFSC. Magnes did not mince words: "A large part of the responsibility for the hostility of indifference of the American people to suffering in Soviet Russia is ... to be borne by the two greatest of American relief organizations, the American Red Cross and the American Relief Administration" and other religious organizations, except the AFSC.[49]

By 1921, some Western health authorities determined that new waves of typhus would continue to disrupt Poland and threaten all of Europe if humanitarian aid was not directed toward Russia, the source of typhus. Famine relief provided the reason for entry. Fridtjof Nansen's International Committee for Russian Relief (Nansen Action) began in August 1921 (before Nansen became High Commissioner for Russian Refugees). With the ICRC in Geneva, Nansen Action provided a coordinating structure for European international aid organizations: German groups, Ica, and Werelief.[50] Nansen's famine relief seemed like it might even hold the key to normalizing relations with Russia, which seemed crucial to European reconstruction efforts.[51]

Although Nansen appealed for food in Russia, Rajchman, who became head of the new League of Nations Health Section, turned to the epidemic. Rajchman's Epidemic Commission diverted its operations to Russia, sending a special commission to Moscow to tour famine areas in Ukraine and the Caucasus to study the prevalence of disease and distribute supplies. Rajchman then sent a medical officer, Dr. Farrar, to represent the League's Epidemic Commission on the Nansen Action in Moscow, but Farrar succumbed to typhus not long after. Rajchman was a universalist, an orientation perhaps derived from his Jewish background and family connections across Europe in addition to his strong feelings for Poland, and he was determined to attack the epidemic at its source. There are no indications, however, that Farrar was replaced or that the Nansen Action pursued a program to improve health in Russia.

In 1922, Rajchman pushed for an international solution to the typhus epidemic through the cooperation of governments, not just private associations, that would include assistance to Russia and Ukraine. Yet financial support promised by governments failed to materialize. With his ambitions fading, Rajchman did not push through a League of Nations Health Section–Soviet cooperation.[52] By 1922, Werelief began to work with the Nansen Action and the ICRC to provide food and clothing to famine sufferers in Russia, creating ambulatories and polyclinics to fight typhus in the process.[53] The Nansen Action was the closest the League system came to working with the Soviet regime, and it concentrated more on famine than on typhus.

Simultaneously, the United States decided to address Bolshevism through Hoover's ARA–led famine relief program in autumn 1921, hoping that through stability, it could stymie the forces of Bolshevik anarchy. The ARA distributed up-to-date scientific literature to Russian medical personnel, and the Rockefeller Foundation underwrote bulk ARA remittances of food and clothing relief directly to physicians and nurses. Typhus threatened ARA personnel, since there was no way to inoculate them, and they developed an aloof reputation as they took prophylactic measures to protect only themselves. Deemed too difficult, plans for an ARA delousing campaign in the Volga famine region were abandoned in favor of importing soap and other disinfectants that institutions could immediately put to use. The ARA medical program expanded into Ukraine in 1922. When Bogen finally reached Ukraine under the auspices of the ARA, he focused on preventing another epidemic the following winter. He made sure the population was fed, clothed, and sheltered, and sought to restore medical services, a process that will be discussed later in this chapter. With the end of famine, typhus cases declined after 1922 and European foreign relief teams withdrew.[54]

The struggle to negotiate a collaboration to fight typhus launched international Jewish health care by Jews and for Jews. The JDC could not heal Jews dying from typhus or contain epidemics, and it could not make governments or international organizations care, but it could promote health among Jews. Jewish social medicine looked inward for strength and strived for self-sufficiency, while crossing geopolitical borders. Rather than joining the projects of research and standardization that became the focus of many international health organizations in the interwar period, Jewish organizations did more of what states had started doing since the late nineteenth century: extending social health measures beyond epidemic control to Jewish health promotion more generally.

Elevation through Social Medicine

Despite the ills it presented for European Jews, the war catalyzed a broad program of international and local Jewish health activity that reignited social changes that swept Eastern European Jewish society before the war. Before 1860, an eclectic approach to medicine and health reigned in the Pale of Settlement. Traditionally, local organizations that were built into the fabric of Eastern European Jewish communities, including the *hekdesh* to house sick and destitute people, and charitable societies such as Bikur Cholim, Ezras Cholim, and Linas Hatsedek, dealt with sickness. Yet, Jews tended to avoid the hekdesh, which rarely healed, resorting instead to self-treatment and folk remedies. Beginning in the mid-nineteenth century in Russia, an unprecedented number of Jewish men and women entered medicine, while health care became a modernizing force for Jews in the Pale of Settlement. The idea of ameliorating the general status of Jews in modern society through improved hygiene was incorporated into the agenda of the *maskilim* (leaders of the Haskalah, the Jewish enlightenment movement).[55] In the run-up to the Great War, modern philanthropic activity had only just been organized around Jewish health: OZE was founded in St. Petersburg in 1912 and Hadassah sent a handful of American nurses to focus on maternal and child health in the Yishuv in 1913. The war was merely a setback to this nascent activity – Hadassah's nursing station in Palestine shut down in 1915 and OZE switched to emergency response mode. The upsurge in American Jewish humanitarianism ushered in a golden age of Jewish social medicine, or the social relations of health and disease, in the interwar period.

Jewish social medicine stayed far from Jewish politics, even if it had an ideological bent, and more within the realm of Jewish professional debates. Social hygiene, preventative medicine, state medicine, sanitary engineering, public health, and medical sociology have all been terms used to describe social medicine.[56] By definition, social medicine is about social, public relations, and not private, clinical medicine. But exactly *how* public and *which* social relations were involved were open questions hashed out in the political arenas of Western states starting in the nineteenth century. Jewish social medicine in the interwar period lacked a unifying state around which to base this discussion. For Russian Jewish intellectuals, social medicine looked like a path to such a state, or at least toward recognition of a Jewish national solidarity that transcended political boundaries. American Jews, steeped in Progressive American public health ideas, faced the self-prescribed challenge of raising the health of the Jews to prove the fitness of Jews as a people and themselves as capable leaders, within the multiple state frameworks in which Jews lived. For Hadassah women, public health initiatives would be a practical way to lay the foundations for a Jewish national home in Palestine, proving Jews capable of self-governance. The JDC was less ideologically ambitious. Dr. Plotz wrote in his first report: "I think that it is important for our people to learn the value of cleanliness. Should they adopt some of these simple measures, I feel certain that much of the prejudice would be removed."[57] Plotz was determined to lift up Jewish society in East Central Europe by reforming the entire health system (what remained after the war) for Poland's Jews.

Jewish social medicine made a convincing project for Jewish self-improvement. Jewish social scientists sought explanations for the myriad ways in which Jews were supposedly healthier than non-Jewish populations, for example, succumbing to typhus less often and having a lower infant mortality rate. Still, Jews and gentiles alike accepted that Jews had a number of pathologies or were affected by and spread certain diseases at a rate high above their neighbors. While some Western scientists engaged in racial scientific theories such as Darwinism, eugenics, and degeneracy, Jewish social scientists adopted social and environmental factors to explain Jewish illness.[58] If society and the environment were responsible for Jewish disease, then it followed that Jewish disease could be reduced or prevented by changing the environment and practices of the Jewish people. So-called Jewish pathologies such as tuberculosis, favus, typhus, and trachoma became the prime targets of Jewish social welfare organizations. Jewish self-help organizations, local and international, sought to civilize and transform Jews into acceptable modern citizens through health.

Improving the health of the Jewish people coincided with the general postwar shift from charitable medicine for the sick to community and preventative health measures for all, and from domestic programs to at least some international projects. Jewish relief synced with the contemporary interests of international organizations and with a particularly American Progressive concern with public health. It was clear by the 1920s that America had become the heavyweight in public health practices and was eager to spread the gospel to less civilized parts of the world, which now included Europe. This was epitomized by the far-reaching medical philanthropy and biomedical research programs of the Rockefeller Foundation (RF).[59] The American Red Cross and its broad medical program and postwar relief work in East Central Europe was another example. The ARC was on a quest to bring European citizens into line with American social and medical ideas and guide and uplift them in pursuit of long-term European stability that required no American governmental intervention.[60] The League of Nations Health

Organisation (LNHO), formed in 1921, included indirect but significant participation from the Assistant US Surgeon-General, Hugh S. Cumming, and considerable financial support from the RF.[61]

Given the status of social medicine at the time, the argument for particular Jewish public health and medical programs was easy. For example, treating an epidemic through education and personal interventions required Yiddish-speaking doctors and nurses. And fortunately, since medical doctors were indeed a common profession among Jews, there was also the potential for more built-in communal expertise than there was within most humanitarian relief organizations, aside from the medically driven ARC or RF. Although the JDC was unsuccessful at mitigating the typhus epidemic, its attempts placed it in the orbit of international health work. The JDC and Hadassah redirected their efforts to preventing Jewish disease and improving Jewish fitness in what they saw as the redeemable Jewish backwaters of the East (Palestine, Poland, and Ukraine). Meanwhile, the RF and ARC put their dollars and expertise into lifting up other "less-established civilizations" than their own and expanding American medical hegemony into Europe.

Upbuilding Palestine through Health

In the former Ottoman Empire, the postwar situation was dire. Famine, disease, and hard labor pummeled society far beyond the large number of military casualties. Russian refugees, prisoners, and fleeing civilians poured into Constantinople. Britain, France, and the new state of Turkey controlled different parts of the land. Within the British Mandate, post-Balfour Declaration, a Jewish national home in Palestine seemed within reach, rather than a utopian Zionist fantasy. Suddenly, American Zionist plans for building up Palestine gained traction. Hadassah, which had spearheaded experimental maternal and child welfare nursing services just before the war, had been waiting for the opportunity to send a unit of American medical professionals to Palestine. They would build the new Jewish nation through a modern health care system, supporting the ideal of healthy and strong Jewish bodies. Before Bogen set foot in Poland, a group of American Jewish doctors and nurses had already reached Palestine. So had the American Red Cross. Almost immediately after World War I, American Jews began to create a new health organization in Palestine that would serve as a social welfare foundation for the proto-state and an example of how American–style Jewish social medicine might look.

Since 1914, medical relief for Palestine was high on the agenda of American Jews. Before that, Henrietta Szold founded Hadassah in

1912 to bring American medical achievements to the Jews of Palestine. Hadassah sent a few nurses to run a child welfare and visiting nurse service in 1913 in Palestine, on Nathan Straus' bill, and supported the work of pediatrician Dr. Helena Kagan throughout the war.[62] American Zionist women used war relief work for Jews in Palestine to promote Zionist ideology at home, expending little energy on non-Jewish relief. Hadassah's committed fundraising efforts in 1915–16 brought in one-eighth of the total collected for the Palestine Emergency Fund.[63] In 1916, Hadassah announced plans to send a medical unit and supplies to Palestine on a boat chartered jointly by the ARC and the American Committee for Armenian and Syrian Relief.[64] America's declaration of war rendered that impossible, and Americans in Jerusalem, including Hadassah's nurses, pulled out, entrusting the JDC's and Zionist relief work to the Dutch banker, Siegfried Hoofien.[65] Although Hadassah's medical unit never made it to Palestine during the war, this did not keep Hadassah and other Zionist organizations from actively planning postwar activities.

The ARC was also in Palestine during the period of American neutrality and cooperated closely with the Near East Relief (then the American Committee for Armenian and Syrian Relief), to aid civilians during the war. From New York, the ARC deployed a commission to the Eastern Mediterranean to work alongside British occupying forces, which arrived in Beirut in June 1918. Those who traveled with the ARC to Palestine in 1918 were mostly health professionals who pursued projects to combat cholera, typhus, malaria, and famine.[66] One such professional was Solomon Lowenstein, who joined the ARC mission to Palestine as an unofficial representative of the JDC.[67] From Lowenstein's reports it became clear that the JDC would have to contend with the Zionist Commission, the group of British Zionists in Palestine chaired by Chaim Weizmann that would become the Jewish Agency under the Palestine Mandate.[68] There were few entrenched local interests, however. In June 1918, the Zionist Commission took over administration of the JDC's funds for relief work.[69] Lowenstein assured Warburg that the relief committee still disbursed in a nondiscriminatory and nonpartisan manner. Lowenstein further reported that the prevailing situation was normal poverty exacerbated by war conditions, barely comparable to places that had been occupied by invading armies.[70] The JDC thus determined that Palestine was not a high priority for its relief work.

Yet in June 1918, the American Zionist Medical Unit (AZMU) set sail from New York, with the JDC paying a quarter of the $400,000 budget. Hadassah had assembled equipment and goods and appointed as its head the experienced child welfare worker Alice Seligsberg. Hadassah's leaders had already gained some practical experience in relief work from prior collaboration with the JDC and the Zionist Organization of America (ZOA) faction led by Louis Brandeis, and both the JDC and the ZOA were partners in the AZMU.[71] They also had the ARC mission nearby, connected by Lowenstein, from which they could gather standards and prices, cooperate on relief, purchase supplies, and learn from its relationship with governing authorities.[72] The British Mandate was more than willing to let Jews take care of themselves and be relieved of that duty, and the World Zionist Organization also let the AZMU work autonomously. In its first months, the AZMU triaged only the most urgent medical issues, but by November, it embarked on its planned social medical program, opening hospitals, laboratories, clinics, and dispensaries in urban centers, including revitalizing the Rothschild hospital in Jerusalem and adding a nursing school. It also opened or reopened hospitals in Jaffa, Tiberias, Haifa, and Safed. The organization's first medical director was Dr. Isaac Max Rubinow, a Russian-born physician and a socialist whose interests focused on health insurance. Under Rubinow, each patient's financial situation determined hospitalization fees, a policy he took from the mutual aid tradition of the Jewish community.[73]

Figure 4.2 Hadassah medical unit to Palestine. The American Zionist Medical Unit in June 1918 posing in New York before sailing to Palestine. Unit members, mostly physicians, wear typical military uniforms with Star of David armbands and sit behind an American and proto-Israeli flag.
(JDC, NY_04926)

The medical unit traveled with forty-four physicians, nurses, and social workers. They were like the ARC's professionals dispatched to Europe and the Eastern Mediterranean, except they were Jews who focused their professional practice on helping Jewish immigrants. Even more specifically, they were Zionists. Unlike ARC medical professionals with training in urgent medical work in the field, AZMU personnel went mostly without prior experience in emergency field work.[74] Jewish residents of Palestine did not regard the AZMU as another ARC – for example, the workers' sick funds society, known as Kupat Holim, appealed to the AZMU for assistance in its capacity as a messenger of Zionism and part of the Jewish community. Rubinow's reaction was to absorb the medical services of the Kupat Holim, which needed outside financial assistance, on the AZMU's terms. These agricultural workers resisted Rubinow's administrative demands and paternalistic attitude, but had no choice but to comply.[75]

In fact, this disagreement suggests the extent to which this was a Progressive-era, liberal project despite Rubinow's own socialist, Russian background. The ideal of efficiency was met through professionalization of health-care workers, administrative centralization, prioritization based on medical statistics and quantified need, extensive records, and concentrating in urban centers. The AZMU, like the ARC's Child Health Program for Eastern Europe, bore a strong resemblance to Progressive community health programs in the United States through its strategies of surveillance by medical experts, holistic approaches to health, and collection of data.[76] Both Hadassah and the ZOA Brandeis group believed Americans should retain control over the funds they donated and should do so according to Progressive standards of efficiency and organization.[77]

The Wilsonian liberalism of Louis Brandeis reoriented the growing American Zionist movement as a whole after the war toward labor Zionism. In June 1918 in Pittsburgh, Brandeis and philosopher Horace Meyer Kallen extended agricultural colonization, the late nineteenth-century Jewish self-help panacea, to Palestine. This American liberal Zionist vision preferred economic and land development projects over strong political claims of Palestine as the authentic home of the Jewish nation. Even some non-Zionist leaders of the JDC could imagine Palestine as an extension of liberal America and thus support this kind of relief and welfare project. Hadassah's plans for social medicine sat at the margins of this romantic vision. Whether public health work was "productive" or "unproductive," contributed to state-building or maintained dependence, and was thus worthy of Zionist effort, was a matter of debate. Either way, many Jewish Zionists and Progressives came to believe that Palestine could function as a testing ground for social experiments that were impossible to implement in the United States.[78] In the case of the AZMU, which asserted its autonomy from Palestine's Jewish communal structures, governing authorities, and the World Zionist Organization, the opportunity for American Jews to apply the precepts of social medicine without political interference was unparalleled. As the 1920s wore on, debates within the Zionist movement, as well as the JDC's refusal to commit to long-term philanthropy, especially in Palestine, would prove a greater challenge to the autonomy and continuation of the program, but still one Hadassah was able to meet.

Although American Jewish women gained ground in Jewish and women's public roles before the war, like Western women generally, they largely played a secondary role in war relief work in the hopes that they would reap some returns, like suffrage, in its aftermath. This became frustrating for some women, especially in the Zionist movement, where men took it for granted that women had achieved equality in the movement, but women felt there had been no return on their acquiescence. Tensions between practice versus rhetoric regarding gendered participation in the United States and Palestine surfaced toward the end of the war. Hadassah did not appreciate being in the position of turning over its carefully raised funds to a different organization (the Zionist Organization of America) with which it was supposed to be equal but by which it was subsumed. The AZMU gave Hadassah members a chance to show how women could contribute to nation building in Palestine.[79] Hadassah's "Zionist maternalism," like the maternalist rhetoric used by contemporary women activists in the West, was a way of carving out and maintaining a public sphere that seemed appropriate for women and allowed them to autonomously pursue political agendas. Zionist maternalism held that social welfare work was the province of women, and that social welfare in Palestine was the province of Zionist women.[80]

The leadership and programming of activities in Palestine betrayed this Progressive Zionist maternalist underpinning. Lillian Wald's Henry Street Settlement and Visiting Nurses Association, funded by Jacob Schiff, would guide the work of American professional women as they traveled to Palestine.[81] Not only did Hadassah send American nurses to Palestine before the war, and then in greater number than physicians with the AZMU, but also it prioritized establishing a nursing school in Jerusalem after the war. Hadassah wished to inculcate the idea, as JDC physician J. J. Golub later wrote, that "Medical service and programs of preventative medicine are unthinkable without nurses."[82] In the Ottoman Empire, nursing was considered less a profession than a tradition, handed down by apprenticeship. Hadassah, however, urgently needed more nurses to expand the AZMU's activity into rural areas. Hadassah also required a professional, educated workforce with wide-ranging skills and high standards to act as the backbone of its medical service. The Hadassah Nursing School, founded in Jerusalem in 1918, was the first professional school of any kind for women in Palestine. It aspired to do for the Yishuv what American professional nurses did in city slums; nurses were emissaries for Western liberal and Progressive culture. Like a modern American nursing school, Hadassah's was managed by a committee of elite, nonprofessional women engaged in public works, in this case, Hadassah women in America, who formed a bridge to Columbia University's nursing school, the foremost institution of its kind. Carried out by American registered nurses, training adhered to the standard curriculum of the National League of Nursing Education in the United States. By 1928, Hadassah's nursing school trained 135 graduates and started coursework for male orderlies to serve traditional men who did not want to be seen by women nurses.[83]

Hadassah's Zionist exertions targeted mothers and children, particularly through social medicine. In this area, the JDC and Hadassah were accompanied by the ARC, which was carrying out a long-term civilian aid program focused on child health in Europe. The medicalization of childcare and motherhood had long been apparent in Jewish social medicine, as the next chapter will explore in more depth. For Hadassah, Zionist maternalism included mothering children, and by extension, the entire Jewish people and the land of Palestine. Hadassah's first activity in Palestine was to send two American nurses to the Yishuv in 1913 to care for expecting and new mothers and their families through a Maternal and Infant Welfare Center. In North America and Western Europe, motherhood was a unifying theme for Progressive-era voluntary associations that argued that women were a reservoir of expertise on the needs of other women and children. A related strand of Progressive thought concerned what constituted proper childhood development, which was said to be achieved through the application of biomedical, social scientific, and public health expertise. These combined in Palestine with Jewish social scientific ideas: Jewish health was determined by environmental factors and the promise of social medicine to elevate Jewish society through self-help. Hadassah's program, centered on mothers and children, launched an assault on high infant mortality rates, childhood diseases, malnutrition, and physical weakness, all perceived as pervasive in Palestine, and featured American solutions including everything from medical clinics to playgrounds, school lunches, child colonies, milk stations, and child rearing and sanitary education for mothers.[84]

The AZMU set up modern hospitals, the nursing school, pasteurized milk stations, sanitary supervision of schools, maternal and child welfare centers, health screening for incoming immigrants, and public health education programs within the first few years of its existence, as Jewish anti-epidemic efforts in Eastern Europe floundered. When the British Mandate shifted from military to civilian rule in 1920, it adopted a policy not to interfere with the development of health services in the Yishuv, and to concentrate instead on the Arab community, which lacked outside support.[85] Accordingly, the AZMU was asked to assist in founding a health system to provide continuing care to the Jewish community in Palestine, although it also lost some of its most public functions like sanitary inspections, street cleaning, and patrolling cisterns for mosquitoes.[86] The 1921 World Zionist Congress in Carlsbad turned the AZMU into an independent medical organization, subordinate to Hadassah: the Hadassah Medical Organization (HMO).[87] The HMO constructed a joint medical school with the new Hebrew University in 1925, into which the nursing school was eventually integrated. Hadassah in the 1920s undertook campaigns against specific diseases, malaria in particular, adapting the plan of the RF's International Health Board.[88] Hadassah assisted with land reclamation projects, like reforestation, to reduce malaria. When the Mandate government took over routine mosquito-elimination projects, it relied on Hadassah-trained professionals.[89] This was carried out with the financial support of American Jews, through JDC and Zionist appeals, including the United Palestine Appeal fundraising scheme, beginning in 1925. From 1917 to 1922, the JDC alone provided $700,000 to the AZMU.[90]

The HMO was a nongovernmental health agency. But its external funding, hiring doctors on salary, eschewing private practice, and sliding scale fees resembled a public health system rather than a mutual aid organization. Yet Rubinow wrote to the JDC that the HMO, despite comparisons to a health department, simply did not have the governmental authority to do "real public health work," which required changing the social conditions such as housing, wages, or sanitation.[91] In reality, the HMO was somewhere in-between: a modern, international mutual aid organization from America acting like a national medical service for Jews in Palestine. Hadassah had put some basic structures of self-government in place, through a diaspora social welfare arrangement, decades before the declaration of the State of Israel.

Suffering from volatile funding in the 1920s as organizational donors cut back, by 1928, Hadassah became the sole funder of the HMO. In an ongoing debate about how much American Jewish reconstruction money should be directed toward Europe versus Palestine, and the JDC's overall attempt to limit its long-term commitments, the JDC attempted to reduce its funding of the HMO. The JDC managed its contribution to the HMO as part of its broader Palestine relief and then medical program. Although the JDC was a major funder of the HMO, with a representative on its executive committee, JDC delegates traveled to Palestine independently or with other American organizations, not under the banner of the HMO.[92]

To deal with HMO work in Palestine, the JDC called on Bernard Flexner, a Zionist in the Brandeis group and a prominent lawyer who replaced Friedlander and Cantor after their murders in Eastern Europe.[93] Bernard was a brother of two RF leaders and his connections for chairing the JDC's Medical Committee were impeccable. He facilitated a visit to Palestine by Dr. Victor Heiser, Director for the East of the RF International Health Board, to consult on the start of the HMO's anti-malaria work. Heiser additionally reported back to the JDC that the HMO was conducting excellent work, but "on a scale that was really not necessary, according to European standards," with the Jerusalem hospital as modern as the best in the United States.[94] The JDC, uninterested in the project of making medicine in Palestine as good as that in New York, insisted on the HMO's liquidation or transfer to another financial backer starting in 1922. It simultaneously worked to liquidate its European programs, which were not in nearly as good shape.[95] Although Flexner followed JDC liquidation protocol, noting that the HMO always seemed to be enlarging its scope, he was sympathetic to the Zionist cause and advocated for continued JDC input in Palestine.[96] Therefore, despite official JDC non-Zionism, as Derek Penslar has argued, "the yearning to bring about a change in the Jews' occupational structure and economic behavior, was realized most fully in Palestine," due to "areas of concord, cooperation, and overlap," which existed between Zionism and Jewish philanthropy generally, despite the fact that most histories separate these issues or highlight their conflicts.[97]

Hadassah was also engaged in a long struggle for autonomy within the Zionist movement, which resulted in the ZOA's and Keren Hayesod's (the development foundation fund run by the World Zionist Organization) withdrawals of funding in 1927. For Hadassah, these conflicts looked suspiciously like the Zionist movement was pulling support from social welfare work that was absolutely essential to the Zionist cause, simply because men derided it as perpetuating the Yishuv's dependence. Hadassah's reaction was to double down on its commitment to manage the HMO; Hadassah leaders feared the entire project would crumble under the mismanagement of men. By 1924, Hadassah was already working toward establishing independent finances by building its membership at home and engaging in competitive fundraising. In 1928, when it had regained its independence, it had a dues-paying membership of 36,000.[98] Having its own funding allowed it to continue to expand services, if at a slower pace than it hoped.[99] Regardless, its American funding made it a heavyweight among other decentralized, privatized medical care providers in Palestine.

Hadassah could claim that its focus on healthy bodies, healthy land, and healthy children fit within labor Zionism and liberal Zionism. Both the Balfour Declaration and the war provided the crucial opportunity for American Jewish women, organized by Hadassah, to make the philanthropic move that would set into motion its health infrastructure and state-building project. Hadassah's philanthropic Zionism was essentially American Progressivism exported to Palestine – solutions to health-care problems defined on American terms were addressed in an American way, by Americans, especially in its earliest years. And these solutions were ready to be further socialized, cooperatized, and democratized in Palestine, when political conflicts did not yet appear intractable and reconciliation with Arabs seemed possible. They worked to prevent sickness through a complex framework that addressed root causes, not just existing sickness. They participated in American Zionists' liberal, Progressive dreams of a Jewish model state, spreading the American dream to Palestine in the hopes of a creating a Jewish utopia.[100] And, they would serve as a model for what American Jewish liberals could try to achieve in the far less utopian setting of Eastern Europe.

Medical Work As Reconstruction in Poland

The JDC first sent two doctors to Europe in January 1920 to collect data on Jewish health, distribute sanitary supplies, and report back to New York. Once JDC doctors reached Poland, it did not take them long to dream about long-term social medicine for Jews there. But it was Dr. Plotz, joining them a few months later to focus on epidemic relief, who pushed the JDC's work in Europe toward social medicine. As he struggled to help Poland's Jews fight typhus and was surprised at the sheer inadequacy of international health relief, he could not help but notice the terrible disrepair of Jewish medical institutions and living conditions. He wondered what chance Jews might have stood against the epidemic had they had access to baths and adequate medical care, as well as local support for typhus control. The public health plans he designed encouraged JDC leaders to decide how to conduct a social medical program in Europe. His goals were even more ambitious than emergency epidemic relief, but the rest of the JDC had no intention of installing itself long term in Poland – it was rather hoping to liquidate operations soon. Nevertheless, the JDC was determined to repair the damage of the war and bring lasting medical improvement of some sort to Jews in Eastern Europe. Thus, the JDC's eventual solution was to practice Rockefeller Foundation–style American philanthropy on a short-term basis to demonstrate best practices and build local medical capacity, rather than import Progressive American public health practices wholesale into East Central Europe as Plotz suggested and as Hadassah did in Palestine. The JDC, however, could not contain its medical work to a limited, fully independent local program; instead, public health became an ambitious, demanding local program that looked as much to Jewish medicine in Russia as it did to America for guidance.

Organizing Local Medical Professionals The JDC included medical work as part of its program in Poland starting in 1920. Dr. Meyer I. Leff went as medical director of the JDC's first Overseas Unit to Poland, which was described in Chapter 2. Dr. Charles Spivak, head of the Jewish Consumptive Relief Society in Denver, went as the JDC's special health commissioner to help transition from relief to rehabilitation.[101] Their immediate roles were to do for health work specifically what Bogen had already done for relief in Poland in general: organize local relief efforts and distribute supplies while trying to plan for a more systematic and rehabilitative future. Leff took action at the local level, while Spivak organized a committee of physicians in Warsaw. Collecting data on Jewish health as it did on other subjects, the JDC gathered reports filed from several cities. General JDC relief efforts in Poland, Austria, Czecho-Slovakia, Romania, Lithuania, and Latvia, also included medical work, mostly subsidizing local medical committees.[102] Plotz joined Leff and Spivak, intending to combat contagious diseases. Instead, he proposed a sweeping plan for Jewish sociomedical renewal.

"All forces of destruction seem to have been working in harmony to destroy these people," reported Plotz in October 1920. Beyond typhus, he described how people lived in holes in the ground, in overcrowded conditions, without enough clothing, and severely exposed to the elements. There was no sewage system or garbage disposal, soap or baths, and vermin infestations were rife. There were food shortages. Smallpox, typhoid, dysentery, and tuberculosis ran rampant in Jewish communities, despite vaccines and cures for some of these diseases. Dilapidated hospitals lacked supplies, and he noted that JDC had to find a way to separate the sick to prevent the spread of disease while caring for those who were infected. Pointing out that Jews had been living in such terrible conditions for six years, he blamed the war and its attendant ills for Jewish "lethargy" and the "carelessness" he saw.[103]

The JDC could not simply conduct emergency medical relief, Plotz argued – restoring sanitation and health had to be part of reconstructive work. It should take place in Europe, starting with Poland, and in Palestine. Plotz's plan had three prongs: disseminating propaganda, undertaking constructive work, and collecting vital statistics. Propaganda would involve medical professionals and religious leaders at the local level, exhibitions demonstrating sanitary living, and the publication of pamphlets and newspaper articles. New constructive efforts would include open-air colonies, dispensaries, bringing x-ray machines to treat favus, baths, schools to train Jewish nurses, and athletics. Vital statistics on the Jewish population would have to be systematically collected from a variety of Jewish organizations.[104]

Although Plotz set out an ambitious program that resembled the ambitious AZMU, the JDC Medical Commission saw itself as more limited. By 1921, the JDC struggled to convince American Jews to keep giving. The JDC Medical Commission was to continue the work of Spivak, Leff, and Plotz, reporting, establishing local committees, distributing medical supplies, and building medical facilities and nurses' training centers. There was nothing in its mandate suggesting extensive infrastructure upgrades or far-reaching collaboration with other American organizations.[105] Plotz understood the JDC's uncertain future, but criticized its timidity in undertaking only "the most primitive requisites, and in no sense indicate that we are attempting to build up the sanitary conditions in Poland to anything like those found in other countries." Plotz figured that the best way to spend limited dollars was to repair medical and sanitary infrastructure, like hospital roofs, wells, and baths, and in some cases, build new hospitals, baths, and dispensaries. As Plotz pointed out, "it is useless to preach cleanliness when there is no place to bathe."[106] He sent the Medical Commission around Poland (and one delegate to Romania) to collect hard data on which he could act.[107] Back in New York, however, Herbert Lehman fretted over Plotz's $2 million medical program, writing, "I doubt very much whether even a strong State with great financial resources could hope to put into effect a plan as comprehensive as that outlined by [Plotz]." In Lehman's eyes, this rebuilding program, rather than a modest educational effort, would waste JDC funds or start something that would then have to be ruthlessly cut short.[108]

The JDC sided with Lehman, rejecting Plotz's efforts as over-rationalization and too grand. Even if the JDC had by 1921 switched to rehabilitation rather than relief, the JDC expected Plotz to suggest a typhus relief program, not a comprehensive plan for social medicine – and either way, rehabilitation was supposed to cost less than relief, not more.[109] The JDC had no desire to disrupt the current health system to build from scratch Jewish medical and sanitary work across all of East Central Europe. Yet, Plotz wanted to send Jewish medical professionals from the United States to carry out studies pinpointing exact needs, cross and double-check all activities to avoid making errors, then use huge sums of money to rebuild medical and sanitary work across Poland. He saw local control as "pernicious"[110] and thought the role of American Jews was to make a long-term investment and engage in extensive training of locals. The JDC, by contrast, sought to empower existing local leaders quickly and to make a short-term philanthropic investment that would have ripple effects, hopefully stabilizing the health of Jews in Europe. Lehman suggested to Plotz that rather than repairing and building all over Poland, the JDC might just repair and erect hospitals in circumscribed areas, running a pilot program of sorts, and he emphasized that Plotz should work on forming local committees of medical professionals to take over any sanitary programs.[111] In short, the JDC wanted to run the kind of international philanthropic health work programs that the RF undertook at that time, a private precursor to what would later be called global health development, initiated through the United Nations. But Plotz had in mind something that resembled the scope of Hadassah's efforts, exporting the best of American, Progressive-era public health projects to improve all of Jewish society.[112]

One of the JDC's main objectives was to produce a medical program with "whole-hearted approval and co-operation of the local communities," insisting that the Medical Commission build a health organization of local leaders. In a grudging response, Plotz planned a conference of Jewish medical professionals in Lemberg in June 1921, to elect two doctors from East Galicia who would come together with the Medical Commission. Together, they would discuss what they wished to do and what they could do in East Galicia.[113] The Lemberg event launched a series of conferences facilitated by the JDC to organize medical experts in each district. What the JDC called the "Lemberg Plan" aimed to organize a network of Jewish medical professionals and volunteers across East Central Europe, from the top down instead of working through existing health organizations.[114] At the August conference in Rovno for the Volhyn district, medical experts from Volhynia protested that Plotz got to choose the three members of the central committee created by the conference.[115] In Bialystok, given the rivalry displayed amongst local attendees, Plotz noted, "In this city as in others we feel that the Central

Committee as elected by the people will hardly work. There is a constant effort to receive control of the funds, and the people do not display an interest in the big general problem of their district."[116] In Vilna, delegates had a heated debate about the JDC's expectation that locals take over the work, including financing, pointing out that it was just the places with the worst epidemics and greatest need for help that would be unable to contribute to medical sanitary costs.[117]

While the Lemberg Plan was underway, JDC medical commissioners tentatively began Plotz's program of bath house and hospital repairs and paying physicians to work in small towns. It seemed that locals, medical commissioners, and Plotz could agree on bath house repairs – but crucially, JDC leadership in Paris and New York did not. A major part of Plotz's plans included making sure that Jews who were spread out in small towns, not just urban centers, received medical assistance, but it was difficult for medical commissioners to find a way for places with smaller populations and few medical professionals to find legitimate representation as it turned work over to local actors.[118] At least in the West Galicia district, the new committee formed by Plotz in Krakow was so slow that the JDC physician still had to run all of its activities himself.[119] One JDC physician in Warsaw mused that the other districts seemed to be having similar difficulties.[120] Bath houses were repaired and built very slowly, stalled by weather, money troubles, and disorganization. Plotz's whole program was allotted $300,000.[121] Plotz resigned in September 1921 out of frustration, pronouncing the Lemberg Plan a failure.[122]

The Rockefeller Plan Plotz's resignation was a mixed blessing. The new Medical Affairs Committee chaired by Bernard Flexner at JDC New York wanted to harmonize with the JDC Reconstruction Committee's plans, anyway.[123] The Medical Committee, formed in November 1921, coordinated across regions, but avoided anything to do with Soviet Russia. This was in line with reconstruction plans that also saw the creation of the Refugee Department.[124] Bernard Flexner became chair of the Medical Committee not only because he was interested in the Hadassah Medical Organization as a Zionist, but presumably also because he was the brother of two RF leaders, Abraham and Simon Flexner. Accordingly, the JDC's medical work began to follow the examples of the RF's International Health Board and China Medical Board.[125] Bernard and Simon Flexner suggested to other JDC leaders that it was futile to provide continuous medical assistance to a place that lacked sufficient medical services before the war. A consistent educational approach, modeled on the RF's hookworm campaign, would be preferable. It would be concentrated, not diffuse, and led by an adminis-trator, not a doctor.[126] Flexner's Zionist orientation indicated that he thought JDC medical projects in Palestine and Poland ought to have somewhat different goals and possibilities, and that the scope for Poland should be narrower than for Palestine. Palestine was a nation-building project, whereas Poland needed philanthropy. European Executive Director in Vienna, James N. Rosenberg, concluded: "We must not ... go into the field with an elaborate program. Have something dramatic as Favus, Typhus." And concentrate on one or two specific things, in just a few places. Like the Reconstruction Foundation the JDC was setting up under Herbert Lehman, to be discussed in Chapter 6, the JDC envi-sioned having a "JDC Health Board" arranged as a corporation.[127] The JDC's health philanthropy would be an investment.

And so, in 1922, the JDC's gaze turned entirely to favus. Plotz's plan to build a new society was cast aside, but the RF's hookworm campaign was fully in view. Yet the skeleton of the Lemberg framework remained and with it, the dynamics of Jewish life in Poland. Despite his unhappi-ness with Plotz, Bogen did not appreciate a change that would demoral-ize so many committees and leave smaller places untouched. Plus, focusing on favus, a disease to which Poles were indifferent, seemed misguided. Bogen's advice was mostly ignored in New York.[128] Social worker, rabbi, and former ARC staff member Morris Waldman took over from Plotz. Then, beginning in June 1922, Dr. Jacob J. Golub, a member of the JDC Medical Commission from the start and the only American physician left in the field for the JDC, led medical initiatives from Warsaw.

Under Waldman and Golub's leadership in Europe and the guidance of Flexner's Medical Committee in New York, the JDC helped establish TOZ to build local capacity to fight disease and to redirect responsibility to local organizations. Health priorities shifted to non-life-threatening favus, and to education, including the creation of a nurses training school. Meanwhile, the JDC reluctantly accepted requests to shift build-ing repairs from JDC medical work to the JDC Reconstruction Committee's new engineering department.[129] The center of this European drive remained Poland, especially Warsaw. Minor efforts to undertake similar programs occurred beyond Poland, in Czechoslovakia, Romania, Latvia, and Lithuania.[130] According to Golub, the twin object-ives of the Medico-Sanitary program were to collect information on current and past standards of health and sanitary conditions and to revive or form local voluntary welfare and health institutions with remaining leaders. By doing all this, the JDC hoped to return Jews in Poland and the Baltics to prewar health and sanitary conditions.[131]

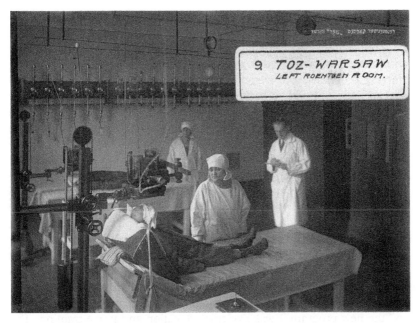

Figure 4.3 X-ray therapy for favus in Warsaw. Children receive x-ray therapy to cure their favus infections in a TOZ x-ray center in Warsaw, equipped by the JDC as part of its health campaign against favus, 1922 or 1923.
(JDC NY_03993)

A long-standing relationship between the JDC and TOZ began with the campaign against favus. In the summer and autumn of 1922, Golub "found" a legal health organization in Warsaw, TOZ, that had gone defunct except on paper. He seized upon this legal structure as a scaffold on which he could build an independent Polish Jewish public health organization that would take over from the JDC Medical Commission. The JDC's new medical program had brought to Poland $175,000 to spend "before we had the organization, instead of as is usually the case of having the organization and not the money." Waldman and Golub brought together the Polish medical delegates established under the Lemberg plan to revise and revive the statutes of TOZ and become district TOZ organizations.[132] The JDC allocated $100,000 for favus work and established relations between districts and the Warsaw center and between the JDC and TOZ.[133]

Favus, a fungal disease of the scalp like ringworm, and endemic in Poland, affected mainly children and was stigmatized as a "Jewish disease" through its links with poverty. It could be treated with x-ray therapy. And so the JDC-TOZ program set up favus clinics where children could stay during treatment, and imported mobile x-ray machines. The favus campaign mobilized local committees, physicians, nursing programs, and hygiene education efforts, all of which the JDC was working to build. Whether the goal was to eradicate the disease or simply reduce its incidence was a matter of discrepancy between locals and the JDC. Kahn, in his typically forceful way, narrowed down the goals and scope of the campaign. Another point of contention was the ownership of the x-ray machines, and in late 1922, the JDC transferred the machines and the program to TOZ. Logistical challenges also appeared, including a lack of cooperation from ordinary Jews, who resisted the idea on many levels and had, of course, faced paternalistic public health propaganda and unknown or rough procedures directed at them since the start of the war. Despite these problems, this collaboration significantly reduced favus. Out of an estimated 15–18,000 affected children, 6,000 were irradiated. After forming a coherent committee to fight a single target, favus, TOZ was off to a good start.[134]

The second part of what I call "the Rockefeller Plan" (the JDC referred to "the new program") was hygienic education and nurse training. The favus campaign underscored the need for modern health principles to reach the Jewish public. While the idea for building nursing capacity and public health education efforts in East Central Europe had been discussed since Plotz went to Poland, it took three years to come to fruition. There simply were no local nurses to restore to their positions, aside from a few women who had trained in accelerated programs in wartime Russia. Although the JDC sought primarily to restore health rather than improve it, public health nurses seemed essential for this task.[135] While the JDC medical commissioners had no troubling assembling Jewish doctors in Polish cities, public health nursing, the face of social medicine in America, was conspicuously rare. In America, the struggle of educated, middle-class women to make nursing a high-status profession preceded the professionalization of nursing in continental Europe, where nurses were still considered bedside helpers rather than educated medical professionals.[136] Lillian Wald's New York idea thus followed the JDC straight from Palestine to Poland. By May 1921, the JDC offered its own six-month training courses in Rovno, Brest-Litovsk, and Lemberg, with hopes for expansion. Plotz hoped Jewish nurses would be accepted to the ARC's new nursing school in Poland – but Jews were barred from attending.[137]

After Plotz abandoned the JDC, Dr. Zofia Syrkin-Binsztejnowa, the physician from Poland in charge of JDC health education, reminded the

JDC that nurses were essential to health education. She argued that it was the JDC's duty to train women not only in preventative medicine and public health education but also in bedside nursing, which would take at least two years of theoretical and clinical study. Syrkin recommended the establishment of a nurses training school next to Warsaw's Jewish Hospital.[138] The Medical Committee in New York pronounced the idea an overextension since "this can hardly be thought of as a war relief measure and ... there was no Jewish nurses' training school in Poland before the war." While waiting for TOZ to get organized, Amelia Greenwald, an American Jewish registered nurse, went to Warsaw in February 1923 to establish and direct the new nursing school.[139] Greenwald had considered going to Palestine as a Hadassah nurse before the war, while working at Columbia's Teachers College and volunteering at Henry Street in public health nursing. Instead, Greenwald became a chief nurse in the AEF/ARC in Verdun, France, during the war and then worked four years for the National Council of Jewish Women.[140] The school finally opened in July, with Greenwald taking the advice of Helen Bridge, the director of the ARC nursing school, that it would take at least five years to graduate enough students to turn it over to local nurses.[141] Based on the New York State University nursing curriculum and experiences related by Bridge, Greenwald built the Jewish School of Nursing with two tracks for nurses: a short, six-month course for public health service and a two-year course for bedside nursing. Local physicians provided instruction. Beginning with a class of twenty nurses, the Warsaw school grew and, by 1928, the JDC turned it over to its own graduates. Three smaller schools for bedside nursing and one in Rovno for training in public health were also established.[142]

An unplanned feature of the JDC's work in Poland was the continuing need to involve government authorities in order to function. From the start, Plotz was adamant that the JDC should not disguise that it was a Jewish organization by claiming to do nonsectarian work, and that it could outright "demand our rights as an American Philanthropic organization." He had discussed this subject with Dr. Rajchman, who backed him fully and promised support.[143] The JDC tried to present whatever would most effectively allow it to carry out its work and protect its recipients from antisemitism. It did not always go well; the JDC felt the Polish government was hostile, while Witold Chodzko, Polish Minister of Health, was at a loss to account for this and said only that the JDC Medical Commission exaggerated its accomplishments.[144] The Medical Commission in Poland was having difficulty getting organizational charters legalized by the government for local committees in any of its districts, until the TOZ solution materialized.[145] To reduce suspicion of local officials, the JDC Medical Commission under Golub appointed liaisons to local government to keep authorities apprised of the work and maintain compliance with local health regulations. While providing data to the central organs of the JDC, the Medical Commission furnished its data on epidemic diseases and vital statistics to local government. In exchange, the JDC received information on diseases, vital statistics, and government efforts in public health from these officials.[146]

Despite the JDC's desire for collaboration beyond the capricious Polish government, in the arena of health care, it mostly kept away from the ARC in Poland after the typhus epidemic had passed. The JDC modeled its non-relief, public health work on that of the Rockefeller Foundation's philanthropy, hoping not to become too deeply involved but still effect change over the long term. After all, it was not even allowed to send Jewish women to the ARC nursing school. While the ARC wrapped up its "long-term" child health programs in 1923, the RF International Health Board began its work in Poland, as it did not earlier feel that it could successfully undertake work in Poland before then. Rajchman finally convinced the RF to help build an institute in Poland for training public health profession-als.[147] In June 1922, the RF's Wickliffe Rose urged the JDC (and Poles) to contribute to the proposed institute and find a way to collaborate with Rajchman, so that there would be "an entering wedge to be used in ameliorating the condition of the Jews."[148] This held the promise of alleviating the need for antisemitism damage control and shifting the medical burden to the untested TOZ. Rajchman was once again enthusi-astic when two JDC Medical Committee men came to see him in Geneva, promising the cooperation of the Polish Public Health Service given the initial JDC contribution of $40,000.[149] Minister Chodzko and the JDC signed a contract for the JDC to cover the cost of purchasing a college building for the new RF Institute's School of Hygiene, a school for fifty students, "open to all Polish citizens irrespective of their religion and/or origin," and soon after the JDC added a $12,000 scholarship fund for Jewish students.[150] For the JDC Medical Committee, this would serve as a litmus test to see how serious the Polish government was about including Jews in the public health sector. As the JDC pointed out, "the School cannot be effective unless the Jewish colonies are penetrated and for this purpose Jewish health workers are indispensable."[151] Though this school got off the ground and was open to Jews, it did not transform the JDC's relationship with the Polish government, the RF, or the League Health Section. The Polish government and Rajchman remained uncomfortable with the exclusivity of the proposed Jewish scholarship fund. At the end of 1923, the JDC still had nearly $98,000 unused that it had set aside for this project, and by 1924, it had nearly lost track of it.[152]

By late 1922, Golub and Kahn were making a concerted effort to liquidate the JDC's medical work in Poland. Making a difference in Jewish health in Poland beyond the JDC's tenure there would require transferring Golub's program (the favus campaign, nurses training school, public health education, and physicians in small towns) to the reorganized TOZ. Provisional committees under TOZ had been established for favus and nurse training, and would hopefully become the core of a legalized TOZ once the JDC departed.[153] Under the directorship of Leon Wulman and guided by Syrkin, who had been JDC employees, TOZ was fully recognized by the Polish government in June 1923, and as the JDC pulled away from Poland in November, all of the JDC's activities except the nursing school were transferred to TOZ.[154]

TOZ quickly grew from five to fifteen branches in its first three years.[155] The JDC had hoped to shed responsibility for the moving target of health in faraway lands, by providing basic relief and then carrying out some closely defined model programs, drawing on RF strategies. The aim was to build local support and to integrate Jewish health care into general health care. However, local support the JDC actually built – in the form of TOZ – seized upon Jewish health work as an opportunity to resist both antisemitism and assimilation, providing a way for Polish Jews to modernize as a distinctive group within Poland. TOZ attempted to carry out the Russian OZE's prerevolutionary vision in independent Poland in concert with OZE's successor in Berlin, as will be discussed shortly. While TOZ utilized methods promoted by the JDC, it had a distinctly Jewish nationalist approach. The favus campaign and Syrkin's emphasis on children blossomed into a child-centric health organization. Though TOZ struggled to keep its financial house in order and expand its program without raising substantial local funds or soliciting much from the JDC, it forged a path into Jewish social statistics and waged a broader campaign for improved Jewish health to "strengthen the general neglected and weakened type of the Jew."[156] Its goals included fighting tuberculosis; lowering infant mortality; improving sanitary conditions in Jewish religious facilities; supervising the hygiene of Jewish religious rituals; and examining emigrants preparing to leave for America, while providing the medical and welfare services the JDC had promoted.[157]

The Medico-Sanitary work of the JDC in Poland was Sisyphean. It moved through several iterations from emergency relief to the top-down provision of emergency medical services and data collection starting in 1920, to broader efforts to repair medical infrastructure and regroup local medical services under the "Lemberg Plan." In 1922, it instituted a program with the intent of transferring it to locals, which finally resulted in a semi-independent TOZ in 1923. The entire medical program was remarkably noncontroversial in the political sphere, despite resistance from nonmedical professional Eastern European Jews. Without governmental authority to force people into quarantine, and knowing that in the end it was up to the Jewish masses to implement health measures for themselves because the JDC would never come up with enough dollars or influence to carry out a top-down program, the organization searched for a way to harness local medical professionals on behalf of Jewish health. Eventually, TOZ became a partner, capable of carrying out the health activities sought by the JDC. After the JDC's departure, TOZ kept running on JDC funds, overseeing Jewish social medicine until the Nazi takeover of Poland.[158]

Propping Up Russian Medicine

If in Palestine the JDC worked mainly through the AZMU/HMO, TOZ/OZE/OSE became the JDC's partners in Europe. With OZE branches in Jewish areas of Russia, a loose East Central European OSE network with Berlin headquarters, and the linked TOZ in Poland, these iterations of OZE reveal Europe's rapidly changing political configuration and the shifting relationship of Jewish social welfare organizations to evolving polities. Although OZE had a strong leadership of medical professionals and a vision of Jewish solidarity and uplift through medicine, its success or failure was almost entirely predicated on its ability to build relationships with other Jewish organizations that could support it financially as it sought to enter into new polities and continued to provide medical assistance at home in Soviet Russia. This is where the JDC came in, but it was a fraught relationship; the late timing of OZE's reconnection with American Jews and disagreement about the donor–recipient relationship undermined what was a shared vision about the need for Jewish social medicine.

Within the Russian Empire, OZE pursued an agenda of social medicine before and during the war. The Bolshevik Revolution cut short these efforts. OZE came into existence in 1912 in St. Petersburg, due to a confluence of factors including the need to protect the professional interests of Jewish doctors, the democratization of Jewish communal organization, and desires to create a prototype for Jewish national autonomy. OZE always saw itself not as improving traditional Jewish medical frameworks but as bringing real change to the Jews, which would require social and preventative medicine on the model of Russian social medicine as practiced by zemstvos. The conditions of war catapulted this nascent Jewish health care organization into an organ of Jewish medical activism. Government organizations were willing to cooperate with it, since it relieved them of responsibility for Jews. During the war, OZE collected data on Jewish health and sanitation as part of EKOPO's overall data collection efforts, which were used to make decisions and demand funding. Jewish physicians toured the Pale of Settlement providing urgently needed care. Because of its dependence on medical professionals, OZE maintained itself as an elite organization. As the war progressed, it responded to Jews deported eastward from the front by sending mobile medical units in train cars to accompany refugees as part of the larger, partly JDC–funded EKOPO operation.[159]

A crucial part of the Russian OZE's wartime program tried to extend the principles of urban social medicine into the realm of Jewish community health, including a focus on children and mothers. The emergency medical response necessitated by the war was an aberration in a broader program of social medicine. As OZE train cars followed Jewish refugees to their new places of settlement, the organization set up a network of medical institutions between 1914 and 1916 that included polyclinics, hospitals, milk stations, nurseries for young children, sanatoriums, playgrounds, medical supervision of schools, and summer colonies for sick children. In effect, OZE, with EKOPO, was creating new Jewish communities for refugees centered around Jewish social welfare organizations. In the process, OZE moved child-rearing out of the family and into the community, but not without controversy. The seeds of a shift to the medicalization of childhood were thus apparent during the war, part of a larger shift in social medicine toward the treatment of children and mothers. A philanthropic focus on children, especially through health initiatives, was also popular with European and American international associations and was an extension of domestic campaigns in social medicine that targeted the urban poor, often immigrants. To some members of OZE, social medicine seemed like a way of civilizing the Jews and cultivating their corporate self-reliance.[160]

After the February Revolution of 1917 and its accompanying Jewish emancipation and political liberalization, OZE defended the need for a continued separate Jewish social medicine that was nonpartisan and served by experts. Yet it was political in the sense that OZE's leaders argued that separate medical institutions for Jews were still necessary to adequately address Jewish physical and social characteristics. In this fleeting moment, Jewish community medicine pursued social reform, but by the end of 1918, the health movement's leaders in Russia had decided to set aside ideological differences and seek accommodation within the Bolshevik regime, because otherwise, it was unable to mobilize resources.[161] The Bolshevik Revolution destroyed OZE's hopes of ascendency. The organization was banned in 1919 as civil society was stifled and officially liquidated when Frank Rosenblatt struggled with Evobshchestkom in 1921 (see Chapter 2). In the Soviet Union, OZE was able to function only half-legally by attaching itself to international humanitarian relief organizations, including the JDC. Besides the attempt to work with the Bolsheviks and the JDC through Evobshchestkom, its leaders, notably Abram Bramson and Moisei Gran, pursued its programs mainly as individuals working in the Soviet health care system.

From 1917 until Nansen and then the JDC arrived with the ARA, OZE endured a tough period, when funds were scarce, and the wounds of war and revolution were fresh. When Dr. William Wovschin served as JDC delegate in late 1920, he focused on epidemics, while outlining a plan for working with OZE and the Narkomzdrav (the Soviet health commissariat) for public medicine. His frank notes betrayed signs of terrible devastation among Russia's Jews. A Jewish health program that extended beyond long-standing Jewish political interests was needed. Besides calls for fuel and medicine in Wovschin's report, he stated that Jews needed American nurses, not doctors. He suggested that American Jewish doctors would not know Russian medical methods or the psychology of their patients. The real issue, however, was that the needs of Russian Jews simply did not match what American medicine might prepare a doctor for. Wovschin, straddling America and Russia as a Jewish doctor, probably felt this without being able to convey it.

Two particular aspects of medical work needed in Ukraine – care for women and children – were particularly unfathomable. First, Wovschin wrote that help was needed for women survivors of rape. Thousands (countless, really) numbers of women were raped in pogroms in Ukraine, starting in 1917. These women had special needs, not least, treatment for venereal and other sexually transmitted diseases. In a sharp departure from the typical discourse of social medicine and Progressive public health measures, Russian Jewish medicine would have to include women not simply as mothers who needed education on child rearing. Women's clinics required a broad gynecological and rehabilitative mandate that extended far beyond maternity.[162]

Children, too, were singled out for relief; but these were no "ordinarily" unfortunate children. Impoverished Jewish orphans roamed Ukraine in the thousands. They had suffered serious dislocations in their short lives. Strikingly, no Jewish children under seven were found among them; the very young had not survived. As Wovschin put it, displacement, war conditions, and pogroms led to "A veritable carnage of the little ones," which constituted an "extermination."[163] One world war later, after the intentional extermination of the Holocaust, surviving Jewish "children" would once again turn out to be older than actual children.[164] With a generation of Russian Jews essentially disappeared, restoring children to health was a top priority. The survival and rehabilitation of children was essential. This explains why in 1920, OZE planned playgrounds even as orphans roamed the streets and people died in refugee camps from hunger, exposure, and disease.[165] The depth of ethno-national violence and corollary needs of Russia's Jews in this hour of social disorder exceeded the bounds of social medicine as it had ever been conceived in the West, or even in Russia. American doctors would hardly be more helpful than Russian Jewish doctors at treating these extenuating conditions. Those needs were rarely met.

Still, in 1922, more than a year after Wovschin's report, the tide turned somewhat in OZE's favor, and presumably in favor of Jewish health. The JDC's famine relief program began with its ARA collaboration in 1922, in which the JDC sought out Jewish institutions. This involved supporting OZE workers to supervise a few dozen medical facilities and childcare institutions in southern Ukraine that the Bolsheviks had leased back to Jewish communities that had once owned them. The Narkomzdrav had given OZE permission to develop activity in regions where there were Jewish pogrom and famine victims, so, in Ukraine, especially. The Narkomzdrav emphasized centralized medicine and exploring the links between disease and changing social conditions as the way forward for science under socialist medicine, but also by cautiously connecting to Western organizations. JDC programs included funding the Narkomzdrav to buy pharmaceuticals, an operating room and x-ray equipment, and establishing courses for young Soviet doctors in thirty-two cities. These operations were conducted with the same workers and committees that had long been part of OZE and made use of ARA-JDC food stocks. Epidemic attachments were planned, but ambulatory and outpatient care centers for children took center stage, which OZE viewed as the easiest way to reach the most people. These were also kernels from which a social medicine program could germinate.[166]

The JDC did try to work with partners besides OZE in Russia but did not make much progress. Bogen pursued independent agreements with Soviet authorities, which amounted to little. A better bet was the ARA, but its program was not devised for complex delousing plans or new institutions (which was deemed impossible in Russia). The ARA's medical program, funded by the ARC, the US government, and the RF, was set up so that the American physicians attached to each ARA district unit only supervised the distribution of ARC medications, giving as many essential supplies to existing institutions as possible. The JDC contributed $25,000 to the ARA's remittance packages program earmarked for Russian doctors and nurses. To little effect, it also tried to get a physician on the ARA's roster. Still, when the ARA departed in June 1923, the JDC was able to distribute some of its surplus medical supplies and its dispensaries in Kiev were turned over to the JDC. The JDC began to concentrate on medical aid instead of food relief. Opening a Medical Commission under Bogen and Rosen in Moscow, the JDC spread its administration beyond Ukraine and Belorussia and worked closely with the Narkomzdrav.[167] Unlike for Palestine or Poland, though, no unit of medical personnel was ever dispatched from New York, not even nurses.

In the intervening period, OZE set up a new base in Berlin, from which it leveraged foreign help for its work in Russia. The Berlin OZE's primary purpose was to keep OZE running by convincing Jews in Western Europe, including Russian emigres, to support Jews suffering in Ukraine.[168] To this end, the Berlin OZE, soon known by its German-language acronym OSE, opened branches in London, Paris, Latvia, Danzig, and Romania. With the Berlin headquarters made up mainly of Russian emigres, such as Moisei Gran, who stayed in close contact with core leaders who remained in Russia, like Abram Bramson, the Berlin OSE and Russian OZE remained tightly linked. In this way, OZE also formed a partnership with Werelief, which was working with the Nansen Action to reach famine sufferers in Russia. Werelief contributed 650,000 francs in 1922 for that purpose to the intergovernmental Nansen Action coordinated by Nansen and the ICRC – an unusual act for a private association. Funds brought in through the Nansen Action and the International Save the Children Union and provided to OZE were also used to operate the medical and childcare facilities OZE had leased from the government in 1922 and 1923. OSE credited these European donors, especially the London War Victims Fund, Werelief, Ica, the Alliance Israélite, and also the Ukrainian Federation of Africa (probably a federation of landsmanshaftn in South Africa), with $170,000 of the $215,000 it had put to use for health work from 1922 to 1924.[169]

Bogen eventually concluded an agreement with the Narkomzdrav and high-ranking Ukrainian health officials regarding medical work for 1924, for which the JDC first allocated $150,000 and donated nearly $500,000 by February of that year.[170] The resulting "Joint OZE Commission" was directed by Abram Bramson as the JDC's medical representative in Russia.[171] By early 1923, Bogen was able to report back to New York that while most medical work in Russia was at a standstill, at least the "the medical needs of Jews of Kiev are fairly well supplied."[172] Bogen also found reason for optimism, despite limiting circumstances, because the Soviet government did not discriminate against Jews as was the case in Poland.[173] Like in Poland, favus treatment was a pet project of JDC medical relief in Russia – a wedge for the JDC, and an opening for

OZE.[174] From Bogen's perspective, the JDC's medical work in Russia through the remnants of OZE was "especially encouraging" and needed a continual infusion of funds.[175]

The Berlin OSE was not as successful at fundraising with the JDC, though – Bernard Kahn's firm support of JDC liquidation from East Central Europe after 1923 led him to tell the OSE that it should not expect more funds, even though Kahn believed OZE to be an "able and honest organization." As the JDC prepared to pull out in 1923 from East Central Europe, the European OSE Federation was just getting established and starting its program. It begged for help by contacting JDC leaders in New York, circumventing Kahn's authority. The JDC liquidated its general relief work in Russia in November 1923, and Bogen left Moscow in mid-1924, reconnecting the Russia OZE and Berlin OSE as he departed, and leaving the medical work in Bramson's charge.[176] Bogen agonized to Lewis Strauss that the JDC was already pulling out, "I am still of the opinion that this liquidation should not have taken place now, as long as there is a single farthing left in the J.D.C. or as long as the American Jews are still able to contribute even a pittance towards the very serious situation in Russia."[177]

Moisei Gran and two other representatives of OSE Berlin traveled to New York in 1925 to seek funding from American Jews for the Joint-OZE Commission. Although the JDC typically ostracized European Jews coming to America to seek funds directly rather than through the rationalized auspices of the JDC, Boris Bogen went out of his way to support OZE. Bogen praised Abram Bramson to his colleagues within the JDC, explaining that Bramson's efforts had resulted in the special Joint-OZE Commission that could take charge of work subsidized by foreign organizations.[178] Joseph Rosen also wrote from Moscow in support of the OSE, suggesting that Kahn allocate funds to these "excellent fully reliable workers."[179] Bogen and Rosen knew from experience that opportunities to reach Jews in Russia were rare, particularly ones involving trustworthy individuals, and that the special commission needed continuous external support to remain operational. The OSE delegation showed up at JDC headquarters in April and May and sent memos urgently requesting funds. They first noted that OZE had helped more than 700,000 people through its 500 institutions since its founding.[180] Gran wrote more personally and explained how the Joint-OZE was having to reduce its activities due to lack of funds, and that it could not rent hospital beds from the government, could not treat thousands of sick people, and could not reopen summer sanatoriums for children.[181] The JDC's reaction was ambivalent and incoherent, differing from city to city in the United States and from member to member. Finally, it reacted at an institutional level by reversing its usual position and folding fundraising for OZE into its general fall 1925 campaign.[182] Regardless, that campaign did not raise enough money for OZE. All told, from 1922 to 1925, the JDC calculated that it had spent a total of $441,000 on Russian medical work.[183]

The JDC was about to launch agricultural colonies in conjunction with Ica in Crimea. James N. Rosenberg suggested immediately after OSE's 1925 appearance in New York that funds ought to come from Joseph Rosen's Agro-Joint project because the JDC Medical Committee in New York no longer had any.[184] There was underlying logic to this argument: the long-standing Jewish self-help remedy that was the Jewish agrarianization movement could easily incorporate the idea that placing Jews on the land would contribute to Jewish health. Promoters of Agro-Joint argued that it would be worthwhile even if the value was just raising "a generation of our urbanised co-religionists upon the soil under sunlight and in fresh air."[185] The usual work of the JDC Medical Committee was thus transferred to Agro-Joint. Agro-Joint funded health care institutions, mostly continuing subsidies to local medical societies in heavily Jewish areas.[186] Although medical aid was officially a Soviet government activity, these institutions only served individuals covered by social insurance, or salaried workers, a group to which the bulk of the poor Jewish population did not belong. Money was needed for the usual dispensaries; campaigns against "social diseases" like tuberculosis, favus, trachoma, and malaria; and infant welfare stations. Starting in 1926, medical work began to also encompass "neuro-psychiatric diseases, which were the result of the difficult past decade."[187] The JDC Medical Commission of Agro-Joint was headed by none other than Abram Bramson, with doctors from Agro-Joint colonies and Kiev also represented.[188] By 1929, Joseph Rosen reported that most medical institutions in cities were able to charge small fees to cover their costs, towns had organized effective mutual aid societies, and the JDC only covered about 25 percent of the budget for Jewish medical work in Russia.[189] Agro-Joint furthermore funded four volumes on Jewish medical particularities in Russia, which made the first inroads into Jewish pathology, using the methods of laboratory sciences.[190] More detail on Agro-Joint follows in Chapter 6.

Meanwhile, although the OSE Federation was organized with the intention of funding health work in Soviet Ukraine, it created a network of Jewish health organizations across Europe. These organizations were, like TOZ in Poland, the inheritors of Jewish social medicine in Europe once the JDC was gone. A report by the JDC medical commissioner in the Vilna district (fought over by Lithuania and Poland at the time) noted that the local OZE and EKOPO branches had managed to carry on through the war and should be "directed and controlled" into a "potential force" to carry out medical work, rather than creating a new organization.[191] And so it was. These reassembled EKOPO/OZE branches were never particularly invested in by the JDC, because they did not fit the narrow and intense program strategy the JDC absorbed from the RF and implemented in Poland. They were instead the direct descendants of the Russian OZE and renewed largely due to the organization's Berlin OSE offspring. The OSE Federation pulled the Polish TOZ into its orbit. By 1925, these branches operated largely on an independent financial basis – OSE claimed that throughout the OSE Federation, 70 percent of budgets came from locals.[192] But the JDC provided OSE branches with support in 1926 and 1927, enabling the growth of an institutional network, mostly directed at child welfare. Reports from Romania, Lithuania, and Latvia in 1927 and 1928 indicated that even if the OSE was unsuccessful in finding financing to put the Joint-OZE on stable footing, it had succeeded within continental Europe.[193] Not that these local OSE branches found themselves in a good position; they wrote of continuing poverty and poor living conditions as much as feeding children in schools, propaganda work, and clinics.[194]

In Russia, then, Jewish social medicine began before the war and revolution and continued after. Western Jewish agencies, including Werelief and the JDC, were interlopers, mainly funders. Bogen and Rosen used American connections and resources to transfer money for desperately needed medical relief, and saw subsidies to medical institutions in Soviet Russia as one way to ensure the continued viability of Jewish life as Jewish in Russia, but never even tried to Americanize the medical work that was carried on by OZE and its related local medical societies. While available statistics regarding medical infrastructure, health campaigns, and Jewish demography do not present a way to understand the effects of the medical work on the health of Russia's Jewish population, what is clear is that OZE effectively maintained a steadfastly Jewish nationalist program that leaked beyond Soviet borders to East Central Europe via the OSE Berlin, under the banner of Jewish health. Far from protesting this arrangement, the JDC continued to fund it, albeit judiciously, accepting that it reflected the new reality of independent, Jewish life in Europe after the war.

International Health for the Jewish Nation

Despite at least a half-century-long relationship between Jews and Western medicine, medicine as Jewish philanthropy came of age due to American Jewish responses to World War I. Launching an international

Jewish health program from America required a general international health effort plus the extremes of an epidemic and rapid demographic restructuring in Jewish life toward further urbanization, fragmentation into independent nation-states, and poverty. These were fundamentally international projects and international health development projects. But as a 1929 appeal by OZE to the RF showed, OZE would never be a candidate for mainstream international health projects, since it was just a semi-legal organization in a system of nation-states, even if it undertook the type of activity the RF supported.[195] Though the RF was crucial to the JDC's philosophy and hopes for postwar reconstructive health work, Jewish health associations never achieved meaningful international collaborations. There was a need for Jewish health care because Jews were discriminated against while asked to rely on antisemitic, or at least, exclusive nationalist governments for their well-being. From immigration restrictions to forced delousing, to the sanitary cordon, the slow response to Jewish epidemics, and the British Mandate in Palestine's focus on Arab health care, it was evident to Jews who were paying attention that Jewish health care had to operate independently of the international and nation-state health regime for Jews to have health care at all.

Though they could continue to seek cooperation, Jewish organizations turned inward because of antisemitism or government unwillingness to engage with non-state actors. The JDC agreed to help stem typhus, and then to repair medical institutions based on these assumptions. Furthermore, Jewish hygiene and health programs served an ideology that suggested that Jews could and should care for the health of other Jews, and that this would improve Jewish solidarity and Jewish status at the same time. Hadassah operated from this perspective. The JDC moved closer to it as it began to support Hadassah, TOZ, and OZE. Two seemingly contradictory principles were at work, often erupting in conflict within the JDC. The JDC wished to act like statesmen, including the hard-boiled realism that funding was limited and that American Jews could neither pour money into Europe indefinitely nor provide endless men on the ground when no other Americans were doing so, a position represented by Kahn, but also Lehman. On the other hand, Bogen especially demonstrated built-in empathy and the duty to help unfortunate Jews in the diaspora.

The JDC sought to improve Jewish life in a way that seemed within reach because it did not depend on unreliable outside forces like changing state borders. Neither did it stir up political controversy. The organization appeared to be a peaceful, stabilizing force for democracy in Europe and for the Jews there. The distortion of Jewish racial science in World War II, which would turn Jewish self-help and Jewish health projects on their heads, could not have been imagined in the 1920s. Improving Jewish health promised a way for Jews in the 1920s to integrate into modern Poland. A program matching a focused and finite Rockefeller campaign, rather than the wholesale exportation of American preventative and curative medicine, seemed the right way to do that. This prototypical American philanthropic project, with its favus campaign, nursing school, and emphasis on education over building institutions, successfully revived dormant capacity for the Jews of Poland, Russia, and then the rest of East Central Europe, to run their own public health affairs. The JDC achieved its goal of turning over a project to locals, who then took it in their own direction: Russian social medicine for the Jewish nation. The OZE-TOZ network, remaining financially dependent on JDC, represented an asymmetrical, negotiated collaboration between Russian and American Jewish understandings of public health. A collectivized vision of Jewish social medicine resulted. This appropriation and reinterpretation of Western culture using American dollars resembled a postcolonial response to development work.

Hadassah never considered its work relief or charity – Hadassah's vision was always one of building up necessary infrastructure and social services in Palestine. Hadassah designed every one of its programs to create a medical system, build local capacity, and allow the Yishuv to take root through social welfare.[196] This put it at odds with one of its major funders, the JDC, which had no interest in creating a medical system. Although the JDC gradually reduced its funding to zero by 1928, the startup funding it provided bought Hadassah the time to increase services in the 1920s by its expanding membership of American Jews, turning public health work into a Zionist and women's cause. Bernard Flexner wrote in late 1922, "That difficult as the Palestine medical situation is, it offers few difficulties, as compared with Poland. The smallness of the country, and the presence of a benevolent government are advantages that make it possible to hope for a demonstration that will be of great value elsewhere."[197] In Poland, Dr. Plotz tried for a year to similarly import the best Progressive New York settlement house strategies, but soon became mired in a web of difficulties in Eastern Europe, where there were more Jews and more hostile governments to impede intervention efforts with less American Jewish will to stay for the long term.

Jewish organizations combined health and medicine into a much larger humanitarian relief and rehabilitation program, an unusual practice given that comparable international organizations at the time, private and governmental, did not typically mix social medicine with other international aid. While Eastern European Jews were in a way colonized, they benefited from emancipated, science-wielding Jews living in Great and Imperial Powers who saw it as their duty to raise up and train their Eastern brethren. As a result, American Jews ended up funding a Jewish nationalist medical program, without any political discussions, that extended from Palestine, to Ukraine, to Poland, and beyond. This international health program was a roadmap to auto-emancipation.

5 Child
Welfare for a Contested Jewish Future

I have seen thousands upon thousands of men mowed down, widows dying of grief, despair and want. I have seen the children – *the real victims of this war*. And I plead for the sake of these children! What will become of them? What will the young generation think of us when it grows up and sees the stamp of Cain upon our brows? ... What a generation will be brought forth, conceived in madness and baptized with blood!
Herman Bernstein, 1916[1].

From the Armenian genocide to evacuations from French cities to famine in Russia, the Great War inflicted trauma on children, including many Jewish children. Poland in 1919 "seemed to be flooded with orphans or lost, refugee children."[2] Jewish orphans in Ukraine were of particular concern to Jewish institutions, in the wake of war, pogroms, and revolution. As Jews fled their towns in a panic, orphans were left behind. Children witnessed violence, lived on the street, begged, or languished in overcrowded, understaffed institutions. In the Rovno region, in the devastated eastern reaches of interwar Poland near Ukraine, where three orphanages were evacuated during the Polish–Soviet War, statistics collected by the JDC in 1921 suggested that anywhere from 11–40 percent of surviving children in any given Jewish community were orphans, and that more were boys than girls.[3] For Ukraine, in particular, outside assistance of every kind seemed necessary for Jewish children, since decimated Jewish communities were unable to take care of them. Compounding the absence of adults was the difficulty of reaching small communities due to ruined infrastructure and the lack of a functioning press. As various towns came under Polish control from Ukraine, the JDC rushed in quickly to see to the care of children.[4] From Ukraine and Belorussia, many children took the initiative to cross borders on their own, appearing as unaccompanied child refugees in Poland and Romania.[5] These child refugees were usually labeled "war orphans." Fighting between Poland and Russia and civil war in Ukraine continued to produce orphans well into the 1920s.

Jewish humanitarians responded to Jewish children affected by the war however they could. The deep emotional investment of Jews around the world produced a humanitarian response even less coherent than usual, while overlapping goals with mainstream humanitarian organizations provided new opportunities. In the immediate postwar period, while the JDC wrestled with this immense Jewish problem and cooperated with the ARA's child feeding program, other Jewish organizations stepped in to help Jewish children. Violence, famine, and epidemics in Ukraine limited relief efforts, even as conditions generated more orphans and refugees. A specific geography of relief emerged just beyond Ukraine's borders. Eventually, the JDC built a cross-cutting child welfare program, the main goal of which was to get children off the street. To do this, the JDC attempted to pass child refugees as regular children, which required negotiations and compromises with pedagogues and child activists in East Central Europe. Distinct child welfare projects began in Palestine and formerly Austrian Poland and spread from there. Yet, the JDC undermined its own efforts as time passed. It was neither willing to abandon Jewish children under its care nor take full responsibility for them. Furthermore, new refugee and orphan welfare projects side-stepped education, which was so controversial among Jews that it had to be institutionally separated and moved into the "cultural" realm. Far from merely "cultural," education was deeply enmeshed in Jewish politics as adults sparred over their children's futures, especially in Poland. It was the only issue that split the JDC into its constituent parts in its overseas work, revealing stark asymmetries between American and Polish Jewry.

Concerns about children were not unique to Jews. Starting in the late nineteenth century, American and European experts focused on children as part of larger questions about labor, science, and crime, viewing childhood as a phenomenon distinct from adulthood. The Great War cast children in the international spotlight as the quintessential victims of war, as Western activists, especially middle- and upper-class women, rallied around them. The war thus marked the moment when children became an object of international relations. While emphasizing the value of children, precisely what *kind* of value they had was debated across states. From a Western perspective, decrying innocent child victims made for successful relief fundraising. Plus, a focus on children narrowed Western commitment to resolve an otherwise overwhelming humanitarian emergency and seemed the surest route to international cooperation in peacetime. Indeed, the ARA and the ARC understood their child-directed programs as creating a foundation for a socially and politically stable Europe. Yet there was also a countervailing view at work that equated children with future national vigor. This redefined children as small soldiers. For Europe, still entangled in nationalist fervor, helping children was synonymous with reconstructing damaged nations and ensuring a successful biological and political future. These ideas were sometimes compatible; for Herman Bernstein, quoted at the beginning of this chapter, children, not nations, were the real victims of war *and* society's future.[6]

While child welfare was the Jewish issue that intersected closely with mainstream humanitarian interests, no charismatic Jewish leader appeared on the international stage. Lillian Wald did not leave Henry Street Settlement to campaign for children the way she had campaigned for peace. The Polish Jewish doctor, writer, and pedagogue, Janusz Korczak, signed the Declaration of the Rights of the Child, spearheaded by Eglantyne Jebb (the British founder of the Save the Children Fund), and adopted by the League of Nations in 1924, but his voice did not carry in Jewish humanitarian circles or outside Poland.[7] Alice Seligsberg, experienced in child welfare, focused on Hadassah's Zionist vision. Instead, the JDC's choice for childcare supervision in the field was a Reform rabbi who suffered a breakdown during his assigned fieldwork. The lack of a compelling international Jewish presence on the issue of child welfare suggested dysfunction: The issue provoked irreconcilable conflict within Jewish institutions and communities, which could not agree on what the Jewish future should look like. Child welfare experts were not able to play a leading role in this highly politicized Jewish setting.

Jewish organizations that sought to take action on behalf of children first had to grapple with what it meant to conduct modern child welfare when traditionally, a Jewish charitable approach to children had lumped together impoverished, sick, uneducated, homeless, and orphan children into one category.[8] The newly drawn political map, the unprecedented scope of violence and suffering, the disruption of local and communal life, and American Jewish involvement in Jewish reconstruction clearly demanded something other than a traditional response. Were homeless or orphaned children refugees, or were they only refugees if adults had carried them across borders? Just how many Jewish children in need were there, anyway? Were these children the future of the nation, or the state, and which nation or state? Whose long-term responsibility were they? What future should be envisioned for them, and what about children who still had relatives to raise them?

To answer these, Jews in America and Europe looked to their neighbors who tackled similar questions and to child pedagogy for guidance. But they discovered a cacophony of possibilities and competing interests, particularly when it came to education. Like with health care, Jewish childcare fared best in Palestine where a proto-state, the Zionist Commission, had been firmly installed and could become part of a nation-building project. The end result fractured humanitarianism for children in Poland, while in Soviet Ukraine, not even childhood survival was a given. However, what emerged institutionally was also remarkably far reaching – even if not by design: The JDC became a transnational welfare state of sorts, funded by American donors for the Jewish diaspora.

Addressing Children

Since medieval times, Jewish societies had cared for orphans in Eastern European Jewish communities as part of an array of charitable societies, including the *talmud torah*, which provided basic Jewish education for poor children, and the *hekdesh*, which housed the sick and homeless. This system began to break down well before the war, as Jewish society transformed in the nineteenth century, and as the number of marginalized Jews outpaced the capacity of traditional Jewish community welfare societies. Large cities in the Russian Empire contended with significant numbers of homeless children begging in the streets. Jewish reformers and *maskilim* pondered the image problem this created and how the situation could be alleviated. Reformers responded by reincarnating traditional institutions as a network of autonomous, supposedly modernized orphanages in the late nineteenth century, often with the aid of Western Jewish organizations such as Ica or the Hilfsverein.[9] By the time displacement and the war's violence further marginalized Eastern European Jews, the issue of orphans had long been on the agenda of the Jewish community.

Whether to cooperate with mainstream humanitarians or take an exclusively Jewish approach to childcare was not only about organizational alliances and posturing. When it came to children, the ARA, the ARC, and the Friends were focused on food, other basic necessities, and general European stability. To Jews, however, Jewish lives, and the Jewish future, were directly at stake, and urgently so. War orphans were a Jewish problem, just as refugees and typhus had become a Jewish problem for Jews to face on their own. A feeding program was helpful, but it could not address that so many Jewish children had nowhere to live, no Jewish community to raise them, and no country desiring their citizenship or planning for their future. Hungry children and war orphans had overlapping but different needs. To reconcile the mainstream humanitarian approach to children and specific Jewish needs, the JDC eventually developed a broad-based childcare program, which deliberately muddled the distinction between orphans and "typical" Jewish children, disguising orphans much as it sought to have adult refugees pass as settled local Jews. How this program evolved is detailed shortly; like with refugees and health, the path was not straight or predetermined. The idea was to pull war orphans, who today would be termed unaccompanied refugee children, into the orbit of local and international humanitarian general childcare services as seamlessly as possible to prevent further stigmatization and exclusion.

Because of Jewish international humanitarianism, child relief never morphed into a policy of child removal, as happened to other minority communities after the war. Armenian and Russian refugee children were most at risk of child removal by humanitarian organizations because they did not have the protective apparatus of a state.[10] Jewish organizations, especially the JDC, stepped in almost like a state, primarily for Russian Jewish child refugees. Even when a Jewish adoption crossed international borders, it remained solidly within the Jewish fold with the goal of international family reunion.

Children or Orphans?

The JDC began to assist Jewish children in Europe as part of the ARA's extensive child feeding operations in 1919. The main focus of the ARA was on feeding children and providing them with other necessities, like basic medical care and clothing – all things the JDC knew Jews desperately needed, in the same places the ARA was headed, namely, Poland.[11] Like with general emergency relief in Poland, the JDC worked in tandem with the ARA's child feeding operation. And so, for a time, the JDC bundled its relief for children into emergency relief. The organization created by the ARA in cooperation with a semi-governmental Polish organization, the Central Committee of Help to Children (CKPD), which became the Polish-American Children's Relief Committee (PAKPD) in 1920, worked closely with Boris Bogen, sharing automobiles and supplies.[12] The JDC and the ARA both channeled the proclivity for rationalization into the management of a vast logistics operation to provide food and clothing to East Europeans.[13]

Herbert Hoover promoted this extensive support to children in Europe as a way to keep Americans safe: saving children now would provide a morally and physically strong basis for the future of European civilization with "the American flag implanted in the hearts of these fifteen million children."[14] Conveniently, it would also limit American involvement in Europe without losing US standing as a humanitarian leader. JDC-supported child welfare institutions purchased food from the

PAKPD to benefit from the subsidies. As the ARA pulled out of Poland, it continued its child feeding operations in 1920, and the JDC continued to take part. Maurice Pate, director of the child program for the ARA Mission in Poland and future first director of UNICEF, had a good relationship with Bogen. For the JDC, this feeding was just the beginning of its child-centered operations. The JDC never saw feeding programs as a long-term solution for Jewish children, but as a way to provide relief to Jews as well as to cooperate with the ARA. But as the ARA's presence became mainly that of the European Children's Fund, an ARA offshoot that extended its stay in Poland, the JDC dallied on organizing its own child relief. It advertised only in the Jewish press, not wanting to undermine its work with the ARA. Because of the ARA's intense focus on childcare and the JDC's need to maintain a good relationship with the ARA, the JDC felt bound to stick to the ARA program instead of duplicating such efforts with an initiative of its own.[15]

Soon after Bogen arrived in Poland, the JDC formed a Standing Committee on Jewish War Orphans in New York to weigh the issue in a "broad and statesman-like manner." First, the JDC had to get a handle on the number of destitute children and orphans, having only some sense that orphans made up about 10 percent of the total Jewish population in Palestine.[16] The JDC began to work on the question of orphans in Palestine and Romania in 1919, leaving childcare work elsewhere in Europe to its collaborative efforts with the ARA.[17] The JDC's desire to come up with a rational, unified plan and to work on the best of terms with the ARA hampered its ability to reach Jewish orphans who were not touched by the ARA, such as in the former Ottoman Empire. It was becoming clear that mainstream humanitarianism's target of "children" was not entirely compatible with Jewish anxieties about "war orphans." The JDC would try to bridge them.

The JDC's decision in 1920 was to provide allowances on a per capita basis for children who were not taken care of. Orphans would thus have money to cover their care and presumably experience life much as regular children. The JDC's experiences feeding children in Poland, plus independent orphan-care work in Palestine, pushed it to create a department that, overseeing both, viewed children's needs as multidimensional. As European Director of Child Care, Simon Peiser was in charge of the whole issue starting in January 1920.[18] Peiser, a Reform rabbi who developed expertise in child welfare while serving as the superintendent of the Jewish Orphan Home of Cleveland, went to Eastern Europe for the JDC as part of the Overseas Unit for Poland.[19] In the summer of 1920, JDC New York grappled with the orphan and childcare question, contemplating various plans, paying for orphans, and creating a childcare bureau to deal with all matters related to children.[20]

As the JDC bided its time with the ARA's child feeding program and considered the child problem comprehensively,[21] other Jewish organizations grew impatient, and stepped in to fill the perceived void in philanthropy. Independently of the JDC, efforts were made to collect funds on behalf of various childcare agencies. Agudas Yisroel, the political organization of religious Jews, wrote from their Netherlands branch that caring for orphans was the "utmost holiest duty."[22] A visit to New York by two Jewish welfare leaders from Ukraine to appeal on behalf of Jewish orphans in their homeland in early 1920 provoked a flurry of activity when the JDC failed to respond immediately.[23]

The first impulse of most Jewish organizations, especially Jewish immigrant groups in the West, was to solve the problem by helping children immigrate. One example was People's Relief, which acted on its own rather than as a constituent part of the JDC. People's Relief set up a special committee on Ukrainian orphans and gathered funds. It wrote to the State Department with a detailed plan to request the admission of orphans in the summer of 1920, assuring the government that People's Relief would ensure adoption.[24] The Canadian government agreed to admit 200 orphans on humanitarian grounds with the Jewish War Orphans Committee of Canada, which inspired other Jewish organizations around the world to seek similar immigration exemptions. Hias also made plans for children to reunite with American relatives as part of its first commission to Europe.[25]

Like in other situations, the JDC repressed appeals to American Jews coming directly from Polish Jewish child welfare organizations seeking to circumvent the JDC. It actively silenced or tried to absorb other American Jewish activities as well.[26] All these non-JDC, orphan-related activities created additional urgency for the JDC on the subject of Jewish war orphans. It sought to maintain its relief monopoly and did not view immigration as a solution.[27] There was a limit, then, to how far the JDC could move toward mainstream collaboration before its constituency decided it was not fulfilling its Jewish mandate. When it came to children, however, the JDC was simultaneously under pressure to cooperate exclusively with the ARA. The JDC thus chose to coordinate with the Jewish War Orphans Committee of Canada, supporting its initiative to bring children from Ukraine to Canada.[28] Bogen recommended that the JDC do as much for other organizations planning what he called "the wholesale exportation of orphans from Poland," including cooperating with Werelief. Bogen argued that the neglect of children by the JDC would be unpardonable.[29] Through the assistance of Anita

Müller-Cohen of Vienna, a prominent social worker dedicated to child welfare and a Zionist activist, Werelief hoped to place orphans in Jewish communities around the world, including sending 100 to Buenos Aires for adoption.[30] In the spring of 1921, in the southeastern part of Poland that was formerly Ukraine, a number of Jewish delegations not affiliated with the JDC simply showed up to take children with them, including representatives from South Africa, Palestine, and from Werelief.[31]

It did not help that the JDC lacked women within its ranks. Even more than with medical care, women were deeply involved in childcare in the Jewish philanthropic world. Maternalist discourse and Progressive-era reforms of the settlement house, which middle-class American Jews were engaged in, put them at the center of mothering the future Jewish people.[32] Unlike with medical care, there was no layer of male medical doctors with which women leaders had to contend. For example, Hadassah women began preparing for child welfare work immediately after the war. Child welfare expert Alice Seligsberg had warned during the war that American Jews would have to think about war orphans in Europe and Palestine, and had by 1917 already laid out a broad, statesman-like plan of the kind the JDC was trying to generate in 1920. Seligsberg prophesied a "world-wide Jewish organization administering the work of reconstruction and relief; one portfolio in its cabinet ... will be given to a secretary of child-welfare."[33] Soon after the war, Jewish women sought inclusion, reminding the JDC of the experience of women welfare workers.[34] Once the JDC finally organized its own child relief, it sought out women's help, recruiting from Hadassah and reaching out to women's organizations to ask for their financial support, including Hadassah and the Council of Jewish Women (NCJW), whose local chapters began collecting money.[35] Special women's fundraising campaigns had proven the potential for success.[36] Although the JDC New York Committee on Jewish War Orphans began with only one woman on it – Harriet Lowenstein – others joined following the committee's outreach efforts.[37]

Because war orphans sparked separate campaigns undertaken by American Jewish organizations, it seemed as if the issue might end up fracturing into separate initiatives. The American Jewish Relief Committee even appointed representatives of an adoption committee along the lines of the Central Relief and People's Relief orphan adoption committees.[38] Responding to this pressure, and the ARA's impending withdrawal from Poland, the Joint launched its childcare bureau focusing mainly on orphans in autumn 1920, which evolved into a comprehensive childcare program.[39]

Attempting to wrest Jewish children and war orphans from fragmented feeding and overseas adoptions initiatives, the JDC brought on board celebrity cantor Josef Rosenblatt to support the cause. Rosenblatt sang

Figure 5.1 Sheet music cover of "Shomer Israel" by Cantor Josef
Rosenblatt, a new setting of weekday liturgy composed in 1921. In the
art nouveau aesthetic of E. M. Lilienthal and fusing Judeo-Christian
tropes, it demonstrates the sacredness of Jewish children via a circle of
ragged orphans facing an ark with a mother and children, rather than a
Torah, inside of it. Listen to Rosenblatt's recording at rsa.fau.edu/
album/36760.

benefit concerts for Jewish relief around the United States and dedicated a song to the cause of the war orphans with the Hebrew liturgy, "Oh Guardian of Israel, save the remnants of Israel."[40] But who was the guardian of Jews in this turbulent time? If the Guardian of Israel could not intervene from on high to help the child "remnants," the answer could only be American Jews.

Adoptions and "Adoptions"

Besides the idea of supporting children in their "native environment" with general relief dollars, the JDC and other Jewish organizations pondered bringing orphan children to the West for adoption. Despite the clamor of other organizations to adopt children into Jewish communities far from Eastern Europe, the JDC remained skeptical as it reflected on past experience. After the Kishinev pogroms a decade and a half earlier – a small tragedy compared to the Great War – enough American Jewish interest was aroused that efforts began to adopt orphaned children. Fifty Jewish children from Kishinev, then part of the Russian Empire, were adopted in America. Boris Bogen himself adopted seven child victims, and James Becker remarked that only Bogen's adopted children were happy among the fifty. The JDC did not have enough social workers for mass international adoption to be in the best interests of children, aside from the legal and political difficulties this presented. Yet, American Jewish interest was such that in late 1919, the JDC asked the State Department whether it was feasible. The JDC outlined a plan to gather statistics on how many children could be cared for in America, establish a receiving station in New York, and investigate how many children in Europe and Palestine could be sent across the Atlantic.[41]

Jewish organizations considered international adoption while other American groups also clamored for war orphan adoption. Although rare in practice, American adoptions of Eastern European children after the war sought to remove children from their national and familial contexts supposedly to provide a more peaceful, non-Bolshevik, American future while preserving a modicum of European difference.[42] American Jews joined the American clamor for international adoptees, but family reunion and the Jewish collectivity were at the heart of all Jewish adoption plans. Many Jewish immigrants believed that Jewish orphans would be better off outside Eastern Europe. All of these Jewish organizations tended to think in terms of family and Jewish futures, even as they differed in how important they deemed geographical origin versus Western safety. Unlike its peer humanitarian organizations, the JDC was the most cautious and the most committed to preventing international adoption.

JDC helped bring some children to the United States by supporting family reunions and cooperating with Hias and the NCJW. Family reunions reflected a judicious approach, somewhere in between a full-scale communal adoption program and ignoring ceaseless calls for international adoption, which would have only strengthened competing Jewish organizations. At first, reunions were undertaken in an ad hoc manner, with the New York office occasionally calling on JDC representatives in Poland to track down children whose parents or relatives could support their passage to America.[43] Peiser looked for ways to connect children to their overseas relatives.[44] By early 1921, Hias teamed up with the JDC since it was, after all, a matter of immigration assistance.[45] The NCJW sent a representative, Dr. Margaret C. Paukner, to the JDC in Poland just to assist orphans who were preparing to travel to America.[46] Paukner oversaw the JDC Child Care Department in Warsaw's procedures to reunite orphan children, which involved locating a given child through a district office; examining the child; obtaining the necessary documents from Poland and the United States; providing the child with a place to stay and transportation in Warsaw; reserving a ticket on a steamer; escorting the child to Danzig; and then allowing Hias to oversee the rest of the child's journey.[47] In the summer of 1921, she personally accompanied the first transport of these children, fifteen of them, on a ship to America.[48] This was the first of several such transports, which were usually accompanied by a young female escort.[49] In 1922, the JDC facilitated about 500 such reunions. Hias and the NCJW were essential at the receiving end, too, since they had already established special privileges at Ellis Island. NCJW representatives also had the task of following up with these families and reporting on the children to JDC.[50]

When it came to legal adoptions by nonrelatives in America, the JDC sent and received applications in the United States, and JDC workers in Poland tried to organize a list of adoptable children from local communities. But these adoptions were mired in legal problems.[51] The JDC never invested in this effort, not wanting to get involved in immigration matters and recognizing the difficulty of finding homes for foreign Jewish children brought to the United States.[52] The mere prospect of finding homes for Jewish orphans in the United States, however, pushed the JDC to develop a childcare department that was not unidirectional, with Americans simply funding projects abroad. It briefly presented the very real possibility of relief work reaching American shores and Jewish communities across the United States, and the JDC outlined its plans accordingly, with a childcare program destined to operate at home and abroad.[53]

Yet, ever-increasing restrictions on immigration ensured that the JDC's childcare work remained remote. People's Relief urged the Secretary of State to consider the issue from a "humanitarian standpoint," and to follow the precedent of US exemptions for Belgian, French, and Serbian orphans.[54] But US immigration laws only became more closed to humanitarian and refugee considerations with the passage of time, and Jewish orphans were hardly as desirable as Belgian children. Undersecretary of State Norman H. Davis replied unsympathetically: "The humanitarian project you have in mind is not one concerning which the Department can express an opinion."[55] By 1921, instead of working with Hias to bring transports of children to the United States, Jessie Bogen was responding to inquiries regarding adoption: "the Joint Distribution Committee is in no position to offer financial assistance for the transportation of anyone to America as this would be a violation to the Immigration Laws. None of the funds of the Joint Distribution Committee can be used for immigration purposes."[56] The JDC decided to focus on Jewish orphans and children as targets for relief and constructive work, but not to bring them to the United States.

Given the circumstances, the JDC began to encourage "financial adoption," or child sponsorship schemes in which American Jews chose individual children abroad to support with direct financial subsidies. From the beginning, the JDC knew that the bulk of its work on behalf of children would have to take place within the borders of European countries and Palestine. In 1920, the Bogens fleshed out a plan that would allow children to remain where they lived, supported by American Jewish donors.[57] Earlier, other child welfare organizations introduced child sponsorship, notably the ARC and Save the Children Fund, in an effort to redirect popular demand for adoptions they could not facilitate.[58] Even the ARA adopted this strategy in December 1920, extolling President Wilson's commitment to "adopt" twenty children with $200, and exhorting Americans to invite "invisible child guests" into the "circles around their Christmas trees."[59] In early 1919, Albert Lucas suggested adapting this scheme for French and Belgian war orphans to the JDC.[60] Unlike other humanitarian organizations that pursued a variety of causes through sponsorship, the JDC sought to centralize, rationalize, and maximize Jewish orphan welfare, by using inherent diaspora linkages, as it had done in other situations.

Financial adoption involved the immense bureaucratic challenge of keeping track of children and their sponsors. It would also require good salespeople – Boris Bogen joked at the Vienna Conference that he was "sorry that Mrs. Troper is here; she ought to be in the United States selling babies." Boris Bogen instructed a JDC worker in Warsaw to begin collecting not just numbers but also names, other data, and a photo. Jessie Bogen returned to New York from her task of preparing JDC publicity in Poland to run the financial adoption program, starting in the fall of 1920 with the launch of the Childcare Department. The JDC hoped that some of the relationships that developed between children and their sponsors would result in legal adoption.[61]

Financial adoption was largely a fundraising maneuver. Children made for good fundraising. As we have seen, adults cared about children and could project meaning onto them. As Becker pointed out, "The appeal of the children is naturally stronger than that of any other group."[62] Moving to financial adoption would allow the JDC to capitalize on the fundraising potential. A major point was not simply to replace funding for children with new, direct, and inspired donors but also to expand the number of children the JDC could reach. Financial adoption funds were separated from general JDC accounts, intended to directly finance and expand the per capita subsidy scheme developed in 1920 to support needy children living in private homes.[63] While JDC subsidies to orphanages might suffice in Poland, the financial adoption plan was targeted to Jewish orphans in what the JDC continued to think of as Ukraine, although it was now part of Poland, where capacity to help orphans had to grow without increasing the institutional burden on surviving adults. Peiser agonized that the JDC could not cover all the children in need, despite the immense efforts toward financial sponsorship.[64] Now under Soviet control, Ukraine was out of the question for financial adoption programs, since the Soviets would never accede to what was required institutionally.

At least American Jews, by now accustomed to sending remittances and food packages to relatives and friends or hometowns in the old country, seemed primed to enthusiastically take part in such a plan. Like with remittances, the JDC would have to trace links between individuals on different continents.[65] Additionally, the plan would keep existing immigrants and landsmanshaftn invested in the JDC's work. By late 1920, JDC workers in Poland complained of the naivete and inexperience of various landsmanshaft "delegates" streaming to East Central Europe to help their hometowns, and asked the JDC for help on the ground. Jessie Bogen argued that the JDC should make use of "this element of sentiment and local ties" and direct it toward sending remittances and food to localities, encouraging relief campaigns within local East European Jewish communities, and providing for specific children, "rather than to await its birth with apprehension and to attempt to control it, once it has expressed itself in the establishment of separation [sic] organization, the launching of separate plans and, it must be

admitted, the centralizing of authority in separate hands."[66] Jewish financial adoption relied on Jewish diaspora networks, the resources and
networks of the state, and other American private organizations.

Jessie Bogen saw financial adoption as a way for the JDC to organize
"Jewish child-care in Europe through American Jewish women." Even in
choosing Bogen to run the program, Warburg, at least, felt that if the
JDC were to reach out to Jewish Americans to ask them to adopt
children, it ought to have women leading the campaign, since women
were the potential adopters.[67] Following the French–Belgian adoption
scheme, Bogen suggested it involved "the payment by American
women and women's organizations, of a given sum of money for a child
cared for in a private home or institution in Poland."[68] Despite complicated logistics and the necessary mastery of finance, financial adoption
was seen as women's work. Women and women's organizations had,
after all, proved quite effective in fundraising on behalf of war relief
efforts across the United States. By including two disenfranchised
populations within American Jewish politics – women and immigrants –
financial adoption bolstered the JDC. In the field, too, women were
routinely expected by the JDC to assume the burden of childcare and
financial adoption at the local level, sharing the reconstruction of Jewish
life and welfare work with Jewish men who were focused on issues
besides children.[69]

Modeling Child Welfare in Palestine

Like with healthcare, the JDC's first experiment in childcare abroad was
really its orphan work in Palestine, where it bundled its child relief into
the activities of the Zionist Commission rather than the ARA. The JDC
counted about 3,000 war orphans in Palestine.[70] Later, it was estimated
that war orphans constituted about 7.5 percent of Palestine's surviving
Jewish population. The JDC's orphan programs began under the prescient Alice Seligsberg, who traveled for Hadassah to Palestine and Egypt
near the end of the war, in charge of the AZMU's personnel and the
execution of its venture. As a graduate-educated child welfare worker
who founded and ran a social center for orphans in New York called
Fellowship House from 1913 to 1918, Seligsberg prepared during the
war for the large number of orphans that would inevitably result from it.
She called on American Jews to establish a Fund for the Children of our
People, for an international commission to collect data on the situation,
and to work on the legal questions involved in adopting children into the
United States. "The solution of the problem will depend mainly on
money and on social vision" in the West, she stated.[71]

When Seligsberg arrived in Palestine, she noticed that the Zionist Commission was unable to provide for Jewish orphans, and that the entire child population was languishing in poor conditions. Hadassah and the Zionist Commission set about clothing children and counting orphans, who seemed to Seligsberg nearly indistinguishable from children with parents.[72] Seligsberg became the director of the Orphan Bureau of the Zionist Commission in May 1919, supervising all Jewish orphans in Palestine. The JDC War Orphans Committee soon informed her that more funding would arrive, and that it wished that she remain in charge of orphan work for a committee responsible to the JDC.[73] Although the JDC was reluctant to take on much work in Palestine since it felt that various Zionist bodies worked adequately, Cyrus Adler wrote from Paris to encourage the JDC to take care of these orphans, because "it would be a danger and a scandal to Judaism if this were not done."[74]

So with the Zionist Commission, the JDC set up a joint orphans committee: the Palestine Orphan Committee (POC) codirected by Seligsberg and Col. Norman Bentwich.[75] The POC made a concerted effort at the beginning to look after children in private homes, "placing out" orphans to private homes when possible while providing subsidies, home visits, and a system for supervision and control, and to use institutions only for "full orphans" (who had no surviving parents).[76] Seligsberg set about creating a network of orphan relief committees, connecting them to the Zionist Commission's relief organization, standardizing orphan care, and establishing the POC's semi-autonomy.[77]

When Sophia Berger Mohl took over the POC after Seligsberg left Palestine, she asked the JDC to continue and even expand its contributions for orphans.[78] Berger was a Hadassah leader and social worker who was the superintendent of the Young Women's Hebrew Association in New York. During the war, she organized ARC canteens for soldiers in France. The ARC also brought her to Palestine to run an ARC workroom in Jerusalem.[79] Seligsberg, in the meantime, began to serve on the JDC's Palestine and orphan committees at its headquarters in New York, reading every relevant document and pushing the JDC to keep child welfare going. She acted as an intermediary between New York's formal committees and her former colleagues in childcare in Palestine.[80]

While the goals of the JDC, the Zionist Commission, and Hadassah were broadly shared when it came to children, there were differences in long-term visions. The JDC sought to pull support from Palestine as soon as possible, whereas the Zionist organizations would expand social services to build an infrastructure approaching that of a social welfare state to prepare for more immigrants. As part of that quest, one of Berger's first initiatives was to press Sir Herbert Samuel, the first

British High Commissioner of Palestine, to draft legislation to protect women and children. She recommended that the POC assume legal guardianship over orphans and a compulsory school law.[81] The JDC continued with its planned cuts despite pleas to the contrary, setting the POC searching for ways to trim its budget. In the meantime, Hadassah organized its own financial adoption scheme, creating Junior Hadassah branches for young American Jewish women to "adopt" orphans in Palestine.[82] Established in 1920, Junior Hadassah contributed over $13,000 by the end of 1923.[83] In its expectations that America's youth would develop a sense of obligation and fund faraway youth welfare projects, this program was likely established on the precedent of the ARC's Junior Red Cross, which was just three years old.[84] Alongside public health initiatives by Hadassah women who had the support of the JDC, the financial adoption program centered on women and children.

JDC work in Palestine was thus Jewish and child-centered from the start. Though not all American Jews shared the goal of Zionist state-building, undertaking child welfare in a Progressive manner appealed to the JDC and Western-led Zionist social programs in Mandate Palestine. Zionists and Jewish political and philanthropic institutions shared an interest in social policy, despite a celebrated history of conflict between them.[85] A broad liberal reorientation and expansion of Zionism in America during and after the war under Brandeis' leadership made room for pragmatic cooperation for the purposes of relief. Hadassah women, Seligsberg in particular, exported their child-centric views from the American Progressive settlement house to Jerusalem, and all the Joint had to do was provide dollars.[86]

Systematizing Child Welfare

The possibility that the JDC might undertake adoption work begun by other Jewish organizations was discarded in light of the rising nativist climate in the United States that resulted in the 1921 Quota Act.[87] By 1923, the JDC resolved that orphan transports of any kind were not good for the transported children, that these children were not fit for the journey, and that local Jews actually wanted children to remain in place.[88] The JDC planned to continue exporting American Progressive attitudes to Poland, emphasizing the need for expert planning, modern hygiene, secular education, family life, putting the child's perceived interests over parental or community interests, and the rational distribution of funding. And because it was ultimately the JDC that ended up running the child welfare program, and not Hias, the NCJW, or Werelief, there was a determined effort to support these orphans and other children where they already lived, in the most innovative, rational way possible.

Although the JDC led the way, women played significant roles in all childcare activities. Ideas about how to promote child welfare were centered around health, but many of these activities, squarely in the niche of social medicine, were open to women's leadership. Local women led child welfare and pedagogy in many places: Anita Müller-Cohen in Vienna; Stefania Wilczyńska with Korczak in Warsaw; Anna Braude Heller also in Warsaw; Zofia Syrkin in West Galicia; Mrs. Abramowicz in Polish Galicia; Cecylja Klaftenowa in Lemberg; and Mrs. Saslavskaya in Ukraine.[89] American Jewish nurses brought their expertise to bear, training a generation of Jewish nurses in child welfare and public health and, in Palestine, practicing as nurses. In these positions helping women and children, American and local Jewish women enjoyed autonomy.

If the JDC's original comprehensive plan was to pay out subsidies on a per capita basis to needy Jewish children in Poland,[90] the work of the JDC and other American Jewish organizations on behalf of children turned out to be far less systematic, child-centric, and individualized. Since Poland was no longer in a state of emergency by the time JDC launched its full childcare program, locals were in a position to push back. American Progressives met resentment in Poland, just as Jewish immigrants in New York had resisted settlement houses and visiting nurses.[91] In Vilna, for example, the local EKOPO branch announced that the JDC would have to cooperate on its terms to conduct child relief, which would require the JDC to organize a network of institutions for a designated number of years.[92] Besides the funding it infused into existing childcare programs, the JDC mainly succeeded in getting local Jewish child activists to coordinate their work and in obliging aid recipients to adopt the principle of cooperation and non-duplication of relief.[93] Poland functioned as the focal point of the JDC's childcare efforts, but the JDC also worked on similar projects in Austria, Czecho-Slovakia, Latvia, Lithuania, Romania, and Turkey.[94] Within Poland, Bogen and Peiser agreed that the starting point for childcare should be Polish Galicia, where "former Austrian training" meant that Jews were better organized. When forced to choose, the JDC often preferred to support currently needy, yet formerly modernized or comfortable Jews because it felt that this would increase the chances it would see a return on its philanthropic investment.[95]

Homing or Institutionalizing Children?

For several reasons, the JDC's programs for children were closely tied to its efforts to figure out a plan for orphans. First, the JDC needed a plan that would at least be as suitable as those of its many competitors. Second, it was difficult to define an orphan given that many children had some kind of living relatives, had become separated from parents whose whereabouts were unknown, or had close family members who were incapable of fully supporting them. Given the confusion, it made sense to intermingle programs for all children, including orphans, like the JDC's original per capita subsidy idea. Third, the JDC thought that shifting responsibility for war orphans to the communities in which they arrived, as they did for adult refugees, was best accomplished as part of a broader child welfare program. JDC leaders assumed that if they stopped distinguishing war orphans from regular children or orphans, locals would as well.[96] Fourth, the JDC followed precedents set by the ARA and the ARC, which also found it difficult to estimate and categorize numbers of children in need. They were feeding over a million children by 1920, and recognized that there were still more children, perhaps another million, going hungry.[97] In general, the international, Western discourse on child welfare changed after the war from a typology of "abnormal children," such as orphans or refugees, to a broader one in which even the "normal child," in a stable, middle-class family, also needed specialized initiatives to live a sheltered, whole life.[98] The ARC, in particular, invested in comprehensive child welfare and social medicine focused on children.[99]

In Poland, the JDC was supporting nearly 5,000 orphans by mid-1921, at a cost of about $20,000 per month in direct subsidies.[100] Yet the shift to supporting orphans on a per capita basis via financial adoption meant that although the JDC continued its support of these individual children long term, it pulled away support for local institutions that took care of children. The JDC claimed, after its 1920 Vienna Conference, that it was trying to turn institutions back over to community control and local fundraising.[101] This JDC aversion to a long-term commitment in Europe, coupled with the knowledge that financial adoption was by definition a long-term arrangement, made the JDC even more determined to stop supporting childcare institutions well into the 1920s. The JDC's hope was that local communities would take responsibility for institutions, and eventually for individual war orphans, even though local Jews continued to resist the notion that child refugees were their long-term responsibility.[102] Meanwhile, such difficult work in Eastern Europe made Peiser so ill that he had to step down as director of the Child Care Department after a year and a half on the job. He was replaced by Morris Waldman in the fall of 1922 and joined by Abraham Shohan, a seasoned relief worker from the first overseas mission to Poland, and newly married to Jessie Bogen, who accompanied him to Vienna.[103]

Table 5.1 *The JDC's estimated number of war orphans, April 1921*[104]

Congress Poland	15,000
Galicia	20,000
White Russia	20,000
Polish Ukraine	30,000
Romania	8,000
Palestine	4,000
Lithuania	4,000
Soviet Ukraine	80,000

One of the JDC's main contributions to child welfare, once it finally began, was to push already existing child welfare organizations to unite their activities.[105] They came together under the Federation of Orphan Welfare Organizations in Poland (CENTOS), an umbrella organization of child welfare organizations in Poland that coordinated local programs. In 1921, the JDC established a childcare bureau in Warsaw, dividing the administrative responsibilities for childcare, much like its regular relief, among its main office, district offices, provincial offices, and sometimes small-town offices. Simultaneously, the JDC worked toward the establishment of local children's committees that would interface between branch office JDC workers and children. The idea was that every local general relief committee would have a subsidiary branch – a local children's committee – that registered all orphans requiring care, found out who had relatives in America, and placed orphans in private homes if funding could be secured through financial adoption. In addition, these committees were to develop what the JDC now called "personal service," which was dedicated to connecting relatives and providing assistance with paperwork so that orphans might be adopted by American relatives.[106] This was part of a continuing effort at family reunification undertaken with Hias, despite stricter immigration requirements. CENTOS grew to have 349 committees operating in 335 towns by 1926, though it continued to require the JDC's support.[107]

Shohan considered the JDC's main contributions to include raising awareness of the issue, confronting local Jews with this responsibility, setting minimum standards of childcare, and preventing local factionalization from impeding welfare work. In the Bialystock district, Shohan presided over a conference on childcare that passed a resolution that served as a guide, reflecting Progressive ideas on a child's best interest that were imported by the JDC, but tempered by the reality of the situation. As much as possible, orphans near Bialystock were to live in private homes, attend school with other children, learn a trade if older than fourteen years, maintain legal status and property rights, and receive care from trained personnel at institutions where minimum sanitary, cultural, and pedagogic standards were to be met.[108] Despite efforts to include all factions on the Bialystock childcare committee, workmen boycotted it, which was typical, according to Shohan.[109] The JDC encountered difficulties that varied from place to place, usually having to do with partisan bickering and lack of funds. CENTOS and its committees actively promoted child welfare and provided opportunities for Jewish child welfare leaders to discuss their views.[110]

Although the prescriptions suggested that children should be placed in homes rather than new orphanages built for them, the orphanages mostly won out. It was the preference of the community and, besides, the war's destruction had turned home placements into an impossible standard.[111] Locals in charge of childcare usually ended up raising Jewish children collectively and to some extent, continuing familiar prewar traditions of charity. The general Jewish public wanted to see their funds at work and to retain control over the Jewish national future. For educated Jewish welfare workers in Poland, this question was a matter of continuous negotiation, but the extreme disruption of family life and community preference made it difficult to launch new, idealistic programs for foster care, despite the theoretical financial savings on overhead costs.[112] In America, programs to remove children from oppressive institutions into family homes also had not worked; even there, Progressive ideals consistently outpaced resources.[113] Jewish social workers in the Untied States had already had this debate with inconclusive results.

Financial adoption by Americans to provide per capita subsidies to individual children living in family homes was designed by the JDC to support home life over institutional life.[114] In a 1921 JDC report from Volhynia, which the JDC called Ukraine but was legally Poland, a JDC representative wrote that he was trying to secure the "actual or financial adoption" of children there to "bring up the children in a family atmosphere." There were complications: "In spite of the fact that the costs of maintaining the children were being refunded to the families, the public were reluctant to fully act as guardians for the children, as they were unable and unwilling fully to realize the importance of such action."[115]

Financial adoption did see some success in Europe; 800 children living with family members received support in 1924. The previous year, child orphans in Palestine received financial sponsorship through the fundraising efforts of Junior Hadassah under Seligsberg's guidance.[116] Kahn claimed that 80 percent of the orphans cared for by the JDC were, in fact, in private homes.[117] Yet subsidies intended for individuals to care for orphans could go awry. Because only poor families needed these subsidies, the care of poor children was simply outsourced to families who desperately needed the extra income.[118]

The goal of the JDC, however, was to provide any home, institutional or private, and to remove children from the streets one by one.[119] Though it failed to place all orphans in family homes, the JDC steadfastly refused to fund the creation of new orphanages, recoiling, for example, when Margaret Paukner, the NCJW's delegate, suggested opening an institution in Lublin.[120] Yet even in orphanages, the JDC conceded (and bragged), children who were financially adopted through the JDC indirectly raised the living conditions of the entire place. Furthermore, institutions did have the benefit of leaders, usually women whom the JDC could train and expect to popularize "modern methods of childcare" taught by "specialists in education and in child diseases."[121] Seligsberg wrote that while private home placement was best, the question of what kind of child was under consideration and the available money also had to be considered.[122]

By 1923, the JDC had firm policies in place not to create new institutions, nor to allow the "transfer of children from one community to another community, thus creating a direct obligation on the part of the JDC." The purpose of the latter was to help local communities solve a problem the JDC saw as belonging to the local community, even as it expressed its own moral obligation to sustain children until they became self-supporting.[123] By then, Bernard Kahn, as the director of the JDC European Executive Committee, was playing an active role in childcare alongside Abraham Shohan. He insisted, characteristically, despite Shohan's plea to stick to the moral obligation of long-term child support, that the JDC turn over childcare to local committees and announce that it would liquidate the program at the start of 1926.[124] Yet, it was starting to dawn on the JDC that these unaccompanied children were indeed refugees whose ongoing dependence on philanthropy could not be denied in the same way it might be for adults. Shohan had directed refugee relief in Poland before moving to childcare. He noticed how refugee and childcare programs began to conflict with each other on the ground.[125]

Child Health from Poland to Palestine

Since the JDC and Hadassah wanted to do more than simply find homes for orphans, they introduced various programs to promote child health and welfare. The JDC European Executive Council pointed out in February 1921: "All American organizations in Poland are now concentrating on a medical Child Care and Child Welfare program." Unlike its peer humanitarian organizations, the JDC saw no need to restrict its activities to children. It continued to seek cooperation opportunities with American organizations where possible, the ARA and the ARC, which meant taking a health-centered approach to general child welfare. The JDC looked favorably upon the ARA and the ARC's programs for nurseries; infant feeding; clinics for children; sanitation, feeding, and medical examinations in schools, orphanages, clinics, and homes; visiting nurses; and introducing hygienic measures.[126] Emulating that approach, the JDC ran feeding programs in East Central Europe, milk

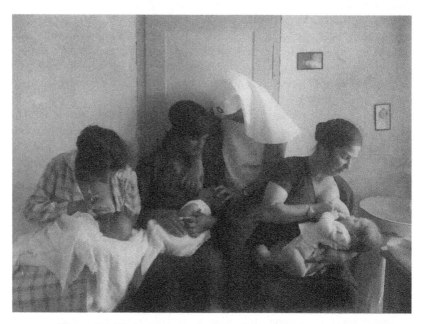

Figure 5.2 Hadassah breastfeeding clinic. A Hadassah nurse wearing her Star of David cap instructs breastfeeding babies and mothers at an infant welfare center in Palestine. In the photo album presented to Edmond de Rothschild by the Hadassah Medical Organization c. 1925. (Waddesdon, The Rothschild Collection (The National Trust), PIC20/45 Yad Hanadiv)

stations in Poland and Europe, summer colonies, and year-round colonies for orphans in Palestine. These projects further blurred the lines between regular children and orphans. The ARC's, ARA's, and JDC's programs all conveyed the purported superiority of American childcare practices and the need to spread these practices by transforming European methods.[127] And like social medicine and child welfare in the West, these programs deepened the distinction between children and adults, seeking to transform and uplift an entire society through raising children freed from the yolk of family and tradition.

As we have seen, child feeding was the JDC's first child-specific activity and the primary focus of mainstream humanitarian organizations. The ARA set up a network of milk stations and kitchens for children across Poland, some of which the JDC operated. Milk stations ran according to the model established by American settlement houses with generous funding by Nathan Straus. Yet these were not entirely foreign to Poland; westward-looking doctors and hygienists had built some milk stations in Galicia and Russian Poland before the war, which were popular among Jews.[128] Intended to reduce infant mortality, milk stations provided clean, subsidized milk for infants and small children who did not have enough breast milk. This was a defining feature of activity for Hadassah in Palestine, as well, where Tipat Halav (Drop of Milk) stations served poor families.[129]

The ARA required that food be distributed to children regardless of their identity, forming a network of local Polish committees of the CKPD/PAKPD to carry out distribution, each filled out with representatives of all local nationalities, religions, and classes. This pluralist idea was not easily accepted by Eastern Europeans, but the ARA made food conditional on cooperation, a powerful incentive. The JDC relied on the ARA for this feeding program, and was not eager to replace it with an independent initiative once the ARA began to pull out of Poland in 1920. Jessie Bogen worried that "the cutting down of the rations by the A.R.A. spells a catastrophe far-reaching in its effects." Although the ARA gradually transferred power to the Polish side of the PAKPD, it did not fully withdraw from Poland until spring 1922.[130]

Despite ARA policy, local PAKPD distribution committees sometimes lacked Jewish representatives, which worried the JDC because it meant that small Jewish communities might not receive attention. The JDC was thus invested in making sure ARA, ARC, and PAKPD activities served Jews, or it helped assemble separate institutions in places where it knew Jews would otherwise not be assisted. In the town of Piotrkow, where a third of the population was Jewish, it came to the JDC inspector's attention that the PAKPD committee there had set up a milk station for Catholics. Debate within the JDC and with the ARC followed as to whether the ARC should insist on integrating the milk station or allow the creation of a separate Jewish milk station. In the end, the JDC arranged with the ARC to provide equipment for a milk station run by the Piotrkow Jewish community. In this way, some ARA/PAKPD kitchens in Poland became Jewish, and the JDC also made sure that Jews who lived in smaller towns organized kitchens so that their children could receive ARA foodstuffs. As usual, the JDC made heavy contributions to the ARA alongside the American and Polish governments for child relief to negotiate such favorable terms. In the spring of 1921, the JDC worked out a plan whereby the ARA furnished milk and food supplies to the JDC's child clinics, and the JDC's Medical Commission would join the PAKPD, ARA, and ARC in their child welfare work. Jewish institutions in areas without Jewish representatives on the local PAKPD committee were instructed to send duplicates of requests to the committee straight to the JDC's Medical Commission, which passed these onto the ARC to cross-check with supply requests coming from local PAKPDs.[131]

For the ARA and Hadassah, children had to eat on site to prevent adults from sharing the ration. The ARA and the Friends also ran closely supervised kitchens, mostly in urban centers, to prepare and dispense their food products to older children, on-site. This consume-on-site rule was difficult to enforce, given pushback from adults and local committee leaders who were uninterested in following the procedure.[132] The JDC's food, clothing, and medical care distribution was also carried out through Jewish school networks. In Palestine, Hadassah's Palestine School Luncheon Fund provided one hot meal ("penny lunches") to schoolchildren using the collected pocket change of American Jewish children. Whether in East Central Europe or Palestine, schools were essential to child relief as places where children were naturally grouped and could be reached without parental interference. The ARA, JDC, and Hadassah's primary goal was to maintain quality control and ensure that their resources were directed toward their object: children. Grouping children qua children and feeding and educating them separately from adults reflected the hope that the children would in turn educate their parents. The message was that American, scientifically backed institutions should have more control than parents and the local community over children and the distribution of resources. Schools proved more effective at this than child-only kitchens.[133]

Milk stations, especially in Palestine, served a primary function as infant and maternal welfare centers, as well. Milk distribution encouraged women to come for pregnancy and childrearing advice from nurses. Before babies were old enough to bring home their learning from school, nurses and professionals dispensed advice to new mothers based on American scientific childrearing expertise and tried to disabuse them of traditional practices and beliefs.[134] Middle-class American Jews promoting childcare in Eastern Europe and Palestine felt the American model was best and should be shared with locals to improve society as a whole. In fact, weak government oversight meant that there was more latitude to experiment and improve upon New York models. For Seligsberg, how to care for orphans in an acceptable way while not improving the living standard of their friends who still had homes and parents presented a conundrum. She determined, "no doubt we should have a hard fight to change the point of view of mothers and foster mothers in regard to living conditions and the care of children."[135]

Since the ARC made child health its primary postwar reconstructive activity in Europe, it was a natural partner for the JDC. Although the JDC and ARC had an inconsistent, fraught relationship, the organizations worked out limited cooperation on behalf of children in 1921. This allowed the JDC to work with another American organization on a broad program of child relief and make a smoother transition from the ARA's narrow focus on feeding. The ARC focused on children but as a medicine and health-oriented organization, it interfaced with the JDC's medical unit, as it had since battling typhus. Although the ARC would not accept combining its childcare program with the JDC, it was sensitive to claims that Jews in Poland were receiving supplies from both the JDC and ARC. In March, the two organizations planned their work as if it were a single program, ensuring that the JDC would not duplicate the ARC's work.[136] The JDC concluded an arrangement with the ARC, through Col. Olds, on the basis of funds that were collected through a joint European Relief Council drive. The ARC was to pay the JDC $400,000 in New York and provide an additional $400,000 in medical supplies in Europe, all for the JDC to carry out child health work. This would necessitate close cooperation between representatives of both organizations within Latvia, Lithuania, Czechoslovakia, Austria, Hungary, Romania, and Constantinople. Despite enjoying good relations in Paris, the ARC struggled to convey the agreement to its field workers, who were loath to provide dwindling supplies to JDC field workers. Still, Plotz was satisfied with the ARC's effort to live up to the agreement.[137] Additionally, the ARC agreed in spring 1921 to cross-checking incoming supply requests from the PAKPD and the JDC Medical Commission regarding requests from local Jewish institutions.[138]

Child colonies were another "health" program touted by the JDC, set up in great numbers but difficult to maintain in practice. In the summer of 1919, the JDC established its first child colonies in Poland to care for

25,000 children. "American experience" indicated to the JDC that it was "preferable to bring up children in the country rather than in the city."[139] These were institutions in rural settings, like summer camps, seen as a healthful, temporary alternative to conditions at inner city orphanages. One press release extolled the virtues of these small, rural, child-centered utopias, explaining, "all summer long a stream of crippled bent little old people went out, to return as happy, growing children."[140] Child colonies were not especially American or new to Europe; pedagogues and medical professionals removed poor children from urban environments and sent them to summer colonies as part of the health movement spanning Europe since the late nineteenth century.[141] Local pediatrician Dr. Anna Braude Heller, however, set up the first Jewish child colony postwar near Warsaw, a model then copied across East Central Europe.[142]

As part of the planned transition from relief to reconstruction in 1921, the JDC planned to drop its subsidies of the summer colonies it had set up the previous year, leaving it to local communities to continue them if

Figure 5.3 A JDC summer colony in Poland. Young children sunbathing in lawn chairs in a JDC-supported summer colony in Poland, with adults looking on. Jewish childcare initiatives evolved far beyond basic food provision. In the JDC's 1926 "Child Care Department" album.
(YUA, Wiernik Collection, Box 8, Folder 1)

possible. It had the idea of encouraging landsmanshaftn to support these and other childcare institutions as a bridge between local and JDC support. Long-term plans for summer colonies, where children could escape the urban slum, withered as soon as the JDC expected locals to provide funding.[143] This aspect of the JDC's work suggested a shift in its attention from life-sustaining child relief to programs seeking to enrich and restore Jewish life through Jewish children. One can imagine that local Jews saw a luxury they could hardly afford. Thus, the JDC found itself pumping money into children's summer colonies in East Central Europe, year after year, providing 40–70 percent of their budgets.[144]

These child welfare programs were largely absorbed by the initiatives of the OSE Federation in Europe and TOZ in Poland, especially after JDC medical work liquidated in Europe after 1923. TOZ launched school supervision programs, infant welfare stations, sports programs in schools, and school ambulatories, and extended JDC-initiated summer colony and favus work. Both TOZ and OSE became child-focused organizations that incorporated a broad, social definition of child health. In fact, the JDC continued to subsidize all facets of child welfare, not just "luxuries" like summer camps, to see them continue, but the extensive, transborder OZE/OSE/TOZ network proved a capable partner, meaning the JDC did not have to run the programs. The network's concentration on child health over adult health was also a part of population politics, a way of raising a healthy Jewish generation. Its focus on using schools as the medium offered time and space to work on children away from the unhealthy example of their parents.

Economic crisis, especially in Poland starting in 1925, and widespread poverty necessitated and stymied these programs – for example, OSE and TOZ reverted to large school child-feeding programs. Until 1928, OSE reported on infant welfare stations, school medical supervisions, and summer colonies in the Baltics, Romania, Poland, and Danzig. These all depended on the continued flow of JDC money for maintenance, and especially for growth.[145] By World War II, OSE morphed entirely into a child-saving organization rather than one focused on the health of Jews.[146]

In Palestine, too, Hadassah and the JDC set up a couple of year-round, experimental child colonies under the Palestine Orphan Committee. One was called Meir Shfeye, originally established with Ica and Rothschild money as a farming colony before the war and still in existence today. Sophia Berger helped turn Meir Shfeye into a haven for about 100 formerly urban orphan girls from Palestine, training them to become farmers' wives and eventually including farm training for boys. Berger explained to the first president of Junior Hadassah that the point of these children's villages was to educate children through apprenticing in agricultural work and related trades, alongside academic study.[147]

Meanwhile, 120 Jewish orphans, mostly boys, came to Palestine from Ukraine, sponsored by the United South African Jewish Relief, Reconstruction, and Orphan Fund. The original plan was to expand Meir Shfeye for them, and Sophia Berger received permission to go to Ukraine on behalf of the JDC and the "Durban Committee" to retrieve these children. With the approval of authorities in Palestine, the US government facilitated her entrance into Odessa in 1923.[148] These Ukrainian Jewish orphans were placed in a new, separate colony called Givat Hamoreh, founded on land acquired by the Jewish National Fund.[149]

The JDC covered some of the overhead for child colonies in Palestine, and its Palestine Orphan Committee directed the work. Berger's idea was to move orphans from urban orphanages to the countryside to learn a farm lifestyle. By then, most institutionalized Palestine orphans were funded through the financial adoption programs of the Junior Hadassah and the ARC. Junior Hadassah thus covered the costs of Jewish childcare institutions that the JDC would not, funding about 10 percent of orphans cared for by the POC. Through 1924, the POC still had JDC support for 80 percent of the remaining 1,300 children in its care and 60 percent of its total budget. In 1925, Junior Hadassah fully took over funding children's villages.[150]

Berger felt that her and Seligsberg's work directing the POC was not mere philanthropy. Children's villages taught children to work on the land, for the land, and as such, child welfare became national work. Children were to self-govern and form a republic, a small agricultural utopia of orphans, although this ideal was never realized.[151] Orphan colonies in Palestine were clearly not just about child health – they attempted to go much further than Jewish summer colonies in Europe toward shaping the collective lives of children. They offered an alternative to the homing or institutionalizing question and were more than a temporary reprieve, like European summer colonies. They combined the ideas of general child welfare and raising orphans into one radical experiment. In removing orphans from urban institutions and foster homes, these colonies positioned children to become the collective future Jewish nation, in the image of the Zionist ideal of agrarian labor.

Unmet Needs in Ukraine

When it came to Jewish children under Soviet control in Ukraine, the JDC tried to find ways to reach them. People's Relief worried that there were 75,000–100,00 Jewish orphans in the region.[152] These homeless or abandoned Jewish children were just some of the hundreds of thousands of Soviet street children who were victims of broken families resulting from war, famine, and epidemics. These homeless waifs, termed *besprizorniki* in Russian, visible in their makeshift camps and notorious for their criminal behavior, became an object of early Soviet policy in 1918, which aimed to socialize childcare, replacing the family with the state. Yet provisions for material welfare, let alone education, fell far short of what was needed. The limited plans concocted by the Soviet state and Russian pedagogues to coordinate relief activities, such as evacuating besprizorniki to farmlands, providing soup kitchens, and rounding them up in institutions, disintegrated under the New Economic Policy and were unofficially abandoned by the mid-1920s.[153]

Aware of suffering Jewish children and the Kremlin's inability to assist them, the JDC pressed on with its search to enter Ukraine. In the fall of 1921, Jessie Bogen wrote the AFSC to see if the Quaker unit in Soviet Russia could assist the JDC in bringing orphan children to America or in delivering remittances. The AFSC declined, suggesting that such a complex problem "ought to be handled by people who are able to speak Russian, and perhaps by those … who understand something about the local situation."[154] Unfortunately for American Jews, as discussed in Chapter 2, the JDC had no better alternative. The best the Friends could do was to deliver food paid for by the JDC to general feeding points and children's institutions in areas of Ukraine and around Minsk where they operated.[155]

When Bogen first traveled to Ukraine under the auspices of the ARA in April 1922, his first glimpse of the pitiable state of children horrified him. He sent an urgent cable through the ARA to Lewis Strauss that it was impossible for him to stand the sight of thousands of children "absolutely naked," unable to leave institutions or recover from disease. He frantically requested a rush order by wire for clothes in London to be shipped to Odessa.[156] Strauss hastily purchased 20,000 outfits, which were on a ship to Odessa by mid-May through the ARA.[157] More clothing followed.

While the JDC eventually managed to assist some Jewish children in Soviet Ukraine, its efforts resembled the urgent relief and feeding programs in East Central Europe in 1919–20 rather than its comprehensive child welfare programs centered in Galicia, Poland. The aid effort was clearly targeted at orphans and the homeless, not all children. Cash transfers to individual recipients were out of the question, and Bogen flatly dismissed the possibility that any children could be transported from Soviet Russia to America.[158] Although the JDC could reach Ukraine by 1922, strained relations with Soviet authorities meant that the JDC could not transplant its orphan work from Poland to Ukraine; it

could not undertake extensive child programming nor extend its financial adoption scheme.[159] Given the limitations, the JDC in the Soviet
Union financed the construction of new children's institutions (called
"internats" in Soviet Russia). While not formally designated as Jewish,
the internats cared for large numbers of Jewish children and received
equipment, bed linens, clothing, supplementary feeding, shoes, and
winter fuel from the JDC.[160]

The JDC claimed to be assisting 80,000 children in Soviet Russia in
1923.[161] Since American Jews were unable to offer more comprehensive
Jewish child relief, Werelief and Lucien Wolf also looked for openings to
reach children through interwar European relief networks. Werelief and
Ica teamed up with the International Save the Children Union (IUSE),
which opened a series of kosher kitchens through its representative in
Ukraine under Werelief's name in a number of towns starting in 1922,
including Kiev, Zhytomyr, and Berdychiv.[162] In 1923 and 1924, 10,000
Jewish children were fed through these 31 kitchens and homes, according
to Werelief, although IUSE struggled to maintain separate Jewish

Figure 5.4 Children in an Agro-Joint colony. Mountain Jew children sit
on farm machinery at an Agro-Joint colony near Yevpatoria, in Crimea,
c. 1925. Child welfare became a component of Agro-Joint, the main
JDC initiative in the USSR, after 1923.
(JDC, NY_44675)

kitchens, especially in non-famine areas.[163] Werelief promised to "devote
its attention to these children [orphaned in the famine] till the last day of
its activity."[164] IUSE's kitchens belonged to decentralized famine relief
operations under the banner of the Nansen Action's activities.[165] Wolf
also promised to sponsor four additional kosher kitchens along railways,
and the IUSE likewise promised to deliver food to orphanages in Jewish
quarters.[166]

In Petrograd, Jewish children from Ukraine lived in internats that were
steadily improving, and infrastructure was paid for by the Soviets, through
Evobshchestkom. Life in cities also began to improve by 1923, which
Bogen attributed to the JDC's representatives and Evobshchestkom's
"working hand-in-hand." In western and northern Ukraine, along the
Polish and Romanian borders, where Jews had congregated as refugees
but there was no urban infrastructure to support them, the situation
remained dire, with orphans having nowhere to go.[167] In 1924, the JDC
supported 25,157 children at 470 institutions, providing about a fifth of
the sum supplied by the Soviet government.[168] Starting in 1925, the JDC
began to liquidate its childcare programs in Soviet Russia, turning its
attention to the Agro-Joint colonization project, although reports indicate
that as late as 1927, the JDC still supported nearly 2,000 children.[169] The
JDC planned for Agro-Joint to improve the lives of children, too, keeping
families and generations of Jews united by working the land; read more
about Agro-Joint in Chapter 6.[170]

A Moral and Financial Conundrum

As time went on, Jewish childcare programs developed and shrank.
Emergency relief did not end, either; Bernard Kahn found himself
cabling New York in 1922 for help with child refugees who were being
repatriated from Russia to Poland and the Baltics and who lost parents en
route, and then again with the refugee crisis in Romania in 1923.[171] Yet
Kahn was determined to shut down or shrink the childcare program as
quickly as was morally justifiable. Starting in 1924, the JDC struggled to
reconcile the goal of pulling out of Europe with its continuing obligation
to Jewish children. The JDC understood that it could stretch its budget
by covering more children for a short period, or fewer children for a
longer period.[172] In 1926, the JDC Childcare Department wrote as it
prepared to fundraise, that although it hoped that local Jewish communities would be able to care for "their" orphans without outside aid, these
expectations were unmet. Rather, Jewish communities "are facing still,
or perhaps again, a very critical time."[173] TOZ and OSE branches in East
Central Europe put JDC dollars to use for programs the JDC had set up,

but required infusions of funds.[174] Landsmanshaftn picked up some of the work to compensate for lack of JDC input, which merely shifted the burden from a centralized American institution to many smaller ones. They had already been crucial in supporting childcare efforts in small, outlying places.[175] The Palestine Orphan Committee had fewer war orphans to look after each year as these children grew older or were successfully adopted. At the beginning of 1928, the committee officially dissolved, though Sophia Berger volunteered her time to help those still in need.[176]

All told, the JDC spent over $4 million on childcare between 1922 and 1931. Poland alone absorbed nearly $2.5 million. Jews across East Central Europe took on a greater proportion of funding childcare, carrying 85.5 percent of the burden in Poland by 1929. Yet the figures indicate that total expenditures on childcare contracted, with local absolute funding remaining almost constant from year to year as the JDC withdrew its support.[177] So while locals took on a greater portion of the financial burden, that was only because JDC funding was slashed, not because locals contributed more money, although in its propaganda, the JDC played up the ways that locals took over the work. Either the Jews of Eastern Europe did not like the JDC's programs, children grew out of them, or, most likely, were never able to come up with the funds to support these foreign programs. Kahn claimed in 1928 that some, though not all, local communities took on the burden and tried to keep standards high.[178]

In the late 1920s, while some children had aged out of the system, many parentless children remained refugees of sorts, even without experiencing severe dislocation, and despite JDC presence in childcare. Continuing crises coupled with long-term dependencies created a sense of ongoing failure and need. CENTOS leaders bemoaned their lack of funds and decried the wretched state of Jewish children in 1927, arguing that helping children was a rational Jewish national duty, not just a charitable activity.[179] In early 1929, the directors of CENTOS prepared a trip to the United States to plead for additional JDC and landsmanshaft funding for the orphan federation, even though the JDC considered its childcare work successfully complete and an obligation that the Jews of Poland had already assumed.[180] In fact, CENTOS produced its own long and statistically detailed reports for the JDC, suggesting that it had transitioned to an independent child welfare organization in cooperation with TOZ; it merely lacked consistent funding.[181]

In the end, the JDC pursued all reasonable options. It pushed the Jewish child welfare system into a nationally conscious, goal-oriented system in Poland and other parts of Europe it could reach.[182] Its

Figure 5.5 War orphans in Romania. War orphans gather on the steps of the
JDC's "Marmarosh-Sighet District" office in 1919. JDC reports described
once-Habsburg Sighetu Marmației, Romania's Jewish communities as
"medieval": the most isolated, neglected, and perhaps poorest in Europe.
Sighet's Jews had no provisions for orphans until the JDC arrived.
(JDC, NY_00976)

children's bureau in Warsaw had someone to arrange financial adoption, legal adoption, and to connect relatives. It reached Romania, Austria, and Bulgaria, where orphanages received subsidies starting in 1919. In the field, especially in Poland and Palestine, the JDC administered and supervised a vast network of child-centered programs, first through the ARA's child feeding operations, and then independently, with an eye to the ARC.

But children's needs extended beyond health, shelter, and food; children needed to grow up. Schools were a site of relief but also a major consideration of postwar childcare. By 1920, Norman Bentwich had concluded that Palestine's schools had to support the moral and intellectual growth of children, at least as much as the Catholics' schools did.[183] Similarly, in 1921, after a visit to Rovno, Peiser deemed it unacceptable for orphaned children to be growing up illiterate; education had to be part of the JDC's plan for children.[184] Yet, questions about how to pay for education and what form this would take outgrew the boundaries of child welfare work. The JDC was loath to admit it, preferring to calculate the costs of food, shelter, and health programs for children. Education, according to Frank Rosenblatt was a "tremendous problem" when it came to orphans, since it dragged the JDC into the bitter political and partisan discussions that accompanied any conversation about Jewish education.[185]

Education As Battleground

One group would have in mind under the word Cultural, synagogues and religious schools ... while another group might support schools which are the antithesis of these. On the one side the religious schools would be viewed as relics of superstition, on the other side the radical schools would be considered as subversive of Judaism ... [A] permanent committee on Cultural Activities ... would only involve its membership in continuous debate ... On the other hand, [it] was felt that it is only by maintaining the spirit of our brethren in Eastern Europe that their life is worth preserving to them and that education and the provision for a continued leadership is as essential as food and clothing.

With those words, the Committee on Cultural Activities of the JDC New York, with Cyrus Adler presiding, recommended in autumn 1920 that it should not exist. Feelings ran so high on this issue in New York and Poland that the JDC concluded that a united American Jewish position on education abroad was impossible.[186] As indicated, gaps between American and Eastern European ways of undertaking relief and reconstruction work after the war were typical. Religious and political tension among Jews prevailed. However, compromises usually emerged for the purposes of relief – after all, the JDC sought to make local institutions independent again, if also modernized. But this system of compromise and plurality broke down when it came to Jewish education.

International child relief organizations did not have education on the agenda, other than to encourage states to educate their citizens. But as Morris Waldman stated at a 1925 conference of American Jewish social workers, the war had resulted in "a recognition of Jewish education as the most vital element in the preservation of the Jewish people."[187] For Jewish organizations, education was the battleground between Jewish autonomy and state control, particularly in light of stipulations in the Minorities Treaties regarding schooling. Education was also an internal battle over the hearts and minds of the future Jewish people. That internal Jewish battle was confused, given the mismatch between the ideological composition of American Jewish givers versus East European Jewish receivers; there was discord on both sides, but that discord took different forms.

The idea that children, or at least boys, should go to primary school was widely accepted by Jews. The central institution embodying traditional Jewish education in Europe was the ubiquitous *cheder*, a one-room school for boys who studied sacred Jewish texts. While Tsarist Russia focused on educating elite Russians, Jews in the Russian Pale of Settlement developed educational institutions that they had brought from medieval Western Europe. All Jewish communities, no matter how small, had a cheder, and larger towns sponsored religious primary schools for poor boys called the talmud torah. Jewish law mandated religious education for boys, and literacy among Jews was high, even for women. The Haskalah had created pathways for Jews to acculturate in the West and eventually brought reform to Jewish schools in the Pale in the nineteenth century by introducing secular subjects and vocational training, and by including women. Maskilim felt that orphans and poor Jewish children needed a modern education to become useful citizens. Traditional Jews had begun to organize in response to modernization by the end of the century, as modernizers formed into competitive groups. Education was already politicized terrain on the eve of war, even as the majority of Jewish boys in Russia still attended the cheder.[188]

For American Jews thinking about Eastern Europe, the question was not how to get children out of the labor force and into school, as it was in New York,[189] but what kind of school children should attend, and for how long. Jewish men, who traditionally occupied the spheres of education and politics, were to ponder these questions. The debate was most intense in connection with Poland, where Jewish life had undergone extensive, rapid transformation as part of the new Polish state, bringing freedoms, changed incentives, and access to the West that had long been out of reach in the Pale of Settlement or even in the eastern reaches of the Austro-Hungarian Empire. Jewish political and cultural activity, banned under the Russian Tsars, began to flourish in what became Poland by the end of the war, starting in 1915, when the Central Powers invaded Russian territory and emancipated Jews to win their support. In Poland, Jewish schools needed to meet state standards while upholding the Minorities Treaty and a new, liberal constitution. Jewish education was therefore reordered in new states after the war. With the default no longer being the cheder, alternatives proliferated. What was at stake was first a question of Jewish continuity and which traditions to preserve, and second, how to educate children for a successful economic future. Although most Polish Jews attended public elementary schools established by the new state of Poland, which taught in Polish and at no cost, Jewish nationalists, Bundists, Orthodox, Yiddishists and Hebraists scrambled to obtain a slice of the future Jewish collective at school.[190] In Soviet Russia, in a complete upending of the traditional educational system, Jewish children attended state Jewish schools, where the language of instruction was Yiddish but any religious teachings were forbidden.[191] There was little debate or room to maneuver in the Soviet system.

The JDC uncomfortably lumped education into its "cultural" work, which included subsidizing rabbis, university students, and some crucial cultural institutions, including libraries and theaters. As Cyrus Adler indicated, no one was clear on what Jewish culture meant or how much the JDC should emphasize it to the detriment of more basic human needs – better to reduce its involvement in politicized posturing and let the locals sort it out by themselves. Whereas the Alliance Israélite and the Hilfsverein had long established their own Westernized Jewish schools in the empires and Palestine, Hias and Hadassah did not enter the education business. Neither did mainstream humanitarian organizations at the time; the ARA, ARC, RF, and others left new European states to manage primary education and instead returned to domestic questions on schooling and how to improve nutrition science internationally. Yet the pesky question of primary education, at the very least for the children the JDC was paying to raise, was impossible to ignore.

As the JDC moved into child welfare work, the Yiddish press filled with demands that the organization take a stand on how the Jewish children it helped should be raised.[192] The JDC never did. Still, the various educational institutions in Poland and elsewhere in East Central Europe appealed to the JDC and their contacts in America on

behalf of their vision of the Jewish future and in light of tough competition from free Polish schools. These appeals sparked so much political
fervor within the JDC's constituent groups in America that in the end,
the JDC abandoned its core principle of pluralist unity by allowing each
constituent to fund its own favored schools as "cultural" rather than
"childcare" work. The three constituent committees of the JDC – the
People's Relief, Central Relief, and American Jewish Relief
Committees – would designate institutions to which no more than a
third of their total funds would go, thus providing direct contributions
for "cultural" purposes via the JDC's logistical machinery.[193]

Sometimes the question of educational upbringing threatened to derail
local child welfare efforts, as in the case of Brest-Litovsk, where the
refugee issue compounded the problem. Abraham Shohan explained
how in the winter of 1922, thousands of Jewish refugees returned to
Brest-Litovsk. Given inadequate housing and the JDC Childcare
Department's policy to not build orphanages, local Jews instead appealed
to the JDC Refugee Department for a new orphanage. This appeal came
from younger, nationalist, secular Jews. New orphanages and programs
funded by the JDC Refugee Department began to compete with the
town's preexisting orphanage, run by religious Jews. Orthodox dissatisfaction increased especially as the JDC Childcare Department began to
subsidize children in these newer programs. Orthodox Jews in the town,
including the authoritative and far-reaching voice of a Soloveitchik within
the famous rabbinic dynasty of that name, protested widespread secular
upbringing. Although the JDC mediated negotiations to reconstitute a
more representative childcare committee, only "moderates" who were
willing to work with one another remained on the committee.[194]

Examining a debate among Jews in Poland and New York and considering the practical outcomes shines light both on American Jews,
Polish Jews, and the troubled nature of their connection. Of all the arenas
in which American Jews played a role in postwar Jewish life abroad,
education was probably the most broadly American Jewish project of
all. It was clearly not the project of a handful of elite American Jews who
would sometimes cave under pressure, but truly a project in which many
kinds of American Jews participated (with the exception of women), from
fundraising to distribution and even decision-making. The example of
education demonstrates that the JDC was not always a top-down organization; in this case it neither dictated to regular American Jews from
above, nor from New York to Poland. We have seen in past chapters that
the JDC's core leadership was somewhat responsive to constituent
demands, knowing it needed to make some modifications to maintain
overall control over American Jewish relief efforts. There was always

room for change from below because JDC leadership was so averse to public controversy.

Facing demands to deal with education, Adler proposed dividing decision-making on education among its constituent committees but uniting the logistics under JDC bureaucracy.[195] With the international banking system up and running by 1921, however, there was little incentive for People's Relief or Central Relief to take advantage of the JDC bureaucracy, and the separate committees sent the money however they wanted.[196] The JDC Cultural Committee and the JDC's constituent organizations eventually agreed to disagree, decentralizing control over Jewish education policy as determined in New York. The "joint" aspect of the JDC seemed to become an afterthought soon after its creation, other than for fundraising. But on everything education related, it reverted to its "joint" constituency of three committees and thereby became "disjointed."

This fundamentally Polish Jewish debate over education and Jewish cultural, national, and religious continuity took on a new and distinct life in the American context. The American Jewish domestic education conversation was barely linked; the Bureau of Jewish Education in New York was not a formal party to the debate about what should happen overseas, for example.[197] Instead, the formal parties were the constituent committees of the JDC, whose ideologies mirrored those that immigrants had brought with them to America from Russia before the war. Since those immigrants had not experienced political factionalization, new nation-building projects, and cultural flourishing opened by the war, however, the various ideological camps in America did not match those in Poland. Context mattered: American Jews attracted to free public schools in America might support Jewish schools in Poland. Not to mention that there were Jews in America, often in the most prominent positions, whose origins were not in the Pale of Settlement at all. Those involved in Jewish educational assistance programs from America referred to "mixed-type" schools, code for schools that did not fit the American Jewish ideological typology and were therefore difficult to delegate to a constituent committee. Polish Jews would not have thought of them as "mixed" but as fully independent, coherent school alternatives within their present ideological spectrum. Only vocational training, which fit into the long-standing Jewish enlightenment, self-help ideal of productivizing the Jew, was broadly appealing, and will be discussed in the next chapter.

That the JDC would not fund educational institutions and the fact that such institutions should apply directly to People's Relief or Central Relief was advertised in the Polish Jewish press in early 1921. People's Relief soon noticed that there were three major groups of schools applying for assistance, not two – and that third did not "belong" to the ideology of People's Relief or Central Relief.[198] The American Jewish Relief Committee, which by that time had become indistinguishable from the JDC, regrouped to act as the third constituent committee.[199] Education support was then split between the constituent committees of the JDC, with People's Relief funding labor-oriented, Yiddishist schools; Central Relief, religious schools; and, in a twist of irony, the American Jewish Relief Committee paid for Zionist schools since no other organization would, as well as assimilationist schools.[200]

The JDC continued to subsidize children, leaving it to locals and relatives to determine what school each child should attend. This put the onus on Polish Jews to compete for the resources of the three constituent committees. In this way, American Jewish organizations encouraged the factionalization of Polish Jewish society and provided an impetus for ever-more energy to be spent sparring rather than putting it to productive use. Furthermore, it disadvantaged schools in peripheral locations outside Warsaw, since neither Central Relief nor People's Relief had the infrastructure to reach them, nor did small schools have a fair chance to compete in urban Jewish politics.[201]

Somehow, this system worked. The JDC was able to educate over 10,000 war orphans in Poland in 1923; 82 percent of those in its care, in a talmud torah, Yiddish school, Hebrew school, public elementary school, or high school, in proportions that resembled other countries.[202] And although People's Relief only distributed to labor-oriented schools, Barnet Zuckerman, its general manager who was also dedicated to the JDC (he was the JDC's man on the ground during the Pinsk pogrom and kept the People's Relief attached to the JDC when there was pressure to secede after Dubrowsky's installation of the New York Evobshchestkom), seemed genuinely concerned that every Jewish educational institution should be supported in some way. He initiated efforts to coordinate the work of the various JDC constituent committees.[203] So while each committee supposedly struck out in an antagonistic and independent manner to support only the cultural and educational institutions aligned with the ideology of its own committee, in fact, coordination occurred among them. Further, the AJRC took on a role to support any school which did not correlate to institutionalized American Jewish political ideology, whereas it might have been expected to support only assimilationist institutions given the identity of its leaders. Still, a fragmented system for the support of educational institutions did generate confusion as information remained limited in New York and came from multiple sources; paperwork increased for all the committees, which all had to parse requests and divide the work, while operating from separate New York offices.[204] Constituent committee by constituent committee is how one has to understand American Jewish organizational interference in educational, cultural, and religious life in 1920s Poland.

The People's Relief was a socialist and Yiddishist organization. Its education funds went to the Workmen's Relief Committees in Poland, not directly to any schools or educational institutions at all.[205] It was only indirectly allied with Tsisho, the network of Yiddishist, socialist schools that promoted a national, diaspora-centered, secular Jewish culture.[206] People's Relief viewed all kinds of workers' institutions as appropriate targets for cultural subsidies, not just schools supported by the Jewish labor movement.[207] These Workmen's Committees were essentially the Polish Jewish equivalent of the People's Relief; rather than undermine them, the People's Relief gave funds to them to distribute.

Central Relief, on the other hand, saw its role as pushing for traditional or religious Jewish education. It sent what it called "remittances for cultural work" to talmud torahs and yeshivas, particularly in Poland, Lithuania, and Palestine.[208] For Central Relief, cultural work was synonymous with religious work and extended the boundaries of education strictly defined; all contributions for religious purposes counted.[209] These were remittances in the sense that they were provided in direct response to requests from primary and secondary religious schools. Central Relief did not overly concern itself with secular institutions to manage these distributions but sent funds directly to the schools with which it had contact.

Central Relief said it would see to it that the JDC's War Orphans Bureau ensured that children would be brought up in a manner meeting the requirements of traditional Judaism "and thus save them from being weaned away from the spiritual food that they are entitled to."[210] To the Jews who made up Central Relief, children had not only the right to a home, food, and healthcare but also a right to learn about Judaism as part of their education and heritage. Warburg tried to make a case for drawing a distinction between the two issues of child welfare and education to Leon Kamaiky, the chairman of the Central Relief after his stint as Hias commissioner to Warsaw, but to no avail.[211] Central Relief was incensed when the JDC created Evobshchestkom and turned over its child relief to it, with the full knowledge that Evobshchestkom would not provide a religious education.[212]

Finally, the American Jewish Relief Committee set up its own cultural committee in February 1921.[213] Cyrus Adler, encouraged by People's Relief and Boris Bogen, guided the AJRC to allot dollars to educational institutions that were not supported by People's Relief or Central Relief.[214] It pushed toward Jewish pluralism, the ideology of the JDC. In fact, the AJRC had become so powerful within the JDC that the two had trouble sorting out the differences between them – who, for example, was treasurer of the AJRC: the treasurer of the JDC, or someone else?[215] Jewish institutional candidates who did not find sympathy with People's Relief or Central Relief could expect the support of the AJRC, and there was "no lack of applications."[216] To be sure, the AJRC had to provide for assimilationist schools where the language of instruction was Polish, because that did not meet the standards of People's Relief or Central Relief. But the other category of schools that fell through the cracks was Hebrew-language schools with a secular, Zionist ideology.[217] In the name of pluralism, the AJRC found itself providing funding largely for Zionist and Hebrew-language secular Tarbut schools, despite the AJRC's non-Zionist stance. The AJRC also provided funding for Jewish schools of various kinds in Central Europe that did not fit the Polish Jewish ideological framework and culturally resembled the Jewish leadership of the AJRC.[218]

Although Poland was the wellspring of American Jewish controversy over education, the JDC and its constituent committees were actively involved elsewhere, from Austria to Palestine, and later even Russia. The JDC, always limited in its capacity to work under the Soviets but dedicated to helping Jews continue a real Jewish life, also made an unpublicized and "extra-legal" commitment to supporting Jewish education there.[219] Because Jewish life and culture were intimately bound up in religion, work, and study, Bolshevik anti-religious policies tore apart the fabric of Jewish life.[220] In one clandestine operation to counter these policies, the Rebbe Yosef Yitzchak Schneersohn courted the JDC once its palliative relief ended in the USSR, arguing against focusing on productivization at the expense of Jewish religious life. Felix Warburg himself and the JDC's main cultural committee became involved; there was otherwise very little discussion about it within the JDC or its constituent committees. The Lubavitch sect of Chasidism, and in particular, its leader Schneersohn, began distributing JDC money in 1926, keeping a form of religious Judaism alive through his networks. The JDC facilitated Schneersohn's escape from Soviet Russia to Riga in autumn 1927, helping him as he moved money across the border in support of continued religious education among his followers and network. Once the JDC decided that it compromised its legitimacy, it severed the relationship. Even then, the JDC continued its commitment to religious life in Russia through Joseph Rosen's agreement to distribute funds for religious purposes.[221]

In East Central Europe and Palestine after the Great War, education was not about welfare at all, but about the collective future. Nationalism in Europe was often contested through children, who were seen as national property and the future of the nation. Children and parents were thus seen as objects of welfare and politics, not as agents in their own right. Parents were mostly indifferent to schemes to bring up Jewish children in various communal, national, or productive educational institutions. Competing for attention, funds, and student enrollment, activist pedagogues tried to win over Jewish parents to Jewish schools and trade education. But parents overwhelmingly sent their children to free Polish schools and preferred academic educations that would allow their children to professionalize.[222] In Palestine, Sophia Berger was not able to find modern educators who could inspire the orphans of child villages to become agricultural workers; the best educators only caused the girls at Meir Shfeye to wish to pursue higher learning.[223]

The opinions of the children and youth in question were not considered, though they, too, were affected by the war. The first Jewish generation to live in a democratic Poland, they had firsthand knowledge of total violence and the deprivations of war. Rapidly acculturated in the new Polish state, Jewish youth were drawn to joining their peers in newly formed youth groups. Youth received an informal education through the libraries and networks of their youth movements, which were inherently political. The JDC, working through local organizations and for youth, but not *with* youth, was both faceless and ubiquitous from a child's perspective, unable to effect change in their lives. Many children survived on their own in groups on the streets, without adults, especially in Russia, and sometimes crossed borders to find relief. The notion of the sheltered childhood, that children needed protection, education, and welfare until they were adults, was still an idea rather than a self-evident truth.[224]

Institutionalizing Welfare in Dispersion

The JDC's narrative of progress was more narrative than reality. While it hoped to improve the prospects of Jewish children throughout East Central Europe through its summer colonies and educational opportunities, it met resistance from locals and immigrants in the United States, and from within its own ranks regarding its role. American responses to Jewish children who had suffered in the war were influenced by general trends of child welfare and internationalist and nationalist sentiment at the time, and by the ideological fragmentation of Eastern European Jews in the interwar period. American ideas of rational child welfare espoused by the JDC, in which experts were supposed to collaborate, but children were to be addressed as individuals within family units, clashed with collectivist continental pedagogy, in which various Jewish projects and personalities competed to collect as many Jewish children into their particular, ideological institutions as possible.

What did it mean to export American Progressivism when there was no state that might absorb the programs of reformers, and when Progressivism was evaporating in America? American Jewish Progressives assumed that Americanizing Eastern Jews was synonymous with making them suitable citizens of their modern states, although those states were unequipped to take on these projects themselves and were not taking shape along American lines. The entire Progressive model American Jews emulated was based on encouraging states to take over social welfare. Although the JDC followed the "classic progressive reform strategy: start with privately supported demonstration projects, then secure government funding to expand services,"[225] it was unclear what government or higher order would provide this long-term funding.

The reality was that no one was willing or able to fund these programs on a long-term basis. The JDC's assumption was always that the economic situation in Eastern Europe would improve, while reality said otherwise. Approaches to childcare in particular highlighted the extent to which Jewish organizations had internalized and simply could not reconcile competing visions of what it meant to build for the Jewish future according to best practices. The JDC therefore cordoned off education into a mostly separate, limited realm, where Jewish politics remained intense, and brought its scientific Americanism to bear on the rest of child welfare, focusing on orphans in their "native environments."[226]

The JDC's childcare program was designed to modernize Jewish childcare locally and to pass the responsibility for child refugees to Jewish communities in East Central European states, especially in Poland. With eugenics and national competition dominating the discourse of child welfare at the time, it was never a question that the JDC would cede Jewish childcare to any state, and it felt morally compelled to remain involved. And yet, the inability of locals to even maintain programs the JDC had set up, let alone expand them, meant that the JDC reluctantly acted as a social welfare state. In 1927, JDC reported that nine years after the war, it was not still doing war orphan relief as its critics claimed, but rather, bringing up Jewish children through "modern, social childcare."[227]

This was all made plain in 1921 when Morris Waldman sent a list of questions to JDC New York requesting clarification on core issues in childcare, from how long the JDC was responsible; to the age limits of children; to whether the JDC or locals should define minimum standards; and to whether the JDC should cooperate with other organizations for out-of-country adoptions. He concluded: "Are we correct in believing that in contributing towards the support of children, we desire to do this indirectly, leaving the responsibility with the local institutions and organizations, and providing our own administrative force only for the necessary supervision ... It is quite apparent that this is not altogether the conception of the local people interested in this work, but they look upon the adoption of the children as a direct responsibility of the J.D.C. for an indefinite period."[228] Solomon Lowenstein, who headed the Childcare Committee in New York, sidestepped the question of long-term responsibility in his answer: "Eager as we might be to maintain our children on the standards which our American viewpoint would demand of us, we must remember that whatever steps we take in this work will be only part of the general orphan care program in the community and that the care of a limited number of orphans on a standard especially established for them would be contrary ultimately to the good of the community."[229]

The Jewish Question and the meaning and future of minority rights were brought to the fore by the challenges of raising the next generation and by competing visions over the future of Jewish life. If in Palestine, the JDC retreated because there was a proto-state to absorb programming, in the diaspora, the JDC reinforced Jewish solidarity and turned itself into something resembling a social welfare state, sharing resources with the American government, and taxing the Jewish citizens of America for redistribution to Europe's needy Jews. Yet neither in this Jewish welfare diaspora state nor in the United States did everyone agree on a sheltered and education-focused childhood for all.

6   The Impoverished
Credit As Reconstruction

Hoping for a restoration of economic liberalism after the war's economic mayhem, Max Warburg noted in 1919, "The long duration of the war, the enormous calamity caused by it, makes its liquidation all the more difficult."[1] It is by now well understood by historians that the economic consequences of the war and subsequent peace resulted in the Great Depression, which pulled Europe back into war. Wartime animosities were enshrined in economic nationalism. Nationalist and racist convictions became central features of the organization of the postwar European economy.

Jews were squeezed out of struggling national economies across Central and Eastern Europe. Intractable poverty among the Jews of Eastern Europe did not begin with the war but was a decades-long crisis entangled with antisemitism. After the war, economic difficulties were compounded with general struggles. Rampant inflation led to great suffering among urban and mercantile Jews, whose wealth, which existed in money rather than physical assets, made them vulnerable to every economic fluctuation. And not only was the entire Russian market no longer available to Soviet Jews, but Polish Jews could no longer trade there or produce handicrafts they could expect to sell there. Similarly, Jews in Romania and Czechoslovakia were separated from crucial prewar markets in Hungary and Austria.[2] While economic desperation had been an important push factor for Jewish emigration from the Pale for a half century, emigration was no longer a widely available option for economic alleviation.

Jewish humanitarians led by the JDC aimed to reconstruct and secure the long-term Jewish future by supporting economic development within target Jewish communities. It involved two main parts: (1) vocational-educational work to develop productive Jews and (2) economic efforts based on Jewish mutual aid.[3] The program featured housing reconstruction, vocational training, agricultural colonization projects, and loans that were collectively designed to recreate Jewish spaces, improve the Jewish body, overcome historic lack of access to guilds and land, and provide transnational, low-interest communal funding to make this possible. It immediately began absorbing refugee, public health, and child welfare activities as well, becoming heir to the activities of all the other departments.[4]

This was selfish and practical: The JDC wished to make itself, and thus ongoing American Jewish fundraising redundant, putting an end to donor fatigue by removing the need to donate. Like wartime Jewish humanitarianism, this project was based on using and moving money creatively through Jewish financial networks. The strategy was for Jewish humanitarianism to function like an international business but with philanthropic goals rather than capital accumulation.[5] The idea was to rehabilitate Jews who suffered as a result of the war by rapidly developing industry and commerce. Jewish reconstruction offered no new radical or transformative social vision, and sought to avoid intensive, overt interventions. Since it would need to rely on the infrastructure, experiences, and abilities of Eastern European Jews, reconstruction used multiple strategies that came primarily from the nineteenth-century Jewish social policy playbook.

The plan, however, was not entirely conservative, despite its nineteenth-century trappings. It was impossible to restore Jewish society to what it had been before the war; too much had changed. At a JDC meeting with Warsaw Jews in April 1921, it was decided that "an attempt must be made not only to improve the economic status of the Jews and bring it to its prewar level, but must go far beyond that. The political and economic changes following the war must be accompanied by corresponding changes in the structure of Jewish economic life. It must be made more productive [and] stand on its own feet."[6] As usual, the JDC inventively deployed its strengths and knowledge of the Jewish diaspora to launch something that superficially appeared to be merely reconstructing the prewar situation but was actually designed to propel its recipients into modernity, without any overt articulation of drastic change.

The restructuring of the Jewish economy in places where Jews already lived – as a concerted, international Jewish effort – was at the heart of the reconstruction program. Underpinning it was the transformation of the credit cooperative movement into the political economy of the Jews, via international Jewish philanthropy. There was no vision of Jewish political economy per se that was put forward as Jewish ideology, but the tools of liberal international finance, immigrant banking, and revolutionary cooperative banking met here. Indeed, humanitarian remittance cash transfers undertaken by Hias and the JDC had foreshadowed this development. The JDC's understated political ambitions lay in building an international and centralized Jewish cooperative banking system.

The first ambition was to bring together the fractured and dispersed Jewish world by interlinking its economy and institutionalizing its ethnic separateness from other political economies. The second was to create a self-sustaining, pluralist, cooperative social system to carry out the work indefinitely.

Economic reconstruction was the most particularly Jewish field of humanitarian activity; other humanitarians dared not or could not enter this realm. It required a high level of trust and collaboration with locals, risked the possibility of seeming to conduct humanitarian aid for profit, and proved a long-term commitment to socioeconomic change. Yet for American Jewish humanitarians, this was the most feasible way to actually restructure Jewish life in Europe, making it economically viable and adapting it to war-changed surroundings. Seeking to provide the economic advantages of Western-style emancipation to the Jews of Eastern Europe, this route also played across class and national lines to an imagined Jewish masculine financial prowess. In doing so, it largely neglected Jewish women's historic and continued participation in economic life. These women moved toward opportunities on the radical left.

Creating the JDC Reconstruction Department was no simple matter – it was established in 1921 and only rolled out in 1922, last among the JDC's major programs, but quickly its favorite.[7] Herbert Lehman chaired the Reconstruction Committee in the JDC New York office. A colonel in the war and recent treasurer of the JDC, Lehman was also a partner in the Lehman Brothers bank. He would be elected governor of New York State in 1932, replacing Franklin D. Roosevelt who became president, and then would institute Roosevelt's New Deal. In the field, Alexander Landesco generated the Reconstruction Department from his base in Romania shortly after the war by launching a housing reconstruction program. Leonard Robinson, a leader in the US Jewish cooperative movement, took over from him in 1922. Bernard Kahn kept a close eye on the entire project as European director, and then as director of the American Joint Reconstruction Foundation.

The JDC relied on ORT and Ica for every aspect of reconstruction; despite an infusion of American wealth and know-how, reconstruction was an international, collaborative effort. Before the war, Ica supported cooperatives, agricultural colonies, and trade schools in the Pale of Settlement from its Paris headquarters through its Russian branch. ORT's prewar, elite leaders believed their work could become a mass Jewish movement for social change, capable of bringing about reforms that would support Jewish national autonomy and would modernize Jewish life in the Russian Empire. After the war, Ica carried on much as before, somewhat diminished relative to the JDC but with an intact endowment. Reconstruction was more transformative for ORT, however, which grew into a transnational, multilevel network of social and political actors: the World ORT Union. Similar to the transformation of the Russian OZE into the international OSE Federation, the JDC facilitated ORT's internationalization through the provision of crucial funds. The World ORT Union brought together financial organizations, trade corporations, political establishments, vocational schools, and branches and regional committees of ORT volunteer societies. Reconstruction incorporated preexisting Jewish economic strategies and organizations such that in target regions of Jewish development, the Jewish political economy would seem to locals to be a differently configured version of its prewar self.[8]

A subtle restructuring of the three humanitarian theaters also occurred. The Soviet Union remained altogether separate but opened in this moment to an expansive reconstructive project that met its terms: agricultural colonization. East Central Europe remained the region at the center of Jewish humanitarianism, Poland especially. Interestingly, Jews in South East Europe became absorbed into the East Central European theater, even though credit cooperation was not native to these regions. Even as Christian Europe may have felt itself more fragmented than ever before, Jews operated with an expanded notion of "Europe," acknowledging new regimes but building right across them. Yet Palestine increasingly became a distinct entity on the Jewish humanitarian map. The British Mandate and its opportunity to build a Jewish national home saw the emergence of a directly related but distinctly Zionist humanitarian cooperative movement.

Mirroring the JDC's two-part reconstruction, this chapter begins with an outline of vocational training and agricultural colonization projects. Even these fields, which appeared to revise prewar Jewish social policy for new political and legal regimes, took on totally different forms after the war. The second half tells the story of the creation of the interwar, non-state, transnational Jewish political economy, as it took shape through an unprecedented system of federated Jewish cooperatives welded to American creditor foundations. This was an integrated economic development plan, not to just restore economic life but also to bring all the cooperative initiative and technical and financial know-how from Jews in the West to bear on a diaspora-wide, grassroots project. It aimed to restructure Jewish economic life in Europe and in Palestine to realize the dream of economic normalization and modernization of Jewish bodies and institutions in the postwar landscape without the need of a state.

Developing the Jew

Maskilim had long searched for an answer to the Jewish Question from within the community, suggesting that remaking backward Jews and reforming their ways would lift Jews out of their miserable, marginal situation. Modern Jewish philanthropic organizations in Europe, from the Alliance Israélite to the Russian ORT, had been founded on this very premise – that there was something Jews could do to improve Jewish life, and that the Haskalah held the keys to this improvement. Actual economic opportunities grounded in reality were not necessarily under consideration so much as Jewish self-identity.[9] Of course, the leaders of all this philanthropic activity themselves were intellectuals, industrialists, and financiers without experience in or personal connections to vocational training, manual labor, artisan crafts, farming, or the like.

Ica and ORT, both long-established in Jewish productivization, led the way. Working with Ica was, according to the JDC, "a blending of the viewpoint of the old world and the new." Ica had traditions and history, while the JDC was "a virile democracy of the young." The JDC put up required funds to attend to war damage, but the "permanent" Ica would look after trade education in the long term by repairing, equipping, and supervising their schools.[10] Although ORT was cash-poor, it was a leading force in the reconstructive project. One could argue that ORT itself drove reconstruction, especially the practical elements, while the JDC merely provided funds and access to American Jews and American political leadership. The JDC regarded the impoverished ORT as the JDC's own agency, at least at first.

Russian ORT leaders in Ukraine in 1917 created a foreign delegation to raise money; such foreign delegations were common practice. ORT Delegation Abroad was led by Leon Bramson, older brother of the OZE's Abram Bramson and former member of the First Russian State Duma, and David Lvovitch, a prominent territorialist. They traveled to the United States and circulated amongst leaders of the JDC and the Jewish labor movement. In 1920, the delegation opened a new office in Paris. From there, it built connections with Western European Jewish philanthropic and labor organizations. Garnering Werelief's support at its Carlsbad Conference in 1920, the delegation then reached out to Russian Jewish emigrants and founded branches in Paris, London, and Berlin, creating a transnational European, "national" Russian Jewish institution constituted by Russian Jewish emigres.[11]

These branches and nine new societies from East Central Europe collected formally into the World ORT Union in 1921, committing themselves to pursuing agricultural work, supporting artisans, and developing vocational training among Jews. Like the transformation of OZE to OSE, former branches of the Russian ORT maintained the old mission under new regimes and became affiliated with the World ORT Union once they were cut off from the old center by new borders and the Soviet state. In 1921, World ORT joined Hias leaders to form the American ORT branch and fundraise, and in 1923, the American ORT briefly merged with the People's Relief. By 1922, World ORT had collected $180,000 from its Western partners. Settling into Berlin head-quarters in 1921, it rolled out an ambitious program to fundraise in the West, cooperate with the JDC, Ica, and local communal institutions, and extend its activities to Russian Jewish emigres, not just within Soviet Russia. In the mid-1920s, World ORT worked with its two "sister organizations," OSE and Emigdirect, to fundraise and grow their programs. It also sought government and municipal assistance to help Jews integrate into the economic life of their countries, which highlighted the ambivalent nature of such a transnational organization, without an obvious government to call upon.[12]

JDC reconstructive work got underway on a large, institutional scale in 1922. That year, the JDC funded programs in Lithuania, Latvia, Czechoslovakia, Hungary, Turkey, Palestine, Austria, Romania, and Poland. These were mostly run by ORT and Ica, allowing the JDC to maintain only a light presence in these regions. Across South East Europe, however, in the former Ottoman Empire, in Constantinople (Istanbul), Salonika (Thessaloniki), and Smyrna (Izmir), the JDC struggled to switch from relief to reconstruction. Given years of war, partitions, and multilayered refugee crises, and without a prewar tradition of receiving international Jewish philanthropy, it was not so simple to absorb these regions into a European reconstruction program. Meanwhile, Joseph Rosen was creating an entirely separate plan in the USSR, based on agricultural colonization, that would rival the Jewish reconstruction program for Europe. And in Palestine, Zionist philanthropies and the Zionist labor movement focused, as they had since the previous century, on expanding Jewish trade and agricultural opportunities, but this was a specific state-building program that was not the focus of Jewish humanitarianism. This first section of the chapter will explore housing construction before moving to trade education and then agrarianization projects.

Rebuilding the Shtetl

The sheer loss of housing, businesses, baths, and other communal institutions in war, revolution, and pogroms – the destruction of the shtetl itself – meant that alongside addressing refugees, health, and children starting in 1921, the JDC sought to rebuild infrastructure in East Central Europe. Jewish reconstruction began and sometimes ended with a home rebuilding project carried out across East Central Europe to restore damaged private homes, to rebuild the spaces for future Jewish life at home in the diaspora.

Independent, small-scale reconstructive efforts began around 1920, with Jewish communities and JDC representatives organizing housing loans. Formal housing reconstruction started in Romania – this was the first reconstruction project after the war, out of which the larger program grew. Alexander Landesco, JDC representative in Romania, made a study of destroyed Jewish property, especially housing, and then tightly connected the revival of Jewish credit organizations to the financing of house rebuilding projects through local loans.

In Lithuania, the occupying German army destroyed Jewish homes in 1915, and as early as 1916, Jewish returnees who were evacuated into the Russian Empire returned to find themselves homeless. Repairing and rebuilding homes remained at the top of the JDC's agenda in 1922, when this task absorbed three quarters of the JDC budget for reconstruction in Lithuania. In Salonika, the great fire of 1917 had wiped out 17,000 homes in the trading quarter – meaning Jews were its primary victims in this very Jewish city. Smyrna's 1922 fire destroyed wealthier Jewish homes located in the European quarter. Deviating from its stated position of war-relief organization, the JDC provided rebuilding loans in the mid-1920s to these fire-devasted places.

Poland also saw the rebuilding of destroyed homes starting in late 1922, despite technical and legal difficulties. The JDC lobbied successfully to convince the Polish Ministry of Reconstruction to focus on urban spaces, not just rural places, in its program, which enabled Jewish home rebuilders to take advantage of the government's provision of building materials. In a few months' time, 2,000 homes were built. Still, by the time the JDC intervened to make the Polish government's reconstruction programs accessible to Jews, both the Polish Reconstruction Bank and the budget set aside for this purpose were nearly exhausted – so Jewish reconstruction happened largely apart from that effort. Yet the JDC also found itself absorbed into the Polish reconstruction program, advancing money within that system for reconstruction loans for Jewish housing. Loans made to war sufferer homeowners to rebuild were undertaken by local Jewish credit cooperatives when possible, and in some cases, to create new local building cooperatives. In this way, a shtetl completely razed by war was able to rise again, through JDC houses.

Yet the housing problem was enmeshed with the unresolvable refugee issue and the mass abandonment of the shtetl for urban places during the war. A pilot program in one shtetl could not simply create every razed shtetl anew, though partial investment could be enough to spur the rest of a town into action and provide a solid foundation for rebuilding a given locale. Nor did newly urbanized Jews necessarily find themselves willing and able to return wholesale to their shtetlekh. The JDC and its derivative cooperatives might have been able to finance thousands of rebuilt homes but could not build millions. It was also particularly difficult to find a way to house repatriates who had been tenants, not homeowners, of no-longer-existent buildings, in places such as Lithuania, even though the JDC would rather support poorer than better-off Jews. As such, the JDC prioritized home rebuilding in places that were more than 50 percent destroyed, more than 40 percent Jewish, and that had an ongoing stream of homeless repatriated refugees.[13]

The dearth of stable, safe housing played a large role in the continued precariousness of Jewish life in this era. This chapter picks up after the initial project of reconstruction, which greatly improved the lives it touched without reaching the vast majority of homeless Jews. Ambition aside, the JDC was not able to rebuild the shtetl; this had to be about building for a different future.

Handicrafts and Industries

Vocational education was integral to the reconstruction program. The goal was to raise the standards of Jewish artisans and manufacturers and extend trade education to the Jewish masses to create more opportunities for Jews to be in "productive" occupations, while taking into consideration "the special needs of the Jewish population." Since the nineteenth century, Jewish philanthropists had embraced trade education. This was because in the maskilic mindset, trade education was the physical enactment of productivization, which promised to create a Jewish working class. Therefore, beginning in 1922, the JDC, Ica, and ORT cooperated to set up technical schools, specialized workshops, and private establishments for training children. Many existed before the war but had to be rebuilt and equipped by the JDC, ORT, and Ica. The JDC, having no intention to run its own schools, worked to expand trade education while Ica and ORT were left to run schools. The JDC was content to provide land and buildings, paying up to 50 percent of the total cost of a given school, as long as local communities fundraised and contributed to their construction. For schools maintained by Ica, the JDC helped pay for equipment. And since the impoverished, postrevolutionary ORT had no funds of its own, it continued with JDC funding.[14]

This vocational training program was entwined with the Joint's work for Jewish children and youth. Unlike the ARA or the ARC, the Near East Relief (NER) similarly ended up with a long-term reconstruction program that focused on trade schools, especially for orphans.[15] For the JDC, trade education was understood as the "most important work of the child care activity," which it hoped would enable children to be self-supporting.[16] American Jewish philanthropists, as both American Progressives and heirs to the Haskalah, not surprisingly supported the idea that diligence and hard work were necessary for poor children.[17] As the JDC struggled with the perceived moral obligation to continue helping Jewish children despite its simultaneous goal of leaving Europe as quickly as possible, its long-term approach to helping children was through productive training. Orphans, in particular, were to receive vocational training, and the JDC even helped some children move to cities to receive it.[18] In the 1920s, it seemed the best way to get orphans and children without sufficient family support off philanthropic hands, and quickly.

The JDC prioritized moving children off welfare and to independent status through vocational work as quickly as possible – like the NER. Hoping to limit its long-term involvement in child welfare without having moral qualms, the JDC settled on age fourteen as the marker for the end of childhood and its attendant benefits, agreeing upon the Polish legal standard dating from 1919 that mandated education until age fourteen.[19] Unlike the JDC, the ARA started with fourteen as the age until which children could qualify for their feeding programs, but ended up raising the age limit, feeling that fourteen was too young to fend for oneself to cover basic needs.[20] The ARA, however, never expanded far beyond feeding programs, so the conditions are not entirely comparable. The goal for the JDC was that, by fourteen, Jewish adolescents should have finished primary education and should be prepared to earn their own wages in a productive way. This strategy seemed so durable and sound that, while liquidating all other forms of institutionalized child welfare after 1925, the JDC prepared to educate young Jews in various trades indefinitely, and by 1929, it was the only form of childcare the JDC was willing to undertake, as set forth by Bernard Kahn.[21]

Despite clear pressure from JDC New York, Ica, ORT, and local communities to point youth toward vocational education and set up trade schools, in 1922, JDC social workers in Europe debated their relative importance. They regarded them as the JDC's "stepchild," never receiving proper attention or money. While frustrated at letting ORT take the lead, social workers felt that the schools turned out too many half-baked artisans who would never be competitive; that orphanages receiving support simply hoped for side income, making pretenses at education when there was dubious educational content; and that sinking resources into a project the Jews had been focused on for centuries to little effect was futile. They wanted to provide something new that would change Jewish trade education and give it an "American stamp."[22] Still, trade school was seen as one of the most critical long-term investments Jewish international humanitarians could make to ensure a future for Jewish youth, and thus, a Jewish future sum told. ORT and Ica were happy to press onward with this familiar project dressed in interwar clothes. In Poland, it seemed necessary to create pathways for Jews in manual labor so they could take part in the rapidly industrializing economy and overcome economic discrimination.[23] And the last thing the JDC wanted was to grow a competitor organization in ORT, which proved itself good at fundraising – several times in the 1920s, the JDC paid ORT to stop fundraising separately.[24] By the middle of the decade, however, the JDC, less interested in maintaining trade schools, left this task to the transformed ORT and Ica.[25]

In 1923, Kahn listed just 1,736 orphans in Poland receiving vocational education out of the 10,067 attending some kind of school.[26] In early 1924, there were 65 trade schools with almost 4,500 students.[27] By 1925, claimed Kahn, the JDC had supported the training of 3,409 children throughout East Central Europe, 1,655 of whom had already become self-supporting.[28] In 1926, the JDC supported 121 orphanages, 20 vocational schools, 54 professional schools and workshops, and 43 summer colonies, assisting a total of 18,891 orphans.[29] The popularity of the new Beis Yakov schools for religious girls in Poland seemed to indicate that even forward-looking Orthodox Jewish leaders accepted the precepts of productivization and were willing to modernize by adding vocational training to a religious upbringing.[30] The Tsisho Yiddishist schools also moved in this direction.[31] In rural regions like East Slovakia and Sub-Carpathia, the JDC made an effort in 1922 to establish three such (sewing) schools and "workshops" from nothing. In Libau, Latvia (Liepāja), the JDC bent over backward to establish a trade school due to premonitions that the port town was dying.[32] In Palestine, too, orphans were pushed toward technical education, and the Palestine Orphan Committee happily celebrated success when hundreds of its charges became self-supporting in the trades they had been taught.[33]

Even in the USSR, internats housing Jewish children were equipped with trade workshops by Evobshchestkom and supplied by the JDC.[34] Rosen reported in August 1922 that more than 120 trade and agricultural schools were operating in Soviet Russia under ORT, Ica, or local communities. That year, Rosen had $200,000 allotted to him by the JDC to provide vocational training. Ica was an important partner since it also received permission to work in the USSR.[35] This was for 42 schools with about 4,000 youth trainees, including garment workers, iron workers, shoemakers, carpenters, and was designed to advance new fields with imported Western equipment. ORT continued to support artisans in cities by importing Western machinery and tools and providing instructors to advise artisans and help them acquire new skills. ORT worked with Soviet authorities to establish new industrial undertakings that would include Jews, and as Rosen argued, the local population trusted ORT. It also continued to support vocational schools, even after these schools were absorbed into the state, by providing after-hours training in Yiddish for teachers.[36] The JDC did not trust ORT enough to turn over work to it as its contractor, but the JDC did continue to provide appropriations on the scale of tens of thousands of dollars per year – much less than the JDC gave Rosen.[37] Once Agro-Joint was established in the USSR, about which there will be more in the following section, the JDC was able to support vocational training for farmers on its colonies but also for Jews in urban centers in Ukraine and Belorussia.[38]

To emphasize the ways in which Jewish children were being trained to become productive, independent citizens of their new nation states, some of these training programs focused on teaching children the handicrafts of their respective countries. In Romania, for example, Jewish children learned a "native art" – weaving brightly colored rugs, and to make horse harnesses like Ruthenian peasants, gold Viennese cushions, and Bulgarian inlaid wood furniture.[39] But artisanal training was not easy to carry out, since Jews were not part of the guild systems in most countries and it was hard to find Jewish artisans to teach the younger generation.[40] Furthermore, who were Jews to make the "native" luxury goods of their neighbors? The market was already saturated given that most luxuries were wiped out by war. Still, Jewish organizations seemed intent on creating a future in which Jews could make claims on "native" national cultures, which were being reworked in any case.

One exceptional school, the Jewish Girls Vocational School in Lwów (Lemberg), made "Jewish native art." Students produced textiles, ritual objects, and banners for Jewish professional organizations. It was run by Dr. Cecylja Klaftenowa, a PhD in zoology, who had served on the local Jewish relief committee during the war and ran its soup kitchen. She created the local branch of CENTOS and started a crafts workshop for girls from which the Jewish Girls Vocational School grew. It was a handicrafts school filled, unsurprisingly, with refugee youth. According to Klaftenowa, the purpose of the school was educational, not merely to train future employees. Students learned art, plus a mix of standard secular and Jewish education, in Polish, and the in-house Rimon Studio allowed graduating students to transition into professional artisanry. A mix of feminist, patriotic, and Jewish values underpinned this school. Handicrafts potentially bought these women independence, while keeping them within Judaism and away from factories and revolutionary spaces that appealed to poor young Jewish women. The Jewish current was ever present in the art they produced. But it was also remarkably feminist and subversive to have a girls' school producing original Jewish ritual items and teaching girls to develop the genre according to their artistic sensibilities. This school was modernizing Judaic culture through the modernization of the production process. It seems unlikely, however, that anyone would have expected the economy to support a huge expansion in Judaica artisans, and this particular school was indeed rare.[41]

Certainly, most programs were not dedicated to "native art." Rather, the overwhelming majority of trade schools focused on teaching "modern" handicrafts, like building buses, making prosthetics, and using sewing machines. Even if sewing was hardly a new trade, sewing schools had machines, and Jewish women were using the latest techniques and fashions. Gender norms shifted in this process; girls filled the most artisanal roles, doing fine artistic work, including Judaica, while boys created machines and other items with wheels. Previously, most Jewish women in handicrafts were seamstresses, while men had a far greater range. Now men were prepared for the factory, and women were trained as more independent artisans connected to "native" traditions, Jewish and otherwise. As part of the productivization and enrooting of Jewish youth in their new national cultures and economies, it seemed that gendered social reform brought Jewish socioeconomic roles in line with gendered roles in their broader societies. Except for a few spots within the educational realm, such as Klaftenowa's or Beis Yakov schools, girls and women were made secondary objects of Jewish economic reform as it was internationalized, rather than maintaining their role as central participants in its transformation.

Deeply proud of its productivization work with children, the JDC organized a special childcare exhibition in Berlin in September 1925, intended to exhibit the strides it had made in trade education. The exhibition opened at the JDC Berlin headquarters on Knesebeckstrasse to a large crowd of ambassadors, including the American ambassador and ambassadors from various Eastern European countries, Jewish organizational representatives, and government officials. This was not

Figure 6.1 Auto mechanic trade school in Czechoslovakia. Boys
learning to build an automobile at a JDC-supported auto mechanic
trade school in Czechoslovakia. In the JDC's 1926 "Child Care
Department" album.
(YUA, Wiernik Collection, Box 8, Folder 1)

the only exhibition of this kind – as early as 1923, children's artwork went
on display in Central Europe, including in Vienna, and in the United
States to fundraise for humanitarian child feeding purposes.[42] In Berlin,
seven booths were arranged inside a large room with a Victorian glass
ceiling in what appeared to be a cross between a teenage art show, with
plaster bust sculptures and photographs bearing the names and bio-
graphical information of their respective child artists, and a serious
display of artisanal handicrafts from lace, to rugs, dresses, harnesses,
furniture, and synagogue ornaments – the latter, the exhibit's centerpiece,
produced by the Jewish Girls Vocational School of Lwów. The statistical
division booth was lined with large, hand-drawn maps displaying JDC
activities and data regarding its philanthropic activity. It recalled both the
home industries exhibitions and colonial exhibitions popular across
Europe at the turn of the century. Kahn reported that Jacob Gould
Schurman, American ambassador to Germany, expressed his admiration
for the results achieved and his pride for his "Jewish co-citizens."[43]

Harriet Lowenstein oversaw the exhibit's tour to the United States, with stops in New York's Grand Central Palace and in Philadelphia in 1927, at great expense.[44]

The traveling exhibit included a photo album of the JDC's child welfare activities, beginning with mug shots of tiny, sad war orphans and moving to photos of children engaged in trades, being fed at their tidy orphanages, and squinting in the sun at summer colonies. It ended with mug shots of war orphans showing off their successful trades and businesses. The Berlin office sent about 170 of these books to America.[45] The effort and dollars behind this childcare exhibit indicates that the JDC was particularly proud of putting orphans into trades and summer colonies – and collecting data. The exhibit's narrative portrayed a Jewish childhood in Eastern Europe that had become more sheltered and sanitary, despite the war, with children passing successfully into adulthood through Jewish self-help activities.

These handicrafts could also travel. The children had no chance of getting to America, with the doors to immigration firmly shut in the 1920s. But the handicrafts they produced could, and they could attract donations from American benefactors, Jewish and probably Christian. The goods were not sold in the United States; in fact it was difficult for the Joint to liquidate the exhibition. In general, the JDC was much more engaged in creating Jewish artisans than creating meaning with handicrafts or generating any kind of market. Material handicrafts and the transformation they embodied were a symbol of the progress of the JDC's entire humanitarian project and goals of restructuring of Jewish life, connecting donors to its long-term success.

These trade schools taught children to sew with fast machines, put together automobiles, weave beautiful rugs, and design intricate synagogue textiles. The actual material being generated seems entirely beside the point, except for perhaps in the case of the Lwów girls' school, where the handicraft had deep Jewish meaning. But did that also mean that the only "Jewish" native art could lie in the religious sphere? Probably not, as the diversity of these Jewish schools shows. Though the choice of craft demonstrated modernity or various forms of belonging, such choice seemed fleeting in terms of the organizations' understandings of their own programs. How students themselves understood their work or their handiwork is unclear. Skill-building and a broader education were important, and students wanted to attend these schools in the interwar period, more than they had before the war. Their training seemed to provide them with something valuable, more so than standard Polish or traditional Jewish schooling. Specifically, Jewish trade schools allowed Jews to observe the Sabbath, which instantly made Jewish trade schools preferable to public trade schools. In Hungary, Jewish trade schools allowed Jews to continue training in trades when state schools adopted *numerus clausus*. The process was central and optimistic, demonstrating a way for Jews to become part of their nation-states, culturally and economically, without assimilating and losing their Jewishness.

The head of JDC reconstruction in Poland, Michael Freund, declared the artisan the "most productive element of the Jewish population." He noted that it was important that artisans be able to buy raw material and tools and find a market to sell their finished products. Supporting artisans was not limited to children – equipment was necessary for established artisans to take up their trade once again. In fact, ORT reconstituted itself as the World ORT Union through an international tool and equipment fundraising campaign.[46] And thus, the creation of schools and handicrafts alone was not enough; artisans' cooperatives were needed to organize and finance materials and sales.[47]

Agriculture

Before the war, most Jews in the Pale of Settlement were not allowed to farm land. During the war, artisans and merchants had no market for their wares, but food was scarce and land was plentiful. Jews in shtetlekh began to farm during the war. After the war, legal restrictions returned but so did the dream of Jewish farming. Jewish elites felt that they could not let the "spontaneous movement of the Jews towards the land" go to waste.[48] These elites were heirs to Haskalah thought and late nineteenth-century initiatives that held that a return to the land would develop the bodies, minds, and spirits of Eastern European Jews, lifting them from economic and moral decay. In other words, Western Jewish elites thought that agrarianization would reverse poverty and political victimization among poor Eastern European Jews.[49] More generally, soon after the war, rural populations and agricultural workers became international issues, especially under the auspices of the International Labour Organization. The potential sociopolitical power of peasants, especially in the wake of the Russian Revolution, was apparent, as were the possibilities for rural land management.[50] Yet, this idea of agrarianization *as social reform* remained unique to Jewish humanitarians, as other rehabilitative humanitarian organizations such as the NER sought to *maintain* and modernize an agricultural economy and prevent urbanization.[51]

In most cases, the JDC did not prioritize agrarianization. But since agrarianization offered some opportunity, it seemed worthy of some JDC support. Rural colonization projects within states, as a form of sociopolitical change, occurred elsewhere, not just among Jews. In particular, in the Soviet Union, agrarianization emerged as the main long-term opportunity for the JDC to remain involved in the country. Interwar Jewish agrarianization thus built on a process that had been developing among Jewish philanthropies for the previous five decades, now adapted to a new project in Crimea and drawing on a wealth of contemporary ideas about agricultural colonization. But in East Central Europe, the idea of Jewish agrarianization post-Pale was also something new, raising questions about the place of Jews within their new nation-states.

In East Central Europe, the JDC invested first in farmers who had farmed before the war, rather than on new colonization experiments, because of its limited interest in developing agricultural work beyond prewar levels. Ica and ORT, meanwhile, planned to expand agrarianization, and as the most interested parties, accepted the JDC funds and designs to do so. Ica and ORT possessed expertise and networks in philanthropic agrarianization, and the JDC followed its usual practice of supporting preexisting or home-grown initiatives where possible. ORT and the JDC cooperated closely; the JDC supported Jewish farming initiatives by extending hundreds of thousands of dollars in credit to the projects ORT had already undertaken. ORT further acted as the JDC's agent for agricultural loans in Poland and Lithuania. Indeed, the JDC recognized "there [was] only one organization who has the machinery to carry out special agricultural work, and that is the ORT."[52] ORT needed only funding – it already functioned as something of a producer cooperative, purchasing agricultural supplies in bulk.

Yet American Jews were not entirely outside their own realm of experience. Hias and other North American Jewish philanthropies closely linked to the JDC, especially the Industrial Removal Office (IRO) and the Jewish Agricultural Society (JAS), had been agrarianizing Eastern European Jewish immigrants within the United States. The JDC leaders and personnel Felix Warburg, Julius Rosenwald, Cyrus Adler, Lewis Strauss, Joseph Rosen, Boris Bogen, Morris Waldman, and others donated funding, directed or served on boards of, or acted in professional capacities for the IRO or the JAS. The JDC's links to Hias were personal and organizational. The JDC was able to deploy years of experience in American Jewish agrarianization with Agro-Joint in the USSR, as well as toward colonies in East Central Europe and Palestine. This included viewing agrarianization as reconstruction, not charity, and providing instruction from trained agronomists.[53] Agricultural colonies, like the rest of the JDC's work, were to be overseen by local offices whose workers made day-to-day decisions on their own.

Since Jews in prewar Austrian Galicia had owned agricultural land and farmed at rates that were at least double or more those in the Russian

Empire, this seemed an operable model to revive and possibly expand across East Central Europe. In Bessarabia, Romania, for example, the JDC worked to revive the prewar Jewish farming scene, in which Ica was involved. This involved bringing in the cooperative banking union it was organizing to credit farmers but also establishing a legal aid bureau. The legal aid bureau would ensure that Jewish farmers were included in the land redistribution process, since in 1922, the Romanian government began redistributing land it seized from private estates. The JDC estimated that between 4,000 and 5,000 Jewish farmers were granted land, a turning point in Bessarabia that made agrarianization a significant economic force. Working together, JDC and Ica discovered that Jewish farmers had almost no equipment with which to work; hence the importance of extending credit so that the farmers could actually work their land. By 1923, these several thousand farmers were cultivating their land, directed by eighteen cooperatives in areas where they were concentrated, with Ica furnishing machinery and stock and guiding farmers to new forms of agricultural activity.[54]

Like other Jewish social welfare projects in which professionals circulated among humanitarian theaters, the same was true for agrarianization programs. In particular, many pre- and postwar agricultural colonies were founded to train Zionist pioneers (chalutzim) before they went to establish agricultural colonies in Palestine. Professionals and administrators trained and employed by European Jewish agricultural philanthropies also immigrated to Palestine, and in some cases, took up roles in the Zionist agricultural administration and the Histadrut (the institutionalized Zionist labor movement founded in 1920). In short, Eastern European Jews, although still funded by Western European Jews, had become transnational exporters of agricultural expertise by the 1920s.

Joseph Rosen and the JDC supported colonies, even Zionist ones, because they contributed to the productivization of the Jews.[55] Although ORT concentrated on territorialism, and in this way, seems ideologically to have had a strong connection to labor Zionism, the relationship between ORT and Zionist organizations was complicated. Chalutzim trained at ORT model farms or, more often, at Zionist training farms with ORT's support before emigrating to agricultural colonies in Palestine. Ultimately, ORT was a diasporist organization, despite sharing many practical goals and strategies with the Zionist movement. As such, ORT was happy for Zionist organizations to join it, as part of a diaspora movement – much like the JDC's own relationship to Zionism.

In Palestine, agricultural colonies were a long-standing form of practical Zionist work. Jewish bodies worked and developed the land using

Western technologies that Zionist philanthropies could import.[56] The Palestine-oriented branch of Ica, known as PICA, along with a variety of Zionist organizations, provided land, Jewish labor, and equipment; chalutzim had often trained on Zionist colonies in Europe. Meir Shfeye and Givat Hamoreh children's colonies in Palestine primarily focused on agricultural training for children, who were to govern and run their own farm settlements under adult supervision. In the Palestine-centric vision for Jewish life, agriculture was the primary way forward, rather than handicrafts or industry. All were about developing and productivizing the Jew and the body, but the humanitarian project was not especially concerned with this core Zionist program because it was about the imagined Palestine future, not reconstructing Jewish lives after war. There was little room for common ideological ground, even if the JDC, ORT, and Ica collectively worked on almost the same activities in Europe, drawing on shared practices, expertise, and labor. Still, the JDC-run Central Bank of the Palestine Economic Corporation, which will be covered later in this chapter, advanced credit to agricultural cooperatives, enabling them to build on purchases of seed, livestock, equipment, buildings, irrigation systems, and the like.

Although agrarianization was never the highest priority for any Jewish organization in East Central Europe in this period, in which trade and industry seemed the clearest path to Jewish modernization, this was not the case in the Soviet Union. There, agriculture was to be the main avenue to provide relief and future possibilities for Jews. Under Soviet authorities, complete civil rights were granted only to productive workers, and thus Jews had to be urgently moved out of petty trade and from owning small artisan workshops. At the end of the Russian Civil War, thousands of Jews managed to transition to the new order by obtaining plots of land attached to the shtetl as they organized themselves into agricultural cooperatives. ORT did what it could to support old and new agricultural colonies in Ukraine and Belorussia, even as fighting continued and Russia fragmented. ORT's foreign delegation fundraised for new farmers and sent seed, grain, and tools purchased from AEF surplus.[57]

The tide shifted toward Jewish agrarianization in the Soviet Union as a state-sponsored Jewish agricultural colonization project developed in Crimea. When Boris Bogen's cooperation with the ARA ended, Joseph Rosen took over the JDC's program in the USSR. Rosen, too, was involved as an ARA agronomist and informal JDC representative during the famine, but his expertise and networks took the JDC to an entirely different place within Soviet Russia. This collaboration between Jewish humanitarians, Soviet commissars, and American statesmen has been described as an "unlikely triangle" by Jonathan Dekel-Chen, on whose research this section relies.[58]

By 1922, Rosen had an enormous appropriation of $800,000 for agricultural work.[59] The JDC, wanting the World ORT Union and the Russian ORT to remain distinct, provided Rosen with JDC money instead of sending too much to ORT. In particular, it did not want to do anything that would help ORT to appear to be "legatees or successors of the J.D.C."[60] By spring 1922, remaining Jewish colonists in Ukraine were receiving American aid as JDC funds and material aid arrived. The colonists creatively traded them for agricultural goods and borrowed against promises of future donations to secure Soviet seeds. Rosen used the allocation to bring in American tractors and tools, import high-yield grain and breeding stock, and assist settlers with land development. Ica joined in funding the new Agricultural Commission, sending grain seed with the Nansen Action, for example, and then vine shoots from France to develop viniculture. Western expertise and equipment allowed the Jewish colonists to make new products and make them available at faraway markets. This aroused suspicion; the matter was discussed within the Evsektsiia (the Jewish section of the Party).[61]

Rosen and Bogen convinced the rest of the JDC to embark on a massive project: Beginning in 1923–24, Rosen launched the Joint Agricultural Corporation of the American Jewish Joint Distribution Committee (Agro-Joint). Seeing the chalutzim's agricultural communes in Crimea, they were convinced that agrarianization of the Jewish masses could work under proper conditions. And addressing the crisis of Soviet Jewry required creative solutions. Agro-Joint replaced the JDC Committee on Russia, taking over all Russia-related work. Reaching Soviet Jews with any large-scale humanitarian activity required bravery.

The JDC had to try to function legally within a chaotic country, with which the United States still had no formal diplomatic relations, and without the buffer of the ARA. Agro-Joint offered a way to bridge the divide between capitalist humanitarians (JDC) and the Bolsheviks. For the Kremlin, continued cooperation with the JDC meant a window to the United States would remain open allowing the acquisition of American technical expertise and products. Not to mention that both late Tsarist Russia and Bolshevik ideology aimed to productivize impoverished Jews from the Pale. The NEP was well underway by 1923, meaning that the chances of JDC success in the Soviet Union were much higher than a few years prior. Although agrarianization was hardly at the top of the agenda, the JDC would have broad access to Soviet Jews without having to operate through the Friends, the ARA, Evobshchestkom, or ORT. With several years of experience negotiating with Soviet authorities behind them, and Joseph Rosen's rekindling of revolutionary friendships from his youth, which now linked him to medium-level comrades in the Soviet administration, the JDC was ready to try to renegotiate a deal with the Soviets that would work better than the Fisher-Pine Agreement of 1920. Starting in 1924, Agro-Joint signed a series of contracts with the Kremlin that institutionalized and expanded colonization, with Soviet authorities providing free land, plus transportation, tax exemption, and fuel.

Agro-Joint leadership had clear ideas about what to do when starting new colonies in Crimea. They knew that: The ideal starting size was 30–50 families; Jewish farmers would agree to take on daring projects that had a comparative advantage in a region full of traditional farmers who found new ventures unappealing; Jewish farmers needed winter employment; and reducing social and cultural isolation was essential to retain colonists. How to finance the colonies through loans was also at the center of JDC thinking: Credit cooperatives would provide low-interest loans. This fit the rest of the JDC's program and seemed like it would prevent defaults on loans, a persistent problem in previous Jewish agrarianization efforts. Rosen hired the sons of JAS colonists in America

Figure 6.2 *On the Jewish Fields of the Ukraine* by Issachar Ryback. This particular sketch, "Fetching Water," was part of the artist's booklet of images portraying everyday agricultural life in the new Agro-Joint colonies in Crimea.
(JDC, Album-17_Ukraine-1926_050)

as instructors for the colonies, while most Russian-Jewish personnel and managers had experience with Jewish colonies in Ukraine and had been trained or involved in ORT or Ica agrarianization programs.[62]

Agro-Joint was not alone; Zionist agricultural cooperatives continued to exist in the Soviet Union until the authorities became suspicious of their nationalism. By the mid-1920s, World ORT had an income of nearly $1 million over three years, but over 60 percent came from Americans, and of that, half was from the JDC. To get ORT to stop raising money in America, the JDC agreed to support ORT's projects in the USSR, where the focus was to connect agricultural cooperatives and artisans to Western Jewish funding to import tools of all kinds. It used a remittance-like program for sending and distributing domestic and agricultural implements. ORT also vaguely endorsed the Soviet plan for Jewish colonization in the Far East, in Birobidzhan, once it was announced in 1928.[63] ORT's successful colonization work was like "a modest version of Agro-Joint."[64]

The JDC provided $16 million for Agro-Joint – a sum much larger than any other Jewish philanthropy or the Soviet state provided. Finally, Agro-Joint could put significant resources toward Soviet Jews. Given that this was how the JDC spent its money for Soviet Jewry as a whole, the enormous sum is less surprising. This was *the* JDC's effort to reconstruct Soviet Jews, with trade education, loans, child welfare, and health bundled into the Agro-Joint program in the USSR. Between its establishment in 1924 and its end in 1937, Agro-Joint employed 3,000 workers at its peak in offices throughout Crimea and southern Ukraine, established and supervised 200 new colonies, helped thirty preexisting colonies, and provided guidance, equipment, and loans to 200,000 farmers over one million acres of land. Like the JDC did in most of its work outside Russia, Agro-Joint outfitted these farms with state-of-the-art, mechanized equipment and taught advanced techniques. With Joseph Rosen as expert agronomist and JDC personnel, Agro-Joint pioneered experimental techniques that had not always been tested in the United States, using implements and practices that were even more cutting-edge than what the JDC provided in East Central Europe. It helped that American businessmen hoped to sell their latest equipment to Russian farmers and that Agro-Joint was the most reliable potential customer.[65]

As JDC New York leaders visited Agro-Joint colonies and met with Soviet statesmen, JDC attitudes warmed to the USSR. JDC delegations returned energized and convinced that the Kremlin was committed to solving the Jewish Question via Agro-Joint. This position on US–Soviet relations was controversial. Among American Jews, Zionists wondered why money would go to Crimea that could otherwise go to Palestine, and considered all Russians, including the Bolsheviks, inherently antisemitic. In typical fashion, the JDC was criticized from across the Jewish spectrum for not negotiating a better deal. Jews were fundamentally divided as to whether it made sense for Russian Jews to leave the Pale of Settlement and strike out en masse for Crimea, which was unknown territory for Jews. Ica refused to commit to Agro-Joint despite the JDC's exhortations, frustrating the JDC and prompting its 1925 United Jewish Campaign for another $15 million.[66] JDC leadership was not naive about the limits of solving the Jewish Question. Rosen said while promoting Agro-Joint in 1925, "it would be a ridiculous contention to claim that any single measure could untie the complex agglomeration of economic, social, political and cultural knots that go to make up the so-called Jewish problem." Yet there were precious few alternatives, especially in the USSR, so all the JDC could do was try and try again, and as the United Jewish Campaign put it: "Give them a chance to help themselves."[67]

The JDC's relations with the USSR were particularly sensitive because of the charged public debate occurring within the Jewish community and everywhere outside it. For example, Ukrainian emigres attacked the Soviet regime by inveighing against the JDC for plotting against the Ukrainian people. The JDC had learned from its experience managing its image around Soviet relations, and this time avoided confrontation and deflected criticism.[68] Furthermore, Evobshchestkom had dissolved, and David Dubrowsky's disruptive American office had closed.[69] The Soviets had no reason to undermine the JDC. In fact, the Kremlin probably overestimated Agro-Joint and what real influence the JDC had in America. In an antisemitic, fantastical projection of power onto a Jewish organization, the Kremlin granted the JDC more power.

Although the JDC downplayed its role as much as possible within the United States, Agro-Joint was cautiously diplomatic, far beyond its initial agreements with the Kremlin. Agro-Joint mediated between the colonies and Soviet agencies, insulating settlers from Soviet rule. It also assumed informal administrative authority for Jewish farmers and non-Jewish peasantry where it worked. And indeed, it acted as a window for the Soviets to the United States, bringing American businessmen to the USSR and improved diplomatic relations. The Soviet press, in turn, publicized Agro-Joint as a conduit to Washington, and Maxim Litvinov approached James Rosenberg in 1926 with a plan to repay Soviet debts in exchange for diplomatic recognition. Such requests continued through the next few years. Felix Warburg and Rosenberg, who served respectively as JDC executive director and president of Agro-Joint, became ardent spokesmen for US diplomatic recognition of the USSR for practical reasons, though the State Department did not respond.[70]

This institutional behavior was also not unprecedented. Although the JDC resolutely claimed that it was nonpolitical, it was always a political actor. Its behavior was closer to diplomacy and social welfare advocacy than congressional or partisan politics. It was much simpler for the JDC, however, to shift public focus toward its humanitarian, philanthropic, and productivist goals over political connections and whatever Soviet influence it might have held. The JDC continued its long-standing practice of remaining within legal bounds, minimizing risks by checking with Washington for approval before taking action in Russia. Though the State Department never gave its approval, it agreed not to intervene and was always apprised of what the JDC was doing in the USSR. State Department Russianists opposed diplomatic recognition of the USSR, while officials worried that Agro-Joint was ill-conceived and harbored doubts about the JDC's purpose and diplomatic tendencies. The contacts that Boris Bogen, and the JDC generally, made via cooperation with the ARA, along with professional and political contacts that JDC New York had always cultivated, continued to provide necessary nodes of support throughout the US bureaucracy and in other elite institutions. In return, the State Department garnered crucial intelligence about conditions in Soviet Russia through Agro-Joint, tracking its activities and debriefing Rosen and other JDC personnel, just as it had done with the ARA and still did with other private American businesses in Russia. The JDC supplied expert, durable information on rural Russia that was not available anywhere else.[71]

Agro-Joint provided unmatched services, offering integrated agricultural operations to an entire region. Jewish life thrived within Agro-Joint colonies more than anywhere in the USSR. Colonists had a more prosperous, shielded life than their neighboring peasants, who were directly exposed to Soviet brutality and economic conditions without Agro-Joint's insulating effect. While there was never more than 9 percent of Soviet Jews working as colonists at any given time, Agro-Joint settled more Jews on Russian soil than had been settled in Palestine in twenty-five years.[72] Agro-Joint's successes forged a new Jewish identity in Russia and allowed the JDC as a whole to stay involved in Jewish life in Soviet Russia for many years, providing a full range of services to all kinds of Jews through the Agro-Joint framework. Dekel-Chen's eloquent book makes it clear that Agro-Joint was a central, durable feature of Jewish international development work. When Rosen and Agro-Joint ceased operations in 1937, as the JDC focused on seeking refuge from the Nazi threat outside Central and Eastern Europe, it left behind eighty-six Jewish colonies prospering in Crimea. Former colonists ascended ladders in Soviet society. Agro-Joint's colonies seemed to be on track to solve the Jewish Question in the USSR. But in the autumn of 1941, the Crimean agrarianization project ended abruptly with Nazi conquest of the colonies.[73]

Developing Jewish Society: Microcredit Cooperatives

When the Great War began in 1914, American Jews reacted to the suffering of fellow Jews in the only way they could: sending cash through the neutral US diplomatic pouch and Jewish banking and institutional networks for humanitarian purposes. The banking and merchant networks that linked the Jewish world also enabled philanthropy to move seamlessly through those networks. The JDC and Hias made ample use of this built-in feature of Jewish philanthropy since the war years, exchanging currencies and funding projects through trusted Jewish banking houses. As we have seen, most Jews experienced this direct humanitarian connection to the banking world through "individual relief" (remittances, food packages, emigration cases, financial adoption). There was, however, a final and crucial program of the Joint Distribution Committee that utilized these same networks, launched by Jewish American bankers and future politicians: the Lehman brothers. This new American Joint Reconstruction Foundation and the credit cooperative movement it nurtured represented a remarkable fusion of postwar Central and Eastern European economic nationalist tactics, Jewish self-help ideology deriving from the nineteenth century, and the security of American Jewish banking elites in the new American international financial center. Rather than individual relief, it was about individual development. It was, in other words, an extremely innovative proto-international development policy, unique to Jewish humanitarianism.

The credit cooperative idea grew out of medieval guild *kassas*.[74] In the late nineteenth century, cooperatives were founded across rural Europe as a means of self-help, or mutual aid, for farmers and artisans. The principle was simple: A group of people jointly contributed to help one another in times of difficulty. If others wanted to open an account with the cooperative, they had to contribute to the capital by buying membership shares. Although the cooperative *movement* was international, members of a given cooperative typically belonged to the same ethnic group. As such, cooperatives could be used not only as economic self-help but also for national liberation movements against elites, such as in Prussian Poland.[75] Jews, too, built credit cooperatives in the nineteenth century, some 700 of them within the Pale of Settlement. Most received support from Ica, which consulted with them and provided credit but did not actually manage them.[76]

After the Great War, new nationalist state economies absorbed cooperatives, and cooperatives became tools for segregation along national lines. Providing economic support for individuals in an ethnic group, cooperatives offered ideal conditions for pursing ethnic aims. Minorities could make use of cooperatives, which offered a stable organizational structure, against the states in which they lived. And so ethnic Germans used cooperatives across the new states of East Central Europe. They were subsidized by a hidden German state policy to support ethnic Germans living in territories lost by Germany in the war.[77] Jews in Transylvania, Romania, in particular, noted the organized mutual aid and banks of other minorities before the war, and the way these banks held together minorities.[78] It was clear that cooperatives could also work to keep Jews, who were squeezed out of nationalist economies across East Central Europe, economically viable. Yet Jews did not have a state to subsidize Jewish cooperatives.[79] Here, then, entered the Joint Distribution Committee, which followed the German example as a model.[80]

Alexander Landesco, who spearheaded JDC reconstruction efforts after the war through his initiatives in Romania, counted the revival of 24 out of 37 prewar credit cooperatives in Bessarabia by 1921. From these initial efforts, the JDC created a federated Jewish cooperative banking system in Poland by 1922 and deployed the American Joint Reconstruction Foundation in 1924 to make it sustainable in the long term, from both American and Polish perspectives. In 1921, the Palestine Cooperative Company, in partnership with the JDC, set up a similar cooperative system to develop the Jewish economy in Palestine, becoming the Palestine Economic Corporation in 1925. American leadership of the American Joint Reconstruction Foundation and the Palestine Economic Corporation and its predecessor organizations overlapped, sharing many goals and cultural assumptions. These were exclusively male domains, even though presumably women were frequently, if indirectly, cooperative members through their husbands.

American Jews were no strangers to the cooperative movement; Leonard Robinson, European Director for JDC Reconstruction, boasted in his 1914 *A Credit Union Primer* that the only American credit union among farmers had been established by the Jewish Agricultural and Industrial Aid Society.[81] Working-class Jews had already been organizing cooperatives throughout Eastern Europe and the Americas. Elite, liberal German and Italian Jews had approved and proposed the cooperative movement, especially in credit union form, as a liberal alternative to radical socialism in the nineteenth century.[82] Ica had supported cooperatives in the Pale before the war. Elite American Jews, familiar with the European cooperative movement and old world struggles to improve the

Jewish condition via cooperatives, were already sponsors of Jewish cooperative farming projects in the Americas. Integrating cooperatives as part of a new international Jewish humanitarianism proved a small leap in imagination.

Other humanitarians did not conceive of cooperative banking as a tool: It was a distinctively American Jewish invention. Functioning alongside state welfare provision on a number of fronts, cooperatives became a manifestation of transnational Jewish self-determination. Despite the existence of dollar diplomacy, in-kind food and health-related humanitarianism, and occasional trade education provided by other American humanitarians in this era, the creation of long-term, transnational financial networks was not in the "standard" humanitarian repertoire. Nor was it in the standard Jewish repertoire. Reliance on business and instilling a work ethos to generate progress, wealth, and independence came from the American Puritan tradition. Furthermore, it was an American commitment to the decentralization of the economy, in which a mosaic of small economic units contributed to the development of the economy as a whole, that was applied to this Jewish, cooperative, grassroots humanitarianism.[83] Similarly, the cooperatives' democratic principles, local nature, and pluralist aims embodied the American Progressive ethos. Indeed, a particular goal of reconstruction was "to leave with [European Jews], as a guide in their work, the American social vision." The JDC felt it would be remembered not by the concrete contributions of money or institutions but by having taught European Jews the methods of American social work: how to organize efficiently for common cause.[84]

Some years later, philosopher Horace Kallen wrote definitively:

[T]he source and stimulus of the co-operative interest among Jews in Palestine and in Europe ... is American. Co-operation was laid down as a principle of Palestinian development in the "Pittsburgh Program" adopted by the Zionist Organization of America in 1917 and later implemented by the Palestine Development Corporation. In Poland and elsewhere it was fostered, particularly in the matter of credit, by the Joint Distribution Committee. But Jews have not been disposed spontaneously to employ co-operative association in large numbers.[85]

Like a central bank with transnational reach, the cooperative movement allowed Jews to compete economically as individuals but also as a national minority group. The point was not profit, but rather to enable impoverished loanees to eventually become self-supporting and eligible for ordinary commercial credit. It allowed Jews to do any productive work they deemed fit, and not to be chained to certain forms of labor. In these ways, the cooperative movement was a forerunner of microfinance, which emerged in the 1990s. At least in Poland, trade cooperatives could become a legal entity if no refusal was made within two months of registration in a district court, making it just the kind of everyday business activity that would stay out of political controversies but quietly allow the JDC to restructure Jewish life. In contrast to credit and trade cooperatives, the JDC hesitated to support consumer cooperatives, worrying that these often became overtly political, even while counteracting some of the problems that depreciation created for credit cooperatives.[86] These internationally credited credit cooperatives were experimental, and, as Kallen acknowledged, "varied so radically from established, standard, co-operative practice."[87]

Cooperation beyond Relief

Prior to the war, there were many credit cooperatives, Jewish and otherwise, across Eastern Europe. Bessarabia alone had thirty-seven. In a place where private banks were essentially nonexistent, cooperatives became default banks. Before the war remade the borders of Romania and Ukraine, Bessarabia's cooperatives were linked to the metropole of Odessa and were assisted by Ica. In 1920, Alexander Landesco decided to revive these cooperatives and draw them into a union/syndicate, even though Bessarabia remained under martial law. The JDC provided the loan that underpinned this union of twenty-four cooperatives, and Landesco's successor in Romania labored to stabilize and enroot the cooperatives. He also grappled with whether it made sense to maintain the syndicate, which cost money to maintain but served as a middleman between the JDC and the cooperatives. These questions, raised first in Romania, became crucial everywhere the Jewish reconstructive project went.

In the Bukovina region, Landesco created a limited stock company with a central office in Czernowitz and appointed Orthodox, labor, and B'nai Brith representatives to run it. While supposed to provide loans to rebuild housing, it was clearly just a philanthropic organization that extended credits; it was not a bank and it did not reclaim loans. From the JDC's perspective, it had to become a credit cooperative to become self-sustaining.

As becomes clear from these early reconstruction efforts in postwar Romania, for the JDC, credit cooperatives made sense because of their democratic nature. Of course, there were employees and hierarchy, but all members within a cooperative were fundamentally equal. They could not so easily be taken over by specific religious, class, or political groups, and they did not require extensive top-down engineering on the part of the JDC to have this inclusive Jewish format. Cooperatives, in short, institutionalized pluralism and held together local Jewish communities in self-sustaining perpetuity – out of the spotlight of politics and away from increasingly politicized Jewish philanthropy. The JDC planned for credit cooperatives where each member had an equal vote, rather than limited stock companies, where votes would be unequal and the JDC could have maintained greater control. There was no single path to reviving or creating cooperatives, and ethical issues would obviously have to be weighed carefully and continuously. Still, even if credit cooperatives were not possible everywhere – even within Romania, they were banned in Transylvania – they would be the goal.

Everywhere Jewish credit cooperatives took root they were dependent on the state and its currency but also freed from it. In Romania, the JDC employed the slogan "Save for the future" to attract local deposits for cooperative banks. Noting that the state provided no insurance for unemployment, sickness, or anything else, the JDC argued that cooperatives with a strong deposit base of individual members who used the bank to save would stabilize the lives of members, along with the cooperatives themselves. So in 1922, the cooperative banking initiative in Romania enrooted locals in Bessarabia's long-term future, in a decidedly optimistic vision that valued individual savings deposits. It would reduce reliance on the Romanian state to integrate its Jews into a future economy. Yet Romanian Jews were less optimistic, pointing out that mutual savings funds for burial and dowry societies, to which they had contributed to for years, were destroyed in the war. Looking at their political situation, locals hesitated to invest their savings and rely on Romanian stability in any way.[88]

The Jewish National Council of Lithuania, through which the JDC carried out relief during the war, organized cheap credit self-help almost immediately, and put JDC funds toward that economic vision long before the JDC centrally organized its own reconstruction department. In January 1920, it organized Jewish volksbanks, depositing JDC funds in amounts equal to what the cooperative community could raise. With nearly 10,000 members, the almost seventy banks created the Jewish Central Cooperative Bank for Lithuania in late 1921. But in October 1922, when the Lithuanian lito replaced the German mark, Jewish banks could no longer get credit from German banks. The volksbanks had to rely on one government-authorized bank in Lithuania. The Lithuanian ethno-national banking system became a serious rival to Jewish cooperative banking, and the new currency depreciated so quickly that just a few months later, the Jewish credit cooperatives lost all their savings and accumulations.[89] Grassroots Jewish credit cooperatives could not change their situation from within, it seemed.

Figure 6.3 Jewish cooperative bank in Lithuania. This volksbank, pictured in 1923, was owned cooperatively by and made loans to Jews in the town of Kėdainiai and surrounding villages, supported by the JDC. (JDC, NY_07381)

Ideally, the role of the JDC was to promote local organizational and financial resources and to assist them by providing cheap credit. In reality, the JDC also bailed out failing cooperatives that could not ride out economic shocks, as in Lithuania. Each kassa was designed as a local community institution "founded upon the most democratic principles ... by the people themselves," and was meant to be permanent in a way that no relief committees ever were. The JDC determined that existing cooperatives would have to organize their own federations, each with a central reconstruction bank. The central bank would supply the federated cooperatives with credits, coordinate and regulate them, and interface between the cooperatives and the JDC. Though Romania and Lithuania began reconstructive work in 1920, the JDC's usual East Central European target, Poland, did not. The idea was established early in 1921 but soon ran into problems: The Polish government would not grant a charter for a central bank. By the end of 1922, there were more credit cooperatives – 205 – in Poland than there had been before the war. By then, the JDC had also set up a credit institution in Vienna.[90]

Even as the credit cooperative movement expanded, how exactly the JDC should interact with it was undetermined. The war had destroyed the prewar Jewish cooperative movement. From 236 loan and saving societies in what became Poland, the few that survived the war had no funds. The JDC could not credit institutions that were no longer there; first it had to revive them. As usual, the JDC was committed not simply to creating new organizations where preexisting ones could be revived; making new institutions meant making them pluralist, with representatives of "all the elements of the Jewish population" carrying out a united program. In Hungary, where JDC relief committees were liquidated in June 1921, the JDC's work had to be entirely revived through this project. In Poland, the JDC first trained instructors to help credit cooperatives. Simultaneously, it created the Central Credit Kassas (known as KKS) in Warsaw, Bialystok, and Vilna to finance and coordinate among cooperatives across Poland. The Warsaw location became the central focus of the JDC's program, and the JDC and Ica established a managing board for the KKS. Launched in May 1922, the Warsaw KKS expanded quickly, distributing nearly a billion Polish marks by the end of the year, for which it had been credited about $200,000 by the JDC and Ica. Around 75,000 households had received loans within the first sixth months of the KKS through its member kassas.

Although the JDC came up with the idea of institutionalizing credit cooperation as Jewish political economy though the short-term injection of generous international philanthropy, Ica had invested in the cooperative movement and sought to continue doing so. The JDC always sought to fuse its interests with prewar initiatives, the better to set its recipients on a path to independence. So when the KKS in Galicia had trouble getting organized, since Ica held the majority stock of the kassas and new Polish laws had to be met, the JDC and Ica had to reach an understanding, even if cooperation did not come easily.[91] The JDC felt that while it tried to create independent, local, democratic cooperatives and entrusted its personnel to make decisions, Ica wanted to micromanage cooperatives, reviewing all decisions in Paris. These fundamental differences made it difficult for the JDC and Ica to work together. For example, in the Eastern Mediterranean, the JDC hoped to establish kassas but struggled given divisions amongst Jews, broader instability in the region, and limited commercial opportunities. Refugee relief demanded attention first. Then, in Constantinople, the JDC allowed a separate Russian Refugee Division of loan kassas to come into existence to counter Ica's proposal to create a kassa exclusively for refugees. The JDC realized that catering to an exclusive and marginal group was a "poor investment" but had to manage its interorganizational relations.[92]

To what purposes were all these loans headed? In short, these were loans designed for artisans and farmers – the productive workers at the ideological heart of the reconstructive project. In some cases, there were also home rebuilding loans taken out by whole households, usually with a man as cooperative member and loan applicant. There were loans for tradesmen to buy new equipment and raw material to carry out their work. Producer cooperatives were also set up for designated trades and agricultural ventures: for tailors, joiners, wheelmakers, electricians, chalutzim, and the like.

Michael Freund argued that the new Jewish cooperative movement was no longer made of up of limited loan and saving societies but represented "real financial centers" that acted as banks that served small businesses and artisans instead of big merchants and manufacturers. Among their duties were attending to remittances and providing loans for rebuilding houses. Through these, the KKS were connected to the banking and credit world beyond internal membership or their international Jewish crediting organizations. The KKS could generate income not just off interest on loans but also from other banking functions. What the JDC and Ica provided was startup capital to serve as credit. This infusion of credit into the Polish economy in 1922 actually reduced the overall market rate for loans by a few points.[93]

By establishing a network of credit cooperatives, the JDC was trying to raise the economic floor. Cooperatives were not meant for the indigent, homeless, or unskilled, and they were not handouts but loans to be repaid. They included the lowest class of workers from which they were to create a larger middle class. They were also not intended to pull down wealthier Jews who received no special treatment outside the regular market. The JDC made efforts to bring them into the project to redistribute wealth. The goal was to have a variety of loans available for different needs, all far below the prevailing rates charged by reputable banking houses. The JDC social workers discussed class issues at length to try to find the right balance: Its cooperative work was designed for personal reconstruction loans and the smallest of businesses, but there was recognition that without bringing in capital from established merchants and industrialists, it would be difficult to keep the credit cooperatives running.

For the poorest Jews left out of the cooperative system, there was the traditional Eastern European Jewish communal institution of the *gemilut chesed*, the free loan society. Organized in Poland in 1926 by the CEKABE (Central Organization of Societies for the Support of Non-Interest Credit and Promotion of Productive Work), it was largely for petty traders. CEKABE provided the JDC its main channel for funneling support to indigent Jews.[94] The JDC counted 1,013 places in Poland with more than 300 Jews, and in 722 of these, the JDC helped establish gemilut chesed kassas.[95] These, however, were an afterthought as far as the Jewish humanitarians were concerned.

In the meantime, the JDC had plenty to contend with as Jewish cooperatives struggled to get off the ground in Czechoslovakia. The new state pushed together four regions of Jews that did "not hang together" and that were "cut ... off from its former life blood centres, Vienna and Budapest." There were no institutions whatsoever that connected these Jews. Several factions – Orthodox Jews, Chasidim, Zionists, and assimilated Hungarians – refused to interact. While the JDC struggled, the common purpose of creating credit did help unite Jews. Accordingly, the JDC began to form a "national" Jewish constituency, building from the ground up: identifying the largest Jewish population centers; allowing local control in exchange for pluralist participation in local committees; and slowly bringing together regional cooperative initiatives. By 1923, fourteen kassas were established in the most difficult regions, East Slovakia and Sub-Carpathia.[96] Here, too, Jewish merchants faced opposition from non-Jewish consumer cooperatives, which sought to eliminate the middleman – who was usually Jewish. This was not a phenomenon confined to this region; it was an antisemitic weapon widely perceived as ethical and often supported by governments in East Central Europe.[97] This was the central reason why the JDC did not enthusiastically establish many consumer cooperatives, and turned to producer cooperatives to fulfill some of the same functions; they would have pitted some Jews against others.[98]

Polish reconstruction developed unevenly. The Warsaw KKS quickly grew, like the reincarnation of the prewar Vilna KKS, while the Bialystok one floundered. Each needed different approaches and support, all of which was carried out by JDC's traveling staff of nine instructor-bookkeepers. Locals were expected to run things on their own. Still unable to form a new central financial institution that the Polish government would approve of, the JDC cleverly worked around this obstacle. It acquired Bank dla Spółdzielni, a private bank, and transformed it into a public bank to support Polish Jewish cooperatives. (This process was similar to the JDC's takeover of TOZ on its way to reviving the Jewish health movement in Poland through preexisting, legal, but nearly defunct institutions.) But in 1923, depreciation happened so quickly that despite locally raised funds, the kassas could not keep pace, and their reserves dropped precipitously. The Polish mark collapsed, and Poland transitioned to the zloty. This did not save the financial situation, and Ica, worried about its own stability and on a limited endowment, pulled out. The JDC swooped in to save the kassas, loaning to Bank dla Spółdzielni to distribute to them, and the cooperatives established new guidelines. Fifty kassas still had to close, and the three KKS were made redundant by dla Spółdzielni. With their diffuse membership of small loanees and lack of connection to big, bankrupted firms, the remaining Polish Jewish kassas held on amid depression and economic instability.[99]

The JDC and Ica were pouring in money to such an extent that Ica felt it had to leave the project. How was it possible to create a banking system that would continue to function without continuous credits? Devising the answer was difficult when Poland, Lithuania, Hungary, and elsewhere were experiencing depreciation or currency fluctuation, while the United States and Western Europe were more stable.[100] In Lithuania, the JDC first tried to stipulate repayment for loans in dollars, but depreciation made this far too burdensome on loanees.[101] In Hungary, the JDC saw no way of safeguarding its funds if it wanted to keep its work going; therefore it simply had to "take a chance." The JDC required mere proof of intent of repayment and that the funds would be used for productive purposes, which was much more suggestive of a humanitarian, philanthropic endeavor than a business one. And in Poland, the JDC bailed out the kassas in 1923 even as Ica pulled out.[102] Was the JDC like a welfare state? Was it a philanthropy with a business foundation? A business institution with a social character?

In the USSR, although reconstruction was the linchpin of all JDC aid, an overtly capitalist solution to reconstruction could not be the approach; Jewish reconstruction was happening through agrarianization. The credit cooperative, however, was still relevant to Soviet Jews. From 1922, Rosen's budget included $250,000 for credit cooperatives, when the JDC obtained Soviet permission to organize a low-interest credit bank for peasant and handicraft cooperatives. Together, the JDC and Ica funded a variety of cooperatives that tended to provide loans in the form of raw materials or equipment in exchange for future produce, sureties, or were secured on household goods. By August 1923, there were seventy-six loan agencies. They were locally rooted and, other than repayment in kind rather than cash, functioned much like contemporary Jewish cooperatives in East Central Europe, with funding coming through membership fees and loans of the JDC and Ica. The JDC also made its funding contingent on the cooperatives' willingness to assist old age homes, orphanages, kindergartens, clinics, and hospitals. In other words, the JDC expected their cooperative work to interact with and directly support the full system of social work and development. Unsurprisingly, the Evsektsiia was suspicious that this project was linked to the restoration of traditional Jewish community.[103]

A cornerstone of Agro-Joint's work was credit cooperation that provided low-interest loans to colonists. Rather than institutionalizing reconstruction through federating or centralizing the cooperative movement itself, in the USSR, the future of cooperatives was to be a sub-activity of Agro-Joint, part of an array of services for colonists. As elsewhere, these loans were primarily designated to purchase farm equipment, to support vocational schools and artisans, and to construct homes. The difference was that in the USSR, cooperatives were subsumed into the agrarianization infrastructure, instead of existing as separate, mutually beneficial entities. Agro-Joint gave agricultural settlers three years to repay loans, so as to provide opportunities for the colonies to establish themselves and avoid loan defaults.[104] Like cooperatives in East Central Europe, the idea was business methods but with humanitarian motivation; the purpose was to help the colonies and the colonists, since building the economy could certainly not be a goal. ORT, too, used Jewish cooperatives throughout this period to distribute loans to Jewish agricultural settlers.[105]

Yet overall, the Jewish cooperative movement under Agro-Joint was more closely tied to cooperative colonies than credit banks. The JDC discovered that it was much easier to provide agricultural supervision to a centralized, collectivist model of agricultural colonies over household, village-centered colonies. This was the same logic as federating credit cooperatives in Poland but remade for an agricultural society. Jewish colonists voluntarily reconstituted collective bodies between 1926–28 as land settlement, production, and consumer *artels* (Soviet cooperatives) to make the best use of labor, equipment, and purchasing power. Agro-Joint colonies thus operated as cooperative collectives on private land, thus exceeding rural norms for cooperation.[106]

Finally, economic development in Palestine was a central part of the international Jewish reconstructive project and also distinct. Unlike in East Central Europe, the cooperative movement in Palestine became directly related to Jewish state-building and the formation of Jewish national institutions.[107] Still, the private credit cooperatives so common in the Yishuv were not a local invention – like agricultural colonies, they traveled there with Eastern European Jews.[108] In Palestine, credit cooperatives did *not* already dot the landscape of the Yishuv prior to the war. Yet philanthropists who took up the credit cooperative cause after the war were primarily American. In July 1920, Louis Brandeis made a comprehensive economic plan for the upbuilding of Palestine to complement Hadassah's medical work. It could not be an economy run on donations and had to bring in the wealthy non-Zionist crowd (like several key JDC leaders).[109] His liberal American Zionist followers enacted just that plan, founding the Palestine Cooperative Company and bringing English Jewish elites on board as well. The Jewish economy in Palestine thus diverged from the JDC-ORT-Ica directed Europe, in a transnational partnership of four American-Anglo Jewish organizations with a clear Zionist bent. In 1922, the Central Bank of Cooperative Institutions in Palestine was founded by the JDC, the Economic Board for Palestine of London, the Palestine Jewish Colonization Association (PICA), and the Palestine Development Council, with each holding equal shares.

The Central Bank, registered in Palestine, began to lend to credit unions and agricultural cooperatives; supporting agriculture was its target. Its vision mirrored the central/regional crediting banks the JDC was organizing across East Central Europe: providing a place to unify the cooperatives enough to allow the Palestine Cooperative Company to interact with them at scale, rather than individually. Rather than a credit cooperative, however, it was a limited stock company, with shares held by the supporting philanthropies – a status that gave it an ambivalent relationship to the cooperatives.[110] The Central Bank was explicitly designed to provide long-term loans for cooperative agricultural colonies in Palestine, most of which had been previously funded by the Zionist Organization or PICA. Agricultural colonists were supposed to set up their own cooperatives to receive credit through the Central Bank.[111] The Central Bank's leadership (including Bernard Flexner, Herbert Lehman, Julian Mack, Bernard Kahn from Europe, and other JDC leaders) struggled to keep the bank's work separate from that of the Zionist Organization, and, simultaneously, to keep its methods closer to the business and less on the charitable side of things. Both tasks were difficult given the circumstances of the colonies applying for loans.[112] In practice, the bank still extended credit and advice to risky cooperative undertakings and thereby stimulated and supported the growth of the cooperative movement in Palestine.

The JDC also ran Kupath Milveh, founded in 1921. This banking activity began with war relief but then became part of the JDC's general reconstruction activities absorbed under the auspices of the Palestine Cooperative Company. It resembled the economic relief the JDC set up in Ukraine for pogrom sufferers, not originally designed to be self-sustaining or locally run.[113] Kupath Milveh granted small loans to borrowers who could not easily obtain credit from commercial banks, like artisans, teachers, shopkeepers, tradesmen, and clerks. It was to develop small-scale industry in Palestine. By 1924, the JDC had expended more than $260,000 on the Kupath Milveh.[114] While it was clearly designed for Jews, Kupath Milveh occasionally provided loans to non-Jews; this was in keeping with the JDC's approach to benefiting some non-Jewish locals wherever it worked.[115] Whereas the Palestine Cooperative Company was inclined to devote resources toward the chalutzim due to

Zionist ideals, the JDC agreed jointly to establish the Central Bank with the Palestine Development Council and other philanthropies, and otherwise struck out on its own to provide loans to make sure that the Yishuv would be developing a well-rounded Jewish economy. This supplementation, like the JDC's balancing of the books against forms of individual relief elsewhere, equalized aid everywhere while allowing individuals to direct their own resources. Interestingly, in Palestine, the JDC's self-guided reconstructive work through credit institutions supported the usual "productive" suspects, trades and agriculture, but only in Palestine did it use separate institutions because of the ideological interests involved.

This whole economic venture, while in many ways revolutionary, was also intended by its American Jewish architects to be conservative by design. It was meant to deflect attention, and, as Leonard Robinson noted in 1922, the point of the Reconstruction Department was not to disburse funds, but to *conserve* them: "The Reconstruction Fund ... does not belong to any particular class or country. It is a legacy from American Jewry to our war stricken brothers and the heritage of Jewry the world over. It is a sacred trust to be husbanded and conserved for all time."[116] It was experimental and grand, meant to have staying power. Just how it would, however, was yet to be determined.

Two Central Banks for the Jewish People

If cooperatives were meant to be local and democratic, left to develop according to their own environments and traditions, the JDC needed to find some way of maintaining a link to them – to provide credit in a standardized, centralized way without assuming the risks or control of the cooperatives. Regional banks in East Central Europe and even Palestine's Central Bank of Cooperative Institutions did not serve as the central banks that the JDC hoped they could become. To be more like a central bank, they needed reserve funds and credit, which in lieu of a state, would here have to come from more prosperous Jews in the West. American Jews, however, aspired to end their fundraising; elite leaders hoped they could simply manage revolving funds in conjunction with Western European Jewish partners. The proposed solution for creating transnational central banks for the Jewish people, making the most of the diaspora without drawing too heavily on the American Jewish public, was to weld Western Jewish creditor foundations to Eastern Jewish regional cooperative banks. Thus, Jewish humanitarians created the American Joint Reconstruction Foundation ("the Foundation") and the Palestine Economic Corporation, attaching them to local cooperative banks through East Central Europe and Palestine, respectively. These high finance-cooperative amalgamations were like "real" central banks.

In their transnational dimensions, however, these organizations, especially the Foundation, also resembled what the Jewish liberal Italian Finance Minister Luigi Luzzati had proposed in the nineteenth century: permanent, international cooperation between central banks. This idea was directly taken up by the internationalist milieu in the 1920s, and resulted in the creation of the Bank for International Settlements in 1930 in Basel, Switzerland.[117] In general, the League of Nations, in particular through its Economic and Financial Organisation (EFO), was becoming deeply invested in creating international monetary cooperation to support global capitalism and stabilize the world economy, which was in a constant state of quasi emergency.[118] The goal of international cooperation among central state banks was evident, but it was not humanitarians or non-state groups of any kind that EFO technocrats had in mind, even though League efforts to address refugees, children, and public health involved non-state actors.

The JDC was neither a successor state nor, like the EFO, did it carry any international authority. What it did have was international financial know-how, rooted in its small group of politically savvy, Jewish international financiers. For instance, Paul Warburg, Felix's and Max's brother, was known as a fierce advocate for an American central bank (the Federal Reserve) before the war and was the founding director of the Council on Foreign Relations. By 1924, as economic reconstruction seemed destined to take over American Jewish humanitarianism, People's Relief and Central Relief dissolved. Their small-donor fundraising bases had grown weary, distinctive educational programs were no longer required, and the Dubrowsky branch of Evobshchestkom no longer needed to be countered by People's Relief. The JDC's landsmanshaft bureau also closed down. The JDC shrank to the size of the AJRC: Its future would be governed by a small group of New York financiers who retained a few key professional personnel.

Though ideas for a central bank were circulating as early as 1920, JDC discussions for a new organization that would handle the reconstructive work of the JDC began in earnest in 1923. The plan was to make the work long lasting while allowing the JDC to liquidate or at least scale back. Herbert Lehman argued that if the JDC simply turned over its assets to the Jewish cooperatives' regional banks, the money would simply evaporate. Lehman thus set about making a plan for a new organization that would take over the JDC's reconstructive work and permanently bring in Ica, "the only rich organization abroad," as a partner in European Jewish reconstruction. Indeed, Ica had an endowment, while the JDC had no permanent financial base nor a plan to develop one. Bernard Kahn would be placed at its head – in every way he seemed perfect for the role: knowledgeable, diplomatic, and conservative. Ica's Louis Oungre would supervise from Paris. Not everyone in the JDC was happy; they felt Ica was too committed to itself, its endowment, and its own program, and that the JDC would be strengthening Ica and giving it control over JDC funds. The much less wealthy ORT was better liked by some. Various compromises were floated to include diverse religious and political opinions and geographical bases, so that the new organization would be even more "joint" than the JDC, including representative men from the Hilfskomite, ORT, and London War Victims Fund, but still with the JDC and Ica mostly in charge.[119] There was some concern that Ica would reject ORT's participation, and that ORT was in any case taking advantage of American Jewish funds to inflate its own importance.[120]

In short, the risk and cost of long-term Jewish cooperative banking would not be borne by the JDC alone, but spread out over Western Jewish humanitarian organizations, and Jews in East Central Europe would still collectively determine how and where credit was used. The careful titration of representation on the organization's governing body was the issue at hand. With this new institution, combined with the federated cooperatives system growing in Poland and elsewhere in East Central Europe, there might be a permanent, stable central bank of the Jewish people. It would rely on the presumed stable currency after the war: the US dollar. The JDC would provide money in installments to the Foundation as it did for its other programs, continuing to fundraise in the United States while keeping the money from depreciating by shifting it to an Eastern European currency.

By early 1924, the JDC Reconstruction Department was liquidating itself across East Central Europe, writing up final reports, conducting financial audits, and turning over its local assets and work to the most centralized local institutions like the Bank dla Spółdzielni.[121] By then, over $2 million had gone for reconstructive purposes to East Central Europe and South East Europe, and another $1 million to Russia.[122] Ten central/regional banks provided credit to 362 local kassas. After conversations between Ica and JDC representatives in Paris, joint terms were negotiated for the Foundation, as well as for Ica's financial support for Agro-Joint. Bernard Flexner went abroad to seal the deal with Ica's Louis Oungre and Franz Phillipson, which was signed in March 1924. The JDC would infuse more than $1 million into the Foundation "for the relief of the poor and needy Jews in Europe and elsewhere," which would "stimulate activities and agencies which tend to make the people self-supporting." These funds would sit in depositories in the United States, and if JDC was liquidated in the future, trustees would be appointed to act in the JDC's capacity. A twenty-man board of directors would feature JDC and Ica nominees plus "the proper representation of the interests ... of Jewry of Eastern and Central Europe." Ica would contribute $500,000 up front and collaborate on an ongoing, ad hoc basis, essentially acting as junior partner to the JDC. Kahn and Oungre would be co-managing directors.[123]

This American Joint Reconstruction Foundation "radiated power and optimism" with its far-reaching and audacious plans.[124] Although it was incorporated in London and meetings were held in Paris, it was most connected to the JDC, and specifically, to Bernard Kahn. Its governing council included 20 men: 6 from the JDC and 6 from Ica, and 8 Eastern European Jewish leaders, including Leon Bramson of ORT. This new arrangement, never explicitly stated, allowed for just a few exceptionally wealthy Western Jewish philanthropists to give occasional, significant donations to prop up the poorest parts of the Jewish world, rather than relying on middle- and working-class Jews in the West to donate small funds en masse to this project. Rather than the JDC having to fundraise from Jewish immigrants in America, immigrants returned to sending remittances through the banking system – now of the Jewish cooperatives. It was hoped that eventually, Eastern Jews would accumulate and concentrate their own capital (made in part of received remittances) in their cooperatives and become independent of the Foundation.

The problems of continuous currency depreciation in East Central Europe, alongside a banking system dependent on currencies beyond the control of these "Jewish central banks" came to a head shortly after the Foundation's creation. In Poland and Lithuania in 1925, Jewish cooperative movements nearly broke down. In Poland, the kassas actually accumulated deposits during inflation in 1924–25 as public confidence in private banks fell, even as Jewish members shared in economic misery. The kassas could not, however, escape the effects of the plummeting currency at the end of 1925. The Foundation did not want to expose itself to such an unstable currency, but once credit seemed to stabilize again in mid-1926, the Foundation provided close inspection for kassas, created new kassas, and consolidated business practices, and then infused more credit into the system. In Lithuania, which was low on reserves, the Central Bank could not cope when the national currencies suddenly depreciated, and depositors made a run on the bank. The bank became insolvent, threatening the cooperatives in their networks and membership – and the economic status of Lithuanian and Polish Jewry. Local community and business leaders came to the rescue alongside the

Foundation, which offered more credit, accepted delayed repayment, and forced the Central Bank to restructure and become more like a commercial bank. As that bank then overcompensated, reducing its support to cooperatives to support itself, the Foundation became uninterested, severed ties, and began to build a new relationship directly with the cooperatives and their union.

During currency difficulties, the Jewish cooperative movement in each country kept going with help from the Foundation, while shifting with the economic and political tides in various ways. In Poland, the Jewish cooperatives formed a union, due to Polish law requiring a supervisory union for cooperatives in 1922. This Union of Jewish Cooperatives, rather than the KKS or Central Bank, liaised with the Foundation and the Bank dla Spółdzielni. Dla Spółdzielni was allowed in 1924 to take on regular banking operations so it could increase revenue without applying to the Foundation to do what it was meant to: offer low interest rates to cooperatives. When dla Spółdzielni's shares were transferred to the Jewish cooperative movement in 1925, the Union became the owner of the Bank dla Spółdzielni. Though having this additional central bank between the Foundation and the individual cooperatives meant that rates were higher, they were still lower than the general banking system. It acted as a "powerful Jewish economic bulwark ... with which other economic organizations must reckon." Dla Spółdzielni could thus obtain credits not just from the Foundation but also from the Bank of Poland and the Polish Postal Savings Bank. The Foundation could then step back from tight control and allow the Union and its bank to function normally.[125]

Although the relationship of the Foundation to the local Jewish cooperative movement in each region and country was different, regional credit banks were gradually replaced by associations or unions of Jewish credit cooperatives that functioned as intermediaries between the Foundation (and other economic institutions) and Jewish cooperatives. In 1927, both the JDC and Ica agreed to invest another $600,000 over four years. Even the Jews of Turkey had credit kassas in Constantinople, Adrianople, and Smyrna, as the JDC prevailed upon them and worked around Turkey's lack of a cooperative law by creating it as a stock company. In Poland, the cooperative movement had started experimenting with consumer and producer cooperatives under the JDC's initiative. By 1931, the American Joint Reconstruction Foundation was connected to 756 Jewish credit cooperatives through their centralized organizations, with 539 alone in Poland, and the rest spread out across Austria, Bulgaria, Czechoslovakia, Estonia, Latvia, Lithuania, Romania, and Turkey.[126]

For Palestine, there was a separate organization that was similar in concept, but it evolved differently in form and function in the context of the Yishuv. Palestine did not come under the "reconstructive" mandate anymore; and what was happening there was less reconstruction, and more construction of a Jewish state. Herbert Lehman wrote, "it would not be wise to include our ventures in Palestine in the Foundation"; Ica directly opposed the Foundation's extension to Palestine. As the Reconstruction Department was being liquidated in 1924, the JDC tried to determine what to do with its assets in Palestine, hoping to hand them off to another American Jewish organization.[127] In 1925, Bernard Flexner proposed forming a company to take over the Palestine Cooperative Company's and the JDC Reconstruction Department in Palestine's assets and activities. He had always been a committed liberal Zionist and paid special attention to Hadassah's work, and had been vice chair of the JDC's Reconstruction Committee and a board member of the Joint Reconstruction Foundation. This new organization, the Palestine Economic Corporation (PEC), was formally incorporated in the United States in 1926, with Flexner as its first president and, until 1944, as chairman of its board. PEC took over the merged Palestine assets of the JDC and the Palestine Cooperative Company in 1926, namely operations of the Central Bank as well as the Kupath Milveh.[128]

The formation of a network of private credit cooperatives with the help of the PEC represented the economic powerhouse of Jewish Palestine, rather than the quasi-public-sector institutions represented by the Keren Hayesod, the Histadrut, and the labor movement that are typically identified.[129] The British administration in Palestine, its commitment to a Jewish national home, and its law governing credit cooperatives allowed for the growth of the Jewish political economy. Mandatory law favored private credit cooperatives because it protected private property and was based on a liberal worldview, allowing the cooperative movement autonomy for collective development.[130] A 1920s wave of Eastern European immigrants to Palestine brought the experience of active participation in the cooperative movement, which was helpful for establishing credit cooperatives in their new home. And Harry Viteles, former chief of the Reconstruction Department in the JDC's central European office in Vienna, moved to Jerusalem in 1925 to run the Jewish cooperative movement in Palestine and was eager to bring a Progressive social vision there.

As the Jewish cooperative movement in Palestine mushroomed, cooperatism did not grow among proximate Arabs, who retained a more traditional economy. Though the Central Bank's leaders thought it would be a good idea for the Arabs to have their own cooperative movement, it did not feel it could create such a movement, and instead encouraged the mandate government to create a cooperative bureau that would benefit both Arab and Jewish initiatives based on business considerations. Viteles considered that the Central Bank could become the central financial institution for all types of cooperative societies, or at least advise a nascent Arab movement, but that plan did not go anywhere.[131] Mandate Palestine's economy was effectively divided between Jewish and Arab, with only Jews bringing expertise and funding from around the Jewish world to catapult the Jewish economy into modernity.[132]

As part of the new PEC, starting in 1924, the Kupath Milveh sought to be regarded as a business venture, known as Loan Bank, rather than a charitable organization. The idea, under its new board of governors, was to maintain "small industrial credits" through a central bank.[133] Loan Bank granted three-to-five-year credits to small manufacturers and small loans to borrowers who were ignored by commercial banks, such as artisans, teachers, shopkeepers, tradesmen, and clerks. While its borrowers benefited, Loan Bank did not become an influential institution, nor did it have any particular link to the cooperative movement. Its manager attempted to give local branches of the bank more autonomy and suggested changing its name to "the People's Bank," but these ideas did not come to fruition.[134]

Meanwhile, the Central Bank served as the unloved backbone of the cooperative movement in Palestine. In 1927, it had a capital of £100,000. It financed credit cooperatives, agricultural cooperatives, and individuals who needed loans larger than what Loan Bank provided. There were twenty-nine cooperative credit societies in the Yishuv, some rural and others urban, with some 17,500 members. Each was based on a local initiative, with only a loose federation among them and weak oversight from creditors. One critic suggested that what was needed was centralized, objective government oversight over the cooperative movement, or alternatively, more democratic governance of the Central Bank elected from the cooperative membership.[135]

Instead, however, the Merkaz, the Central Institution of Credit and Saving Institutions in Palestine, was established in 1924 by urban cooperatives as a grassroots alternative to Loan Bank and the Central Bank. These urban workers were suspicious of both the PEC and the top-down labor movement associated with the Histadrut and agricultural colonies, while still preferring a cooperative ethos. The Merkaz became an audit and supervisory union and represented the cooperatives to external bodies. Eventually, the Merkaz became the center of the private credit cooperative movement, presenting a challenge to Loan Bank, which felt that its role had been usurped by the rise of urban coopera-tives.[136] Yet, the PEC had in mind a socioeconomic arrangement beyond government oversight that would jumpstart a grassroots cooperative movement without being controlled by it – and it appeared to be succeeding.

The Central Bank's New York leadership was not entirely pleased, worrying about the bank's losses and that it had no reserves from which to lend to struggling, worthy cooperatives. Perhaps, there should be no Loan Bank, but simply one central cooperative bank, like its European counterparts, that would lend to cooperative banks only, not private individuals, in the city and on the land.[137] Furthermore, the banks' leadership agreed that they needed to be closer to the cooperatives, provide more auditing, and support cooperatives' pressure on the gov-ernment. The prevailing dualism of Loan and Central Bank, the alter-native organized urban credit cooperatives, and the inability of either PEC bank to become part of the fabric of the cooperative movement in Palestine, despite having been crucial to starting that movement, was much debated.[138] It was unclear how to responsibly transition away from their joint-stock, philanthropic roots and merge them into a cooperative effort, while retaining urban and agricultural loans. Viteles, Central Bank's manager, suggested that the bank allow the cooperatives to buy shares, but New York was against the idea since the cooperatives did not have sufficient funds. The Central Bank sought to diversify its advisory committee in Palestine to be more representa-tive of the cooperatives rather than the founding philanthropies. Its New York governors, however, were resolutely opposed to giving too much power over to the cooperatives. Opposition to the bank could destroy it, since many locals were ideologically driven by colonization rather than business pragmatism.[139]

Except for the Soviet Union, building and sustaining the Jewish cooperative movement throughout Europe and the Eastern Mediterranean became the legacy of Jewish humanitarian war relief work. An international central bank for the Jewish people, linking finan-ciers with unionized credit cooperatives and philanthropy with small loans proved especially successful across East Central Europe. The micro-finance-like system, however, was never successfully implemented in Palestine, even though its beginnings spurred the cooperative move-ment into existence. By the late 1920s, the Yishuv could no longer be addressed as just one point in the diaspora. There were too many competitors, local and far away, vying to accelerate the Yishuv into nationhood. At this moment, within the development and international banking initiative, the split between the diaspora and Palestine was institutionalized. Held together through a common project, plan, and leadership throughout the 1920s, these Jewish economic development organizations (the PEC and the Foundation) were nevertheless set on two separate institutional pathways that would never again meet, but would instead lay the groundwork for an enduring cleavage in the Jewish international political fabric. Three humanitarian theaters were collapsed into two: Europe (including East Central Europe, the Soviet Union, and South East Europe) and Palestine; Diaspora and National Home. Condoned and promoted by pluralist, liberal Western Jewish leadership, Jewish philanthropy focused on practical work and cooperation in Palestine made a separatist, territorialist Jewish nationalism acceptable within even the most liberal of international Jewish political circles. Although two banking foundations institutionalized a split in international Jewish politics, both brought the JDC into the Zionist fold, where it would remain for the next century: simultaneously Zionist and Diasporist.

Between Welfarism and Development

[Is JDC] satisfied merely with helping to readjust the economic life of the Jews so that it should always approximate as far as possible the pre war status ... or does it go beyond that in an attempt to fill in those gaps which probably should have been filled in before the war? ... Are we going to limit our work to particular elements of society and say we have nothing to do with the rest, or is it our point of view to be that of the State, embodying all types of cases and activities in our activities—work for the entire Jewish people.[140]

Michael Freund's perceptive questions went straight to the heart of the matter. What was the JDC and what was Jewish humanitarianism, by intention and in practice? Freund had his own answer:

The local population must ... marshall its own social, organizational and financial resources. The function of the J.D.C. in the scheme would be two-fold ... to act in the capacity of promoter and creditor, and to do for the economically unadjusted Jewish population what under normal conditions would have been generally done for them by the State.[141]

That the JDC worked for all Jews, and was "indirectly concerned with everything Jewish," especially the "little fellows," was noncontroversial within the JDC. Still, its professional leaders never publicly articulated such basic values, and that, of course, was in keeping with the JDC's own pretenses at staying above ideology, dogma, and politics. Yet, the question suggests that the comparison of the JDC to the state is appropriate. The point of all of this economic activity was to provide enormous sums of money and absorb all the risk to change and improve Jewish life along every dimension. Reconstruction might have been done through business methods, but a capitalist return on investment was certainly not the goal. In 1929, about 10 percent of Jewish income in Poland was internally redistributed from the upper income half to the lower income half of the Jews.[142] By the mid-1920s, sustainable, long-term social transformation of the Jews by this non-state, welfare-state-like mosaic of Jewish organizations became the goal.

Removing the history of interwar Jewish international reconstruction from its usual place within regional histories provides a different and much more contradictory picture of events. It is simplistic, though tempting, to see cooperative and reconstructive activity happening in East Central Europe as defensive on one hand, with cooperative and reconstructive activity in Palestine as offensive on the other. Bringing territorialist Jewish agricultural colonies in Russia into the frame weakens this binary. More significantly, reconstructive activities were almost identical by leadership and across states and humanitarian theaters, if slightly adapted to local conditions. As such, the entire enterprise and its goals cannot be fully comprehended when siloed into various local contexts. Rather, since international Jewish humanitarianism came to define the contours of the diaspora itself, it must be understood as a diasporic phenomenon. Wherever reconstruction went, it was committed to a distinct Jewish body politic, transcending geopolitical borders while working everywhere to enroot Jews in their localities. It should be understood everywhere as an offensive, politicized Jewish response to the Jewish Question, intentionally understated everywhere but Palestine.

International Jewish reconstruction, as seen through the prism of international banking, was local, national, transnational, and international – all at once. Its inherent diasporist dimension made it quite unlike a social welfare state as normally understood. Jewish humanitarianism had none of the sovereignty or peer recognition of a state but carried out many welfare state functions, down to stabilizing currency and restructuring the economy. Jewish humanitarianism does not adhere to the story that is usually told and that is centered around state-building, migration, nationalism, and imperialism. When it comes to imperial entanglement, Jews drew on Western expertise and imperial influence, bringing the most modern equipment and techniques and, as Western imperialists often did with their colonial subjects, sought to transform people and territories under their reach. Yet, Jews harnessed these networks through the multilayered Jewish diaspora to uplift and develop the most needy Eastern parts of that same Jewish diaspora. This long-term, economic, reconstructive project in its transnational dimensions might also be understood as a precursor of international development, a phenomenon that would reach the rest of the world only in the wake of decolonization a half century later.

In all the places it reached, Jewish humanitarianism after the Great War was both welfare-state-building and international development. Between 1924 and 1929, Jewish humanitarianism appeared as a major force that was reconstructing a simultaneously national and transnational Jewish society. Jewish diaspora nationalism through humanitarianism and international development seemed to be succeeding, including its burgeoning cultural center in Palestine, where private credit cooperatives held about 44 percent of the deposits market and a third of loans in the Jewish economy at its 1935 peak.[143] Since there was vanishingly little time for optimism, it is difficult to assess this long-term plan with historical hindsight; so much was destroyed in the following decade. Yet the JDC's revolving funds kept cooperative lending afloat, even as it staggered into impossibly difficult years, with a resolute Kahn at its helm.

Epilogue

"I could write and speak about the duties and opportunities of American Jewry in Israel's present crisis without end. The amazing thing is how people can find the self-complacency to enjoy a life of ease and extravagance and not be haunted," wrote Felix Warburg in late 1919.[1] The plight of Jews outside America weighed on Warburg, motivating him to put extensive personal resources into rescuing them, when he could himself have enjoyed a life of ease. As early as 1919, he saw international Jewish humanitarianism as a duty – Jewish solidarity demanded that much. But there were also opportunities for American Jews in international humanitarianism.

In 1921, the JDC still saw itself as a "war organization," which, by definition, was temporary.[2] Proving the point that American Jewish organizations were only incidentally committed to foreign work abroad, JDC leaders had not yet internalized the shift in power globally and in the Jewish world, from Europe to America. Keeping Jewish life going did not seem to be a long-term American Jewish responsibility, but a short-term emergency need. Looking at other American humanitarian organizations, the ARA and the ARC, for example, JDC leaders saw how those groups were planning their exits. As it turned out, however, this moment marked a turning point that was hardly anything like an end point.

In late 1920, the League of Nations was starting in Geneva, while the Whites and the Reds ceased the struggle over Ukraine. In early 1921, as the Polish–Soviet War ended, international relief organizations spread across Europe and began pouring funds and expertise into civilian relief. The Nansen Action and the ARA were helping the Soviet government deal with its famine; Nansen initiated his work as the High Commissioner for Russian Refugees while listening to Lucien Wolf's advice; and the Zionist Commission in Palestine gained governing authority under the British Mandate under its new title of Palestine Zionist Executive. While these were all promising developments, the stalwart Jacob Schiff passed away in 1920; America voted its first immigration quotas into existence; the Minorities Treaties were proving ineffective at ending flagrant abuses against Jews in countries that had signed them; and famine and epidemic were wiping out Jews or sending them fleeing still. Though late 1921 was already three years after the armistice, the JDC had just started its field work after wiring money overseas during the war, diplomatic negotiations in Paris in 1919, and tentative surveys and emergency relief in war-torn eastern zones in 1920. The JDC simply could not abandon its aid recipients.

Instead, in the autumn of 1920, the JDC reconfigured itself to undertake what it hoped would serve as reconstructive and rehabilitative work to restore European Jews to their prewar status and still allow the JDC to liquidate itself within a few years. Rather than organizing its efforts along geographic lines, with country directors dispensing food, medicine, and clothing to local Jewish inhabitants, the JDC addressed issues thematically and systematically. Boris Bogen, the genial mediator and broker who entered destroyed regions, pulled together bedraggled Jewish populations and advocated for Jewish relief to the necessary authorities – first in Poland, then in Russia. To coordinate refugee work, public health, child welfare, and economic stabilization across Europe, Bernard Kahn, the steely pragmatist, rose to dominate JDC work.

After 1921, American Jewish philanthropy was arranged with a fundraising engine in the United States, powered by elite New York Jewish leadership, landmanshaft involvement, the JDC's three constituent committees, and a nationwide network of women's and urban fundraising units. Kahn, based in Central Europe and reporting back to New York, supervised thematic departments operating throughout East Central Europe with a special eye to the hub of postwar Jewish Europe: Poland. Soviet Russia's reconstructive phase, lagging a few years behind and never entirely open to Western philanthropy, was directed by Joseph Rosen, who also reported to New York. Work in Palestine was funded in part by the JDC but delegated to Hadassah when possible. Hias served as the "travel department," moving Jews in trouble from one place to the next and connecting wanderers to one another.

The idea was to use this humanitarian machine to motivate local philanthropy, show the possibilities open to Jews if they sufficiently helped themselves, and create local partners to take over the work once the JDC departed: in short, to remake the international Jewish philanthropic map for the postwar political order. It was a difficult, frustrating undertaking for all parties concerned, to be sure – slow, risky, uncertain, controversial, grueling, expensive, unyielding, and infinitesimal – but the many hardships seemed worth the effort. This was all done under the assumption that liberalism in Europe would prevail, and in the hope that Jews in Russia would be allowed to operate somewhat autonomously; if society as a whole improved, surely this would assure that Jews would rise with it.

American Jewish organizations remained committed to Jews in Russia, Palestine, and East Central Europe much longer than postwar relief operations by all other American international organizations. This commitment showed the extent to which American Jews felt morally obligated to rehabilitation and development work on behalf of faraway Jews.[3] Although JDC employees nearly all left Europe by 1923 (Kahn remained in Europe, Rosen in Russia, and Hadassah workers in Palestine), and the AJRC's "joint" American constituents, the Central Relief and People's Relief, disbanded by 1924, the JDC did not yet succeed in turning over its work to locals. While organizations like the OZE network, CENTOS, ORT, and Emigdirect/Hicem were capable of carrying out Jewish welfare activities, demonstrating the significant successes of American Jewish reconstructive work, they were never able to manage fundraising. Ica would only provide funds in concert with the JDC. The rosy view of the future of Europe and the JDC's conservative estimates of how much aid Jews would need meant that when economic crisis hit Poland from 1924–26 and turned into a permanent recession, the JDC was unprepared. Children, in particular, held the JDC's attention, as it was their economic future at stake.

The JDC continued to dole out money, though it was back to working through European Jewish partners as it had during the war, now for the purposes of childcare, loan institutions, medical work, and the occasional refugee crisis.[4] While weary, donors recognized that Eastern European Jews truly needed help, which coincided with the assumption that American prosperity would continue, and so the JDC allowed its work to drag on. The hope was that an international, low-interest, small-loan Jewish banking system would keep the heart of the Jewish world running without too much input from American Jews beyond occasional infusions of funding and management. It was not until 1927 that the JDC finally moved to recognize its own permanence, when Louis Marshall suggested reorganizing for that purpose.[5] The JDC had come to aspire to a system for redistributing wealth, resources, and responsibility among Jews. It provided a safety net for the weak, no matter where they lived, and in that way, it began to resemble a social welfare state more than a typical humanitarian organization. Between 1914 and 1931, the JDC disbursed more than $80 million, a sum equivalent to well over a billion dollars today.[6]

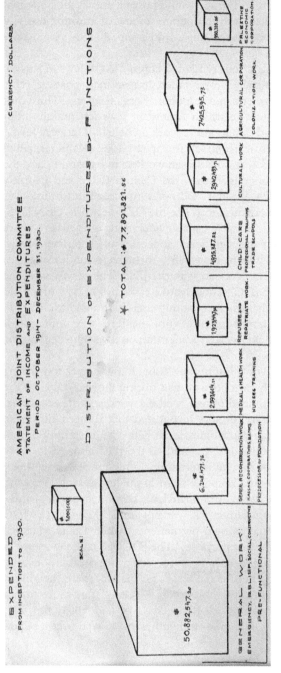

Figure E.1 Visualizations of JDC expenditures, by departmental theme (this page) and by country (over the fold), 1914–1930. Together, these show the breadth of welfare the JDC undertook, in many regions simultaneously, with an annual budget averaging $4.2 million. The JDC was precise in accounting and enumerating its work, and in not overspending what it raised. It regularly presented data in hand-drawn graphics, displaying its exacting professionalism. ("Data Relating to Its Operations," March 1932, at YUA, Wiernik Collection, Box 15)

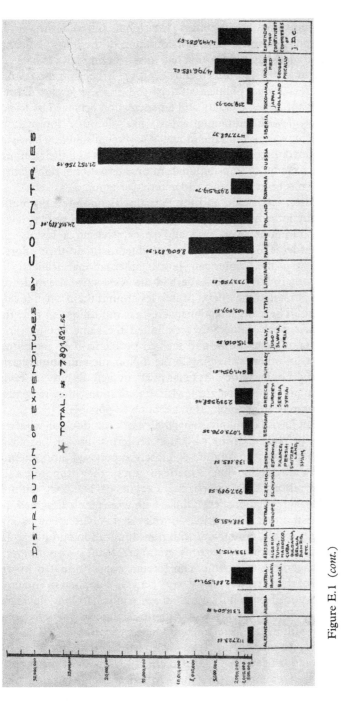

Figure E.1 (*cont.*)

Like international Jewish diplomacy, Jewish humanitarianism was fundamentally connected to the diaspora condition of the Jewish collective and statist, nationalist ambitions that had arisen among Jews to solve the Jewish Question in the late nineteenth century. It became the primary vehicle of a larger Jewish political strategy to bring the Jews of Eastern Europe the advantages of equality and emancipation achieved by Jews in the West. Yet, Jewish humanitarianism, like all other international humanitarianism, was built on the model of sovereign states by non-state actors who defined themselves with and through states and their empires. It was far less a model of transnationalism or international non-statism, even though it has been typically understood (or ignored) as such.

The JDC, Hias, Hadassah, and the Palestine Economic Corporation were profoundly influenced by the larger environment as well as Jewish philanthropic traditions over time and space, sharing a history that reached back at least to the European Enlightenment. In their effort to rehabilitate Jewish life, American Jewish international leaders, like maskilim and other elite Jewish leaders in the West since the mid-nineteenth century, imitated the liberal principles around them when it came to social policy.[7] These organizations were thus not unique in how they carried out their work; rather, they exploited the same opportunities, deployed the same techniques, and tackled problems they categorized in the same way as others struggling in the diplomatic and humanitarian arenas. They did not try to be particular at all; in fact, despite preserving their right to maintaining separate Jewish organizations, they were more likely to deliberately work to blend in as much as possible.

For American Jewish humanitarians, their work was done on what they perceived and helped to define as American terms: liberal, pluralistic, professional, benevolent, harmonious, closely supervised, and scientific by design. To maintain that American aura, they supported the American war effort; sidestepped the League of Nations; faithfully abided by all legal regulations, even those with which they disagreed, like immigration restrictions; and partnered with other American humanitarians whenever possible, complying with non-duplication and nonsectarian agreements even while under pressure to create their own programs. Sustained engagement with American foreign policy, initiated in wartime, also meant that American Jews were actively complicit in American imperial expansion. Jewish humanitarian ambitions had long dovetailed with imperial ambitions, not just with America's imperialism of free trade but previously with British, French, and German aspirations.[8] The sheer ubiquity and persistence of American Jewish work abroad meant, in fact, that it was American Jews who most seemed to represent the interwar face of American empire, rather than American soldiers, Red Cross workers, missionaries, or businessmen.[9] It was also American Jews who carried the torch of Progressivism to their target lands, keeping its spirit alive long after Progressivism flagged within the United States.

Still, differences in intention and composition meant that American Jewish organizations were in some ways quite distinct from their non-Jewish, humanitarian peers. For example, being an organized minority targeting the same organized minority abroad, they had a built-in though finite donor, supporter, and recipient base. They struggled alongside other humanitarian organizations with how to define and measure "need" to spread thin resources as equitably as possible, but there was never any question about from whom the money was collected or for whom it would be spent. Second, American Jewish organizations were more concerned with defining themselves against one another than distinguishing themselves among non-Jewish organizations, since the real competition for authority was internal to the Jewish community and part of a vigorous debate about Jewish continuity in modernity. Thus, nuances between Jewish and gentile or mainstream organizations went unaddressed by the organizations. Meanwhile, the sudden dependence of Eastern European Jews on American Jews had a striking impact on Jewish political and social circles. A third major difference was the fact that they were always operating in environments they assumed to be antisemitic, and thus they were engaged in an exercise as to how to be as unobtrusive as possible while accomplishing their work efficiently and effectively. They had to operate from a minority and private position, finding ways of appearing to have authority without any guaranteed weight of authority behind them. This was often accomplished by making financial contributions to state welfare and mainstream international humanitarian projects that were enormous relative to the size of the Jewish population.

Finally, unlike most other American humanitarian organizations, Jewish organizations had deep connections to their targeted recipients, including family, business, and cultural ties. With JDC, Hadassah, and Hias constituencies largely made up of first-generation immigrants, there were particular results. Remittances became a beloved form of efficient relief, from cash to food to financial adoption to tracing services, and moved from the sphere of immigrant activity into mainstream humanitarian relief via the JDC. Information on what was happening on the ground was readily available from multiple, unofficial, and closely proximate, if still biased, sources. Aid recipients had ways of resisting, negotiating, circumventing, or co-opting aid programs because they had lines of connection to their donors, including organized landsmanshaftn, and American Jewish leaders reacted accordingly. Jewish professionals sent to Europe for social work often had expertise and contextual knowledge of the places and the people with whom they were working that far exceeded that of monolingual Americans who outfitted the ARA, ARC, NER, AFSC, or RF, which occasionally made them valuable partners for these latter organizations.

American Jews were unconcerned with the motivations of other American or international relief organizations; any collaboration with them was built on mutual necessity rather than shared objectives. The JDC sought to fill the vacuum of governance in recent war zones not with international government or sovereign state government, but by developing and creating links across Jewish civil society. American Jewish organizations upheld a strict agenda of Jewish solidarity, actively working against East European Jews' limited rights and restricted access to welfare in the postwar order by nurturing political, social, cultural, and economic growth through the transnational Jewish collective. They felt morally obligated to remain involved, at least financially, for the long haul. In turn, the whole political economy of Jewish humanitarianism in this moment ran counter to US isolationism, making American Jewish civic postures seem "abnormal" to the American mainstream. Jewish imperial ambitions for America were thus limited to what American hegemony could provide in terms of access to faraway, beleaguered Jewish populations. It was imperialism at the scale of the Jewish world. Jewish state-building was linked, like Jewish humanitarianism overall, to imperialism, but Jewish humanitarianism in Palestine was not motivated by state-building. Zionism, too, was conceived as an answer to the Jewish Question, a route to auto-emancipation and the decolonization and liberation of Eastern Europe's Jews. American Jewish nationalists, those most likely to be found in the People's Relief wing of the JDC and in the American Jewish Congress, understood from the war that relief work had the end goal of national rights for Jews.[10] The JDC's more elite leadership did not overtly share this goal. But as Penslar has written, "International Jewish social policy attempted to create a blueprint for a new type of Jew, both in the Diaspora and in Palestine."[11] Humanitarianism modeled on American social welfare became Jewish social policy and the blueprint for overcoming the horrors of the Great War. Disastrously, the diaspora Jewish social welfare state was not to last beyond 1929.

In 1929, the world in which international Jewish humanitarianism emerged came crashing down.[12] By then, the Jews of the United States had come to dominate 17 million Jews around the world, largely due to the deflating effect of the war on Europe's Jews and the American Jewish international projects that followed. The steady and solid upward economic mobility of American Jews that enabled these humanitarian and Zionist projects throughout the 1920s screeched to a halt, and the finances of the Joint Distribution Committee, already overextended, now shriveled. Louis Marshall, the great advocate for Jewish rights, died suddenly on a trip to Europe, just when he was to attend the constituent assembly establishing the Jewish Agency for Palestine, and where he was to discuss the gravity of the onset of the "Hitlerite danger in Germany" with Max Warburg.[13] Meanwhile, the consolidation of power in the hands of Joseph Stalin in the Soviet Union created a dogmatic regime, intolerant of its Jewish branches, forcing Jewish activists to choose between Communism and the Jews inside and outside Russia. While Agro-Joint colonies survived forced collectivization, the world changed. In Palestine, Arab rioting shook the Jewish world, underscoring the vulnerability of the Zionist state-building project. The World Zionist Organization established the Jewish Agency, forging a more coherent Jewish community in Palestine under the British Mandate and bringing a wide range of non-Zionist philanthropists and Jews of Middle Eastern and North African origins into the Zionist project. As participants in the transnational Jewish community of politics, philanthropy, culture, and economy, but also subject to the winds of global change and the policies of their home countries, the fate of the Jews was linked. This study ends here, at this pivotal moment in the Jewish world, and indeed, the whole world.

The Long Century of Jewish Aid

Like the map of Europe that is recognizable today, the map of international Jewish humanitarianism was forged during and after the Great War. One hundred years after the remarkable project at the center of this book, it is possible to look back over a long century of international Jewish humanitarianism. The humanitarian project worked differently in its various theaters: in one, entirely collapsing in the Holocaust, in another, purged and expunged over the lifetime of the Soviet Union, and in still another, dispossessing a different people from the land and the economy under the British Mandate and thereby successfully consolidating economic power into a Jewish sovereign state.

Fascism, racialized antisemitism, genocide, poverty, more refugees, and the seeds of another global war were sewn in the Great War and the years that followed. Jewish international organizations already struggled through devastation, attending to repeated calamities affecting their brethren that destroyed all notions that Jewish life in Eastern Europe might improve. American Jewish and Zionist organizations would soon have to address the cataclysm waiting on their doorstep, against which whatever political leverage they had accumulated would prove ineffectual. Jewish social policy plans, so carefully built over the 1920s to reconstruct Jewish life, proved inadequate, lacking as they did

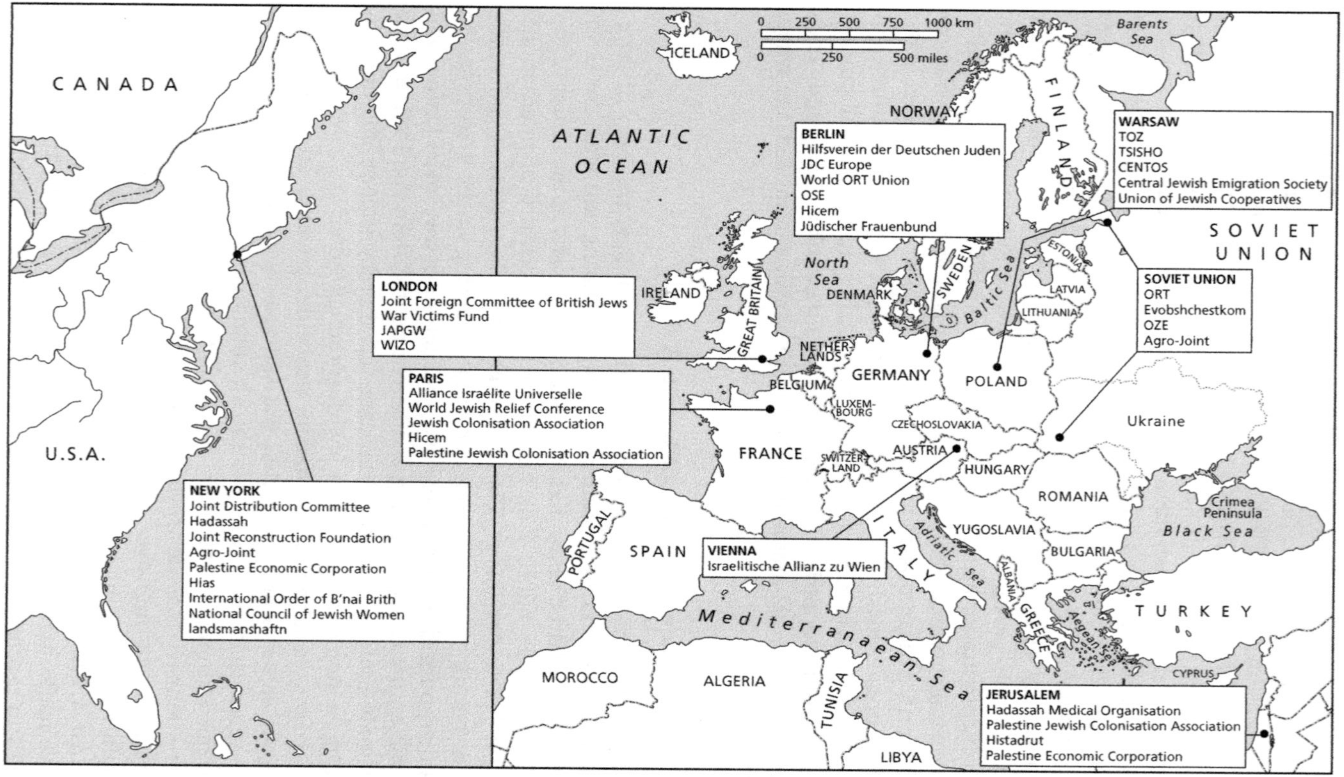

Map E.1 Map of interwar Jewish humanitarian mosaic

the resources to stem even the unstoppable, escalating refugee crisis. "Soft" Jewish transnational political power was soft indeed; the means to counter fascism amid financial crisis on behalf of endangered Jews was simply not there. Even if it had been, the JDC was ill prepared to be truly the only available Jewish humanitarian organization, or to suddenly switch ideological courses and support mass migration and resettlement programs.[14] Every option pursued by Jewish humanitarian organizations quickly closed or became terribly insufficient, from emigration to agrarianization to long-term development projects to financial support. Although the JDC, Ica, and the Jewish Agency urgently tried them all, for the Jews of Europe and their organizations, their crises would end overwhelmingly in the death camps and pits in the Bloodlands.

As Jewish humanitarian institutions, they would emerge on the other side relatively unscathed. The continuities are startling, given that the tragedy and changes in Jewish life have been so vast. As individual philanthropists, social workers, and activists, the younger individuals among them would rise to lead New Deal programs (Henry Alsberg), head important US government and international initiatives (Herbert Lehman, Lewis Strauss), take up prominent roles in Palestine (Judah Magnes), or remain somewhere in the world of Jewish communal service (Boris Bogen, Morris Waldman, Stephen Wise, Jacob Billikopf, Alice Seligsberg) if not within the JDC itself (Felix Warburg, Bernard Kahn, Harriet Lowenstein). These trajectories demonstrate the deep commitment made by the JDC's elite and middle-class leaders of the Great War era to liberal American ideas and to the future of Jewish life in America and outside it.

The JDC and Hias have helped Jewish refugees survive wars and civil unrest until the present day: They have been there through the Holocaust; the expulsion of Jews from the Arab world; anti-Zionist campaigns and Polish Jewish emigration; the fall of the Berlin Wall and the exodus of Soviet Jews; and the Yugoslav Wars. The JDC was there to make sure Jews made it through the crisis in Ukraine beginning in 2014, and Hias helped immigrants of all kinds make it in America despite bans under the Trump administration. Hadassah and the Palestine Economic Corporation have meanwhile become integrated into the fabric of Israel. The National Council of Jewish Women finally formed a standing international organization with Jewish women around the world, the International Council of Jewish Women, which has both supported human rights and Zionism, despite an international climate that has long seen these goals as opposed. Even the World ORT has carried on as an educational and vocational organization in America, Israel, and elsewhere. New Jewish humanitarian organizations have emerged: World Jewish Relief, starting as the Central British Fund for Jewish Refugees in the 1930s, and the American Jewish World Service, which works with non-Jewish, grassroots NGOs on development projects. The Israeli state began international development projects of its own, especially in Africa, soon after its founding.

Unlike the Red Cross, rushing from crisis to crisis around the world, or UN peacekeepers, their blue uniforms signaling their belonging and peaceful intentions, the JDC has never enjoyed a neutral reputation. Nor has it, like most every NGO or state humanitarian aid project of the last half century, dedicated itself to a single political or social cause, or to one particular region, or to acting as a relief agency only in times of crisis. Despite their Americanness, and the degree of security that it has assured, these Jewish humanitarian organizations have not had an easy history. Indeed, the JDC has conducted economic, material, and cultural aid inside fully functioning sovereign states until to the present. To maintain its extraordinary non-state foreign relations, the JDC has continued its understated, two-way relationship with the US federal government, as informant, listening post, and humanitarian ambassador.

Its publicity and methods have kept up to date, but the JDC has remained an organization committed to the Jewish collective, wherever Jews may live, for however long they live there, ready to spring into action wherever the next crisis for Jews appears. The JDC knows that the past has not gone anywhere; it keeps its own archive and looks to it to guide its future. The JDC is here to remind us that Westerners have forgotten that Jews still live in poverty in small towns in Eastern Europe. That antisemitism has a past, a present, and likely a future, but that antisemitism cannot be an excuse for inaction. But the JDC has also continually reminded political authorities and antisemites of these very same things. Even as Jewish humanitarian organizations aid non-Jewish populations in need, their persistent insistence that Jewish lives still hang in the balance and still matter has repeatedly made them the suspect.

The JDC has always been the object of antisemitic fantasies about American power and its nefarious Jewish embodiment. As in its earliest days, American Jews who sporadically show up in Poland with American money, claiming to be there for independent humanitarian purposes but then ask for Jewish memorials, make claims on the JDC's reputation but do not share the JDC's history. The complex memory politics of Eastern Europe include the figures of the Jewish humanitarian and the posturing Jewish humanitarian. And current American xenophobia continues to feature the stock Jewish philanthropist who places international Jewish interests above supposedly American ones. Indeed, eleven people were murdered in the Tree of Life synagogue in 2018 on the pretense that

American Jews, overall, and Hias specifically, were responsible for migrants attempting to cross into the United States. The Jewish international humanitarian, an export of the liberal, wealthy West interfering in local matters, or alternatively, nefariously shaping American foreign relations, has in other words, become its own antisemitic trope.

The Paradigm and the Exception

Addressing People's Relief shortly after the Bolshevik revolution, Judah Magnes said:

There *is* the Jewish International, the International of the spirit, an International more subtle than any freemasonry, an International that thinks but little of material forms for its expression. It is that quality that makes Jew understand Jew regardless of the lands and languages of their nativity, or of the occupations upon which they are engaged ... In a world in which internationalism is suspect, what a blessing that this international people lives and has the will to develop its International in common with every other International of the spirit.[15]

Magnes was a pacifist and Reform rabbi, who listened to immigrants and their radical politics, journeyed into the Eastern war zones to see the plight of the Jews, and moved to Palestine and became first president of the Hebrew University. Magnes believed in the unity of the Jewish people across time and space.

This international unity, which the JDC tried to develop, could be intellectually deployed like the Socialist or Communist International, as Magnes made clear. Of course, it usually was not much like socialism – Jewish internationalism was more liberal and ameliorative than radically transformative. The point is that international Jewish humanitarianism in the age of the Great War can be understood within several categories: as an international political movement; a (diaspora) social welfare state; a proto international development project; or a piece of American imperialism. Yet while Jewish humanitarianism can function as historical archetype, this plurality suggests that Jewish humanitarianism simultaneously sits outside all of these categories. While this might seem contradictory, it exemplifies the modern Jewish condition as both paradigm and exception.

When international historians write about the early interwar period, they focus on state-building, migration, and nationalism. There are few themes about American international development work or narratives of American international ascendancy; this story created a space to think about them. When international historians focusing on the 1930s onward write about welfare states, human rights, decolonization, and American hegemony, they do not necessarily have a vision for what transnationalism looked like, or how non-state interactions with global power functioned a few years earlier. This hard focus on governments – national and imperial – prior to the middle of the twentieth century fails to engage in this non-state story that emerged well before the middle of the twentieth century. Yet Jewish humanitarianism, which amounted to much more than the war relief undertaken by the United States and other nation states after the Great War, outlived and outdid the activities carried out by states. Jewish international history in the twentieth century is far more than migration and Israel alone.

This history captures a moment of transition between nineteenth- and twentieth-century models. It demands recognizing the full dimensions of what modern transnational action undertaken by non-state actors could be, exposing links between geography and power in an unevenly structured, globalizing world. Understanding transnational Jewish activism in this moment is crucial for thinking about the twentieth century – American, Jewish, and European. In the age of the Great War, there was a capacious notion of what welfare could be, and who could deliver it and where. Although Jewish humanitarianism drew on its nineteenth-century past, it was less strictly yoked to the formal imperial order, and rather more like an internationalized American Progressivism applied to the Jews of Europe. While affirming the centrality of the national idea in Europe in this moment, including among Jews, Jews ran with it in a particular way, internationalizing and liberalizing the national idea. International humanitarianism provided a way for Jews to escape their ascribed "national minority" status, offering instead a liberal diaspora nationality.

This book imagines a world in which the Jewish diaspora ran its own affairs across vast geographic distances, rather than through territorial settlement. The diaspora dimension that characterized Jewish life so thoroughly, so normatively that it is often invisible, is what makes Jewish humanitarianism so incomparable. This world is a mosaic of Jewish humanitarian projects and organizations, with the JDC as its connective thread. It is pluralistic and liberal, with space for many kinds of Jews but with American Jews as its financial guardians. In this world, Palestine is a cultural center, one Jewish hub among America, East Central Europe, and Russia. The Great War and its aftermath, the Holocaust before the Holocaust, brought this world, this Israel before Israel, to life for a tantalizing instant. It glimmered and then, it was gone.

Notes

Preface

1. The history of Jewish archives and Jewish scholarship is vast and fascinating. See, for example, Leff, *Archive Thief*; Kuznitz, *Scholarship for the Yiddish Nation*; Kassow, *Who Will Write Our History?*

Introduction

1. J. Becker to Abraham G. Becker and Kate Friedman (of A. G. Becker & Co. bank). Jan. 8 [1920] Folder 1. AJA, Becker Papers.
2. Then in Romania, now Chernivtsi in western Ukraine.
3. Duker, "Jews in the World War," 29.
4. Ibid., 17.
5. Snyder, *Bloodlands*; Bugge, "Shatter Zones"; Bartov and Weitz, *Shatterzone of Empires.*
6. American Jewish Committee, *Jews in the Eastern War Zone*, 7, 9.
7. Frankel, "Paradoxical Politics of Marginality," 6.
8. Gatrell, *A Whole Empire Walking*; American Jewish Committee, *Jews in the Eastern War Zone*, 8, 63; Rabinovitch, *Jewish Rights, National Rites*, 170–3; Bernstein, *Les Persécutions Des Juifs En Roumanie*; Goldin, "Deportation of Jews by the Russian Military."
9. Duker, "Jews in the World War," 10–12.
10. J. Marcus, Reconstruction Conference, Vienna. Dec. 1922. Folder 141. item=319064. JDC, NY: 21–32.
11. Goldin, "Deportation of Jews by the Russian Military"; Lohr, *Nationalizing the Russian Empire.*
12. Bernstein, *Les Persécutions Des Juifs En Roumanie*, 10–11.
13. McGeever, *Antisemitism and the Russian Revolution.*
14. Bernstein, *Les Persécutions Des Juifs En Roumanie*, 30.
15. Duker, "Jews in the World War," 14–16.
16. Hagen, *Anti-Jewish Violence in Poland.*
17. Frankel, "Paradoxical Politics of Marginality," 6–7; Hanebrink, *Specter Haunting Europe.*

18. Astashkevich, *Jewish Women in the Pogroms*; Veidlinger, *Pogroms of 1918–1921*; Bemporad, *Legacy of Blood*; Budnitskii, *Jews between the Reds and Whites*; Miller, "Forgotten Pogroms"; Hagen, *Anti-Jewish Violence in Poland*; Prusin, *Nationalizing a Borderland*; Bloxham, *The Final Solution*, Chapter 2.
19. Jacobson, *From Empire to Empire*.
20. Duker, "Jews in the World War," 18–20; Frankel, "Paradoxical Politics of Marginality," 6.
21. Penslar, *Jews and the Military*.
22. Cooperman, *World War I and Religious Pluralism*.
23. Elbogen, *A Century of Jewish Life*, 455.
24. Roskies, *Against the Apocalypse*, 84; Zavadivker, "Rescue and Representation."
25. Duker, "Jews in the World War," 8–10, 13–14; Roskies, *Against the Apocalypse*, 135–41; Penslar, *Jews and the Military*.
26. Peter Gatrell describes the widespread displacement as "a whole empire walking." The borders of Russia did not contain the Jewish refugee crisis, however. *A Whole Empire Walking*.
27. Engel, "World War I and Its Impact on the Problem of Security," 17.
28. American Jewish Committee, *The Jews in the Eastern War Zone*, 8.
29. Gerwarth and Horne, eds., *War in Peace*.
30. Engel, "World War I and Its Impact on the Problem of Security," 17.
31. Fink, *Defending the Rights of Others*, 9.
32. This story is told by Fink, *Defending the Rights of Others*; Levene, *War, Jews, and the New Europe*; Janowsky, *Jews and Minority Rights*.
33. Case, *Age of Questions*.
34. A history of the slogan "Jewish Question" or "*Judenfrage*" is in Toury, "The Jewish Question."
35. H. Morgenthau to J. Schiff. n.d. Folder 1.1. item=11. JDC, NY:14–18.
36. L. Marshall to N. Leven. Sept. 14, 1914. Series II. Box 9. Folder 1. AJ Committee, Correspondence.
37. 1914. n.d. Folder 1.1. item=19. JDC, NY:14–18.
38. Penslar, *Shylock's Children*, 226; Leff, *Sacred Bonds of Solidarity*.
39. On the development of Jewish international organizations, see: Green, *Moses Montefiore*; Frankel, *The Damascus Affair*; Leff, *Sacred Bonds of Solidarity*.
40. Penslar, *Shylock's Children*, 243.
41. Pak, *Gentlemen Bankers*, 4, 49, 80.
42. Ibid., 76–8.
43. Birmingham, *Our Crowd*; Supple, "A Business Elite."
44. See Green, "Liberals, Socialists, Internationalists, Jews" on the trajectories of children of 1848.
45. On the Protestant aristocracy in America, see Baltzell, *The Protestant Establishment*; Pak, *Gentlemen Bankers*.
46. Pak, *Gentlemen Bankers*, 92.
47. The idea and practice of immigrant foreign relations is articulated in Gabaccia, *Foreign Relations*.
48. See Green, "Remembering the Plutocrat and the Diplomat."
49. On the American Jewish Committee, see Cohen, *Not Free to Desist*; Silver, *Louis Marshall*, chapters 3–5.

50. For summaries of American Jewish politics, philanthropy, and communal organizations in this period, see Diner, *Jews of the United States*, chapter 5; Raphael, "Origins of Organized National Jewish Philanthropy in the United States."

51. McCune, *Whole Wide World*; Klapper, Melissa R., *Ballots, Babies, and Banners*.

52. Deutsch, "Hias 1909–1939"; Wischnitzer, *Visas to Freedom*.

53. Raider, *American Zionism*, 13–28.

54. Goren, *New York Jews and the Quest for Community*; Kotzin, *Judah L. Magnes*.

55. Frankel, "American Jewish Congress Movement"; Loeffler, "Nationalism without a Nation?"

56. Stein, "Jewish Social Work," 13–14. Stein includes the JDC, Hias, and Hadassah as Jewish social work in America.

57. Balogh, *Associational State*, 23–47.

58. Wiebe, *The Search for Order*, 111–21.

59. Rosenberg, *Financial Missionaries to the World*; Gabaccia, *Foreign Relations*; Tyrrell, *Reforming the World*.

60. Simmons, *Hadassah and the Zionist Project*.

61. On American Jewish diplomatic and philanthropic activity from the late nineteenth century to the Great War, see: Best, *To Free a People*; Penslar, *Jews and the Military*, 145–9; Cohen, *Not Free to Desist*; Wilson, "Taking Liberties Abroad"; Feingold, *Zion in America*, 244–7; Best, "Financing a Foreign War"; Sarna, *When General Grant Expelled the Jews*; Adler and Margalith, *With Firmness in the Right*; Silver, *Louis Marshall*; Kohler and Wolf, *Jewish Disabilities in the Balkan States*.

62. Kohler, "Wolf's Notes on the 'Diplomatic History of the Jewish Question.'"

63. Frankel wrote of the "high degree of continuity that marks what can be best seen, perhaps as a thirty-years' war" in "Paradoxical Politics of Marginality," 3–4.

64. On Jewish solidarity, see Leff, *Sacred Bonds of Solidarity*.

65. Penslar, *Shylock's Children*, 226–31.

66. Kallen, *Culture and Democracy in the United States*; Greene, *The Jewish Origins of Cultural Pluralism*.

67. Bulmer, "Mobilising Social Knowledge for Social Welfare"; Watenpaugh, *Bread From Stones*; Akçapar, *Indian Medical Mission*; Framke, "War and Political Humanitarianism in South Asia."

68. Kuznitz, *Scholarship for the Yiddish Nation*.

69. Gillerman, *Germans into Jews*, 14.

70. Penslar, *Zionism and Technocracy*.

71. Grachova, "Pathologies of Civility," 213–14; Zavadivker, "Jewish Aid Work in the Russian Civil War."

72. Global historians have begun to challenge the assumptions that humanitarians were always, or even primarily, connected to Christian imperialism. They explore the role of non-Christian, non-Europeans in producing alternative forms of political humanitarianism globally. See Konishi, "Emergence of an International Humanitarian Organization in Japan"; Akçapar, *Indian Medical Mission*; Framke, "War and Political Humanitarianism in South Asia."

1 War Sufferers

1. Frankel, "Paradoxical Politics of Marginality," 10.
2. M. Waldman to D. Brown. Sept. 4, 1922. Folder 53a. item=307225. JDC, NY:21–32;
3. Curti, *American Philanthropy Abroad*, 239–56; Irwin, *Making the World Safe*, 57–65.
4. Statement showing the appropriation made by the Joint Distribution Committee since the Beginning of the War to November 15, 1918. Folder 12. item=581. JDC, NY:14–18. This would value about $250 million today. According to the "Summary of Relief Operations" compiled in Bane and Lutz, eds., *Organization of American Relief in Europe 1918–1919*, 721, private charity by American relief organizations to Europe totaled $30 million during the war, indicating that the JDC's efforts could have amounted to nearly half of *all* American private relief at the time. Amounts cited by Curti, *American Philanthropy Abroad*, 239–48, indicate that the sums the JDC disbursed were higher than similar ethnic and religious American relief organizations, such as the Polish Victims Relief Fund Committee, the Serbian and Roumanian relief committees, the Committee of Mercy, and the American Committee for Armenian and Syrian Relief. Further, the JDC did not disburse all the funds it raised due to the War Trade Board's restrictions, nor did it include the individual remittances in this reckoning.
5. Cohen, *Not Free to Desist*, 81; Goren, *New York Jews and the Quest for Community*, 228–9; Rappaport, *Hands Across the Sea*, 20–71; Klapper, Melissa R., *Ballots, Babies, and Banners*, 111–14; Panter, *Jüdische Erfahrungen Und Loyalitätskonflikte*; Sterba, *Good Americans*.
6. Frankel, "Paradoxical Politics of Marginality," 7–8.
7. Conference of National Jewish Organizations. Oct. 25, 1914. Bound Minutes 1914–1915. JDC, NY:14–18.
8. McCune, *Whole Wide World*.
9. The JDC's founding is documented in: American Jewish Committee, "Jewish War Relief Work," 196–203; Szajkowski, "Concord and Discord in American Jewish Relief," 99–112; Karp, *UJA in the American Jewish Community*, 45–50; Silver, *Louis Marshall*, 259–65.
10. On the development of American international private associations due to the Great War, see Curti, *American Philanthropy Abroad*; Little, "Humanitarian Relief in Europe and the Analogue of War"; Irwin, *Making the World Safe*; Rodogno, *Night on Earth*; Little, ed., "Humanitarianism in the First World War"; Piller, "American War Relief."
11. Stein, "Jewish Social Work," 47.
12. F. Warburg, L. Marshall correspondence. Oct. 27, Dec. 18, 1914. Box 166. Folder 10. AJA, Warburg Papers.
13. Including the Roumanian Relief Committee of America, the Serbian Relief Committee, the Committee of Mercy, the Polish Victims Relief Fund Committee, and the Smith College Relief Unit. Curti, *American Philanthropy Abroad*, 229, 239–48.

14. Wilson's contacts included Oscar Straus, Henry Morgenthau, Abram Elkus, Herbert Lehman, Stephen Wise, Herman Bernstein, Nathan Straus, Paul Warburg, and Louis Brandeis.
15. Silver, *Louis Marshall*.
16. Best, *To Free a People*.
17. Cohen, *Jacob H. Schiff*.
18. Agar, *The Saving Remnant*, 19.
19. Chernow, *The Warburgs*, 163–5.
20. Cowett, "Jacob Billikopf."
21. Kobrin, "American Jewish Philanthropy, Polish Jewry"; Soyer, *Jewish Immigrant Associations*.
22. Silver, *Louis Marshall*, 263.
23. By the President of the United States of America: A Proclamation. Jan. 1,1916. Folder 38. item=5106. JDC, NY:14–18.
24. On the complexities of fundraising, see: Rosenfelt, *This Thing of Giving*; Szajkowski, "Concord and Discord in American Jewish Relief."
25. Cowett, "Jacob Billikopf," 53–4.
26. McCune, *Whole Wide World*.
27. On the American Jewish Congress, see: Frommer, "The American Jewish Congress," Fink, *Defending the Rights of Others*; Raider, *American Zionism*; Frankel, "American Jewish Congress Movement"; Loeffler, "Nationalism without a Nation?"
28. On Zionism in America and Hadassah in the Great War era, see: Gal, *Envisioning Israel*; Raider, *American Zionism*; McCune, *Whole Wide World*; Simmons, *Hadassah and the Zionist Project*; Katzburg-Yungman, *Hadassah*.
29. Karp, *UJA in the American Jewish Community*, 59–73.
30. On Hias, see Deutsch, "Hias 1909–1939"; Wischnitzer, *Visas to Freedom*.
31. Kobrin, "American Jewish Philanthropy, Polish Jewry."
32. Bremner, *American Philanthropy*, 116–35; Zunz, *Philanthropy in America*, 56–72.
33. On transatlantic Progressivism, see Rosenberg and Foner, *Spreading the American Dream*; Rodgers, *Atlantic Crossings*.
34. Panter, *Jüdische Erfahrungen Und Loyalitätskonflikte*.
35. Silver, *Louis Marshall*, 36.
36. Młynarski, *Protest and Appeal*, 1.
37. Transcript of Vienna Conference, 21. Nov. 15–19, 1920. Folder 64. item=208783. JDC, NY:19–21.
38. Report of the Committee on Conference by Julian Leavitt. Aug. 10, 1919. Folder 4. item=200078. JDC, NY:19–21.
39. On the difficulties of getting American relief to Poland, see: Fisher and Brooks, *America and the New Poland*, 78–91; Biskupski, "Diplomacy of Wartime Relief" and "Wartime Relief of Belgium, Serbia, and Poland"; Szajkowski, "Private and Organized American Jewish Overseas Relief (1914–1938)."
40. Duker, "Jews in the World War," 14–16, 20–1; Davis, *Home Fires Burning*, 132–6; Elbogen, *A Century of Jewish Life*, 462, 516.

41. W. Phillips to F. Brylawski. Feb. 27, 1915. Folder 35.1. item=2296. JDC, NY:14–18.
42. Hyman, *American Aid to Jews Overseas*, 14.
43. This estimate was based on a 1916 report of the Hilfskomite, which noted that local distributors reported providing about one mark monthly per person. American Jewish Committee, "Jewish War Relief Work," 206–13.
44. On the Warburg bank and family, see: Chernow, *The Warburgs*; Rosenbaum and Sherman, *M. M. Warburg & Co.*
45. Chernow, *The Warburgs*, 162.
46. M. Warburg to F. Warburg. Jan. 4,1915. Folder 18.1. item=1103. JDC, NY:14–18.
47. AJRC to M. Warburg. Jan. 19, 1915. Folder 18.1. item=1109. JDC, NY:14–18.
48. Felix Warburg's papers do not show a significant trace of correspondence with his brothers, and papers on this subject in JDC archives are on Kuhn Loeb letterhead. One might infer that this transfer of funds within the family was entirely conducted in business transactions from Kuhn Loeb, New York, to M. M. Warburg & Co., Hamburg.
49. AJRC treasurer to F. Brylawski. Feb. 24, 1915. Folder 129.1. item=9133. JDC, NY:14–18; Minutes of the JDC. March 1, 1915. Bound Minutes 1914–1915. JDC, NY:14–18.
50. Minutes of the JDC. March 1, 1915. Bound Minutes 1914–1915. JDC, NY:14–18.
51. Minutes of the AJRC. June 2, 1916. Folder 3.2. item=160. JDC, NY:14–18.
52. Minutes of the JDC of the AJRC. June 20, 1916. Folder 3.2. item=161. JDC, NY:14–18.
53. Fink, *Defending the Rights of Others*, 73–4, 82–3.
54. On the jockeying over distribution of American Jewish funds in American, German, and Polish Jewish communities, see: Aschheim, "Eastern Jews, German Jews"; Szajkowski, "Jewish Relief in Eastern Europe 1914–1917"; Jahr, *Paul Nathan*, 171–222; Silber, "A Joint Political Program for the Jews of Poland during World War I."
55. Hyman, *American Aid to Jews Overseas*, 14; Szajkowski, "Jewish Relief in Eastern Europe," 36.
56. E. Lewin-Epstein to JDC. March 17, 1916. Folder 129.2. item=9141. JDC, NY:14–18.
57. Translation of an abstract of a report of the Hilfsverein. May 26, 1916. Folder 129.2. item=9184. JDC, NY:14–18.
58. Over four months, Magnes went to Warsaw, Radzimin, Vilna, Kovno, Lodz, Lublin, Lemberg, and Vienna. Report to the JDC by Magnes and Dushkin. March 24, 1917. Folder 155. item=155106. JDC, NY:14–18.
59. Kotzin, *Judah L. Magnes*; Goren, *New York Jews and the Quest for Community*.
60. J. Magnes to F. Warburg. Sept. 24, 1916. Box 168. Folder 20. AJA, Warburg Papers.
61. Preliminary Report of the Chairman, Commission of the American Jewish Relief Funds. Sept. 24, 1916. Folder 18.3. item=1322. JDC, NY:14–18.
62. Szajkowski, "Jewish Relief in Eastern Europe," 42–3.

63. Goren, *New York Jews and the Quest for Community*, 217.
64. Koss, "Jewish Vilna, 1914–1918," 48–63; Tessaris, "War Relief Work in Poland and Lithuania," 131–2.
65. Rechter, David, *Jews of Vienna*, 83–90; Rozenblit, *Reconstructing a National Identity*, 65–81; Szajkowski, "Jewish Relief in Eastern Europe," 44–5.
66. J. Magnes to F. Warburg. Sept. 24, 1916. Box 168. Folder 20. AJA, Warburg Papers.
67. Szajkowski, "Private and Organized American Jewish Overseas Relief (1914–1938)."
68. Little, "Humanitarian Relief in Europe and the Analogue of War."
69. Secretary's report of subjects to be discussed. Oct. 21, 1915. Box 166. Folder 27. AJA, Warburg Papers.
70. W. Phillips to F. Brylawski. Feb. 27, 1915. Folder 35.1. item=2296. JDC, NY:14–18.
71. Minutes of the JDC Executive Committee. Jan. 11, 1916. Bound Minutes 1916. JDC, NY:14–18.
72. Farley, *To Cast Out Disease*, 45.
73. J. Magnes to F. Warburg. Sept. 24, 1916. Box 168. Folder 20. AJA, Warburg Papers.
74. Memorandum: Assistance to Jews during the First Two Years of the European War Rendered by State Department. July 26, 1916. 861.4016/ 215. NARA, State Dept.
75. Duker, "Jews in the World War," 12–13; American Jewish Committee, *Jews in the Eastern War Zone*, 20–36, 61–2; Goldin, "Deportation of Jews by the Russian Military."
76. National Workmen's Committee on Jewish Rights, *The War and the Jews in Russia*, 102–4; Report on the Treatment of Jews in Poland and the Occupied Provinces of Galicia by the American Consulate in Russia. June 10, 1915. 861.4016/182. NARA, State Dept.
77. Pipes, *Russia under the Bolshevik Regime*, 100.
78. Duker, "Jews in the World War," 13–14.
79. Standing Committee on Russia and Occupied Territories recommendations. 27 May 1918. Folder 10. item=457. JDC, NY:14–18.
80. Ica Petrograd (Marc A. Varshavsky, David Feinberg) to Ica Paris. July 30 and Aug. 28, 1914. Folder 39/2. Russie Emigration du 29 Mai 1914 au 27 Fevrier 1918 No. 111–224. CAHJP, JCA/Lon Num.
81. Penslar, *Shylock's Children*, 228. On Ica, see: Norman, *Outstretched Arm*.
82. Zipperstein, "Politics of Relief," 23, 27–8.
83. Report of the Central Jewish Committee for Relieving the Victims of the War from the Beginning of its Activities (August 1914) to the 30th of June, 1917. Folder 143.3. Digital ID 10135. JDC, NY:14–18.
84. Zipperstein, "Politics of Relief," 23.
85. Ibid., 26.
86. Rabinovitch, *Jewish Rights, National Rites*, 181.
87. On prerevolutionary, Jewish St. Petersburg, see: Beizer, *The Jews of St. Petersburg*; Epstein, "Caring for the Soul's Home"; Horowitz, *Jewish Philanthropy and Enlightenment*; Norman, *Outstretched Arm*; Shapiro, *History of ORT*.

88. Zipperstein, "Politics of Relief," 27.

89. Zavadivker, "Jewish Aid Work in the Russian Civil War."

90. Agar, *The Saving Remnant*, 27.

91. JDC Treasurer to National City Bank. Dec. 2, 1914. Folder 143.1. item=9926. JDC, NY:14–18.

92. Letters from JDC Treasurer to National City Bank. 1914–1915. Folder 143.1. JDC, NY:14–18.

93. American Jewish Committee, "Jewish War Relief Work," 14; Notice Regarding Remittances. Sept. 2, 1915. Box 166, Folder 27. AJA, Warburg Papers.

94. Folder 39/2. Russie Emigration du 29 Mai 1914 au 27 Fevrier 1918 No. 111–224. CAHJP, JCA/Lon Num; Cables from AJRC to EKOPO, Petrograd. May to Nov. 1915. Box 166, Folder 27. AJA, Warburg Papers; Cables from AJRC to Ica, Petrograd. Jan. to April 1916. Box 168, Folder 20. AJA, Warburg Papers.

95. Zavadivker, "Jewish Aid Work in the Russian Civil War."

96. Special Conference for the Organization of War Refugees. March 1, 1916. Folder 143.2. item=10010. JDC, NY:14–18; Report of the Central Jewish Committee for Relieving the Victims of the War from the Beginning of its Activities (August 1914) to the 30th of June, 1917. Folder 143.3. item=10135. JDC, NY:14–18. Although British Jews could send private funds to Russian Jews, French and British Jewish leaders failed to convince their own governments to pressure their Russian ally to stop persecuting its Jews, see Fink, *Defending the Rights of Others*, 78–9.

97. American Jewish Committee, "Jewish War Relief Work," 205.

98. Report of the Central Jewish Committee for Relieving the Victims of the War from the Beginning of Its Activities (August 1914) to the 30th of June, 1917. Folder 143.3. item=10135. JDC, NY:14–18; Translated letter from D. Feinberg to F. Warburg. Feb. 26, 1915. Box 167, Folder 16. AJA, Warburg Papers.

99. Information received by the Petrograd Committee of Relief. Dec. 17, 1915. Folder 143.1. item=9981. JDC, NY:14–18; Special Conference for the Organization of War Refugees. March 1, 1916. Folder 143.2. item=10010. JDC, NY:14–18; Beizer, *The Jews of St. Petersburg*, 130–2, 141.

100. Evreyskaya Nedelia 18–33. Summer 1916. Folder 143.2. item=10077. JDC, NY:14–18.

101. JDC Press Notice. Jan. 22, 1917. Box 174, Folder 4. AJA, Warburg Papers.

102. Report of the Central Jewish Committee for Relieving the Victims of the War from the Beginning of Its Activities (August 1914) to the 30th of June, 1917. Folder 143.3. item=10135. JDC, NY:14–18.

103. Rabinovitch, *Jewish Rights, National Rites*, 186.

104. Memorandum: Assistance to Jews during the First Two Years of the European War Rendered by State Department. July 26, 1916. 861.4016/215. NARA, State Dept.

105. D. Francis to P. Warburg. May 15, 1916. Folder 143.2. item=10026. JDC, NY:14–18.

106. Ambassador D. Francis to Secretary of State R. Lansing and Russian Minister of Foreign Affairs B. Sturmer. Aug. 1916. 861.4016/227–9. NARA, State Dept.

107. Cables from AJRC to EKOPO, Petrograd. July 1 and Sept. 8, 1915. Box 166, Folder 27. AJA, Warburg Papers.

108. Translated letter from D. Feinberg to F. Warburg. Feb. 26, 1915. Box 167, Folder 16. AJA, Warburg Papers.

109. Report of the Central Jewish Committee for Relieving the Victims of the War from the Beginning of Its Activities (August 1914) to the 30th of June, 1917. Folder 143.3. item=10135. JDC, NY:14–18.

110. Minutes of the JDC Executive Committee. Jan. 11, 1916. Bound Minutes 1916. JDC, NY:14–18; Report of the Central Jewish Committee for Relieving the Victims of the War from the Beginning of Its Activities (August 1914) to the 30th of June, 1917, 2. Folder 143.3. item=10135. JDC, NY:14–18.

111. Rabinovitch, *Jewish Rights, National Rites*, 185.

112. On Jewish war relief in Russia including Soviet archival evidence, see Beizer, *Russian Jewry and the Joint*, part I.

113. *Chalukah* was an international Jewish philanthropic network of rabbinic emissaries from Palestine focused on raising and sending funds from abroad to maintain the Jewish community in Palestine. This charitable giving from diaspora Jews to Jews in Palestine existed from the eighteenth century, engaging first the Sephardic diaspora and by the nineteenth century, Ashkenazim. Lehmann, *Emissaries From the Holy Land*; Green, "Old Networks, New Connections."

114. Tanielian, *Charity of War*; Jacobson, *From Empire to Empire*.

115. Duker, "Jews in the World War," 18–20; Frankel, "Paradoxical Politics of Marginality," 6.

116. April 1917. *Bulletin of the JDC*; Statement of Relief Funds Forwarded by JDC for Relief of Jews in Palestine. n.d. Folder 12. 519. JDC, NY:14–18.

117. During the Great War, the World Zionist Organization shifted from its European base to America. The Provisional Zionist Committee was the temporary home in America of the Zionist Organization during World War I. The JDC and PZC were able to cooperate on a practical, mutually beneficial level to send emergency relief to Palestine, but the non-Zionist JDC never attempted to absorb the PZC into its own organization because of ideological conflict.

118. Karp, *UJA in the American Jewish Community*, 45–6; American Jewish Committee, "Eighth Annual Report of the American Jewish Committee," 360–5.

119. American Relief Fund, Jerusalem: Report of the Work of the Committee for the Month of October. Oct. 1914. File 1021. CAHJP, Magnes Papers.

120. Silver, *Louis Marshall*, 260.

121. Penslar, *Zionism and Technocracy*, 145.

122. A. Ruppin to H. Morgenthau. Oct. 1, 1914. File 1021. CAHJP, Magnes Papers.

123. A. Ruppin to J. Magnes. 15 Nov. 1914. File 1021. CAHJP, Magnes Papers.
124. Frankel, "Paradoxical Politics of Marginality," 10.
125. H. Bernstein, J. Daniels correspondence. Jan.–March 1915. Box 5, Folder 153. YIVO, Bernstein Papers; Memorandum: Assistance to Jews during the First Two Years of the European War Rendered by State Department. July 26, 1916. 861.4016/215. NARA, State Dept.
126. J. Magnes to F. Warburg. Feb. 26, 1915. Box 166. Folder 27. AJA, Warburg Papers.
127. Memorandum: Assistance to Jews during the First Two Years of the European War Rendered by State Department. July 26, 1916. 861.4016/215. NARA, State Dept; Bauer, *My Brother's Keeper*, 7.
128. State Department to F. Brylawski. Dec. 4, 1915. Box 166, Folder 27. AJA, Warburg Papers; Memorandum: Assistance to Jews during the First Two Years of the European War Rendered by State Department. July 26, 1916. 861.4016/215. NARA, State Dept; Jacobson, *From Empire to Empire*, 46.
129. Friedman, *Germany, Turkey, and Zionism*, 195.
130. Memorandum: Assistance to Jews during the First Two Years of the European War Rendered by State Department. July 26, 1916. 861.4016/215. NARA, State Dept; April–Aug. 1915. Box 9. Folders 1–3. YUA, Central Relief; First Meeting of the AJRC. Nov. 22, 1914. Bound Minutes 1914–1915. JDC, NY:14–18.
131. Sufian and Shvarts, "'Mission of Mercy' and the Ship That Came Too Late," 389–92; Memorandum: Assistance to Jews during the First Two Years of the European War Rendered by State Department. July 26, 1916. 861.4016/215. NARA, State Dept.
132. Sufian and Shvarts, "'Mission of Mercy' and the Ship That Came Too Late," 393–5. See also Watenpaugh, *Bread From Stones*; Tanielian, *Charity of War*.
133. Jackson, "Transformative Relief"; Tanielian, *Charity of War*; Watenpaugh, *Bread From Stones*.
134. Memorandum: Assistance to Jews during the First Two Years of the European War Rendered by State Department. July 26, 1916. 861.4016/215. NARA, State Dept.
135. Brecher, *Reluctant Ally*, 2–11; Jacobson, *From Empire to Empire*, 47; Jacobson, "American 'Welfare Politics,'" 57–63; Oren, *Power, Faith, and Fantasy*, 357; Letter from O. Glazebrook to L. Levin. Aug. 30, 1915. File 1021. CAHJP, Magnes Papers.
136. April–Aug. 1915. Box 9. Folders 1–3. YUA, Central Relief; Brecher, *Reluctant Ally*, 2–4; Oren, *Power, Faith, and Fantasy*, 327.
137. Oren, *Power, Faith, and Fantasy*, 333.
138. The Effects of the War on Palestine. n.d. 1915. File 1021. CAHJP, Magnes Papers.
139. Szajkowski, "Private and Organized American Jewish Overseas Relief (1914–1938)."
140. H. Lowenstein to F. Warburg. Aug. 1, 1916. Folder 36.1. item=3045. JDC, NY:14–18; Articles in Scrapbook. Box 1. AJHS, Lowenstein Papers.

141. Ica (S. Yanovsky) cable to JDC, Dec. 11, 1917. Box 174, Folder 4. AJA, Warburg Papers.
142. H. Lowenstein to F. Warburg. Aug. 1, 1916. Folder 36.1. item=3045. JDC, NY:14–18.
143. Press notice regarding remittances. Nov. 27, 1916. Folder 36.1. item=3091. JDC, NY:14–18.
144. A. Lucas to F. Warburg, H. Lehman, and H. Fischel. Nov. 23, 1916. Box 170. Folder 17. AJA, Warburg Papers.
145. Press notice regarding remittances. Nov. 27, 1916. Folder 36.1. item=3091. JDC, NY:14–18.
146. JDC Press Notice. Jan. 19, 1917. Box 174. Folder 4. AJA, Warburg Papers.
147. American Jewish Committee, "Jewish War Relief Work," 207–8.
148. Memorandum: Assistance to Jews during the First Two Years of the European War Rendered by State Department. July 26, 1916. 861.4016/215. NARA, State Dept.
149. H. Lowenstein to F. Warburg. Aug. 1, 1916. Folder 36.1. item=3045. JDC, NY:14–18; J. Magnes to F. Warburg. Sept. 24, 1916. Box 168, Folder 20. AJA, Warburg Papers; Folder 39/2. Russie Emigration du 29 Mai 1914 au 27 Fevrier 1918 No. 111–224. CAHJP, JCA/Lon Num.
150. Harriet Lowenstein to F. Warburg. Jan. 22, 1915. Box 166. Folder 27. AJA, Warburg Papers.
151. Szajkowski, "Private and Organized American Jewish Overseas Relief (1914–1938)," 70–83.
152. Sanders, Ronald, Shores of Refuge, 289–94; Szajkowski, "Private and Organized American Jewish Overseas Relief (1914–1938)," 67–9; Wischnitzer, Visas to Freedom, 78–82.
153. Nov. 1915. Jewish Immigration Bulletin; Tartakower manuscript, 23. 1939. 245.4.26. xxvi–1. YIVO, HIAS.
154. Szajkowski, "Private and Organized American Jewish Overseas Relief (1914–1938)," 67–9.
155. Cables from I. Hershfield to Hias NY. Feb. –March 1916. 245.4 XII-Germany-0. YIVO, HIAS; May 1916. Jewish Immigration Bulletin; Memorandum concerning American Relief Work in Poland. June 2, 1917. 861.48/320. NARA, State Dept.
156. May 1916. Jewish Immigration Bulletin; Wischnitzer, Visas to Freedom, 80–1.
157. Folder 39/2. Russie Emigration du 29 Mai 1914 au 27 Fevrier 1918 No. 111–224. CAHJP, JCA/Lon Num.
158. Wischnitzer, Visas to Freedom, 80–1.
159. Soyer, Jewish Immigrant Associations, 166–70.
160. Ibid., 163–7.
161. Ibid., 162.
162. Minutes of Executive Committee. 1917. Folder 3.1. item=152. JDC, NY:14–18.
163. Examples: Isidore Hershfield of Hias came to an AJRC meeting in June 1916, having returned to the United States. The AJRC questioned him regarding the relief money it had sent, asking if he thought the number of dependents were correct, if people thought funds were distributed fairly,

and if there was any discrimination by the German government regarding relief. Minutes of the American Jewish Relief Committee. June 2, 1916. Folder 3.2. item=160. JDC, NY:14–18. In another example, Elie Lewin-Epstein, treasurer of the PZC and active in relief work went to Poland in 1916, and expressed to the JDC his dissatisfaction with Hilfsverein's work. E. Lewin-Epstein to JDC. March 30, 1916. Folder 129.2. item=9159. JDC, NY:14–18; E. Lewin-Epstein to JDC. March 17, 1916. Folder 129.2. item=9141. JDC, NY:14–18. Both accounts prompted the JDC to push for Magnes to visit Poland. In the case of Bernard Flexner, who went to Romania as part of the ARC, he reported his findings back to the ARC *and also* the JDC. He had spoken with the American minister Vopicka in Jassy and a local Jewish leader, pronouncing them both efficient and capable of organizing relief, and also sent two men to Odessa to obtain supplies on the JDC's bill. Minutes of the JDC. Dec. 18, 1917. Box 174. Folder 4. AJA, Warburg Papers. When it came to former US Ambassador Abram Elkus, a JDC Executive Committee meeting was called in July 1917 so he could report on Jews in the Ottoman Empire. Minutes of the JDC. July 17, 1917. Folder 3.1. item=156. JDC, NY:14–18.

164. Irwin, *Making the World Safe*, 105–40.
165. Secretary of State to the Ambassador in Spain and Secretary of State to the Treasurer of the JDC. Feb.–April 1917. 861.48/252,255,448. United States Department of State, *FRUS 1918, the World War*, 498–9; W. Phillips and H. Lehman. April 1917. Folder 35.2. item=2345, 2347. JDC, NY:14–18.
166. Summary of JDC communications regarding transmission of funds by H. Lehman. April–May 1917. Folder 35.2. item=2353. JDC, NY:14–18; The Secretary of State to the Charge in the Netherlands. May 1917. 861.48/300a, 308. Ibid., 501–2; Documents pertaining to transmission of funds. May–June 1917. Folder 35.2. item=2355. JDC, NY:14–18; S. Wise to H. Lehman. July 6, 1917. Folder 35.2. item=2366. JDC, NY:14–18; JDC Press Notice. July 2, 1917. Box 174. Folder 4. AJA, Warburg Papers.
167. Bogen, *Born a Jew*, 96–106; Report of B. Bogen and M. Senior to State Department. Feb. 18, 1918. Folder 129.5. item=9388. JDC, NY:14–18.
168. Bogen, *Born a Jew*, 106.
169. Letter to the Secretary of State. Feb. 19, 1918. Folder 38. item=5131. JDC, NY:14–18; Story of Holland Commission by M. Senior. April 1918. Folder 1.2. item=91. JDC, NY:14–18.
170. Report of B. Bogen and M. Senior to Secretary of State. Feb. 19, 1918. Folder 38. item=5131. JDC, NY:14–18; Story of Holland Commission by M. Senior. April 1918. Folder 1.2. item=91. JDC, NY:14–18; Affidavit, Agreement and Guarantee. Dec. 21, 1917. Folder 17.1. item=934. JDC, NY:14–18; JDC Netherlands to Central Committee Warsaw. Dec. 26, 1917. Folder 17.1. item=946. JDC, NY:14–18; American Jewish Committee, "Jewish War Relief Work," 206.
171. Davis, *Home Fires Burning*.
172. Memorandum concerning American Relief Work in Poland. June 2, 1917. 861.48/320. NARA, State Dept.
173. W. Phillips to R. Lansing. May 17, 1917. 861.48/301. NARA, State Dept.

174. Memorandum concerning American Relief Work in Poland. June 2, 1917. 861.48/320. NARA, State Dept.

175. Synopsis of a Report of the Distribution of Relief Funds. Feb.–Aug. 1917. Box 174, Folder 4. AJA, Warburg Papers.

176. Jacobson, "American 'Welfare Politics,'" 62–4; Statement of Relief Funds Forwarded by JDC for Relief of Jews in Palestine. n.d. Folder 12. Item ID 519. JDC, NY:14–18; S. Hoofien to F.S. Van Nierop. Aug. 10, 1917. Folder 35.2. item=2383. JDC, NY:14–18; F Brylawski to J. Grew. Aug. 23, 1917. Folder 35.2. item=2385. JDC, NY:14–18.

177. Penslar, *Zionism and Technocracy*, 145–6.

178. Jacobson, *From Empire to Empire*, 141–2.

179. Removal of Racial and Religious Limitations. April 18, 1917. Folder 143.3. item=10125. JDC, NY:14–18.

180. Zavadivker, "Jewish Aid Work in the Russian Civil War."

181. Szajkowski, *Mirage of American Jewish Aid in Soviet Russia*, 7.

182. Standing Committee on Russia and Occupied Territories recommendations. May 27, 1918. Folder 10. item=457. JDC, NY:14–18.

183. Ibid.

184. A. Lucas draft letter to R. Lansing, Secretary of State. June 27, 1918. Folder 10. item=461. JDC, NY:14–18.

185. Rosenson was presumably an American Jew sharing personal networks with JDC leaders. Minutes of a Meeting of the Standing Committee on Russia and Occupied Territories. Aug. 20, 1918. Folder 10. item=481. JDC, NY:14–18; B. Bogen to S. Rosenson. Aug. 12, 1918. Folder 1.2. item=97. JDC, NY:14–18.

186. Szajkowski, *Mirage of American Jewish Aid in Soviet Russia*, 8.

187. Irwin, *Making the World Safe*, 105, 112–13; Polk, *Constructive Efforts*; Standing Committee on Russia and Occupied Territories recommendations. May 27, 1918. Folder 10. item=457. JDC, NY:14–18; Minutes of a Meeting of the Standing Committee on Russia and Occupied Territories. Aug. 20, 1918. Folder 10. item=481. JDC, NY:14–18.

188. Communications regarding Russian and Polish relief. n.d. [summer 1918]. Folder 10. item=456. JDC, NY:14–18.

189. Standing Committee on Russia and Occupied Territories recommendations. May 27, 1918. Folder 10. item=457. JDC, NY:14–18.

190. Szajkowski, "Private and Organized American Jewish Overseas Relief (1914–1938)," 84.

191. Statement of Appropriations Made by the Joint Distribution Committee. Dec. 20, 1918. Folder 12. item=586. JDC, NY:14–18.

192. Szajkowski, "Private and Organized American Jewish Overseas Relief (1914–1938)," 87.

193. Adler and Margalith, *With Firmness in the Right*, 147–8; L. Marshall to President W. Wilson. May 4, 1918. Folder 38. item=5138. JDC, NY:14–18.

194. Adler and Margalith, *With Firmness in the Right*, 142–7.

195. Telephone message from A. Lucas for F. Warburg. Nov. 1, 1917. Box 174. Folder 5. AJA, Warburg Papers; Minutes of the Joint Distribution Committee. Nov. 7, 1917. Folder 3.1. item=157. JDC, NY:14–18.

196. Communications regarding Russian and Polish relief. n.d. [summer 1918]. Folder 10. item=456. JDC, NY:14–18.
197. W. Phillips to R. Lansing. May 17, 1917. 861.48/301. NARA, State Dept; Memorandum concerning American Relief Work in Poland. June 2, 1917. 861.48/320. NARA, State Dept.
198. For example, Lucas noted that Warburg thought it "would not be wise for us to put ourselves in the position of having an official application declined by the State Department," suggesting that Brylawski first ask around to see if semi-official credentials for Bogen and Senior's trip to Holland would be welcomed. A. Lucas to F. Brylawski. July 1, 1917. Folder 38. item=5119. JDC, NY:14–18.
199. W. Phillips to A. Lucas. Dec. 6, 1918. Folder 38. item=5146. JDC, NY:14–18.
200 May 1917. *Bulletin of the JDC*.

2 The Hungry

1. F. Warburg to M. Warburg. Nov. 15, 1918. Box 10. Folder 27. AJHS, Strauss Papers.
2. F. Warburg to Jewish leaders in Europe. Nov. 15, 1918. Box 10. Folder 27. AJHS, Strauss Papers.
3. Pfau, *No Sacrifice Too Great*, 10–17. On Hoover and the US Food Administration, see: Veit, *Modern Food, Moral Food*; Mullendore, *History of the U.S. Food Administration*; Little, "Humanitarian Relief in Europe and the Analogue of War"; Nash and Clements, *Life of Herbert Hoover*; Surface and Bland, *American Food in the World War*.
4. F. Warburg to Jewish leaders in Europe. Nov. 15, 1918. Box 10. Folder 27. AJHS, Strauss Papers; Pfau, *No Sacrifice Too Great*, 16–17.
5. Gerwarth and Horne, eds., *War in Peace*.
6. Veit, *Modern Food, Moral Food*, 58–76.
7. Statement Furnished by Messrs. Hoover and Davis. Dec. 10, 1918. Bane and Lutz, eds. *Organization of American Relief in Europe 1918–1919*, 83.
8. Veit, *Modern Food, Moral Food*, 73–5.
9. The President's Proposal for a Congressional Appropriation of One Hundred Million Dollars for European Relief. Jan. 1, 1919. Bane and Lutz, eds., *Organization of American Relief in Europe 1918–1919*, 139–40.
10. For histories of this moment see Fink, *Defending the Rights of Others*; Janowsky, *Jews and Minority Rights*; Levene, *War, Jews, and the New Europe*; Adler and Margalith, *With Firmness in the Right*; Loeffler, "Between Zionism and Liberalism."
11. B. Bogen to JDC NY. Jan. 29, 1919. Folder 61.1. item=207888. JDC, NY:19–21.
12. Box 8. Folder 2. AJHS, Strauss Papers.
13. H. Lowenstein to F. Warburg. April 30, 1919. Folder 61.2. item=208004. JDC, NY:19–21.
14. Harriet Lowenstein (Goldstein) created the JDC Transmission Bureau, set up the JDC's European operations postwar in Europe, served as the JDC's

comptroller, acted as Warburg's philanthropic adviser, and was both an accountant and lawyer by training. She is a forgotten figure, though in her time, she featured in profiles of Jewish leaders in the Jewish press; see Box 1. Scrapbook 1917–1955. AJHS, Lowenstein Papers. Lowenstein functioned in the world of leading Jewish men, rather than working among Jewish women of her time, as did Henrietta Szold, Janet Roberts, or Rebekah Kohut. She seemed to arrive at her positions, which carried real responsibility but little publicity, by sheer force of dedication and talent.

15. Hoover set up a complete, secure telegraph system connecting European capital cities with American military operators at the clearing points. Willis, *Herbert Hoover and the Russian Prisoners of World War I*, 5.

16. Landman, "Send a Woman for It: The Story of a Job in France and How It Was Done."

17. H. Lowenstein to Capt. Schumann. April 7, 1919. Folder 61.2. item=207951. JDC, NY:19–21; C. Adler to F. Warburg. April 9, 1919. Folder 61.2. item=207954. JDC, NY:19–21.

18. A. Lucas to H. Lowenstein. May 17, 1919. Folder 61.2. item=208045. JDC, NY:19–21.

19. F. Warburg to B. Bogen. Jan. 23, 1919. Folder 61.1. item=207876. JDC, NY:19–21.

20. Transcript of Meeting of the JDC, 21. Aug. 10, 1919. Folder 4. item=200080. JDC, NY:19–21.

21. Adler recommended that minutes could travel safely only "by hand of some discreet friend who is going over to America." H. Lowenstein to JDC NY. n.d. [late April/early May] 1919. Folder 61.2. item=208006. JDC, NY:19–21.

22. Weindling, "From Sentiment to Science," 204–6; Cabanes, *The Great War and the Origins of Humanitarianism*, 228.

23. The delegate was a Sephardic rabbi, David de Sola Pool, who had worked in Hoover's Food Administration, in the JWB, as the US representative of the Zionist Commission to Jerusalem, and then as the JDC's regional director for Palestine and Syria. Transcript of Vienna Conference, 40–1. Nov. 15–19, 1920. Folder 64. item=208783. JDC, NY:19–21.

24. Veit, *Modern Food, Moral Food*, 35–8, 51.

25. J. Goldman to F. Warburg. Feb. 18, 1920. Folder 63.1. item=208235. JDC, NY:19–21; LBI, Kahn Memoir, 62.

26. Klapper, "American Jewish Women's International Travel."

27. L. Gonsolin to H. Lowenstein. Sept. 15, 1919. Folder 62. item=208190. JDC, NY:19–21.

28. LBI, Kahn Memoir, 70–1.

29. Stenographer's Transcript of Meeting of the JDC, 5. Dec. 12, 1920. Folder 6. item=200102. JDC, NY:19–21.

30. Appointment of an American Food Mission to Poland. Hoover to Kellogg. Dec. 23, 1918. Bane and Lutz, eds., *Organization of American Relief in Europe 1918–1919*; Fisher and Brooks, *America and the New Poland*, 124–6; Lerski, *Herbert Hoover and Poland*, 5–8.

31. Veit, *Modern Food, Moral Food*, 74.

32. Rodogno, "Humanitarian Politics & Policies in Asia Minor and Greece," 85.

33. Biskupski, "Diplomacy of Wartime Relief."
34. Transcript of Vienna Conference, 5. Nov. 15–19, 1920. Folder 64. item=208783. JDC, NY:19–21.
35. Heller, *On the Edge of Destruction*.
36. Bogen, *Born a Jew*, 125.
37. B. Bogen to JDC NY. Jan. 4, 1919. Folder 61.1. item=207864. JDC, NY:19–21.
38. L. Strauss to B. Bogen. Jan. 3, 1919. Box 9. Folder 4. AJHS, Strauss Papers; B. Bogen to JDC NY. Jan. 11, 1919. Folder 61.1. item=207867. JDC, NY:19–21; Bogen, *Born a Jew*, 126–7.
39. B. Bogen to JDC NY. Feb. 11, 1919. Box 183. Folder 2. AJA, Warburg Papers.
40. Wentling, "The Engineer and the Shtadlanim," 405.
41. B. Bogen to JDC NY. 20 Jan. 1919. Folder 61.1. item=207878. JDC, NY:19–21.
42. B. Bogen to JDC NY. 29 Jan. 1919. Folder 61.1. item=207888. JDC, NY:19–21.
43. Becker, "James Becker and East European Jewry after World War I," 279.
44. Bogen, *Born a Jew*, 130.
45. Bogen, *Born a Jew*, 132; B. Bogen cable to JDC NY. Feb. 15, 1919. Folder 61.1. item=207894. JDC, NY:19–21.
46. Bogen, *Born a Jew*, 147–8.
47. J. Becker to parents. Feb. 9, 1919. Folder 2. AJA, Becker Papers.
48. J. Becker to parents. March 28, 1919. Folder 2. AJA, Becker Papers.
49. The Polish Relief Committee covered the other half.
50. Surface and Bland, *American Food in the World War*, 57.
51. B. Bogen to L. Strauss. Feb. 29, 1919. Box 10. Folder 28. AJHS, Strauss Papers.
52. Wentling, "The Engineer and the Shtadlanim," 383.
53. B. Bogen to L. Strauss. March 6, 1919. Box 10. Folder 28. AJHS, Strauss Papers.
54. L. Strauss to F. Warburg. March 15, 1919. Box 10. Folder 23. AJHS, Strauss Papers.
55. J. Becker to parents. April–May 1919. Folder 2. AJA, Becker Papers.
56. Folder 68.1. JDC, NY:19–21.
57. Fisher and Brooks, *America and the New Poland*, 138.
58. B. Bogen to H. Lowenstein. April 11, 1919. Folder 61.2. item=207973. JDC, NY:19–21.
59. He asked for a minimum of $500,000 immediately for relief, describing the ravages of typhus due to lack of soap, linen, food, and medicine. Cable from H. Lowenstein to JDC NY. April 18, 1919. Folder 61.2. item=207978. JDC, NY:19–21.
60. For more on Pinsk and the reverberations it had in Paris, see: Fink, *Defending the Rights of Others*, 173–202; Pease, "The United States and the 'Polish Pogroms'"; Wentling, "The Engineer and the Shtadlanim," 383–90; Engel, "What's in a Pogrom"; June–July 1919. 860c.4016/99–104, 120. NARA, State Dept; Interview with Hoover, L. Strauss, C. Adler, L. Marshall, H. Lowenstein. April 19, 1921. Folder 187.1. item=224033. JDC, NY:19–21.

61. H. Lehman to Secretary of War. Oct. 9, 1920. Folder 29. Digital ID 202402; H. Cutler to F. Warburg. Sept. 4, 1919. Folder 29. Digital ID 202372. JDC, NY:19–21; Uniforms for JDC Personnel. Folder 29. Digital ID 202368. JDC, NY:19–21.

62. H. Lowenstein to JDC NY. April 18, 1919. Folder 61.2. item=207978. JDC, NY:19–21.

63. I. Hershfield to H. Gibson. April 10, 1921. Folder 29. item=202416. JDC, NY:19–21; M. Baynton to JDC NY. March 26, 1921. Folder 29. item=202415. JDC, NY:19–21.

64. B. Bogen to H. Lowenstein. April 27, 1919. Folder 61.2. item=208007. JDC, NY:19–21.

65. Bogen, *Born a Jew*, 161–3, 180–9.

66. Ibid., 162.

67. A. Lucas to H. Lowenstein. July 3, 1919. Folder 62. item=208140. JDC, NY:19–21.

68. S. Bero to P. Wiernik, E. Troper to S. Bero. Nov. 10–11, 1922. Box 10. Folder 3. YUA, Wiernik Collection; L. Strauss with B. Zuckerman. May 16 and 19, 1922. Vol. B. CAHJP, People's Relief.

69. A. Lucas to H. Lowenstein. May 17, 1919. Folder 61.2. item=208045. JDC, NY:19–21.

70. I. Hershfield, B. Zuckerman, C. Adler to JDC NY. May 21, 1919. Folder 61.2. item=208056. JDC, NY:19–21; Transcript of Meeting of the JDC, 4–8. Aug. 10, 1919. Folder 4. item=200080. JDC, NY:19–21.

71. L. Marshall, C. Adler, N. Sokolow to B. Bogen. July 11, 1919. Folder 189. item=224177. JDC, NY:19–21.

72. Transcript of Meeting of the JDC. Aug. 10, 1919. Folder 4. item=200080. JDC, NY:19–21.

73. Statement by F. Warburg. Nov. 7, 1919. Folder 62. item=208217. JDC, NY:19–21.

74. Edited for clarity, I. Hershfield to F. Warburg. Oct. 1, 1920. Folder 62. item=208207. JDC, NY:19–21.

75. B. Bogen to J. Goldman. Jan. 18, 1920. Folder 68.1. item=209050. JDC, NY:19–21.

76. Overseas Unit 1, Report 1. Jan. 25, 1920. Folder 68.1. item=209055. JDC, NY:19–21.

77. Information Service Letter 7. Dec. 24, 1919. Folder 68.1. item=209017. JDC, NY:19–21.

78. Draft press release on Polish Unit. n.d. [Dec. 1919/Jan. 1920]. Folder 68.1. item=209043. JDC, NY:19–21.

79. Permanent Assignments. March 1, 1920. Folder 68.1. item=209069. JDC, NY:19–21.

80. Bogen, *Born a Jew*, 216–17.

81. Transcript of Meeting of the JDC. Aug. 10, 1919. Folder 4. item=200080. JDC, NY:19–21.

82. W. P. Fuller (ARA Warsaw) to W. L. Brown (ARA London). May 20, 1920. Box 85. Folder 3. HIA, ARA Europe.

83. Draft letter A. Elkus to F. Polk. March 1, 1920. Folder 68.1. item=209068. JDC, NY:19–21.

84. A. Lucas to B. Bogen. March 25, 1920. Folder 68.1. item=209074. JDC, NY:19–21.
85. Minutes of Meeting of Committee on Remittances and Finance. Jan. 16, 1920. Folder 24.2. item=201469. JDC, NY:19–21.
86. Report of Finance Committee to the JDC. Dec. 12, 1920. Folder 24.2. item=201486. JDC, NY:19–21.
87. Report of the Committee on Food, Clothing, and Transportation. Aug. 10, 1919. Folder 23.1. Digital ID 201229. JDC, NY:19–21.
88. These kinds of packages become known as CARE packages after World War II, rebranded by former ARA men who moved to lead CARE (Cooperative for American Remittances to Europe). Farré, *Colis De Guerre*, 66–7, 232–53.
89. Taylor, A. E. "Principles of the Food Draft." Oct. 15, 1920. 2.2. *ARA Bulletin*; Transcript of Vienna Conference, 124. Nov. 15–19, 1920. Folder 64. item=208783. JDC, NY:19–21; Cox, *Hunger in War and Peace*, 275–8.
90. Overseas Unit 1, Report 1. Jan. 25, 1920. Folder 68.1. item=209055. JDC, NY:19–21; W. P. Fuller (ARA Warsaw), B. Bogen, WL Brown (ARA London) correspondence. Jan. 1920. Box 85. Folder 3. HIA, ARA Europe.
91. Transcript of Vienna Conference, 124–5. Nov. 15–19, 1920. Folder 64. item=208783. JDC, NY:19–21.
92. Draft letter A. Elkus to F. Polk. March 1, 1920. Folder 68.1. item=209068. JDC, NY:19–21.
93. "Summary Statement on the European Children's Fund and American Relief Administration Warehouses." Oct. 15, 1920. 2.2. *ARA Bulletin*.
94. ARA Childfund Warehouse to ARA New York. June 7, 1920. Box 505. Folder 3. HIA, ARA Europe.
95. One can assume that all kosher packages were intended for Jews, but some Jews may have bought ordinary packages, as well. The percentage of kosher packages should be seen as a low estimate of the percentage of all ARA food packages destined for Jews.
96. Transcript of Vienna Conference, 30. Nov. 15–19, 1920. Folder 64. item=208783. JDC, NY:19–21.
97. Bicknell, *With the Red Cross in Europe*, 347–8.
98. July–Sept. 1920. Box 1. Folder 3. AJA, Bogen Papers.
99. Beizer, "Who Murdered Friedlaender and Cantor."
100. Stenographer's Transcript of Meeting of the JDC, 5. Dec. 12, 1920. Folder 6. item=200102. JDC, NY:19–21.
101. Minutes of JDC Executive Committee. March 10, 1921. Folder 21. item=200982. JDC, NY:19–21; J. N. Rosenberg to JDC NY. April 4, 1922. Folder 488. item=355402. JDC, NY:21–32.
102. Abramson, *Prayer for the Government*, 110.
103. Studies of the pogroms include: Astashkevich, *Jewish Women in the Pogroms*; Dekel-Chen, Meir, and Gaunt, eds. *Anti-Jewish Violence*; Bemporad, *Legacy of Blood*; Veidlinger, *Pogroms of 1918–1921*; Bemporad and Chopard, eds., "Pogroms of the Russian Civil War"; Budnitskii, *Jews between the Reds and Whites*; McGeever, *Antisemitism and the Russian Revolution*.

104. The exact number remains unknown: 50,000 is the minimum. A contemporaneous report provides horrifying samples of testimonies and estimates 120,000 Jewish dead and 50–60,000 orphans due directly to these pogroms: Heifetz, *Slaughter of the Jews*.

105. Report on Medico-Sanitary Conditions by William Wovschin, July 15, 1920. March 7, 1921. March 25, 1921. Folder 255.1. item=233238-9. JDC, NY:19–21.

106. Report on the Condition of Jews in Ukrainia by Kass and Leff. n.d. [July 1920]. Folder 247.2. item=232045. JDC, NY:19–21.

107. Report of Commission Appointed by the JDC to Investigate the Conditions of and Establish Relief Committee for the Jewish War Sufferers in Russia and Ukraina. n.d. [July 1920]. Folder 247.2. item=232041. JDC, NY:19–21.

108. For example, Patenaude, *Big Show in Bololand*, 96–101; Fisher, *Famine in Soviet Russia*, 246–66.

109. See Dekel-Chen, "Crimea 2008."

110. A. Lucas to Otto Rosalsky. Nov. 20, 1919. Folder 68.1. item=209005. JDC, NY:19–21.

111. Draft press release on Polish Unit. n.d. [Dec. 1919/Jan. 1920]. Folder 68.1. item=209043. JDC, NY:19–21.

112. B. Bogen via ARA London. Feb. 25, 1920. Box 85. Folder 3. HIA, ARA Europe; Report on Ukraine by Leo Gerstenzang. April 15, 1920. Folder 247.2. item=232009. JDC, NY:19–21; Relief Work Organized in Soviet Russia. June 1, 1920. Folder 45. item=205376. JDC, NY:19–21.

113. JDC had a district office in Rovno headed by Abraham Shohan of the Overseas Unit, with a warehouse and garage, which coordinated efforts in areas of Ukraine accessible from Poland. J. Goldman to JDC NY. May 25, 1920. Folder 247.2. item=232022. JDC, NY:19–21; Report on Volhynia by Voorsanger and Spivak. June 9, 1920. Folder 247.2. item=232026. JDC, NY:19–21; Report on the Condition of Jews in Ukrainia by Kass and Leff. n.d. [July 1920]. Folder 247.2. item=232045. JDC, NY:19–21; Information Service Letter 4. Oct. 20, 1920. Folder 247.2. item=232057. JDC, NY:19–21.

114. Newsletter. May 10, 1920. Folder 247.2. item=232021. JDC, NY:19–21; Meeting of the JDC Executive Committee, 29–31. Feb. 26, 1920. Folder 19.1. item=200920. JDC, NY:19–21.

115. The information blockade fell in late 1921. Patenaude, *Big Show in Bololand*, 8.

116. Report from Judge Harry M. Fisher and Mr. Max Pine. April 6, 1920. Folder 247.2. item=232006. JDC, NY:19–21.

117. H. Fisher to F. Warburg. Jan. 29, 1920. Folder 247.2. item=231969. JDC, NY:19–21.

118. Henry Alsberg wrote from Bucharest in December 1919, "I repeat, the situation in Southern Russia of the Jews beats anything for misery I have seen anywhere. And you know I have seen about every kind of misery to be seen in Europe and Eastern Asia." He pleaded for the JDC to prepare to "go in big now" and passed along reports of pogroms from a Jewish committee in Kiev. H. Alsberg to L. Strauss. Dec. 30, 1919. Folder 247.2. item=231975. JDC, NY:19–21.

119. H. Sliosberg to JDC NY. Received March 9, 1920. Folder 247.2. item=231980. JDC, NY:19–21.

120. Transcript of Vienna Conference, 27–32. Nov. 15–19, 1920. Folder 64. item=208783. JDC, NY:19–21.

121. Correspondence in 1919. 860E.4016/6. NARA, State Dept; Correspondence in 1919–20. 860E.48/a-17. NARA, State Dept.

122. B. Richards, R. Lansing correspondence. 3, Dec. 5, 1919. 860E.4016/6. NARA, State Dept; L. Marshall to Secretary B. Colby. May 21, 1920. 860E.4016/18. NARA, State Dept.

123. Dec. 1919. 860E.4016/9–17. NARA, State Dept.

124. Szajkowski, *Mirage of American Jewish Aid in Soviet Russia*, 9–12, 15–20; Fisher, *Famine in Soviet Russia*, 1–48; Patenaude, *Big Show in Bololand*, 34–8.

125. Memorandum of Conversation with Mr. Allex Wardwell by J. L. Magnes. Jan. 27, 1920. Folder 247.2. item=231972. JDC, NY:19–21.

126. F. Polk to L. Marshall. March 25, 1920. Folder 248. item=232122. JDC, NY:19–21.

127. J. Goldman to F. Warburg. March 9, 1920. Folder 247.2. item=231981. JDC, NY:19–21; Interview of Dr. J. Goldman and Miss Hetty Goldman with Mr. Litvinov. April 24, 1920. Folder 247.2. item=232015. JDC, NY:19–21; Report from Judge Harry M. Fisher and Mr. Max Pine. April 6, 1920. Folder 247.2. item=232006. JDC, NY:19–21.

128. H. Fisher and M. Pine to JDC NY. n.d. [May–July 1920]. Folder 247.2. item=232036. JDC, NY:19–21.

129. JDC Minutes of Executive Committee. June 10, 1920. Folder 19.2. item=200932. JDC, NY:19–21.

130. Soviet Ukraine had a contested status as a sovereign state, with its own government – it was not merely a federated republic within Soviet Russia – and thus relief to Ukraine had to be approved both in Moscow and in Ukraine. Patenaude, *Big Show in Bololand*, 100–1.

131. Cable from J. Goldman to JDC NY. June 15, 1920. Folder 247.2. item=232029. JDC, NY:19–21.

132. To the JDC. July 1, 1920. Folder 18. item=200800. JDC, NY:19–21.

133. Evobshchestkom is a Russian acronym, or Yidgeskom in Yiddish. It was later renamed the All Russian Jewish Public Committee.

134. J. Goldman to H. Lehman. Sept. 15, 1920. Folder 248. item=232181. JDC, NY:19–21.

135. Report of Commission Appointed by the JDC to Investigate the Conditions of and Establish Relief Committee for the Jewish War Sufferers in Russia and Ukraina (including the Agreement Regulating the Work United Jewish Committee for Relief to Victims of Pogroms). n.d. [July 1920]. Folder 247.2. item=232041-232044. JDC, NY:19–21.

136. Information Service Letter 4. Oct. 20, 1920. Folder 247.2. item=232057. JDC, NY:19–21.

137. JDC correspondence. April–July 1921. Folder 249.1. JDC, NY:19–21.

138. McGeever, *Antisemitism and the Russian Revolution*.

139. Report of Commission Appointed by the JDC to Investigate the Conditions of and Establish Relief Committee for the Jewish War Sufferers in Russia and Ukraina. n.d. [July 1920]. Folder 247.2. item=232041. JDC, NY:19–21; Zavadivker, "Jewish Aid Work in the Russian Civil War."

140. Report of Commission Appointed by the JDC to Investigate the Conditions of and Establish Relief Committee for the Jewish War Sufferers in Russia and Ukraina (including the Agreement Regulating the Work United Jewish Committee for Relief to Victims of Pogroms). n.d. [July 1920]. Folder 247.2. item=232041-232044. JDC, NY:19–21.

141. F. Rosenblatt to JDC NY via J. Goldman. Aug. 25, 1920. Folder 247.2. item=232051. JDC, NY:19–21.

142. J. Goldman to H. Lehman. Sept. 19, 1920. Folder 251.2. item=232768 JDC, NY:19–21.

143. Chairman Report on Soviet Russia. n.d. [Oct. 1920]. Folder 27.3. item=202259. JDC, NY:19–21.

144. F. Rosenblatt to F. Warburg. Dec. 8, 1920. Folder 247.2. item=232059. JDC, NY:19–21; Agreement. n.d. [Jan. 1921]. Folder 249.2. item=232429. JDC, NY:19–21; Minutes of JDC Executive Committee. March 10, 1921. Folder 21. item=200982. JDC, NY:19–21; Szajkowski, *Mirage of American Jewish Aid in Soviet Russia*, 54–6; Zavadivker, "Jewish Aid Work in the Russian Civil War,"

145. Zosa Szajkowski examined the JDC, People's Relief, Judah Magnes, Yiddish press, and State Department records (Evobshchestkom's archives were not available). I summarize his findings, having seen many of the cited documents: *Mirage of American Jewish Aid in Soviet Russia*, 21–59. On the broader context of the Soviet Bureau in New York as an unrecognized embassy, see Pfannestiel, "The Soviet Bureau."

146. Coudreau, "L'Action Nansen Et Les Bolcheviks," 56–7.

147. In the moment, Soviet propaganda made it unclear if the Dubrowsky route did actually provide relief to pogrom victims, or if the money was absorbed by the Soviets. Beizer has found that packages did mainly go toward relief, though occasionally they did not reach their intended recipients, *Russian Jewry and the Joint*, 116–27.

148. On Jews and the Red Scare, see: Szajkowski, *Impact of the Red Scare on American Jewish Life*; Fischer, *Spider Web*; Michels, *A Fire in Their Hearts*; Silver, *Louis Marshall*, 459–62.

149. L. Marshall's Report on JDC and Dubrowsky relationship. Dec. 9, 1920. 861.48/1325 NARA, State Dept.

150. Bogen, *Born a Jew*, 272–4.

151. Szajkowski, *Mirage of American Jewish Aid in Soviet Russia*, 60–2.

152. Minutes of JDC Executive Committee. March 10, 1921. Folder 21. item=200982. JDC, NY:19–21.

153. Minutes of JDC Executive Committee. April 5, 1921. Folder 21. item=200984. JDC, NY:19–21; A. Kahn to D. Dubrowsky. April 11, 1921. Folder 249.1. item=232263. JDC, NY:19–21; Record of Administration Committee. June 2, 1921. Folder 14. item=200537. JDC, NY:19–21.

154. F. Warburg to B. Bogen. April 6, 1921. Folder 249.1. item=232281. JDC, NY:19–21.

155. F. Rosenblatt to J. Becker. April 22, 1921. Folder 73.2. item=209836. JDC, NY:19–21; Conference held in the Office of the AFSC. April 28, 1921. Folder 73.2. item=209837. JDC, NY:19–21.

156. JDC telegram. n.d. [April 1921]. YM/MfS/FEWVRC/MISSIONS/7/5/5/2. Library of Friends.

157. Interview with Friends in London. May 7, 1921. Folder 259. item=234284. JDC, NY:19–21; F. Rosenblatt, J. Norton correspondence. 23, June 28, 1921. Folder 259. item=234332, 234293. JDC, NY:19–21; Szajkowski, *Mirage of American Jewish Aid in Soviet Russia*, 63–5.

158. F. Rosenblatt to AFSC. Aug. 23, 1921. Folder 91b. item=311792. JDC, NY:21–32; W. Thomas to F. Warburg. Nov. 20, 1921. Folder 91b. item=311798. JDC, NY:21–32.

159. Minutes of JDC Executive Committee. March 10, 1921. Folder 21. item=200982. JDC, NY:19–21.

160. Patenaude, *Big Show in Bololand*, 37–48.

161. The ARA representatives negotiated with the same Maxim Litvinov with whom Goldman had spoken in Denmark. Litvinov was "the assistant people's commissar of foreign affairs, a formidable negotiating talent with ample experience at playing a weak hand." Patenaude, *Big Show in Bololand*, 39.

162. Felix Warburg, James N. Rosenberg (the new European director of the JDC), and Lewis Strauss (now serving on the JDC's Committee on Russia in New York) represented the JDC. Minutes of the European Relief Council. Aug. 24, 1922. Folder 488. item=355353. JDC, NY:21–32.

163. Patenaude, *Big Show in Bololand*, 50–1.

164. Bauer, *My Brother's Keeper*, 57–8; Dekel-Chen, *Farming the Red Land*, 2–4, 26; Silver, *Louis Marshall*, 491.

165. J. N. Rosenberg to JDC NY. April 4, 1922. Folder 488. item=355402. JDC, NY:21–32. Rosenberg complained that Rosen had not been given due credit. Such oversight has remained, including in Patenaude, *Big Show in Bololand*, 145–71.

166. B. Bogen to JDC Committee on Russia. Dec. 5, 1921. Folder 483. item=355090. JDC, NY:21–32.

167. Distribution in White Russia by Cornell Hewson. Feb. 20, 1922. Folder 488. item=355372. JDC, NY:21–32.

168. Hoover, Herbert. "Food Drafts for Russia." Oct. 17, 1921. 2.18. *ARA Bulletin*.

169. Farré, *Colis De Guerre*, 83.

170. Patenaude, *Big Show in Bololand*, 96–101.

171. ARA NY to ARA London. March 24, 1922. Box 505. Folder 3. HIA, ARA Europe.

172. Memorandum of Discussion between Rosenberg and Brown. Oct. 20, 1921. Folder 488. item=355356. JDC, NY:21–32;

173. W. L. Brown to W. Haskell. Oct. 27, 1921. Folder 488. item=355357. JDC, NY:21–32; J. N. Rosenberg to W. L. Brown. Feb. 1, 1922. Folder 488. item=355365. JDC, NY:21–32; Patenaude, *Big Show in Bololand*, 53–4.

174. J. N. Rosenberg to F. Warburg. March 17, 1922. Folder 488. item=355384. JDC, NY:21–32; J. Rosen to JDC NY. March 21, 1922. Folder 488. item=355388. JDC, NY:21–32. Existing ARA histories remark upon the strange nature of the Ukraine famine having been hidden from the ARA, while the Volga famine elicited an international call for help, crediting JDC and American Jewish food remittances purchased for Ukraine for bringing it to the ARA's attention: Fisher, *Famine in Soviet Russia*, 246–66; Patenaude, *Big Show in Bololand*, 96–101. But Jews in Ukraine were suffering the same hunger and violence they had been suffering, and copious remittances directed there indicated a long-awaited opportunity of American Jews to send them. The JDC did not know anything about a famine in rural Ukraine; it was an accident that the ARA discovered famine in Ukraine while there investigating.

175. Fisher, *Famine in Soviet Russia*, 246–66; Patenaude, *Big Show in Bololand*, 96–101.

176. Minutes of the JDC Executive Committee. March 14, 1922. Folder 447. item=352741. JDC, NY:21–32; JDC NY to J. N. Rosenberg. March 16, 1922. Folder 488. item=355382. JDC, NY:21–32; Cable on ARA–JDC Conference. March 28, 1922. Folder 488. item=355392. JDC, NY:21–32.

177. H. Hoover to W. L. Brown and W. Haskell. March 14, 1922. Folder 488. item=355381. JDC, NY:21–32; J. N. Rosenberg to JDC NY. April 4, 1922. Folder 488. item=355402. JDC, NY:21–32.

178. F. Warburg to J. N. Rosenberg. March 20, 1922. Folder 488. item=355389. JDC, NY:21–32.

179. J. N. Rosenberg to W. L. Brown. Feb. 1, 1922. Folder 488. item=355365. JDC, NY:21–32.

180. J. N. Rosenberg to JDC NY. March 17, 1922. Folder 488. item=355383. JDC, NY:21–32; Agreement Reached at Moscow between Representatives of the ARA and JDC. June 19, 1922. Folder 488. item=355446. JDC, NY:21–32; Patenaude, *Big Show in Bololand*, 51.

181. Surface and Bland, *American Food in the World War*, 914–15.

182. J. N. Rosenberg to F. Warburg. March 17, 1922. Folder 488. item=355384. JDC, NY:21–32.

183. J. N. Rosenberg, F. Rosenblatt, J. Rosen to JDC NY. March 20, 1922. Folder 488. Digital ID 355386. JDC, NY:21–32; J. N. Rosenberg to JDC NY. April 4, 1922. Folder 488. Digital ID 355402. JDC, NY:21–32.

184. Bogen, *Born a Jew*, 291.

185. J. N. Rosenberg to JDC NY. March 18, 1922. Folder 488. Digital ID 355385. JDC, NY:21–32; J.N. Rosenberg to JDC NY. April 4, 1922. Folder 488. Digital ID 355402. JDC, NY:21–32.

186. ARA NY to ARA London. March 24, 1922. Box 505. Folder 3. HIA, ARA Europe.

187. J. N. Rosenberg to JDC NY. April 4, 1922. Folder 488. item=355402. JDC, NY:21–32.

188. Surface and Bland, *American Food in the World War*, 145, 259; Lowe, "Red Cross and the New World Order," 272–3.

189. Patenaude, *Big Show in Bololand*, 181; Folder 488. JDC, NY:21–32.

190. Bogen, *Born a Jew*, 300; Cable L. Strauss to J. N. Rosenberg. May 23, 1922. Folder 488. item=355413. JDC, NY:21–32; Cable J. N. Rosenberg to L. Strauss. May 25, 1922. Folder 488. item=355414. JDC, NY:21–32.

191. J. N. Rosenberg to B. Bogen. June 6, 1922. Folder 488. item=355436. JDC, NY:21–32;

192. Condensed Report of the Relief Activities of the JDC in Russia, Nov. 1, 1922 to Oct. 31, 1923. Nov. 8, 1923. Folder 457. item=353358. JDC, NY:21–32.

193. J. N. Rosenberg to JDC NY. April 4, 1922. Folder 488. item=355402. JDC, NY:21–32.

194. Conference of Herter, Logan, Kahn, Rosenberg. June 3, 1922. Folder 488. item=355425. JDC, NY:21–32; Description of plan agreed upon by JDC and ARA. June 9, 1922. Folder 488. item=355444. JDC, NY:21–32.

195. Moscow News Item. July 25, 1922. Folder 488. item=355462. JDC, NY:21–32.

196. Friends International Service. Nov. 11, 1922. Folder 91b. item=311832-6. JDC, NY:21–32.

197. Patenaude, *Big Show in Bololand*, 96–101.

198. Trott, "American Philanthropy and Soviet Medical Research," 134.

199. Condensed Report of the Relief Activities of the JDC in Russia, Nov. 1, 1922 to Oct. 31, 1923, 2. Nov. 8, 1923. Folder 457. item=353358. JDC, NY:21–32; The American Jewish Joint Distribution Committee in Russia, 3. Jan. 1924. Folder 457. item=353359. JDC, NY:21–32.

200. H. Bernheim to C. Adler. July 5, 1922. Folder 488. item=355457. JDC, NY:21–32.

201. Patenaude, *Big Show in Bololand*, 178–9; Trott, "American Philanthropy and Soviet Medical Research," 134.

202. J. M. Naishtut to B. Bogen. May 4, 1922. Box 3. Folder 2. AJA, Bogen Papers; I. M. Naischtut, L. Strauss, B. Bogen, H. Hoover correspondence. June–July 1922. Box 1. Folder 5. AJA, Bogen Papers; B. Bogen to E. Morrissey. June 20, 1923. Box 1. Folder 6. AJA, Bogen Papers; Conference of Herter, Logan, Kahn, Rosenberg. June 5, 1922. Folder 488. item=355425. JDC, NY:21–32.

203. How Your Contributions Are Helping. Oct. 20, 1922. Folder 489. item=355542. JDC, NY:21–32; Essential Points in Dr. Bogen's Letters. Sept. 19, 1922. Folder 448. item=352876-7. JDC, NY:21–32.

204. W. Grove to J. N. Rosenberg. June 24, 1922. Folder 488. item=355452. JDC, NY:21–32; W. Grove to L. Strauss. July 8, 1922. Folder 488. item=355461. JDC, NY:21–32; L. Strauss to W. Grove. Aug 10, 1922. Folder 489. item=355477. JDC, NY:21–32; Report of Committee on Russia from Minutes of Executive Committee. Oct. 24, 1922. Folder 449. item=352912. JDC, NY:21–32; J. N. Rosenberg to L. Strauss. Oct. 27, 1922. Folder 49. item=305544. JDC, NY:21–32.

205. B. Bogen to L. Strauss. Aug. 14, 1922. Folder 448. item=352841. JDC, NY:21–32.

206. Patenaude, *Big Show in Bololand*, 51, 90–1, 181, 600, 633; Fisher, *Famine in Soviet Russia*, 429, 437–8; L. Strauss to B. Bogen. Oct. 4, 1922. Folder 449. item=352896. JDC, NY:21–32; Extract from minutes of dinner meeting. Dec. 5, 1922. Folder 479. item=354912. JDC, NY:21–32.

207. B. Bogen to H. Lehman. Aug. 31, 1922. Folder 448. item=352854. JDC, NY:21–32.

208. Condensed Report of the Relief Activities of the JDC in Russia, Nov. 1, 1922 to Oct. 31, 1923, 2. Nov. 8, 1923. Folder 457. item=353358. JDC, NY:21–32; The American Jewish Joint Distribution Committee in Russia, 38. Jan. 1924. Folder 457. item=353359. JDC, NY:21–32.

209. Agreement regarding Operations in the Ukraine and White Russia between the JDC and the ARA. Aug. 14, 1922. Folder 489. item=355481. JDC, NY:21–32; L. Marshall, H. Lehman, J. N. Rosenberg, L. Strauss cable to W. Grove, B. Bogen. Aug. 18, 1922. Folder 489. item=355490. JDC, NY:21–32.

210. J. N. Rosenberg to W. L. Brown. Sept. 14, 1922. Folder 489. item=355490. JDC, NY:21–32; L. Strauss to B. Bogen. Aug. 29, 1922. Folder 448. item=352852. JDC, NY:21–32; Report of Committee on Russia from Minutes of Executive Committee. Oct. 24, 1922. Folder 449. item=352912. JDC, NY:21–32; Minutes of Meeting between Representatives of the ARA and JDC. Dec. 11, 1922. Folder 449. item=352925. JDC, NY:21–32.

211. Sample agreements of Mennonites, Friends. Folder 456. item=353316, 353320. JDC, NY:21–32; B. Bogen to L. Strauss. Sept. 11, 1922. Folder 448. item=352863. JDC, NY:21–32; L. Strauss to JDC NY. Oct. 20, 1922. Box 1. Folder 5. AJA, Bogen Papers.

212. J. Rosen to L. Strauss. Nov. 27, 1922. Box 1. Folder 5. AJA, Bogen Papers; Temporary Agreement. Sept. 22, 1922. Folder 456. item=353315. JDC, NY:21–32.

213. Memorandum from B. Kahn. Nov. 6, 1922. Folder 456. item=353326. JDC, NY:21–32.

214. Bogen, *Born a Jew*, 336; C. Adler to L. Strauss. Oct. 23, 1922. Folder 449. item=352913. JDC, NY:21–32.

215. Condensed Report of the Relief Activities of the JDC in Russia, Nov. 1, 1922 to Oct. 31, 1923. Nov. 8, 1923. Folder 457. item=353358. JDC, NY:21–32; B. Bogen to L. Strauss re: Evobshestkom. Oct. 25, 1922. Folder 449. item=3529167. JDC, NY:21–32.

216. The JDC in Russia [by B. Bogen]. n.d. [1923]. Folder 457. item=353357. JDC, NY:21–32; Patenaude, *Big Show in Bololand*, 82–6.

217. Bogen, *Born a Jew*, 335–6.

218. J. N. Rosenberg to W. L. Brown. Feb. 3, 1922. Folder 488. item=355366. JDC, NY:21–32; Condensed Report of the Relief Activities of the JDC in Russia, Nov. 1 1922 to Oct. 31, 1923, 2. Nov. 8, 1923. Folder 457. item=353358. JDC, NY:21–32; The American Jewish Joint Distribution Committee in Russia, 30. Jan. 1924. Folder 457. item=353359. JDC, NY:21–32; Final Agreement Signed by Mr. Strauss. Sept. 25, 1922. Folder 489. item=355517. JDC, NY:21–32; B. Bogen to JDC NY Committee on Russia. March 5, 1923. Folder 489. item=355594–5. JDC, NY:21–32; B. Bogen to JDC NY. Nov. 4, 1922. Folder 91b. item=311830. JDC, NY:21–32; Memorandum of Matters taken up with Mr. Rosenberg. Sept. 16, 1922. Folder 448. item=352874. JDC, NY:21–32.

219. The JDC in Russia [by B. Bogen]. n.d. [1923]. Folder 457. item=353357. JDC, NY:21–32.

220. Bogen, *Born a Jew*, 318.
221. Memorandum re: agreement with ORT on seeds signed F. Hardy. March 24, 1922. Folder 483. item=355091. JDC, NY:21–32; L. Strauss to J. Rosen. July 10, 1922. Folder 483. item=355114. JDC, NY:21–32; S. Arons to J. Hyman. Resume of the work done for Dr. Rosen. Dec. 1, 1922. Folder 483. item=355142. JDC, NY:21–32.
222. L. Cohan to J. N. Rosenberg and L. Strauss. Aug. 28, 1922. Folder 448. item=35280. JDC, NY:21–32; Ch. Rakowsky to J. Rosen. July 20, 1922. Folder 448. item=352881–2. JDC, NY:21–32.
223. S. Arons to J. Hyman. Shipment of machinery and seeds to Russia. Dec. 26, 1922. Folder 483. item=355150. JDC, NY:21–32; S. Arons to J. Rosen. Dec. 21, 1922. Folder 483. item=355156. JDC, NY:21–32; Sowing Campaign. Translation from Zwezda. March 2, 1923. Folder 483. item=355174. JDC, NY:21–32.
224. H. Lehman to J. Rosen. Sept. 21, 1922. Folder 483. item=355128. JDC, NY:21–32; J. Rosen to J. N. Rosenberg. Dec. 4, 1922. Folder 483. item=355146. JDC, NY:21–32.
225. The American Jewish Joint Distribution Committee in Russia, 6–7. Jan. 1924. Folder 457. item=353359. JDC, NY:21–32.

3 Refugee

1. Marrus, *Unwanted*, 9–10.
2. Gatrell and Zhvanko, eds., *Europe on the Move*, 2–3.
3. Marrus, *Unwanted*, 7–8, 51.
4. Cohen, *In War's Wake*, 59.
5. Marrus, *Unwanted*, 61–2.
6. Ibid., 27–39; Penslar, *Shylock's Children*, 195–205.
7. Ica as discussed here is both the Western European, management face of the organization of elite French and British Jews, and also the Russian technical training and emigration support side discussed in the first chapter. The Russian Ica branches that found themselves in the new states of East Central Europe continued their prewar work, sometimes morphing considerably in their new environments (as did the other Russian Jewish philanthropic organizations). Its independent source of funding and its plutocratic leadership meant that Ica was largely immune to public opinion and regained its footing quickly after the war. Leading figures included Franz M. Phillipson, Lucien Wolf, Louis Oungre, Edouard Oungre, and Arnold Netter.
8. Werelief was a relief body that in 1920 grew out of the Committee of Jewish Delegations from the Paris peace negotiations. It had no steady source of funding, but its leadership of Eastern European Jewish nationalists living in Western Europe was strongly committed to its own independent existence, thereby challenging the hegemony of liberal Jewish diplomacy from the West. Neither the Committee of Jewish Delegations nor Werelief have known organizational archives. Leading figures included Leo Motzkin, Yisroel Efroikin, Vladimir Tiomkin, Nahum Sokolow, and Leon Bramson.

It held big conferences in Czechoslovakia in 1920, 1921, 1923, and 1924. The World Jewish Relief Conference was referred to as the Carlsbad Committee, the Conférence Universelle Juive de Secours, the Yidisher Velt Hilf Konferents, the Jüdische Welthilfskonferenz, Werelief, or some combination or alternate spelling thereof. Its Paris telegraph address was "Wereliew." The Committee of Jewish Delegations eventually beget the World Jewish Congress and Werelief beget Emigdirect and later HICEM.

9. Engel, "World War I and Its Impact on the Problem of Security," 17–18.
10. Jones, *American Immigration*, 270.
11. See Porter, *Benevolent Empire*, chapter 1.
12. Gatrell, *The Making of the Modern Refugee*, 55.
13. 14th Annual Hias Report 1922, 8. March 11, 1923. 245.4 I-42. YIVO, HIAS.
14. Skran, *Refugees in Inter-war Europe*, 1.
15. Statement by Felix Warburg. Nov. 7, 1919. Folder 62. item=208217. JDC, NY:19–21.
16. Cohen, *In War's Wake*, 61.
17. Gatrell, *The Making of the Modern Refugee*, 30–1; *Europe on the Move*, 5–6.
18. Refugee reports are within: Transcript of Meeting of the JDC. Aug. 10, 1919. Folder 4. item=200080. JDC, NY:19–21; Transcript of Vienna Conference. Nov. 15–19, 1920. Folder 64. item=208783. JDC, NY:19–21.
19. Summary of Vienna Conference. Nov. 15–19, 1920. Folder 64. item=208782. JDC, NY:19–21; Transcript of Vienna Conference. Nov. 15–19, 1920. Folder 64. item=208783. JDC, NY:19–21.
20. JDC correspondence. Jan.–March. 1921. Box 1. Folder 4. AJA, Bogen Papers.
21. Penslar, *Shylock's Children*, 201–2.
22. Ibid., 195–205.
23. Transcript of Vienna Conference, 82. Nov. 15–19, 1920. Folder 64. item=208783. JDC, NY:19–21.
24. Bauer, *My Brother's Keeper*, 21–2.
25. Penslar, *Shylock's Children*, 236–7.
26. Transcript of Vienna Conference, 32. Nov. 15–19, 1920. Folder 64. item=208783. JDC, NY:19–21.
27. Preliminary Report on the Refugee Problem. B. Kahn. n.d. [Nov. 1, 1921] Folder 433. item=351737. JDC, NY:21–32.
28. Summary of Vienna Conference. Nov. 15–19, 1920. Folder 64. item=208782. JDC, NY:19–21.
29. Draft letter C. Sulzberger to L. Levin. March 23, 1922. Folder 95a. item=313398. JDC, NY:21–32.
30. Summary of Vienna Conference. Nov. 15–19, 1920. Folder 64. item=208782. JDC, NY:19–21; Preliminary Report on the Refugee Problem. B. Kahn. n.d. [Nov. 1, 1921] Folder 433. item=351737. JDC, NY:21–32.
31. Transcript of Vienna Conference, 82. Nov. 15–19, 1920. Folder 64. item=208783. JDC, NY:19–21.
32. Report on the Condition of Jews in Ukrainia by Kass and Leff. n.d. [July 1920]. Folder 247.2. item=232045. JDC, NY:19–21.

33. Transcript of Vienna Conference, 163. Nov. 15–19, 1920. Folder 64. item=208783. JDC, NY:19–21.
34. As in Penslar, *Shylock's Children*, 103.
35. Refugees Budget. n.d. [early 1921] Folder 161. item=320056. JDC, NY:21–32; H. Gans to J. Rosenberg. Oct. 7, 1921. Folder 161. item=320064. JDC, NY:21–32.
36. B. Kahn and A. Landesco to JDC NY. Nov. 14, 1921. Folder 161. item=320068. JDC, NY:21–32.
37. Preliminary Report on the Refugee Problem. B. Kahn. n.d. [Nov. 1, 1921] Folder 433. item=351737. JDC, NY:21–32.
38. Summary of Vienna Conference. Nov. 15–19, 1920. Folder 64. item=208782. JDC, NY:19–21; Abstract of Preliminary Report on the Refugee Problem. B. Kahn. Nov. 1, 1921. Folder 161. item=320060. JDC, NY:21–32.
39. Extract from Minutes of European Executive Council. Nov. 10, 1921. Folder 161. item=320067. JDC, NY:21–32; Cable F. Warburg to J. Rosenberg. Nov. 18, 1921. Folder 161. item=320070. JDC, NY:21–32.
40. Report on Ica Conference at Paris Oct. 30, 1921 by B. Kahn. Nov. 11, 1921. Folder 161. item=320081. JDC, NY:21–32; Eurexco to JDC NY. Nov. 21, 1921. Folder 161. item=320071. JDC, NY:21–32.
41. Preliminary Report on the Refugee Problem. B. Kahn. n.d. [Nov. 1, 1921] Folder 433. item=351737. JDC, NY:21–32.
42. B. Bogen to H. Gans. Jan. 13, 1922. Folder 161. item=320127. JDC, NY:21–32; R. Breckler to J. Schweitzer. Jan. 15, 1922. Folder 161. item=320131. JDC, NY:21–32; Publicity Statement by the Various Departments in Warsaw. n.d. [Dec. 1921] Folder 161. item=320075. JDC, NY:21–32.
43. B. Bogen to H. Gans. Jan. 13, 1922. Folder 161. item=320127. JDC, NY:21–32.
44. D. W. Senator to B. Kahn. Nov. 7, 1921. Folder 161. item=320066. JDC, NY:21–32; Brinkmann, "From Immigrants to Supranational Transmigrants and Refugees"; Committee on Work in Foreign Countries Meeting Minutes. June 6, 1923. 245.1.14. YIVO, HIAS.
45. Work of the European Executive Council and the Management of the European Field. Feb. 17, 1921. Box 1. Folder 4. AJA, Bogen Papers.
46. Cretu, "Romanian Nation-Building and American Assistance," 215–18.
47. Abstract of Preliminary Report on the Refugee Problem. B. Kahn. Nov. 1, 1921. Folder 161. item=320060. JDC, NY:21–32.
48. Preliminary Report on the Refugee Problem. B. Kahn. n.d. [Nov. 1, 1921] Folder 433. item=351737. JDC, NY:21–32.
49. Transcript of Vienna Conference, 92, 166. Nov. 15–19, 1920. Folder 64. item=208783. JDC, NY:19–21. Nestor is the transliterated Yiddish name for the Dniester River.
50. Cretu, "Romanian Nation-Building and American Assistance," 204–7.
51. Agenda Refugees. Nov. 28, 1921. Folder 161. item=320079. JDC, NY:21–32.
52. A. Held to J. Bernstein. Oct. 31, 1921. 245.4 XII-Europe-5. YIVO, HIAS.

53. Cretu, "Romanian Nation-Building and American Assistance," 204.
54. B. Kahn to JDC NY. Nov. 28, 1921. Folder 161. item=320084. JDC, NY:21–32.
55. Outline of Hias Work in Europe. Feb. 15, 1922. Folder 95a. item=313392. JDC, NY:21–32; A. Held to J. Bernstein. Oct. 31, 1921. 245.4 XII-Europe-5. YIVO, HIAS.
56. Cretu, "Romanian Nation-Building and American Assistance," 205–6.
57. W. Bacilieri to T. F. Johnson. Oct. 19, 1922. Registry Files. R1727/45/24387x/15127. LNA, Nansen Fonds; Ukrainian Refugees in Rumania and Bessarabia: Second Report by Dr. Vladimir Tjomkin. n.d. Series 7. Folder 125. YIVO, Wolf-Mowschowitch Papers.
58. B. Bogen to C. Sulzberger. Dec. 20, 1921. Folder 161. item=320103. JDC, NY:21–32; B. Bogen to H. Gans. Jan. 13, 1922. Folder 161. item=320127. JDC, NY:21–32; C. Sulzberger to B. Kahn. Jan. 24, 1922 Folder 161. item=320138. JDC, NY:21–32.
59. B. Bogen to H. Gans. Jan. 13, 1922. Folder 161. item=320127. JDC, NY:21–32.
60. B. Kahn to JDC NY. Jan. 8, 1922. Folder 161. item=320141. JDC, NY:21–32.
61. Draft statement on refugee work by D. Bressler. Sept. 10, 1925. Folder 163. item=320313. JDC, NY:21–32;
62. B. Kahn to JDC Committee on Refugees NY. March 6, 1923 Folder 163. item=320268. JDC, NY:21–32; B. Kahn to D. Bressler. Aug. 30, 1923 Folder 433. item=351810. JDC, NY:21–32.
63. B. Kahn to D. Bressler. July 30, 1924. Folder 163. item=320302. JDC, NY:21–32;
64. B. Kahn to JDC Committee on Refugees NY. March 6, 1923. Folder 163. item=320268. JDC, NY:21–32; P. Baerwald to D. Bressler. July 25, 1924. Folder 163. item=320301. JDC, NY:21–32;
65. B. Kahn to Hicem. July 5, 1927. Folder 29.3. item=302680. JDC, NY:21–32.
66. Best, *To Free a People*; Berkowitz, "Between Altruism and Self-Interest."
67. Tartakower manuscript, 19. 1939. 245.4.26. xxvi-1. YIVO, HIAS.
68. Zolberg, *Nation by Design*, 19–23; Bon Tempo, *Americans at the Gate*.
69. As in Wyman, *Paper Walls*.
70. On the concept of "remote control," see Zolberg, *Nation by Design*, 9.
71. See Chapters 1 and 2 on wartime Hias and on Hershfield. Hias' archives have few overseas records from this period to follow affiliations with Jewish migration offices, but see: A. Adee to F. Warburg. Aug. 25, 1916. Folder 35.1. item=2298. JDC, NY:14–18; Wischnitzer, *Visas to Freedom*, 78–80.
72. Torpey, *Invention of the Passport*, 111–12.
73. Hias committee meeting minutes from 1909–1922 in 245.4 I-1 to I-31 and from 1920-on in 245.1.12-20. YIVO, HIAS.
74. Nov. 1917. *Jewish Immigration Bulletin*.
75. Schiff had long-standing ties in the Far East: Best, "Financing a Foreign War"; Cohen, *Jacob H. Schiff*, 33–9.
76. Nov. 1917, May 1918, Sept. 1918. *Jewish Immigration Bulletin*.

77. Tartakower manuscript, 24. 1939. 245.4.26. xxvi–1. YIVO, HIAS.
78. May, Sept. 1918. *Jewish Immigration Bulletin*. The Central Information Bureau and its branches soon became independent from Hias and corresponded with American associations, including the ARC, Hias, JDC, People's Relief, and NCJW. It provided an essential service connecting relatives between the Far East and Eastern Europe, via New York. It is best known for facilitating the entry of German Jewish refugees into Shanghai in 1939–40. CAHJP, DAL; YIVO, Birman Papers.
79. Sept. 1918, 9. *Jewish Immigration Bulletin*.
80. March 1919. *Jewish Immigration Bulletin*.
81. Torpey, *Invention of the Passport*, 111–17.
82. Dec. 1919. *Jewish Immigration Bulletin*.
83. May, Dec. 1919. *Jewish Immigration Bulletin*; Irwin, "The Great White Train."
84. May, June 1918. *Jewish Immigration Bulletin*.
85. Dec. 1919. *Jewish Immigration Bulletin*. Irwin interprets Mason's remark to the ARC that relief should "not smack of alms or charity" to mean that the ARC saw this is a guiding principle concerning reconstructive philanthropy, *Making the World Safe*, 154. Yet these are not the words of an ARC man, but a Hias man. This quotation was rather a guiding principle of American Jewish organizations, as they tried to appeal to and expand the definition of mainstream American humanitarianism. The ARC never used banking as Hias suggested it do; Jews did – see Chapter 6.
86. Journalist Herman Bernstein (see Chapter 1) was in Siberia on behalf of philanthropist Nathan Straus. Dec. 1919. *Jewish Immigration Bulletin*. The JDC delegate was Frank Rosenblatt, who would soon be running the Ukraine operation (see Chapter 2).
87. Beizer, "Frank Rosenblatt's Mission in Siberia"; Committee on US Immigration Stations and Work in Foreign Countries Meeting Minutes. July 22, 1920. 245.4 I-15. YIVO, HIAS. Relief of Jewish political prisoners in Siberia was handled along with the rest of the refugee issue. On prisoners in Siberia, see further: Willis, *Herbert Hoover and the Russian Prisoners of World War I*; Szajkowski, *Kolchak, Jews, and the American Intervention in Siberia*.
88. Committee on Foreign Relations Meeting Minutes. March 4, June 26, 1919. 245.4 I-14. YIVO, HIAS; Executive Committee Meeting Minutes. March 27, 1919. 245.4 I-8. YIVO, HIAS.
89. April, June–Aug. 1919. *Jewish Immigration Bulletin*.
90. Committee on US Immigration Stations and Work in Foreign Countries Meeting Minutes, 3–4. Oct. 28, 1919. 245.4 I-14. YIVO, HIAS.
91. Committee on Foreign Relations Meeting Minutes. Oct. 2, 1919. 245.4 I-14. YIVO, HIAS.
92. Tartakower manuscript, 24. 1939. 245.4.26. xxvi–1. YIVO, HIAS; YUA, Central Relief.
93. Kamaiky Report on European Commission, 14–17. Aug. 1, 1920. 245.4 XII-Europe-1. YIVO, HIAS; Minutes of a Board of Directors Meeting. [Aug. 12, 1919.] 245.4 XII-Europe-1. YIVO, HIAS.

94. April 1920. *Jewish Immigration Bulletin*; Kamaiky Report on European Commission, 12–20. Aug. 1, 1920. 245.4 XII-Europe-1. YIVO, HIAS.

95. April, Oct. 1920. *Jewish Immigration Bulletin*; Committee on Foreign Relations Meeting Minutes. Sept. 17 n.d. [1919]. 245.4 I-16. YIVO, HIAS; Kamaiky Report on European Commission, 15–17. Aug. 1, 1920. 245.4 XII-Europe-1. YIVO, HIAS.

96. Breitman and Kraut, "Antisemitism in the State Department."

97. Confidential State Department, Labor Department, correspondence. July 20, 1920. 150.60c66/orig. NARA, State Dept; Korman, "When Heredity Met the Bacterium," 262–8.

98. Confidential State Department, Labor Department, correspondence. Dec. 1920–Feb. 1921. 150.60c66/2 and /4. NARA, State Dept.

99. L. J. Keena (American Consul General, Warsaw) to Secretary of State. Nov. 16, 1921. 150.60c66/8. NARA, State Dept.

100. Memorandum in the Matter of the Alleged Conspiracies to Bring into the United States Jews from Russian Poland and Other Eastern European Countries, 2, 8. May 27, 1921. 150.60c66/7. NARA, State Dept.

101. Korman, "When Heredity Met the Bacterium," 267.

102. Bendersky, *The "Jewish Threat."*

103. Massel Report on European Commission, 6–7. [late 1921]. 245.4 XII-Europe-1. YIVO, HIAS.

104. Kamaiky Report on European Commission, 17–24. Aug. 1, 1920. 245.4 XII-Europe-1. YIVO, HIAS; Minutes of a Board of Directors Meeting. [Aug. 12, 1919.] 245.4 XII-Europe-1. YIVO, HIAS.

105. Hias List of Local Committees. Nov. 23, 1921. Folder 95a. item=313410. JDC, NY:21–32.

106. Kobrin, "Jewish Immigrant 'Bankers.'"

107. Tevis, "Hebrews Are Appearing in Court."

108. Minutes of a Board of Directors Meeting. [Aug. 12, 1919.] 245.4 XII-Europe-1. YIVO, HIAS.

109. Confidential State Department, Labor Department correspondence. Oct.–Dec. 1920. 150.60c66/1. NARA, State Dept.

110. Confidential State Department, Consul in Warsaw correspondence. June 1922–Jan. 1923. 150.60c66/9 to 150.60c66/20. NARA, State Dept.

111. Marrus, *Unwanted*, 65.

112. Committee on US Immigration Stations and Work in Foreign Countries Meeting Minutes. July 22, 1920. 245.4 I-15. YIVO, HIAS; Apr., Sept., Oct. 1920. *Jewish Immigration Bulletin*; Minutes of a Board of Directors Meeting. [Aug. 12, 1919.] 245.4 XII-Europe-1. YIVO, HIAS; Report of E. Rosenblum of Trip to Danzig. July 22, 1920. Box 1. Folder 3. AJA, Bogen Papers.

113. Committee on US Immigration Stations and Work in Foreign Countries Meeting Minutes. May 20, 1920. 245.4. I-15. YIVO, HIAS; J. Bernstein to L. Marshall. June 7, 1922 Folder 95a. Digital ID 313434. JDC, NY:21–32; Terrible Plight of Refugees in Danzig. n.d. [Aug. 1920]. 245.4 XII-Europe-9. YIVO, HIAS; Tartakower manuscript, 22. 1939. 245.4.26. xxvi-1. YIVO, HIAS.

114. Personnel for Work Abroad. n.d. [1921]. 245.4 XII-Europe-8. YIVO, HIAS.
115. Report to John Bernstein, 3. n.d. [Oct. 1921]. 245.4 XII-Europe-1. YIVO, HIAS.
116. Kass to J. Fain. Aug. 28, 1921. 245.4 XII-Europe-8. YIVO, HIAS; A. Held and J. Bernstein. 1921. 245.4 XII-Rumania-1. YIVO, HIAS.
117. Hias Statement of Expenses. March 27, 1922. Folder 95a. item=313406. JDC, NY:21–32.
118. Draft letter C. Sulzberger to L. Levin. March 23, 1922. Folder 95a. item=313398. JDC, NY:21–32.
119. Abstract of Preliminary Report on the Refugee Problem. B. Kahn. Nov. 1, 1921. Folder 161. item=320060. JDC, NY:21–32.
120. Summary of Vienna Conference. Nov. 15–19, 1920. Folder 64. item=208782. JDC, NY:19–21.
121. L. Marshall to S. Goldenson. Sept. 12, 1927. Folder 95a. item=313459. JDC, NY:21–32.
122. Oct. 1918, 9. *Jewish Immigration Bulletin.*
123. Committee on Foreign Relations Meeting Minutes. March 4, June 26, July 30, Oct. 28, 1919. 245.4 I-14. YIVO, HIAS; Executive Committee Meeting Minutes. Oct. 21, 1919. 245.4 I-8. YIVO, HIAS.
124. Lederhendler, "HIAS under Pressure," 105.
125. Torpey, *Invention of the Passport*, 119–20.
126. Massel Report on European Commission. [late 1921]. 245.4 XII-Europe-1. YIVO, HIAS; Committee on Work in Foreign Countries Meeting Minutes. June 6, 1923. 245.1.14. YIVO, HIAS.
127. L. Marshall to J. Bernstein. April 1, 1922 Folder 95a. item=313417. JDC, NY:21–32; National Budgeting Study Dealing with Hias. May 10, 1922. Folder 95a. item=313420. JDC, NY:21–32. On Hias' struggles, see: Deutsch, "Hias 1909–1939," chapter 3; Lederhendler, "HIAS under Pressure"; Sanders, Ronald, *Shores of Refuge*, 367–415; Wischnitzer, *Visas to Freedom*, 91–129.
128. The Influence of Organizations in Immigration from Poland and Adjoining Sections of Russia by L. J. Keena. Nov. 16, 1921. 150.60c66/8. NARA, State Dept.
129. Mr. Leon Kamaiky Returns to America. [July 1920]. 245.4 XII-Europe-9. YIVO, HIAS.
130. Bendersky, *The "Jewish Threat."*
131. M. Wischnitzer interview with A. Held. Oct. 9, 1953. 245.4.26. xxvi-7. YIVO, HIAS.
132. On this idea with respect to Jews in Germany after the Great War: Aschheim, "Eastern Jews, German Jews."
133. Sarna, *American Judaism*, 215–23.
134. Memorandum in the Matter of the Alleged Conspiracies to Bring into the United States Jews from Russian Poland and other Eastern European Countries by Robe Carl White. May 27, 1921. 150.60c66/7. NARA, State Dept.

135. 15th Annual Hias Report 1923, President's Message. 1924. 245.4 I-41. YIVO, HIAS.

136. L. Marshall to S. Goldenson. Sept. 12, 1927. Folder 95a. item=313459. JDC, NY:21–32.

137. Rapport sur l'activite de la Hias-J.C.A.-EMIGDIRECT 1927-1928. 245.4 II-1. YIVO, HIAS.

138. The Foreign Relations Department. n.d. [1921]. 245.4 I-16. YIVO, HIAS.

139. Committee on Work in Foreign Countries Meeting Minutes. June 5, 1922. 245.1.13. YIVO, HIAS.

140. 17th Annual Hias Report 1925, President's Message. April 11, 1926. 245.4 I-42. YIVO, HIAS.

141. Work of the European Executive Council and the Management of the European Field. Feb. 17, 1921. Box 1. Folder 4. AJA, Bogen Papers.

142. Preliminary Report on the Refugee Problem. B. Kahn. n.d. [Nov. 1, 1921] Folder 433. item=351737. JDC, NY:21–32.

143. A. Held to J. Bernstein. Oct. 31, 1921. 245.4 XII-Europe-5. YIVO, HIAS; Letter from the Central Committee for the Relief of Ukrainian Refugees in Romania. 1922.5.18. Folder 433. Digial ID 351796, 351797. JDC, NY:21–32.

144. Terms of Agreement between JDC and Hias. Sept. 13, 1921. Folder 95a. item=313388. JDC, NY:21–32.

145. J. Bernstein to F. Warburg. Feb. 15, 1922. Folder 95a. item=313391. JDC, NY:21–32.

146. A. Held to J. Bernstein. n.d. [March 1922] 245.4 XII-Europe-5. YIVO, HIAS; B. Bogen to L. Levin. March 8, 1922. Folder 95a. item=313396. JDC, NY:21–32; L. Marshall to J. Bernstein. April 1, 1922 Folder 95a. item=313417. JDC, NY:21–32.

147. Agreement of JDC and Hias. May 11, 1922 Folder 95a. item=313433. JDC, NY:21–32; J. Bernstein to L. Marshall. June 26, 1922. Folder 95a. item=313441. JDC, NY:21–32.

148. Deutsch, "Hias 1909–1939," chapter 3; Wischnitzer, *Visas to Freedom*, 106–7; 14th Annual Hias Report 1922, Report of the Treasurer. March 11, 1923. 245.4 I-42. YIVO, HIAS; 15th Annual Hias Report 1923, Report of the Treasurer. 1924. 245.4 I-41. YIVO, HIAS.

149. L. Marshall to J. Bernstein. June 29, 1922. Folder 95a. item=313442. JDC, NY:21–32.

150. Committee on Work in Foreign Countries Meeting Minutes. June 5 1922. 245.1.13. YIVO, HIAS; J. Bernstein to L. Marshall. June 7, 1922 Folder 95a. item=313434. JDC, NY:21–32; 17th Annual Hias Report 1925, President's Message. April 11, 1926. 245.4 I-42. YIVO, HIAS.

151. Committee on Work in Foreign Countries Meeting Minutes. Jan. 11, 1923. 245.1.13. YIVO, HIAS; Committee on Work in Foreign Countries Meeting Minutes. June 6, 1923. 245.1.14. YIVO, HIAS.

152. Abraham Herman's Report on Trip Abroad, 11–12. Sept. 22, 1927. 245.4 XII-Europe-1A. YIVO, HIAS.

153. 20th Annual Hias Report 1928, President's Message. 1929. Box 105. YUA, Central Relief.
154. A. Held to J. Bernstein. June 9, 1921. 245.4 XII-Europe-3. YIVO, HIAS; [L. Marshall] to J. Bigart. June 1, 1920. Series II. Box 9. Folder 1. AJCommittee, Correspondence; Werelief, JFC, AJC correspondence. Jan.–March 1920. Series 8. Folder 175. YIVO, Wolf-Mowschowitch Papers; A. Held to J. Bernstein. Oct. 31, 1921. 245.4 XII-Europe-5. YIVO, HIAS; Report on Ica Conference at Paris Oct. 30, 1921 by B. Kahn. Nov. 11, 1921. Folder 161. item=320081. JDC, NY:21–32; Cable B. Kahn to JDC NY. Nov. 29, 1921. Folder 161. item=320082. JDC, NY:21–32.
155. A rare, accurate summary of Emigdirect in this era: Elbogen, *A Century of Jewish Life*, 502.
156. 17th Annual Hias Report 1925, President's Message. April 11, 1926. 245.4 I-42. YIVO, HIAS.
157. Rapport sur l'activite de la Hias-J.C.A.-EMIGDIRECT 1927–1928, 2–3. 245.4 II-1. YIVO, HIAS; Bulletin of the Executive Committee of the Jewish World Relief Conference. Sept. 20, 1921. Box 7. Folder 6. YUA, Wiernik Collection; Sanders, Ronald, *Shores of Refuge*, 392–3.
158. 17th Annual Hias Report 1925, President's Message. April 11, 1926. 245.4 I-42. YIVO, HIAS; Marrus, *Unwanted*, 67–8.
159. Administrative Committee Minutes. 1924. Box 2. Folder 2. AJHS, AJCongress; Report of Executive Committee. Oct. 25–26 1925. Box 5. Folder 9. AJHS, AJCongress; 17th Annual Hias Report 1925. April 11, 1926. 245.4 I-42. YIVO, HIAS.
160. B. Kahn to D. Bressler. July 30, 1924. Folder 163. item=320302. JDC, NY:21–32.
161. P. Baerwald to B. Kahn. Aug. 21, 1924. Folder 163. item=320305. JDC, NY:21–32; L. Marshall to Goldenson. Sept. 12, 1927. Folder 95a. item=313459. JDC, NY:21–32.
162. 17th Annual Hias Report 1925, President's Message. April 11, 1926. 245.4 I-42. YIVO, HIAS; Report of Executive Committee. Oct. 25–26 1925. Box 5. Folder 9. AJHS, AJCongress; Report of Executive Committee. Feb. 20, 1927. Box 5. Folder 11. AJHS, AJCongress.
163. Memorandum on activities of HICEM 1927–43. 245.4 II-3. YIVO, HIAS; Rapport sur l'activite de la Hias-J.C.A.-EMIGDIRECT 1927–1928. 245.4 II-1. YIVO, HIAS; Abraham Herman's Report on Trip Abroad. Sept. 22, 1927. 245.4 XII-Europe-1A. YIVO, HIAS; 22nd Annual Hias Report 1930, Report of the General Manager. 1930. Box 105. YUA, Central Relief; Jewish Telegraphic Agency, "Ica Reports on Progress of Jewish Colonization Work in Russia"; Lederhendler, "The Interrupted Chain"; Wolff, "New Destinations in Jewish Migration."
164. Abraham Herman's Report on Trip Abroad, 7–8. Sept. 22, 1927. 245.4 XII-Europe-1A. YIVO, HIAS.
165. B. Kahn to Hicem. July 5, 1927. Folder 29.3. item=302680. JDC, NY:21–32.
166. On "immigrant foreign relations," see Gabaccia, *Foreign Relations*, 1.

167. 15th Annual Hias Report 1923, President's Message. 1924. 245.4 I-41. YIVO, HIAS.

168. 21st Annual Hias Report 1929, President's Message. 1930. Box 105. YUA, Central Relief; Correspondence between L. Marshall and M. Waldman. July 1929. Series I. Box 1. Folder 175. AJCommittee, Correspondence.

169. "Jewish diplomacy" is the accepted way to describe this phenomenon. Lucien Wolf described himself in these words, in the context of "A New Jewish Diplomacy" suggested by the Russian Jewish historian Simon Dubnow. L. Wolf to editors of the *Jewish Guardian*. Oct. 23, 1928. Series 6. Folder 91. YIVO, Wolf-Mowschowitch Papers.

170. Granick, "Les Associations Juives à la Société des Nations"; Fink, *Defending the Rights of Others*.

171. Piana, "International Refugee Regime," 115–17, 132.

172. Ibid., 130–5; LNA, CRR.

173. Registry Files. R1732/45/16224/16224. LNA, Nansen Fonds; Conférence des réfugiés russes. Sept. 16, 1921. C.R.R./2nd Session/P.V.I. LNA, CRR.

174. Piana, "International Refugee Regime," 118, 122–3.

175. Registry Files. R1734/45/16650/16650. LNA, Nansen Fonds; Registry Files. R1732/45/16224/16224. LNA, Nansen Fonds.

176. See Schoeni and Natchkova, "L'Organisation Internationale Du Travail, Les Féministes"; Wikander, "Demands on the ILO."

177. Minutes of the Second Session of the Advisory Committee of Private Organisations for the Relief of Russian Refugees. Nov. 24, 1921. C.C.R.R./O.P./P.V.2. LNA, CRR; World Jewish Relief Conference Press Bulletin No. 43. n.d. [Dec. 1921]. Series 7. Folder 125. YIVO, Wolf-Mowschowitch Papers.

178. Report on Ica Conference at Paris Oct. 30, 1921. B. Kahn. Nov. 11, 1921. Folder 161. item=320081. JDC, NY:21–32.

179. Piana, "International Refugee Regime," 122.

180. On Lucien Wolf, see Fink, *Defending the Rights of Others*; Levene, *War, Jews, and the New Europe*; Granick, "Les Associations Juives à la Société des Nations."

181. Commission Files. C1409/R404/1/25/1. Original File 45/16225/16225x. LNA, Nansen Fonds; Minutes of the Meeting of the Advisory Committee of Private Organisations for the Relief of Russian Refugees. May 29, 1922. C.C.R./O.P./P.V.1. LNA, CRR.

182. Ica Diplomatic Report. 1925. Series 8. Folder 183. YIVO, Wolf-Mowschowitch Papers.

183. L. Wolf correspondence. Nov. 1926 and Jan. 1927. R1165–1166/14/48711/54529x. LNA, Secretariat.

184. Wolf, *Report at Seventh Assembly*, 10–11; Siegelberg, *Statelessness*.

185. L. Wolf correspondence. Nov. 1926 and Jan. 1927. R1165–1166/14/48711/54529x. LNA, Secretariat.

186. Granick, "Les Associations Juives à la Société des Nations."

187. L. Wolf, T. F. Johnson, F. Nansen, A Thomas correspondence. 1925–1927. Commission Files. C1409/R404/1/25/1. LNA, Nansen Fonds.

188. Executive Committee Minutes. 1925–1927. Box 5. Folders 9–11. AJHS, AJCongress.

189. B. Kahn to JDC NY. Jan. 8, 1922. Folder 161. item=320141. JDC, NY:21–32.
190. E. A. Frick tó L. Wolf. Nov. 18, 1921. Series 6. Folder 84. YIVO, Wolf-Mowschowitch Papers; Commission Files. C1409/R404/1/25/1. Original File 45/16225/16225x. LNA, Nansen Fonds.
191. On the refugee situation in Romania, see Cretu, "Romanian Nation-Building and American Assistance," chapter 3; Guzun, *Indezirabilii*.
192. Cable of B. Kahn to JDC NY. Nov. 28, 1921. Folder 161. item=320084. JDC, NY:21–32; Minutes of Meeting of the Committee on Refugees. Dec. 12, 1921. Folder 161. item=320095. JDC, NY:21–32; E. A. Frick to Swiss Legation, Bucharest. Nov. 10, 1921. Registry Files. R1738/45/18065/18065x. LNA, Nansen Fonds; List of Wolf's activities regarding Jews in Bessarabia, 1923–1924. B CR 123/49. ICRC; Piana, "International Refugee Regime," 125–6; Cretu, "Romanian Nation-Building and American Assistance," 213; W. Bacilieri to T. F. Johnson. Oct. 19, 1922. Registry Files. R1727/45/24387x/15127. LNA, Nansen Fonds; Ica Diplomatic Report. 1925. Series 8. Folder 183. YIVO, Wolf-Mowschowitch Papers; E. Frick to F. Nansen. Dec. 23, 1921. Registry Files. R1727/45/18335x/14682. LNA, Nansen Fonds; 1922 conversation on coordination orgs. Series II. Box 14. Folder 10. AJCommittee, Correspondence.
193. E. A. Frick and L. Wolf Correspondence. Oct.–Nov. 1921. Series 6. Folder 84. YIVO, Wolf-Mowschowitch Papers; Commission Files. C1409/R404/1/25/1. Original File 45/16225/16225x. LNA, Nansen Fonds; Minutes of the Second Session of the Advisory Committee of Private Organisations for the Relief of Russian Refugees. Nov. 24, 1921. C.C.R.R./O.P./P.V.2. LNA, CRR; I. Efroikin to E. A. Frick. March 8, 1922. P. Noel-Baker to C. de Watteville. March 18, 1922. Registry Files. R1739/45/189761/18976x. LNA, Nansen Fonds.
194. Aschheim, "Eastern Jews, German Jews," 362.
195. J. N. Rosenberg to JDC NY. April 4, 1922. Folder 488. item=355402. JDC, NY:21–32.
196. Marrus, *Unwanted*, 51–2.

4 The Sick

1. Transcript of Meeting of the JDC. Aug. 10, 1919. Folder 4. item=200080. JDC, NY:19–21. On the ARC in Palestine, see Rodogno, "International Relief Operations in Palestine."
2. Borowy and Gruner, eds. *Health in Europe in the Interwar Years*.
3. From the nineteenth century, Jews used the tools of European science, especially biology and medicine, to socially define and categorize Jews on their own terms. Hart, *Social Science and Modern Jewish Identity*; Efron, *Defenders of the Race*.
4. Davidovitch and Zalashik, "Air, Sun, Water," 129.
5. Patterson, "Typhus and Its Control in Russia"; Weindling, *Epidemics and Genocide in Eastern Europe*, 73–108.

6. Rosenthal, "Confronting the Bacterial Enemy"; Weindling, *Epidemics and Genocide in Eastern Europe*, 73–108.
7. Kraut, *Silent Travelers*, 4.
8. Markel, *Quarantine!*; Kraut, *Silent Travelers*, 139–40; Weindling, *Epidemics and Genocide in Eastern Europe*, 70–3; Brinkmann, "From *Hinterberlin* to Berlin."
9. Cohen, *Jacob H. Schiff*, 161; Eisenberg, *Jewish Agricultural Colonies in New Jersey*, 72–4.
10. Committee on US Immigration Stations and Work in Foreign Countries Meeting Minutes. July 22, 1920. 245.4 I-15. YIVO, HIAS; April, Sept., Oct. 1920. *Jewish Immigration Bulletin*; Minutes of a Board of Directors Meeting. [Aug. 12, 1919.] 245.4 XII-Europe-1. YIVO, HIAS; Report of E. Rosenblum of Trip to Danzig. July 22, 1920. Box 1. Folder 3. AJA, Bogen Papers.
11. JDC Eurexco to JDC NY re. Medical Program. Jan. 26, 1921. Folder 210.1. item=227919. JDC, NY:19–21.
12. Balinska, "Epidemic Commission of the League of Nations," 82–3; Cornebise, *Typhus and Doughboys*, 153; Dubin, "The League of Nations Health Organisation," 57–8; Piana, "Le Typhus En Pologne," 35; Weindling, *Epidemics and Genocide in Eastern Europe*, chapter 6.
13. Message from F. Brylawski. Feb. 28, 1919. Folder 75. item=209967. JDC, NY:19–21; P. Ross to A. Lucas. April 4 1919. Folder 75. item=209970. JDC, NY:19–21.
14. Transcript of Meeting of the JDC, 46, 51–2. March 11, 1920. Folder 19.2. item=200923. JDC, NY:19–21.
15. Report from Dr. Goldman. Feb. 18, 1920. Folder 63.1. item=208238. JDC, NY:19–21; Transcript of Meeting of the JDC, 48–53. March 11, 1920. Folder 19.2. item=200923. JDC, NY:19–21.
16. Conference between F. C. Keppel, ARC, F. Warburg and J. Magnes. Feb. 10, 1920. Folder 75. item=209983. JDC, NY:19–21.
17. Message from A. Lucas. April 28, 1920. Folder 72.3. item=209766. JDC, NY:19–21.
18. J. Goldman to F. Warburg. Feb. 18, 1920. Folder 63.1. item=208235. JDC, NY:19–21; J. Goldman to F. Warburg. Feb. 19, 1920. Folder 63.1. item=208237. JDC, NY:19–21.
19. J. Goldman to F. Warburg. 19 Feb. 1920. Folder 63.1. item=208237. JDC, NY:19–21.
20. Statement Re Poland. 8 March 1920. Folder 27.1. item=202085. JDC, NY:19-21.
21. Transcript of Meeting of the JDC, 46. March 11, 1920. Folder 19.2. item=200923. JDC, NY:19–21.
22. J. Goldman to F. Warburg. Feb. 18, 1920. Folder 75. item=209995. JDC, NY:19–21.
23. Report from Dr. Goldman. Feb. 18, 1920. Folder 63.1. item=208238. JDC, NY:19–21; Agreement Made by JDC through Dr. Goldman with Col. Gilchrist of the American Typhus Mission. Feb. 25–26, 1920. Folder 63.1. item=208251-2. JDC, NY:19–21.

24. "Dr. Harry Plotz, Expert on Typhus."
25. Report of Dr. Harry Plotz to F. Warburg. Oct. 20, 1920. Folder 92. item=214545. JDC, NY:19–21.
26. Ibid.
27. Weindling, *Epidemics and Genocide in Eastern Europe*, 145.
28. Cornebise, *Typhus and Doughboys*, 64, 66, 117.
29. JDC Information Service Letter No. 17. March 1, 1921. Folder 92. item=214548. JDC, NY:19–21.
30. Golub, "The J.D.C. and Health Programs in Eastern Europe," 294.
31. Memo to Mr. Lucas. Dec. 7, 1920. Folder 93. item=214629. JDC, NY:19–21.
32. Report on Epidemic at Mosciska by Dr. Irvin Michlin. May 15, 1921. Folder 92. item=214576. JDC, NY:19–21.
33. Aschheim, "Eastern Jews, German Jews," 364–5.
34. Weindling, *Epidemics and Genocide in Eastern Europe*, 144–8.
35. Report of medical activities in East Galicia, by R. Kohn. July 1921. Folder 357. item=2001012. JDC, NY:21–32.
36. JDC Eurexco to JDC NY. March 4, 1921. Folder 210.1. item=227928. JDC, NY:19–21.
37. Trott explains that the Russian medical science community kept up with research in Western Europe and built their own scientific institutes and public health projects in "American Philanthropy and Soviet Medical Research," 126–7; Patterson, "Typhus and Its Control in Russia."
38. Grachova, "Pathologies of Civility," 216–32.
39. Patterson, "Typhus and Its Control in Russia"; Report on Medico-Sanitary Conditions by William Wovschin, July 15, 1920–March 7, 1921. March 25, 1921. Folder 255.1. item=233238-9. JDC, NY:19–21; Address by J. L. Magnes at Meeting for Medical Relief for Soviet Russia. Jan. 18, 1921. Folder 255.1. item=233235. JDC, NY:19–21; Trott, "American Philanthropy and Soviet Medical Research," 128.
40. Weindling, *Epidemics and Genocide in Eastern Europe*, 148–53.
41. Irwin, "The Great White Train."
42. Medical Relief for Russia by J. L. Magnes. Sept. 2, 1920. Folder 255.1. item=233225. JDC, NY:19–21.
43. H. Fisher to F. Rosenblatt. March 1920. Folder 255.1. item=233190. JDC, NY:19–21.
44. Report of Dr. Harry Plotz to F. Warburg. Oct. 20, 1920. Folder 92. item=214545. JDC, NY:19–21.
45. Report to Julius Goldman. June 18, 1920. Folder 255.1. item=233205. JDC, NY:19–21.
46. List of Medical and Hospital Supplies for the Ukraine. April 19, 1920. Folder 255.1. item=233191. JDC, NY:19–21; Telegram from JDC NY to JDC Paris. June 2, 1920. Folder 255.1. item=233201. JDC, NY:19–21.
47. W. Wovschin to F. Rosenblatt. Dec. 5, 1920. Folder 255.1. item=233230. JDC, NY:19–21; Report on Medico-Sanitary Conditions by William Wovschin, July 15, 1920–March 7, 1921. March 25, 1921. Folder 255.1. item=233238-9. JDC, NY:19–21.

48. F. Rosenblatt to H. Plotz. June 16, 1921. Folder 255.1. item=233243. JDC, NY:19–21.
49. Address by J. L. Magnes at Meeting for Medical Relief for Soviet Russia. Jan. 18, 1921. Folder 255.1. item=233235. JDC, NY:19–21.
50. Weindling, *Epidemics and Genocide in Eastern Europe*, 164.
51. Lowe, "Red Cross and the New World Order," 236.
52. Weindling, *Epidemics and Genocide in Eastern Europe*, 167–71; Balinska, "Epidemic Commission of the League of Nations," 96–8; Coudreau, "L'Action Nansen Et Les Bolcheviks"; Borowy, *League of Nations Health Organisation*, 89–90.
53. B. Bogen to JDC NY. June 13, 1923. Folder 481. item=355004. JDC, NY:21–32; Report by the Delegation in Russia of the Jewish World Relief conference on its activity in Russia during 1922–24. Series 7. Folder 125. YIVO, Wolf-Mowschowitch Papers.
54. Trott, "American Philanthropy and Soviet Medical Research," 133–5; Patenaude, *Big Show in Bololand*, 236–43; Fisher, *Famine in Soviet Russia*, 437–8; Patterson, "Typhus and Its Control in Russia," 381; Weindling, *Epidemics and Genocide in Eastern Europe*, 170–1, 181.
55. Epstein, "Caring for the Soul's Home."
56. Porter and Porter, "What Was Social Medicine?"
57. Report of Dr. Harry Plotz to F. Warburg. Oct. 20, 1920. Folder 92. item=214545. JDC, NY:19–21.
58. Hart, *Social Science and Modern Jewish Identity*. This is not to say that Jewish scientists never veered towards eugenics – enthusiasts founded an OZE branch in Poland in 1918. Davidovitch and Zalashik, "Air, Sun, Water," 135.
59. Weindling, *International Health Organisations*; Borowy, *League of Nations Health Organisation*; Farley, *To Cast Out Disease*; Weindling, "American Foundations and the Internationalizing of Public Health."
60. Irwin, "Sauvons Les Bébés."
61. Dubin, "The League of Nations Health Organisation."
62. *Hadassah Bulletin*. Volumes 1–4, Issues 1–45. Sept. 1914–March 1918. RG 17. AJHS, Hadassah; Katzburg-Yungman, *Hadassah*, 25–8; Kagan, *The Voice That Called*.
63. McCune, *Whole Wide World*, 51–3, 60.
64. "Palestinian Medical Unit: Hadassah Starts Campaign to Raise $100,000 for Sending of Corps of Physicians to Holy Land."
65. First Annual Report of the Palestine Orphan Committee by Alice Seligsberg. [Oct.] 1920. File 1044. CAHJP, Magnes Papers.
66. Rodogno, "International Relief Operations in Palestine"; Davison, *The American Red Cross in the Great War*, 261–6; Irwin, *Making the World Safe*, 114.
67. Boris Bogen looked to this example as he tried right after the armistice to get to Poland. B. Bogen to JDC NY. Jan. 23, 1919. Folder 75. item=209963. JDC, NY:19–21.
68. Transcript of Meeting of the JDC. Aug. 10, 1919. Folder 4. item=200080. JDC, NY:19–21.

69. First Annual Report of the Palestine Orphan Committee by Alice Seligsberg. [Oct.] 1920. File 1044. CAHJP, Magnes Papers.
70. S. Lowenstein to F. Warburg. Aug. 23, 1918. Folder 120.10. item=8707. JDC, NY:14–18.
71. McCune, *Whole Wide World*, 61.
72. AZMU Executive Committee Minutes. Sept. 30, 1918 Box 80. Folder 1. RG 2. AJHS, Hadassah; S. Lowenstein to JDC NY. Aug. 27, 1918. Folder 120.10. item=8711. JDC, NY:14–18; I. M. Rubinow to H. Szold. Aug. 1, 1919. Folder 1436. CZA, HMO.
73. Shvarts and Brown, "Experiment to Establish Health Care Services in Palestine," 32–5.
74. Ibid, 31.
75. Ibid., 38–42.
76. Irwin, "Sauvons Les Bébés," 60.
77. McCune, *Whole Wide World*, 99; I. M. Rubinow to J. de Haas. Aug. 24, 1919. Box 1. Folder 1. RG 2. AJHS, Hadassah.
78. Sarna, "Zion in the Mind's Eye of American Jews"; Raider, *American Zionism*, 28, 43; Simmons, *Hadassah and the Zionist Project*, 24–6.
79. McCune, *Whole Wide World*, 62, 64, 72, 91–111.
80. Shvarts and Shehory-Rubin, "On Behalf of Mothers and Children in Eretz Israel," 181; Simmons, *Hadassah and the Zionist Project*.
81. Simmons, *Hadassah and the Zionist Project*, 13–17; Bartal, "A Nursing School in Jerusalem," 199; Ḳatzburg-Yungman, *Hadassah*, 25–6.
82. Golub, "The J.D.C. and Health Programs in Eastern Europe," 300.
83. Bartal, "A Nursing School in Jerusalem"; Shvarts and Brown, "Experiment to Establish Health Care Services in Palestine," 34; McCune, *Whole Wide World*, 92.
84. Irwin, "Sauvons Les Bébés"; Simmons, *Hadassah and the Zionist Project*, 47–79.
85. Ḳatzburg-Yungman, *Hadassah*, 32.
86. I. M. Rubinow to B. Flexner. Feb. 7, 1922. Folder 947. CZA, HMO.
87. Shvarts and Brown, "Experiment to Establish Health Care Services in Palestine," 43.
88. Third Report, Sept. 1920–Dec. 1921. 1922. Box 57. Folder 4. RG 2. AJHS, Hadassah; Notes on meeting of Committee on Medical Affairs. Jan. 16, 1922. Folder 33. item=303382. JDC, NY:21–32.
89. McCune, *Whole Wide World*, 92–3.
90. I. M. Rubinow to A. Cohen. Sept. 4, 1922. Folder 948. CZA, HMO.
91. I. M. Rubinow to B. Flexner. Feb. 7, 1922. Folder 947. CZA, HMO.
92. Report on Palestine (draft) by Aaron Teitelbaum. Sept. 1919. Folder 167.2. item=222079. JDC, NY:19–21.
93. Jewish Relief News, Vol. 1 No. 6. July 25, 1920. Folder 45. item=205424. JDC, NY:19–21.
94. Notes on meeting of Committee on Medical Affairs. Jan. 16, 1922. Folder 33. item=303382. JDC, NY:21–32.
95. I. M. Rubinow to B. Flexner. June 1, 1922. Folder 947. CZA, HMO.
96. B. Flexner to F. Warburg. May 18, 1922. Folder 33. item=303414. JDC, NY:21–32; B. Flexner to the JDC Executive Committee. Dec. 1922. Folder 34. item=303473. JDC, NY:21–32.

97. Penslar, *Shylock's Children*, 232.
98. R. Jacobs to R. Szold. Feb. 2, 1928. Box 1. Folder 1. RG 2. AJHS, Hadassah.
99. McCune, *Whole Wide World*, 92–111; Simmons, *Hadassah and the Zionist Project*, 23–9.
100. Sarna, "Zion in the Mind's Eye of American Jews."
101. Draft press release on Polish Unit. n.d. [Dec. 1919/Jan. 1920]. Folder 68.1. item=209043. JDC, NY:19–21.
102. H. Plotz to H. Lehman. April 6, 1921. Folder 92. item=214560. JDC, NY:19–21.
103. Report of Dr. Harry Plotz to F. Warburg. Oct. 20, 1920. Folder 92. item=214545. JDC, NY:19–21.
104. An outline of work in Europe and Palestine by H. Plotz. Sept. 13, 1920. Folder 92. item=214544. JDC, NY:19–21.
105. JDC Information Service Letter No. 17. March 1, 1921. Folder 92. item=214548. JDC, NY:19–21.
106. H. Plotz to H. Lehman. March 16, 1921. Folder 92. item=214552. JDC, NY:19–21.
107. H. Plotz to H. Lehman. April 6, 1921. Folder 92. item=214560. JDC, NY:19–21; Progress of Medical Work. April 6, 1921. Folder 93. item=214687. JDC, NY:19–21.
108. H. Lehman to H. Gans. March 17, 1921. Folder 92. item=214553. JDC, NY:19–21.
109. Transcript of Meeting of the Executive Committee of the JDC. April 1, 1920. Folder 19.2. item=200925. JDC, NY:19–21.
110. H. Plotz to H. Lehman. April 6, 1921. Folder 92. item=214560. JDC, NY:19–21.
111. H. Lehman to H. Plotz. March 30, 1921. Folder 92. item=214559. JDC, NY:19–21.
112. Schneider describes the programs of the RF as "the product of reaction and empiricism rather than a new, full-blown grand strategy" in "The Men Who Followed Flexner," 8.
113. Report on the Medical and Sanitary Program. H. Plotz to F. Warburg. May 2, 1921. Folder 357. item=2001005. JDC, NY:21–32; Summary of Conference upon Medical Program Between Dr. Plotz, Dr. Bogen, Mr. Landesco and Mr. Gans. May 4, 1921. Folder 357. item=2001004. JDC, NY:21–32; I. Michlin to H. Plotz. Sept. 20, 1921. Folder 357. item=2001043. JDC, NY:21–32; JDC; Memorandum for guidance of the members of the Medical Commission. May 23, 1921. Folder 210.1. item=227947. JDC, NY:19–21.
114. Local Contributions As Fixed by the District Conferences; District Committee Organization. n.d. [Sept. 1921]. Folder 357. item=2001049. JDC, NY:21–32.
115. Report of First Conference of the Central Committee for Wolyn at Rowno on August 8th and 9th. Aug. 17, 1921. Folder 357. item=2001029. JDC, NY:21–32.
116. Bialystok Medical Conference. Sept. 14, 1921. Folder 357. item=2001041. JDC, NY:21–32.
117. Report of the Medical Sanitary Conference in Wilna. Sept. 21–22, 1921. Folder 357. item=2001044. JDC, NY:21–32.

118. Report of medical activities in East Galicia. R. Kohn. July 1921. Folder 357. item=2001012. JDC, NY:21–32; 108 Bath Houses and 28 Hospitals Repaired and Newly Constructed in Poland. n.d. [Aug. 1921]. Folder 357. item=2001037. JDC, NY:21–32; Baths Hospitals Ambulatories Etc. 19 Sept. Folder 357. item=2001042. JDC, NY:21–32.

119. I. Michlin to H. Plotz. Sept. 20, 1921. Folder 357. item=2001043. JDC, NY:21–32.

120. Progress of Work in Poland. S. M. Schmidt. Oct. 19, 1921. Folder 358. item=2001053. JDC, NY:21–32.

121. Minutes of Meeting of Medical Committee. Nov. 20, 1922. Folder 34. item=303461. JDC, NY:21–32.

122. H. Plotz to F. Warburg. July 2, 1921. Folder 129. item=318037-9. JDC, NY:21–32; F. Warburg to H. Plotz. July 4, 1921. Folder 129. item=318041. JDC, NY:21–32; H. Plotz to F. Warburg. Sept. 30, 1921. Folder 357. item=2001048. JDC, NY:21–32.

123. B. Flexner to J. N. Rosenberg. Dec. 2, 1921. Folder 129. item=318116. JDC, NY:21–32.

124. Minutes of the first meeting of the Committee on Medical Affairs. Nov. 28, 1921. Folder 33. item=303339. JDC, NY:21–32.

125. On the RF, see: Tournès, "La Fondation Rockefeller"; Farley, *To Cast Out Disease*; Ma, "Rockefeller Foundation's Medical Programs in China." Physician Simon Flexner was the director of the Rockefeller Institute for Medical Research and an active proponent of scientific medicine: Ross, "Simon Flexner and Experimental Medicine at the Rockefeller Institute." Abraham Flexner was a leading scholar of education and became an officer in the RF's General Education Board after his 1910 report on medical education: Bonner, *Abraham Flexner*; Schneider, "The Men Who Followed Flexner."

126. Farley, *To Cast Out Disease*, 27–43, 61–74; B. Bogen to M. Waldman. Oct. 26, 1921. Folder 129. item=318062. JDC, NY:21–32.

127. J. N. Rosenberg to F. Warburg. Oct. 13, 1921. Folder 129. item=318081. JDC, NY:21–32.

128. B. Bogen to M. Flexner. Dec. 8, 1921. Folder 129. item=318126. JDC, NY:21–32.

129. Minutes of the meeting of the Committee on Medical Affairs. March 19. 1922. Folder 33. item=303390. JDC, NY:21–32; Summary of Meetings of the Medical Committee. Nov. 14–29, 1922. Folder 34. item=303458. JDC, NY:21–32.

130. Conference with Dr. Golub. Nov. 28, 1922. Folder 34. item=303468. JDC, NY:21–32; Agenda for Meeting of Committee on Medical Affairs. March 1, 1923. Folder 34. item=303482. JDC, NY:21–32.

131. Golub, "The J.D.C. and Health Programs in Eastern Europe," 294–5.

132. Minutes of Meeting of Medical Committee. Nov. 20, 1922. Folder 34. item=303461. JDC, NY:21–32.

133. Minutes of Meetings of the Committee on Medical Affairs. Nov. 28, 1922. Folder 34. item=303467. JDC, NY:21–32.

134. Zalashik, "The Anti-Favus Campaign in Poland."

135. Golub, "The J.D.C. and Health Programs in Eastern Europe," 300.

136. Bartal, "A Nursing School in Jerusalem," 197–8. However, Russian Jewish women went to Switzerland and Germany to train as physicians since the late nineteenth century: Hirsch, *From the Shtetl to the Lecture Hall*.

137. JDC Eurexco to JDC NY. Feb. 3, 1921. Folder 210.1. Digital ID 227925. JDC, NY:19–21; Report on the Medical and Sanitary Program. H. Plotz to F. Warburg. May 2, 1921. Folder 357. item=2001005. JDC, NY:21–32; Memorandum of interview with Miss Bridge in re Nurses Training School. Jan. 17, 1922. Folder 33. item=303394. JDC, NY:21–32. On the ARC nursing program, see Irwin, *Making the World Safe*, 181–2.

138. Z. Syrkin on Nurses' Training Schools. Dec. 29, 1921. Folder 129. item=318142. JDC, NY:21–32; Golden, "Syrkin-Binsztejnowa's Health Work in Early Interwar Poland," 146–51.

139. Minutes of Meetings of the Committee on Medical Affairs. Nov. 27–28, 1922. Folder 34. item=303466-7. JDC, NY:21–32; Agenda for Meeting of Medical Committee. Dec. 21, 1922. Folder 34. item=303471. JDC, NY:21–32.

140. Minutes of the Meeting of the Committee on Medical Affairs. Dec. 21, 1922. Folder 34. item=303472. JDC, NY:21–32; Mayer, "Jewish Experience in Nursing in America," 64–88.

141. Agenda for Meeting of Committee on Medical Affairs. Oct. 9, 1923. Folder 34. item=303488. JDC, NY:21–32.

142. Mayer, "Jewish Experience in Nursing in America," 64–88; Golub, "The J.D.C. and Health Programs in Eastern Europe," 300–1; Medical Appropriate Relief. Sept. 15, 1925. Folder 34. item=303509. JDC, NY:21–32.

143. Report on the Medical and Sanitary Program and Budget Proposed for Poland. H. Plotz to F. Warburg. May 2, 1921. Folder 357. item=2001005. JDC, NY:21–32.

144. C. J. Liebman to B. Flexner. Oct. 9, 1922. Folder 34. item=303443. JDC, NY:21–32.

145. Minutes of Meeting of Medical Committee. Nov. 20, 1922. Folder 34. item=303461. JDC, NY:21–32.

146. Summary of Meetings of the Medical Committee. Nov. 14–29, 1922. Folder 34. item=303458. JDC, NY:21–32; Golub, "The J.D.C. and Health Programs in Eastern Europe," 296–7.

147. Balinska, *Ludwik Rajchman, Medical Statesman*, 71–2.

148. Suggestions for Plans for work to be undertaken by the Medical Committee. June 8, 1922. Folder 33. item=303420. JDC, NY:21–32.

149. L. Rajchman to A. Cohn and C. J. Liebman. Aug. 12, 1922. Folder 34. item=303430. JDC, NY:21–32.

150. Agreement between the Republic of Poland and the American Joint Distribution Committee. Sept. 8, 1922. Folder 34. item=303440. JDC, NY:21–32; Agreement between the Republic of Poland and the American Joint Distribution Committee. Feb. 27, 1923. Folder 363. item=2001250. JDC, NY:21–32.

151. Minutes of the meeting of the Committee on Medical Affairs. Oct. 11, 1922. Folder 34. item=303450. JDC, NY:21–32; C. J. Liebman to B. Flexner. Oct. 9, 1922. Folder 34. item=303443. JDC, NY:21–32.
152. Medical Department Statement of Appropriations. Nov. 27, 1923. Folder 34. item=303494. JDC, NY:21–32; B. Flexner and L. Rajchman Correspondence. May 29, June 28, 1924. Folder 363. item=2001281-2. JDC, NY:21–32; C. J. Liebman to B. Flexner. Oct. 3, 1925. Folder 363. item=2001288. JDC, NY:21–32.
153. Summary of Meetings of the Medical Committee. Nov. 14–29, 1922. Folder 34. item=303458. JDC, NY:21–32; Minutes of Meeting of the Committee on Medical Affairs. Nov. 27, 1922. Folder 34. item=303466. JDC, NY:21–32;
154. J. J. Golub to B. Kahn. June 29, 1923. Folder 363. item=2001269. JDC, NY:21–32; Dr. Kahn's Report on the Medical Activities of the Joint Distribution Committee. Nov. 1923. Folder 34. item=303495. JDC, NY:21–32; Golden, "Syrkin-Binsztejnowa's Health Work in Early Interwar Poland," 149–51.
155. Wulman, "Social Medical Work for Jews in Poland," 268.
156. Five Years of "TOZ" Activity 1922–1926. 1927. Folder 369. item=333377. JDC, NY:21–32.
157. Zalashik, "The Anti-Favus Campaign in Poland."
158. Wulman, "Social Medical Work for Jews in Poland"; Golub, "The J.D.C. and Health Programs in Eastern Europe."
159. Hobson Faure, Gardet, Hazan, and Nicault, eds., L'Oeuvre de Secours aux Enfants; Zavadivker, "Rescue and Representation"; Grachova, "Pathologies of Civility," 216–32.
160. Zavadivker, "Rescue and Representation"; Grachova, "Pathologies of Civility," 232–38.
161. Ibid., 214–15, 263–4.
162. Report on Medico-Sanitary Conditions by William Wovschin, July 15, 1920–March 7, 1921. March 25, 1921. Folder 255.1. item=233238-9. JDC, NY:19–21; Astashkevich, Jewish Women in the Pogroms.
163. Report on Medico-Sanitary Conditions by William Wovschin, July 15, 1920–March 7, 1921. March 25, 1921. Folder 255.1. item=233238-9. JDC, NY:19–21.
164. Zahra, Lost Children.
165. Oze Ukrainian Branch Monthly Budget on Kiev. Folder 255.1. item=233212-7. JDC, NY:19–21.
166. Grachova, "Pathologies of Civility," 279; Memorandum for organizing through the Berlin Committee of the Oze. June 22, 1922. Folder 102. item=312625-6. JDC, NY:21–32; Trott, "American Philanthropy and Soviet Medical Research," 128–30, 138.
167. Extract from Minutes of Dinner Meeting. Dec. 5, 1922. Folder 479. item=354912. JDC, NY:21–32; Patenaude, Big Show in Bololand, 90–1; Fisher, Famine in Soviet Russia, 429, 437–8, 443; B. Bogen to J. N. Rosenberg. July 2, 1923. Folder 479. item=354919. JDC, NY:21–32; Trott, "American Philanthropy and Soviet Medical Research," 138.

168. Memorandum for organizing through the Berlin Committee of the Oze. June 22, 1922. Folder 102. item=312625-6. JDC, NY:21–32; B. Kahn to Eurexco. May 15, 1923. Folder 102. item=312632. JDC, NY:21–32.

169. B. Bogen to JDC NY. June 13, 1923. Folder 481. item=355004. JDC, NY:21–32; Golub, "OSE–Pioneer of Jewish Health," 369–70; CISR, procès-verbal, Jan. 25–26, 1922, CR87, ACICR. Quoted in Lowe, "Red Cross and the New World Order," 283; Memorandum of the OSE Delegation to the JDC Executive Committee. April 4, 1925. Folder 102. item=312639. JDC, NY:21–32; Report by the Delegation in Russia of the Jewish World Relief conference on its activity in Russia during 1922–24. Series 7. Folder 125. YIVO, Wolf-Mowschowitch Papers.

170. B. Bogen to L. Strauss. Aug. 29, 1923. Box 19. Folder 1. AJHS, Strauss Papers; Trott, "American Philanthropy and Soviet Medical Research," 138.

171. B. Bogen to J. Billikopf. April 14, 1925. Box 3. Folder 5. AJA, Bogen Papers.

172. B. Bogen to JDC NY Committee on Russia. Feb. 3, 1923. Folder 479. item=354920. JDC, NY:21–32.

173. Extract from minutes of dinner meeting. Dec. 5, 1922. Folder 479. item=354912. JDC, NY:21–32.

174. Present State and Prospects for the Future Medical Relief Given to the Needy, Declassed Jewish Population of the USSR, 8–9. July 1926. Folder 479. item=354937-42. JDC, NY:21–32.

175. B. Bogen to H. Alsberg. July 23, 1923. Box 1. Folder 1. AJA, Bogen Papers.

176. B. Kahn to Eurexco. May 15, 1923. Folder 102. item=312632. JDC, NY:21–32; M. Kreinin Fundraising Letter to JDC members. Nov. 19, 1923. Folder 102. item=312634-5. JDC, NY:21–32; B. Kahn to W. J. Mack. April 1, 1924. Folder 102. item=312637. JDC, NY:21–32.

177. B. Bogen to L. Strauss. Nov. 18, 1923. Box 1. Folder 6. AJA, Bogen Papers.

178. B. Bogen to J. Becker. March 15, 1925. Box 3. Folder 5. AJA, Bogen Papers; Bogen, Warburg, Lehman, and Morrissey correspondence. Nov. 1924. Folder 479. item=354930-2. JDC, NY:21–32.

179. J. Rosen to JDC NY. April 8, 1925. Folder 102. item=312643. JDC, NY:21–32.

180. Memorandum of the OSE Delegation to the JDC Executive Committee. April 4, 1925. Folder 102. item=312639. JDC, NY:21–32.

181. M. Gran to JDC Executive Committee. May 12, 1925. Folder 102. item=312644. JDC, NY:21–32.

182. B. Bogen, J. Billikopf correspondence. April 14, May 6, 1925. Box 3. Folder 5. AJA, Bogen Papers; Conference between members of the OSE delegation and Mr. Hyman. May 21, 1925. Folder 481. item=355026. JDC, NY:21–32.

183. "The Progress of the Jewish Farm Colonies in Russia," Report by Joseph A. Rosen, 9–10. Oct. 22–23, 1927. Folder 457a. item=353375. JDC, NY:21–32.

184. J. N. Rosenberg to J. C. Hyman. April 7, 1925. Folder 102. item=312642. JDC, NY:21–32.

185. "The Jewish Situation in Eastern Europe," Report by Jacob Billikopf, Dr. Maurice B. Hexter, 32. Oct. 9–10, 1926. Folder 457a. item=353369. JDC, NY:21–32.

186. "The Present Status of Russian Jewish Agricultural Colonization and the Outlook." By Joseph A. Rosen, 11–12. Oct. 9–10, 1926. Folder 457a. item=353369. JDC, NY:21–32; "The Progress of the Jewish Farm Colonies in Russia." Report by Joseph A. Rosen, 9–10. Oct. 22–23, 1927. Folder 457a. item=353375. JDC, NY:21–32.

187. Reports of JDC medical work in Russia. 1926–28. Folder 479. item=354937-42. JDC, NY:21–32; Reports of JDC medical work in Russia. 1926–29. Series III. Subseries 3. Folder 293. YIVO, Joseph Rosen Papers.

188. J. Becker Russia diary. May 9, 1927. Folder 457a. item=353374. JDC, NY:21–32.

189. Dr. Rosen's Report. Sept. 20, 1929. Folder 457a. item=353380. JDC, NY:21–32.

190. Grachova, "Pathologies of Civility," 282–3.

191. Z. A. Bonoff to M. Waldman. Sept. 7, 1921. Folder 357. item=2001039. JDC, NY:21–32.

192. Memorandum of the OSE Delegation to the JDC Executive Committee. April 4, 1925. Folder 102. item=312639. JDC, NY:21–32.

193. Summary of the Activities of the "OZE" during the years 1926–28. Folder 102. item=312667. JDC, NY:21–32.

194. OSE reports. April 4, 1925. Folder 102. item=312664-6. JDC, NY:21–32.

195. Zalashik, "Jewish American Philanthropy and the Crisis of 1929," 101.

196. Simmons, *Hadassah and the Zionist Project.*

197. B. Flexner to the JDC Executive Committee. Dec. 1922. Folder 34. item=303473. JDC, NY:21–32.

5 Child

1. Bernstein, *In Sackcloth and Ashes.*

2. Fisher and Brooks, *America and the New Poland*, 215.

3. Report of Rowno Branch. March 13, 1921. Folder 207. item=227423. JDC, NY:19–21.

4. S. Peiser to War Orphan Committee JDC NY. May 19, 1921. Folder 207. item=227454. JDC, NY:19–21; Report of the Orphans' Relief Section in Volhynia. July 1, 1921. Folder 207. item=227466. JDC, NY:19–21.

5. Conference between Dr. Rosenblatt and Mr. Rosenberg, 19. Sept. 10, 1921. Folder 88.1. item=213926. JDC, NY:19–21.

6. Cabanes, *The Great War and the Origins of Humanitarianism*, 260–70; Zahra, *Lost Children*, 19–21, 27; Marshall, "Children As an Object of International Relations"; Marshall, "Humanitarian Sympathy for Children in Times of War," 184–6; Irwin, "Sauvons Les Bébés"; Bernstein, *In Sackcloth and Ashes.*

7. Lifton, *Biography of Janusz Korczak.*

8. Meir, "From Communal Charity to National Welfare," 20–6.

9. Ibid.

10. Baughan, "International Adoption," 204–13.

11. B. Bogen to H. Lowenstein. April 27, 1919. Folder 61.2. item=208007. JDC, NY:19–21.

12. T. Cawlikowski to ARA Mission to Poland. Aug. 18, 1919. Folder 207. item=227360. JDC, NY:19–21.

13. Weindling, "From Sentiment to Science," 206.

14. Hoover, Herbert. "The Children Must Be Saved." Feb. 1, 1921. 2.9. *ARA Bulletin*.

15. Marshall, "Humanitarian Sympathy for Children in Times of War," 185; Rodogno, Piana, and Gauthier, "Shaping Poland"; B. Bogen to JDC NY. Nov. 4, 1920. Folder 207. item=227408. JDC, NY:19–21.

16. A. Lucas to F. Warburg. May 5, 1919. Folder 25.2. item=201682. JDC, NY:19–21; JDC NY to H. Lowenstein. May 28, 1919. Folder 207. item=227356. JDC, NY:19–21.

17. War Orphans Committee Statement to the Public. Oct. 6, 1919. Folder 25.2. item=201706. JDC, NY:19–21.

18. B. Bogen to L. Gerstenzang. July 6, 1920. Folder 207. item=227388. JDC, NY:19–21.

19. Polster, *Cleveland Jewish Orphan Asylum*, 163–76.

20. J. Goldman to F. Warburg. Aug. 4, 1920. Folder 207. item=227389. JDC, NY:19–21; Minutes of the Committee on War Orphans. Aug. 25, 1920. Folder 25.2. item=201726. JDC, NY:19–21; Additional memorandum on Jewish Child-Care. n.d. [Aug. 1920] Folder 25.2. item=201728. JDC, NY:19–21.

21. A. Lucas to F. Warburg. May 5, 1919. Folder 25.2. item=201682. JDC, NY:19–21.

22. The War Orphans Stock of Agudas Isroel. April 10, 1919. Folder 207. item=227354. JDC, NY:19–21.

23. Minutes of Meeting of Committee on War Orphans. Sept. 8, 1920. Folder 25.2. item=201736. JDC, NY:19–21.

24. People's Relief to Sec. of State. Aug. 17, 1920. 860E.4016/23. NARA, State Dept; Minutes of Meeting of Committee on War Orphans. Sept. 8, 1920. Folder 25.2. item=201736. JDC, NY:19–21.

25. Committee on Foreign Relations Meeting Minutes. Sept. 17, n.d. [1919]. 245.4 I-16. YIVO, HIAS; Kamaiky Report on European Commission, 16–17. Aug. 1, 1920. 245.4 XII-Europe-1. YIVO, HIAS.

26. War Orphans Committee Statement to the Public. Oct. 6, 1919. Folder 25.2. item=201706. JDC, NY:19–21; JDC EEC to JDC NY. April 28, 1921. Folder 207. item=227428. JDC, NY:19–21; Report on the War Orphans Bureau. Jan. 16, 1921. Folder 207. item=227418. JDC, NY:19–21; Minutes of Meeting of Committee on War Orphans. Sept. 8, 1920. Folder 25.2. item=201736. JDC, NY:19–21.

27. Additional Memorandum on Jewish Child-Care. n.d. [Aug. 1920] Folder 25.2. item=201728. JDC, NY:19–21.

28. Draft of the Arrangement between the Canadian Orphan Organization and our Orphan Committee. Jan. 12, 1921. Folder 88.1. item=213877. JDC, NY:19–21.

29. B. Bogen to Child Care Committee JDC NY. March 18, 1921. Folder 88.1. item=213890. JDC, NY:19–21.
30. T. Efroykin to B. Bogen. May 18, 1921. Folder 88.1. item=213894. JDC, NY:19–21.
31. Report of the Orphans' Relief Section in Volhynia. July 1, 1921. Folder 207. item=227466. JDC, NY:19–21.
32. See: McCune, *Whole Wide World*; Kuzmack, *Woman's Cause*; Klapper, *Ballots, Babies, and Banners.*
33. Seligsberg, "Jewish War Orphans."
34. McCune, *Whole Wide World*, 84–6.
35. Report on the War Orphans Bureau. Jan. 16, 1921. Folder 207. item=227418. JDC, NY:19–21.
36. McCune, *Whole Wide World*, 58–65.
37. Committee on Jewish War Orphans. n.d. [summer 1919]. Folder 25.2. item=201680. JDC, NY:19–21.
38. L. Marshall to H. Rosenfelt. Feb. 11, 1921. Folder 90.1. item=214302. JDC, NY:19–21.
39. Additional Memorandum on Jewish Child-Care. n.d. [Aug. 1920] Folder 25.2. item=201728. JDC, NY:19–21. For mainstream international organizations, interest in children abroad waned quickly after the war and activity returned to domestic child concerns as the decade wore on. Marshall, "Humanitarian Sympathy for Children in Times of War," 186.
40. Announcement 1. n.d. [Feb. 1921]. Folder 109. item=314213. JDC, NY:21–32.
41. Standing Committee on War Orphans Report to the Executive Committee. Nov. 25, 1919. Folder 25.2. item=201714. JDC, NY:19–21; J. Becker to F. Warburg. Nov. 6, 1920. Folder 207. item=227410. JDC, NY:19–21.
42. Baughan, "International Adoption," 181–94.
43. H. Lowenstein to I. Hershfield or B. Bogen. Aug. 27, 1919. Folder 207. item=227361. JDC, NY:19–21.
44. S. Peiser to War Orphan Dept JDC NY. Feb. 18, 1921. Folder 88.1. item=213886. JDC, NY:19–21.
45. Report on the War Orphans Bureau. Jan. 16, 1921. Folder 207. item=227418. JDC, NY:19–21; M. Raskin to JDC NY. Aug. 5, 1921. Folder 339. item=332763. JDC, NY:19–21.
46. She was entrusted additionally to take charge of the childcare work in Congress Poland. Report of Activities. M. Paukner to S. Peiser. May 20, 1921. Folder 207. item=227453. JDC, NY:19–21; Annual Meeting of Board of Managers of the Council of Jewish Women Proceedings. Dec. 1, 1921. Box I:2. LOC, NCJW; Sternberger, "At the Gates of Hope." On the NCJW European reconstruction unit, see McCune, *Whole Wide World*, 84–91.
47. Programme of reuniting the orphan children to their relatives in America. June 21, 1921. Folder 339. item=332758. JDC, NY:19–21.
48. JDC Warsaw to War Orphans Department JDC NY. June 23, 27, 1921. Folder 207. item=227460-1. JDC, NY:19–21.
49. War Orphans' Bureau JDC NY to JDC Eurexco. Dec. 23, 1921. Folder 339. item=332818. JDC, NY:21–32.

50. Report of War Orphans Bureau. Dec. 1922. Folder 107. item=314076. JDC, NY:21–32; L. Strauss, E. J. Henning correspondence. Sept. 2, Oct. 4, 1921. Box 14. Folder 15. AJHS, Strauss Papers.

51. Report on the War Orphans Bureau. Jan. 16, 1921. Folder 207. item=227418. JDC, NY:19–21.

52. Transcript of Vienna Conference, 133. Nov. 15–19, 1920. Folder 64. item=208783. JDC, NY:19–21.

53. Minutes of Meeting of Committee on War Orphans. Sept. 15, 1920. Folder 25.2. item=201741. JDC, NY:19–21.

54. People's Relief to Sec. of State. Aug. 17, 1920. 860E.4016/23. NARA, State Dept.

55. N. H. Davis to People's Relief. Aug. 20, 1920. 860E.4016/23. NARA, State Dept.

56. J. Bogen to I. Werlin. March 25, 1921. Box 108. Folder 3. YUA, Central Relief.

57. Transcript of Vienna Conference, 128–32. Nov. 15–19, 1920. Folder 64. item=208783. JDC, NY:19–21; Standing Committee on War Orphans Report to the Executive Committee. Nov. 25, 1919. Folder 25.2. item=201714. JDC, NY:19–21.

58. Baughan, "International Adoption," 194–204; Cox, *Hunger in War and Peace*, 314–25.

59. "Appeal by President Wilson," Dec. 31, 1920. 2.7. *ARA Bulletin*.

60. A. Lucas to F. Warburg. May 5, 1919. Folder 25.2. item=201682. JDC, NY:19–21.

61. Transcript of Vienna Conference, 129–32. Nov. 15–19, 1920. Folder 64. item=208783. JDC, NY:19–21; Minutes of Meeting of the Committee on War Orphans. Nov. 5, 1920. Folder 25.2. item=201754. JDC, NY:19–21.

62. J. Becker to F. Warburg. Nov. 6, 1920. Folder 207. item=227410. JDC, NY:19–21.

63. Transcript of Vienna Conference, 129–30. Nov. 15–19, 1920. Folder 64. item=208783. JDC, NY:19–21; JDC New York to JDC Paris re: Financial Adoption. 13 Jan. 1921. Folder 88.1. item=213880. JDC, NY:19–21.

64. S. Peiser to War Orphan Committee JDC NY. May 19, 1921. Folder 207. item=227454. JDC, NY:19–21.

65. Transcript of Vienna Conference, 129. Nov. 15–19, 1920. Folder 64. item=208783. JDC, NY:19–21.

66. Report of Jessie Bogen. Jan. 6, 1921. Folder 190.1. item=224330. JDC, NY:19–21.

67. F. Warburg to H. Lowenstein. Sept. 20, 1920. Folder 25.2. item=201742. JDC, NY:19–21.

68. Report of Jessie Bogen. Jan. 6, 1921. Folder 190.1. item=224330. JDC, NY:19–21.

69. S. Peiser to JDC NY. April 27, 1921. Folder 88.1. item=213907. JDC, NY:19–21.

70. A. Lucas to F. Warburg. May 5, 1919. Folder 25.2. item=201682. JDC, NY:19–21.

71. Simmons, *Hadassah and the Zionist Project*, 59; Jacobs, "Alice. L Seligsberg 1873–1940"; Seligsberg, "Jewish War Orphans."
72. Statement concerning Orphans by Alice Seligsberg. Feb. 10, 1919. File 1042. CAHJP, Magnes Papers.
73. Minutes of the Meeting of the Sub-committee on Jewish War Orphans. July 1, 1919. Folder 25.2. item=201684. JDC, NY:19–21; A. Seligsberg to E. Rothschild. July 3, 1919. File 1042. CAHJP, Magnes Papers.
74. C. Adler to F. Warburg. April 9, 1919. Folder 210.2. item=227788. JDC, NY:19–21.
75. Minutes of the Meeting of the Standing Committee on War Orphans. Aug. 15, 1919. Folder 25.2. item=201696. JDC, NY:19–21; Palestine Orphan Committee First Meeting Minutes. Aug. 1, 1919. File 1042. CAHJP, Magnes Papers.
76. Palestine Orphan Committee Fourth Meeting Minutes. Aug. 17, 1919. File 1042. CAHJP, Magnes Papers.
77. Palestine Orphan Committee Meeting Minutes. 1919. File 1042. CAHJP, Magnes Papers; First Annual Report of the Palestine Orphan Committee by Alice Seligsberg. [Oct.] 1920. File 1044. CAHJP, Magnes Papers.
78. S. Berger to A. Lucas. Aug. 15, 1920. File 1043. CAHJP, Magnes Papers.
79. Feinberg, "Jewish Women with the A.E.F"; "Women's Share in the Campaign."
80. A. Seligsberg to S. Berger. Feb. 27, 1921. Reel 1. Folder 4. RG 19. AJHS, Hadassah.
81. First Annual Report of the Palestine Orphan Committee by Alice Seligsberg, 31. [Oct.] 1920. File 1044. CAHJP, Magnes Papers; S. Berger to H. Samuel. July 16, 1920. File 1044. CAHJP, Magnes Papers.
82. Palestine Orphan Committee Meeting Minutes. Oct. 19, 1920–Jan. 27, 1922. File 1044. CAHJP, Magnes Papers.
83. Simmons, *Hadassah and the Zionist Project*, 67.
84. Irwin, "Sauvons Les Bébés," 54–5.
85. Penslar, *Shylock's Children*, 223.
86. See Simmons, *Hadassah and the Zionist Project*, 47–86.
87. See correspondence about visas and paperwork from Hias, the JDC, and the US government scattered throughout Folder 340. JDC, NY:21–32.
88. A. Shohan to B. Kahn. Nov. 7, 1922 [or 1923]. Folder 107. item=314066. JDC, NY:21–32.
89. [A. Teitelbaum] to S. Lowenstein. Sept. 3, 1920 Folder 25.2. item=201735. JDC, NY:19–21; S. Peiser to War Orphans Committee JDC NY. 15 Nov. 1921. Folder 339. item=332789. JDC, NY:19–21; Childcare report. 1924. Folder 112. item=314344. JDC, NY: 19–21; Golden, "Syrkin-Binsztejnowa's Health Work in Early Interwar Poland."
90. Report on the War Orphans Bureau. Jan. 16, 1921. Folder 207. item=227418. JDC, NY:19–21.
91. On resentment in New York, see Fromenson, "East Side Preventative Work," 118–19; Tomes, *The Gospel of Germs*, 188–95.
92. A. Shohan to M. Waldman, 14. Oct. 28, 1921. Folder 339. item=332781. JDC, NY:19–21.

93. Meir, "From Communal Charity to National Welfare," 28.
94. Data Relating to Its Operations. March 1932. Box 15. YUA, Wiernik Collection.
95. S. Peiser to War Orphans Committee JDC NY. Nov. 15, 1921. Folder 339. item=332789. JDC, NY:19–21.
96. Conference between Dr. Rosenblatt and Mr. Rosenberg, 19. Sept. 10, 1921. Folder 88.1. item=213926. JDC, NY:19–21.
97. Fisher and Brooks, *America and the New Poland*, 215.
98. Rooke and Schnell, "'Uncramping Child Life,'" 177–8.
99. Irwin, "Sauvons Les Bébés."
100. Table of Orphans under the Care of the JDC: Poland. May 26, 1921. Folder 207. item=227455. JDC, NY:19–21.
101. B. Bogen to JDC NY. June 28, 1921. Folder 207. item=227462. JDC, NY:19–21.
102. Conference between Dr. Rosenblatt and Mr. Rosenberg, 19. Sept. 10, 1921. Folder 88.1. item=213926. JDC, NY:19–21.
103. S. Peiser to J. Bogen. 19 May 1921. Folder 339. item=332754. JDC, NY:21–32; Story about Shohan's appointment. Nov. 25, 1921. Folder 339. item=332792-3. JDC, NY:19–21.
104. The Problem of War Orphans. April 1921. Folder 88.1. item=213891. JDC, NY:19–21. Geographical divisions reflect a Jewish sense of space as opposed to the recognized political borders of nation-states in 1921.
105. Meir, "From Communal Charity to National Welfare," 28.
106. JDC New York to JDC Paris re: Financial Adoption. Jan. 13, 1921. Folder 88.1. item=213880. JDC, NY:19–21.
107. Bar-Yishay and Web, "Care of Orphans and Child Welfare in Poland," 112; Martin, "How to House a Child," 5.
108. A. Shohan to B. Kahn. Bialystock District Conference. Sept. 5, 1922. Folder 340. item=332913-7. JDC, NY:21–32.
109. A. Shohan to B. Kahn. Nov. 10, 1922. Folder 340. item=332924. JDC, NY:21–32.
110. Martin, "How to House a Child," 7.
111. Report of Rowno Branch. March 13, 1921. Folder 207. item=227423. JDC, NY:19–21; Ibid., 2.
112. Martin, "How to House a Child," 7, 10–11.
113. Macleod, *The Age of the Child*, 14–18.
114. JDC New York to JDC Paris re: Financial Adoption. Jan. 13, 1921. Folder 88.1. item=213880. JDC, NY:19–21.
115. Report of the Orphans' Relief Section in Volhynia. July 1, 1921. Folder 207. item=227466. JDC, NY:19–21.
116. Simmons, *Hadassah and the Zionist Project*, 67; Jacobs, "Alice. L Seligsberg 1873–1940"; E. Morrissey to S. Lowenstein. Dec. 11, 1924. Folder 108. item=314180. JDC, NY:21–32.
117. Dr. Kahn's Report on Child Care Activities Abroad to the Committee on War Orphans. Nov. 7, 1923. Folder 108. item=314162. JDC, NY:21–32.

118. Martin, "How to House a Child," 7.
119. Transcript of Vienna Conference, 127. 15–19 Nov. 1920. Folder 64. item=208783. JDC, NY:19–21; B. Bogen to JDC NY. Oct. 12, 1920. Folder 207. item=227392. JDC, NY:19–21.
120. JDC Paris to J. Bogen. April 28, 1921. Folder 88.1. item=213905. JDC, NY:19–21.
121. How the 100,000 Orphans in Poland Are Provided For. n.d. [1922]. Folder 340. item=332898. JDC, NY:21–32.
122. Seligsberg, "Jewish War Orphans."
123. A. Shohan to B. Kahn. March 26, 1923. Folder 108. item=314121. JDC, NY:21–32.
124. B. Kahn to Committee on War Orphans NYC. April 17, 1923. Folder 108. item=314130. JDC, NY:21–32.
125. A. Shohan to War Orphans Committee JDC NY. Jan. 31, 1923. Folder 108. item=314105. JDC, NY:21–32; A. Shohan to B. Kahn. March 26, 1923. Folder 108. item=314121. JDC, NY:21–32.
126. JDC Eurexco to JDC NY. Feb. 3, 1921. Folder 210.1. item=227925. JDC, NY:19–21.
127. Irwin, "Sauvons Les Bébés," 41.
128. Kuzma-Markowska, "From 'Drop of Milk' to Schools for Mothers."
129. McCune, *Whole Wide World*, 93.
130. Report of Jessie Bogen. Jan. 6, 1921. Folder 190.1. item=224330. JDC, NY:19–21; Fisher and Brooks, *America and the New Poland*, 223–6, 298.
131. Report on the Medical and Sanitary Program. H. Plotz to F. Warburg. May 2, 1921. Folder 357. item=2001005. JDC, NY:21–32; Correspondence on Milk Station in Piotrkow. Aug. 9–Sept. 29, 1921. Folder 357. item=2001013-9. JDC, NY:21–32; Report of Rowno Branch. March 13, 1921. Folder 207. item=227423. JDC, NY:19–21; JDC Eurexco to JDC NY. Feb. 3, 1921. Folder 210.1. item=227925. JDC, NY:19–21; Fisher and Brooks, *America and the New Poland*, 230–1.
132. Fisher and Brooks, *America and the New Poland*, 228; Cox, *Hunger in War and Peace*, 307–8.
133. Levine, *School Lunch Politics*, 22–3; Simmons, *Hadassah and the Zionist Project*, 47–71.
134. Shvarts and Shehory-Rubin, "On Behalf of Mothers and Children in Eretz Israel."
135. Statement concerning Orphans by Alice Seligsberg. Feb. 10, 1916. File 1042. CAHJP, Magnes Papers.
136. JDC Eurexco to JDC NY. March 4, 1921. Folder 210.1. item=227929. JDC, NY:19–21.
137. H. Plotz, M. Emerson, R. E. Olds correspondence. May–Aug. 1921. Folder 92. item=214578-601. JDC, NY:19–21; Minutes of JDC Executive Committee Meeting. June 27, 1921. Folder 21. item=201005. JDC, NY:19–21.
138. Report on the Medical and Sanitary Program. H. Plotz to F. Warburg. May 2, 1921. Folder 357. item=2001005. JDC, NY:21–32.

139. S. Lowenstein to A. Lucas. Sept. 22, 1919. Folder 25.2. item=201697. JDC, NY:19–21.

140. Children's Colonies. April 21, 1920. Folder 207. item=227381. JDC, NY:19–21.

141. Pomfret, *Young People and the European City*, 199–242.

142. Childcare report. 1924. Folder 112. item=314344. JDC, NY: 19–21.

143. JDC EEC to JDC NY. April 20, 1921. Folder 207. item=227442. JDC, NY:19–21.

144. Remarks on the activities of the AJDC in Eastern European Countries. n.d. [early 1926]. Folder 108. item=314207. JDC, NY:21–32.

145. Five Years of "TOZ" Activity 1922–1926. 1927. Folder 369. item=333377. JDC, NY:21–32; Summary of the Activities of the "OZE" during the years 1926–1928. Folder 102. item=312667. JDC, NY:21–32; Wulman, "Social Medical Work for Jews in Poland."

146. Hobson Faure, Gardet, Hazan, and Nicault, eds., *L'Oeuvre de Secours aux Enfants*.

147. S. Berger to F. Ullian. Dec. 4, 1925. Box 7. Folder 17. RG 15. AJHS, Hadassah.

148. G. C. Cobb to Sec. of State. June 5, 1923. 860E.4016/30. NARA, State Dept.

149. Palestine Orphan Committee 1919–1924. n.d. [1925]. Folder 108. item=314185. JDC, NY:21–32.

150. S. Berger to S. Lowenstein. March 26, 1923. Folder 108. item=314124. JDC, NY:21–32; Palestine Orphan Committee 1919–1924. n.d. [1925]. Folder 108. item=314185. JDC, NY:21–32; Partial POC report. n.d. [1929]. Box 7. Folder 17. RG 15. AJHS, Hadassah.

151. S. Berger to F. Ullian. Dec. 4, 1925, April 4, 1926. Box 7. Folder 17. RG 15. AJHS, Hadassah.

152. People's Relief to Sec. of State. Aug. 17, 1920. 860E.4016/23. NARA, State Dept.

153. Goldman, *Women, the State, and Revolution*, 59–100.

154. W. K. Thomas to J. Bogen. Nov. 28, 1921. Folder 91b. item=311796. JDC, NY:21–32.

155. W. K Thomas to F. Warburg. Nov. 30, 1921. Folder 91b. item=311798. JDC, NY:21–32.

156. B. Bogen to L. Strauss. April 25, 1922. Folder 471. item=354149. JDC, NY:21–32.

157. ARA telegram. May 15, 1922. Folder 471. item=354154. JDC, NY:21–32.

158. B. Bogen to A. Kottler. Dec. 15, 1922. Folder 471. item=354158. JDC, NY:21–32.

159. Report of David A. Brown to the Special Commission of the AJRC, 26–7. 1922. Folder 457. item=353356. JDC, NY:21–32.

160. B. Bogen to L. Strauss. Oct. 5, 1922. Folder 471. item=354157. JDC, NY:21–32.

161. Condensed Report of the Relief Activities of the JDC in Russia, Nov. 1, 1922–Oct. 31, 1923, 2. Nov. 8, 1923. Folder 457. item=353358. JDC, NY:21–32.

162. S. Ferrière to L. Wolf. 24, July 19, 1922. Series 7. Folder 125. YIVO, Wolf-Mowschowitch Papers; Z. Aberson to J. de Watteville. March 15, 1922. Registry Files. R1727/45/18335x/14682. LNA, Nansen Fonds.
163. Werelief cover letter for IUSE annual report. May 1923. Folder 308b. CAHJP, ORT.
164. Report by the Delegation in Russia of the Jewish World Relief conference on its activity in Russia during 1922–1924. Series 7. Folder 125. YIVO, Wolf-Mowschowitch Papers.
165. Lowe, "Red Cross and the New World Order," 284; Breen, "Save the Children's Russian Relief."
166. S. Ferrière, L. Wolf correspondence. Dec. 13, 1922–Feb. 4, 1923. Series 7. Folder 125. YIVO, Wolf-Mowschowitch Papers.
167. B. Bogen to JDC NY Russian Committee. Jan. 24, Feb. 5, 1923. Folder 471. item=354160-1. JDC, NY:21–32.
168. Schedule of relief activities of Joint in Russia: children's institutions by F. Rosen-Lev. 1924. Folder 471. item=354182. JDC, NY:21–32.
169. Summarized Statement to the Report of Relief Dep't Agrojoint in USSR. 1927. Folder 471. item=354186. JDC, NY:21–32.
170. "The Jewish Situation in Eastern Europe including Russia and the Work of the JDC." Joint Report by Jacob Billikopf and Dr. Maurice B. Hexter, 32. 9–10 Oct. 1926. Folder 457a. item=353369. JDC, NY:21–32.
171. B. Kahn to JDC NY. Feb. 28, 1922. Folder 340. item=332771. JDC, NY:19–21; Block to A. Kottler. Jan. 10, 1923. Folder 108. item=314094. JDC, NY:21–32.
172. I. Speiser to S. Lowenstein. Aug. 17, 1922. Folder 340. item=332898. JDC, NY:21–32.
173. Remarks on the activities of the AJDC in Eastern European Countries. n.d. [early 1926]. Folder 108. item=314207. JDC, NY:21–32.
174. Summary of the Activities of the "OZE" during the years 1926–1928. Folder 102. item=312667. JDC, NY:21–32.
175. B. Bogen to JDC NY Committee on Russia. March 26, 1923. Folder 471. item=354167. JDC, NY:21–32.
176. Summary Report of the Palestine Orphan Committee. March 1, 1929. Box 5. Folder 4. YUA, Wiernik Collection.
177. Data Relating to Its Operations. March 1932. Box 15. YUA, Wiernik Collection.
178. E. Morrissey to J. Hyman. April 18, 1929. Folder 341. item=333008. JDC, NY:21–32.
179. Shniurson, ed., *Dos Elendste Kind.*
180. J. Hyman regarding the Federation of Jewish Orphan Care Committees in Poland. Jan. 7, 1929. Folder 341. item=333004. JDC, NY:21–32; J. Hyman to M. Schneerson. April 1, 1929. Folder 341. item=333007. JDC, NY:21–32.
181. CENTOS reports (in Yiddish). 1929–32. Folder 341. item=333013-23. JDC, NY:21–32.
182. Meir, "From Communal Charity to National Welfare," 29.
183. N. Bentwich to A. Lucas. Aug. 15, 1920. File 1043. CAHJP, Magnes Papers.

184. Report of Rowno Branch. March 13, 1921. Folder 207. item=227423. JDC, NY:19–21.

185. Conference between Dr. Rosenblatt and Mr. Rosenberg, 19–21. Sept. 10, 1921. Folder 88.1. item=213926. JDC, NY:19–21.

186. Committee on Cultural Activities Report to the Executive Committee. Nov. 18, 1920. Folder 22.2. item=201157. JDC, NY:19–21.

187. Waldman, "New Issues in Federation," 175.

188. Adler, *In Her Hands*, 13–27; Meir, "From Communal Charity to National Welfare," 20–2.

189. Youcha, *Minding the Children*, 115–33; Macleod, *The Age of the Child*.

190. Martin, *Jewish Life in Cracow*, 121–87; Mendelsohn, *Jews of East Central Europe*, 63–7; Weiser, *Jewish People, Yiddish Nation*, 120–217.

191. Report of the Relief Activities of the JDC in Russia, Nov. 1, 1922 to Oct. 31, 1923, 35–9. 1923. Folder 458. item=353399. JDC, NY:21–32.

192. Eurexco to JDC NY. July 27, 1921. Folder 339. item=332765-6. JDC, NY:19–21.

193. Committee on Cultural Activities Report to the Executive Committee. Nov. 18, 1920. Folder 22.2. item=201157. JDC, NY:19–21.

194. Correspondence concerning protest against JDC orphan work in Brest-Litovsk. Dec. 7, 1922–April 10, 1923. Folder 340. item=332945-52. JDC, NY:21–32.

195. Committee on Cultural Activities Report to the Executive Committee. Nov. 18, 1920. Folder 22.2. item=201157. JDC, NY:19–21.

196. Cultural Activities. April 26, 1921. Folder 90.1. item=214367. JDC, NY:19–21.

197. See Krasner, *Benderly Boys*.

198. B. Zuckerman to JDC NY. Feb. 4, 1921. Folder 90.1. item=214294. JDC, NY:19–21.

199. A. Lucas to B. Zuckerman. Feb. 11, 1921. Folder 90.1. item=214299. JDC, NY:19–21.

200. Cultural Activities. April 26, 1921. Folder 90.1. item=214367. JDC, NY:19–21.

201. B. Bogen to C. Adler. March 26, 1921. Folder 90.1. item=214338. JDC, NY:19–21;

202. Dr. Kahn's Report on Child Care Activities Abroad to the Committee on War Orphans. Nov. 7, 1923. Folder 108. item=314162. JDC, NY:21–32.

203. B. Zuckerman to H. Rosenfelt. Feb. 15, 1921. Folder 90.1. item=214304. JDC, NY:19–21; B. Zuckerman to A Lucas. Feb. 24, 1921. Folder 90.1. item=214313. JDC, NY:19–21.

204. J. Magnes to C. Adler. April 18, 1921. Folder 90.1. item=214354. JDC, NY:19–21.

205. B. Zuckerman to A. Lucas. Feb. 14, 1921. Folder 90.1. item=214300. JDC, NY:19–21.

206. Founded in 1921, Tsisho oversaw a network of about 130 primary schools. Mendelsohn, *Jews of East Central Europe*, 64–5; Weiser, *Jewish People, Yiddish Nation*, 189.

207. Cultural Activities. April 26, 1921. Folder 90.1. item=214367. JDC, NY:19–21.
208. Central Committee's Direct Remittances for Cultural Work. Dec. 21, 1920. Folder 90.1. item=214309. JDC, NY:19–21; Direct Remittances Made by Central Relief Committee for Cultural Work. April 1, 1921. Folder 90.1. item=214343. JDC, NY:19–21.
209. Cultural Activities. April 26, 1921. Folder 90.1. item=214367. JDC, NY:19–21.
210. S. Bero to J. Bogen. May 5, 1921. Box 108. Folder 3. YUA, Central Relief.
211. F. Warburg to L. Kamaiky. Jan. 5, 1922. Box 109. Folder 1. YUA, Central Relief.
212. "Central Relief Conference Decides on Campaign to Raise $600,000 for Religious Culture." *Morning Journal.* Jan. 8, 1923. Folder 91a. item=311778. JDC, NY:21–32.
213. L. Marshall to H. Rosenfelt. Feb. 11, 1921. Folder 90.1. item=214302. JDC, NY:19–21.
214. C. Adler to A. Lehman. March 27, 1921. Folder 90.1. item=214339. JDC, NY:19–21;
215. C. Adler to H. Rosenfelt. March 14, 1921. Folder 90.1. item=214329. JDC, NY:19–21.
216. H. Rosenfelt to C. Adler. Feb. 25, 1921. Folder 90.1. item=214312. JDC, NY:19–21.
217. B. Bogen to C. Adler. March 26, 1921. Folder 90.1. item=214338. JDC, NY:19–21; Subventions for cultural institutions of the Hebrew and mixed types. March 20, 1921. Folder 90.1. item=214336. JDC, NY:19–21.
218. C. Adler to A. Lehman. April 13, 1921. Folder 90.1. item=214350. JDC, NY:19–21.
219. C. Adler to E. Morrissey. July 22, 1927. Folder 473. item=354437. JDC, NY:21–32; J. Hyman to C. Adler. Sept. 16, 1927. Folder 473. item=354463. JDC, NY:21–32; Bemporad, "JDC in Minsk," 52–5.
220. Pipes, *Russia under the Bolshevik Regime,* 362–6.
221. Dekel-Chen, *Farming the Red Land,* 79–82; J. I. Schneerson's letters, reports. 1927. Folder 473. item=354336. JDC, NY:21–32; JDC correspondence regarding J. I. Schneerson. 1928. Folders 474–5. item=354441, 354494. JDC, NY:21–32.
222. Weiser, *Jewish People, Yiddish Nation,* 188–9; Martin, *Jewish Life in Cracow,* 184–7; Zahra, *Kidnapped Souls.*
223. S. Berger to F. Ullian. April 4, 1926. Box 7. Folder 17. RG 15. AJHS, Hadassah.
224. Shandler, *Awakening Lives*; Mendelsohn, *Jews of East Central Europe,* 59. On interwar youth in Poland, see Kijek, *Dzieci Modernizmu.*
225. Macleod, *The Age of the Child,* 27, 66.
226. Standing Committee on War Orphans Report to the Executive Committee. Nov. 25, 1919. Folder 25.2. item=201714. JDC, NY:19–21.
227. Excerpts from Report on the Activities of the JDC at Chicago: Child-Care. Oct. 23, 1927. Folder 108. item=314208. JDC, NY:21–32.

228. Questions of Policy Requiring Enlightenment from New York by M. Waldman. Sept. 14, 1921. Folder 339. item=332771. JDC, NY:19–21.
229. S. Lowenstein to M. Waldman. Sept. 14, 1921. Folder 339. item=332795. JDC, NY:19–21.

6 The Impoverished

1. Quoted in Kreutzmüller, "Racist Fault Lines," 1–2.
2. Report of Activities, 1924–26. Folder 156. item=319987. JDC, NY:21–32.
3. M. Freund, Reconstruction Conference, Vienna. Dec. 1922. Folder 141. item=319064. JDC, NY:21–32.
4. L. Robinson, Reconstruction Conference, Vienna. Dec. 1922. Folder 141. item=319064. JDC, NY:21–32.
5. Ibid.
6. M. Freund, Reconstruction Conference, Vienna. Dec. 1922. Folder 141. item=319064. JDC, NY:21–32.
7. L. Robinson, Reconstruction Conference, Vienna. Dec. 1922. Folder 141. item=319064. JDC, NY:21–32.
8. Ivanov, "Activities of the World ORT Union."
9. For an intellectual history of this discourse: Penslar, *Shylock's Children*.
10. Reconstruction Conference, Vienna. Dec. 1922. Folder 141. item=319064. JDC, NY:21–32.
11. Ivanov, "Activities of the World ORT Union"; Estraikh, "From Foreign Delegation to World ORT Union"; Reconstruction Conference, Vienna. Dec. 1922. Folder 141. item=319064. JDC, NY:21–32.
12. Ivanov, "Activities of the World ORT Union"; Estraikh, "From Foreign Delegation to World ORT Union."
13. Reconstruction Conference, Vienna. Dec. 1922. Folder 141. item=319064. JDC, NY:21–32; Report of Activities, 1924–26. Folder 156. item=319987. JDC, NY:21–32.
14. M. Freund, Reconstruction Conference, Vienna. Dec. 1922. Folder 141. item=319064. JDC, NY:21–32; Remarks on the activities of the AJDC in Eastern European Countries. n.d. [early 1926]. Folder 108. item=314207. JDC, NY:21–32; Excerpts from Report on the Activities of the JDC at Chicago: Child-Care. Oct. 23, 1927. Folder 108. item=314208. JDC, NY:21–32.
15 Rodogno, *Night on Earth*.
16. Remarks on the activities of the AJDC in Eastern European Countries. n.d. [early 1926]. Folder 108. item=314207. JDC, NY:21–32.
17. Youcha, *Minding the Children*, 124.
18. Report of Rowno Branch. March 13, 1921. Folder 207. item=227423. JDC, NY:19–21.
19. Rodogno, *Night on Earth*; Conference Between Dr. Rosenblatt and Mr. Rosenberg, 19. Sept. 10, 1921. Folder 88.1. item=213926. JDC, NY:19–21; Kijek, *Dzieci Modernizmu*.
20. Thank you to Melissa Hibbard for this comparison.

21. Excerpts from Report on the Activities of the JDC at Chicago: Child-Care. Oct. 23, 1927. Folder 108. item=314208. JDC, NY:21–32; E. Morrissey to J. Hyman. April 18, 1929. Folder 341. item=333008. JDC, NY:21–32.

22. Reconstruction Conference, Vienna. Dec. 1922. Folder 141. item=319064. JDC, NY:21–32.

23. Kijek, *Dzieci Modernizmu*.

24. Estraikh, "From Foreign Delegation to World ORT Union," 89.

25. Report of Activities, 1924–26. Folder 156. item=319987. JDC, NY:21–32.

26. Dr. Kahn's Report on Child Care Activities Abroad to the Committee on War Orphans. Nov. 7, 1923. Folder 108. item=314162. JDC, NY:21–32.

27. Assets of Foundation. April 8–9, 1924. Folder 147. item=319186. JDC, NY:21–32.

28. B. Kahn to S. Lowenstein. Sept. 10, 1925. Folder 113. item=314360. JDC, NY:21–32.

29. Short Remarks in Regard to the Articles of the Exhibit. Oct. 7, 1926. Folder 113. item=314374. JDC, NY:21–32.

30. Mendelsohn, *Jews of East Central Europe*, 66.

31. Weiser, *Jewish People, Yiddish Nation*, 129.

32. Reconstruction Conference, Vienna. Dec. 1922. Folder 141. item=319064. JDC, NY:21–32.

33. Palestine Orphan Committee 1919–1924. n.d. [1925]. Folder 108. item=314185. JDC, NY:21–32.

34. Internate and Workshops of the Home of Jewish Young Workers. Folder 502. item=356702. JDC, NY:21–32.

35. H. Zoellner, Reconstruction Conference, Vienna. Dec. 1922. Folder 141. item=319064. JDC, NY:21–32.

36. Shapiro, *History of ORT*, 150–2.

37. Beizer, *Russian Jewry and the Joint*, 180–2.

38. Dekel-Chen, "Unlikely Triangle," 357.

39. "What Is Becoming of the Eastern War Orphans?" Sept. 12, 1925. *Vossische Zeitung* (trans. from German). Folder 113. item=314364. JDC, NY:21–32; "Jewish Orphans in Manual Trade." Sept. 10, 1925. *Berliner Tageblatt* (trans. from German). Folder 113. item=314365. JDC, NY:21–32.

40. Dr. Kahn's Report on Child Care Activities Abroad to the Committee on War Orphans. Nov. 7, 1923. Folder 108. item=314162. JDC, NY:21–32.

41. Zarrow, "Jewish Girls in Interwar Lwów."

42. Cox, *Hunger in War and Peace*, chapter 9.

43. Child Care Department: A Few Illustrations of Articles Exhibited at Headquarters Typical of the Trade Education. 1926. Box 8. Folder 2. YUA, Wiernik Collection; B. Kahn to S. Lowenstein. Sept. 10, 1925. Folder 113. item=314360. JDC, NY:21–32; Short Remarks in Regard to the Articles of the Exhibit. Oct. 7, 1926. Folder 113. item=314374. JDC, NY:21–32; Excerpts from Report on the Activities of the JDC at Chicago: Child-Care. Oct. 23, 1927. Folder 108. item=314208. JDC, NY:21–32.

44. D. J. Schweitzer to J. Hyman. Oct. 8, 1926. Folder 113. item=314367. JDC, NY:21–32; Child Care Exhibit Statement of Expenses. Jan. 31, 1927. Folder

113. item=314384. JDC, NY:21–32; H. Goldstein to J. Hyman. March 23, 1927. Folder 113. item=314389. JDC, NY:21–32.

45. Child Care Department: Its Activities in Pictures. 1926. Box 8. Folder 1. YUA, Wiernik Collection; Short Remarks in Regard to the Articles of the Exhibit. Oct. 7, 1926. Folder 113. item=314374. JDC, NY:21–32.

46. Ivanov, "Activities of the World ORT Union."

47. M. Freund at the Reconstruction Conference, Vienna. Dec. 1922. Folder 141. item=319064. JDC, NY:21–32.

48. Ibid.

49. Dekel-Chen, "One Big Agrarianizing Family."

50. Van de Grift and Ribi Forclaz, eds., *Governing the Rural*.

51 Rodogno, *Night on Earth*.

52. M. Freund, Reconstruction Conference, Vienna. Dec. 1922. Folder 141. item=319064. JDC, NY:21–32.

53. Dekel-Chen, "One Big Agrarianizing Family."

54. I. Rubinstein, Reconstruction Conference, Vienna. Dec. 1922. Folder 141. item=319064. JDC, NY:21–32; Report of Activities, 1924–26. Folder 156. item=319987. JDC, NY:21–32.

55. Dekel-Chen, "One Big Agrarianizing Family," 271–4; Beizer, *Russian Jewry and the Joint*, 227–8.

56. Schayegh, "Imperial and Transnational Developmentalisms"; Karlinsky, "Jewish Credit Cooperatives."

57. Estraikh, "From Foreign Delegation to World ORT Union."

58. See especially Dekel-Chen, *Farming the Red Land*.

59. H. Zoellner, Reconstruction Conference, Vienna. Dec. 1922. Folder 141. item=319064. JDC, NY:21–32.

60. J. N. Rosenberg to J. Becker. March 7, 1924. Folder 147. item=319151. JDC, NY:21–32.

61. Beizer, *Russian Jewry and the Joint*, 218–27.

62. Dekel-Chen, "One Big Agrarianizing Family," 269–70.

63. Ivanov, "ORT in the Soviet State"; Estraikh, "From Foreign Delegation to World ORT Union."

64. Dekel-Chen, *Farming the Red Land*, 85–6.

65. Dekel-Chen, "Unlikely Triangle," 356–8.

66. Dekel-Chen, "Unlikely Triangle"; Dekel-Chen, *Farming the Red Land*, 83–5.

67. Report of Dr. Joseph A. Rosen on Jewish Colonization Work in Russia. 9–10 Oct. 1925. Folder 457a. item=353366. JDC, NY:21–32.

68. Dekel-Chen, "Unlikely Triangle."

69. Beizer, *Russian Jewry and the Joint*, 233.

70. Dekel-Chen, "Unlikely Triangle."

71. Ibid.

72. Dekel-Chen, *Farming the Red Land*, 77.

73. Dekel-Chen, "Unlikely Triangle," 375.

74. The JDC interchangeably used the words "kassas," "credit cooperatives," and "loan and saving societies."

75. Kreutzmüller, "Racist Fault Lines."

76. Karlinsky, "Jewish Credit Cooperatives," 151.

77. Kreutzmüller, "Racist Fault Lines."
78. I. Rubinstein, Reconstruction Conference, Vienna. Dec. 1922. Folder 141. item=319064. JDC, NY:21–32.
79. Robionek, "Ethnic-German Cooperatives."
80. M. Freund, Reconstruction Conference, Vienna. Dec. 1922. Folder 141. item=319064. JDC, NY:21–32.
81. Ham and Robinson, *Credit Union Primer.*
82. Fleck, *Sozialliberalismus Und Gewerkschaftsbewegung*; Alessandrini, Barco and Battalani, *Co-operative Model in Trentino*, 9–23.
83. Gal, "Brandeis's View on the Upbuilding of Palestine." Gal writes about Brandeis' vision for the Jewish economy in Palestine; it in fact applies far more broadly for the American Jewish vision of the Jewish economy throughout Europe and Palestine in the 1920s.
84. Reconstruction Conference, Vienna. Dec. 1922. Folder 141. item=319064. JDC, NY:21–32.
85. Kallen, "Review of the Cooperative Credit Movement in Palestine."
86. M. Freund, Reconstruction Conference, Vienna. Dec. 1922. Folder 141. item=319064. JDC, NY:21–32.
87. Kallen, "Review of the Cooperative Credit Movement in Palestine."
88. I. Rubinstein, Reconstruction Conference, Vienna. Dec. 1922. Folder 141. item=319064. JDC, NY:21–32.
89. J. Marcus, Reconstruction Conference, Vienna. Dec. 1922. Folder 141. item=319064. JDC, NY:21–32.
90. Reconstruction Conference, Vienna. Dec. 1922. Folder 141. item=319064. JDC, NY:21–32.
91. M. Freund, Reconstruction Conference, Vienna. Dec. 1922. Folder 141. item=319064. JDC, NY:21–32.
92. W. Montesor, Reconstruction Conference, Vienna. Dec. 1922. Folder 141. item=319064. JDC, NY:21–32.
93. M. Freund, Reconstruction Conference, Vienna. Dec. 1922. Folder 141. item=319064. JDC, NY:21–32.
94. Marcus, *History of the Jews in Poland*, 140–1.
95. Free Loan Kassas in Poland, 1926–35. Folder 399. item=335308. JDC, NY:21–32.
96. Reconstruction Conference, Vienna. Dec. 1922. Folder 141. item=319064. JDC, NY:21–32; Report of Activities, 1924–26. Folder 156. item=319987. JDC, NY:21–32.
97. Gröschel, "Anti-semitism in Interwar Polish Cooperatives," 2006.
98. Reconstruction Conference, Vienna. Dec. 1922. Folder 141. item=319064. JDC, NY:21–32.
99. Report of Activities, 1924–26. Folder 156. item=319987. JDC, NY:21–32.
100. M. Freund, Reconstruction Conference, Vienna. Dec. 1922. Folder 141. item=319064. JDC, NY:21–32.
101. J. Marcus, Reconstruction Conference, Vienna. Dec. 1922. Folder 141. item=319064. JDC, NY:21–32.
102. Report of Activities, 1924–26. Folder 156. item=319987. JDC, NY:21–32.

103. Beizer, *Russian Jewry and the Joint*, 216–18.
104. Dekel-Chen, "One Big Agrarianizing Family," 270.
105. Shapiro, *History of ORT*, 149.
106. Dekel-Chen, *Farming the Red Land*, 108–11.
107. Ziv, "Credit Cooperatives in Early Israeli Statehood," 216.
108. Karlinsky, "Jewish Credit Cooperatives," 149.
109. Gal, "Brandeis's View on the Upbuilding of Palestine," 222–5.
110. H. Zoellner, Reconstruction Conference, Vienna. Dec. 1922. Folder 141. item=319064. JDC, NY:21–32; Gal, "Brandeis's View on the Upbuilding of Palestine," 222–5.
111. Minutes of the Governing Board of Kupath Milveh. Jan. 27, 1925. Box 65. NYPL, PEC.
112. General Correspondence, 1924–25. Box 39. NYPL, PEC.
113. Kupat-Milveh & Central Bank. 1924. Box 65. NYPL, PEC.
114. Report of the Activities of the American Joint Reconstruction Foundation. July 24, 1929. Folder 156. item=319990. JDC, NY:21–32.
115. Minutes of the Governing Board of Kupath Milveh. Jan. 27, 1925. Box 65. NYPL, PEC.
116. Reconstruction Conference, Vienna. Dec. 1922. Folder 141. item=319064. JDC, NY:21–32.
117. Giovanoli, "Role of the Bank for International Settlements."
118. Clavin, *Securing the World Economy*.
119. Minutes of Reconstruction Meeting. Aug. 14, 1923. Folder 38. item=303773. JDC, NY:21–32.
120. B. Kahn to JDC NY. March 6, 1924. Folder 147. item=319151. JDC, NY:21–32.
121. L. Robinson to H. Lehman. Jan. 9, 1924. Folder 147. item=319151. JDC, NY:21–32.
122. Assets of Foundation. April 8–9, 1924. Folder 147. item=319186. JDC, NY:21–32.
123. Memorandum of Agreement. Feb. 14, 1924. Folder 147. item=319156–7. JDC, NY:21–32; American Joint Reconstruction Foundation Report. Aug. 28, 1929. Folder 156. item=319989. JDC, NY:21–32.
124. Karlinsky, "Jewish Credit Cooperatives."
125. Report of Activities, 1924–26. Folder 156. item=319987. JDC, NY:21–32.
126. Report of Activities, 1924–26. Folder 156. item=319987. JDC, NY:21–32; American Joint Reconstruction Foundation Report. Aug. 28, 1929. Folder 156. item=319989. JDC, NY:21–32; Data Relating to Its Operations. March 1932. Box 15. YUA, Wiernik Collection.
127. J. Hyman to J. Mack. April 11, 1924. Folder 147. item=319186. JDC, NY:21–32.
128. PEC, *Ten Years of the Palestine Economic Corporation*.
129. Karlinsky, "Jewish Credit Cooperatives," 163.
130. Ziv, "Credit Cooperatives in Early Israeli Statehood," 221.
131. Arab Cooperative Societies 1928–1930. Box 39. NYPL, PEC.

132. Metzer, *Divided Economy*; Karlinsky, "Private Cooperative in the Mandate Period."
133. Minutes of the Governing Board of Kupath Milveh. Jan. 27, 1925. Box 65. NYPL, PEC.
134. Agenda of the Governing Board of Kupath Milveh. May 15, 1924. Box 65. NYPL, PEC.
135. Report of the Activities of the American Joint Reconstruction Foundation. July 24, 1929. Folder 156. item=319990. JDC, NY:21–32; J. Ben-David articles in "Davar," May 27, June 21. General Correspondence, 1927–28. Box 39. NYPL, PEC.
136. Karlinsky, "Private Cooperative in the Mandate Period."
137. Kupat-Milveh & Central Bank. 1924. Box 65. NYPL, PEC.
138. The Loan Bank. Credit Union Activities, 1926. Box 65. NYPL, PEC.
139. General Correspondence, 1927–30. Box 39. NYPL, PEC.
140. M. Freund, Reconstruction Conference, Vienna. Dec. 1922. Folder 141. item=319064. JDC, NY:21–32.
141. Ibid.
142. Marcus, *History of the Jews in Poland*, 144.
143. Karlinsky, "Jewish Credit Cooperatives."

Epilogue

1. Warburg is referring to the Jews, not the state of Israel. F. Warburg to F. Levy (Chicago Rabbinical Association). Nov. 28, 1919. Box 182. Folder 2. AJA, Warburg Papers.
2. Conference between Dr. Rosenblatt and Mr. Rosenberg, 7–8. Sept. 10, 1921. Folder 88.1. item=213926. JDC, NY:19–21.
3. This is with the notable exceptions of the RF and the NER, also invested in rehabilitative work.
4. "The Jewish Situation in Eastern Europe including Russia and the work of the JDC." Joint Report by Jacob Billikopf and Dr. Maurice B. Hexter, 42. Oct. 9–10, 1926. Folder 457a. item=353369. JDC, NY:21–32.
5. Reincoporation did not actually happen until 1931. Bauer, *My Brother's Keeper*, 27.
6. Data Relating to Its Operations. March 1932. Box 15. YUA, Wiernik Collection.
7. Penslar, *Shylock's Children*, chapter 3.
8. Wilson, "Taking Liberties Abroad"; Leff, *Sacred Bonds of Solidarity*; Green, "The British Empire and the Jews."
9. Rebecca Kobrin explores the theme of Jews as interwar American empire builders and Polish perceptions of them in *Jewish Bialystok and Its Diaspora*.
10. Rabinovitch, *Jewish Rights, National Rites*, 189.
11. Penslar, *Shylock's Children*, 240.
12. Hasia Diner, David Engel, Gennady Estraikh, Tobias Brinkmann, Rebecca Kobrin, and Rakefet Zalashik chronicle the tragic litany of events that

coalesced around the collapse of financial markets in Diner and Estraikh, eds., *1929: Mapping the Jewish World.*

13. Correspondence of L. Marshall with M. Waldman. July–Sept. 1929. Series I. Box 1. Folder 8. AJCommittee, Correspondence.

14. Dekel-Chen, "Transnational Intervention and Its Limits," 5–6.

15. J. Magnes Speech to People's Relief Conference. Dec. 29, 1917. File 904. CAHJP, Magnes Papers.

Bibliography

Archives Consulted

American Jewish Archives, Cincinnati, OH (AJA)

MS-536. James H. Becker Papers
MS-900. B'nai Brith International Archives
MS-3. Boris D. Bogen Papers
MS-2. Henry Hurwitz Papers
MS-359. Louis Marshall Papers
MS-23. Morris Waldman Papers
MS-457. Felix M. Warburg Papers

American Jewish Committee Archives, AJC Headquarters, New York

Series I General Correspondence Files 1906–1946
Series II General Correspondence Files 1906–1946

American Jewish Historical Society, New York (AJHS)

I-77. American Jewish Congress Records
P632. Admiral Lewis Lichtenstein Strauss Papers
P31. Harriet Lowenstein Goldstein Papers
P140. Marvin Lowenthal Papers
I-13. People's Relief Committee
I-83. American Jewish Relief Committee
P686. Abram Elkus Papers
Stephen S. Wise Collection (microfilm copies from Brandeis University)
Hadassah Collections

Central Archive for the History of the Jewish People, Jerusalem (CAHJP)

World ORT Union head office
P 3. Judah Leib Magnes Papers
JCA/Lon Num. Jewish Colonization Association Head Office Numeric Files
RI-41 (DAL/). The Far Eastern Jewish Central Information Bureau (DALJEWCIB): Harbin-Shanghai
US 160. People's Relief Committee
Central Zionist Archives, Jerusalem (CZA)
J113. Hadassah Medical Organization.
A95. Sigmund Hoofien

A216. E. Lewin-Epstein
A192. David Idelovitch

Columbia University Manuscript Library

American Relief Administration
Paul Baerwald Papers
Herbert Lehman Papers
Lillian D. Wald Papers

Hoover Institution Archives, Stanford University (Hoover)

American Relief Administration European Operations Records
American Relief Administration Russian Operational Records

Houghton Library, Harvard University

Ms Am 2232. William Phillips

International Committee of the Red Cross Archives, Geneva (ICRC)

B CR 123. Expulsion of the Jews 1923–1939
B CR 163. Stateless Persons 1926–1945
B Mis. Missions Files 1919–1923
CR 87/5. Russian Refugees

International Labour Organization Historical Archives, Geneva (ILO)

File-Series, A. Closed Series: Diplomatic, Emigration, Information, League of
    Nations, Refugees
File-Series, B. Continuing Series: External collaboration

Joint Distribution Committee Archives, New York (JDC)

Photographs of the American Jewish Joint Distribution Committee, New York.
Records of the New York Office of the American Jewish Joint Distribution
    Committee, 1914–1918.
Records of the New York Office of the American Jewish Joint Distribution
    Committee, 1919–1921.
Records of the New York Office of the American Jewish Joint Distribution
    Committee, 1921–1932.

League of Nations Archives, Geneva (LNA)

Commission des Réfugiés Russes (Bound Volume of Procès-Verbaux)
Refugees Mixed Archival Group (Nansen Fonds)
Secretariat

Leo Baeck Institute Archives, New York (LBI)

ME 344a. Bernhard Kahn Memoirs 1914–1921

Library of Congress, Washington, DC (LOC)

MSS61810. National Council of Jewish Women Records
MSS33498. Henry Morgenthau Papers

Library of the Society of Friends, London (Friends)

YM/MfS/FEWVRC/MISSIONS/7/3-8/3. Society of Friends. London Yearly Meeting. Friends Emergency and War Victims Relief Committee (1919–1923). Post-revolution Russia: relief work.

London Metropolitan Archives

4175. British Women's International Zionist Organisation

National Archives and Records Administration II, College Park, MD (NARA II)

RG 59. General Records of the Department of State

New York Public Library Manuscripts and Archives Division, New York (NYPL)

MssCol 2326. Palestine Economic Corporation

Waddesdon Archive, Waddesdon Estate, UK

Palestine Jewish Colonisation Association records

Yeshiva University Archives, New York (YUA)

1963.099. Records of the Central Relief Committee
1966.098. Peter and Bertha Wiernik Collection

YIVO Institute for Jewish Research, New York (YIVO)

RG 352. Papers of Meir Birman
RG 713. Papers of Herman Bernstein
RG 245. Hebrew Immigrant Aid Society (HIAS) Archive
RG 358. Papers of Joseph A. Rosen
RG 348. Papers of Lucien Wolf and David Mowshowitch

Primary Sources

Adler, Cyrus, ed. *Jacob H. Schiff: His Life and Letters*. New York: Doubleday, Doran, 1929.
Bulletin of the American Schools of Oriental Research, no. 68 (1937): 2–4.
Adler, Cyrus, and Aaron M. Margalith. *With Firmness in the Right: American Diplomatic Action Affecting Jews, 1840–1945*. Philadelphia: Jewish Publication Society, 1946.
American Jewish Committee. "Eighth Annual Report of the American Jewish Committee." In *American Jewish Year Book*, edited by Joseph Jacobs. Philadelphia: Jewish Publication Society of America, 1915.
The Jews in the Eastern War Zone. New York: American Jewish Committee, 1916.
"Jewish War Relief Work." In *American Jewish Year Book*, edited by Samson D. Oppenheim. Philadelphia: Jewish Publication Society of America, 1917.
American Relief Administration Bulletin. New York: American Relief Administration.
Ancel, Jean, ed. *Filderman, Wilhelm: Memoirs and Diaries: Volume 1, 1900–1940*. Tel Aviv: Tel Aviv University, 2004.

An-Ski, S. *The Enemy at His Pleasure: A Journey through the Jewish Pale of Settlement During World War I. Khurbn Galitsye,* translated by Joachim Neugroschel. New York: Metropolitan Books, 2002.

Bane, Suda Lorena, and Ralph Haswell Lutz, eds. *Organization of American Relief in Europe 1918–1919, Including Negotiations Leading Up to the Establishment of the Office of Director General of Relief at Paris by the Allied Powers: Documents.* Stanford, CA: Stanford University Press, 1943.

Barton, James L. *The Story of Near East Relief: An Interpretation.* New York: Macmillan, 1930.

Bein, Alex, ed. *Arthur Ruppin: Memoirs, Diaries, Letters.* London: Weidenfeld and Nicolson, 1971.

Bernstein, Herman. *In Sackcloth and Ashes: The Tragedy of Belgium, Poland and the Jews.* New York, 1916.

"The History of American Jewish Relief: An Account of the Activities and Achievements of the Joint Distribution Committee." In JDC Archives, 1928.

Bernstein, Simon. *Les Persécutions des Juifs en Roumanie.* Copenhagen: Bureau de l'Organisation Sioniste, 1918.

Bicknell, Ernest Percy. *With the Red Cross in Europe, 1917–1922,* edited by Grace Vawter Bicknell. American National Red Cross, 1938.

Bogen, Boris David, and Alfred Segal. *Born a Jew.* New York: Macmillan, 1930.

Bulletin of the Joint Distribution Committee. New York: Joint Distribution Committee.

Davison, Henry Pomeroy. *The American Red Cross in the Great War.* New York: Macmillan, 1919.

"Dr. Harry Plotz, Expert on Typhus." *New York Times,* January 7, 1947.

Duker, Abraham G. "Jews in the World War: A Brief Historical Sketch." *Contemporary Jewish Record* 2, no. 5 (1939): 6–29.

Engelman, Morris. *Fifteen Years of Effort on Behalf of World Jewry.* New York: Ference Press, 1929.

Feygenberg, Rakhel. *Bay di Bregen fun Dnyester [On the Banks of the Dniester].* Warsaw: Tsentral, 1925.

Feinberg, Zelda. "Jewish Women with the A.E.F." *The American Hebrew & Jewish Messenger (1903–1922),* April 11, 1919.

Fisher, Harold Henry. *The Famine in Soviet Russia, 1919–1923: The Operations of the American Relief Administration.* Stanford, CA: Stanford University Press, 1935.

Fisher, Harold Henry, and Sidney Brooks. *America and the New Poland.* New York: Macmillan, 1928.

Fromenson, A. H. "East Side Preventative Work." In *Trends and Issues in Jewish Social Welfare in the United States, 1899–1952: The History of American Jewish Social Welfare, Seen through the Proceedings and Reports of the National Conference of Jewish Communal Service,* edited by Robert Morris and Michael Freund. Philadelphia: Jewish Publication Society of America, 1966.

Golub, J. J. "OSE–Pioneer of Jewish Health." *The Jewish Social Service Quarterly* 14, no. 4 (1938): 365–71.

"The J.D.C. and Health Programs in Eastern Europe." *Jewish Social Studies* 5, no. 3 (1943): 293–304.

Guzun, Vadim, ed. *Rusia Înfometată: Acțiunea Umanitara Europeana Documente Din Arhivele Romanesti 1919–1923 [Starved Russia: The European Humanitarian Action Documents from the Romanian Archives 1919–1923].* Grupul Filos, 2014.

Ham, Arthur Harold, and Leonard George Robinson. *A Credit Union Primer: An Elementary Treatise on Cooperative Banking, Containing Questions and Answers concerning Methods of Organization and Operation, Necessary Books and Forms, Suggested By-Laws and the Credit Union Law of New York.* New York: Russell Sage Foundation, 1914.

Heifetz, Elias. *The Slaughter of the Jews in the Ukraine in 1919.* New York: Thomas Seltzer, 1921.

Hyman, Joseph Charlap. *Twenty-Five Years of American Aid to Jews Overseas: A Record of the Joint Distribution Committee.* American Jewish Joint Distribution Committee, 1939.

Jacobs, Rose. "Alice. L Seligsberg 1873–1940." In *American Jewish Year Book*, edited by Harry Schneiderman. Philadelphia: Jewish Publication Society of America, 1942.

Jewish Immigration Bulletin. New York: Hebrew Sheltering and Immigrant Aid Society of America.

Jewish Telegraphic Agency. "Ica Reports on Progress of Jewish Colonization Work in Russia." *Jewish Daily Bulletin*, 1927.

Kagan, Helena. *The Voice That Called.* In London Metropolitan Archives: WIZO 4175/03/02/03/001, 1978.

Kallen, Horace Meyer. *Culture and Democracy in the United States.* Boni and Liveright, 1924.

Kohler, Max J. "Wolf's Notes on the 'Diplomatic History of the Jewish Question.'" *The Jewish Quarterly Review* 11, no. 1 (1920): 120–4.

Kohler, Max J., and Simon Wolf. *Jewish Disabilities in the Balkan States: American Contributions toward Their Removal, with Particular Reference to the Congress of Berlin.* Publications of the American Jewish Historical Society 24. Baltimore: Lord Baltimore Press, 1916.

Landman, Isaac. "Send a Woman for It: The Story of a Job in France and How It Was Done." *The American Hebrew & Jewish Messenger (1903–1922)*, June 6, 1919.

Młynarski, Feliks. *Protest and Appeal in Re American Relief Action for Poland: Filed with the Department of State of the United States of America.* New York, 1916.

Morgenthau, Henry, and French Strother. *All in a Life-Time.* Garden City, NY: Doubleday, Page and Company, 1922.

Morris, Robert, and Michael Freund, eds. *Trends and Issues in Jewish Social Welfare in the United States, 1899–1952: The History of American Jewish Social Welfare, Seen through the Proceedings and Reports of the National Conference of Jewish Communal Service.* Philadelphia: Jewish Publication Society of America, 1966.

National Workmen's Committee on Jewish Rights. *The War and the Jews in Russia.* New York: 1916.

Palestine Economic Corporation. *A Brief Outline of the Ten Years of Activities of the Palestine Economic Corporation.* New York: 1936.

"Palestinian Medical Unit: Hadassah Starts Campaign to Raise $100,000 for Sending of Corps of Physicians to Holy Land." *The American Hebrew & Jewish Messenger (1903–1922)*, December 29, 1916.

Rosenfelt, Henry H. *This Thing of Giving: The Record of a Rare Enterprise of Mercy and Brotherhood.* New York: Plymouth Press, 1924.

Seligsberg, Alice L. "Jewish War Orphans." *The Maccabaean*, February 1918.

Shandler, Jeffrey, ed. *Awakening Lives: Autobiographies of Jewish Youth in Poland before the Holocaust*. New Haven, CT: Yale University Press, 2002.

Shniurson, M., ed. *Dos Elendste Kind*. Warsaw: CENTOS, 1927.

Sternberger, Estelle. "At the Gates of Hope." *The American Hebrew*, April 22, 1921.

Straus, Lina Gutherz. *Disease in Milk: The Remedy, Pasteurization; The Life Work of Nathan Straus*. New York: Dutton, 1917.

Strauss, Lewis L. *Men and Decisions*. New York: Doubleday, 1962.

Surface, Frank Macy, and Raymond L. Bland. *American Food in the World War and Reconstruction Period: Operations of the Organizations under the Direction of Herbert Hoover, 1914 to 1924*. Stanford, CA: Stanford University Press, 1931.

United States Department of State. *Papers Relating to the Foreign Relations of the United States, 1918. Supplement 2, the World War*. U.S. Government Printing Office, 1933.

Waldman, Morris D. *Nor by Power*. New York: International Universities Press, 1953.

"New Issues in Federation." In *Trends and Issues in Jewish Social Welfare in the United States, 1899–1952: The History of American Jewish Social Welfare, Seen Through the Proceedings and Reports of the National Conference of Jewish Communal Service*, edited by Robert Morris and Michael Freund. Philadelphia: Jewish Publication Society of America, 1966.

Wolf, Lucien. *Russo-Jewish Refugees in Eastern Europe: Report on the Fourth Meeting of the Advisory Committee of the High Commissioner for Russian Refugees of the League of Nations*. London: Joint Foreign Committee, 1923.

Report of the Secretary and Special Delegate of the Joint Foreign Committee on Questions of Jewish Interest at the Sixth Assembly of the League. London: Joint Foreign Committee of the Board of Deputies of British Jews and the Anglo-Jewish Association, 1925.

Report of the Secretary and Special Delegate of the Joint Foreign Committee on Questions of Jewish Interest at the Seventh Assembly of the League. London: Joint Foreign Committee of the Board of Deputies of British Jews and the Anglo-Jewish Association, 1926.

"Women's Share in the Campaign." *The American Hebrew & Jewish Messenger (1903–1922)*, September 12, 1919.

Wulman, Leon. "Between Two Wars: A Review of Social Medical Work for Jews in Poland, 1919–1939." *The Jewish Social Service Quarterly* 16, no. 3 (1940): 267–73.

Secondary Sources

Abramson, Henry. *A Prayer for the Government: Ukrainians and Jews in Revolutionary Times, 1917–1920*. Cambridge, MA: Harvard University Press, 1999.

Adler, Eliyana R. *In Her Hands: The Education of Jewish Girls in Tsarist Russia*. Detroit: Wayne State University Press, 2011.

Agar, Herbert. *The Saving Remnant: An Account of Jewish Survival*. New York: Viking Press, 1960.

Akçapar, Burak. *People's Mission to the Ottoman Empire: M.A. Ansari and the Indian Medical Mission, 1912–13*. New Delhi: Oxford University Press, 2014.

Alessandrini, Sergio, Samuel Barco, and Patrizia Battalani. *The Co-operative Model in Trentino (Italy): A Case Study*, edited by Alessandra Proto. OECD Working Papers, 2014.

Aschheim, Steven E. *Brothers and Strangers: The East European Jew in German and German Jewish Consciousness, 1800–1923*. Madison: University of Wisconsin Press, 1982.

"Eastern Jews, German Jews and Germany's Ostpolitik in the First World War." *Leo Baeck Institute Yearbook* 28, no. 1 (1983): 351–65.

Astashkevich, Irina. *Gendered Violence: Jewish Women in the Pogroms of 1917–1921*. Boston: Academic Studies Press, 2018.

Balinska, Marta Aleksandra. "Assistance and Not Mere Relief: The Epidemic Commission of the League of Nations, 1920–1923." In *International Health Organisations and Movements, 1918–1939*, edited by Paul Weindling, 81–108. Cambridge: Cambridge University Press, 1995.

For the Good of Humanity: Ludwik Rajchman, Medical Statesman. New York: Central European University Press, 1998.

Balogh, Brian. *The Associational State: American Governance in the Twentieth Century*. Philadelphia: University of Pennsylvania Press, 2015.

Baltzell, E. Digby. *The Protestant Establishment: Aristocracy & Caste in America*. New York, Random House, 1964.

Bar-Yishay, Nina, and Marek Web. "Yesoymim-Farzorgung un Kindershuts in Poyln (1919–1939)" [Care of Orphans and Child Welfare in Poland]. In *Studies on Polish Jewry 1919–1939: The Interplay of Social, Economic and Political Factors in the Struggle of a Minority for Its Existence*, edited by Joshua A. Fishman, 99–136. New York: YIVO Institute for Jewish Research, 1974.

Bartal, Nira. "Establishment of a Nursing School in Jerusalem by the American Zionist Medical Unit, 1918: Continuation or Revolution?" In *Jewish Women in Pre-state Israel: Life History, Politics, and Culture*, edited by Ruth Kark, Margalit Shilo, and Galit Hasan-Rokem, 193–201. Waltham, MA: Brandeis University Press, 2008.

Bartov, Omer, and Eric D. Weitz. *Shatterzone of Empires: Coexistence and Violence in the German, Habsburg, Russian, and Ottoman Borderlands*. Bloomington: Indiana University Press, 2013.

Bauer, Yehuda. *My Brother's Keeper; a History of the American Jewish Joint Distribution Committee, 1929–1939*. Philadelphia: Jewish Publication Society of America, 1974.

Baughan, Emily. "International Adoption and Anglo-American Internationalism, c. 1918–1925." *Past & Present* 239, no. 1 (2018): 181–217.

Becker, Hortense. "James Becker and East European Jewry after World War I." *American Jewish Archives* 46, no. 2 (1994): 279–312.

Beizer, Michael. *The Jews of St. Petersburg: Excursions through a Noble Past*. Translated by Michael Sherbourne. Philadelphia: The Jewish Publication Society, 1989.

"Who Murdered Professor Israel Friedlaender and Rabbi Bernard Cantor: The Truth Rediscovered." *American Jewish Archives Journal* 55, no. 1 (2003): 63–113.

"Restoring Courage to Jewish Hearts: Frank Rosenblatt's Mission in Siberia in 1919." *East European Jewish Affairs* 39, no. 1 (2009): 35–56.

Relief in Time of Need: Russian Jewry and the Joint, 1914–24. Bloomington: Slavica Publishers, Indiana University, 2015.

Bemporad, Elissa. "JDC in Minsk: The Parameters and Predicaments of Aiding Soviet Jews in the Interwar Years." In *The JDC at 100: A Century of Humanitarianism*, edited by Avinoam Patt, Atina Grossmann, Linda G. Levi, and Maud S. Mandel, 41–59. Detroit: Wayne State University Press, 2019.

Legacy of Blood: Jews, Pogroms, and Ritual Murder in the Lands of the Soviets. New York: Oxford University Press, 2020.

Bemporad, Elissa, and Thomas Chopard, eds. "The Pogroms of the Russian Civil War at 100: New Trends, New Sources." *Quest. Issues in Contemporary Jewish History* 15 (2019).

Bendersky, Joseph W. *The "The Jewish Threat": Anti-Semitic Politics of the U.S. Army.* New York: Basic Books, 2000.

Berkowitz, Michael. "Between Altruism and Self-Interest: Immigration Restriction and the Emergence of American-Jewish Politics in the United States." In *Migration Control in the North Atlantic World: The Evolution of State Practices in Europe and the United States from the French Revolution to the Inter-war Period*, edited by Andreas Fahrmeir, Olivier Faron, and Patrick Weil, 253–70. New York: Berghahn Books, 2003.

Best, Gary Dean. "Financing a Foreign War: Jacob H. Schiff and Japan, 1904–5." *American Jewish Historical Quarterly* 61, no. 4 (1972): 313–24.

To Free a People: American Jewish Leaders and the Jewish Problem in Eastern Europe, 1890–1914. Westport, CT: Greenwood Press, 1982.

Birmingham, Stephen. *Our Crowd: The Great Jewish Families of New York.* Syracuse, NY: Syracuse University Press, 1996.

Biskupski, Mieczysław B. "The Diplomacy of Wartime Relief: The United States and Poland, 1914–1918." *Diplomatic History* 19, no. 3 (1995): 431–52.

"Strategy, Politics, and Suffering: The Wartime Relief of Belgium, Serbia, and Poland, 1914–1918." In *Ideology, Politics, and Diplomacy in East Central Europe*, edited by Mieczysław B. Biskupski and Piotr Stefan Wandycz, 31–57. Rochester, NY: University of Rochester Press, 2003.

Bloxham, Donald. *The Final Solution: A Genocide.* Oxford: Oxford University Press, 2009.

Bon Tempo, Carl J. *Americans at the Gate: The United States and Refugees during the Cold War.* Princeton, NJ: Princeton University Press, 2008.

Bonner, Thomas Neville. *Iconoclast: Abraham Flexner and a Life in Learning.* Baltimore: Johns Hopkins University Press, 2002.

Borowy, Iris. *Coming to Terms with World Health: The League of Nations Health Organisation 1921–1946.* Frankfurt: Peter Lang, 2009.

Borowy, Iris, and Wolf D. Gruner, eds. *Facing Illness in Troubled Times: Health in Europe in the Interwar Years, 1918–1939.* Frankfurt: Peter Lang, 2005.

Brecher, Frank W. *Reluctant Ally: United States Foreign Policy toward the Jews from Wilson to Roosevelt.* New York: Greenwood Press, 1991.

Breen, Rodney. "Saving Enemy Children: Save the Children's Russian Relief Operation, 1921–23." *Disasters* 18, no. 3 (1994): 221–37.

Breitman, Richard D., and Alan M. Kraut. "Antisemitism in the State Department, 1933–44: Four Case Studies." In *Anti-Semitism in American History*, edited by David A. Gerber, 167–98. Urbana: University of Illinois Press, 1986.

Bremner, Robert H. *American Philanthropy*. Chicago: University of Chicago Press, 1988.

Brinkmann, Tobias. "From *Hinterberlin* to Berlin: Jewish Migrants from Eastern Europe in Berlin before and after 1918." *Journal of Modern Jewish Studies* 7, no. 3 (2008): 339–55.

"From Immigrants to Supranational Transmigrants and Refugees: Jewish Migrants in New York and Berlin before and after the Great War." *Comparative Studies of South Asia, Africa and the Middle East* 30, no. 1 (2010): 47–57.

Budnitskii, Oleg. *Russian Jews between the Reds and the Whites, 1917–1920*. Translated by Timothy J. Portice. Philadelphia: University of Pennsylvania Press, 2011.

Bugge, Peter. "'Shatter Zones': The Creation and Re-creation of Europe's East." In *Ideas of Europe since 1914*, edited by Menno Spiering and Michael Wintle, 47–68. London: Palgrave Macmillan, 2002.

Bulmer, Martin. "Mobilising Social Knowledge for Social Welfare: Intermediary Institutions in the Political Systems of the United States and Great Britain between the First and Second World Wars." In *International Health Organisations and Movements, 1918–1939*, edited by Paul Weindling, 305–25. Cambridge: Cambridge University Press, 1995.

Cabanes, Bruno. *The Great War and the Origins of Humanitarianism, 1918–1924*. Cambridge: Cambridge University Press, 2014.

Case, Holly. *The Age of Questions: Or, a First Attempt at an Aggregate History of the Eastern, Social, Woman, American, Jewish, Polish, Bullion, Tuberculosis, and Many Other Questions over the Nineteenth Century, and Beyond*. Princeton, NJ: Princeton University Press, 2018.

Chernow, Ron. *The Warburgs: The Twentieth-Century Odyssey of a Remarkable Jewish Family*. New York: Random House, 1993.

Clavin, Patricia. *Securing the World Economy: The Reinvention of the League of Nations, 1920–1946*. Oxford: Oxford University Press, 2013.

Cohen, Gerard Daniel. *In War's Wake: Europe's Displaced Persons in the Postwar Order*. New York: Oxford University Press, 2012.

Cohen, Naomi Wiener. *Not Free to Desist: The American Jewish Committee, 1906–1966*. Philadelphia: Jewish Publication Society of America, 1972.

Jacob H. Schiff: A Study in American Jewish Leadership. Hanover, NH: Brandeis University Press, 1999.

Cooperman, Jessica. *Making Judaism Safe for America: World War I and the Origins of Religious Pluralism*. New York: New York University Press, 2018.

Cornebise, Alfred E. *Typhus and Doughboys: The American Polish Typhus Relief Expedition, 1919–1921*. Newark, DE: University of Delaware Press, 1982.

Coudreau, Marin. "Le Comité International de Secours à la Russie, l'Action Nansen et les Bolcheviks (1921–1924)." *Relations Internationales* 151 (2012): 49–61.

Cowett, Mark. "Jacob Billikopf: A Jewish Social Worker in America, 1900–1950." *American Jewish Archives Journal* 68, no. 2 (2016): 35–89.

Cox, Mary Elisabeth. *Hunger in War and Peace: Women and Children in Germany, 1914–1924*. Oxford: Oxford University Press, 2019.

Cretu, Doina Anca. "'For the Sake of an Ideal': Romanian Nation-Building and American Foreign Assistance (1917–1940)," diss., Graduate Institute of International and Development Studies, 2018.

Curti, Merle Eugene. *American Philanthropy Abroad*. New Brunswick, NJ: Transaction Books, 1988.

Davidovitch, Nadav, and Rakefet Zalashik. "'Air, Sun, Water': Ideology and Activities of OZE (Society for the Preservation of the Health of the Jewish Population) during the Interwar Period." *Dynamis* 28 (2008): 127–49.

Davis, Belinda Joy. *Home Fires Burning: Food, Politics, and Everyday Life in World War I Berlin.* Chapel Hill: University of North Carolina Press, 2000.

Dekel-Chen, Jonathan L. "An Unlikely Triangle: Philanthropists, Commissars, and American Statesmanship Meet in Soviet Crimea, 1922–37." *Diplomatic History* 27, no. 3 (2003): 353–76.

Farming the Red Land: Jewish Agricultural Colonization and Local Soviet Power, 1924–1941. New Haven, CT: Yale University Press, 2005.

"JCA-ORT-JAS-JDC: One Big Agrarianizing Family." *Jewish History* 21, no. 3 (2007): 263–78.

"Crimea 2008: A Lesson about Uses and Misuses of History." *East European Jewish Affairs* 39, no. 1 (2009): 101–5.

"Defusing the Ethnic Bomb: Resolving the Local Conflict through Philanthropy in the Interwar USSR." In *Anti-Jewish Violence: Rethinking the Pogrom in East European History,* edited by Jonathan L. Dekel-Chen, Natan M. Meir, and David Gaunt, 186–203. Bloomington: Indiana University Press, 2010.

"Transnational Intervention and Its Limits: The Case of Interwar Poland." *Journal of Modern Jewish Studies* 17, no. 3 (2018): 1–22.

Dekel-Chen, Jonathan L., Natan M. Meir, and David Gaunt, eds. *Anti-Jewish Violence: Rethinking the Pogrom in East European History.* Bloomington: Indiana University Press, 2010.

Deutsch, Zeev. "Hias–the Hebrew Sheltering and Immigrant Aid Society 1909–1939" [Hebrew], diss., Hebrew University, 2003.

Diner, Hasia R. *The Jews of the United States, 1654 to 2000.* Berkeley: University of California Press, 2004.

Diner, Hasia R., and Gennady Estraikh, eds. *1929: Mapping the Jewish World.* New York: New York University Press, 2013.

Dubin, Martin David. "The League of Nations Health Organisation." In *International Health Organisations and Movements, 1918–1939,* edited by Paul Weindling, 81–108. Cambridge: Cambridge University Press, 1995.

Efron, John M. *Defenders of the Race: Jewish Doctors and Race Science in Fin-de-siècle Europe.* New Haven, CT: Yale University Press, 1994.

Eisenberg, Ellen. *Jewish Agricultural Colonies in New Jersey: 1882–1920.* Syracuse, NY: Syracuse University Press, 1995.

Elbogen, Ismar. *A Century of Jewish Life.* Philadelphia: Jewish Publication Society of America, 1945.

Engel, David. "What's in a Pogrom? European Jews in the Age of Violence." In *Anti-Jewish Violence: Rethinking the Pogrom in East European History,* edited by Jonathan L. Dekel-Chen, Natan M. Meir, and David Gaunt, 19–37. Bloomington: Indiana University Press, 2010.

The Assassination of Symon Petliura and the Trial of Scholem Schwarzbard 1926–1927: a Selection of Documents. Göttingen: Vandenhoeck & Ruprecht, 2016.

"World War I and Its Impact on the Problem of Security in Jewish History." In *World War I and the Jews: Conflict and Transformations in Europe, the Middle East, and America,* edited by Marsha L. Rozenblit and Jonathan Karp, 17–31. New York: Berghahn Books, 2017.

Epstein, Lisa. "Caring for the Soul's Home: The Jews of Russia and Health Care 1860–1914," diss., Yale University, 1995.

Estraikh, Gennady. "From Foreign Delegation to World ORT Union." In *Educating for Life: New Chapters in the History of ORT*, edited by Rachel Bracha, Adi Drori-Avraham, and Geoffrey Yantian, 76–94. London: World ORT, 2010.

Farley, John. *To Cast Out Disease: A History of the International Health Division of the Rockefeller Foundation (1913–1951)*. Oxford: Oxford University Press, 2004.

Farré, Sébastien. *Colis de Guerre: Secours Alimentaire et Organisations Humanitaires (1914–1947)*. Rennes: Presses universitaires de Rennes, 2014.

Feingold, Henry L. *Zion in America: The Jewish Experience from Colonial Times to the Present*. New York: Twayne Publishers, 1974.

Fink, Carole. *Defending the Rights of Others: The Great Powers, the Jews, and International Minority Protection, 1878–1938*. New York: Cambridge University Press, 2004.

Fischer, Nick. *Spider Web: The Birth of American Anticommunism*. Urbana: University of Illinois Press, 2016.

Fleck, Hans-Georg. *Sozialliberalismus Und Gewerkschaftsbewegung: Die Hirsch-Dunckerschen Gewerkvereine 1868–1914*. Köln: Bund-Verlag, 1994.

Framke, Maria. "'We Must Send a Gift Worthy of India and the Congress!' War and Political Humanitarianism in Late Colonial South Asia." *Modern Asian Studies* 51, no. 6 (2017): 1969–98.

Frankel, Jonathan. "The Jewish Socialists and the American Jewish Congress Movement." *YIVO Annual* 16 (1976): 202–341.

"An Introductory Essay – the Paradoxical Politics of Marginality: Thoughts on the Jewish Situation during the Years 1914–21." In *Studies in Contemporary Jewry: Volume IV: The Jews and the European Crisis, 1914–1921*, edited by Jonathan Frankel, Peter Y. Medding, and Ezra Mendelsohn, 3–21. New York: Oxford University Press, 1988.

The Damascus Affair: "Ritual Murder," Politics, and the Jews in 1840. Cambridge: Cambridge University Press, 1997.

Friedman, Isaiah. *Germany, Turkey, and Zionism 1897–1918*. Oxford: Clarendon Press, 1977.

Frommer, Morris. "The American Jewish Congress: A History, 1914–1950," diss., Ohio State University, 1978.

Gabaccia, Donna R. *Foreign Relations: American Immigration in Global Perspective*. Princeton, NJ: Princeton University Press, 2012.

Gal, Allon. "Brandeis's View on the Upbuilding of Palestine, 1914–1923." *Journal of Israeli History* 3, no. 2 (1982): 211–40.

ed. *Envisioning Israel: The Changing Ideals and Images of North American Jews*. Jerusalem: Magnes Press, Hebrew University, 1996.

Gatrell, Peter. *A Whole Empire Walking: Refugees in Russia during World War I*. Bloomington: Indiana University Press, 1999.

The Making of the Modern Refugee. Oxford: Oxford University Press, 2015.

Gatrell, Peter, and Liubov Zhvanko, eds. *Europe on the Move: Refugees in the Era of the Great War*. Manchester: Manchester University Press, 2017.

Gerwarth, Robert, and John Horne, eds. *War in Peace: Paramilitary Violence in Europe after the Great War*. Oxford: Oxford University Press, 2012.

Gillerman, Sharon. *Germans into Jews: Remaking the Jewish Social Body in the Weimar Republic*. Stanford, CA: Stanford University Press, 2009.

Giovanoli, Mario. "The Role of the Bank for International Settlements in International Monetary Cooperation and Its Tasks Relating to the European Currency Unit." *International Lawyer* 23, no. 4 (1989): 841–64.

Golden, Juliet D. "'Show That You Are Really Alive': Sara-Zofia Syrkin-Binsztejnowa's Emergency Medical Relief and Public Health Work in Early Interwar Poland and the Warsaw Ghetto." *Medizinhistorisches Journal* (2018): 125–62.

Goldin, Simeon. "Deportation of Jews by the Russian Military Command, 1914–1915." *Jews in Eastern Europe* 41, no. 1 (2000): 40–73.

Goldman, Wendy Z. *Women, the State, and Revolution: Soviet Family Policy and Social Life, 1917–1936*. New York: Cambridge University Press, 1993.

Goren, Arthur A. *New York Jews and the Quest for Community: The Kehillah Experiment, 1908–1922*. New York: Columbia University Press, 1970.

Grachova, Sofiya. "Pathologies of Civility: Jews, Health, Race and Citizenship in the Russian Empire and the Bolshevik State, 1830–1930," diss., Harvard University, 2014.

Granick, Jaclyn. "Les Associations Juives à la Société des Nations, 1919–1929: L'accès sans l'influence." *Relations Internationales* 151 (2012): 103–13.

Green, Abigail. "The British Empire and the Jews: An Imperialism of Human Rights?" *Past & Present* 199, no. 1 (2008): 175–205.

Moses Montefiore: Jewish Liberator, Imperial Hero. Cambridge, MA: Harvard University Press, 2010.

"Old Networks, New Connections: The Emergence of the Jewish International." In *Religious Internationals in the Modern World: Globalization and Faith Communities since 1750*, edited by Abigail Green and Vincent Viaene, 53–81. Palgrave Macmillan, 2012.

"Remembering the Diplomat and the Plutocrat." *Jewish Review of Books* 10, no. 4 (Winter 2020): 41–4.

"Liberals, Socialists, Internationalists, Jews." *Journal of World History* 31, no. 1 (2020): 11–41.

Greene, Daniel. *The Jewish Origins of Cultural Pluralism: The Menorah Association and American Diversity*. Bloomington: Indiana University Press, 2011.

Grift, Liesbeth Van De, and Amalia Ribi Forclaz, eds. *Governing the Rural in Interwar Europe*. London: Routledge, 2017.

Gröschel, Cornelius. "Causes and Applications of Anti-Semitism in Interwar Polish Cooperatives." In *Cooperatives in Ethnic Conflicts: Eastern Europe in the 19th and Early 20th Century (4)*, edited by Torsten Lorenz, 283–306. 2006.

Guzun, Vadim. *Indezirabilii: Aspecte Mediatice, Umanitaire Si De Securitate Privind Emigratia Din Uniunea Sovietica in Romania Interbelica [The Outcasts: Media, Humanitarian and Security Aspects about the Emigration from Soviet Union to Romania during the Interwar Period]*. Grupul Filos, 2014.

Hagen, William W. *Anti-Jewish Violence in Poland, 1914–1920*. Cambridge: Cambridge University Press, 2018.

Hanebrink, Paul A. *A Specter Haunting Europe: The Myth of Judeo-Bolshevism.* Cambridge, MA: Harvard University Press, 2018.

Hart, Mitchell Bryan. *The Healthy Jew: The Symbiosis of Judaism and Modern Medicine.* New York: Cambridge University Press, 2007.

Social Science and the Politics of Modern Jewish Identity. Stanford, CA: Stanford University Press, 2000.

Heller, Celia Stopnicka. *On the Edge of Destruction: Jews of Poland between the Two World Wars.* New York: Columbia University Press, 1977.

Heller, Daniel. "The Gendered Politics of Public Health: Jewish Nurses and the American Joint Distribution Committee in Interwar Poland." *Jewish History* 31, no. 3–4 (2018): 319–52.

Hirsch, Luise. *From the Shtetl to the Lecture Hall: Jewish Women and Cultural Exchange.* Lanham, MD: University Press of America, 2013.

Hobson Faure, Laura, Mathias Gardet, Katy Hazan, and Catherine Nicault, eds. *L'Oeuvre De Secours aux Enfants et les Populations Juives au Xxe Siècle: Prévenir et Guérir dans un Siècle de Violence.* Paris: Armand Colin, 2014.

Horowitz, Brian. *Jewish Philanthropy and Enlightenment in Late-Tsarist Russia.* Seattle: University of Washington Press, 2009.

Irwin, Julia F. "The Great White Train: Typhus, Sanitation, and US International Development during the Russian Civil War." *Endeavour* 36, no. 3 (2012): 89–96.

"Sauvons Les Bébés: Child Health and U.S. Humanitarian Aid in the First World War Era." *Bulletin of the History of Medicine* 86, no. 1 (2012): 37–65.

Making the World Safe: The American Red Cross and a Nation's Humanitarian Awakening. New York: Oxford University Press, 2013.

Ivanov, Alexander. "ORT in the Soviet State, 1917–1938." In *Educating for Life: New Chapters in the History of ORT*, edited by Rachel Bracha, Adi Drori-Avraham, and Geoffrey Yantian, 76–94. London: World ORT, 2010.

"From a Russian-Jewish Philanthropic Organization to the 'Glorious Institute of World Jewry': Activities of the World ORT Union in the 1920s–1940s." In *The Russian Jewish Diaspora and European Culture, 1917–1937*, edited by Jörg Schulte, Olga Tabachnikova, and Peter Wagstaff, 387–416. Brill, 2012.

Jackson, Simon. "Transformative Relief: Imperial Humanitarianism and Mandatory Development in Syria-Lebanon, 1915–1925." *Humanity: An International Journal of Human Rights, Humanitarianism, and Development* 8, no. 2 (2017): 247–68.

Jacobson, Abigail. *From Empire to Empire: Jerusalem between Ottoman and British Rule.* Syracuse, NY: Syracuse University Press, 2011.

"American 'Welfare Politics:' American Involvement in Jerusalem during World War I." *Israel Studies* 18, no. 1 (2013): 56–76.

Jahr, Christoph. *Paul Nathan: Publizist, Politiker Und Philanthrop 1857–1927.* Göttingen: Wallstein Verlag, 2018.

Janowsky, Oscar Isaiah. *The Jews and Minority Rights (1898–1919).* New York: Columbia University Press, 1933.

Johnson, Sam. "Breaking or Making the Silence? British Jews and East European Jewish Relief, 1914–1917." *Modern Judaism* 30, no. 1 (2010): 95–119.

Jones, Maldwyn Allen. *American Immigration.* Chicago: University of Chicago Press, 1960.

Kallen, Horace M. "Reviewed Work: *The Cooperative Credit Movement in Palestine* by Manoah L. Bialik." *Jewish Social Studies* 3, no. 1 (1941): 107–8.

Karlinsky, Nahum. "The Private Cooperative in the Mandate Period: Credit and Savings." In *Economy and Society in the Mandate Period: 1918–1948* [Hebrew], edited by Avi Bareli and Nahum Karlinsky, 239–90. Sede Boker: Ben-Gurion University of the Negev, 2003.

"Jewish Philanthropy and Jewish Credit Cooperatives in Eastern Europe and Palestine up to 1939: A Transnational Phenomenon?" *Journal of Israeli History* 27, no. 2 (2008): 149–70.

Karp, Abraham J. *To Give Life: The UJA in the Shaping of the American Jewish Community*. New York: Schocken Books, 1981.

Kassow, Samuel D. *Who Will Write Our History? Emanuel Ringelblum, the Warsaw Ghetto, and the Oyneg Shabes Archive*. Bloomington: Indiana University Press, 2007.

Katzburg-Yungman, Mira. *Hadassah: American Women Zionists and the Rebirth of Israel*. Translated by Tamar Berkowitz. Portland: Littman Library of Jewish Civilization, 2012.

Kijek, Kamil. *Dzieci Modernizmu: Swiadomosc Kultura I Socjalizacja Polityczna Mlodziezy Zydowskiej W Ii Rzeczypospolitej [Children of Modernism]*. Wrocław: Wydawnictwo Uniwersytetu Wrocławskiego, 2017.

Klapper, Melissa R. *Ballots, Babies, and Banners of Peace: American Jewish Women's Activism, 1890–1940*. New York: New York University Press, 2013.

"American Jewish Women's International Travel and Activism at the Turn of the Twentieth Century." *Journal of Modern Jewish Studies* 21, no. 1 (2022).

Kobrin, Rebecca. *Jewish Bialystok and Its Diaspora*. Bloomington: Indiana University Press, 2010.

"American Jewish Philanthropy, Polish Jewry and the Crisis of 1929." In *1929: Mapping the Jewish World*, edited by Hasia R. Diner and Gennady Estraikh, 73–92. New York: New York University Press, 2013.

"Currents and Currency: Jewish Immigrant 'Bankers' and the Transnational Business of Mass Migration, 1873–1914." In *Transnational Traditions: New Perspectives on American Jewish History*, edited by Ava F. Kahn and Adam D. Mendelsohn, 84–104. Detroit: Wayne State University Press, 2014.

Konishi, Sho. "The Emergence of an International Humanitarian Organization in Japan: The Tokugawa Origins of the Japanese Red Cross." *The American Historical Review* 119, no. 4 (2014): 1129–53.

Korman, Gerd. "When Heredity Met the Bacterium: Quarantines in New York and Danzig, 1898–1921." *Leo Baeck Institute Yearbook* 46, no. 1 (2001): 243–76.

Koss, Andrew Noble. "World War I and the Remaking of Jewish Vilna, 1914–1918," diss., Stanford University, 2010.

Kotzin, Daniel P. *Judah L. Magnes: An American Jewish Nonconformist*. Syracuse, NY: Syracuse University Press, 2010.

Koven, Seth, and Sonya Michel. "Womanly Duties: Maternalist Politics and the Origins of Welfare States in France, Germany, Great Britain, and the United States, 1880–1920." *The American Historical Review* 95, no. 4 (1990): 1076–1108.

Krasner, Jonathan B. *The Benderly Boys and American Jewish Education*. Waltham, MA: Brandeis University Press, 2011.

Kraut, Alan M. *Silent Travelers: Germs, Genes, and the "Immigrant Menace."* Baltimore: Johns Hopkins University Press, 1995.

Kreutzmüller, Christoph. "Introduction: The Eruption of Racist Fault Lines in Central European Economy 1918–1933." In *National Economies: Volks-Wirtschaft, Racism and Economy in Europe between the Wars (1918–1939/45)*, edited by Christoph Kreutzmüller, Michael Wildt, and Moshe Zimmermann, 1–17. Newcastle upon Tyne: Cambridge Scholars Publishing, 2015.

"Jewish Credit Cooperatives in Berlin, 1927–1938." *Shofar* 35, no. 2 (2017): 1–19.

Kuzma-Markowska, Sylwia. "From 'Drop of Milk' to Schools for Mothers–Infant Care and Visions of Medical Motherhood in the Early Twentieth Century Polish Part of the Habsburg Empire." In *Medicine within and between the Habsburg and Ottoman Empires: 18th–19th Centuries*, edited by Teodora Daniela Sechel and Gülhan Balshoy, 131–47. Bochum: Dieter Winkler, 2011.

Kuzmack, Linda Gordon. *Woman's Cause: The Jewish Woman's Movement in England and the United States, 1881–1933*. Columbus: Ohio State University Press, 1990.

Kuznitz, Cecile Esther. *YIVO and the Making of Modern Jewish Culture: Scholarship for the Yiddish Nation*. New York: Cambridge University Press, 2014.

Lazaroms, Ilse Josepha. "As the Old Homeland Unravels: Hungarian-American Jews' Reactions to the White Terror in Hungary, 1919–24." *Austrian History Yearbook* 50 (2019): 150–65.

Lederhendler, Eli. "Hard Times: Hias under Pressure, 1925–26." *YIVO Annual* 22 (1995): 105–29.

"The Interrupted Chain: Traditional Receiver Countries, Migration Regimes, and the East European Jewish Diaspora, 1918–39." *East European Jewish Affairs* 44, no. 2–3 (2014): 171–86.

Leff, Lisa Moses. *Sacred Bonds of Solidarity: The Rise of Jewish Internationalism in Nineteenth-Century France*. Stanford, CA: Stanford University Press, 2006.

The Archive Thief: The Man Who Salvaged French Jewish History in the Wake of the Holocaust. New York: Oxford University Press, 2015.

Lehmann, Matthias B. *Emissaries From the Holy Land: The Sephardic Diaspora and the Practice of Pan-Judaism in the Eighteenth Century*. Stanford, CA: Stanford University Press, 2014.

Lerski, Jerzy Jan. *Herbert Hoover and Poland: A Documentary History of a Friendship*. Stanford, CA: Hoover Institution Press, 1977.

Levene, Mark. *War, Jews, and the New Europe: The Diplomacy of Lucien Wolf, 1914–1919*. Oxford: Littman Library of Jewish Civilization, 1992.

Levin, Marlin. *Balm in Gilead: The Story of Hadassah*. New York, Schocken Books, 1973.

Levine, Susan. *School Lunch Politics: The Surprising History of America's Favorite Welfare Program*. Princeton, NJ: Princeton University Press, 2008.

Levitt, Peggy, and Deepak Lamba-Nieves. "Social Remittances Revisited." *Journal of Ethnic and Migration Studies* 37, no. 1 (2011): 1–22.

Lifton, Betty Jean. *The King of Children: A Biography of Janusz Korczak*. New York: Schocken Books, 1988.

Little, John Branden. "Humanitarian Relief in Europe and the Analogue of War, 1914–1918." In *Finding Common Ground: New Directions in First World War Studies*, edited by Jennifer D. Keene and Michael S. Neiberg, 139–58. Leiden: Brill, 2011.

ed. "Special Issue: Humanitarianism in the Era of the First World War." *First World War Studies* 5, no. 1 (2014): 1–129.

Loeffler, James. "Between Zionism and Liberalism: Oscar Janowsky and Diaspora Nationalism in America." *AJS Review* 34, no. 2 (2010): 289–308.

"Nationalism without a Nation? On the Invisibility of American Jewish Politics." *The Jewish Quarterly Review* 105, no. 3 (2015): 367–98.

Rooted Cosmopolitans: Jews and Human Rights in the Twentieth Century. New Haven, CT: Yale University Press, 2018.

Lohr, Eric. *Nationalizing the Russian Empire: The Campaign against Enemy Aliens during World War I*. Cambridge, MA: Harvard University Press, 2003.

Lowe, Kimberly. "The Red Cross and the New World Order, 1918–1924," diss., New Haven, CT: Yale University, 2013.

Ma, Qiusha. "The Peking Union Medical College and the Rockefeller Foundation's Medical Programs in China." In *Rockefeller Philanthropy and Modern Biomedicine: International Initiatives From World War I to the Cold War*, edited by William H. Schneider, 159–83. Bloomington: Indiana University Press, 2002.

Macleod, David I. *The Age of the Child: Children in America, 1890–1920*. New York: Twayne, 1998.

Marcus, Joseph. *Social and Political History of the Jews in Poland, 1919–1939*. Berlin: Mouton Publishers, 1983.

Markel, Howard. *Quarantine! East European Jewish Immigrants and the New York City Epidemics of 1892*. Baltimore: Johns Hopkins University Press, 1997.

Marrus, Michael R. *The Unwanted: European Refugees in the Twentieth Century*. Oxford: Oxford University Press, 1985.

Marshall, Dominique. "The Construction of Children As an Object of International Relations: The Declaration of Children's Rights and the Child Welfare Committee of League of Nations, 1900–1924." *The International Journal of Children's Rights* 7 (1999): 103–47.

"Humanitarian Sympathy for Children in Times of War and the History of Children's Rights, 1919–1959." In *Children and War: A Historical Anthology*, edited by James Alan Marten, 184–200. New York: New York University Press, 2002.

Martin, Sean. *Jewish Life in Cracow 1918–1939*. London: Vallentine Mitchell, 2004.

"How to House a Child: Providing Homes for Jewish Children in Interwar Poland." *East European Jewish Affairs* 45, no. 1 (2015): 26–41.

Mayer, Susan Lee Abramson. "The Jewish Experience in Nursing in America: 1881 to 1955," diss., Columbia University, 1996.

McCune, Mary. *The Whole Wide World, without Limits: International Relief, Gender Politics, and American Jewish Women, 1893–1930*. Detroit: Wayne State University Press, 2005.

McGeever, Brendan. *Antisemitism and the Russian Revolution*. Cambridge: Cambridge University Press, 2019.

Meir, Natan. "From Communal Charity to National Welfare: Jewish Orphanages in Eastern Europe before and after World War I." *East European Jewish Affairs* 39, no. 1 (2009): 19–34.

Mendelsohn, Ezra. *The Jews of East Central Europe between the World Wars.* Bloomington: Indiana University Press, 1983.

Metzer, Jacob. *The Divided Economy of Mandatory Palestine.* Cambridge: Cambridge University Press, 1998.

Michels, Tony. *A Fire in Their Hearts: Yiddish Socialists in New York.* Harvard University Press, 2009.

Miller, Michael L. "The Forgotten Pogroms, 1918." *Slavic Review* 78, no. 3 (2019): 648–53.

Mullendore, William Clinton. *History of the United States Food Administration, 1917–1919.* Stanford, CA: Stanford University Press, 1941.

Nash, George H., and Kendrick A. Clements. *The Life of Herbert Hoover: Master of Emergencies 1917–1918.* New York: W. W. Norton, 1996.

Norman, Theodore. *An Outstretched Arm: A History of the Jewish Colonisation Association.* London: Routledge & Kegan Paul, 1985.

Oren, Michael B. *Power, Faith, and Fantasy: America in the Middle East, 1776 to the Present.* New York: W. W. Norton & Co, 2007.

Pak, Susie J. *Gentlemen Bankers: The World of J. P. Morgan.* Cambridge, MA: Harvard University Press, 2013.

Panter, Sarah. *Jüdische Erfahrungen Und Loyalitätskonflikte Im Ersten Weltkrieg.* Göttingen: Vandenhoeck & Ruprecht, 2014.

Patenaude, Bertrand M. *The Big Show in Bololand: The American Relief Expedition to Soviet Russia in the Famine of 1921.* Stanford, CA: Stanford University Press, 2002.

Patterson, K. David. "Typhus and Its Control in Russia, 1870–1940." *Medical History* 37, no. 4 (1993): 361–81.

Pease, Neal. "'This Troublesome Question': The United States and the 'Polish Pogroms' of 1918–1919." In *Ideology, Politics, and Diplomacy in East Central Europe*, edited by Mieczysław B. Biskupski and Piotr Stefan Wandycz, 58–79. Rochester, NY: University of Rochester Press, 2003.

Penslar, Derek J. *Zionism and Technocracy: The Engineering of Jewish Settlement in Palestine, 1870–1918.* Bloomington: Indiana University Press, 1991.

Shylock's Children: Economics and Jewish Identity in Modern Europe. Berkeley: University of California Press, 2001.

Jews and the Military: A History. Princeton, NJ: Princeton University Press, 2013.

Pfau, Richard. *No Sacrifice Too Great: The Life of Lewis L. Strauss.* Charlottesville: University Press of Virginia, 1984.

Piana, Francesca. "Humanitaire et Politique, *In Medias Res*: Le Typhus en Pologne et l'Organisation Internationale d'Hygiène de la SDN (1919–1923)." *Relations Internationales* 138 (2009): 23–38.

"At the Origins of Humanitarian Diplomacy: The International Refugee Regime (1918–1930)," diss., Graduate Institute of International and Development Studies, 2012.

Piller, Elisabeth. "American War Relief, Cultural Mobilization, and the Myth of Impartial Humanitarianism, 1914–17." *The Journal Of The Gilded Age And Progressive Era* 17, no. 4 (2018): 619–35.

Pipes, Richard. *Russia under the Bolshevik Regime*. New York: A. A. Knopf, 1993.

Pfannestiel, Todd. "The Soviet Bureau: Bolshevik Strategy to Secure U.S. Diplomatic Recognition through Economic Trade." *Diplomatic History* 27, no. 2 (2003).

Polk, Jennifer Ann. "Constructive Efforts: The American Red Cross and YMCA in Revolutionary and Civil War Russia, 1917–1924," diss., University of Toronto, 2012.

Polster, Gary Edward. *Inside Looking Out: The Cleveland Jewish Orphan Asylum, 1868–1924*. Kent, OH: Kent State University Press, 1990.

Pomfret, David M. *Young People and the European City: Age Relations in Nottingham and Saint-Etienne, 1890–1940*. Burlington, VT: Ashgate, 2004.

Porter, Dorothy, and Roy Porter. "What Was Social Medicine? An Historiographical Essay." *Journal of Historical Sociology* 1, no. 1 (1988): 90–106.

Porter, Stephen R. *Benevolent Empire: U.S. Power, Humanitarianism, and the World's Dispossessed*. Philadelphia: University of Pennsylvania Press, 2017.

Prusin, Alexander Victor. *Nationalizing a Borderland: War, Ethnicity, and Anti-Jewish Violence in East Galicia, 1914–1920*. Tuscaloosa: University of Alabama Press, 2005.

Rabinovitch, Simon. *Jewish Rights, National Rites: Nationalism and Autonomy in Late Imperial and Revolutionary Russia*. Stanford, CA: Stanford University Press, 2014.

Raider, Mark A. *The Emergence of American Zionism*. New York: New York University Press, 1998.

Raphael, Marc Lee. "The Origins of Organized National Jewish Philanthropy in the United States, 1914–1939." In *The Jews of North America*, edited by Moses Rischin. Detroit: Wayne State University Press, 1987.

Rappaport, Joseph. *Hands across the Sea: Jewish Immigrants and World War I*. Lanham, MD: Hamilton Books, 2005.

Rechter, David. *The Jews of Vienna and the First World War*. London: Littman Library of Jewish Civilization, 2001.

Roberts, Priscilla. "Jewish Bankers, Russia, and the Soviet Union 1900–1940: The Case of Kuhn, Loeb and Company." *American Jewish Archives Journal* 69 (1997): 9–37.

Robionek, Bernd. "Ethnic-German Cooperatives in Eastern Europe between the World Wars: The Ideology and Intentions behind an Ethnic Economy." In *National Economies: Volks-Wirtschaft, Racism and Economy in Europe between the Wars (1918–1939/45)*, edited by Christoph Kreutzmüller, Michael Wildt, and Moshe Zimmermann, 212–28. Newcastle upon Tyne: Cambridge Scholars Publishing, 2015.

Rodgers, Daniel T. *Atlantic Crossings: Social Politics in a Progressive Age*. Cambridge, MA: Belknap Press, 1998.

Rodogno, Davide. "The American Red Cross and the International Committee of the Red Cross' Humanitarian Politics & Policies in Asia Minor and Greece (1922–1923)." *First World War Studies* 5, no. 1 (2014): 83–99.

"Non-state Actors' Humanitarian Operations in the Aftermath of the First World War." In *The Emergence of Humanitarian Intervention: Ideas and Practice from the Nineteenth Century to the Present*, edited by Fabian Klose, 185–207. Cambridge: Cambridge University Press, 2015.

"International Relief Operations in Palestine in the Aftermath of the First World War: The Discrepancy between International Humanitarian Organisations' Visions, Ambitions, and Actions." *Journal of Migration History* 6 (2020): 16–39.

Night on Earth: A History of International Humanitarian Relief and Rehabilitation in the Near East. Cambridge: Cambridge University Press, 2021.

Rodogno, Davide, Francesca Piana, and Shaloma Gauthier. "Shaping Poland: Relief and Rehabilitation Programmes Undertaken by Foreign Organizations, 1918–1922." In *Shaping the Transnational Sphere: Experts, Networks and Issues from the 1840s to the 1930s*, edited by Davide Rodogno, Bernhard Struck, and Jakob Vogel, 259–78. New York: Berghahn Books, 2014.

Rojanski, Rachel. "The Influence of American Jewry on the Establishment of the Jewish Welfare System in Poland, 1920–1929" [Hebrew]. *Gal'ed* 11 (1989): 59–86.

Rooke, Patricia T., and Rudy L. Schnell. "'Uncramping Child Life': International Childrens' Organisations, 1914–1939." In *International Health Organisations and Movements, 1918–1939*, edited by Paul Weindling, 176–202. Cambridge: Cambridge University Press, 1995.

Rosenbaum, Eduard, and Ari Joshua Sherman. *M. M. Warburg & Co., 1798–1938: Merchant Bankers of Hamburg.* London: C. Hurst, 1979.

Rosenberg, Emily S. *Financial Missionaries to the World: The Politics and Culture of Dollar Diplomacy, 1900–1930.* Cambridge, MA: Harvard University Press, 1999.

Rosenberg, Emily S., and Eric Foner. *Spreading the American Dream: American Economic and Cultural Expansion, 1890–1945.* New York: Hill and Wang, 1982.

Rosenthal, Daniel. "Confronting the Bacterial Enemy: Public Health, Philanthropy, and Jewish Responses to Typhus in Poland, 1914–1921." In *World War I and the Jews: Conflict and Transformations in Europe, the Middle East, and America*, edited by Marsha L. Rozenblit and Jonathan Karp, 131–50. New York: Berghahn Books, 2017.

Roskies, David G. *Against the Apocalypse: Responses to Catastrophe in Modern Jewish Culture.* Cambridge: Harvard University Press, 1984.

Ross, Karen Deane. "Making Medicine Scientific: Simon Flexner and Experimental Medicine at the Rockefeller Institute for Medical Research, 1901–1945," diss., University of Minnesota, 2006.

Rozenblit, Marsha L. *Reconstructing a National Identity: The Jews of Habsburg Austria during World War I.* Oxford: Oxford University Press, 2001.

Sanders, Ronald. *Shores of Refuge: A Hundred Years of Jewish Emigration.* New York: Schocken, 1988.

Sarna, Jonathan. "A Projection of America As It Ought to Be: Zion in the Mind's Eye of American Jews." In *Envisioning Israel: The Changing Ideals and Images of North American Jews*, edited by Allon Gal, 41–59. Jerusalem: Hebrew University, 1996.

American Judaism: A History. New Haven, CT: Yale University Press, 2004.

When General Grant Expelled the Jews. New York: Schocken Books, 2012.

Schayegh, Cyrus. "Imperial and Transnational Developmentalisms: Middle Eastern Interplays, 1880s–1960s." In *The Development Century: A Global History*, edited by Stephen J. Macekura and Erez Manela, 61–82. Cambridge: Cambridge University Press, 2018.

Schilde, Kurt, and Dagmar Schulte. *Need and Care: Glimpses into the Beginnings of Eastern Europe's Professional Welfare*. Opladen: Barbara Budrich Publishers, 2005.

Schneider, William H. "The Men Who Followed Flexner: Richard Pearce, Alan Gregg, and the Rockefeller Foundation Medical Divisions." In *Rockefeller Philanthropy and Modern Biomedicine: International Initiatives from World War I to the Cold War*, edited by William H. Schneider, 7–60. Bloomington: Indiana University Press, 2002.

Schoeni, Céline, and Nora Natchkova. "L'organisation Internationale Du Travail, Les Féministes Et Les Réseaux D'expertes. Les Enjeux D'une Politique Protectrice (1919–1934)." In *L'Organisation Internationale Du Travail: Origine, Développement, Avenir*, edited by Isabelle Lespinet-Moret and Vincent Viet, 39–52. Rennes: Presses Universitaires de Rennes, 2011.

Shapiro, Leon. *The History of ORT: A Jewish Movement for Social Change*. New York: Schocken Books, 1980.

Shvarts, Shifra, and Theodore M. Brown. "Kupat Holim, Dr. Isaac Max Rubinow, and the American Zionist Medical Unit's Experiment to Establish Health Care Services in Palestine, 1918–1923." *Bulletin of the History of Medicine* 72, no. 1 (1998): 28–46.

Shvarts, Shifra, and Zipora Shehory-Rubin. "On Behalf of Mothers and Children in Eretz Israel: The Activity of Hadassah, the Federation of Hebrew Women, and WIZO to Establish Maternal and Infant Welfare Centers–Tipat Halav, 1913–1948." In *Jewish Women in Pre-state Israel: Life History, Politics, and Culture*, edited by Ruth Kark, Margalit Shilo, and Galit Hasan-Rokem, 180–92. Waltham, MA: Brandeis University Press, 2008.

Siegelberg, Mira L. *Statelessness: A Modern History*. Cambridge: Harvard University Press, 2019.

Silber, Marcos. "The Development of a Joint Political Program for the Jews of Poland During World War I – Success and Failure." *Jewish History* 19, no. 2 (2005): 211–26.

Silver, Matthew M. *Louis Marshall and the Rise of Jewish Ethnicity in America: A Biography*. Syracuse, NY: Syracuse University Press, 2013.

Simmons, Erica. *Hadassah and the Zionist Project*. Lanham, MD: Rowman & Littlefield Publishers, 2006.

Skran, Claudena M. *Refugees in Inter-War Europe: The Emergence of a Regime*. Oxford: Oxford University Press, 1995.

Snyder, Timothy. *Bloodlands: Europe between Hitler and Stalin*. New York: Basic Books, 2010.

Soyer, Daniel. *Jewish Immigrant Associations and American Identity in New York, 1880–1939*. Cambridge, MA: Harvard University Press, 1997.

Stein, Herman D. "Jewish Social Work in the United States, 1654–1954." In *American Jewish Year Book 57*, edited by Samson D. Fine, 3–98. Philadelphia: Jewish Publication Society of America, 1956.

Sterba, Christopher. *Good Americans: Italian and Jewish Immigrants during the First World War*. New York: Oxford University Press, 2003.

Sufian, Sandy, and Shifra Shvarts. "'Mission of Mercy' and the Ship That Came Too Late: American Jewish Medical Relief to Palestine during World War I." In *Jewish Studies at the Turn of the Twentieth Century: Proceedings of the 6th EAJS Congress, Toledo, July 1998*, edited by Judit Targarona Borrás and Angel Sáenz-Badillos, 389–98. Leiden: Brill, 1999.

Supple, Barry E. "A Business Elite: German-Jewish Financiers in Nineteenth-Century New York." *The Business History Review* 31, no. 2 (1957): 143–78.

Szajkowski, Zosa. "Jewish Relief in Eastern Europe 1914–1917." *The Leo Baeck Institute Yearbook* 10, no. 1 (1965): 24–56.

"Private and Organized American Jewish Overseas Relief (1914–1938)." *American Jewish Historical Quarterly* 57, no. 1 (1967): 52–106.

"Private and Organized American Jewish Overseas Relief and Immigration (1914–1938)." *American Jewish Historical Quarterly* 57, no. 2 (1967): 191–253.

"Private American Jewish Overseas Relief (1919–1938): Problems and Attempted Solutions." *American Jewish Historical Quarterly* 57, no. 3 (1968): 285–348.

"Budgeting American Jewish Overseas Relief (1919–1939)." *American Jewish Historical Quarterly* 59, no. 1 (1969): 83–113

"Concord and Discord in American Jewish Overseas Relief, 1914–1924." *YIVO Annual of Jewish Social Science* 14 (1969): 134–35.

"American Jewish Relief in Poland and Politics, 1918–1923" [Hebrew]. *Zion* 34 (1969): 219–60.

"'Reconstruction' vs. 'Palliative Relief' in American Jewish Overseas Work (1919–1939)." *Jewish Social Studies* 32, no. 1 (1970): 14–42.

"'Reconstruction' vs. 'Palliative Relief' in American Jewish Overseas Work (1919–1939) (Part II)." *Jewish Social Studies* 32, no. 2 (1970): 111–47.

The Impact of the 1919–20 Red Scare on American Jewish Life. New York: KTAV, 1974.

"Western Jewish Aid and Intercession for Polish Jewry, 1919–1939." In *Studies on Polish Jewry 1919–1939: The Interplay of Social, Economic and Political Factors in the Struggle of a Minority for Its Existence*, edited by Joshua A. Fishman, 150–241. New York: YIVO Institute for Jewish Research, 1974.

Kolchak, Jews, and the American Intervention in Northern Russia and Siberia, 1918–20. self-published, 1977.

The Mirage of American Jewish Aid in Soviet Russia, 1917–1939. self-published, 1977.

Tanielian, Melanie S. *The Charity of War: Famine, Humanitarian Aid, and World War I in the Middle East*.

Tessaris, Chiara. "The War Relief Work of the American Jewish Joint Distribution Committee in Poland and Lithuania, 1915–18." *East European Jewish Affairs* 40, no. 2 (2010): 127–44.

Tevis, Britt P. "'The Hebrews Are Appearing in Court in Great Numbers': Toward a Reassessment of Early Twentieth-Century American Jewish Immigration History." *American Jewish History* 100, no. 3 (2016): 319–47.

Tomes, Nancy. *The Gospel of Germs: Men, Women, and the Microbe in American Life*. Cambridge, MA: Harvard University Press, 1998.

Torpey, John. *The Invention of the Passport: Surveillance, Citizenship, and the State*. Cambridge: Cambridge University Press, 2000.

Tournès, Ludovic. "La Fondation Rockefeller et la Naissance de l'Universalisme Philanthropique Américain." *Critique Internationale* 35, no. 2 (2007): 173–97.

Toury, Jacob. "'The Jewish Question' – A Semantic Approach." *Leo Baeck Institute Yearbook* 11 (1966): 85–106.

Trott, Margaret A. "Passing Through the Eye of the Needle: American Philanthropy and Soviet Medical Research in the 1920s." In *Rockefeller Philanthropy and Modern Biomedicine: International Initiatives from World War I to the Cold War*, edited by William H. Schneider, 125–158. Bloomington: Indiana University Press, 2002.

Tyrrell, Ian R. *Reforming the World: The Creation of America's Moral Empire*. Princeton, NJ: Princeton University Press, 2010.

Veidlinger, Jeffrey. *In the Midst of Civilized Europe: The Pogroms of 1918–1921 and the Onset of the Holocaust*. New York: Metropolitan Books, 2021.

Veit, Helen Zoe. *Modern Food, Moral Food: Self-Control, Science, and the Rise of Modern American Eating in the Early Twentieth Century*. Chapel Hill: University of North Carolina Press, 2013.

Watenpaugh, Keith David. *Bread from Stones: The Middle East and the Making of Modern Humanitarianism*. Oakland: University of California Press, 2015.

Weindling, Paul. "From Sentiment to Science: Children's Relief Organisations and the Problem of Malnutrition in Inter-war Europe." *Disasters* 18, no. 3 (1994): 203–12.

ed. *International Health Organisations and Movements, 1918–1939*. Cambridge: Cambridge University Press, 1995.

Epidemics and Genocide in Eastern Europe, 1890–1945. New York: Oxford University Press, 2000.

"American Foundations and the Internationalizing of Public Health." In *Shifting Boundaries of Public Health: Europe in the Twentieth Century*, edited by Susan Gross Solomon, Lion Murard, and Patrick Zylberman, 63–86. Rochester, NY: University of Rochester Press, 2008.

Weiser, Keith Ian. *Jewish People, Yiddish Nation: Noah Prylucki and the Folkists in Poland*. Toronto: University of Toronto Press, 2011.

Wentling, Sonja P. "*The Engineer and the Shtadlanim*: Herbert Hoover and American Jewish Non-Zionists, 1917–28." *American Jewish History* 88, no. 3 (2000): 377–406.

Werner, Morris R. *Julius Rosenwald: The Life of a Practical Humanitarian*. New York: Harper & Bros, 1939.

Wiebe, Robert H. *The Search for Order, 1877–1920*. London: Macmillan, 1967.

Wikander, Ulla. "Demands on the ILO by Internationally Organized Women in 1919." In *ILO Histories: Essays on the International Labour Organization and Its Impact on the World during the Twentieth Century*, edited by Jasmien van Daele, Magaly Rodriguez Garcia, and Geert van Goethem, 73–90. Bern: Peter Lang, 2010.

Willis, Edward F. *Herbert Hoover and the Russian Prisoners of World War I.* Stanford, CA: Stanford University Press, 1951.

Wilson, Ann Marie. "Taking Liberties Abroad: Americans and International Humanitarian Advocacy, 1821–1914," diss., Harvard University, 2010.

Wischnitzer, Mark. *Visas to Freedom: The History of Hias.* Cleveland: World Publishing Company, 1956.

Wolff, Frank. "Global Walls and Global Movement: New Destinations in Jewish Migration, 1918–1939." *East European Jewish Affairs* 44, no. 2–3 (2014): 187–204.

Wulman, Leon. *In Fight for the Health of the Jewish People: 50 Years of OSE.* New York: World Union OSE and the American Committee of OSE, 1968.

Wyman, David S. *Paper Walls: America and the Refugee Crisis, 1938–1941.* New York: Pantheon Books, 1985.

Youcha, Geraldine. *Minding the Children: Child Care in America From Colonial Times to the Present.* New York: Scribner, 1995.

Zahra, Tara. *Kidnapped Souls: National Indifference and the Battle for Children in the Bohemian Lands, 1900–1948.* Ithaca, NY: Cornell University Press, 2008.

The Lost Children: Reconstructing Europe's Families after World War II. Cambridge, MA: Harvard University Press, 2011.

Zalashik, Rakefet. "Jewish American Philanthropy and the Crisis of 1929: The Case of OZE-TOZ and the JDC." In *1929: Mapping the Jewish World*, edited by Hasia R. Diner and Gennady Estraikh, 93–106. New York: New York University Press, 2013.

"The Anti-Favus Campaign in Poland: Jewish Social Medicine." In *Polin: Studies in Polish Jewry. Jews in the Kingdom of Poland, 1815–1918* 27, edited by Glenn Dynner, Antony Polonsky, and Marcin Wodzinski, 369–84. Oxford: Littman Library of Jewish Civilization, 2015.

Zarrow, Sarah Ellen. "From Relief to Emancipation: Cecylia Klaftenowa's Vision for Jewish Girls in Interwar Lwów" Forthcoming in *Polin: Studies in Polish Jewry. Jewish Childhood, Children and Child Rearing in Eastern Europe*, 36, edited by Natalia Aleksiun. Oxford: Littman Library of Jewish Civilization, 2024.

Zavadivker, Polly. "Fighting 'On Our Own Territory': The Relief, Rescue, and Representation of Jews in Russia during World War I." In *Russia's Home Front in War and Revolution, 1914–22; Book 2: The Experience of War and Revolution*, edited by Adele Lindemeyr, Christopher Read, and Peter Waldron, 79–106. Bloomington: Slavica Publishers, Indiana University, 2016.

"Contending with Horror: Jewish Aid Work in the Russian Civil War Pogroms." *Quest. Issues in Contemporary Jewish History* 15 (2019).

Zipperstein, Steven J. "The Politics of Relief: The Transformation of Russian Jewish Communal Life during the First World War." In *Studies in Contemporary Jewry: Volume IV: The Jews and the European Crisis, 1914–1921*, edited by Jonathan Frankel, Peter Y. Medding, and Ezra Mendelsohn, 22–40. New York: Oxford University Press, 1988.

Ziv, Neta. "Credit Cooperatives in Early Israeli Statehood: Financial Institutions and Social Transformation." *Theoretical Inquiries in Law* 11, no. 1 (2010): 209–46.

Zolberg, Aristide R. *A Nation by Design: Immigration Policy in the Fashioning of America.* Cambridge: Harvard University Press, 2006.

Zunz, Olivier. *Philanthropy in America: A History.* Princeton, NJ: Princeton University Press, 2012.

Index

Please note that page numbers in bold direct the reader to images.